California Wills and Trusts

California Wills and Trusts

Cases, Statutes, Problems, and Materials

Peter T. Wendel

PROFESSOR OF LAW
PEPPERDINE UNIVERSITY SCHOOL OF LAW

Robert G. Popovich

PROFESSOR OF LAW
PEPPERDINE UNIVERSITY SCHOOL OF LAW

CAROLINA ACADEMIC PRESS
Durham, North Carolina

ISBN 978-1-61163-674-1
eISBN 978-1-5310-0840-6
LCCN 2015955457

Carolina Academic Press, LLC
700 Kent Street
Durham, North Carolina 27701
Telephone (919) 489-7486
Fax (919) 493-5668
www.cap-press.com

Printed in the United States of America

To the lovely Gerri—asking you to marry me was the best question I've ever asked;
To my children (Carolyn, Paul, John, and Kristin) and grandchildren
(Quinn and Ronan)—the pride and joy of my life; and
To my students—from whom I've learned so much.

Peter T. Wendel

To my two sons, Mark and Brian—you give me immeasurable love and pride
To my students; past, present and future—
you are my family who gives me purpose in work
To my colleague and friend Peter—you gave me years of friendship and
the chance to work with you on this book

Robert G. Popovich

Contents

Table of Cases

Table of Statutory Material

Preface

The study of Wills, Trusts, and Estates is a methodical, mostly logical, and dare we say "fun" journey. The issue in the course can be reduced to a simple question: "who gets your property when you die?" The answer, like the answer to most questions in law school, is "it depends." What it depends on, and what it *should* depend on, will take a whole semester to analyze. You will learn the foundational rules to make sure that your client's property goes where, and to whom, he or she wants. Sadly, many of the cases one finds in Wills, Trust and Estates casebooks provide illustrations on how *not* to do things. Learn from the mistakes of others.

The Wills, Trusts & Estates course is an introductory course. If you think you might be interested in practicing in this area of law, there are a number of additional courses that you should take (if you law school offers them). At a minimum, most scholars and practitioners would recommend the Estate & Gift Tax course and the Estate Planning course (so too Probate Administration, but that course is not offered at many law schools these days). In addition, it is probably a good idea to also take Family Law, Community Property (if you plan on practicing in a community property state), and Business Associations (to facilitate the estate planning needs of clients who own small businesses and plan to pass them on to family members). This course is not intended to qualify you to practice in this area of law; it is merely the introductory course. You would be well-advised to take at least some of these additional courses if you are thinking about practicing in this area of law.

There are a number of good Wills, Trusts & Estates casebooks in the market already; why one more? Virtually all the other casebooks are written for a national audience. Accordingly, the books assume a non-community property approach and use the Uniform Probate Code to teach the material. The problem is that California is a community property state, and the law of wills and intestacy are intensely state-specific areas of law. While one can use any probate code to teach the issues and basic approach to this area of law, inasmuch as most students who attend a California law school plan on practicing in the state, we thought it would be helpful to have a casebook that focuses on the California Probate Code and the California approach to the issues.[1]

There is no escaping the fact that this course deals primarily with property issues relating to death. The authors apologize, in advance, if any of the material in the book appears insensitive with respect to the issues surrounding death. While one of

---

1. For a variety of reasons, however, we decided to adopt more of a generic approach to trusts portion of the casebook.

our goals was to make the course an enjoyable experience, we realize that sooner or later the emotional, practical, and legal issues surrounding death touch all of us. Life, unfortunately, is not put on "pause" while in law school, and some of the topics discussed in this course may "hit close to home." Please know that your professor grieves with you and never wishes to be hurtful when discussing the scenarios, issues and doctrines faced in a Wills, Trusts and Estates course.

We want to thank our research assistants over the years for their invaluable help in the research and writing of the casebook: Lauren Cleland, Katelin Eastman, Katherine, Kilmer, Danielle Lewis, Chelsea McGrath, Edrina Nazaradeh, Kelley Owen, Monica Paladini, Sara Puls, and Emily Speier. In addition, we want to express our gratitude to the wonderful people at Carolina Academic Press whose support, assistance and patience made this book possible. In particular, we'd like to acknowledge Ryland Bowman, Elisabeth ("Biz") Ebben, Beth Hall, and Grace Pledger for their help in the editing and production process; and a special "shout-out" to Roberta O'Meara of Carolina Academic Press, our long-time friend whose confidence in us paved the way for this project.

PETER T. WENDEL

ROBERT G. POPOVICH

California Wills and Trusts

Chapter 1

Introduction and the
Wills & Trusts Landscape

I. The Subject of Wills and Trusts

The study of wills, trusts, and other time-of-death transfers is a methodical, mostly logical, and often interesting journey. The primary question underlying the course is "*Who gets your property when you die?*" Almost everyone agrees that the decedent's wishes should control who gets the decedent's property when he or she dies. The issue then becomes what should a decedent have to do to properly express his or her wishes to ensure that the law will honor those wishes upon his or her death. As you will see, scholars and jurisdictions disagree on the answer to that question.[1]

II. Quick Overview:
Probate versus Nonprobate

Historically, the most common instrument an individual used to express their testamentary wishes was a last will and testament (more commonly called, simply, "a will"). An individual who executes a valid will is called a *testator*.[2] A will, however, applies only to a decedent's *probate property*. Probate property refers to the decedent's property that passes by way of a state court supervised "probate" procedure. It is also possible, however, for one to hold *nonprobate property*. A decedent's nonprobate property bypasses the probate process when it makes the journey from the decedent to the intended recipients. Thus, classifying property as "probate" versus "nonprobate"

---

1. Having said that, the material in this book will focus on how California answers this question. To the extent the book covers other approaches, it does so because either (1) the California approach to the particular issue is the default approach, but a party can opt out of it with proper drafting so the "other" approaches are viable options; or (2) knowing the historical evolution of the law in the area and/or the different possible approaches will help you better understand the California approach. With respect to how much of the non-California law you are responsible for, take your cues from your professor.

2. At common law, if the decedent who died with a will was a female she was called a *testatrix*. The modern trend uses the term *testator* to refer to a decedent of either gender.

distinguishes how the property will make its way, at time of death, from the decedent to the intended beneficiaries. In addition, classifying property as "probate" versus "non-probate" is important because different rules often apply to the different types of property.

A. Probate Property

The probate process is the default system. Upon an individual's death, all of his or her property will fall into probate unless the person takes the necessary steps, while he or she is alive, to shift the property from probate property to nonprobate property. Because it is assumed that most people die with at least some probate property, following a decedent's death the first step is to "open" probate. Typically, a family member will take a copy of the decedent's death certificate to the appropriate state court (usually referred to as the probate court or the probate division of a standard state civil court system). The probate court will then appoint someone to administer the decedent's probate estate. This appointed person essentially has three duties: (1) ascertain the scope of the decedent's *probate* property (i.e., inventory the decedent's property that will be passing through the probate process); (2) give notice to the decedent's creditors to assert their claims as part of the probate process[3] — and pay those claims that are properly asserted; and (3) distribute the remaining probate property to the parties who are entitled to receive it.

The official title of the person appointed by the probate court to administer the decedent's probate property varies depending on the jurisdiction and the circumstances. If the decedent dies *testate* (i.e., with a valid will) and the will names the person to be appointed, the person is typically called "the *executor*." If the decedent died *intestate* (i.e., without a valid will) — or if he or she died testate but the will does not name a person to administer the estate — the person appointed by the probate court is typically called "the *administrator*." The modern trend prefers to minimize legalese — legal terminology that is confusing to laypeople. Accordingly, the modern trend uses the term "*personal representative*" to describe the person appointed by the probate court to administer the decedent's probate estate regardless of whether the decedent named the party or the probate court selected the party.

Who is entitled to receive the decedent's probate property depends on whether the decedent dies testate or intestate. The primary purpose of a will is to express one's wishes with respect to who should get one's probate property when the party dies. If a person dies testate, the will directs to whom the decedent's probate property should be distributed. Historically, a gift of real property in a will was called a *devise* (it can also be used as a verb — "the testator *devised* Greenacres to Gerri"). If the gift was an item of personal property or money, historically it was called a *bequest* or *legacy* (it can also be used as a verb — "the testator *bequeathed* his stamp collection

---

3. Creditors must assert their claims in a timely manner in probate court or their claims can be extinguished.

to Carolyn"). In the interest of minimizing legalese, the modern trend uses the term "devise" to describe a gift of any type of property, real or personal. If a person dies intestate, the decedent's property will be distributed to his or her heirs according to the state's statute of intestate succession.

A full discussion of a typical state probate process is well beyond the scope of a basic wills and trusts course, but we would be remiss if we did not discuss one more issue. Many people have a negative view of probate. That view distorts the typical layperson's view of probate. Many people believe that probate is nothing more than an expensive, time-consuming form of state interference with the transfer of the decedent's property. Not so. Not all families and loved ones are as functional and/or honest as the decedent may have assumed. Probate is a form of protection for the decedent. The probate process ensures judicial supervision over distribution of the decedent's property. The judge serves as a disinterested third party who is there to ensure that (a) creditor claims against the decedent are properly resolved, (b) the estate's personal representative properly performs his or her duties, and (c) the decedent's assets are distributed according to the testator's wishes (as expressed in his or her will or as presumed under the state's intestate succession laws).

B. Nonprobate Property

For a variety of reasons beyond the scope of this course material, it has become generally accepted that probate is a "bad" way of transferring one's assets at death (though that is not always the case). The most common rationales for this view are that probate is costly, too invasive, takes too long, and/or it delays distribution of the decedent's assets.[4] Individuals increasingly are opting out of probate by putting their assets into nonprobate arrangements. The four classic nonprobate arrangements that de facto transfer property at time of death are (1) transferring the property to an *inter vivos* trust, (2) putting the property into joint tenancy, (3) purchasing a life insurance policy (where the time of death benefits are paid to the policy beneficiary pursuant to the terms of the insurance contract), and/or (4) creating a legal life estate and remainder.

Of the four classic nonprobate arrangements, in recent decades two have assumed an increasingly important role in estate planning. The first is the "revocable living trust." A revocable living trust is functionally similar to a will (i.e., created *inter vivos*, revocable until death, and transfers property to the beneficiaries identified in the instrument at time of death), but it accomplishes the time of death transfer via a different mechanism. It is the paradigm "will substitute": it functions like a will in that for all practical purposes it transfers property at death, but it is actually a will *substitute* because of its ability to avoid probate. Each of the nonprobate arrangements constitutes a will substitute, and collectively they are often referred to as "the will substitutes."

---

4. In Chapter 11, we explore these common beliefs in more detail.

The second increasingly important nonprobate method of transferring property at time of death is the contractual time of death transfer. The modern trend takes the traditional nonprobate exception that was limited to the life insurance contract and expands it to include any and all contracts with a payment on death clause. Increasingly, in many jurisdictions, bank accounts, pension plans, and/or brokerage accounts now can be valid nonprobate transfers simply by including in the contractual agreement a payment on death clause that directs to whom the funds should be paid at time of the party's death.

To the extent the overarching question in the course is "who gets your property when you die?" one way to analyze this issue is to focus on how the decedent holds the property. The decedent may hold probate and nonprobate property, and how the decedent holds the asset can affect who gets the asset. A table of a decedent's possible assets, grouped by probate and nonprobate arrangements, and how that affects who gets the property might look like this:

Probate Property	_Nonprobate Property_
A Will—Property passes to others through the terms of the decedent's will.	_Property passing by Operation of Law_—Joint tenancy property, with its "right of survivorship" attribute, is the traditional and most common example of this type of property,[5] where at death of the first cotenant, his or her interest is extinguished and the surviving cotenant(s)' shares are re-calculated (or as some prefer to think of it, the property "passes," by law, to the surviving cotenant(s)).
No Will—Property passes to others by intestacy.	_Property passing by Contract_—A life insurance policy is the traditional and most common example of this type of property. In many jurisdictions the modern trend is to expand this exception to include other contractual instruments with a named beneficiary or beneficiaries. Common examples include pension and retirement plans, savings accounts, checking accounts, and other _payable on death_ (POD) or _transfer upon death_ (TOD) type accounts.
	Trusts—There are various forms of trusts with the revocable living trust being the most common (and acting most like a will), where property passes pursuant to the terms of the trust instrument.

---

5. This can also include "Community Property with right of survivorship" as well as certain property interests created with legal life/income and remainder interests.

Nonprobate methods of transferring property at time of death are explored in greater detail in Chapter 11. Each of the nonprobate transfers has the practical effect of transferring a property interest to another party at time of death. Thus, laypeople perceive them as functioning very much like a will. Some, but not all, nonprobate transfers occur more quickly (and cheaper) than probate transfers. Hence the modern trend "nonprobate revolution." Today, more assets are transferred via nonprobate instruments than through wills; however, the use of wills continues to be an important vehicle for the disposition of one's estate.

III. An Estate Planning Perspective

As most people age, they begin to contemplate the question that is the focus of this course, though they phrase it a bit differently: "Who *should* get my property when I die?"[6] Most individuals do not have much trouble answering that question. For example, the person may decide: "I want $10,000 to go to Alice, my house to Bob, my car to Carol, $15,000 to Children's Hospital, and the rest of my assets to my children, in equal shares." Deciding who should get their property is generally not difficult for the average individual. What is difficult, however, is knowing what must be done to ensure that his or her wishes are given legal effect.

Historically, most people would consult a lawyer[7] — ideally, one who specializes in estate planning — for help with the time-of-death transfer process. The client, of course, wants to decide who gets the property — or "direct" his or her at-death distributions — and that may be his or her sole focus (as least at first). There are, however, many possible means of accomplishing the client's wishes. The Probate Code tends to refer to the different means of transferring property at death in terms of the probate versus nonprobate process discussed above. Estate planners, on the other hand, tend to think of the different means of transferring property at death in terms of "directed" versus "non-directed" means.

---

6. As the material progresses, we will ask you to think about the difference between the original phrasing of the issue in the course and the client's phrasing. Should the two be identical? To what extent should the law be concerned with who *should* get the decedent's property? Should that be the *only* public policy consideration underlying probate law? To what extent should the law be willing to go to determine who *should* get the decedent's property? Who should make that determination? What other public policy considerations are relevant, and why? To the extent there are other public policy considerations, are they all equal or should some be given greater weight than others? How should the different policy considerations be balanced?

7. The terms *lawyer* and *attorney* are used interchangeably throughout the book as they minimize legalese and are perceived to be synonymous to the general public. As used historically, however, a lawyer was someone who had studied the law (e.g., graduated from law school) but was not qualified to practice law in that jurisdiction, while an attorney was a lawyer who had also met the added requirements to practice law in a particular state (i.e., passed the bar exam and met a state's licensing requirements).

Using the same probate and nonprobate terms set forth in the table above, a table of a decedent's assets grouped by directed and non-directed means might look like this:

Directed Dispositions

A Will—Property passes to others through the decedent's will. The decedent directs, via the will provisions, to whom (along with when and how) his or her property passes to others (the beneficiaries).

Property passing by Contract—A life insurance policy is the traditional and most common example of this type of property. In many jurisdictions the modern trend is to expand this exception to include other contractual instruments with a named beneficiary or beneficiaries. Common examples include pension and retirement plans, savings accounts, checking accounts, and other *payable on death* (POD) or *transfer upon death* (TOD) type accounts.

Trusts—There are various forms of trusts, with the inter vivos revocable living trust being the most common (and acting the most like a will), where property passes pursuant to the terms of the trust instrument.

Property Passing by Operation of Law—Joint tenancy property, with its "right of survivorship" attribute, is the traditional and most common example of this type of property,[8] where at the death of the first cotenant, his or her interest is extinguished and the surviving cotenant(s)' shares are re-calculated (or as some prefer to think of it, the property "passes," by law, to the surviving cotenant(s)).[9]

Non-Directed Dispositions

No Will or nonprobate instrument—Property passes to others by intestacy (i.e., there is no will or other instrument disposing of property).

This course will focus on covering the basics of the different methods (or "vehicles") that can be used to transfer one's property at time of death, how to properly create them, and what happens if a party fails to properly create them (i.e., does not validly create one of the instruments listed in the *directed* disposition column). Each of these transfer options is, in essence, a tool that a good estate planner has at his or her disposal to express a client's estate planning wishes. Which vehicle(s) *should* be used, and why, is a more difficult question. The planning professional's analysis involves a number of variables that are beyond the scope of an introductory wills and trusts

---

8. This can also include "Community Property with right of survivorship" as well as certain property interests created with legal life/income and remainder interests.

9. *See* Chapter 11. Passing by operation of law can be viewed as a "directed" form of distribution, but has more limitations than the other distribution methods listed.

course.[10] Which estate planning vehicle(s) is/are the most appropriate for the disposition of the client's property at time of death is the focus of the upper-level estate planning course.

Problems

Bob died earlier today. In each of the following scenarios, to whom do the assets go? In particular, analyze which assets are probate versus nonprobate assets, as well as which assets are being disposed of by directed versus non-directed means. Do you see a pattern of how the matrices overlap? Can you spot any potential issues or problems?

1. Bob, a single individual, has a valid will and the will provisions specify that at his death each student in his most recent "Wills & Trusts" class is to receive $20,000 in cash. The will also provides that his remaining assets are to be distributed, outright and in equal shares, to his two sons, Mark and Brian.

2. Assume the same facts as Problem 1, except Bob also has a $2 million life insurance policy (he is the insured) with his son, Brian, as the named beneficiary.

3. Assume the same facts as Problem 2, except that the primary beneficiary of Bob's life insurance policy is his father, George, if living at Bob's death. If not, the policy lists "Bob's estate" as the secondary, or contingent, beneficiary.

4. Assume the same facts as Problem 3, except that Bob married Claudia over a recent holiday weekend. His will was executed a year ago and prior to his marriage. Bob did not have the time to amend his will or make a new one.

5. Assume the same facts as Problem 1, except that Bob's sons, Mark and Brian, contest the will, claiming that the students in his most recent "Wills & Trusts" class exerted undue influence in the making of his will. The court agrees and sustains Mark and Brian's assertion.

6. Bob and Hannah, who are unrelated, own a parcel of prime beachfront land in Malibu as joint tenants. The land is worth $10 million at Bob's death (Hannah survives Bob).

   a. Bob's will does not address his interest in this land.

   b. Bob's will states that his undivided one-half joint interest in the Malibu land goes to his friend and colleague, Pete.

7. Bob does not have a will, but he established a revocable living trust during his life. During his life, he transferred all of his assets to the trust. Bob was the trustee of this trust, and his sister, Marcee, is named as successor trustee. The trust provides that at Bob's death, all of the trust property goes, outright, to his two sons — Mark and Brian.

---

10. These variables include tax considerations, potential creditor(s)' claims, family considerations (i.e., are there minor children or other dependents who cannot/should not hold the property), and/or asset considerations (in what form is the property currently held and whether that makes a difference — e.g., a family farm or closely held business, out-of-state real property, etc.).

8. Assume the same facts as in Problem 7, except that during his lifetime, Bob forgot about the 10,000 shares of ABC stock that he owned and failed to transfer them to his trust. Would there be a difference if the stocks were held in a brokerage/investment account with a transfer upon death (TOD) provision? What if the account has a TOD provision, but the individual named as beneficiary has predeceased Bob?

9. Assume the same facts as Problem 7, except that Bob's other sister, Melinda, files a lawsuit to set aside the trust claiming that Bob was incompetent when he established the trust. The court agrees, finding that Bob did not have the requisite mental capacity when establishing the trust.

10. Assume the same facts as Problem 1, except that Bob's will provides that the remainder of his assets (after the bequests/devises to his Wills & Trusts students) be held in trust with trust income payable to his two sons, Mark and Brian, in equal shares for a period of 10 years. At the end of 10 years, the trust principal/corpus is to be distributed, outright and in equal shares, to Mark and Brian.

If you find it helpful, the same probate versus nonprobate, directed versus non-directed analytical approach can be applied to cases:

In re Succession of Plummer

847 So.2d 185 (La. App. 2003)

KOSTELKA, Judge Pro Tempore.

In this disputed succession case, the brothers and sisters of the decedent, Ronald R. Plummer, appeal the judgment of the trial court holding that the document presented for probate is not a valid olographic will.[11] ...

FACTS

In 1999, Ronald R. Plummer ("Mr. Plummer") attempted to create an inter vivos trust for the management and distribution of his assets using a printed form with the caption "Revocable One-Party Living Trust". ... In one section of the trust instrument entitled "Schedule of Beneficiaries and Distributive Shares," handwritten instructions designate the beneficiaries and direct the management and division of the trust property upon his death. Mr. Plummer was divorced with no children from the

---

11. An olographic will is more commonly known as a holographic will. The classic will is an attested will—one that is signed by the testator in the presence of two witnesses who then sign the will as witnesses. The prototypical attested will is prepared by an attorney who usually supervises the execution ceremony (the ceremony where the testator and the witnesses sign the will). Some jurisdictions also recognize holographic wills. A holographic will is essentially a homemade will—a will that typically is created by the testator, without the help of an attorney, and it does not require witnesses. While it does not have to be witnessed to be valid, it typically has to be in the testator's handwriting to be valid. The differences between attested wills and holographic wills are covered in Chapter 6.

marriage. He named his brothers and sisters, Carl Plummer, Donald Plummer, Sheryl Plummer and Doris Plummer ("the appellants"), all of whom live in Adams County, Mississippi, as beneficiaries to the trust. The document is dated June 25, 1999 and signed "Ronald R. Plummer." Mr. Plummer died on April 9, 2000 without having completed the inter vivos trust.[12]

Besides his brothers and sisters, Mr. Plummer was survived by his ten-year-old daughter, Cheronda Leshay Thomas. On September 4, 2001, Cheronda's mother, Cynthia Thomas ("Thomas"), filed a petition on behalf of her daughter to open the succession of Mr. Plummer and to have Mr. Plummer's succession declared intestate. In response, the appellants filed a "Petition to Probate Olographic Testament" on January 28, 2002 alleging that Mr. Plummer had a Last Will and Testament. The alleged will consisted of two unusually numbered pages, K105-3 and K105-3-1, annexed to the petition. The "will" was, in fact, the "Schedule of Beneficiaries and Distributive Shares" (hereinafter "Exhibit A") from the inter vivos trust instrument.

After an evidentiary hearing and argument on May 10, 2002 and a second oral argument on August 1, 2002, the court issued its Ruling on September 4, 2002, holding that the document was not a valid olographic will. The court specifically found that the testamentary intent of the document was not "unmistakable," and that the signature to the document had not been proven authentic.

The appellants filed ... [an] appeal....

DISCUSSION

...

There are two essential requirements for a valid will: the act must be in valid form and the clauses it contains, or the manner in which it is made must clearly establish that it is a disposition of last will. *Hendry v. Succession of Helms*, 557 So.2d 427 (La.App. 3d Cir.02/07/90), *writ denied*, 560 So.2d 8 (La.1990).

Formal Requisites of an Olographic Testament

An olographic testament is that which is entirely written, dated, and signed by the testator. The olographic testament is subject to no other form. La. C.C. art. 1575. The olographic testament must be proved by two credible witnesses testifying that the handwriting on the instrument is that of the testator. La. C.C.P. art. 2883. *Succession of Calhoun*, 28,233 (La.App.2d Cir.04/03/96), 674 So.2d 989. The jurisprudence interpreting La. C.C.P. art. 2883 has held that the phrase "credible witness" includes individuals who are familiar with the testator's handwriting, as well as handwriting experts. *In re Succession of Jones*, 356 So.2d 80, 82 (La.App. 1st Cir.1978), *writ denied*,

---

12. The court does not elaborate on what it means when it says that Mr. Plummer did not "complete" the trust. One of the requirements for the creation of a valid trust is that the settlor (the party creating the trust) must transfer property to the trust. Apparently Mr. Plummer did not transfer any property to the trust.

357 So.2d 1168 (La.1978). Thus, proof that an alleged olographic will was entirely written, dated and signed in the testator's handwriting is not limited to handwriting experts. A credible individual familiar with decedent's handwriting is competent to serve as a credible witness pursuant to La. C.C.P. art. 2833. *Succession of Lirette,* 5 So.2d 197 (La.App. 1st Cir.1941).

The courts, over the years, have lessened the formalities of olographic wills, i.e., using slash dates instead of writing out the date, *Succession of Boyd,* 306 So.2d 687 (La.1975); writing the will in part pencil, part ink, *Succession of Smart,* 214 La. 63, 36 So.2d 639 (1948); and, in *Oroszy v. Burkard,* 158 So.2d 405 (La.App. 3d Cir.1963), the court held that an olographic will does not, in its entirety, have to all be written on the same date. Nevertheless, the basic formal requisites have remained in place, i.e., a valid olographic testament must be written, dated and signed in the handwriting of the testator.

In this case, the trial court concluded that Exhibit A does not survive as an olographic will because the "testamentary intent is not unmistakable," citing *Succession of Burke,* 365 So.2d 858 (La.App. 4th Cir.1978). In *Burke, supra,* the court held that the trial court did not err in finding a valid will, where the testamentary intent was unmistakable in the words that the decedent wrote using a printed will form in which he filled in the blanks in his own handwriting, and the essential formalities of an olographic will were present.

Appellants argue that *Succession of Burke, supra* requires the court to disregard the printed form words in the document in construing the will. If the printed language is ignored, appellants argue, the type of printed form document used has no significance for purposes of testamentary intent, and hence the case *sub judice* is not distinguishable from *Succession of Burke.* Therefore, if there is testamentary intent present in confecting the document and such intent is demonstrated by the language written by the testator, they argue the document survives as a will.

. . .

It is clear from ... [the] cases that the presence of extraneous printed material such as a personal or business letterhead will not defeat the formal requisites of an olographic will provided that the testament itself is entirely written, dated and signed in the handwriting of the testator. Thus, our courts have ignored those printed words whose presence on the document is incidental. An exception has evolved with respect to partially printed dates. In those cases that have upheld the will in spite of the fact that a portion of the date was printed, the rule is that the handwritten portion of the date must be sufficient to be certain of the date when the printed numbers are ignored. *Succession of Heinemann, supra.* In other words, the ignored numerals are not essential to a determination of the date.

In this instance, however, the complete inter vivos trust instrument filled out by Mr. Plummer consists of several pages of printed words that are an essential part of the trust instrument. Exhibit A, the Schedule of Beneficiaries and Distributive Shares, consisting of pages K105-3 and K105-3-1, is inseparable from Exhibit J-1, consisting of pages K105-1A thorough D and K105-2, and all pages are essential to the confection of the trust document. Exhibit A was no doubt intended by Mr. Plummer to be part of the overall trust document. Unlike the cases using mere stationery or letterhead upon which a testament was written, we cannot ignore the printed words on the trust document because they are inextricably tied to and form an integral part of the entire document, thus negating the formal requirement that the will be entirely written in the hand of the testator. We, therefore, hold that the trial court correctly concluded that the document did not constitute a valid olographic will.

. . .

Testamentary Intent

The trial court recognized that Exhibit A was actually a part of the main document entitled a "Revocable One-Party Living Trust," Exhibit J-1. This is plainly evidenced by the page numbering style connecting the two documents. The trial court concluded that when Exhibit A is taken into account with Exhibit J-1 and *Succession of Burke, supra,* it cannot be said that the testamentary intent is unmistakable. We interpret the court to mean that when the trust instrument is considered as a whole, testamentary intent is lacking. The trial court distinguished the facts of *Succession of Burke, supra,* in which the decedent used a printed statutory will form instead of a "Revocable One-Party Living Trust" form as used in the case *sub judice.* The trial court concluded that the nature of the printed form casts doubt as to the testamentary intent of the document. We agree.

In *Succession of Patterson,* 188 La. 635, 177 So. 692, 694 (1937), our supreme court quoted approvingly from 28 Ruling Case Law, § 3, p. 59 as follows:

> In the interpretation of acts of last will, the intention of the testator must principally be endeavored to be ascertained, without departing, however, from the proper signification of the terms of the testament. Article 1712. But … Furthermore, *the animus testandi must exist when the instrument is executed or acknowledged, and the intent must apply to the particular instrument produced as a will. A paper is not established as a man's will merely by proving that he intended to make a disposition of his property similar to or even identically the same as that contained in the paper. It must satisfactorily appear that he intended the very paper to be his will.* … (Emphasis ours.)

Here, the document submitted for probate contains no actual bequests. Virtually all expressions or words by Mr. Plummer regarding the disposition of his property involve directions for the management of the trust property by his brothers and sisters. He names them as the beneficiaries and to act on his behalf after he has died. He directs them to sell the home, but does not bequeath them the proceeds of the sale. He directs them to divide the contents of the home among themselves, to use the $10,000 life insurance policy for his funeral, and if the costs exceed the policy, then to use money from his checking/savings account. He directs them to take the remainder of the money and put it in a savings account along with the money from the sale of the home. He directs them to roll over the interest into the account. He grants the beneficiaries the power to manage his debts and whatever other finances he leaves upon his death. He then grants them "full usage of the money" in the account "to solve what problems they encounter." Even with regard to his truck, he instructs his brothers and sisters to decide who will receive it. Finally, Mr. Plummer states that his daughter, Cheronda, will receive his retirement pension from the City of Monroe. It is not clear if this is a bequest.

Even if we were to conclude that the document is in valid form, being entirely written, dated and signed by the decedent, the document fails as a valid will because it lacks the necessary *animus testandi*. Despite the fact that the document contains expressions which reflect Mr. Plummer's intention to direct the division of his property upon his death, there are few words, if any, signifying bequests. Accordingly, we conclude that the trial court was correct in concluding that the document did not evidence testamentary intent.

Signature of the Testator

The trial court concluded that the legal proof required to authenticate Mr. Plummer's signature had not been met. Because we have determined that the document presented for probate fails as an olographic testament both in form and substance, it is unnecessary to decide this issue.

CONCLUSION

Accordingly, the trial court did not err in concluding that the document presented for probate did not constitute a valid olographic will. The judgment of the trial court is affirmed at appellants' costs.

———————

Notes

1. *Probate versus nonprobate/directed versus non-directed*: Which type of disposition did Mr. Plummer apparently wish to make, directed or non-directed? Which type of transfer would that have been, probate or nonprobate? The bulk of the court's analysis concerns itself with which type of transfer? Why? Ultimately, how was Mr. Plummer's estate disposed? Why was Mr. Plummer's apparent intent not honored?

2. *Intent versus formalities*: The study of wills and trusts is primarily a study of the formalities the law requires before a decedent's testamentary wishes will be honored. How high should the "formalities" bar be set before the law will recognize a decedent's wishes? In this book, we explore the foundational laws and rules that are *designed* to ensure that a decedent's property goes to whom he or she wishes. Nevertheless, this book is replete with examples of people's intent not being honored because of a mistake in the execution of the instrument that purported to express the party's testamentary wishes. In many instances, the mistake is one that easily could have been avoided. The conflict between the decedent's intent and the required formalities inevitably raises the issue of whether society should lower the bar to make it easier for individuals to express their testamentary wishes — or would low-

ering the bar create problems in terms of increased potential for fraud and/or increased litigation.

IV. Professional Responsibility — Ethical Issues

Legal malpractice claims typically are based on either a breach of contract claim or a negligence claim. Historically, the problem with either approach is that in the estate planning field, the claims did not fit very well. To maintain a breach of contract claim, the plaintiff had to establish that he or she was in privity of contract with the defendant. In the typical estate planning context, the decedent is the party who was in privity of contract with the attorney. Accordingly, only the decedent's estate (i.e., his or her personal representative) had standing to maintain an action against the drafting attorney. Similarly, if the plaintiff preferred a torts-based approach and claimed negligence, the first requirement is that the plaintiff must show that the defendant owed the plaintiff a duty. Again, historically that posed problematic when applied to the estate planning context. Virtually all courts held that while the drafting attorney owed a duty to the client—the testator/transferor—the drafting attorney did *not* owe a duty to any other party. Under such an approach, *only* the decedent's personal representative could bring a negligence claim on behalf of the estate—no one else could.

While such a narrow approach might initially sound overly protective of estate planners, the courts feared that if they were to open the doors and grant standing to "any intended beneficiary," then anyone who knew the decedent and expected to receive a gift when the decedent died but did not could come running into court to assert a malpractice claim against the drafting attorney ("The decedent told me he/she was going to leave me a gift, so the only reason I wasn't mentioned in the decedent's estate plan must be due to the attorney's malpractice!"). In balancing the competing options and public policy concerns, the more traditional approach clearly took a narrower approach to the issue of standing, thereby granting generous protection to an estate planner. Over time, however, that approach has come under increasing attack.

Lucas v. Hamm
56 Cal.2d 583 (1961)

GIBSON, C. J.

Plaintiffs, who are some of the beneficiaries under the will of Eugene H. Emmick, deceased, brought this action for damages against defendant L. S. Hamm, an attorney at law who had been engaged by the testator to prepare the will. They have appealed from a judgment of dismissal entered after an order sustaining a general demurrer to the second amended complaint without leave to amend.

The allegations of the first and second causes of action are summarized as follows: Defendant agreed with the testator, for a consideration, to prepare a will and codicils thereto for him by which plaintiffs were to be designated as beneficiaries of a trust provided for by paragraph Eighth of the will and were to receive 15% of the residue as specified in that paragraph. Defendant, in violation of instructions and in breach of his contract, negligently prepared testamentary instruments containing phraseology that was invalid by virtue of section 715.2 and former sections 715.1 and 716 of the Civil Code relating to restraints on alienation and the rule against perpetuities. Paragraph Eighth of these instruments "transmitted" the residual estate in trust and provided that the "trust shall cease and terminate at 12 o'clock noon on a day five years after the date upon which the order distributing the trust property to the trustee is made by the Court having jurisdiction over the probation of this will." After the death of the testator the instruments were admitted to probate. Subsequently defendant, as draftsman of the instruments and as counsel of record for the executors, advised plaintiffs in writing that the residual trust provision was invalid and that plaintiffs would be deprived of the entire amount to which they would have been entitled if the provision had been valid unless they made a settlement with the blood relatives of the testator under which plaintiffs would receive a lesser amount than that provided for them by the testator. As the direct and proximate result of the negligence of defendant and his breach of contract in preparing the testamentary instruments and the written advice referred to above, plaintiffs were compelled to enter into a settlement under which they received a share of the estate amounting to $75,000 less than the sum which they would have received pursuant to testamentary instruments drafted in accordance with the directions of the testator.

...

It was held in *Buckley v. Gray*, 110 Cal. 339, 42 P. 900, 31 L.R.A. 862, that an attorney who made a mistake in drafting a will was not liable for negligence or breach of contract to a person named in the will who was deprived of benefits as a result of the error. The court stated that an attorney is liable to his client alone with respect to actions based on negligence in the conduct of his professional duties, and it was reasoned that there could be no recovery for mere negligence where there was no privity by contract or otherwise between the defendant and the person injured. 110 Cal. at pages 342–343, 42 P. 900. The court further concluded that there could be no recovery on the theory of a contract for the benefit of a third person, because the contract with the attorney was not expressly for the plaintiff's benefit and the testatrix only remotely intended the plaintiff to be benefited as a result of the contract. 110 Cal. at pages 346–347, 42 P. 900....

The reasoning underlying the denial of tort liability in the *Buckley* case, i.e., the stringent privity test, was rejected in *Biakanja v. Irving*, 49 Cal.2d 647, 648–650, 320 P.2d 16, 65 A.L.R.2d 1358, where we held that a notary public who, although not authorized to practice law, prepared a will but negligently failed to direct proper attestation was liable in tort to an intended beneficiary who was damaged because of the invalidity of the instrument. It was pointed out that since 1895, when *Buckley* was decided, the rule that in the absence of privity there was no liability for negligence committed in the performance of a contract had been greatly liberalized. 49 Cal.2d at page 649, 320 P.2d 16. In restating the rule it was said that the determination whether in a specific case the defendant will be held liable to a third person not in privity is a matter of policy and involves the balancing of various factors, among which are the extent to which the transaction was intended to affect the plaintiff, the foreseeability of harm to him, the degree of certainty that the plaintiff suffered injury, the closeness of the connection between the defendant's conduct and the injury, and the policy of preventing future harm. 49 Cal.2d at page 650, 320 P.2d 16. The same general principle must be applied in determining whether a beneficiary is entitled to bring an action for negligence in the drafting of a will when the instrument is drafted by an attorney rather than by a person not authorized to practice law.

Many of the factors which led to the conclusion that the notary public involved in *Biakanja* was liable are equally applicable here. As in *Biakanja*, one of the main purposes which the transaction between defendant and the testator intended to accomplish was to provide for the transfer of property to plaintiffs; the damage to plaintiffs in the event of invalidity of the bequest was clearly foreseeable; it became certain, upon the death of the testator without change of the will, that plaintiffs would have received the intended benefits but for the asserted negligence of defendant; and if persons such as plaintiffs are not permitted to recover for the loss resulting from negligence of the draftsman, no one would be able to do so, and the policy of prevent future harm would be impaired.

Since defendant was authorized to practice the profession of an attorney, we must consider an additional factor not present in *Biakanja*, namely, whether the recognition of liability to beneficiaries of wills negligently drawn by attorneys would impose an undue burden on the profession. Although in some situations liability could be large and unpredictable in amount, this is also true of an attorney's liability to his client. We are of the view that the extension of his liability to beneficiaries injured by a negligently drawn will does not place an undue burden on the profession, particularly when we take into consideration that a contrary conclusion would cause the innocent beneficiary to bear the loss. The fact that the notary public involved in *Biakanja* was guilty of unauthorized practice of the law was only a minor factor in determining that he was liable, and the absence of the factor in the present case does not justify reaching a different result.

It follows that the lack of privity between plaintiffs and defendant does not preclude plaintiffs from maintaining an action in tort against defendant.

Neither do we agree with the holding in *Buckley* that beneficiaries damaged by an error in the drafting of a will cannot recover from the draftsman on the theory that they are third-party beneficiaries of the contract between him and the testator. Obviously the main purpose of a contract for the drafting of a will is to accomplish the future transfer of the estate of the testator to the beneficiaries named in the will, and therefore it seems improper to hold, as was done in *Buckley*, that the testator intended only "remotely" to benefit those persons. It is true that under a contract for the benefit of a third person performance is usually to be rendered directly to the beneficiary, but this is not necessarily the case. (See Rest., Contracts, § 133, com. d; 2 Williston on Contracts (3rd ed.1959) 829.) For example, where a life insurance policy lapsed because a bank failed to perform its agreement to pay the premiums out of the insured's bank account, it was held that after the insured's death the beneficiaries could recover against the bank as third-party beneficiaries. *Walker Bank & Trust Co. v. First Security Corp.*, 9 Utah 2d 215, 341 P.2d 944, 945 et seq. Persons who had agreed to procure liability insurance for the protection of the promisees but did not do so were also held liable to injured persons who would have been covered by the insurance, the courts stating that all persons who might be injured were third-party beneficiaries of the contracts to procure insurance. *Johnson v. Holmes Tuttle Lincoln-Merc., Inc.*, 160 Cal.App.2d 290, 296 et seq., 325 P.2d 193; *James Stewart & Co. v. Law*, 149 Tex. 392, 233 S.W.2d 558, 561–562, 22 A.L.R.2d 639. Since, in a situation like those presented here and in the *Buckley* case, the main purpose of the testator in making his agreement with the attorney is to benefit the persons named in his will and this intent can be effectuated, in the event of a breach by the attorney, only by giving the beneficiaries a right of action, we should recognize, as a matter of policy, that they are entitled to recover as third-party beneficiaries. See 2 Williston on Contracts (3rd ed. 1959) pp. 843–844; 4 Corbin on Contracts (1951) pp. 8, 20.

Section 1559 of the Civil Code, which provides for enforcement by a third person of a contract made "expressly" for his benefit, does not preclude this result. The effect of the section is to exclude enforcement by persons who are only incidentally or remotely benefited. *See Hartman Ranch Co. v. Associated Oil Co.*, 10 Cal.2d 232, 244, 73 P.2d 1163; cf. 4 Corbin on Contracts (1951) pp. 23–24. As we have seen, a contract for the drafting of a will unmistakably shows the intent of the testator to benefit the persons to be named in the will, and the attorney must necessarily understand this.

Defendant relies on language in *Smith v. Anglo-California Trust Co.*, 205 Cal. 496, 502, 271 P. 898, and *Fruitvale Canning Co. v. Cotton*, 115 Cal.App.2d 622, 625, 252 P.2d 953, that to permit a third person to bring an action on a contract there must be "an intent clearly manifested by the promisor" to secure some benefit to the third person. This language, which was not necessary to the decision in either of the cases, is unfortunate. Insofar as intent to benefit a third person is important in determining his right to bring an action under a contract, it is sufficient that the promisor must have understood that the promisee had such intent. (Cf. Rest., Contracts, § 133, subds. 1(a) and 1(b); 4 Corbin on Contracts (1951) pp. 16–18; 2 Williston on Contracts (3rd ed. 1959) pp. 836–839). No specific manifestation by the promisor of an intent to benefit the third person is required. The language relied on by defendant is disapproved to the extent that it is inconsistent with these views.

We conclude that intended beneficiaries of a will who lose their testamentary rights because of failure of the attorney who drew the will to properly fulfill his obligations under his contract with the testator may recover as third-party beneficiaries.

However, an attorney is not liable either to his client or to a beneficiary under a will for errors of the kind alleged in the first and second causes of action.

The general rule with respect to the liability of an attorney for failure to properly perform his duties to his client is that the attorney, by accepting employment to give legal advice or to render other legal services, impliedly agrees to use such skill, prudence, and diligence as lawyers of ordinary skill and capacity commonly possess and exercise in the performance of the tasks which they undertake. *Estate of Kruger*, 130 Cal. 621, 626, 63 P. 31; *Moser v. Western Harness Racing Ass'n*, 89 Cal.App.2d 1, 7, 200 P.2d 7; *Armstrong v. Adams*, 102 Cal.App. 677, 684, 283 P. 871; see Wade, The Attorney's Liability for Negligence (1959) 12 Vanderbilt Law Rev. 755, 762–765; 5 Am.Jur. 336. The attorney is not liable for every mistake he may make in his practice; he is not, in the absence of an express agreement, an insurer of the soundness of his opinions or of the validity of an instrument that he is engaged to draft; and he is not liable for being in error as to a question of law on which reasonable doubt may be entertained by well-informed lawyers. *See Lally v. Kuster*, 177 Cal. 783, 786, 171 P. 961; *Savings Bank v. Ward*, 100 U.S. 195, 198, 25 L.Ed. 621; 5 Am.Jur. 335; 7 C.J.S. Attorney and Client § 143, p. 980. These principles are equally applicable whether the plaintiff's claim is based on tort or breach of contract.

The complaint, as we have seen, alleges that defendant drafted the will in such a manner that the trust was invalid because it violated the rules relating to perpetuities and restraints on alienation. These closely akin subjects have long perplexed the courts and the bar. Professor Gray, a leading authority in the field, stated: "There is something in the subject which seems to facilitate error. Perhaps it is because the mode of reasoning is unlike that with which lawyers are most familiar. * * * A long list might be formed of the demonstrable blunders with regard to its questions made by eminent men, blunders which they themselves have been sometimes the first to acknowledge; and there are few lawyers of any practice in drawing wills and settlements who have not at some time either fallen into the net which the Rule spreads for the unwary, or at least shuddered to think how narrowly they have escaped it." Gray, The Rule Against Perpetuities (4th ed. 1942) p. xi; see also Leach, Perpetuities Legislation (1954) 67 Harv.L.Rev. 1349 (describing the rule as a "technicality-ridden legal nightmare" and a "dangerous instrumentality in the hands of most members of the bar"). Of the California law on perpetuities and restraints it has been said that few, if any, areas of the law have been fraught with more confusion or concealed more traps for the unwary draftsman; that members of the bar, probate courts, and title insurance companies make errors in these matters; that the code provisions adopted in 1872 created a situation worse than if the matter had been left to the common law, and that the legislation adopted in 1951 (under which the will involved here was drawn), despite the best of intentions, added rurther complexities. (See 38 Cal.Jur.2d 443; Coil, Perpetuities and Restraints; A Needed Reform (1955) 30 State Bar J. 87, 88–90.)

In view of the state of the law relating to perpetuities and restraints on alienation and the nature of the error, if any, assertedly made by defendant in preparing the instrument, it would not be proper to hold that defendant failed to use such skill, prudence, and diligence as lawyers of ordinary skill and capacity commonly exercise. The provision of the will quoted in the complaint, namely, that the trust was to terminate five years after the order of the probate court distributing the property to the trustee, could cause the trust to be invalid only because of the remote possibility that the order of distribution would be delayed for a period longer than a life in being at the creation of the interest plus 16 years (the 21-year statutory period less the five years specified in the will). Although it has been held that a possibility of this type could result in invalidity of a bequest (Estate of Johnston, 47 Cal.2d 265, 269–270, 303 P.2d 1; Estate of Campbell, 28 Cal.App.2d 102, 103 et seq., 82 P.2d 22), the possible occurrence of such a delay was so remote and unlikely that an attorney of ordinary skill acting under the same circumstances might well have "fallen into the net which the Rule spreads for the unwary" and failed to recognize the danger. We need not decide whether the trust provision of the will was actually invalid or whether, as defendant asserts, the complaint fails to allege facts necessary to enable such a determination, because we have concluded that in any event an error of the type relied on by plaintiffs does not show negligence or breach of contract on the part of defendant. It is apparent that plaintiffs have not stated and cannot state causes of action with respect to the first two counts, and the trial court did not abuse its discretion in denying leave to amend as to these counts.

. . .

The judgment is affirmed.

Notes

1. *California's role in developing the modern trend approach*: California courts have played an important role in the modern trend estate planning malpractice revolution. The traditional common law privity requirement made it impossible for intended beneficiaries to bring a claim against the testator's/transferor's attorney despite how blatant the attorney's error was and no matter how much they were damaged. With the Court's holding in *Lucas*, California became the first state to abolish the privity requirement, thereby permitting disappointed beneficiaries to bring a malpractice claim against the decedent's estate planning attorney. By the turn of the century only a handful of states still followed the traditional common law rule that a lack of privity was an absolute bar to intended beneficiaries being able to bring a suit against the drafter.

2. *The modern trend approach*: While almost all states have followed California's lead and have abolished the privity requirement as it relates to standing to bring a cause of action for malpractice against the decedent's attorney, not all jurisdictions agree on what should be the new test. The California approach may constitute the broadest approach. It grants standing to virtually all third parties (so long as they can show they were an "intended beneficiary") who have been injured as a result of an error committed by the decedent's attorney during the drafting phase.

Some states, however, have expressed concerns about the effect that such an approach would impose on the legal profession, particularly on estate planners. Some courts and scholars have expressed the concern that such an approach would expose estate planners to an increased risk of malpractice claims, thereby increasing the costs of their malpractice insurance, which in turn will increase the costs of practicing estate planning, which in turn will increase the costs of estate planning legal services, which in the long run will hurt the consumer and hurt society by increasing the number of people who die intestate—which will increase administrative costs associated with the probate process.

In response to these public policy concerns about the potential increased costs of administration associated with the approach California adopted, some courts have modified it slightly:

> An attorney preparing a will has a duty not only to the testator-client, but also to the testator's intended beneficiaries, who may maintain a legal malpractice action against the attorney on theories of either tort (negligence) or contract (third-party beneficiaries). However, liability to the testamentary beneficiary can arise only if, due to the attorney's professional negligence, the testamentary intent, *as expressed in the will,* is frustrated, and the beneficiary's legacy is lost or diminished as a direct result of that negligence.

DeMaris v. Asti, 426 So.2d 1153, 1154 (Fla. Dist. Ct. App. 1983) (emphasis in original; citations omitted); *see also Schreiner v. Scoville,* 410 N.W.2d 679, 683 (Iowa 1987); *Mieras v. DeBona,* 550 N.W.2d 202 (Mich. 1996). Some courts have de facto achieved the same result by adopting the third-party beneficiary approach and limiting standing to third parties where the intent to benefit the third party is "clear"—i.e., because the third party is named in the testamentary instrument. *See Guy v. Liederbach,* 459 A.2d 744, 746 (Pa. 1983); Fabian v. Lindsay, 765 S.E.2d 132 (S.C. 2014)

3. *Estate planning and tax liability*: To re-emphasize the point, an estate planner faces potential liability anytime he or she drafts an estate planning instrument and an intended beneficiary does not receive as much as he or she could have received without the attorney's drafting error. In the *Lucas* case, the intended beneficiaries claimed they were injured as a result of the language the attorney included in the will with respect to when the trust ended. The court ultimately held that the attorney was not liable essentially because the Rule Against Perpetuities is so difficult to understand that as a matter of law it is not malpractice to misunderstand it. That part of the court's opinion, however, has been criticized and other courts have declined to follow it (even if the Rule Against Perpetuities is that difficult, most estate planning instruments routinely include a "saving clause" that automatically terminates the interest before it violates the Rule Against Perpetuities just in case the attorney has made a mistake—so at a minimum the attorney should have been liable for failing to include a savings clause).

More important, however, is the big picture. Beneficiaries under an estate planning instrument typically receive their benefits only after taxes are paid. Accordingly, the size of their gift is subject to tax liability issues. If the decedent could have paid lower estate and gift taxes, the beneficiaries could have received more. If the failure to include appropriate tax avoidance clauses causes the estate or decedent to incur greater tax liability, the beneficiaries whose shares are reduced as a result of the increased taxes have a malpractice claim against the drafting attorney. Drafting estate planning documents without a comprehensive understanding of estate and gift tax issues is a risky business that is generally not recommended.

4. *Other wills and trusts "ethical" issues*: Throughout this book, we will see many other areas where ethical issues come to light in the context of an attorney's work in the area of wills and trusts (commonly referred to as "estate planning"). Some of the more common ethical issues that estate planners face include: (1) what is the attorney's role is assessing the requisite cognitive capacity of the client to execute the document; (2) can an attorney represent both spouses and draft the corresponding testamentary documents for both even though their dispositive wishes may be in conflict; and (3) can an attorney draft a document in which he or she is a beneficiary? These are but a handful of the interesting yet complex ethical issues that can arise in the estate planning field.

V. A Brief Word about Estate Planning

Notwithstanding the ever-present shroud of death in the study of wills and trusts, the subject can be a fascinating one. An interest in the subject often leads to thoughts of possibly practicing law in the area of estate planning. One's initial thoughts of such practice are, perhaps, morbid and not very exciting. This cannot be further from the truth. In the practice of estate planning, the lawyer and client typically have a very close and rewarding relationship. The client is meeting with *you*, typically unaccompanied by his or her representatives, entourage, or another attorney. It is just you and your client discussing "life-important" matters. The estate planning lawyer is one part lawyer, dealing with very complex legal matters, and one part counselor. The best estate planners not only have the necessary technical prowess, but they also have superb "people skills"—they are adept at listening and being sensitive to what are often very private and difficult real-life issues.

The personal and professional rewards from this area of practice can be greater than in many other areas of legal practice. Unfortunately, so can the pitfalls. There is a reason why malpractice insurance rates for attorneys practicing estate planning are among the highest in the legal profession. Simply put, it is a complex area of practice and it is exceptionally easy to make mistakes—far-reaching and very costly mistakes.

The core components of the material in this course are just the beginning of what is necessary to practice in the area of estate planning. An effective estate planning attorney, to avoid malpractice, requires more. An absolutely integral part of estate planning is an in-depth knowledge of federal estate and gift taxes (including the very draconian and complex subject of "generation skipping transfer taxes"), as well as federal income taxes (and any corresponding state and local taxes). The typical law school courses in *federal estate and gift taxation* and *income taxation* are good starting points. A *community property* class is also essential for an estate planning practice in California (or other community property states). If available, an estate planning course would be a great addition.

VI. But What if ...

The primary focus of any Wills, Trusts, and Estates course is on the different legal mechanisms that one can use to make a valid disposition of his or her assets through one or more of the methods listed in the directed distribution column. There is always the risk, however, that one will fail to make a valid directed disposition. What happens to one's property at death if there is no will (or will substitute, or other form of non-probate disposition)? Recent surveys indicate that approximately 50–60 percent of American adults do not have a will (or will substitute).[13] In addition, as you will see throughout this book, some of the people who think they have a will (or trust or other nonprobate instrument) will have it declared invalid (in whole or in part) for one reason or another.

What if there is no will (or other dispositive vehicle)? Who gets the decedent's assets?

---

13. A 2013 Harris Poll conducted for Rocket Lawyer had the number at 61 percent, while a 2007 Harris Poll conducted by Martindale-Hubbell/LexisNexis had the number at 55 percent.

Chapter 2

The California Intestate Scheme

I. Overview:
What Is an Intestate Scheme?

Who gets your property when you die? The prevailing answer is "whoever you wish." That answer (that the decedent's intent should control), however, assumes that the decedent has properly expressed his or her intent. What if the decedent did not properly express his or her intent? Should the probate court hold a hearing to determine the decedent's intent — or at least the decedent's *probable* intent? Most scholars agree that doing so would be prohibitively expensive and would open the probate process to the potential for fraud.

When a decedent fails to properly express his or her testamentary wishes with respect to the decedent's probate property, the property passes pursuant to the state's statutes of descent and distribution,[1] more commonly known as the state's "intestate succession laws" or the state's "intestate scheme" (the phrases, and derivatives thereof, are used interchangeably). A party dies intestate to the extent he or she dies with probate property that passes through the state's intestacy scheme. The most common example of this is when an individual dies without a will.[2]

---

1. The phrase "descent and distribution" implicitly recognizes that at early common law real property and personal property were treated differently. At death, the decedent's real property was said to descend to the appropriate takers under the canons of descent. Under the rule of primogeniture, real property descended to the decedent's sons, who inherited before — and to the exclusion of — the decedent's daughters; and if the decedent had more than one son, the real property passed to the eldest son. In contrast, at very early common law, the decedent's personal property was used by the administrator to pay the decedent's debts, and then the administrator kept any personal property left over. The English Statute of Distribution was adopted in 1670 to rein in the abuses of the administrators. The Statute of Distribution granted a right to family members to receive the personal property. The Statute of Distribution has been called the "father" — or perhaps more appropriately, the "grandfather" — of the typical American intestate scheme because the order of who takes under most state intestate statutes these days is very similar to the order under the Statute of Distribution. The principal change in the law is that that the canons of descent have been abolished — folded into the statute of distribution, in essence. Hence, today a decedent's real and personal property passes under the state's statute of descent and distribution, but that statute is based upon the English Statute of Distribution, not the canons of descent.

2. In later chapters we explore the application of intestate succession acting as a "backstop" default for other situations. These scenarios include, among others, a decedent dying with a will but a court finds it to be partially or wholly invalid, or where the testator has a valid will but thereafter he or she

Inasmuch as a state's intestate scheme controls in the event a decedent did not properly express his or her testamentary wishes, what should be the approach of a state's intestate succession laws? Should a state's intestate succession laws reflect the presumed intent of a typical decedent, or does dying without a will indicate that the decedent did not care who took his or her property, thereby leaving the state free to dispose of the decedent's property according to the state's preferred intent? If a decedent fails to properly express his or her intent, should that reduce the traditional notions of private property and support a greater role for the notion of communal property?

Lastly, from an estate planning perspective, starting with the intestate scheme is a bit odd. The job of an estate planner is to *avoid* intestacy. An estate planner's job is to ascertain the client's intent, properly draft the appropriate instruments to effectuate the client's intent (i.e., will, non-probate instrument, or some combination thereof), and ensure that the instruments are properly executed. Nevertheless, inasmuch as the intestate scheme is the default in the absence of proper estate planning, and inasmuch as approximately 50 percent of all decedents die intestate, the intestate scheme is the most logical place to start one's study of this area of law.

II. The California Intestate Scheme: Who Takes How Much[3]

Unlike most first-year courses, which are primarily common law-based (judge-made law), Wills, Trusts, and Estates consists primarily of statutory law. It is important to develop the skill of reading and construing statutes. Nowhere is this truer than in the intestate portion of the material. Read and outline the basic intestate scheme set forth in the following core provisions of the California Probate Code (hereinafter "CPC"[4]), sections 6400–6402 below. When reading them, focus on: (1) the order of takers (who takes when), and (2) how much each taker gets.

CPC § 6400. Property subject to the intestacy provisions[5]

Any part of the estate of a decedent not effectively disposed of by will passes to the decedent's heirs[6] as prescribed in this part.

---

marries, or enters into a domestic partnership, or has a child, and the testator dies without revising the will to reflect the change in family status.

3. This is merely the beginning of our trek through California's intestate succession landscape. This chapter focuses on who takes and how much they take. Chapter 3 focuses on who qualifies as an heir; i.e., who qualifies as a spouse, as a parent, as issue, etc.

4. CPC is a commonly used abbreviation for California Probate Code.

5. All statutory provisions will be California Codes unless indicated otherwise.

6. Terminology: Notice that, if used properly, the term "heirs" should be used to refer only to the people who have the right to share in the distribution of a decedent's intestate estate. If you keep that in mind, it should help you analyze the scope of other statutory sections. The terminology used in a statute can help you analyze the scope of the statute.

CPC § 6401. Surviving spouse's intestate share; calculating size of share

(a) As to community property, the intestate share of the surviving spouse is the one-half of the community property that belongs to the decedent under Section 100.

(b) As to quasi-community property, the intestate share of the surviving spouse is the one-half of the quasi-community property that belongs to the decedent under Section 101.

(c) As to separate property, the intestate share of the surviving spouse is as follows:

(1) The entire intestate estate if the decedent did not leave any surviving issue, parent, brother, sister, or issue of a deceased brother or sister.

(2) One-half of the intestate estate in the following cases:

(A) Where the decedent leaves only one child or the issue[7] of one deceased child.

(B) Where the decedent leaves no issue but leaves a parent or parents or their issue or the issue of either of them.

(3) One-third of the intestate estate in the following cases:

(A) Where the decedent leaves more than one child.

(B) Where the decedent leaves one child and the issue of one or more deceased children.

(C) Where the decedent leaves issue of two or more deceased children.

CPC § 6402. Distribution of intestate estate not passing to surviving spouse

Except as provided in Section 6402.5, the part of the intestate estate not passing to the surviving spouse under Section 6401, or the entire intestate estate if there is no surviving spouse, passes as follows:

(a) To the issue of the decedent, the issue taking equally if they are all of the same degree of kinship to the decedent, but if of unequal degree those of more remote degree take in the manner provided in Section 240.

(b) If there is no surviving issue, to the decedent's parent or parents equally.

(c) If there is no surviving issue or parent, to the issue of the parents or either of them, the issue taking equally if they are all of the same degree of kinship to the decedent, but if of unequal degree those of more remote degree take in the manner provided in Section 240.

(d) If there is no surviving issue, parent or issue of a parent, but the decedent is survived by one or more grandparents or issue of grandparents, to the grandparent or grandparents equally, or to the issue of those grandparents if there is no surviving grandparent, the issue taking equally if they are all of the same degree of kinship to the decedent, but if of unequal degree those of more remote degree take in the manner provided in Section 240.

(e) If there is no surviving issue, parent or issue of a parent, grandparent or issue of a grandparent, but the decedent is survived by the issue of a predeceased spouse, to

---

7. Terminology: What is the difference between "child" and "issue"? Notice the significance of that difference as used in this part of the intestate scheme.

that issue, the issue taking equally if they are all of the same degree of kinship to the predeceased spouse, but if of unequal degree those of more remote degree take in the manner provided in Section 240.

(f)   If there is no surviving issue, parent or issue of a parent, grandparent or issue of a grandparent, or issue of a predeceased spouse, but the decedent is survived by next of kin, to the next of kin in equal degree, but where there are two or more collateral kindred in equal degree who claim through different ancestors, those who claim through the nearest ancestor are preferred to those claiming through an ancestor more remote.

(g)   If there is no surviving next of kin of the decedent and no surviving issue of a predeceased spouse of the decedent, but the decedent is survived by the parents of a predeceased spouse or the issue of those parents, to the parent or parents equally, or to the issue of those parents if both are deceased, the issue taking equally if they are all of the same degree of kinship to the predeceased spouse, but if of unequal degree those of more remote degree take in the manner provided in Section 240.

III. The Decedent's Property

A. Overview

If the issue in the course is "who gets the decedent's property when he or she dies," one of the threshold questions is *how* does the decedent hold the property? We saw in the introduction that this is typically viewed in the light of whether it is probate property or non-probate property or, in the alternative, if it is a directed or non-directed disposition. Related to these issues, but distinct, is the question of the *scope* of the decedent's property. Is it the decedent's sole and separate property, or is it concurrently owned, and if so, how should such property be treated? As the Supreme Court of Washington stated in *Olver v. Fowler*, 168 P.3d 348, 356 (Wash. 2007):

> [The argument that the state's intestate scheme alone should control the distribution of the decedent's property] fails to take into account our basic framework for property distribution after death.... First, the decedent's property must be inventoried; a personal representative must determine what property belongs in the decedent's [probate] estate.... Only *after* the contents of the estate are established can the personal representative distribute the contents of the estate according to a valid will or the rules of intestacy. As the Court of Appeals aptly explained, "we do not look to the intestacy statutes to determine what the decedent owned."

1. Single Individual: Separate Property Assumption

From a Property law perspective, the starting assumption is that whatever property an *unmarried* individual owns is held as his or her separate property. Under the bundle of rights approach to property rights, the individual as sole owner has the right to possess the property, to use it, to exclude others from it, and the right to transfer it. The right to transfer is not only *inter vivos* (i.e., during one's life), but also at time of death. If the owner dies testate, he or she can devise the property to whomever he or she wishes.[8] If the owner dies intestate,[9] the property passes pursuant to the state's statute of descent and distribution (i.e., the state's intestate scheme) to the decedent's heirs. Where the property is the decedent's separate property, the starting assumption is that all of the assets in question will be distributed via intestate succession statutes unless the decedent has provided otherwise (i.e., has "directed" the disposition via a valid will or non-probate disposition). In the traditional law school view, this will all be part of the decedent's probate estate (and, additionally, will be controlled by the state's intestacy scheme) unless the decedent took the appropriate steps to hold it as a non-probate asset.

2. Concurrent Estates

In first-year property, you also learned that it is possible for an individual to hold property concurrently with another person or persons. The two most common examples of concurrently held property are: (1) joint tenancy, and (2) tenancy in common. With both forms of concurrent ownership, the parties own the property in whole and in share—each party has the right to possess and enjoy *all* the property in question (he or she owns it in whole), and each party has the right to transfer, *inter vivos*, his or her share. The key distinction between these two forms of concurrent ownership is that a joint tenancy includes the right of survivorship while the tenancy in common does not. The legal significance of that distinction, for purposes of the question "Who gets your property when you die?" is that under the right of survivorship when one joint tenant dies, his or her share is *extinguished* and the shares of the remaining joint tenants are re-calculated. Because the share is extinguished, none of the property goes into the decedent's probate estate. The decedent has no right to transfer the interest to another at death.

The process of each joint tenant's interest being extinguished upon his or her death continues until only one of the original joint tenants survives. At that point, he or she owns the property as his or her separate property. There is no other joint tenant, so the property is no longer concurrently owned. For example, A and B hold a parcel of real property as joint tenants. A dies and, by operation of law, A's share of the parcel immediately goes to B. If A has, for example, a will that states his or her interest in the parcel goes to C, the traditional and still general rule is that this "devise" is irrelevant—C gets no portion of the property as A's share of the joint tenancy property has already been extinguished (i.e., de facto passed to B). This is an example of a

---

8. Historically, the term "devise" applied only to *real* property being transferred under a will to a "devisee." A gift of *personal* property under a will is a "bequest" or a "legacy" to a "legatee." Increasingly, however, the term "devise" is being used to describe any gift under a will, be it real or personal property.

9. For purposes of this discussion, it might be easier to think of the decedent's intestate estate as referring to the property for which the decedent has not made a valid "directed" disposition—by will, or by non-probate disposition. Look back at our tables in the introduction as to when "intestate succession" statutes apply.

non-probate asset and can, alternatively, be viewed as a "directed" disposition (albeit semi-directed—A might have been able to select B as a cotenant in the joint tenancy, thus determining its ultimate disposition in the event that A dies before B; but, unlike a will or most trusts, the selection of B as a recipient is not as easily changed).

On the other hand, if the concurrent estate in question is a tenancy in common, there is no right of survivorship. If there is no right of survivorship, the share of each tenant in common is transferable not only *inter vivos*, but also at time of death. When one tenant in common dies, if he or she has not directed the disposition of such share via a will substitute, such as a trust, then his or her fractional share goes into his or her probate estate. If the deceased tenant died testate, the decedent can devise the property as he or she wishes. If the decedent died intestate, the property will pass pursuant to the state's intestate scheme.

The bottom line is that, if an individual is not married and he or she acquires a dollar, the default assumption is that the dollar is the individual's separate property. Absent affirmative steps to create a concurrent estate (a joint tenancy or a tenancy in common), the dollar is the individual's separate property with all rights to transfer it *inter vivos* or at death as the individual wishes.

What difference, if any, should it make if the individual is married at the time he or she acquires a dollar? Should/does marriage affect a spouse's property rights for purposes of analyzing the scope of the spouse's property upon termination of the marriage (death or divorce)? What is marriage? Is it solely an emotional joining together of two individuals, or is it also a property investment—an economic partnership? If it is a partnership, what is the scope of the partnership? Does it include all of their respective property, whenever and however acquired, or is it limited to a narrower set of assets?

B. Marriage and Property Rights

1. The Non-Community Property Approach

Most of the states in the United States take the view that marriage has no *immediate* effect on a spouse's property rights. Just as a dollar acquired before marriage is that individual's separate property, a dollar acquired after (during) marriage is that spouse's separate property. Marriage has no immediate effect on the classification of the asset when it is acquired, and at time of acquisition the other spouse acquires no interest in the property. That is *not* to say, however, that marriage has no effect upon a spouse's property rights, it simply has no *immediate* effect. In essence, non-community property states treat each spouse as a separate individual with separate property interests for purposes of allocating property interests to property acquired during the marriage.

2. The Community Property Approach

a. The Partnership Model

In contrast, community property states adopt the "partnership model" with respect to marriage. Under the partnership model, marriage has immediate and important consequences with respect to the scope of each spouse's property. Under the partnership model, property acquired as a result of the partnership should be held by the partnership as a form of concurrently owned property, not as separate property. What constitutes "property acquired as a result of the marital partnership" varies from community property jurisdiction to community property jurisdiction. In addition, while historically community property was limited to spouses (which historically was limited to heterosexual couples), community property rights are increasingly being extended to same-sex couples in a legally recognized relationship (marriage, registered domestic partnership, or civil union, depending on the jurisdiction).[10]

California follows the community property approach to marital property. California's approach to community property and separate property is set forth in the California Family Code and is the focus of the Community Property class. Obviously a detailed examination of community property is beyond the scope of this material, but a brief overview is necessary to help you understand what constitutes the scope of the decedent's property if the decedent is married (including same-sex marriages) or in a legally recognized "domestic partnership." Section 760 of the California Family Code states: "Except as otherwise provided by statute, all property, real or personal, wherever situated, acquired by a married person during the marriage while domiciled in this state is community property." Section 770 of the California Family Code, however, provides: "Separate property of a married person includes all of the following: (1) All property owned by the person before marriage. (2) All property acquired by the person after marriage by gift, bequest, devise [under a will], or descent [under the intestate scheme]...."[11] The combined effect of the two sections is to create a general presumption that any property acquired during marriage by either spouse, other than by gift, devise (under the terms of a will), or inheritance (under the intestate scheme), is community property that is owned by the community and held in undivided equal shares (50-50) by the parties.[12]

b. The Classification Process

The process of classifying property as either separate or community property is called the characterization of the property. Property must be characterized as community property or separate property to determine the rights and liabilities of the parties with respect to a particular asset, and is particularly important with respect to the treatment of the asset at death or divorce of the parties. While there are a number of variables that can affect the characterization of an asset, the three most im-

---

10. The inheritance rights of same-sex couples are examined in greater detail in Chapter 3.

11. California Family Code (§ 770, subd. (a).)

12. This general presumption can be rebutted, however, by a number of other doctrines and special presumptions. A common example of this is the doctrine of tracing. Under tracing, the general presumption of community property can be rebutted if the funds used to acquire the asset were separate property funds. The details of tracing, and the other doctrines and special presumptions that can rebut the general presumption of community property, are best left to the Community Property class.

portant factors are: (1) the time of acquisition, (2) the various presumptions that can apply to the acquisition of an asset, and (3) various means of rebutting such presumptions, including whether the party or parties have validly changed ("transmuted") the characterization of the property in question.

Analytically, the threshold question in the characterization process is *"When* was the property acquired?" "The character of the property as separate or community is fixed as of the time it is acquired; and the character so fixed continues until it is changed in some manner recognized by law, as by agreement of the parties."[13] If the asset was acquired during the marriage or registered domestic partnership, the general presumption of community property arises unless the asset was acquired by gift, devise, or via intestacy.

Community property is a fascinating area of law that is complex enough to warrant its own course. The coverage of community property in this class is intended to give you just enough understanding of the basics to understand the most common overlaps between the two areas of law. For purposes of this course, unless your professor tells you otherwise, assume that the initial characterization of the property in question is also the final characterization for death purposes (with the exception of quasi-community property, covered later). A student interested in estate planning as a career would be well advised to take a community property class.

c. Treatment at Death

Community property is a form of marital concurrent ownership. If it helps, think of community property as a concurrent estate where both spouses own the property equally, 50-50. In that respect, it is similar to the concurrent estates you studied in your first-year Property class: joint tenancy and tenancy in common. At time of death, however, community property is more like tenancy in common because there is no right of survivorship.[14] The moment one spouse dies, the deceased spouse's half-interest in each community property asset goes into probate (assuming it has not been put into a valid non-probate arrangement). The surviving spouse holds his or her half-interest in each community property asset as his or her separate property (separate because there is no longer a community—the other spouse is dead). The default assumption and general rule is that the deceased spouse's half-interest in each community property asset is a probate asset.[15]

---

13. Mears v. Mears, 180 Cal. App. 2d 484 (Ct. App. 1960).

14. California Family Code § 682.5 provides for a hybrid form of community property: "Community Property with Right of Survivorship." This is, essentially, a marriage of community property and joint tenancy. It acts like joint tenancy vis-à-vis the right of survivorship, but retains a "community property" character for certain advantageous federal income tax attributes.

15. Although for probate administration purposes California has a special rule that permits universal succession under certain circumstances, that doctrine—like most of probate administration—is beyond the scope of this course.

IV. The Mechanics of the California Intestate Scheme

Above we asked you to read and outline the core provisions of the California intestate scheme, sections 6400–6402, focusing on: (1) the order of takers, and (2) the formula for determining how much each party takes. Use your outline to analyze the following problems.

A. Calculating the Share of the Surviving Spouse

Problems

Hector and Wilma, a married couple, own the following assets:

A.   Greenacre, worth $400,000, which was transferred "to Hector and Wilma as joint tenants with right of survivorship and not as tenants in common."

B.   Hector has $2,000 worth of miscellaneous tangible personal property that he acquired before they were married.

C.   Hector has $10,000 from earnings acquired during the marriage in a certificate of deposit in his name alone.

D.   Hector inherited $400,000 in Amgen stock after he married Wilma.

E.   Wilma has $15,000 worth of miscellaneous tangible personal property that she acquired before they were married.

F.   Wilma has $100,000 from earnings acquired during the marriage in a checking account in her name alone.

G.   Wilma inherited $100,000 in IBM stock after she married Hector.

Who takes Hector's property in the following scenarios?

1.   Hector dies intestate, survived by Wilma, their son, Adan, Adan's two children, Beth and Carl, and Hector's father, Fernando. Who takes Hector's property? How much do they receive?

2.   Hector dies intestate, survived by Wilma, Beth, and Carl, the two children of their predeceased son, Adan (who died with a will giving all of his property to his alma mater, UC-Nirvana), and Hector's mother, Maude. Who takes Hector's property? How much do they receive?

3.   Hector dies intestate, survived by Wilma, their two children, Adan and Yolanda, Adan's two children, Beth and Carl, Yolanda's child, Deirdre, and Hector's father, Fernando. Who takes Hector's property? How much do they receive?

4.   Hector dies intestate, survived by his wife, Wilma, and his sister, Sally. Who takes Hector's property? How much do they receive?

5.   Hector and Wilma never married—why ruin a good relationship with marriage—they just lived together. Hector dies intestate, survived by Wilma, his

son, Adan, Adan's two children, Beth and Carl, and Hector's father, Fernando (*in analyzing the scope of Hector's property, replace all references to their "marriage" in the above fact pattern with references to their "moving-in together" because in this variation they never married—see why that makes a difference in his property?*). Who takes Hector's property? How much do they receive?

6. New couple: Harry and Wanda. Harry and Wanda are married with two children, Ali and Ben. Harry and Wanda own a residence in their joint names as true joint tenants and not as community property. Harry owns stock in X Corporation, worth $10,000, that he acquired before they were married. Harry and Wanda also purchased a boat worth $20,000 with Wanda's earnings acquired during the marriage. Harry dies intestate. What is Harry's property, and how will it most likely be distributed?

B. The In-Law Inheritance Statute

While the base California intestate distribution scheme (CPC sections 6400–6402) is similar to that of other community property states, California has a unique statutory provision, section 6402.5, that needs to be overlapped on the base intestate scheme. Commonly known among practitioners as the "in-law" inheritance statute, section 6402.5 can yield some very odd results. It provides that, under certain circumstances, when a surviving spouse dies, rather than giving all of a decedent's property to his or her relatives, some of the decedent's property should go to his or her former spouse's family (i.e., the decedent's former in-laws). After reading the statute, see if you can determine: (1) when the "in-law" inheritance statute applies; (2) what property is subject to recapture for the in-laws; and (3) who is to receive the recaptured property.

CPC § 6402.5. Portion of decedent's estate attributable to decedent's predeceased spouse; distribution to predeceased spouse's relatives

(a) For purposes of distributing real property under this section if the decedent had a predeceased spouse who died not more than 15 years before the decedent and there is no surviving spouse or issue of the decedent, the portion of the decedent's estate attributable to the decedent's predeceased spouse passes as follows:

  (1) If the decedent is survived by issue of the predeceased spouse, to the surviving issue of the predeceased spouse; ... [the issue take equally as provided in Section 240].

  (2) If there is no surviving issue of the predeceased spouse but the decedent is survived by a parent or parents of the predeceased spouse, to the predeceased spouse's surviving parent or parents equally.

  (3) If there is no surviving issue or parent of the predeceased spouse but the decedent is survived by issue of a parent of the predeceased spouse, to the surviving issue of the parents of the predeceased spouse or either of them, ... [the issue take equally as provided in Section 240].

(4) If the decedent is not survived by issue, parent, or issue of a parent of the prede-ceased spouse, to the next of kin of the decedent in the manner provided in Sec-tion 6402.

...

(b) For purposes of distributing personal property under this section if the decedent had a predeceased spouse who died not more than five years before the decedent, and there is no surviving spouse or issue of the decedent, the portion of the decedent's estate attributable to the decedent's predeceased spouse passes as follows:

(1) If the decedent is survived by issue of the predeceased spouse, to the surviving issue of the predeceased spouse; ... [the issue take equally as provided in Section 240].

(2) If there is no surviving issue of the predeceased spouse but the decedent is sur-vived by a parent or parents of the predeceased spouse, to the predeceased spouse's surviving parent or parents equally.

(3) If there is no surviving issue or parent of the predeceased spouse but the decedent is survived by issue of a parent of the predeceased spouse, to the surviving issue of the parents of the predeceased spouse or either of them, the issue ... [take equally as provided in Section 240].

(4) If the decedent is not survived by issue, parent, or issue of a parent of the prede-ceased spouse, to the next of kin of the decedent in the manner provided in Sec-tion 6402.

...

(e) For the purposes of disposing of property pursuant to subdivision (b), "personal property" means that personal property in which there is a written record of title or ownership and the value of which in the aggregate is ten thousand dollars ($10,000) or more.

(f) For the purposes of this section, the "portion of the decedent's estate attributable to the decedent's predeceased spouse" means all of the following property in the dece-dent's estate:

(1) One half of the community property in existence at the time of the death of the predeceased spouse.

(2) One half of any community property, in existence at the time of death of the pre-deceased spouse, which was given to the decedent by the predeceased spouse by way of gift, descent, or devise.

(3) That portion of any community property in which the predeceased spouse had any incident of ownership and which vested in the decedent upon the death of the predeceased spouse by right of survivorship.

(4) Any separate property of the predeceased spouse which came to the decedent by gift, descent, or devise of the predeceased spouse or which vested in the decedent upon the death of the predeceased spouse by right of survivorship.

(g) For the purposes of this section, quasi-community property shall be treated the same as community property.

Having outlined and analyzed the base California intestate scheme (CPC sections 6400–6402), try to figure out how Section 6402.5 fits into the overall intestate scheme. First, conceptually, what was the California legislature trying to achieve when it adopted Section 6402.5? What is the purpose of the statute? Once you understand the doctrine conceptually, shift your focus to the mechanics of the doctrine. *When* does Section 6402.5 apply? What facts must be present for it to apply? If it applies, what does Section 6402.5 say the probate court should do? The "in-law inheritance" moniker is self-describing, but why do some also use the term "the recapture doctrine" with respect to Section 6402.5? What is it trying to recapture, and why?

At first blush, most students find the in-law inheritance statute strange and unusual (which it is). It is highly unlikely that you will ever encounter a will that makes such gifts to former in-laws. If that is true, why would the legislature include such a provision in the intestate scheme if it does not reflect the intent of a typical decedent? To the extent it is part of the California intestate scheme but it arguably does not reflect the intent of a typical decedent, it is another example of why "directing" where one's property should go at time of death can be so important.

Problems

Assume the same married couple, Hector and Wilma, from the Problem set above (see pages 33–34). Neither of them has any children or issue (what is the difference?) and there has been no change in the assets between their respective deaths.[16] Who takes their property in the following scenarios?

1. Hector dies intestate, survived by his father, Fernando. Twenty years later, Wilma dies intestate, survived by her mother, Mia. (Hector's father, Fernando, is still alive.) Who takes their assets?

2. Hector dies intestate, survived by his father, Fernando. Ten years later, Wilma dies intestate, survived by her mother, Mia. (Hector's father, Fernando, is still alive.) Who takes their assets?

3. Hector dies intestate, survived by his father, Fernando. Three years later, Wilma dies intestate, survived by her mother, Mia. Who takes their assets?

4. In addition to the property in the problem above, assume Hector inherits a farm worth $1 million, which he puts in a trust for his benefit while he is alive. Upon his death, all of the trust property is to be distributed outright to Wilma. In addition, assume Hector executes a will that gives all of his probate property to Wilma. Thereafter, Hector dies, survived by his father, Fernando, and Wilma. Three years later, Wilma dies intestate, survived by her mother, Mia. (Hector's father, Fernando, is still alive.) How will their assets be distributed?

---

16. Granted, that is a very artificial assumption. However, such assumptions are common in law school (and on exams) to limit the nature of the issue(s) that can be examined in the limited time in the class. In the real world, where the assets change in nature, it can raise messy issues of tracing that are beyond the scope of this course.

5. How would your answers change, if at all, in problems 1–4 if Wilma dies testate with a will leaving all of her property to her mother, Mia?

6. How would your answers change, if at all, in problems 1–4 if Wilma dies intestate, but she is survived by a son, Adan?

7. Hector dies intestate, survived by his father, Fernando. Three *days* later, Wilma dies intestate, survived by her mother, Mia. Who takes their assets? Before you answer that question, you might want to consider the survival material below. Is survival purely a question of fact, or is it also a question of law?

Note

Assume that we have a situation where California Probate Code section 6402.5 applies, and we have identified property that is going back to the decedent's former in-laws. What, exactly, is "the property" to be distributed pursuant to this section? Say that an affected asset is stock that has appreciated significantly during the period between the two spouses' deaths — is the entire appreciated value recalled by this statute? Or is it the value of the stock at the first spouse's death? What if the asset is a business and, during the period between the two spouses' deaths, it has appreciated significantly in value — what goes back to the former in-laws? The affected asset is a house with a mortgage loan, and during the intervening years between the two spouses' deaths, the surviving spouse used his or her wages to make payments on the mortgage, reducing its balance (and, at the same time, the house has appreciated in value) — what is pulled back by section 6402.5? What if the asset coming from a predeceased spouse is gone — it has been sold and converted to cash or the proceeds have been used to buy another asset?[17]

V. The Survival Requirement

Should a party have to survive a decedent to take property from the decedent?[18] It is generally assumed that a decedent does not want his or her probate property to go to somebody who is already dead (i.e., one who has predeceased the decedent). Accordingly, there is a general survival requirement placed on any party who claims the right to receive some of the decedent's property.[19] But saying a party must "survive"

---

17. For a riveting analysis of these issues, see: Robert G. Popovich, *It's All Mine — Or at Least Part of It Is: A California Look at Property Apportionment Between the Families of an Intestate and an Intestate's Predeceased Spouse*, 16 Pepp. L. Rev. 3 (1989).

18. If not, the property received by the predeceased party would pass into his or her estate and pass accordingly. If the predeceased party died intestate, it would pass to his or her heirs. If the predeceased party died testate, the property would fall to the residuary clause in the will and pass pursuant to it.

19. Whether the survival requirement should apply to all non-probate transfers as well is not as well accepted. In practice, survivorship requirements are often controlled by the non-probate instrument. For example, a well-drafted *inter vivos* trust (basically, a will substitute) will, undoubtedly, contain some form of survivorship requirement clause.

the decedent begs the question: what does it mean to "survive" the decedent? What should be the survival requirement?

At early common law, before the advent of planes, trains, and automobiles, the question of survival was fairly straightforward, and rarely was at issue. Either the party survived the decedent or the party did not. It was typically a question of pure fact that was fairly easy to analyze. One claiming the right to share in the distribution of the decedent's estate had the burden of proving that he or she "survived" the decedent. Because probate is a matter of civil law, the default burden of proof applied: preponderance of the evidence. With respect to how long one had to survive the decedent, a millisecond technically was enough to support a claim of survival (if one could prove that).

The development of planes, trains, and automobiles, however, led to an increasing number of scenarios involving simultaneous or near-simultaneous deaths between family members. As tragic as such scenarios may be, legally they create a perverse economic incentive for surviving family members to sue each other rather than console each other. In *Unum Life Insurance Company of America v. Craig*, 200 Ariz. 327, 26 P.3d 510 (2001), William and Diane Craig, husband and wife, were involved in a head-on automobile accident. When the responding officer first approached the car, "he was unable to detect any pulse or respiration from William, but heard gurgling and moaning noises from Diane."[20] After securing the accident scene, the officer returned to the car but was unable to detect any signs of life from Diane. The following day, the Medical Examiner who examined the bodies indicated that both parties died at 3:35 p.m., the exact same time. William had two life insurance policies that totaled more than $650,000.00, both of which named Diane as the beneficiary. William was survived by a daughter from a prior marriage, and Diane was survived by two children from a prior marriage. Instead of the respective families consoling each other over the loss of their respective parents, the children ended up fighting in court over whether there was sufficient evidence that Diane survived William. The court noted that too often the outcome of such cases turned:

> ... on fortuitous survival by a moment or two, testified to by medical experts using sometimes gruesome medical evidence to support non-simultaneous death claims. See, e.g., *In re Bucci's Will*, 57 Misc.2d 1001, 293 N.Y.S.2d 994 (Surr.Ct.1968) (husband and wife found dead when removed from wreckage of small airplane, which crashed and burned after colliding with a large airplane; existence of carbon monoxide in wife's blood was found sufficient evidence to establish wife's survival of husband, whose skull was fractured and in whose blood no carbon monoxide was found); *In re Estate of Rowley*, 257 Cal.App.2d 324, 65 Cal.Rptr. 139 (1967) (period of claimed survivorship was 1/150,000 of a second); ...

See *Unum Life Insurance Company of America v. Craig*, 200 Ariz. at 331.

---

20. Unum Life Ins. Co. of Am. v. Craig, 200 Ariz. 327, 328, 26 P.3d 510, 511 (2001).

To counter such messy litigation, the Uniform Law Commission addressed the issue in the Uniform Simultaneous Death Act ("USDA") and, later, the Uniform Probate Code (hereinafter "UPC").[21] Unfortunately, the Uniform Law Commission's response was far from uniform. The Commission has struggled with the appropriate *scope* of the response, wrestling with the following queries: (1) should the enhanced survival requirement apply only to probate intestate property, to all probate property, or to all probate and non-probate property? (2) what should be the survival requirement (and should it be the same for all types of property or should it vary based on the type of property)? and (3) what should be the burden of proof? As a result, a series of responses/approaches emerged over several decades. The first approach applied only to life insurance policies where there was no sufficient evidence that the beneficiary survived the decedent.[22] The second approach applied to all probate intestate property, but not to any directed dispositions (wills or non-probate instruments) and required the heir to prove by clear and convincing evidence that he or she survived the decedent by 120 hours.[23] The third approach applied the clear and convincing evidence standard and 120-hour survival requirement to both intestacy and any "governing instrument," including wills, deeds, trusts, and insurance policies.[24] Depending on when a state's legislature decided to address the issue, different states have adopted different approaches. One must read each state's simultaneous death statutes carefully to see which approach the state has adopted—or if the state has created its own approach.

While the Uniform Law Commission has settled on the 120 hours survival requirement to minimize the incentive for litigation, it is not uncommon for a well-drafted will to impose a much longer survival requirement: six months or longer. The longer survival requirement is not only to reduce the risk of simultaneous death litigation, but also to reduce the risk of double probate and promote the testator's intent. A testator's typical wish and assumption is that a beneficiary will be alive when his or her property is distributed so that the beneficiary will be able to use and enjoy the property. Most testators would *not* want a beneficiary to survive just long only enough to qualify to receive the property but die before distribution. In such cases, de facto all the beneficiary received was the power to redistribute the property to someone else at his or her death. If given the choice, most testators would prefer to be in charge of directing distribution should a beneficiary survive the testator for only a short period. The beneficiary should be alive at time of distribution of the asset or the asset will simply pass from the testator's probate estate to the beneficiary's probate estate, thereby frustrating testator's intent and incurring all the expenses and hassles of double probate. Accordingly, the longer survival requirement is fairly common in most well-drafted estate planning instruments. Should a similar, "longer" survival requirement be the default statutory requirement?

---

21. UPC is a commonly used abbreviation for Uniform Probate Code.
22. Unif. Simultaneous Death Act § 5 (1940).
23. UPC § 2-104 cmt. (amended 1990), 8 (pt. I) U.L.A. 84 (1998).
24. *See* UPC § 1-201(19) (revised 1990, amended 1991, 1993, and 1998), 2-701 (amended 1991), 2-702 (amended 1991 and 1993), 8 (pt. I) U.L.A. 35, 181–82 (1998 & Supp. 2001).

The practical effect of a survival requirement (either statutory or within the directed instrument) is that a party claiming a right to receive the property must prove that he or she not only *factually* survived the decedent, but also that he or she *legally* survived the decedent.

A. The California Survival Approach

The California statutes that address the question of survivorship are set forth below. In analyzing them, keep in mind the key variables: (1) the survival requirement; (2) the scope of the survival requirement (i.e., is it the same for all types of property — probate intestate, probate testate, and non-probate transfers?); and (3) the burden of proof.

CPC § 220. Disposition of property; insufficient evidence of survivorship

Except as otherwise provided in this chapter, if the title to property or the devolution of property depends upon priority of death and it cannot be established by clear and convincing evidence that one of the persons survived the other, the property of each person shall be administered or distributed, or otherwise dealt with, as if that person had survived the other.

CPC Section 6403. Failure to survive decedent by 120 hours; deemed predeceased

(a) A person who fails to survive the decedent by 120 hours is deemed to have predeceased the decedent for the purpose of intestate succession, and the heirs are determined accordingly. If it cannot be established by clear and convincing evidence that a person who would otherwise be an heir has survived the decedent by 120 hours, it is deemed that the person failed to survive for the required period. The requirement of this section that a person who survives the decedent must survive the decedent by 120 hours does not apply if the application of the 120 hour survival requirement would result in the escheat of property to the state.[25]

CPC § 21109. Transferees; failure to survive

(a) A transferee who fails to survive the transferor of an at-death transfer or until any future time required by the instrument does not take under the instrument.

(b) If it cannot be determined by clear and convincing evidence that the transferee survived until a future time required by the instrument, it is deemed that the transferee did not survive until the required future time.

CPC § 223. Joint tenants; "simultaneous death"

(a) As used in this section, "joint tenants" includes owners of property held under circumstances that entitled one or more to the whole of the property on the death of the other or others.

(b) If property is held by two joint tenants and both of them have died and it cannot be established by clear and convincing evidence that one survived the other, the property

---

25. The 120-hour survival requirement is also applicable to a California Statutory Will. *See* CPC § 6211.

held in joint tenancy shall be administered or distributed, or otherwise dealt with, one half as if one joint tenant had survived and one half as if the other joint tenant had survived.

(c) If property is held by more than two joint tenants and all of them have died and it cannot be established by clear and convincing evidence that any of them survived the others, the property held in joint tenancy shall be divided into as many portions as there are joint tenants and the share of each joint tenant shall be administered or distributed, or otherwise dealt with, as if that joint tenant had survived the other joint tenants.

CPC § 103. Community or quasi-community property; "simultaneous death"

... [I]f a husband and wife die leaving community or quasi-community property and it cannot be established by clear and convincing evidence that one spouse survived the other:

(a) One-half of the community property and one-half of the quasi-community property shall be administered or distributed, or otherwise dealt with, as if one spouse had survived and as if that half belonged to that spouse.

(b) The other half of the community property and the other half of the quasi-community property shall be administered or distributed, or otherwise dealt with, as if the other spouse had survived and as if that half belonged to that spouse.

Notes

1. *Scope*: Does the survival requirement apply only to the surviving spouse or to all takers under the California intestate scheme? Does it apply only to intestacy or does it apply to all probate property, testate and intestate? Does it apply only to probate property or does it apply to non-probate property as well?

2. *Questions*: How would the *Craig* case be decided using California law? If you think the outcome is unclear, why? What would the issue be?

In addition to the life insurance policy, assume William had inherited $1 million one year before his death, which he put into a certificate of deposit in his name alone. Assuming both William and Diane died intestate, how would the life insurance policy benefits and the $1 million be distributed under California law?

What if, instead of dying intestate, William died with a validly executed will that left all of his property to his loving wife, Diane (who died intestate)? How would the life insurance policy benefits and the $1 million be distributed under California law?

3. *Heir versus heir apparent; property interest versus expectancy*: One by-product of the survival requirement is that technically it is inappropriate to speak of one's heirs while one is still alive. We cannot determine who will qualify as one's heirs until the person dies because to qualify as an heir, the party claiming to be an heir must meet the survival requirement. Each of us has "heirs apparent" — our family members whom we assume will be our heirs because we assume they will survive us — but technically we cannot determine a person's heirs until that person dies.

Similarly, an heir apparent does not hold a property interest while the person in question is still alive because as long as the person is alive, the heir apparent's interest is not vested. An heir apparent holds an expectancy (the heir apparent "expects" to receive the inheritance, but there is no guarantee—it is not vested). An expectancy is *not* a property interest. Similarly, because a will is not effective until the testator dies, a beneficiary under a will does not hold a property interest. While some refer to a beneficiary's interest in a will as an expectancy (because of the analogous nature of the non-vested interest), technically the term should be used only in connection with an heir apparent.

Because an expectancy is not a property interest, the traditional common law rule was that expectancies are non-transferable. Over time, however, the courts of equity began to enforce contracts that purported to assign an expectancy as long as the contract was "fairly made and not against public policy." California recognizes the assignability of expectancies in equity. *Bridge v. Kedon*, 163 Cal. 493 (1912).

Problems

Return to Hector, Wilma, and their property (see Problems above, on pages 33 and 34).

1. Assume Hector dies intestate, survived by his father, Fernando, and Wilma. Three days later, Wilma dies intestate, survived by her mom, Mia. How will their assets be distributed?

2. Assume Hector and Wilma die in a plane crash. Their bodies are burned beyond recognition. Hector dies intestate, survived by his father, Fernando. Wilma dies intestate, survived by her mom, Mia. How will their assets be distributed?

3. In addition to the property in the problem above, assume Hector inherits $1 million, which he puts in a trust for his benefit while he is alive. Upon his death, all of the trust property is to be distributed outright to Wilma. In addition, assume Hector executes a will that gives all of his probate property to Wilma. Thereafter, Hector dies, survived by his father, Fernando, and Wilma. Three days later, Wilma dies intestate, survived by her mother, Mia. How will their assets be distributed?

4. Assume the same facts as Problem 3, except this time assume that Wilma dies testate, with a will leaving all of her property to her mother, Mia.

5. While out jogging, H is hit by a car and dies intestate. H and W were married. They owned a residence in their joint names as true joint tenants and not as community property.[26] H had stock in the X corporation worth $10,000, and W has stock in the Y corporation worth $10,000, both sets of stock being separate property. H and W owned a boat worth $20,000 as community property. Four days later, at the funeral, under the stress of the situation, W has a heart attack and dies. W also died intestate. H is survived by his father. W is survived by her mother. Under the California Probate Code, what does W's mom receive?

---

26. The "not as community property" portion is a reference to what is the sometimes tricky California issue of whether or not property in joint tenancy is, notwithstanding title, really community property. The nuances of this issue are best left to a community property class.

VI. Calculating the Share of the Issue

Most intestate schemes provide that if there is not a surviving spouse, or if the surviving spouse does not receive all of the decedent's property, the issue of the decedent take next, and they take "equally." Who qualifies as an issue will be explored in the next chapter. For now, focus on what it means to say that the issue will take "equally." At one end of the spectrum of familial scenarios, what it means to say that the issue take equally is as simple and straightforward as it sounds. At the other end of the spectrum of familial scenarios, what it means to say that the issue take equally is much more challenging.

A. The Simple End of the Spectrum: Children Only

Assume the decedent is survived by three children and no one else:

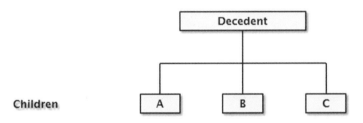

Analyzing what it means to say that the issue take equally is easy — each child receives one-third of the decedent's estate. They receive equal shares not only because it is assumed that the decedent loved each of his or her children equally, but also because they are of the same degree of relationship to the decedent.

1. Calculating One's Degree of Relationship

One's degree of relationship is calculated by counting the "steps" in the family tree between the parties in question. The simplest scenario for counting degrees of relationship is when the parties are in a direct line. Each step occurs when moving from one generation to the next in the family line. For example, counting down from a parent to a child is one step; hence, the parent-child relationship is a relationship within the first degree. The grandparent-grandchild relationship is a relationship within the second degree. In the simple example above, all the surviving issue are of the same degree of relationship to the decedent. There are no other issue, so all take equally, one-third each.

B. The First Variation: Children and Grandchildren

The first variation assumes the same family tree as above, only now assume A has one child, P; B has two children, Q and R; and C has three children, S, T, and U. Assume the decedent dies intestate. Who takes how much?

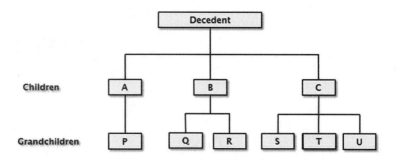

Assuming all of the children and grandchildren are alive, who takes if the decedent dies intestate? Despite the commonly used phrase "the issue take equally," that is, technically, not completely accurate. Once a lineal descendant of a decedent takes, the other issue of that taker do not. Phrased differently, where there are issue at different degrees of relationship to the decedent, those in the more remote degree of relationship will take only if their more immediate ancestors (in the closer degrees of relationship) do not (i.e., if the issue in the closer degree of relationship is dead or treated as if he or she were dead). Here, because A, B, and C are all alive, only A, B, and C will take from the decedent—one-third each—and P, Q, R, S, T, and U will not take at all.

C. Second Variation: Taking by Representation

The second variation assumes the same family tree as immediately above: A has one child, P; B has two children, Q and R; and C has three children, S, T, and U. Now assume A dies first, and then the decedent dies intestate. Who takes how much?

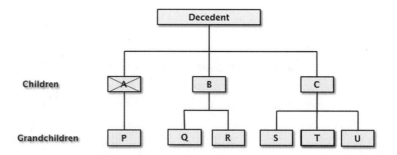

Under the intestate principle of taking by representation, where an issue who otherwise would take predeceases the decedent, if the predeceased party is survived by issue, the issue will represent the predeceased party and take in his or her place. Here, inasmuch as A stood to inherit one-third of the decedent's estate, P would take A's one-third under the principle of taking by representation. Q and R, and S, T, and U are not entitled to take under representation because B and C are alive and take. You may have noticed that the principle of taking by right of representation is the flip side of the principle above in that where there are issue of different degrees of relationship, once a member of a lineal line takes, the issue of that taker do not.

With those simple principles in mind, the legal issues that arise with respect to issue taking are easier to understand.

D. Third Variation: No Live Takers in the First Generation

The third variation assumes the same family tree as above: A has one child, P; B has two children, Q and R; and C has three children, S, T, and U. This time, assume all three children predecease the decedent. A, B, and C all die first, and then the decedent dies intestate. Who takes how much?

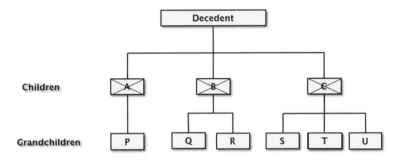

Where should the probate court make the first division in dividing up the decedent's estate? First generation always or first generation where there is a live taker?

Under the traditional or strict per stirpes approach, the first division of a decedent's estate is always at the first generation, regardless of whether anyone is alive at the generation. One share is given to each person alive, and consistent with the principle of taking by right of representation, one share is given to each party in that generation who is dead but survived by issue. The latter shares drop down by bloodline to his or her living issue in the more remote generations.

Under the per capita by representation approach (or, as it is often abbreviated, the per capita approach),[27] the first division of the decedent's property is made at the first generation where there is a live taker. At that generation, one share is given to each person who is alive, and consistent with the principle of taking by right of representation, one share is given to each party at that generation who is dead but survived by issue. The latter shares drop down by bloodline to his or her living issue in the more remote generations.

In the hypothetical above, how would the decedent's property be distributed under the per stirpes approach? How would the decedent's property be distributed under the per capita by representation approach?

---

27. Also known in some jurisdictions as the modern per stirpes because it is more of an American doctrine than the traditional per stirpes, which is more of an English doctrine.

E. Fourth Variation: The Shares for the Deceased Parties Survived by Issue

The fourth variation assumes the same family tree as above: A has one child, P; B has two children, Q and R; and C has three children, S, T, and U. This time, assume only two of the children predecease the decedent. A and C die first, and then the decedent dies intestate. Who takes how much?

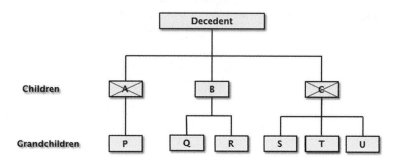

Under both the per stirpes and the per capita by representation approaches, the first division of the decedent's estate should occur at the first generation because there is a live taker at that generation, B. Wherever the first division is made, the formula for how many shares it should be divided into is the same: one share is given to each person alive at that generation, and, consistent with the principle of taking by right of representation, one share is given to each party at that generation who is dead but survived by issue. Here, the decedent's estate would be divided into three shares. B receives a share because B is alive. A and C both receive a share because, although each is dead, each is survived by issue. The question that arises next is: How should the shares for A and C be distributed? For centuries, there was general agreement that the property should be distributed by bloodline: that A's share should fall to A's issue, and that C's share should fall to C's issue. P would take A's one-third, and S, T, and U would take C's one-third. The problem with that approach is although P, S, T, and U are all related to the decedent equally, they are not taking equally. Would the decedent want all those who are equally related to take equally?

In 1990, the Uniform Probate Code embraced the latter position, adopting what is known as the per capita at each generation approach. The first two words signify that the approach adopts the per capita approach to where the first division should be made: at the first generation where there is a live taker. But the last three words of the approach signify that where there is a share for a deceased party that falls to a lower generation, the shares that fall should be "pooled" or combined and re-distributed equally among all the eligible takers at the next generation. In the hypothetical approach, how many shares are falling to a lower generation? Two: A's and C's shares. "Pool" or combine the two shares (1/3 + 1/3 = 2/3), and then divide that pooled amount equally among the eligible takers at the next generation. P, S, T, and U all are eligible takers (Q and R are not because their ancestor has taken a share).

Dividing the pooled shares equally among the eligible takers (2/3 divided by 4 = 2/12 = 1/6) means P, S, T, and U would each take 1/6, taking equally because each is of equal degree of relationship to the decedent.

Although the Uniform Probate Code has adopted the per capita at each generation approach to distributing a decedent's intestate property to his or her issue, the jurisdictions remain split, with some still following the traditional per stirpes approach, some following the per capita by representation approach, and some following the UPC and applying the per capita at each generation approach.

Notes and Problems

1. Assume the following family tree:

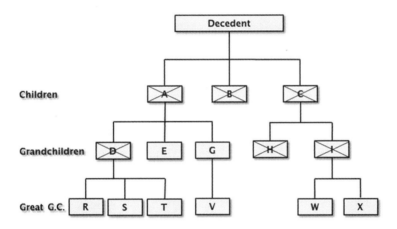

Assume A, B, C, D, H, and I die before the decedent, who dies intestate. Who takes how much of the decedent's property (a) under the per stirpes approach; (b) under the per capita by representation approach; and (c) under the per capita at each generation approach?

2. *California approach:* Which approach has California adopted with respect to how a decedent's intestate property shall be distributed among his or her issue?

CPC § 240. "Equal shares" defined

If a statute calls for property to be distributed or taken in the manner provided in this section, the property shall be divided into as many equal shares as there are living members of the nearest generation of issue then living and deceased members of that generation who leave issue then living, each living member of the nearest generation of issue then living receiving one share and the share of each deceased member of that generation who leaves issue then living being divided in the same manner among his or her then living issue.

CPC § 245. Application of Section 240; express contrary intent

(a) Where a will, trust, or other instrument calls for property to be distributed or taken "in the manner provided in Section 240 of the Probate Code," or where a will, trust, or other instrument that expresses no contrary intention provides for issue or descendants to take without specifying the manner, the property to be distributed shall be distributed in the manner provided in Section 240.

(b) Use of the following words without more, as applied to issue or descendants, is not an expression of contrary intention:

(1) "Per capita" when living members of the designated class are not all of the same generation.

(2) Contradictory wording, such as "per capita and per stirpes" or "equally and by right of representation."

CPC § 246. Distribution in manner provided in Section 246; per stirpes; drafting language

(a) Where a will, trust, or other instrument calls for property to be distributed or taken "in the manner provided in Section 246 of the Probate Code," the property to be distributed shall be divided into as many equal shares as there are living children of the designated ancestor, if any, and deceased children who leave issue then living. Each living child of the designated ancestor is allocated one share, and the share of each deceased child who leaves issue then living is divided in the same manner.

(b) Unless the will, trust, or other instrument expressly provides otherwise, if an instrument ... calls for property to be distributed or taken "per stirpes," "by representation," or "by right of representation," the property shall be distributed in the manner provided in subdivision (a).

…

CPC § 247. Distribution in manner provided in Section 247; per capita at each generation

(a) Where a will, trust, or other instrument calls for property to be distributed or taken "in the manner provided in Section 247 of the Probate Code," the property to be distributed shall be divided into as many equal shares as there are living members of the nearest generation of issue then living and deceased members of that generation who leave issue then living. Each living member of the nearest generation of issue then living is allocated one share, and the remaining shares, if any, are combined and then divided and allocated in the same manner among the remaining issue as if the issue already allocated a share and their descendants were then deceased.

(b) Unless the will, trust, or other instrument expressly provides otherwise, if an instrument calls for property to be distributed or taken "per capita at each generation," the property shall be distributed in the manner provided in subdivision (a).

…

F. Miscellaneous Doctrines Relating to Calculating Shares of Issue

1. Half-Bloods

Hal and Wi are married and have two children, Aki and Bob. Thereafter they divorce, Hal then marries Wendy, and they have a child, Carl. Many years later, after

Hal and Wi die, Aki dies intestate with no surviving spouse or issue. How will his assets be distributed?

The question inherent to the half-blood paradigm is: Where a decedent dies intestate survived by both whole-blooded siblings and half-blooded siblings, should the whole-blooded siblings receive a larger share of the decedent's property or should half-blooded siblings be entitled to an equal share?

CPC § 6406. Relatives of half-blood

> Except as provided in Section 6451 [the CPC section addressing the inheritance rights of adopted individuals], relatives of the halfblood inherit the same share they would inherit if they were of the whole blood.

2. Inheriting through Two Lines

How can one be related to the decedent through two lines? In the next chapter, you will learn that adoption creates a parent-child relationship with the same inheritance rights as a biologically created parent-child relationship. While the traditional rule is that adoption severed the child's relationship with his or her biological parents, that is not is not always the case today. If a young couple were to die, survived by a child, and one set of grandparents adopted the child, legally the child would be both a child and a grandchild of the adopting parents. Assuming one is related to the decedent through two lines, and there are other heirs in both lines (in this hypo, other surviving children and grandchildren of the adopting parent when he or she dies), should the heir be entitled to take both shares?

CPC § 6413. Relation through two lines of relationships; single share

> A person who is related to the decedent through two lines of relationship is entitled to only a single share based on the relationship which would entitle the person to the larger share.

VII. Calculating the Share of the Next of Kin

Under the California intestate scheme, the order of takers is: surviving spouse, issue, parents, issue of parents, grandparents, issue of grandparents, issue of a predeceased spouse, and then "next of kin." Like virtually all intestate schemes, the California intestate scheme starts with those family members assumed to be close to the decedent and moves outward to those family members more remotely associated with the decedent. The scheme starts with what most people would consider one's most immediate family: spouse and issue. Then it moves out to the decedent's second most immediate family: parents and issue of parents. Then it moves out to the next closest family: grandparents and issue of grandparents. The California intestate scheme then takes a turn that most do not—it includes non-blood-related relatives (other than a spouse): issue of a predeceased spouse (stepchildren). Putting aside that step, the California intestate scheme, in its own way, goes by family unit. Instead of continuing with this "parentelic"-like approach after grandparents and issue of grandparents, however, it switches to "next of kin." What is the "next of kin" approach, and how does one calculate who takes and their shares under it?

The following "Table of Consanguinity" may be helpful in determining who is an "heir." The table presents relationships from the perspective of the individual who is typically our decedent—indicated, on the chart, as the "Person." In addition to presenting a useful diagram of one's heirs, it also indicates "degrees of relationship" to the "person" (typically, the decedent). Plus, if you never understood who, exactly, is a "second cousin twice removed," the table of consanguinity will identify him or her.

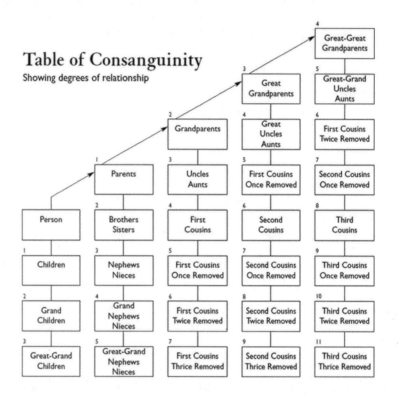

Table of Consanguinity
Showing degrees of relationship

At the national level, there are essentially three approaches to "next of kin." The first is called the parentelic approach. The parentelic approach is based upon the notion that as one ascends "up" a family tree, each ancestral parent is the head of a family line that linearly consists of their issue. If the decedent was married and had issue, the decedent and his or her spouse were the head of their family; but, as one moves out from there, each pair of ancestral parents (on both sides of the decedent) is the head of a parentelic line that includes their issue. The decedent's parents and their issue (the decedent's siblings) are the first parentelic line. The second parentelic line consists of the decedent's grandparents and their issue. The third parentelic line consists of the decedent's great-grandparents and their issue. And so on, line by line, moving out from the decedent with each new set of "parents" constituting the head of a new parentelic line. Under the parentelic approach to next of kin, one keeps going out parentelic line by parentelic line until one finds a live taker in that line. Once there is a live taker in a parentelic line, all of the decedent's intestate property is distributed to the eligible takers in that parentelic line. The parentelic approach is based upon the assumption that those family members in a closer parentelic line probably had a stronger relationship with the decedent compared to those in a more remote parentelic line. It is therefore presumed that the decedent would have wanted to leave his or her property to those collateral relatives with whom he had a closer relationship (those in the closer parentelic line).

The second approach to how to determine "next of kin" is based on the degree of relationship approach. Once one reaches the "next of kin" set of takers under the order of intestate takers, one simply counts the degree of relationship between the decedent and the heir to determine the party's degree of relationship. Calculating degree of relationship is not as easy in the next of kin context because it is typically not as linear in nature as it was above. Instead, calculating degree of relationship in the next of kin context is more collateral (or transverse). Calculating degree of relationship in this scenario is more complex because it involves counting in two directions, with the key being switching directions at the closest common ancestor. The closest common ancestor is the head of the parentelic line in which the party claiming he or she has a right to take falls. The closest common ancestor will always be some degree of "grandparent, or great-grandparent, or ... etc." You can count from either direction, but it might be easier to determine the party's degree of relationship by counting up from the decedent to the closest common ancestor, and then down from the closest common ancestor to the party claiming the right to take from the decedent. The degree of relationship approach is based upon the assumption that those family members with a lower degree of relationship (regardless of his or her parentelic line) probably had a stronger relationship with the decedent as compared to those with a more remote degree of relationship. It is therefore presumed that the decedent would have wanted to leave his or her property to those collateral relatives with whom he had a closer relationship (those in the closer degree of relationship with the decedent).

The third "next of kin" approach is a blending of the two just discussed. It is the degree of relationship approach with a parentelic tiebreaker. Under this approach, first calculate the degree of relationship with respect to all the parties claiming a right to take from the decedent's intestate estate. Those with the lower degree of relationship trump those with a higher degree of relationship. If, however, there is more than one party with the lowest degree of relationship, overlap the parentelic approach on the degree of relationship approach. If the parties with the lowest degree of relationship are in different parentelic lines, it is assumed that those in the closer parentelic line had a stronger relationship with the decedent as compared to those in the more remote parentelic lines, and it is presumed that the decedent would have wanted to leave his or her property to those collateral relatives with whom he had a closer relationship (those in the closer degree of relationship with the decedent and in the closer parentelic line).

A. The California Approach

Based on a general understanding of the three different approaches to determining who qualifies as a next-of-kin taker, you should be able to analyze which approach California has adopted. The California approach is set forth as part of the California's basic intestate statute, Probate Code Section 6402, subsection (f):

> If there is no surviving issue, parent or issue of a parent, grandparent or issue of a grandparent, or issue of a predeceased spouse, but the decedent is survived by next of kin, to the next of kin in equal degree, but where there are two or more collateral kindred in equal degree who claim through different ancestors, those who claim through the nearest ancestor are preferred to those claiming through an ancestor more remote.

Problem

Assume the following family tree (ancestors of the decedent). Assume also (sadly) that the only parties who are alive are V, W, X, and Z. Assume the decedent dies intestate. Who takes how much under the California approach?

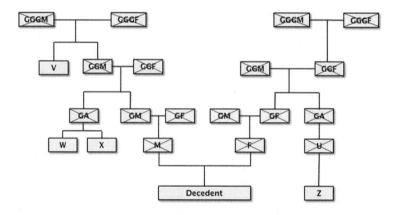

Note

While in theory it is possible to draft around the California approach to the next of kin doctrine, in practice that would be extremely unlikely. Most directed instruments assume that the property being given will be taken well before one were to reach the decedent's next of kin, and if a document were to cover such a contingency, it invariably would simply adopt the California approach. The likelihood that such a scenario would arise under a directed instrument is so unlikely it would hardly be worth the cost of educating the client as to his or her drafting options.

Chapter 3

Who Qualifies as an Heir under the California Intestate Scheme?

I. Overview

At the beginning of the last chapter, the material asserted that the logical answer to the question "Who gets your property when you die?" is "Whoever you wish." How does the typical intestate scheme relate to a decedent's intent? Obviously, it is not the decedent's express intent. Is it appropriate to say that it is the decedent's implied or assumed intent? Implied or assumed based on what? Is that an appropriate basis upon which to imply or assume a decedent's intent? Should the probate court permit evidence that the takers under the intestate scheme are inconsistent with the decedent's intent? Assuming, *arguendo*, that the probate court is not open to such evidence, is the intestate scheme based more on the decedent's intent or on one's legal status vis-à-vis the decedent (i.e., one's legal relationship to the decedent typically based on blood or marriage)?

Most scholars would agree that the more traditional approach to an intestate scheme focused more on status than intent. Is it possible to shift the focus more to intent and still keep the potential for fraud and the costs of administration low? "Legal scholars such as Sir Henry Maine and Emile Durkheim viewed legal development as a movement from the simple to the complex, from relationships of status ... to relationships based on contract [i.e., intent] or achievement."[1] In thinking about who qualifies as an heir under the California intestate scheme, is it based more on status or intent? Is the California approach defensible or outdated?

II. Spouse

The first "taker" under virtually all intestate schemes, including California's, is a "spouse." But that begs the question: who qualifies as a spouse?

---

1. Barbara A. Lavin-McEleney, *Criminality and Democracy in Ancient Systems of Law*, 44 Crim. L. Bull. 6 (2008) (footnotes omitted).

A. Traditional Marriage

Historically, California law defined "marriage" as "a personal relation arising out of a civil contract between a man and a woman, to which the consent of the parties capable of making that contract is necessary. Consent alone does not constitute marriage. Consent must be followed by the issuance of a license and solemnization as authorized by this division...." Cal. Fam. Code § 300 (2015). A legally married husband and wife are, of course, "spouses" for purposes of the California intestate succession statutes.

B. Same-Sex Couples

California, like much of the rest of the country, struggled with, debated, fought over, and litigated the issue of whether the institution of marriage (and/or marital status and spousal benefits) should be extended to same-sex couples.

1. Registered Domestic Partners

California first extended some, but not all, spousal rights and benefits to same-sex couples in 1999 when it permitted same-sex couples to register as domestic partners.[2] The right to inherit from each other under the intestate scheme was granted to domestic partners in 2003.[3] It was not until 2005, with the enactment of the California Domestic Partner Rights and Responsibilities Act, that registered domestic partners were granted *all* the same rights, duties and benefits as spouses under California law:

Family Code § 297.5. Domestic partners; Rights, Benefits, Duties, Status

(a) Registered domestic partners shall have the same rights, protections, and benefits, and shall be subject to the same responsibilities, obligations, and duties under law, whether they derive from statutes, administrative regulations, court rules, government policies, common law, or any other provisions or sources of law, as are granted to and imposed upon spouses.

The recognition of registered domestic partners and granting them spousal status did little, however, to stem the same-sex marriage movement.[4]

2. Same-Sex Marriage

In 2008, the California Supreme Court ruled that the statutory language limiting marriage to "a man and a woman" violated the privacy interests and equal protection

---

2. 1999 Cal. Legis. Serv. Ch. 588 (A.B. 26) (West).

3. 2003 Cal. Legis. Serv. Ch. 447 (A.B. 2216) (West).

4. While same-sex couples represent the majority of domestic partnerships in California, the law also grants domestic partnership status to certain heterosexual couples. For such couples, the law generally requires that one of the parties be at least 62 years of age. For various personal or religious reasons, a widow or widower may wish to have a committed relationship, but is uncomfortable with the thought of remarrying. California Family Code § 297 establishes the criteria required to create a valid domestic partnership.

rights of same-sex couples and therefore was unconstitutional. *In re Marriage Cases*, 76 Cal. Rptr. 3d 683, 183 P.3d 384 (2008). As a result, California began issuing marriage licenses to same-sex couples on June 16, 2008. In November 2008, California voters passed Proposition 8, which amended the California constitution to provide that "only marriage between a man and a woman is valid or recognized in California."[5] The passage of Proposition 8 halted California same-sex marriages on November 5, 2008. While the California Supreme Court upheld the constitutionality of Proposition 8 in 2009,[6] a subsequent federal district court case ruled the proposition unconstitutional and directed that the state officials who were named as defendants, and all persons who were under their control or supervision, be permanently enjoined from enforcing Proposition 8.[7] When the public officials who were enjoined declined to appeal the district court's opinion, the district court permitted Proposition 8's official proponents to intervene and defend it on appeal. The Ninth Circuit then affirmed the district court and held that Proposition 8 was unconstitutional. In *Hollingsworth v. Perry*, 133 S. Ct. 2652 (2013), the U.S. Supreme Court ruled that the petitioners did not have standing to pursue the appeal, thereby vacating the Ninth Circuit's opinion and reinstating the district court's opinion invalidating Proposition 8.

As a result of the above cases, same-sex marriage was once again legal in California. Accordingly, the state began issuing marriage licenses to same-sex couples on June 28, 2013. Therefore, for intestacy and other statutory purposes, a "spouse" is a "spouse" is a "spouse"—the distinction as to gender is, for the most part, irrelevant.[8]

Same-sex marriages became legal nationwide following the U.S. Supreme Court's June 26, 2015, decision in *Obergefell v. Hodges*, 135 S. Ct. 2584. The Supreme Court held that states' bans on same-sex marriages were unconstitutional, violating the Due Process and Equal Protection clauses of the Fourteenth Amendment.

Even though California, as well as the rest of the nation, now recognizes same-sex marriages, registered domestic partnerships still remain a legal option in California. Both registered domestic partners and same-sex spouses have full spousal status, including all spousal rights and benefits under the Probate Code.

C. Putative Spouses

Although the details are best left to the Family Law course, there are a surprising number of scenarios in which a couple might truly believe they are married, but for some reason their marriage is not valid.[9] If the marriage is not valid, the couple tech-

---

5. CAL. CONST. art. I, §7.5 (amended 2008).

6. Strauss v. Horton, 207 P.3d 48 (Cal. 2009).

7. Perry v. Schwarzenegger, 704 F. Supp. 2d 921, 1003 (N.D. Cal. 2010).

8. California also grants spousal status to same-sex couples who move to California who were legally married in another state or country. *See* California Family Code §308 (2015).

9. A marriage may be invalid for a number of reasons, including both technical, filing, logistics-related and, more seriously, invalid due to such matters as a bigamous marriage (often by accident). While we refer to the "couple" here, inferring that both parties thought that they were married, the

nically does not qualify as "spouses" in the true sense of the term. Nevertheless, the courts—and to a lesser degree the California legislature—have been moved by the equities of the situation to grant some benefits to the couple under the "putative spouse" doctrine:

Family Code § 2251. Status of putative spouse; division of quasi-marital property

(a) If a determination is made that a marriage is void or voidable and the court finds that either party or both parties believed in good faith that the marriage was valid, the court shall:

(1) Declare the party or parties to have the status of a putative spouse.

(2) If the division of property is in issue [for dissolution/divorce purposes] that property acquired during the union which would have been community property or quasi-community property if the union had not been void or voidable. This property is known as "quasi-marital property".

...

Note that the statutory putative spouse provision is limited to cases where the marriage ends in divorce. Nevertheless, the courts have extended the putative spouse doctrine to most time-of-death property transfer issues. In *Estate of Leslie*, 37 Cal. 3d 186, 689, P.2d 133, 207 Cal. Rptr. 561 (1984), the California Supreme Court ruled that where there is no competing legal spouse in the picture, a surviving putative spouse steps into the shoes of the legal spouse and receives the same legal rights and benefits of a surviving legal spouse, including the right to inherit the decedent's quasi-marital property and the right to inherit a share of the decedent's separate property.

Notes

1. *Bigamous putative spouse.* The basic putative spouse scenario for a typical wills and trusts course is simple, consisting of just one "marriage." While more complex familial situations involving "bigamous" fact patterns are best left to a proper Community Property class, they can generate fascinating life situations as well as competing intestacy claims.

A "successive bigamous" fact pattern was at play in *Estate of Hafner*, 184 Cal. App. 3d 1371, 229 Cal. Rptr. 676 (1986). Charles married Joan, but the couple later separated (without divorcing). When Charles subsequently "married" Helen, she had no idea that he was still married to Joan. When Charles died *intestate*, the issue was the characterization of the property acquired during this second "marriage" with Helen. Helen, deemed a putative spouse, correctly contended that *from her perspective*: (1) the property in question was quasi-marital property (essentially the same as community property; split 50-50 between the putative spouses); and (2) that as the surviving "spouse" she was entitled to Charles's one-half share (via intestacy), along with

---

concept of a "putative" spouse can refer to situations where only one "spouse" is "innocent" and the other knows the marriage is not valid. This latter situation is generally beyond the scope of this course and is typically covered in the Community Property course.

her one-half share; or 100% of the property. Joan, the surviving legal spouse, also correctly asserted that *from her perspective*: (1) the property in question was Charles's separate property (acquired after their separation); and (2) as the surviving legal "spouse" she and Charles's four children were entitled to receive intestate shares of one-third and two-thirds, respectively. With both "camps" claiming 100 percent of the property and both competitive claims in hopeless conflict, the court reverted to *principles of equity*, effectively giving each party one-half of what would have been their intestacy totals.

In contrast, a "concurrent bigamous" fact pattern was at play in *Estate of Vargas*, 36 Cal. App. 3d 714 (1974). Soon after Juan Vargas died intestate, it was discovered that he had been living a double life as a father and "husband" in two different families—at the same time, just 12 miles apart—for a staggering 24 years! The decedent's intestate property was acquired while "married" to both "spouses," with its proper classification as community property from the perspective of the legal spouse, Mildred, and quasi-marital property from the perspective of the putative spouse, Josephine. Both Mildred and Josephine, as legal and putative spouses, respectively, would have been entitled to their respective one-half share of the property (community and quasi-marital property) and, pursuant to intestate succession as the surviving "spouse," Juan's one-half share of the property (community and quasi-marital). From each "spouse's" perspective, each should end up with 100 percent of the property. Faced again with competing claims in hopeless conflict, the court utilized *equitable principles* and divided the property in equal one-half shares to each "spouse."

2. *Putative domestic partners.* The applicable law for a putative spouse is not limited to traditional marriage scenarios. Because California's "domestic partnership" law effectively incorporates, by reference, all provisions that are applicable to spouses, the putative spouse doctrines apply equally to domestic partners. California courts have, accordingly, recognized "putative domestic partners"—treating them the same as actual domestic partners who, in turn, are treated the same as spouses. *See In re Domestic Partnership of Ellis*, 162 Cal. App. 4th 1000 (Ct. App. 2008).

D. Cohabitants

What about unmarried cohabitants who know they are not legally married yet live together and, perhaps, act as if they are married? Should the law accord spousal benefits to such individuals—at least time-of-death spousal benefits?

A number of states de facto accord spousal status to such couples (including the right to inherit) through the common law marriage doctrine. Common law marriage requires capacity, agreement, cohabitation, and the parties have to hold themselves out to the community as husband and wife so that others regard them as husband and wife.[10] California, however, does not recognize common law marriage.

---

10. Cynthia Grant Bowman, *A Feminist Proposal to Bring Back Common Law Marriage*, 75 Or. L. Rev. 709, 712–13 (1996).

In *Elden v. Sheldon*, 46 Cal. 3d 267 (1988), Plaintiff asked the California Supreme Court to grant spousal status to "de facto spouses." Richard Elden and Linda Ebeling shared an "unmarried cohabitation relationship ... which [he alleged] was both stable and significant and parallel to a marital relationship." In 1982, they were in a serious car accident. Ebeling was thrown from the car and died a few hours later from her injuries. Elden sued Sheldon, the driver of the other car, seeking to recover for negligent infliction of emotional distress, which Elden claimed he suffered as a result of witnessing the injuries to his "de facto spouse." Prior California case law limited standing to invoke the cause of action to cases where the plaintiff and the injured are "closely related." The courts had declined to extend the rule to include "friends or distant relatives of the injured person." Elden claimed that inasmuch as the injured was his "de facto" spouse, he had standing to recover. Although the issue was whether a cohabitant qualified as a spouse for purposes of the doctrine of negligent infliction of emotional distress, the Court's comments speak to the California courts' view of whether cohabitants qualify as spouses for inheritance purposes:

> We have no quarrel with the factual premise of plaintiff's position. There can be no doubt that the last two decades have seen a dramatic increase in the number of couples who live together without formal marriage,[11] that some of these couples are bound by emotional ties as strong as those that bind formally married partners, and that they may share financial resources and expenses in the same manner as married couples. It may well be also that the number of such households has increased to the point that emotional trauma suffered by a partner in such an arrangement from injury to his companion cannot be characterized as "unexpected or remote." Nevertheless, we conclude, for the reasons stated below, that an unmarried cohabitant may not recover damages for emotional distress based on such injury.
>
> ...
>
> There are several policy reasons to justify rejection of plaintiff's claim that he should be allowed to recover damages for emotional distress.
>
> First, ... "spouses receive special consideration from the state, ... Marriage is accorded this degree of dignity in recognition that '[t]he joining of the man and woman in marriage is at once the most socially productive and individually fulfilling relationship that one can enjoy in the course of a lifetime.' [Citation.] Consonant therewith, the state is most solicitous of the rights of spouses. [Citation.] ... Unmarried cohabitants receive no similar solicitous statutory protection, nor should they; such would impede the state's sub-

---

11. The incidence of cohabitation without marriage increased 800 percent between 1960 and 1970 (*see* Marvin v. Marvin, 557 P.2d 106, 109 fn. 1 (Cal. 1976)), and the number of unmarried couple households almost tripled between 1970 and 1984 (U.S. Dept. of Commerce, Current Population Reports (1984) Population Characteristics, series P-20, No. 399, Marital Status and Living Arrangements: Mar. 1984, at p. 7; *see also* Meade, Consortium Rights of the Unmarried: Time for Reappraisal, 15 Fam. L.Q. 223, 224, fn. 6 (1981)).

stantial interest in promoting and protecting marriage." (Nieto v. City of Los Angeles (1982) 138 Cal.App.3d 464, 470–471, 188 Cal.Rptr.31).

…

A second basis for our determination is that the allowance of a cause of action in the circumstances of this case would impose a difficult burden on the courts. It would require a court to inquire into the relationship of the partners to determine whether the "emotional attachments of the family relationship" existed between the parties (Mobaldi, supra, 55 Cal.App.3d at p. 582, 127 Cal.Rptr. 720), and whether the relationship was "stable and significant" (Butcher v. Superior Court (1983) 139 Cal.App.3d 58, 70, 188 Cal.Rptr. 503). Butcher, … suggested that the stability of a cohabitation relationship could be established by evidence of its duration, whether the parties had a contract, the degree of economic cooperation, the exclusivity of sexual relationships, and whether the couple had children. In Norman v. Unemployment Ins. Appeals Board, supra, 34 Cal.3d 1, 8–10, 192 Cal.Rptr. 134, 663 P.2d 904, we commented on the "difficult problems of proof" involved in determining whether a relationship is equivalent to a marriage. Authorities in this state and elsewhere have rejected the Butcher test as inviting "mischief and inconsistent results." … [citations omitted].

…

We hold that plaintiff failed to state a cause of action for negligent infliction of emotional distress and that, therefore, the trial court did not err in sustaining the demurrer to the second cause of action.…

Note

With the extension of spousal status and spousal benefits to same-sex couples now complete, will the next extension of spousal status and benefits be to cohabiting couples in long-term, committed relationships? Opponents to such extension typically cite to the reasons recited by the Court in *Elden*: it would be against public policy, and it would be too difficult administratively to determine who qualifies as a de facto spouse. Yet California's interested drafter statute, which voids gifts to an interested drafter, recognizes an exception for "[a] donative transfer to a person who is related by blood or affinity [i.e., marriage] … to the transferor or is the cohabitant of the transferor." Cal. Prob. Code § 21380. Furthermore, the California Domestic Violence Prevention Act defines "domestic abuse" as "abuse perpetrated against any of the following persons: (a) A spouse or former spouse. (b) A cohabitant or former cohabitant …." Cal. Fam. Code § 6211. If cohabitants can be treated the same as spouses for purposes of these other doctrines, would it really be that difficult to treat cohabitants as spouses for purposes of the intestacy scheme? Is recognition of spousal status for cohabitants just a matter of time?[12]

---

12. Interestingly, the state of Washington, which does not recognize common law marriage, recognizes the doctrine of meretricious partners. Where there exists a long-term, stable, nonmarital

III. Issue

A. Introduction

Inheritance rights go hand-in-hand with a legally recognized parent-child relationship. What constitutes a legally recognized parent-child relationship—and what should constitute a legally recognized parent-child relationship—is primarily a question for Family law. There is obviously quite a bit of overlap in this part of the course between Family law and inheritance rights. An exhaustive study of the issue should accordingly first examine the Family law approach to what constitutes a parent-child relationship, then turn to an exhaustive study of the issue under the Probate Code, and finally conclude with a detailed comparison of the two approaches. Unfortunately (or, perhaps, from a student's perspective, fortunately), time constraints do not permit such an exhaustive approach. References to Family law will be minimized, but even with such minimal coverage most students will see the natural overlap between the two areas of law.[13]

The overlap between Family law and the law of inheritance rights once again highlights the larger issue of whether an intestate scheme should be based on more of an intent-based approach or a status-based approach. To what extent should the Family law basis for a legally recognized parent-child relationship control what constitutes a parent-child relationship for the purpose of succession law? Should the law of succession simply defer to Family law for the answers, or should the Probate Code take its own approach—and, if so, should it be narrower or broader than the Family law basis for a legally recognized parent-child relationship? You should keep these questions in the back of your mind as you move through the material.

Historically, the general approach to inheritance rights reflected more of a straight status-based approach. The modern trend has not been so much to repudiate the status-based approach, but rather to acknowledge that, increasingly, the American family comes in different shapes and sizes, and the law should do more to recognize these changes—i.e., the law should recognize alternative ways of creating a legally recognized parent-child relationship. Yet, instead of throwing down the gauntlet and taking more of an intent-based functional approach to who qualifies as being in a "parent-child" relationship, probate codes are increasingly recognizing different ways in which a legally recognized parent-child relationship can arise. In addition, probate codes are increasingly recognizing different "types" of families—families with more than two parents for certain purposes. You should keep this historical backdrop and evolving modern trend in mind as you study the different California Probate Code

---

family relationship, if the relationship ends, "courts must 'examine the [meretricious] relationship and the property accumulations and make a just and equitable disposition of the property.'" Marriage of Lindsey, 101 Wash. 2d 299, 304 (1984). Subsequently, however, the Court clarified that the doctrine applied only if the meretricious relationship ended in divorce, not death. Peffley-Warner v. Bowen, 113 Wash. 2d 243 (1989). Does that make any sense?

13. If you are considering a career in estate planning, you would be well-advised to take Family Law.

provisions with respect to who qualifies as an issue for purposes of recognizing inheritance rights between the parties.

B. The "Ideal" Nuclear Family

The Millennium issue of the well-respected magazine THE ECONOMIST described the "ideal" nuclear family of northwestern Europe and America as follows: "father at work, mother at home, the pair married since their early 20s and for life, living only with their joint children."[14] Putting aside the propriety of normatively designating such a family as the "ideal nuclear family," this view of what constitutes the ideal family has influenced intestate schemes in these countries as well. The general rule is the moment a child is born to a married couple, the birth automatically establishes a legally recognized parent-child relationship between the child and both parents.[15]

Historically, once there was a legally recognized parent-child relationship, inheritance rights automatically attached themselves to the parties to the relationship. The default set of inheritance rights grants the child the right to inherit "from and through" each natural parent, and each natural parent has the right to inherit "from and through" the child. To appreciate the scope of the inheritance rights, one has to understand what it means to inherit "from and through." For example, if a natural parent were to die intestate, the child could inherit from the parent; and if thereafter the child's grandparent on that side of the family were to die (i.e., the deceased natural parent's parent), the child could inherit through the deceased natural parent from the grandparent. Conversely, though not the norm — and not what any parent would want — the natural parent can inherit from and through the child. The default set of inheritance rights is a full set of inheritance rights — from and through — and the presumption is that these default inheritance rights run in both directions. Although there are countless other possible "from and through" permutations of inheritance, real-life usually presents us with only a few.

The legally recognized parent-child relationship, and the inheritance rights that flow from it, can be diagrammed. The family can be diagrammed as follows:

Parents married, natural conception:

NP   NP

C

---

14. *Anti-nuclear Reaction*, THE ECONOMIST, Dec. 23, 1999.

15. Who qualifies as a child, and whose child it is, are questions primarily for Family Law. This material will cover the overlaps between these issues and Wills, Trusts, and Estates only to the extent necessary for a basic understanding of the issues. If you are interested in these issues, you are encouraged to take the Family Law course. In addition, if you are thinking about practicing estate planning Family Law is a course you should strongly consider taking.

The inheritance rights can be diagrammed as arrows flowing in both directions. The direction of the arrow indicates the direction the property is flowing (i.e., the party to whom the arrow is pointed is the heir who has the right to inherit under the intestate scheme). A "full" arrow indicates full inheritance rights: the right to inherit from and through. Where the parents are married, a child has the right to inherit from and through his or her natural parents.

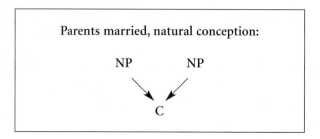

Conversely, where the parents are married, the traditional and general rule is that each natural parent has the right to inherit from and through the child.

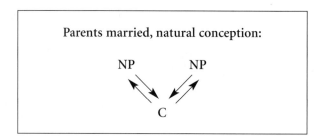

Both biologically, and legally, the starting point for creating a parent-child relationship is the contribution of the genetic material. Under the traditional common law approach, the male who contributed the sperm qualified as the natural father, and the female who contributed the egg qualified as the natural mother.[16] Where the natural father and the natural mother are married, the moment the child is born alive a legally recognized parent-child relationship arises. The moment you have a legally recognized parent-child relationship, inheritance rights attach themselves to that relationship.

While the "biological" approach to the parent-child relationship is the starting point to analyze the parent-child relationship and its concomitant inheritance rights, it is not the only consideration. A plethora of other considerations can affect the parties' rights to inherit from and through each other. Before we are done, you will see

---

16. This approach was reinforced by the fact that, at common law, the party who contributed the egg by definition also had to be the party who gave birth to the child. Due to modern reproductive technology, this is not now always the case. As one would expect, where the party who contributes the egg is not also the party who gives birth to the child, parties argue as to whom should legally be considered the natural parent.

that there are almost a dozen variations on the parent-child relationship that might give rise to a legally recognized parent-child relationship and, accordingly, give rise to some form of inheritance rights.

C. Natural Parents Married

Historically, a key variable in evaluating inheritance rights based on a parent-child relationship was whether the natural parents were married when they had the child. Where a couple is married, a natural presumption arises that the husband is the one who contributed the sperm—but that is obviously not the only possibility. If a third party claims that he is the one who contributed the sperm, who legally should be considered the natural father: the mother's husband or the party who contributed the sperm? What constitutes a "qualifying" parent-child relationship is not purely a question of reproductive biology; it is also a cultural and public policy issue.[17]

Family Code § 7540. Wife's child conclusively presumed husband's

Except as provided in Section 7541,[18] the child of a wife cohabiting with her husband, who is not impotent or sterile, is conclusively presumed to be a child of the marriage.

Because of this presumption in Family Code section 7540, where a child is born to a married couple, a legally recognized parent-child relationship immediately arises and full inheritance rights immediately attach to the relationship. The child can inherit from and through each natural parent, and each natural parent can inherit from and through the child. Thus, for the parent-child relationship to arise and for the inheritance rights to attach, none of the parties has to prove anything other than the birth of the child.

But what if Family Code section 7540 did not apply? What if the natural mother is not married at the time of conception and delivery? Should that affect the child's

---

17. By now you have probably begun to think about how modern reproductive technology plays havoc with this simple nuclear family scenario. No longer is the birthing mother necessarily the woman contributing the egg. Where the two are different parties, which party should be the natural parent—or should both be treated as the natural mother? Legally, should the child have more than one mother? If the husband is infertile, his sperm may have been "blended" with other sperm to increase the chances of conception. Should the use of "blended" sperm call into question the presumption that the husband is the natural father? In addition, California now grants same-sex registered domestic partners the same legal rights as a heterosexual married couple. How does the statutory provision in section 7540, that the presumption of parenthood arises only if the other party "is not impotent or sterile," apply to registered domestic partners? A more detailed discussion of these and other similar issues are best left for the Family Law course, but if you are interested in these types of issues we recommend you start with the following articles: Kristine S. Knaplund, *Children of Assisted Reproduction*, 45 U. MICH. J. L. REFORM 899 (2012), and Kristine S. Knaplund, *Legal Issues of Maternity and Inheritance for the Biotech Child of the 21st Century*, 43 REAL PROP. TR. & EST. L.J. 393 (2008). Our introductory material will focus on the more traditional and common scenarios—at least from a legal perspective—where parent-child and inheritance issues arise.

18. Section 7541 recognizes a limited exception where the presumption can be rebutted, but only if pursued within two years of the child's birth, and only if by the husband or the wife. Michael H. v. Gerald D., 109 S. Ct. 2333, 491 U.S. 110, 105 L. Ed. 2d 91 (1989).

ability to claim inheritance rights with either natural parent? Should that affect the scope of the child's inheritance rights (i.e., should the inheritance rights be "full" inheritance rights or something different)? Conversely, should that affect either natural parent's ability to claim inheritance rights—or the size of the inheritance rights—with respect to the child?

D. Child Born Out of Wedlock

Legally, should the fact that a child is born out of wedlock affect the child's ability to inherit from and through his or her natural parents?

Historically, a child born out of wedlock was frowned upon legally. At common law, an illegitimate child was treated as the legal child of no one: "[A]n illegitimate child was filius nullius and incapable of inheriting from anyone."[19] Many states, in an attempt to ameliorate the harshness of the common law approach, adopted statutes that permitted the child to inherit from and through the natural mother, but nevertheless prohibited the child from inheriting from and through the natural father. As recently as the 1970s, these statutes were widely adopted and accepted. In *Trimble v. Gordon*, however, the U.S. Supreme Court declared these statutes unconstitutional because they violated the Equal Protection Clause of the Fourteenth Amendment by invidiously discriminating on the basis of illegitimacy.[20] At the theoretical level, therefore, the marital status of the natural parents is no longer a variable in the child's right to inherit from and through his or her natural parents.

CPC § 6450. Parent-child relationship

Subject to the provisions of this chapter, a relationship of parent and child exists for the purpose of determining intestate succession by, through, or from a person in the following circumstances:

(a) The relationship of parent and child exists between a person and the person's natural parents, regardless of the marital status of the natural parents.

Although the Supreme Court ruled in *Trimble* that statutes denying children born out of wedlock the right to inherit are unconstitutional, the Court's ruling did not unconditionally grant children born out of wedlock the right to inherit because states have the right to adopt rules setting forth what a child must prove to establish his or her natural parents. Because the married couple parent-child presumption under Family Code section 7540 does not apply to the child born out of wedlock, the parties must prove a legally recognized parent-child relationship before inheritance rights will attach between the parties. In the paradigm "child born out of wedlock" scenario, it is fairly easy to determine who is the natural mother, but determining who is the

---

19. Trimble v. Gordon, 430 U.S. 762, 768 (1976).
20. *Id*. at 765–66.

natural father may not be as straightforward.[21] Here, the California Probate Code defers heavily to the Family Code. California Probate Code section 6453 provides that a natural parent-child relationship is established where the relationship is presumed, and not rebutted, under the Uniform Parentage Act. This presumption of a natural parent-child relationship can arise a number of different ways.[22] Those different ways, however, are best left for the Family law course. In addition, for inheritance purposes, a natural parent-child relationship may be established if a court order declaring paternity was entered during the father's lifetime (section 6453(b)) or if paternity is established by clear and convincing evidence following the natural father's death (section 6453(c)). The heightened burden of proof under the latter provision creates an incentive to bring paternity claims while the alleged natural father is alive and has a chance to respond to the claim.

Once the natural parents of a child born out of wedlock have been established, the child has the right to inherit from and through each natural parent. Should those inheritance rights be reciprocal? Once the natural parent-child relationship is established, should the natural parents have the right to inherit from and through the out-of-wedlock child, or should the natural parents have to prove something else as well?

Estate of Griswold

24 P.3d 1191 (Cal. 2001)

BAXTER, J.

. . .

[On July 12, 1941, in Ashland, Ohio, Betty Jane Morris gave birth to Denis Howard Morris out-of-wedlock. The birth certificate identified John Edward Draves of New London, Ohio, as the father. A week after the birth, Morris filed a "bastardy complaint"[23] and swore under oath that Draves was the child's father. Draves "confessed in Court that the charge ... is true."] The court adjudged Draves to be the "reputed father" of the child, and ordered Draves to pay medical expenses related to Morris's pregnancy as well as $5 per week for child support and maintenance. Draves complied, and for 18 years paid the court-ordered support to the clerk of the Huron County court.

Morris married Fred Griswold in 1942 and moved to California. She began to refer to her son as "Denis Howard Griswold," a name he used for the rest of his life. For many years, Griswold believed Fred Griswold was his father. At some point in time,

---

21. Most state statutes are written generically such that proving who the natural parents are applies to both natural parents, but as a practical matter who is the natural mother is so rarely at issue the material will focus on the paradigm issue — who is the natural father. Technically, though, the identity of both natural parents is an issue.

22. California Family Code §§ 7611–12.

23. A "bastardy proceeding" is an archaic term for a paternity suit. BLACK's LAW DICTIONARY (7th ed. 1999) pp. 146, 1148.

either after his mother and Fred Griswold divorced in 1978 or after his mother died in 1983, Griswold learned that Draves was listed as his father on his birth certificate. So far as is known, Griswold made no attempt to contact Draves or other members of the Draves family.

Meanwhile, at some point after Griswold's birth, Draves married in Ohio and had two children, Margaret and Daniel. Neither Draves nor these two children had any communication with Griswold, and the children did not know of Griswold's existence until after Griswold's death in 1996. Draves died in 1993. His last will and testament, dated July 22, 1991, made no mention of Griswold by name or other reference. Huron County probate documents identified Draves's surviving spouse and two children — Margaret and Daniel — as the only heirs.

[Denis H. Griswold died intestate in 1996, survived by his wife, Norma B. Doner-Griswold. Doner-Griswold petitioned for and received letters of administration and authority to administer Griswold's modest estate, consisting entirely of separate property.

In 1998, Doner-Griswold filed a petition for final distribution, proposing a distribution of estate property, after payment of attorney's fees and costs, to herself as the surviving spouse and sole heir. Francis V. See, a self-described "forensic genealogist" (heir hunter) who had obtained an assignment of partial interest in the Griswold estate from Margaret Loera and Daniel Draves,[24] objected to the petition for final distribution and filed a petition to determine entitlement to distribution.

. . .

Section 6452 of the Probate Code[25] (all statutory references are to this code unless otherwise indicated) bars a "natural parent" or a relative of that parent from inheriting through a child born out of wedlock on the basis of the parent and child relationship unless the parent or relative "acknowledged the child" and "contributed to the support or the care of the child." In this case, we must determine whether section 6452 precludes the half siblings of a child born out of wedlock from sharing in the child's intestate estate where the record is undisputed that their father appeared in an Ohio court, admitted paternity of the child, and paid court-ordered child support until the child was 18 years old. Although the father and the out-of-wedlock child apparently never met or communicated, and the half siblings did not learn of the child's existence

---

24. California permits heirs to assign their interests in an estate, but such assignments are subject to court scrutiny. (See [CPC] § 11604.)

25. [Editors' footnote.] The statute at the time of the case provided as follows:

CPC § 6452. Parent-child relationship of child born out of wedlock
> If a child is born out of wedlock, neither a natural parent nor a relative of that parent inherits from or through the child on the basis of the parent and child relationship between that parent and the child unless both of the following requirements are satisfied:
> (a) The parent or a relative of the parent acknowledged the child.
> (b) The parent or a relative of the parent contributed to the support or the care of the child.

until after both the child and the father died, there is no indication that the father ever denied paternity or knowledge of the out-of-wedlock child to persons who were aware of the circumstances.][26]

...

It is undisputed here that section 6452 governs the determination whether Margaret, Daniel, and See (by assignment) are entitled to inherit from Griswold. It is also uncontroverted that Draves contributed court-ordered child support for 18 years, thus satisfying subdivision (b) of section 6452 [the requirement that the natural parent or relative of that parent contribute to the support or care of the child]. At issue, however, is whether the record establishes all the remaining requirements of section 6452 as a matter of law.... [D]id Draves acknowledge Griswold within the meaning of section 6452, subdivision (a)? ...

...

... On review, we must determine whether Draves acknowledged Griswold within the contemplation of the statute by confessing to paternity in court, where the record reflects no other acts of acknowledgement, but no disavowals either.

...

Although no statutory definition appears, the common meaning of "acknowledge" is "to admit to be true or as stated; confess." (Webster's New World Dict. (2d ed.1982) p. 12; see Webster's 3d New Internat. Dict. (1981) p. 17 ["to show by word or act that one has knowledge of and agrees to (a fact or truth) ... [or] concede to be real or true ... [or] admit"].) Were we to ascribe this common meaning to the statutory language, there could be no doubt that section 6452's acknowledgement requirement is met here. As the stipulated record reflects, Griswold's natural mother initiated a bastardy proceeding in the Ohio juvenile court in 1941 in which she alleged that Draves was the child's father. Draves appeared in that proceeding and publicly "confessed" that the allegation was true. There is no evidence indicating that Draves did not confess knowingly and voluntarily, or that he later denied paternity or knowledge of Griswold to those who were aware of the circumstances. Although the record establishes that Draves did not speak of Griswold to Margaret and Daniel, there is no evidence suggesting he sought to actively conceal the facts from them or anyone else. Under the plain terms of section 6452, the only sustainable conclusion on this record is that Draves acknowledged Griswold.

...

Doner-Griswold disputes whether the acknowledgement required by Probate Code section 6452 may be met by a father's single act of acknowledging a child in court.

---

26. [Editors' footnote.] The three paragraphs in this bracketed section of the opinion are three of the opening paragraphs in the Court's opinion. The authors of the casebook, however, used their editorial discretion to move these paragraphs to the end of the Court's treatment of the facts to facilitate the presentation of the material.

In her view, the requirement contemplates a situation where the father establishes an ongoing parental relationship with the child or otherwise acknowledges the child's existence to his subsequent wife and children....

. . .

Doner-Griswold's authorities do not persuade us that section 6452 should be read to require that a father have personal contact with his out-of-wedlock child, that he make purchases for the child, that he receive the child into his home and other family, or that he treat the child as he does his other children....

. . .

DISPOSITION

" 'Succession to estates is purely a matter of statutory regulation, which cannot be changed by the courts.' " (Estate of De Cigaran, supra, 150 Cal. at p. 688, 89 P. 833.) We do not disagree that a natural parent who does no more than openly acknowledge a child in court and pay court-ordered child support may not reflect a particularly worthy predicate for inheritance by that parent's issue, but section 6452 provides in unmistakable language that it shall be so. While the Legislature remains free to reconsider the matter and may choose to change the rules of succession at any time, this court will not do so under the pretense of interpretation.

The judgment of the Court of Appeal is affirmed.

Concurring Opinion by BROWN, J.

I reluctantly concur. The relevant case law strongly suggests that a father who admits paternity in court with no subsequent disclaimers "acknowledge[s] the child" within the meaning of subdivision (a) of Probate Code section 6452. Moreover, neither the statutory language nor the legislative history supports an alternative interpretation. Accordingly, we must affirm the judgment of the Court of Appeal.

Nonetheless, I believe our holding today contravenes the overarching purpose behind our laws of intestate succession — to carry out "the intent a decedent without a will is most likely to have had." (16 Cal. Law Revision Com. Rep. (1982) p. 2319.) I doubt most children born out of wedlock would have wanted to bequeath a share of their estate to a "father" who never contacted them, never mentioned their existence to his family and friends, and only paid court-ordered child support. I doubt even more that these children would have wanted to bequeath a share of their estate to that father's other offspring. Finally, I have no doubt that most, if not all, children born out of wedlock would have balked at bequeathing a share of their estate to a "forensic genealogist."

To avoid such a dubious outcome in the future, I believe our laws of intestate succession should allow a parent to inherit from a child born out of wedlock only if the parent has some sort of parental connection to that child. For example, requiring a parent to treat a child born out of wedlock as the parent's own before the parent may inherit from that child would prevent today's outcome. (See, e.g., Bullock v. Thomas (Miss.1995) 659 So.2d 574, 577 [a father must "openly treat" a child born out of wedlock "as his own" in order to inherit from that child].) More importantly, such a requirement would comport with the stated purpose behind our laws of succession because that child likely would have wanted to give a share of his estate to a parent that treated him as the parent's own.

Of course, this court may not remedy this apparent defect in our intestate succession statutes. Only the Legislature may make the appropriate revisions. I urge it to do so here.

———————

Notes

1. *Epilogue*: Based on the statutory language and the Court's construction and application of it, did the Court take a status-based approach or an intent-based approach to who qualifies as an heir? Although the California legislature did not revisit Probate Code section 6452 immediately following the *Griswold* opinion, it finally did so in 2013. Did the legislature respond to the Court's request? Would the *Griswold* case come out the same way today?

CPC § 6452. Conditions barring a parent from inheriting from or through a child

(a) A parent does not inherit from or through a child on the basis of the parent and child relationship if any of the following apply:

   (1)   The parent's parental rights were terminated and the parent-child relationship was not judicially reestablished.

   (2)   The parent did not acknowledge the child.

   (3) The parent left the child during the child's minority without an effort to provide for the child's support or without communication from the parent, for at least seven consecutive years that continued until the end of the child's minority, with the intent on the part of the parent to abandon the child. The failure to provide support or to communicate for the prescribed period is presumptive evidence of an intent to abandon.

(b) A parent who does not inherit from or through the child as provided in subdivision (a) shall be deemed to have predeceased the child, and the intestate estate shall pass as otherwise required under Section 6402.

2. *Analyzing the statutory language*: Compare the scope of the "old" Probate Code section 6452 and the current Probate Code section 6452. Is the new provision broader or narrower in scope? Does it make it harder or easier for a court to bar a natural parent from inheriting from his or her child?

3. *Statutory conditions for legally recognized parent-child relationship:* In the "ideal" nuclear family paradigm scenario, a parent-child relationship with full inheritance rights in both directions automatically attaches to the parties the moment the child is born. Every other legally recognized parent-child relationship in California is a variation of that scenario. In each of the other scenarios, however, the California statutory provision that applies requires that some additional condition(s) be proved

before the law recognizes a parent-child relationship for inheritance purposes.[27] In each of the additional scenarios, read the Probate Code section(s) in question carefully to see if you can identify the additional requirement(s) that must be established.

E. Adoption

The general effect of a legal adoption is that it severs the parent-child relationship between the child and his or her natural parents. "The birth parents of an adopted child are, from the time of the adoption, relieved of all parental duties towards, and all responsibility for, the adopted child, and have no right over the child." Cal. Fam. Code § 8617. To the extent a legal adoption severs the parent-child relationship between the child and his or her natural parents, should adoption also sever the child's relationship with his or her natural parents for inheritance purposes under the Probate Code?

CPC § 6450. Parent-child relationship; inheritance rights

Subject to the provisions of this chapter, a relationship of parent and child exists for the purpose of determining intestate succession by, through, or from a person in the following circumstances:

...

(b) The relationship of parent and child exists between an adopted person and the person's adopting parent or parents.

CPC § 6451. Adoption

(a) An adoption severs the relationship of parent and child between an adopted person and a natural parent of the adopted person unless both of the following requirements are satisfied:

(1) The natural parent and the adopted person lived together at any time as parent and child,....

(2) The adoption was by the spouse of either of the natural parents or after the death of either of the natural parents.

(b) Neither a natural parent nor a relative of a natural parent, ... inherits from or through the adopted person on the basis of a parent and child relationship between the adopted person and the natural parent that satisfies the requirements of paragraphs (1) and (2) of subdivision (a), unless the adoption is by the spouse or surviving spouse of that parent.

LAW REVISION COMMISSION COMMENT

In case of an adoption coming within subdivision (a), the adopted child may inherit from or through the adoptive parent, and also from or through the natural parent who

---

27. In the out-of-wedlock scenario, what does the child have to prove to inherit from and through each natural parent? What does the natural parent (or relative of a natural parent) have to prove?

gave up the child for adoption or through the natural parent who died preceding the adoption. The following examples indicate in various situations whether an adopted child or the issue of an adopted child may inherit from or through the child's natural parent.

Example 1. Child never lived with either mother or father. Both parents relinquish child for adoption. The adopted child's relationship with both natural parents' families is severed. The requirements of subdivision (a)(1) are not satisfied.

Example 2. Child's mother and father were married or lived together as a family. Child lives with mother and father. Father dies. Mother relinquishes child for adoption. For the purpose of inheritance, the adopted child remains a member of both the deceased father's family and of the relinquishing mother's family. The requirement of subdivision (a) is satisfied because the adoption was "after the death of either of the natural parents."

...

Under subdivision (a), a non-stepparent adoption severs the relationship between the adopted person and his or her natural "parent." Thus, for example, if a person is adopted by only one adopting parent, that severs the parent-child relationship between the adopted person and his or her natural parent of the same gender as the adopting parent. The parent-child relationship continues to exist between the adopted person and his or her other natural parent.

In case of an adoption described in subdivision (b), the natural relatives cannot inherit from the adopted child, even though under Section 6450(a) the child could inherit from the natural relatives.

Estate of Dye

92 Cal. App. 4th 966 (2001)

MORRISON, J.

This case illustrates the danger of using preprinted wills. Decedent Haskell J. Dye had two natural sons who were adopted away (with his consent) by his first wife's new husband (Arthur Battles) in 1959. Under the law at that time, this cut off their right to inherit from him. The law was changed, effective 1985, to permit some adopted-out children to inherit from their natural parents. In 1989 decedent and his second wife Eleanor signed reciprocal form wills, leaving their property to each other. Eleanor died in January, 1999. Decedent died on June 17, 1999.

Scott Dye, Eleanor's son who had been adopted by decedent, petitioned to probate decedent's estate. Phillip Joe Battles, one of decedent's adopted away natural sons, and some of the issue of the deceased adopted away son (Jimmie Dean Battles) filed an objection, seeking to share in decedent's estate....

DISCUSSION

I.

...

Adoption creates a legal relationship of parent and child, which "implies that the natural relationship between the child and its parents by blood is superseded. The duties of a child cannot be owed to two fathers at the same time." (*Estate of Jobson* (1912) 164 Cal. 312, 316–317, 128 P. 938.) The California Supreme Court reasoned, "From the time of the adoption, the adopting parent is, so far as concerns all legal rights and duties flowing from the relation of parent and child, the parent of the adopted child. From the same moment, the parent by blood ceases to be, in a legal sense, the parent. His place has been taken by the adopting parent." (Id. at p. 317, 128 P. 938.)

. . .

For our purposes, it suffices to begin with former section 257 as it read in 1959, after a 1955 amendment: "An adopted child shall be deemed a descendant of one who has adopted him, the same as a natural child, for all purposes of succession by, from or through the adopting parent the same as a natural parent. An adopted child does not succeed to the estate of a natural parent when the relationship between them has been severed by adoption, nor does such natural parent succeed to the estate of such adopted child." (Stats.1955, ch. 1478, § 1, p. 2690.) This legislation provided that the adopted child had rights of inheritance in and only in the estate of the adoptive parents....

The parties agree that when decedent's sons were adopted by their mother's new husband, this statute cut off their rights to inherit under the intestacy laws at that time. (See *Estate of Hart* (1984) 165 Cal.App.3d 392, 394, fn. 1, 209 Cal.Rptr. 272.)

This rule was changed by a new statute, effective January 1, 1985, which has gone through various amendments. (Former § 6408 Stats.1983, ch. 842, §§ 19, 55, pp. 3024, 3083.) In 1993 the language of the present section 6451 was adopted. (Stats.1993, ch. 529, § 5, p. 2715.) Now an adoption severs the blood relationship "unless both of the following requirements are satisfied: [¶] (1) The natural parent and the adopted person lived together at any time as parent and child[.][¶] (2) The adoption was by the spouse of either of the natural parents[.]" (§ 6451, subd. (a).) California is not alone in providing by statute for adopted-out children to inherit from their natural parents when the adoption was by a stepparent. (See, e.g., *Raley v. Spikes* (Ala.1993) 614 So.2d 1017; *Estate of Carlson* (Minn.App. 1990) 457 N.W.2d 789.)

Before Jimmie Dean and Phillip Joe were adopted out, decedent lived with them, and their adoption was by the new husband of their mother, decedent's former wife. They satisfy the new exception to the statute.

In 1989, after the change in the law, decedent and Eleanor wrote their wills. Eleanor died in 1999, leaving her property to decedent. He died later in 1999, leaving everything to Eleanor....

Where, as here, the decedent has no surviving spouse, the estate passes "To the issue of the decedent, the issue taking equally if they are all of the same degree of kinship to the decedent, but if of unequal degree those of more remote degree take in the manner provided in Section 240." (§ 6402, subd. (a).) ...

. . .

II.

Scott asserts in his brief that decedent and Eleanor did not consult a lawyer and thought he was their only lawful heir, and that decedent never intended to benefit objectors, "some of whom he never even met." Scott urges the case should be remanded so he can introduce evidence to establish decedent's intention regarding the adopted-out children.

A.

Assuming Scott accurately sets forth decedent's wishes, decedent could have expressed such intention by inserting into the will "I disinherit Phillip Joe and Jimmie Dean," or he could have given them each "one dollar." On Eleanor's death he could have written a new will or a codicil naming Scott as sole beneficiary. Decedent did none of these things.

Accordingly, like any other case of intestacy, the courts must apply the default provisions of the intestacy rules set forth by the Legislature. It is presumed citizens know the law, including the intestacy laws, and it is up to any person who does not want those laws applied to his or her estate to opt out by preparing a will setting forth other dispositions. Decedent did not so provide and therefore is presumed to endorse application of the default intestacy laws. This accords with the general rule that the law governing a will is measured as of the date of death, under the fiction that until then, the decedent is presumed to know the law and has the power to change his will....

Here, both the drafting of the will and death occurred after the critical revision to the probate laws.

. . .

Accordingly, we presume decedent was aware of the state of the law in 1989 and understood the possibility all of his natural children would share in his estate. If he wanted to change this result, he could easily have inserted a provision in his will to disinherit any or all of his natural children. He did not....

3.

Scott concludes in part: "It would be a manifest injustice if Haskell's estate were distributed in any part to the Battles when he truly intended the exact opposite." The intestacy laws by their nature will defeat many "true" intentions. Decedent could have prevented such "injustice," if any, by making a new will, or by including in the first will language stating his wishes if Eleanor died first. The objectors have not caused an injustice by invoking applicable law.

DISPOSITION

The order granting the heirship petition is affirmed.

Notes and Problems

1. *Intent versus status*: Based on the court's ruling in *Estate of Dye*, would you say inheritance rights following adoption are based on intent or status? What is the

logic behind permitting the "new" statutory exceptions to the traditional rule that adoption completely severs all inheritance rights between the child and the natural parents?

2. *Negative disinheritance*: The court stated that if Haskell wanted to disinherit an heir (i.e., bar the heir from taking what he or she otherwise would receive under the laws of succession), all the decedent had to do was expressly state as much in his will. Would that have been enough to disinherit the heir?

The traditional and general rule was that an heir could be disinherited *only* if the decedent affirmatively gave away all of his or her probate property so that none of it fell into probate. Any property that fell into intestacy was disposed of pursuant to the terms of the statutory intestate scheme.

The modern trend favors an intent-based approach to disinheritance. The Uniform Probate Code expressly permits negative disinheritance: "A decedent by will may expressly exclude or limit the right of an individual or class to succeed to property of the decedent passing by intestate succession." UPC § 2-101. California has not expressly adopted such statutory language, and while some California courts have expressed, in dicta, an openness to negative disinheritance consistent with the modern trend intent-based approach, other courts and commentators believe California still follows the traditional approach. There are no recent opinions on point.

3. *Visualizing the inheritance rights*: How would you diagram the inheritance rights under CPC section 6451, indicating for each of the following scenarios: (a) who can inherit from whom? (b) do the inheritance rights flow in both directions or only one direction? and (c) what, if anything, has to be proved for the inheritance rights to attach to the parties? (Try to diagram the scenario and diagram the inheritance rights.)

    a.   Pete and Gerri are married and have raised four children. To their surprise, after one particularly passionate night, Gerri learns she is pregnant. They decide to put the child up for adoption. Henry and Wanda, a young couple looking to start a family, adopt the child. Following the adoption, who can inherit from and through whom?

    b.   Pete and Gerri are married. They have one child, Cici. Tragically, Pete and Gerri are killed in a plane crash. Henry and Wanda, a young couple looking to start a family, adopt Cici. Following the adoption, who can inherit from and through whom? What if only Gerri was killed in the plane crash, but Pete decided raising a child as a single parent was too much for him, so he put the child up for adoption and Henry and Wanda adopted Cici? Would the result be any different?

    c.   Pete and Gerri are married. They have one child, Cici. Gerri discovers that Pete is having an affair with Lulu, and she divorces him. Thereafter Gerri marries Bob, and Bob adopts Cici. Following the adoption, who can inherit from and through whom?

    d.   Pete and Gerri are married. They have one child, Cici. Gerri discovers that Pete is having an affair with Lulu, and she divorces him. Thereafter Gerri moves in with Bob, but while they do not marry, Bob adopts Cici. Following the adoption, who can inherit from and through whom?

4. *Same-sex couples*: Would any of the four scenarios above be analyzed differently if either the natural or adopting parent(s) were same-sex parties?

5. *Stepparent versus step-partner*: Is the difference in inheritance rights between the stepparent adoption scenario and the step-partner adoption scenario defensible? Is it simply a variation of the discrimination that once existed against illegitimate children? *See* Peter Wendel, *Inheritance Rights and The Step-Partner Adoption Paradigm: Shades of the Discrimination against Illegitimate Children*, 34 Hofstra L. Rev. 351 (Winter 2005).

F. Intent to Adopt

1. Equitable Adoption

For the most part, there are two ways to have a legally recognized parent-child relationship, either naturally, based on biology (who contributed the sperm or egg), or legally, based on adoption. A majority of jurisdictions, however, also use the doctrine of *equitable* adoption to recognize a parent-child relationship where the parties intended to adopt but failed to do so. Unlike most probate doctrines, it is not statutory but rather judicial in nature. That is also the case in California. Yet because the doctrine is judicial in nature, the exact scope and requirements of the doctrine are not as well defined and accepted as those based on statute.

The doctrine of equitable adoption suffers from something of an identity crisis. Conceptually, as its name implies, the doctrine has one leg firmly planted in equity. The doctrine is an outgrowth of the equitable maxim: "[E]quity regards as done that which ought to be done." It applies where, even though there was no legal adoption, the child ought to be considered adopted. But when should that be the case? Doctrinally, the other leg is firmly planted in contract law. Traditionally, the party invoking the doctrine must prove that the elements of a contract to adopt were performed by all parties except the decedent (who for whatever reason failed to follow through and properly adopt the child), and that the decedent died intestate. The remedy for this breach of contract entitles the child to his or her intestate share of the decedent's estate.

The doctrine's identity crisis is reflected in the court's opinion—and the dissent— in *O'Neal v. Wilkes*, 263 Ga. 850, 439 S.E.2d 490 (1994). Hattie O'Neal was born in 1949. She was born out of wedlock. She did not meet her natural father until she was 21 years old. Her natural mother raised her until she was eight years old, at which time her mother died. Thereafter, Hattie was passed around among several friends and family members until one day she landed in the custody of Estelle Page, her natural father's sister. Estelle heard that Roswell Cook and his wife wanted to adopt a child. The Cooks and Estelle met to discuss the situation, the Cooks agreed to adopt Hattie, and Estelle gave Hattie to the Cooks. They raised her as their own. Roswell often referred to her as his daughter and to her children as his grandchildren, but the Cooks never legally adopted her. Roswell died intestate in 1991. Hattie claimed his estate as his daughter under equitable adoption.

The Georgia Supreme Court applied the traditional approach to the doctrine. The Court's statement of the requirements reflects the contracts-based approach:

> Some showing of an agreement between the natural and adoptive parents, performance by the natural parents of the child in giving up custody, performance by the child by living in the home of the adoptive parents, partial performance by the foster parents in taking the child into the home and treating [it] as their child, and ... the intestacy of the foster parent.[28]

The Court emphasized that the agreement to adopt had to be between parties who were "competent to contract for the disposition of the child."[29] The Court noted that although Estelle had physical custody of Hattie at the time the Cooks took her, Estelle was not her legal custodian. As such, Estelle lacked legal authority to enter into an adoption agreement. The Court ruled the equitable adoption claim failed.

The dissent, authored by Justice Sears-Collins, criticized the majority opinion on two principal grounds. First, she accused the majority of misinterpreting and misapplying the doctrine. She emphasized the doctrine's equitable side and argued that failing to applying the doctrine due to a legal technicality over who had authority to enter into the agreement made no sense. But Justice Sears-Collins did not stop there. She argued that at the doctrinal level the rule should reflect more of its equitable side. She argued for more of an estoppel-based approach to the doctrine: the doctrine should apply anytime a child was led to believe that he or she was adopted. Although Justice Sears-Collins lost in the Georgia Supreme Court that day, she arguably won in the court of academic opinion. Quite a few law review articles were written criticizing the majority's opinion and supporting Justice Sears-Collins's opinion.

A decade later the issue presented itself to the California Supreme Court in Estate of Ford.

Estate of Ford

82 P.3d 747 (Cal. 2004)

WERDEGAR, J.

Terrold Bean claims the right to inherit the intestate estate of Arthur Patrick Ford as Ford's equitably adopted son....

1. FACTUAL AND PROCEDURAL BACKGROUND

Born in 1953, Bean was declared a ward of the court and placed in the home of Ford and his wife, Kathleen Ford, as a foster child in 1955. Bean never knew his natural father, whose identity is uncertain, and he was declared free of his mother's control in 1958, at the age of four. Bean lived continuously with Mr. and Mrs. Ford

---

28. *Wilkes*, 263 Ga. at 851–52.
29. *Id.* at 851.

and their natural daughter, Mary Catherine, for about 18 years, until Mrs. Ford's death in 1973, then with Ford and Mary Catherine for another two years, until 1975.

During part of the time Bean lived with the Fords, they cared for other foster children and received a county stipend for doing so. Although the Fords stopped taking in foster children after Mrs. Ford became ill with cancer, they retained custody of Bean. The last two other foster children left the home around the time of Mrs. Ford's death, but Bean, who at 18 years of age could have left, stayed with Ford and Mary Catherine.

Bean knew the Fords were not his natural parents, but as a child he called them "Mommy" and "Daddy," and later "Mom" and "Dad." Joan Malpassi, Mary Catherine's friend since childhood and later administrator of Ford's estate, testified that Bean's relationship with Mary Catherine was "as two siblings" and that the Fords treated Bean "more like Mary rather than a foster son, like a real son was my observation." Mary Catherine later listed Bean as her brother on a life insurance application.

Bean remained involved with Ford and Mary Catherine even after leaving the Ford home and marrying....

The Fords never petitioned to adopt Bean. Mrs. Ford told Barbara Carter, a family friend, that "they wanted to adopt Terry," but she was "under the impression that she could not put in for adoption while he was in the home." She worried that if Bean was removed during the adoption process he might be put in "a foster home that wasn't safe."

Ford's nearest relatives at the time of his death were the two children of his predeceased brother, nephew John J. Ford III and niece Veronica Newbeck. Neither had had any contact with Ford for about 15 years before his death, and neither attended his funeral....

After trial, the superior court ruled against Bean.... The doctrine of equitable adoption, the trial court found, was inapplicable because "there is no evidence that [Ford] ever told [Bean] or anyone else that he wanted to adopt him nor publicly told anyone that [Bean] was his adopted son." There was thus no clear and convincing evidence of "an intent to adopt."

Bean appealed ... The Court of Appeal affirmed, agreeing with the trial court that equitable adoption must be proven by clear and convincing evidence....

We granted Bean's petition for review.

DISCUSSION

... We ... look to decisional law, rather than statute, for guidance on the equitable adoption doctrine's proper scope and application.

I. Criteria for Equitable Adoption

In its essence, the doctrine of equitable adoption allows a person who was accepted and treated as a natural or adopted child, and as to whom adoption typically was promised or contemplated but never performed, to share in inheritance of the foster parents' property. "The parents of a child turn him over to foster parents who agree to care for him as if he were their own child. Perhaps they also agree to adopt him. They do care for him, support him, educate him, and treat him in all respects as if he were their child, but they never adopt him. Upon their death he seeks to inherit their property on the theory that he should be treated as if he had been adopted. Many courts would honor his claim, at least under some circumstances, characterizing the case as one of equitable adoption, or adoption by estoppel, or virtual adoption, or specific enforcement of a contract to adopt." (Clark, The Law of Domestic Relations in the United States (2d ed.1988) §20.9, p. 925.) The doctrine is widely applied to allow inheritance from the adoptive parent: at least 27 jurisdictions have so applied the doctrine, while only 10 have declined to recognize it in that context. (Annot., Modern Status of Law as to Equitable Adoption or Adoption by Estoppel (1980) 97 A.L.R.3d 347, §3.) ...

In *Estate of Bauer* (1980) 111 Cal.App.3d 554, 168 Cal.Rptr. 743, an inheritance tax case, the court ... aptly summarized the doctrine as it had developed in California: "[E]quitable adoption requires some form of agreement to adopt, coupled with subsequent objective conduct indicating mutual recognition of an adoptive parent and child relationship to such an extent that in equity and good conscience an adoption should be deemed to have taken place." (Id. at p. 560, 168 Cal.Rptr. 743.)

In *Mingo v. Heckler* (9th Cir.1984) 745 F.2d 537, the federal court expanded on *Bauer*'s agreement-plus-conduct analysis, distilling from the California decisions factors tending to show mutual recognition of a parent and child relationship: "[T]he adoptee lived with the adoptive parent for a number of years; the adoptee assumed the adoptive parent's surname; the adoptive parent told the adoptee that he or she was adopted; the adoptive parent publicly acknowledged the adoptee as his or her child; the adoptee considered and conducted himself or herself as a natural child; the adoptee worked or performed services for the adoptive parent; and the adoptive parent attempted legally to adopt or obtained guardianship papers for the child. Because the factors are merely examples of the type of conduct demonstrating an adoptive parent and child relationship, the claimant need not demonstrate that she satisfies every factor." (*Id.* at p. 539.) ...

As reflected in this summary, California decisions have explained equitable adoption as the specific enforcement of a contract to adopt. Yet it has long been clear that the doctrine, even in California, rested less on ordinary rules of contract law than on considerations of fairness and intent for, as Justice Schauer put it, the child "should have been" adopted and would have been but for the decedent's "inadvertence or fault." ...

Bean urges that equitable adoption be viewed not as specific enforcement of a contract to adopt, but as application of an equitable, restitutionary remedy he has identified as quasi-contract or, as his counsel emphasized at oral argument, as an application of equitable estoppel principles. While we have found no decisions articulating a quasi-contract theory, courts in several states have, instead of or in addition to the contract rationale, analyzed equitable adoption as arising from "a broader and vaguer equitable principle of estoppel." (Clark, The Law of Domestic Relations in the United States, supra, at p. 926.) Bean argues Mr. Ford's conduct toward him during their long and close relationship estops Ford's estate or heirs at law from denying his status as an equitably adopted child.

For several reasons, we conclude the California law of equitable adoption, which has rested on contract principles, does not recognize an estoppel arising merely from the existence of a familial relationship between the decedent and the claimant. The law of intestate succession is intended to carry out " 'the intent a decedent without a will is most likely to have had.' " (*Estate of Griswold* (2001) 25 Cal.4th 904, 912, 108 Cal.Rptr.2d 165, 24 P.3d 1191.) The existence of a mutually affectionate relationship, without any direct expression by the decedent of an intent to adopt the child or to have him or her treated as a legally adopted child, sheds little light on the decedent's likely intent regarding distribution of property. While a person with whom the decedent had a close, caring and enduring relationship may often be seen as more deserving of inheritance than the heir or heirs at law, whose personal relationships with the decedent may have been, as they were here, attenuated, equitable adoption in California is neither a means of compensating the child for services rendered to the parent nor a device to avoid the unjust enrichment of other, more distant relatives who will succeed to the estate under the intestacy statutes. Absent proof of an intent to adopt, we must follow the statutory law of intestate succession.

In addition, a rule looking to the parties' overall relationship in order to do equity in a given case, rather than to particular expressions of intent to adopt, would necessarily be a vague and subjective one, inconsistently applied, in an area of law where "consistent, bright-line rules" (*Estate of Furia, supra*, 103 Cal.App.4th at p. 6, 126 Cal.Rptr.2d 384) are greatly needed. Such a broad scope for equitable adoption would leave open to competing claims the estate of any foster parent or stepparent who treats a foster child or stepchild lovingly and on an equal basis with his or her natural or legally adopted children. . . .

While a California equitable adoption claimant need not prove all the elements of an enforceable contract to adopt, therefore, we conclude the claimant must demonstrate the existence of some direct expression, on the decedent's part, of an intent to adopt the claimant. This intent may be shown, of course, by proof of an unperformed express agreement or promise to adopt. But it may also be demonstrated by proof of other acts or statements directly showing that the decedent intended the child to be, or to be treated as, a legally adopted child, such as an invalid or unconsummated attempt to adopt, the decedent's statement of his or her intent to adopt the child, or the decedent's representation to the claimant or to the community at large that the claimant was the decedent's natural or legally adopted child. (See, e.g., *Estate of Rivolo, supra*, 194 Cal.App.2d at p. 775, 15 Cal.Rptr. 268 [parents who orally promised child she would "be their little girl" later told her and others they had adopted her]; *Estate of Wilson, supra*, 111 Cal.App.3d at p. 248, 168 Cal.Rptr. 533 [petition to adopt filed but dismissed for lack of natural mother's consent]; *Estate of Reid* (1978) 80 Cal.App.3d 185, 188, 145 Cal.Rptr. 451 [written agreement with adult child].)

Thus, in California the doctrine of equitable adoption is a relatively narrow one, applying only to those who " "" "though having filled the place of a natural born child, through inadvertence or fault [have] not been legally adopted,'" [where] the evidence establishes an intent to adopt." (*Estate of Furia, supra*, 103 Cal.App.4th at p. 5, 126 Cal.Rptr.2d 384, italics added.) In addition to a statement or act by the decedent un-equivocally evincing the decedent's intent to adopt, the claimant must show the decedent acted consistently with that intent by forming with the claimant a close and enduring familial relationship.[30] That is, in addition to a contract or other direct evidence of the intent to adopt, the evidence must show "objective conduct indicating mutual recognition of an adoptive parent and child relationship to such an extent that in equity and good conscience an adoption should be deemed to have taken place." (*Estate of Bauer, supra*, 111 Cal.App.3d at p. 560, 168 Cal.Rptr. 743.)

II. Standard of Proof of Equitable Adoption

Bean also contends the lower courts erred in applying a standard of clear and convincing proof to the equitable adoption question. We disagree. Most courts that have considered the question require at least clear and convincing evidence in order to prove an equitable adoption. (See Clark, The Law of Domestic Relations in the United States, *supra*, at p. 927; Rein, *supra*, 37 Vand. L.Rev. at p. 780.) Several good reasons support the rule.

First, the claimant in an equitable adoption case is seeking inheritance outside the ordinary statutory course of intestate succession and without the formalities required by the adoption statutes. . . .

Second, the claim involves a relationship with persons who have died and who can, therefore, no longer testify to their intent. As with an alleged contract to make a will (see *Crail v. Blakely* (1973) 8 Cal.3d 744, 750, fn. 3, 106 Cal.Rptr. 187, 505 P.2d 1027), the law, in order to guard against fraudulent claims, should require more than a bare preponderance of evidence. Where "the lips of the alleged adopter have been sealed by death ... proof of the facts essential to invoke the intervention of equity should be clear, unequivocal and convincing." (*Cavanaugh v. Davis* (1951) 149 Tex. 573, 235 S.W.2d 972, 978.)

Finally, too relaxed a standard could create the danger that "a person could not help out a needy child without having a de facto adoption foisted upon him after death." (Rein, *supra*, 37 Vand. L.Rev. at p. 782.) ...

CONCLUSION

Although the evidence showed the Fords and Bean enjoyed a close and enduring familial relationship, evidence was totally lacking that the Fords ever made an attempt to adopt Bean or promised or stated their intent to do so; they neither held Bean out to the world as their natural or adopted child (Bean, for example, did not take the Ford name) nor represented to Bean that he was their child. Mrs. Ford's single statement to Barbara Carter was not clear and convincing evidence that Mr. Ford intended Bean to be, or be treated as, his adopted son. Substantial evidence thus supported

---

30. A close familial relationship sufficient to support the decedent's intent to adopt must persist up to, or at least not be repudiated by, the decedent before the decedent's death.

the trial court, which heard the testimony live and could best assess its credibility and strength, in its finding that intent to adopt, and therefore Bean's claim of equitable adoption, was unproven.

Disposition

The judgment of the Court of Appeal is affirmed.

Notes

1. *The California approach*: Did the California Supreme Court follow the recommendations of the academic community and adopt Justice Sears-Collins's equitable estoppel-based approach to equitable adoption, or did the Court follow the lead of the Georgia Supreme Court? How would the *O'Neal* case come out under the California approach?

2. *Inheritance rights*: Assuming, *arguendo*, one meets the requirements for equitable adoption, equitable adoption does not establish a full parent-child relationship. The equitably adopted party is entitled to inherit only from, but not through, the equitably adoptive parent (except, in many jurisdictions, from a full-blooded sibling). To the extent the child is generally limited to inheriting from the equitably adoptive parent, does the doctrine actually establish a parent-child relationship or is the remedy more consistent with damages for a breach of contract claim?

3. *Visualizing the inheritance rights*: How would you diagram inheritance rights under the California Probate Code with respect to the paradigm equitable adoption scenario? Assume the natural parents are married.

2. Attempted Adoption

While most states require a legally recognized adoption before creating a legally recognized parent-child relationship to which inheritance rights can attach, California statutorily recognizes a special parent-child relationship where there has been an attempted, but *not* legally recognized, adoption.

CPC § 6454. Foster parent or stepparent attempted adoption

For the purpose of determining intestate succession by a person or the person's issue from or through a foster parent or stepparent, the relationship of parent and child exists between that person and the person's foster parent or stepparent if both of the following requirements are satisfied:

(a) The relationship began during the person's minority and continued throughout the joint lifetimes of the person and the person's foster parent or stepparent.

(b) It is established by clear and convincing evidence that the foster parent or stepparent would have adopted the person but for a legal barrier.

Notes

1. *Paradigm scenario*: The paradigm scenario (but not the only scenario) section 6454 was designed to address was the stepparent attempted adoption scenario. For example, Pete and Gerri are married and have one child, Cici. Gerri divorces Pete and marries Bob. Bob wants to make the home environment as close to "one big happy family" as he can, so he tries to adopt Cici. Before the minor child can be adopted, the natural parent whose parental rights will be affected must consent to the adoption. Cal. Fam. Code § 8604 (West 2013). Pete refuses to consent to the proposed adoption. The overwhelming majority of all adoptions and attempted adoptions occur when a child is a minor. The most common legal barrier to an adoption is the natural parent in question refuses to consent. While it is not the only legal barrier, the other possible legal barriers are best left to the Family law course.

2. *Visualizing the inheritance rights*: How would you diagram the inheritance rights under the California Probate Code with respect to the paradigm attempted adoption scenario (assume the natural parents are married)?

3. *Temporal limitation*? What if a relationship begins between a child and a foster parent/stepparent while the child is a minor, the relationship continues throughout their joint lifetimes, and the foster parent/stepparent attempts to adopt the child but the natural parent in question refuses to consent. Twenty-five years later, the foster parent/stepparent dies intestate. Can the child inherit from and through the foster parent/stepparent? Must the legal barrier exist only at the time of the attempted adoption, or must it too continue throughout the joint lifetimes of the child and the foster parent/stepparent?

That issue split the California Courts of Appeal. In *Estate of Stevenson*, 11 Cal. App. 4th 852, 14 Cal. Rptr. 2d 250 (1992), the Sixth Appellate District ruled that the legal barrier needed to exist only at the time adoption was contemplated or attempted. In *Estate of Cleveland*, 17 Cal. App. 4th 1700, 22 Cal. Rptr. 2d 590 (1993), the Second Appellate District ruled that section 6454 requires that the legal barrier or barriers to adoption must have continued until death. The California Supreme Court took up the issue in *Estate of Joseph*.

Estate of Joseph

949 P.2d 472 (Cal. 1998)

MOSK, Justice.

. . .

Petitioner "was taken in by" decedent and his wife, who predeceased him, "and [was] raised by them during the vast period of her minority, from age three on. [They] assisted her after her minority by financing her efforts at San Jose State University and a local junior college. [Decedent] 'gave' [her] away at her wedding. Certainly, the relationship between [decedent and his wife and petitioner] satisfied the common law definition of 'foster child,' at least during the minority and early adulthood of [petitioner], which to simplistically recite [its] shorthand definition means one whose well being is fostered by another person. For a period, at the beginning of the relationship, and during her minority both [decedent and his wife] would from time to time ask [petitioner's] natural parents if they ... could adopt [her]. Each such request was refused. After a while, but still during [her] minority [they] discontinued asking.

...

"Factually, in this case [decedent], the last to die of the [spouses], could have pursued an adult adoption had he really wanted to establish a parent/child relationship with [petitioner]. Additionally, he could have written a will leaving his property to [her] had he intended for her to succeed to his property. (He clearly was aware of the benefits of the use of a will, as he used the services of the [l]awyer who now represents [petitioner] to write a will many years before his death.) We cannot know what [decedent's] intentions were regarding the devolution of his estate, except as he expressed them as to his predeceased spouse when he wrote his will. Although it is not an insignificant fact that he did not express any testamentary intent toward [petitioner] as a successor beneficiary should, as actually happened, his wife have predeceased him. Cleveland ... envisioned just such a case as this when it recognized that any number of reasons could exist for not wanting a 'foster child' to succeed to one's property including loss of affection, disappointment, favoring relatives, dissatisfaction with the choice of the 'foster child's' spouse, to name but a few. In this case [petitioner] obtained her majority age on October 15, 1974, some twenty one years before [decedent's] death. Surely, that passage of time cannot be ignored.... [Decedent and his wife] during their life had ample opportunity to control the outcome and for what ever [sic] reason chose not to. To conclude that [decedent] wanted [petitioner] to inherit his property is presumptuous and not consistent with the Legislature's reasons for enactment of §6454."

...

Our reading of Probate Code section 6454 also suits the purpose that underlies the code generally, that is, to pass the estate of an intestate decedent in accordance with the "intent" that he "is most likely to have had" at the time of death, and to do so in an "efficient and expeditious" manner.

...

Our reading of Probate Code section 6454 also serves the passing of the estate of an intestate foster parent or stepparent efficiently and expeditiously. To quote the Cleveland court again, it "injects a strong dose of certainty into" such matters. (Estate of Cleveland, supra, 17 Cal.App.4th at p. 1712, 22 Cal.Rptr.2d 590.) The provision's mandate that a legal barrier to adoption must have continued until death, together with an intent to adopt, eliminates, or at least reduces, marginal claims, whether genuine or sham, based on little more than an assertion that such a barrier existed only at a time at which adoption was contemplated or attempted. Otherwise, as the Cleveland court explained, there might be "claims by a stepchild or foster child if at any time during his minority the stepparent [or foster parent] expressed a desire to adopt but was denied the consent of the natural parent. Any such child could claim an intestate share of the decedent's estate at his death — no matter how many years elapsed after the removal of the legal impediment. Operating from the stalest sort of evidence, the probate court must then determine whether, "but for" that legal impediment the decedent would have adopted the [child] during his minority and must negate the existence of other reasons for decedent's abandonment of the adoption. In such cases, of course, the decedent is unavailable to rebut these claims asserted by persons with a direct financial interest. Often, the only corroborating testimony is from the nonconsenting [natural] parent who may also be financially interested in the outcome. Typically, there will be no other disinterested third parties to verify the decedent's intent, since the subject matter is commonly considered to be of a highly personal and private nature." (Id. at pp. 1710–1711, 22 Cal.Rptr.2d 590, fn. omitted.) ...

CHIN, Associate Justice, dissenting.

   ...

In disagreeing with the majority, I emphasize the narrowness of the question before us: whether the absence of a legal barrier to petitioner's adoption after she reached the age of majority precludes her, as a matter of law, from establishing that decedent would have adopted her "but for a legal barrier." (§ 6454, subd. (b).) By enacting section 6454, the Legislature indicated that the probate court, as the fact finder, ordinarily should decide whether a decedent would have adopted a foster child or stepchild but for a legal barrier. Contrary to this intent, the majority removes this question from the probate court's consideration in all but the rare cases where both a continuous legal barrier to adoption and a continuous intent to adopt existed. In so doing, the majority weighs certain evidentiary factors in an attempt to make factual determinations about a decedent's likely intent. In my view, this is the function of the probate court considering the entire evidentiary record in a given case, not of this court in the abstract. If the evidence is weak, then the probate court may conclude as a factual matter that the requirements of the statute have not been met. That a legal barrier to adoption did not exist continuously during adulthood is a circumstance for the probate court to weigh in determining whether the foster parent or stepparent would have adopted the child but for a legal barrier. It is not a basis for completely removing the issue from the fact finder's consideration.

   ...

Second, the majority overstates the extent to which the goal of efficiency should guide our inquiry. By opening up a decedent's estate to claims of foster children and stepchildren, and by making these claims depend on proof of highly fact-specific requirements, section 6454, by its very nature, is inconsistent with the goal of efficiency. Had efficiency been the Legislature's sole concern, it would not have enacted section 6454. Instead, it would have left California law unchanged and in accord with that of other states by simply omitting foster children and stepchildren from the intestacy statutes. Thus, by enacting section 6454, the Legislature demonstrated that, at least in this one area, it was not primarily concerned about efficiency....

———————

Notes

1. *Epilogue*: During the appeal process, the California Law Reform Commission initiated procedures to revise Probate Code Section 6454 to reflect the approach adopted by the lower court in *Stevenson*, i.e., that so long as there was clear and convincing evidence that the stepparent or foster parent would have adopted the child but for a legal barrier, the legal barrier did not have to be present at the time the stepparent or foster parent died. The California legislature failed to adopt the proposed amendment to Probate Code Section 6454.

2. *Status vs. intent*: The dissent offered a series of arguments for why efficiency in the distribution of a decedent's estate should not be a relevant variable when considering claims by stepchildren and foster children under Probate Code section 6454. Do you agree or disagree? In doing so, the dissent was implicitly arguing that in adopting Probate Code section 6454 the California legislature adopted which approach to what constitutes a parent-child relationship, at least with respect to the attempted adoption scenario — the status-based approach or the intent-based approach? Do you agree? Does it make sense to apply it only to this scenario and not the other possible parent-child relationship scenarios?

Problem

Andy never married, but he fathered one child (Xavier) with Betty, and two children (Yola and Zack) with Cindy. Andy acknowledged all of his children, and supported them, but the two different families did not know of each other. Thereafter Betty died, then Andy died, and then Xavier died intestate, with no surviving spouse and no surviving issue. Xavier was particularly close to Andy's father, Frank, who had stepped in and raised Xavier after Andy and Betty died. Frank claims Xavier's estate. Only after Andy's death do Yola and Zack learn of their relationship to Xavier. Who takes Xavier's estate, and why?

G. Child Born after Natural Parent's Death

1. Posthumously Born Child

A posthumously born child is a child who was conceived before the natural parent's death but born after the natural parent's death. For inheritance purposes, the common law has always considered a posthumously born child as alive ("in being") from the moment of conception as long as the child is born alive. So long as the child was born within 300 days of the decedent's death, the common law treated the child as an heir of the decedent for inheritance purposes.

California has basically codified the common law approach, with a few extra features included:

Family Code § 7611. Status as natural father; presumption; conditions

> A man is presumed to be the natural father of a child … in any of the following subdivisions:
>
> (a) He and the child's natural mother are or have been married to each other and the child is born during the marriage, or within 300 days after the marriage is terminated by death, annulment, declaration of invalidity, or divorce, or after a judgment of separation is entered by a court.
>
>   …

Probate Code § 6407. Unborn relatives of decedent

> Relatives of the decedent conceived before the decedent's death but born thereafter inherit as if they had been born in the lifetime of the decedent.

Notes

1. *Paradigm scenario*: The paradigm scenario involving the posthumously born child is one where the natural father dies after the child is conceived but before the child is born. At common law, the mother had to be married for the presumption to apply. What was the common law logic behind limiting the doctrine to married couples? Does California limit the doctrine to married couples?

2. *Visualizing the inheritance rights*: How would you diagram the inheritance rights under the California Probate Code with respect to the following paradigm posthumously born scenario? Assume the natural parents are married.

2. Posthumously Conceived Child

While the posthumously born scenario is a relatively old scenario, the posthumously conceived child is a relatively new scenario. While the typical posthumously born scenario involves natural insemination, the posthumously conceived scenario involves artificial insemination. The first reported American case of artificial insemination dates back to the late 1800s. A Quaker couple having trouble conceiving a child met with Dr. William Pancoast, a professor at the Jefferson Medical College in Philadelphia. Dr. Pancoast diagnosed the problem, declaring the husband sterile. Rather than telling the couple, however, he and his six medical students decided "to help out" the couple. They called the woman back in under the pretext of conducting one more test. After anesthetizing her, and without informing the couple or obtaining either party's consent, Dr. Pancoast artificially inseminated the woman using sperm previously collected from one of his students.[31] After the woman became pregnant, the doctor informed the husband how she was impregnated. The husband was so pleased at the thought of having a child that he approved of the procedure so long as they agreed not to tell his wife. It was not until 1909, after Dr. Pancoast died, that one of his students went public with the story.[32]

---

31. Dr. Pancoast and the students agreed they should use the sperm of "the best looking" student — it is not known how that was determined.

32. One of the students involved, Addison Davis Hard, wrote a "tell-all" letter that was published in 1909 in the journal MEDICAL WORLD.

Artificial insemination using sperm donated by someone other than a woman's husband raises many interesting medical, moral, and legal issues. As one might expect with such a medical breakthrough, the first official responses to the practice condemned it. The Pope denounced the practice as sinful, an English Parliamentary Commission that convened to study the practice proposed it be made a crime, and in the United States the initial response of the courts was that even if her husband consented, a wife's use of someone else's sperm was "contrary to public policy and good morals, and considered adultery on the mother's part.... A child so conceived, was born out of wedlock, and therefore illegitimate. As such, it is the child of the mother, and the father has no rights or interest in said child."[33] Like many medical advances, however, opposition waned with time. Yet just as artificial insemination was gaining general social and legal acceptance, another controversial form of reproductive technology evolved: posthumous conception using frozen sperm.

The classic posthumous conception scenario involves the use of a decedent's sperm to artificially inseminate a woman. Posthumous conception necessarily involves artificial insemination, but because sperm has such a short shelf life, posthumous use of sperm was not feasible until the development of cryopreservation—the ability to freeze human tissue and genetic material and thaw it without causing damage. This procedure was mastered in the late 1950s to preserve the sperm of the early astronauts because of uncertainty surrounding the effects of space travel on their health. One of the first publicly covered cases of posthumous conception was in France. Following the successful birth of the posthumously conceived child, the French government called for a gathering of leading experts in medicine, ethics, and reproductive technology. The experts agreed that posthumous conception was against public policy and should be banned—a recommendation the French Parliament adopted that still applies today. In the United States no such ban exists, but issues still remain with respect to the legal status of such children.

Is the posthumously conceived scenario basically the posthumously born scenario taken to the next level due to the advancements in reproductive technology—so the issues and doctrines should basically be the same—or are there meaningful differences between the two scenarios that give rise to different policy considerations, thereby resulting in different doctrines?

Woodward v. Commissioner of Social Security

760 N.E.2d 257 (Mass. 2002)

MARSHALL, C.J.

...

"If a married man and woman arrange for sperm to be withdrawn from the husband for the purpose of artificially impregnating the wife, and the

---

33. Doornbos v. Doornbos, 139 N.E.2d 844 (Ill. App. Ct. 1956).

woman is impregnated with that sperm after the man, her husband, has died, will children resulting from such pregnancy enjoy the inheritance rights of natural children under Massachusetts' law of intestate succession?"

I

The undisputed facts and relevant procedural history are as follows. In January, 1993, about three and one-half years after they were married, Lauren Woodward and Warren Woodward were informed that the husband had leukemia. At the time, the couple was childless. Advised that the husband's leukemia treatment might leave him sterile, the Woodwards arranged for a quantity of the husband's semen to be medically withdrawn and preserved, in a process commonly known as "sperm banking." The husband then underwent a bone marrow transplant. The treatment was not successful. The husband died in October, 1993, and the wife was appointed administratrix of his estate.

In October, 1995, the wife gave birth to twin girls. The children were conceived through artificial insemination using the husband's preserved semen. In January, 1996, the wife applied for two forms of Social Security survivor benefits: "child's" benefits under 42 U.S.C. §402(d)(1) (1994 & Supp. V 1999), and "mother's" benefits under 42 U.S.C. §402(g)(1) (1994).

The Social Security Administration (SSA) rejected the wife's claims on the ground that she had not established that the twins were the husband's "children" within the meaning of the Act....

II

A

We have been asked to determine the inheritance rights under Massachusetts law of children conceived from the gametes of a deceased individual and his or her surviving spouse.

... [T]he parties have articulated extreme positions. The wife's principal argument is that, by virtue of their genetic connection with the decedent, posthumously conceived children must always be permitted to enjoy the inheritance rights of the deceased parent's children under our law of intestate succession. The government's principal argument is that, because posthumously conceived children are not "in being" as of the date of the parent's death, they are always barred from enjoying such inheritance rights.

Neither party's position is tenable. In this developing and relatively uncharted area of human relations, bright-line rules are not favored unless the applicable statute requires them. The Massachusetts intestacy statute does not.

B

... We must therefore determine whether, under our intestacy law, there is any reason that children conceived after the decedent's death who are the decedent's direct genetic descendants — that is, children who "by consanguinity trace their lineage to the designated ancestor"—may not enjoy the same succession rights as children conceived before the decedent's death who are the decedent's direct genetic descendants....

The question whether posthumously conceived genetic children may enjoy inheritance rights under the intestacy statute implicates three powerful State interests: the best interests of children, the State's interest in the orderly administration of estates, and the reproductive rights of the genetic parent. Our task is to balance and harmonize these interests to effect the Legislature's over-all purposes.

1. First and foremost we consider the overriding legislative concern to promote the best interests of children. "The protection of minor children, most especially those who may be stigmatized by their 'illegitimate' status ... has been a hallmark of legislative action and of the jurisprudence of this court." L.W.K. v. E.R.C., 432 Mass. 438, 447–448, 735 N.E.2d 359 (2000). Repeatedly, forcefully, and unequivocally, the Legislature has expressed its will that all children be "entitled to the same rights and protections of the law" regardless of the accidents of their birth. G.L. c. 209C, § 1. See G.L. c. 119, § 1 ... Among the many rights and protections vouchsafed to all children are rights to financial support from their parents and their parents' estates. See G.L. c. 119A, § 1 ("It is the public policy of this commonwealth that dependent children shall be maintained, as completely as possible, from the resources of their parents, thereby relieving or avoiding, at least in part, the burden borne by the citizens of the commonwealth");....

... Posthumously conceived children may not come into the world the way the majority of children do. But they are children nonetheless. We may assume that the Legislature intended that such children be "entitled," in so far as possible, "to the same rights and protections of the law" as children conceived before death. See G.L. c. 209C, § 1.

2. However, in the context of our intestacy laws, the best interests of the posthumously conceived child, while of great importance, are not in themselves conclusive. They must be balanced against other important State interests, not the least of which is the protection of children who are alive or conceived before the intestate parent's death....

The intestacy statute furthers the Legislature's administrative goals in two principal ways: (1) by requiring certainty of filiation between the decedent and his issue, and (2) by establishing limitations periods for the commencement of claims against the intestate estate. In answering the certified question, we must consider each of these requirements of the intestacy statute in turn.

First, ... [b]ecause death ends a marriage, see *Callow v. Thomas*, 322 Mass. 550, 555, 78 N.E.2d 637 (1948); *Rawson v. Rawson*, 156 Mass. 578, 580, 31 N.E. 653 (1892), posthumously conceived children are always nonmarital children. And because the parentage of such children can be neither acknowledged nor adjudicated prior to the decedent's death, it follows that, under the intestacy statute, posthumously conceived children must obtain a judgment of paternity as a necessary prerequisite to enjoying inheritance rights in the estate of the deceased genetic father....

We now turn to the second way in which the Legislature has met its administrative goals: the establishment of a limitations period for bringing paternity claims against the intestate estate.... [T]he limitations question is inextricably tied to consideration of the intestacy statute's administrative goals. In the case of posthumously conceived children, the application of the one-year limitations period of G.L. c. 190, §7 is not clear; it may pose significant burdens on the surviving parent, and consequently on the child. It requires, in effect, that the survivor make a decision to bear children while in the freshness of grieving. It also requires that attempts at conception succeed quickly. Cf. Commentary, Modern Reproductive Technologies: Legal Issues Concerning Cryopreservation and Posthumous Conception, 17 J. Legal Med. 547, 549 (1996) ("It takes an average of seven insemination attempts over 4.4 menstrual cycles to establish pregnancy"). Because the resolution of the time constraints question is not required here, it must await the appropriate case, should one arise.

3. Finally, the question certified to us implicates a third important State interest: to honor the reproductive choices of individuals. We need not address the wife's argument that her reproductive rights would be infringed by denying succession rights to her children under our intestacy law. Nothing in the record even remotely suggests that she was prevented by the State from choosing to conceive children using her deceased husband's semen. The husband's reproductive rights are a more complicated matter.

... [A] decedent's silence, or his equivocal indications of a desire to parent posthumously, "ought not to be construed as consent." ... The prospective donor parent must clearly and unequivocally consent not only to posthumous reproduction but also to the support of any resulting child.... After the donor-parent's death, the burden rests with the surviving parent, or the posthumously conceived child's other legal representative, to prove the deceased genetic parent's affirmative consent to both requirements for posthumous parentage: posthumous reproduction and the support of any resulting child.

...

... It will not always be the case that a person elects to have his or her gametes medically preserved to create "issue" posthumously. A man, for example, may preserve his semen for myriad reasons, including, among others: to reproduce after recovery from medical treatment, to reproduce after an event that leaves him sterile, or to reproduce when his spouse has a genetic disorder or otherwise cannot have or safely bear children. That a man has medically preserved his gametes for use by his spouse thus may indicate only that he wished to reproduce after some contingency while he was alive, and not that he consented to the different circumstance of creating a child after his death. Uncertainty as to consent may be compounded by the fact that medically preserved semen can remain viable for up to ten years after it was first extracted, long after the original decision to preserve the semen has passed and when such changed circumstances as divorce, remarriage, and a second family may have intervened. See Banks, Traditional Concepts and Nontraditional Conceptions: Social Security Survivor's Benefits for Posthumously Conceived Children, 32 Loy. L.A. L.Rev. 251, 270 (1999).

… Where two adults engage in the act of sexual intercourse, it is a matter of common sense and logic, expressed in well-established law, to charge them with parental responsibilities for the child who is the natural, even if unintended, consequence of their actions. Where conception results from a third-party medical procedure using a deceased person's gametes, it is entirely consistent with our laws on children, parentage, and reproductive freedom to place the burden on the surviving parent (or the posthumously conceived child's other legal representative) to demonstrate the genetic relationship of the child to the decedent and that the intestate consented both to reproduce posthumously and to support any resulting child.

C

III

… In the absence of statutory directives … we conclude that limited circumstances may exist, consistent with the mandates of our Legislature, in which posthumously conceived children may enjoy the inheritance rights of "issue" under our intestacy law. These limited circumstances exist where, as a threshold matter, the surviving parent or the child's other legal representative demonstrates a genetic relationship between the child and the decedent. The survivor or representative must then establish both that the decedent affirmatively consented to posthumous conception and to the support of any resulting child. Even where such circumstances exist, time limitations may preclude commencing a claim for succession rights on behalf of a posthumously conceived child. In any action brought to establish such inheritance rights, notice must be given to all interested parties.

Notes

1. *Posthumously conceived parent-child relationship*: One of the traditional maxims is that every child has one mother and one father. Does that maxim automatically and always apply to a posthumously conceived child? Should it? To the extent the child does not meet the requirements as set forth by the Massachusetts Supreme Court, is the child being punished because of the "wrongful" conduct of one of the natural parents? Is that right?

2. *California approach*: The California legislature responded to the *Woodward* opinion and the resulting debate over the legal status of a posthumously conceived child by adopting Probate Code section 249.5. How did the California legislature respond to the concerns raised by the Massachusetts Supreme Court? Did it address all of them?

CPC § 249.5. Posthumously conceived child

For purposes of determining rights to property to be distributed upon the death of a decedent, a child of the decedent conceived and born after the death of the decedent shall be deemed to have been born in the lifetime of the decedent, and after the execution of all of the decedent's testamentary instruments, if the child or his or her representative proves by clear and convincing evidence that all of the following conditions are satisfied:

(a) The decedent, in writing, specifies that his or her genetic material shall be used for the posthumous conception of a child of the decedent, subject to the following:

  (1) The specification shall be signed by the decedent and dated.

  (2) The specification may be revoked or amended only by a writing, signed by the decedent and dated.

  (3) A person is designated by the decedent to control the use of the genetic material.

(b) The person designated by the decedent to control the use of the genetic material has given written notice by certified mail, return receipt requested, that the decedent's genetic material was available for the purpose of posthumous conception. The notice shall have been given to a person who has the power to control the distribution of either the decedent's property or death benefits payable by reason of the decedent's death, within four months of the date of issuance of a certificate of the decedent's death or entry of a judgment determining the fact of the decedent's death, whichever event occurs first.

(c) The child was in utero using the decedent's genetic material and was in utero within two years of the date of issuance of a certificate of the decedent's death or entry of a judgment determining the fact of the decedent's death, whichever event occurs first. This subdivision does not apply to ... human cloning.

3. *Visualizing the inheritance rights*: How would you diagram the inheritance rights under the California Probate Code with respect to the paradigm posthumously conceived child scenario? Assume the natural parents are married.

Chapter 4

Miscellaneous Doctrines That May Affect an Heir's Share

I. Overview

A state's intestate scheme functions as a default will. If a decedent dies without properly executing his or her own valid will, his or her probate property will pass pursuant to the state's intestate scheme. While a valid will can override the intestate scheme, even in the absence of a valid will there are a number of miscellaneous doctrines that can alter or override how much an heir would otherwise take under the intestate scheme.

To the extent the intestate scheme is supposed to reflect the presumed intent of an average decedent, are these doctrines similarly based on presumed intent, or is there something else going on with respect to one or more of these doctrines? Related to that question, some of these doctrines are not limited to heirs and intestate property, but also apply to beneficiaries under a will and/or nonprobate instrument. You should be mindful of the scope of the different doctrines and how that interrelates with the justification for each doctrine.

II. The Advancement Doctrine

The probate scheme provides that if a decedent dies intestate with no surviving spouse, the decedent's property passes to his or her issue *equally*. Why *equally*? No doubt part of the explanation is because the law assumes the decedent loved his or her issue equally. But how far should the "issue should take equally" principle be taken? Should an *inter vivos* gift count against an issue's time of death share?

The common law embraced the principle of equality and took it to its logical extreme. In fact, the common law presumed that a parent's *inter vivos* gifts to a child *should* count against that child's share of the parent's estate. To the extent an *inter vivos* gift counted against the child's share, the *inter vivos* gift basically functioned as an advancement of the child's inheritance; hence the doctrine of advancements. Mechanically, under the doctrine of advancements, all *inter vivos* gifts to the decedent's children are fictionally added back into the decedent's estate as an accounting entry to create what is called "the hotchpot"—a fictional, enhanced probate estate. The hotchpot is then divided equally among the decedent's children. If a child has received an advancement, the advancement is credited against that child's share of the hotchpot to determine the child's actual share of the decedent's actual probate estate. These calculations ensure that, when all is said and done, the decedent's children take equally, taking into consideration the inter vivos advancements.

For example, assume a single parent with two children. The parent gives one child $200,000 to help with college and law school expenses. Thereafter, the parent dies intestate with an estate of $800,000. Under the common law approach, the $200,000 given *inter vivos* to the one child is presumed an advancement of that's child's share of the decedent's intestate estate. To calculate the advancement's effect, add the *inter vivos* gift back in to the probate estate (as an accounting entry only — the child would not be required to pay any money back) to create a "hotchpot" of $1,000,000 ($800,000 + $200,000). This fictional hotchpot estate is then split equally among the decedent's two children, one-half ($500,000) to each, but the advancement is then credited against the one child's share. Therefore, the child who received the $200,000 *inter vivos* gift would receive only $300,000 ($500,000 – $200,000) from the actual probate estate, and the other child would receive the remaining $500,000.

While the common law approach maximizes the principle that children take equally from their parents, it also creates an economic incentive for children to sue each other to increase their own share of the decedent's estate. To the extent a child believes his or her parent favored another child — as children are often tempted to do — the doctrine of advancement gives them an economic incentive to voice their childish claims in the interest of increasing their own share of the parent's estate at the expense of their siblings. The common law approach thus exacerbates natural sibling rivalry. Instead of children consoling and supporting each other following their parent's death, they have an economic incentive to attack and sue each other — which includes high costs of administration, and heightens the potential for fraudulent claims.

The modern trend reverses the traditional approach and arguably remedies most of its adverse consequences. Under the modern trend, a decedent's *inter vivos* gifts to an heir are presumed *not* to count against the heir's share of the decedent's estate. The modern trend presumption is rebuttable. A writing is required to rebut the presumption. Alleged oral declarations by the decedent are not enough. As you might surmise, the modern trend version of the doctrine of advancements drastically reduces how often the doctrine is implicated in actual, real-life intestate succession situations.

There is, however, something of a latent issue lurking in the modern trend approach. What if the parent properly expresses the intent that the *inter vivos* gift should count against the heir's (e.g., the child's) time of death share, but the donee (the child) predeceases the donor (the parent), and the donee's issue (the grandchildren) are entitled to take the donee's (the child's) share by representation. Should the *inter vivos* gift count against the time of death share of the donee's issue (the grandchildren)?

Does California still follow the common law approach, or does it follow the modern trend? How would California answer the "latent issue" above?

CPC § 6409. Inter vivos gifts to decedent's heirs; when constitute advancement against intestate share

(a) If a person dies intestate as to all or part of his or her estate, property the decedent gave during lifetime to an heir is treated as an advancement against that heir's share of the intestate estate only if one of the following conditions is satisfied:

   (1) The decedent declares in a contemporaneous writing that the gift is an advancement against the heir's share of the estate or that its value is to be deducted from the value of the heir's share of the estate.

   (2) The heir acknowledges in writing that the gift is to be so deducted or is an advancement or that its value is to be deducted from the value of the heir's share of the estate.

(b) Subject to subdivision (c), the property advanced is to be valued as of the time the heir came into possession or enjoyment of the property or as of the time of death of the decedent, whichever occurs first.

   …

(d) If the recipient of the property advanced fails to survive the decedent, the property is not taken into account in computing the intestate share to be received by the recipient's issue unless the declaration or acknowledgment provides otherwise.

Notes

1. *The California approach*: How does the California Probate Code answer the question of whether an *inter vivos* gift should affect the donee's time of death share if the donor dies intestate? What is necessary for an *inter vivos* gift to count as an advancement under the California approach? How is the advancement treated if the donee predeceases the donor?

2. *Predeceased donee*: What if a parent properly expresses the intent that the *inter vivos* gift should count against the heir's time of death share, but the donee predeceases the donor, and the donee's issue are entitled to take the donee's share by representation. Should the *inter vivos* gift count against the time-of-death share of the donee's issue?

3. *Advancement versus satisfaction*: The doctrine of "advancements" and California Probate Code Section 6409 apply exclusively to property passing by way of intestate succession. A similar doctrine known as "satisfaction" (or "ademption by satisfaction") applies to directed distributions via will or will substitute (the doctrine of satisfaction is set forth in California Probate Code Section 21135 and discussed in Chapter 9).

Problems

1. Using the numbers from the above common law advancement hypothetical ($200,000 given to one child for college and law school costs, and the single parent's subsequent intestate death with a probate estate of $800,000), how would the decedent parent's estate be distributed pursuant to California intestacy law in the following alternative scenarios?

   a.   Neither the parent nor the child made any oral or written statements, comments, etc. at the time of the *inter vivos* gift, or at any time thereafter, as to whether the $200,000 should count against the recipient child's inheritance.

   b.   What if, at the time of the gift, the parent made a clear oral statement that the $200,000 gift should count against the recipient child's share of the parent's estate? This statement was made in the presence of others who can corroborate it.

   c.   What if the parent expressed in writing that the $200,000 gift should count against the recipient child's share of the parent's estate? Does it matter when the parent creates the writing? What if the parent expressed his or her intent orally (but not in writing), but the recipient child expressed in writing her understanding that the $200,000 gift should count against her share of the parent's estate? Does it matter when the child creates the writing?

   d.   What if, at the time of the gift, the parent's statements were memorialized in a contemporaneous writing, but subsequently—and tragically—the child predeceased the parent. At the parent's death, however, there were living grandchildren (children of the predeceased child). Does the advancement count against the share going to the issue of the predeceased child?

2.   Deb wrote a letter to her nephew, Ned, in which Deb wrote: "I have enclosed a check for $30,000 as a little down payment toward your inheritance. There will be more for you in my estate, but I know you can use this money now." Deb died intestate survived by Ned and two other nieces. Deb's probate estate totals $15,000. How is the $15,000 most likely to be distributed?

III. The Slayer Doctrine

A. Introduction

What difference, if any, should it make if a party otherwise entitled to receive part of the decedent's estate is responsible for the decedent's death? Aside from any criminal punishment that may be imposed, should the slayer's right to receive some of the decedent's property also be affected? Is it right to permit the individual responsible for the decedent's death to receive some of the decedent's property?

In re Mahoney's Estate

126 Vt. 31, 220 A.2d 475 (1966)

SMITH, Justice.

The decedent, Howard Mahoney, died intestate on May 6, 1961, of gunshot wounds. His wife, Charlotte Mahoney, the appellant here, was tried for the murder of Howard Mahoney in the Addison County Court and was convicted by jury of the crime of manslaughter in March, 1962....

… The question submitted is whether a widow convicted of manslaughter in connection with the death of her husband may inherit from his estate.

… The question presented is one of first impression in this jurisdiction.

In a number of jurisdictions, statutes have been enacted which in certain instances, at least, prevent a person who has killed another from taking by descent or distribution from the person he has killed. 23 Am.Jur.2d Descent and Distribution, § 98, p. 841. A statute of this nature, carefully drawn, is considered by many authorities to be the best solution to the problems presented. See "Acquisition of property by wilfully killing another — a statutory solution," 49 Harvard Law Review 715 (1935–1936).

Courts in those states that have no statute preventing a slayer from taking by descent or distribution from the estate of his victim, have followed three separate and different lines of decision.

(1) The legal title passed to the slayer and may be retained by him in spite of his crime. The reasoning for so deciding is that devolution of the property of a decedent is controlled entirely by the statutes of descent and distribution; further, that denial of the inheritance to the slayer because of his crime would be imposing an additional punishment for his crime not provided by statute, and would violate the constitutional provision against corruption of blood. [Citations omitted.]

(2) The legal title will not pass to the slayer because of the equitable principle that no one should be permitted to profit by his own fraud, or take advantage and profit as a result of his own wrong or crime. *Riggs v. Palmer*, 115 N.Y. 506, 22 N.E. 188, 5 L.R.A. 340; *Price v. Hitaffer*, 164 Md. 505, 165 A. 470; *Slocum v. Metropolitan Life Ins. Co.*, 245 Mass. 565, 139 N.E. 816, 27 A.L.R. 1517. Decisions so holding have been criticized as judicially engrafting an exception on the statute of descent and distribution and being "unwarranted judicial legislation." *Wall v. Pfanschmidt, supra.*

(3) The legal title passes to the slayer but equity holds him to be a constructive trustee for the heirs or next of kin of the decedent. This disposition of the question presented avoids a judicial engrafting on the statutory laws of descent and distribution, for title passes to the slayer. But because of the unconscionable mode by which the property is acquired by the slayer, equity treats him as a constructive trustee and compels him to convey the property to the heirs or next of kin of the deceased.

The reasoning behind the adoption of this doctrine was well expressed by Mr. Justice Cardozo in his lecture on "The Nature of the Judicial Process." "Consistency was preserved, logic received its tribute, by holding that the legal title passed, but it was subject to a constructive trust. A constructive trust is nothing but 'the formula through which the conscience of equity finds expression.' Property is acquired in such circumstances that the holder of legal title may not in good conscience retain the beneficial interest. Equity, to express its disapproval of his conduct, converts him into a trustee." See 4 Scott on Trusts (2d ed. 1956) § 402; Bogert, Trusts and Trustees, (2d ed. 1960), § 478. See *Miller v. Belville*, 98 Vt. 243, 247, 126 A. 590.

The New Hampshire court was confronted with the same problem of the rights to the benefits of an estate by one who had slain the decedent, in the absence of a statute on the subject. *Kelley v. State*, 105 N.H. 240, 196 A.2d 68. Speaking for an unanimous court, Chief Justice Kenison said: "But, even in the absence of statute, a court applying common law techniques can reach a sensible solution by charging the spouse, heir or legatee as a constructive trustee of the property where equity and justice demand it." *Kelley v. State, supra,* pp. 69, 70. We approve of the doctrine so expressed.

However, the principle that one should not profit by his own wrong must not be extended to every case where a killer acquires property from his victim as a result of the killing. One who has killed while insane is not chargeable as a constructive trustee, or if the slayer had a vested interest in the property, it is property to which he would have been entitled if no slaying had occurred. The principle to be applied is that the slayer should not be permitted to improve his position by the killing, but should not be compelled to surrender property to which he would have been entitled if there had been no killing. The doctrine of constructive trust is involved to prevent the slayer from profiting from his crime, but not as an added criminal penalty. *Kelley v. State, supra,* p. 70; Restatement of Restitution, § 187(2), comment a.

The appellant here was, as we have noted, convicted of manslaughter and not of murder. She calls to our attention that while the Restatement of Restitution, approves the application of the constructive trust doctrine where a devisee or legatee murders the testator, that such rules are not applicable where the slayer was guilty of manslaughter. Restatement of Restitution, § 187, comment e.

The cases generally have not followed this limitation of the rule but hold that the line should not be drawn between murder and manslaughter, but between voluntary and involuntary manslaughter. *Kelley v. State, supra*; *Chase v. Jennifer*, 219 Md. 564, 150 A.2d 251, 254.

We think that this is the proper rule to follow. Voluntary manslaughter is an intentional and unlawful killing, with a real design and purpose to kill, even if such killing be the result of sudden passion or great provocation. Involuntary manslaughter is caused by an unlawful act, but not accompanied with any intention to take life. *State v. McDonnell*, 32 Vt. 491, 545. It is the intent to kill, which when accomplished, leads to the profit of the slayer that brings into play the constructive trust to prevent the unjust enrichment of the slayer by reason of his intentional killing....

Decree reversed and cause remanded ...

B. The California Approach

As the Court in *Mahoney's Estate* noted, in "a number of jurisdictions, statutes have been enacted which in certain instances, at least, prevent a person who has killed another from taking by descent or distribution from the person he has killed." California is one of those states. It has a rather detailed and extensive approach to its slayer doctrine:

CPC Section 250. Person feloniously and intentionally kills the decedent

(a) A person who feloniously and intentionally kills the decedent is not entitled to any of the following:

  (1) Any property, interest, or benefit under a will of the decedent, or a trust created by or for the benefit of the decedent or in which the decedent has an interest, including any general or special power of appointment conferred by the will or trust on the killer and any nomination of the killer as executor, trustee, guardian, or conservator or custodian made by the will or trust.

  (2) Any property of the decedent by intestate succession.

  (3) Any of the decedent's quasi-community property the killer would otherwise acquire ... upon the death of the decedent.

      ...

(b) In the cases covered by subdivision (a):

  (1) The property interest or benefit referred to in paragraph (1) of subdivision (a) passes as if the killer had predeceased the decedent and Section 21110 does not apply.

  (2) Any property interest or benefit referred to in paragraph (1) of subdivision (a) which passes under a power of appointment and by reason of the death of the decedent passes as if the killer had predeceased the decedent, and Section 673 not apply.

  (3) Any nomination in a will or trust of the killer as executor, trustee, guardian, conservator, or custodian which becomes effective as a result of the death of the decedent shall be interpreted as if the killer had predeceased the decedent.

CPC Section 251. Joint tenants; rights by survivorship

A joint tenant who feloniously and intentionally kills another joint tenant thereby effects a severance of the interest of the decedent so that the share of the decedent passes as the decedent's property and the killer has no rights by survivorship. This section applies to joint tenancies in real and personal property, joint and multiple-party accounts in financial institutions, and any other form of co-ownership with survivorship incidents.

CPC Section 252. Named beneficiaries; felonious and intentional killing of decedent

A named beneficiary of a bond, life insurance policy, or other contractual arrangement who feloniously and intentionally kills the principal obligee or the person upon whose life the policy is issued is not entitled to any benefit under the bond, policy, or other contractual arrangement, and it becomes payable as though the killer had predeceased the decedent.

CPC Section 254. Judgment of conviction as conclusive; preponderance of evidence

(a) A final judgment of conviction of felonious and intentional killing is conclusive for purposes of this part.

(b) In the absence of a final judgment of conviction of felonious and intentional killing, the court may determine by a preponderance of evidence whether the killing was felonious and intentional for purposes of this part. The burden of proof is on the party seeking to establish that the killing was felonious and intentional for the purposes of this part.

Notes

1. *Scope*: These statutes are often collectively referred to as the "slayer" or "killer" statutes. Note that their application is not limited to the distribution of property under intestate succession. This, like many other concepts, spans across both the directed and non-directed spectrums of testamentary dispositions. While we typically do not see the "slayer" statutes at work in movies and television murder mysteries, we often see a basic component of their underlying rationale: "He had a motive — he was the sole beneficiary of the victim's will or life insurance policy."

2. *Should a slayer's children be permitted to take the slayer's share?* Under the California slayer doctrine, do we punish the children for the sins of the parent?

   a. If the decedent died intestate and the killer was one of the decedent's children, do the killer's children take the killer's share pursuant to CPC section 240's per capita by representation?

   b. What if, instead, the decedent died testate (with a will leaving her property to her children equally), and the killer was one of the testator's children and a beneficiary under the will? If a will beneficiary is the killer (in our example, the decedent's child), the statute states that the court should treat the killer as if he or she predeceased the decedent parent. Later in the course, in Chapter 9, you will learn that when a named beneficiary fails to survive the decedent, the devise/bequest fails — or, using proper legal terminology, the gift "lapses." Under common law rules, and absent alternative disposition directed by the will, the predeceased beneficiary's share becomes part of the decedent's residuary estate. If, however, the lapsed gift is to a family member who is survived by issue, many states, including California, have an "anti-lapse" statute that "saves" the otherwise failing gift and gives it to the predeceased beneficiary's issue (CPC §21110 — to be covered in detail in Chapter 9). Circling back to our question: If the killer is the decedent's child, and the killer has issue, do the issue take under anti-lapse, or does California punish the issue for the sins of the parent?

3. *Criminal vs. civil matter*: We see from the statute (CPC §250), that the right to take property terminates for any person who feloniously and intentionally kills the decedent. Does this section apply even if the claimant has not been convicted of, or even charged with, a criminal offense? How so? If the person has been acquitted, is it double jeopardy to raise the issue again? Should the prior ruling have res judicata effect in the subsequent case? What is the applicable burden of proof?

IV. The Disclaimer Doctrine

As you may recall from your first-year Property course, an *inter vivos* gift requires intent, delivery, and acceptance: (1) the donor must intend to relinquish all dominion and control over the property being gifted; (2) the property must be delivered; and (3) the gift must be accepted. Traditional gift law presumes acceptance, particularly where the gift is of value. Acceptance, however, is a rebuttable presumption. That is where the law of disclaimer comes into play.

An inheritance, or a devise under a will or a transfer under a nonprobate instrument, is nothing more than a gift (a time-of-death gift, but nevertheless, still a gift). No heir, devisee, or transferee is *required* to accept property from a decedent at time of the latter's death. The law cannot force someone to accept a gift. A disclaimer is nothing more than a party's way of saying: "No, thank you." The law prefers of a more lawyerly and formal way of saying that, hence the law of disclaimer.

Why would someone "disclaim" property that he or she is entitled to receive? In *Dyer v. Eckols*, below, we see one possible reason.

Dyer v. Eckols
808 S.W.2d 531 (Tex. App. 1991)

MURPHY, Justice.

This is a case of first impression in Texas. The issue is whether the beneficiary of a will can effectively disclaim her inheritance pursuant to § 37A of the Texas Probate Code although disclaiming would defeat the rights of a judgment creditor.

Appellant, Roland Edward Dyer, alleges that appellees conspired to defraud him of the ability to satisfy a default judgment of $1.08 million rendered against appellee Sara M. Croom after Croom's car crashed into an automobile driven by Dyer's mother, causing Mrs. Dyer to burn to death. Prior to being served with citation of the damage suit, Croom, although insolvent, attempted to disclaim a gift of $200,000 which she was to inherit under the will of her recently deceased uncle. By summary judgment, the trial court held as a matter of law that (1) the beneficiary of an estate can defeat a creditor's claim by executing a disclaimer under § 37A of the Texas Probate Code, and (2) Croom's disclaimer was not a "transfer" prohibited by the Texas version of the Uniform Fraudulent Transfer Act, Tex. Bus. & Com. Code Ann. § 24.005(a)(1) (Vernon 1987).... [Dyer is appealing the trial court's ruling.]

Croom's uncle died on November 3, 1987, some four months after the accident in which appellant's mother was killed. In his will, admitted to probate three weeks later, Croom's uncle left her a one-tenth (1/10) share of his estate, valued at $2,013,135. She concedes that "a potential tort claim obviously existed" when she later attempted to disclaim the inheritance by executing an Instrument of Disclaimer and Other Actions. Appellant contends that, in order to prevent him from recovering on the default judgment against her, Croom executed the disclaimer to cause her share of the estate to pass to her uncle's remaining heirs. *Tate v. Siepielski*, 740 S.W.2d 92, 93 (Tex.App.—Fort Worth 1987, no writ). In return, appellant contends, the remaining heirs would "take care" of her. A witness for the appellant testified by affidavit that he confronted appellee Mariann C. Reynolds with this scenario, and Reynolds replied, "You don't think we're going to give our uncle's money to those slobs [the Dyer family], do you?"

Texas law provides that legal title vests in estate beneficiaries immediately upon death of the donor. *Welder v. Hitchcock*, 617 S.W.2d 294, 297 (Tex.Civ.App.—Corpus Christi 1981, writ ref'd n.r.e.). This rule of common law has been enacted into the Texas Probate Code, which provides, in relevant part:

> When a person dies, leaving a lawful will, all of his estate devised or bequeathed by such will ... shall vest immediately in the devisees or legatees of such estate ... subject, however, to the payment of the debts of the testator or intestate ...

Tex. Prob. Code Ann. § 37 (Vernon Supp.1991). Upon this principle has been "superimposed" the disclaimer statute of § 37A. *Welder,* 617 S.W.2d at 297. It provides that a disclaimer, too, is effective as of the death of the decedent:

> Any person ... who may be entitled to receive any property as a beneficiary and who intends to effect disclaimer irrevocably ... of the whole or any part of such property shall evidence same as herein provided. *A disclaimer ... shall be effective as of the death of the decedent and the property ... shall pass as if the person disclaiming ... had predeceased the decedent ...*

(emphasis added.) Tex. Prob. Code Ann. § 37A (Vernon Supp.1991). This "relation back" doctrine is based on the principle that a bequest or gift is nothing more than an offer which can be accepted or rejected. Some form of the doctrine is found in all of the 44 states which have enacted disclaimer statutes.[1]

Nevertheless, appellant contends that as a matter of law, Croom's disclaimer was a "transfer" within the meaning of the Texas fraudulent transfer act, which prohibits "every mode ... of disposing of or parting with an asset or an interest in an asset" — including a release — made with actual intent to hinder, delay, or defraud a claimant. Tex. Bus. & Com. Code Ann. §§ 24.002(12) (defining "transfer"), 24.005(a)(1) (Vernon 1987).

... However, implicit in the act of transferring property is the requirement that the debtor possess the asset: one cannot dispose of something one does not have. "[A] transfer is not made until the debtor has acquired rights in the asset transferred[.]" Tex. Bus. & Com. Code Ann. § 24.007(4) (Vernon 1987). Because disclaimed property passes as if the beneficiary predeceased the testator, the beneficiary never possesses the property. By direction of the legislature, acceptance of the inheritance occurs "only if the person making such disclaimer has previously taken possession or exercised dominion and control of such property in the capacity of beneficiary." Tex. Prob. Code Ann. § 37A(f) (Vernon Supp.1991)....

...

At least six states have legislatively barred, within their disclaimer statutes, the right to disclaim when the rights of the disclaimant's creditors are adversely affected.... California, however, has passed legislation clarifying that "[a] disclaimer is not a fraudulent transfer by the beneficiary." Cal. Prob. Code § 283 (West Supp. 1991). In enacting this provision, the California legislature rejected the holding of *In re Kalt's Estate,* 16 Cal.2d 807, 108 P.2d 401 (1940), that a disclaimer of inherited property could be a fraudulent conveyance....

---

1. [Included within the string cite to the different jurisdictions was a cite to California law: Cal. Prob. Code §§ 275, 282(a) (West 1991).]

Courts have generally taken the position that a creditor cannot prevent a debtor from disclaiming an inheritance. Annotation, *Creditor's Right to Prevent Debtor's Renunciation of Benefit Under Will or Debtor's Election to Take Under Will*, 39 A.L.R. 633 (1985). We adopt the majority view and hold that the "relation back" doctrine prevents a disclaimer from being treated as a transfer under fraudulent transfer acts, absent an express statutory provision to the contrary.

The judgment of the trial court is affirmed.

———————

Notes

1. *California approach*: Note that the Texas court cites and discusses the California approach to the disclaimer doctrine. California has a rather extensive and detailed statutory approach to its disclaimer doctrine:

CPC Section 265. Disclaimer defined

"Disclaimer" means any writing which declines, refuses, renounces, or disclaims any interest that would otherwise be taken by a beneficiary.

CPC Section 278. Disclaimer form requirements

The disclaimer shall be in writing, shall be signed by the disclaimant, and shall:

(a) Identify the creator of the interest.

(b) Describe the interest to be disclaimed.

(c) State the disclaimer and the extent of the disclaimer.

CPC Section 279. Disclaimer filing requirement

(a) A disclaimer to be effective shall be filed within a reasonable time after the person able to disclaim acquires knowledge of the interest.

(b) ... [A] disclaimer is conclusively presumed to have been filed within a reasonable time if it is filed within nine months after the death of the creator of the interest or within nine months after the interest becomes indefeasibly vested, whichever occurs later ...

CPC Section 282. Disclaimant; how treated legally

(a) Unless the creator of the interest provides for a specific disposition of the interest in the event of a disclaimer, the interest disclaimed shall descend, go, be distributed, or continue to be held ... as if the disclaimant had predeceased the creator of the interest.... A disclaimer relates back for all purposes to the date of the death of the creator of the disclaimed interest....

(b) Notwithstanding subdivision (a), where the disclaimer is filed on or after January 1, 1985:

(1) The beneficiary is not treated as having predeceased the decedent for the purpose of determining the generation at which the division of the estate is to be made under Part 6 (commencing with Section 240) or other provision of a will, trust, or other instrument.

> (2)   The beneficiary of a disclaimed interest is not treated as having predeceased the decedent for the purpose of applying subdivision (d) of Section 6409 or subdivision (b) of Section 6410.

2. *Looking a gift horse in the mouth?* Why would anyone (intestate or testate) decline property? We saw in *Dyer* that it may be to prevent attachment by creditors. Can a disclaimer be used for such a purpose in California?

3. *Tax considerations*: Do people actually use disclaimers in real life? Is avoiding creditors the primary reason? Individuals do, in fact, disclaim property. The most common reason for doing so is for tax purposes (primarily federal income and estate and gift taxes). Can you think of why this may be?

The details of tax-related disclaimers are complex and beyond the scope of a typical Wills and Trusts course. The use of disclaimers is an integral part of estate planning and again points to the importance of a comprehensive foundation in income tax, estate and gift taxation, and estate planning to fully grasp their use. Suffice it to say, the California "disclaimer" statutes, above, are circumscribed by federal income tax provisions. Specifically, I.R.C. section 2518 sets out the requirements for a "qualified" disclaimer. Again, while beyond the scope of a Wills and Trusts course, it is very important for a beneficiary's disclaimer to be considered "qualified" for tax purposes; to be otherwise, even if meeting California's statutory disclaimer requirements, can be catastrophic for tax purposes and may expose a supervising attorney to malpractice claims.

4. *California disclaimer qualifiers*: If the effect of a disclaimer is essentially to treat the disclaiming party as if he or she predeceased the decedent, why is the California statute on the effect of a disclaimer so complicated? In particular, what is the purpose of subsection 282(b)(1)? What was the legislature worried about? How did it deal with the concern? What is the purpose of subsection 282(b)(2)? What was the legislature worried about? How did it deal with the concern?

Problems

Below are the family trees of two different California domiciled decedents depicting living and predeceased (crossed-out) descendants.

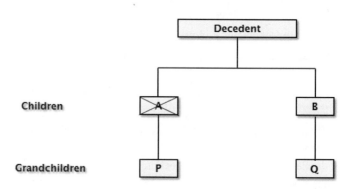

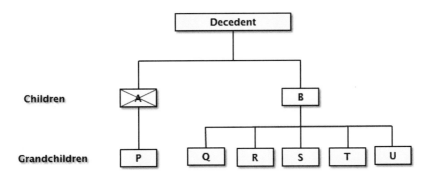

1. In each of the above scenarios, assume that Decedent died *intestate* and no persons have made any valid disclaimers (pursuant to the probate code). Who takes what share of Decedent's property?

2. In each of the above scenarios, assume that Decedent died *intestate*. For this question only, however, assume that B has, pursuant to the California Probate Code, validly disclaimed any rights to Decedent's property. Who takes what share of Decedent's property?

3. Same as question 2, above (B disclaimed any rights to Decedent's property) but for this question only assume that Decedent died *testate*, with a valid will leaving all of his or her property to A and B. In addition, the will specifically provides that should A or B (either or both of them) predecease the Decedent, distribution should be made to Decedent's issue by right of representation utilizing a strict per stirpes method of division. Who takes what share of Decedent's property? Would your answer change if Decedent's will directed that distribution to issue be made on a per capita basis consistent with that in California Probate Code Section 240?

4. In each of the above scenarios, assume that Decedent died *intestate*. Also assume that B has, pursuant to the California Probate Code, validly disclaimed any rights to Decedent's property. Also assume, for this question, that Decedent made an inter vivos gift to B and that such gift constituted a valid *advancement* under California law. Who takes what share of Decedent's property?

Chapter 5

Testamentary Capacity

I. Overview

Who gets the decedent's property when he or she dies? Whoever the decedent wishes. The intestate scheme applies if a decedent has not properly expressed his or her intent. If one does not like the intestate scheme, the traditional way of opting out was to execute a will. Increasingly, however, more and more individuals are opting out by executing "will substitutes," the most common being *inter vivos* trusts,[1] life insurance contracts, and/or joint tenancies. Opting out of intestacy requires us to enter the world of "directed dispositions."[2]

Directed dispositions give an individual the option of exercising *testamentary freedom*:[3] "the ability of a decedent to control the disposition of his property at death."[4] Testamentary freedom is one of the hallmarks of American Wills, Trusts, and Estates law. The testator is free to give his or her property to whomever he or she wishes. At the same time, it is generally accepted that a person should have a certain level of capacity before giving legal effect to his or her actions. To the extent the law requires a person to have capacity before recognizing the validity of his or her will (or will substitute), does that requirement conflict with testamentary freedom? Is there a risk that juries and/or courts will manipulate the capacity doctrines to invalidate a will if the jury/court does not like the intent expressed in the will?[5] Does a decedent really only have as much testamentary freedom as the reviewing jury or court grants? To

---

1. Inter vivos trusts can be either revocable or irrevocable. Assuming they are revocable, they are more commonly known as *revocable living trusts* or just *living trusts.*

2. The first requirement to having a valid directed disposition is that the person in question had the requisite capacity to execute the particular instrument involved. The material in this chapter will examine the doctrines related to the requisite capacity. While many of the capacity-related doctrines covered in this chapter apply to the non-probate will substitute instruments, the introductory course focuses on capacity as it relates to the traditional method of opting out of intestacy: the will. For the most part, the nuanced differences between a will and a will substitute as they relate to the capacity requirements, and which capacity doctrines should be revised to reflect these differences, are best left to the advanced estate-planning course.

3. Most estate planners cling to that phrase with the same passion as Mel Gibson when he cried out at the end of *Braveheart.*

4. Bradley E.S. Fogel, *The Completely Insane Law of Partial Insanity: The Impact of Monomania on Testamentary Capacity*, 42 Real Prop. Prob. & Tr. J. 67, 72 (2007).

5. Beginning in 1989, California law eliminated the availability of jury trials in will contests. *See infra* note 7 and accompanying text.

the extent testamentary freedom and testamentary capacity are circles that overlap, how much overlap should there be, and how should the overlapping lines be articulated to regulate the overlap?

II. General Testamentary Capacity

It arguably is self-evident that the law should require a certain degree of legal capacity before holding an individual accountable for his or her actions, or before giving legal effect to those actions. The more challenging aspects of instituting a legal capacity requirement are: (1) setting the requisite standard of legal capacity, and (2) articulating that standard in a way that is workable in application for a trial court. We have statutes that set forth the broad parameters of testamentary capacity, but they generally do not contain clear definitions or directions for how they apply to particular fact patterns; but, based on the underlying nature of the subject (one's state of mind), this would be difficult to codify. Accordingly, a good portion of the law in this area appears to be case-derived and case-driven. Is that good or bad? Is it inevitable?

CPC § 6100. Persons qualified to make will

(a) An individual 18 or more years of age who is of sound mind may make a will.

(b) A conservator may make a will for the conservatee if the conservator has been so authorized by a court order ...

CPC § 6100.5. Persons not mentally competent to make a will; specified circumstances

(a) An individual is not mentally competent to make a will if at the time of making the will either of the following is true:

(1) The individual does not have sufficient mental capacity to be able to (A) understand the nature of the testamentary act, (B) understand and recollect the nature and situation of the individual's property, or (C) remember and understand the individual's relations to living descendants, spouse, and parents, and those whose interests are affected by the will.

(2) The individual suffers from a mental disorder with symptoms including delusions or hallucinations, which delusions or hallucinations result in the individual's devising property in a way which, except for the existence of the delusions or hallucinations, the individual would not have done.

...

Estate of Mann

184 Cal. App. 3d 593 (1986)

KLINE, Presiding Justice.

FACTS

Hazel Mann, a resident of Mill Valley, California, died on March 22, 1981, at the age of 94 years. At the time of her death, her closest relatives were two nephews, appellant Smith and respondent Van Gorp, who lived in Mill Valley and Missouri, respectively.

Appellant and decedent had a close relationship throughout his life. During his childhood and adolescence appellant lived either with his mother in San Francisco or in foster homes in the San Francisco Bay Area and saw decedent frequently. Beginning with a tour of duty in the Coast Guard in 1960, appellant spent a number of years in Hawaii, corresponding with his aunt by letter and phone. After returning to Mill Valley in 1967, appellant served in the Merchant Marine for several years, staying either with his aunt or with friends when he was not at sea. Thereafter, appellant resided in Marin County and saw decedent on a daily or weekly basis. Appellant testified that his aunt was as close or closer than his mother; a letter from appellant's mother to decedent referred to appellant as "our son." Respondent stipulated that decedent helped raise appellant and that they were very close.

Decedent also had a close and warm relationship with respondent, although she saw him less regularly. Decedent and respondent's mother, Pearl, corresponded almost weekly. In 1926, when respondent was five years old, he spent six months with his mother living in an apartment building in San Francisco owned by decedent and her husband. Other visits occurred in 1940, 1968, 1969, 1972, 1974, and 1978, and respondent telephoned decedent periodically during the 1970s.

In November 1975, appellant became conservator of decedent's person and estate. Appellant testified that he sought the conservatorship on the advice of a social worker and decedent's physician, Dr. Lee; Dr. Lee corroborated this testimony. Respondent also testified that he believed the conservatorship was a good idea. The factors which led to the conservatorship involved decedent's inability to care for herself both financially and personally.... Others testified that prior to the conservatorship decedent was not eating or caring for herself properly; that she was unclean and smelled of urine; that her home was unkempt and her bed filthy; that she did not seem to know how to order the right food from a store; and that she described a toy doll as "me" and seemed "kind of dreamy."

Dr. Lee's notes indicated that in 1979 decedent suffered from senility secondary to arteriosclerosis. He described senile dementia as a gradual progressive disorder with three stages, loss of recent memory, confusion, and dementia or unreality, and placed decedent in the second stage in 1975–1976. According to Dr. Lee, the process occurring during these years was the cause of what he described as decedent's confusion and variable mental state at that time, such as occasionally forgetting dates, the time of year, and what she was doing or eating.

In a declaration filed in the conservatorship proceeding, Lee stated his medical opinion that because of decedent's "present state of mental weakness" she was "unable to rationally and intelligently handle her own affairs." He testified that at this time decedent would sometimes appear extremely senile, sometimes better and more oriented....

Respondent testified that decedent did not recognize him on the phone in mid-1975, and had forgotten that his mother, her sister Pearl, had died two years previously.

On the other hand, several other witnesses testified that decedent was mentally competent and able to carry on a coherent conversation during the 1975–77 time period. John Finn, an accountant with the Internal Revenue Service who helped prepare her annual tax returns, first met decedent in 1960. Finn testified that in 1974 and 1975 decedent had a "pretty good grasp of her financial situation", although he was upset that she left a lot of cash laying around. He also stated that he found decedent's mental condition "considerably improved" after appellant became her conservator.

… Vonnie Adcock, who became decedent's live-in housekeeper a few months prior to the signing of the will, testified that decedent … spent her time sitting at the dining room table looking at the yard, rearranging pictures or watching TV. She had been a poet earlier in life, but no longer read. She did not initiate other activities, and did not like to leave the house. She wanted constant company. She was pleased to have visitors, and tended to be a little flirtatious. Dr. Lee described her as having a characteristic mannerism of pretending not to know people as a means of expressing displeasure with them.

Decedent's will was executed on July 17, 1976. The will was drawn by attorney Robert Williams, a friend of appellant's....

… Appellant brought decedent to Williams' office on what appeared to Williams to be a usual social visit following decedent's appointment at the beauty salon next door. Appellant told Williams decedent had mentioned her need for a will, and Williams agreed to help. The contents of the will were first discussed in a meeting at decedent's home sometime within the next month. Appellant was on the premises but not present for this discussion, during which decedent indicated her desire to give the bulk of her property to appellant.

The subscribing witnesses to the will were Williams, Dr. Lee, and Vonnie Adcock. All testified decedent was alert and knew she was signing a will. Only Dr. Lee specifically remembered decedent discussing the terms of the will. Williams testified that he probably asked decedent to acknowledge that she knew the nature of her estate. Adcock did not remember the will being discussed, but only general conversation and decedent "being pleased that there were men people coming to visit her." …

DISCUSSION

I.

Testamentary Capacity

[The] determinants of testamentary capacity are whether the individual "has sufficient mental capacity to be able to understand the nature of the act he is doing, and to understand and recollect the nature and situation of his property and to remember, and understand his relations to, the persons who have claims upon his bounty and whose interests are affected by the provisions of the instrument." (citations omitted) Testamentary capacity must be determined at the time of execution of the will. (citations omitted) Incompetency on a given day may, however, be established by proof of incompetency at prior and subsequent times. (*Estate of Fosselman* (1957) 48 Cal.2d 179, 185, 308 P.2d 336.) Where testamentary incompetence is caused by senil dementia at one point in time, there is a strong inference, if not a legal presumption, that the incompetence continues at other times, because the mental disorder is a continuous one which becomes progressively worse. (*Estate of Fosselman, supra*, 48 Cal.2d 179, 186, 308 P.2d 336.)

The burden is on the contestant to overcome the presumption that a testator is sane and competent. (*Fritschi, supra*, 60 Cal.2d at p. 372, 33 Cal.Rptr. 264, 384 P.2d 656.) ...

It is well established that "old age or forgetfulness, eccentricities or mental feebleness or confusion at various times of a party making a will are not enough in themselves to warrant a holding that the testator lacked testamentary capacity." (citations omitted) "It has been held over and over in this state that old age, feebleness, forgetfulness, filthy personal habits, personal eccentricities, failure to recognize old friends or relatives, physical disability, absent-mindedness and mental confusion do not furnish grounds for holding that a testator lacked testamentary capacity." (*Estate of Selb* (1948) 84 Cal.App.2d 46, 49, 190 P.2d 277.) Nor does the mere fact that the testator is under a guardianship support a finding of lack of testamentary capacity without evidence that the incompetence continues at the time of the will's execution. (citations omitted)

It must be remembered, in this connection, that "[w]hen one has a mental disorder in which there are lucid periods, it is presumed that his will has been made during a time of lucidity." (*Estate of Goetz* (1967) 253 Cal.App.2d 107, 114, 61 Cal.Rptr. 181.) Dr. Lee testified that decedent's mental state fluctuated and that the conservatorship was established to protect her from the "worst times." Vonnie Adcock testified that even in late 1977 decedent had periods of alertness, as John Finn, decedent's tax accountant, also testified. Thus a finding of lack of testamentary capacity can be supported only if the presumption of execution during a lucid period is overcome.

The witnesses to execution of the will all testified decedent was aware of what she was doing at the time, and that they would not have signed the will if this had not been true. While the jury was free to disbelieve this testimony, "[d]isbelief does not create affirmative evidence to the contrary of that which is discarded." (citations omitted) The only evidence suggestive of decedent's incapacity at the time the will was executed is in fact evidence of her condition at other times. That is, the only bases for the conclusion she lacked capacity at the time of execution would be inferences that the factors leading to the conservatorship rendered her incapable of comprehending the extent of her property and continued to so affect her at the time of the will's execution, and that her senility caused faulty recollection at this time.

There are several problems in the indulging of such inferences. First, the fact that a testator has been placed under a guardianship does not in itself establish testamentary incapacity. (*Estate of Nelson, supra*, 227 Cal.App.2d 42, 55–56, 38 Cal.Rptr. 459; see also, Note, Effect of Adjudication of Mental Incompetency on Power to Make a Will (1943) 16 So.Cal.L.Rev. 355.) Since a conservatorship, unlike a guardianship, does not involve a declaration of incompetence (*Estate of Wochos, supra*, 23 Cal.App.3d 47, 54, 99 Cal.Rptr. 782), a conservatorship raises an even weaker inference of testamentary incapacity.

. . .

Finally, while advanced senility which interferes with the ability to understand the nature of the testamentary act, the extent of one's property and one's relations to those interested in it is sufficient evidence of testamentary incapacity (citations omitted), the evidence in this case is of a much lesser degree of senility at the time of execution. Indeed, the only evidence was of a degree of senility which did not preclude mental alertness, and Dr. Lee, the only witness who testified decedent was medically senile, also stated she was alert when the will was executed and understood the nature and implications of her act. Dr. Lee had known decedent longer than two years at the time the will was executed. His testimony was uncontroverted, and is especially significant as he appears to be one of the few witnesses not aligned with either side to the controversy.

In sum, the evidence of incompetence in this case is much weaker than that held insufficient to justify the setting aside of wills in numerous other cases ... and is simply not enough to overcome the presumption that the testator was sane and competent at the time of the will's execution. (citation omitted).

. . .

For the foregoing reasons, the judgment is reversed. Each party to bear its own costs on appeal.

Notes

1. *Doctrinal questions*: At what point in time is testamentary capacity assessed? What evidence is relevant to the question of testamentary capacity? Who bears the burden of proof with respect to testamentary capacity?

Because of California's presumption of testamentary capacity, a will proponent need not prove capacity—all that needs to be proved is due execution. A standard and completed attestation clause constitutes a prima facie case of due execution. If a party contests the will on lack of capacity grounds (complete incapacity or due to a defect in capacity), the contestant bears the burden of proof.

2. *Different capacity thresholds*: Most law students are first introduced to the notion of legal capacity in their first year Contracts course. Just as an individual must have capacity to enter into a valid contract, he or she must have capacity to execute a valid will. That admission, however, begs the question: what should be the standard for *testamentary* capacity? Should it be the same as contractual capacity? Should it be higher or lower, and why?

First, a few points about contractual capacity as it relates to guardianship and conservatorship. In *Board of Regents v. Davis*, 14 Cal. 3d 333, 120 Cal. Rptr. 407, 410, 414 (1975), the California Supreme Court stated: "A ward under a guardianship lacks the capacity to enter into a contract." California Probate Code Section 1872 states: "[T]he appointment of a conservator of the estate is an adjudication that the conservatee lacks the legal capacity to enter into or make any transaction that binds or obligates the conservatorship estate." Probate Code Section 1870 defines a "transaction" as including making a contract or gift. Based on the court's discussion of guardianships and conservatorships in *Mann*, would you say testamentary capacity is higher or lower than contractual capacity? Does that make sense?

Another important standard of capacity is the capacity required to enter into a marriage. Marriage is an important institution that has many important legal consequences. Should the capacity to enter into a marriage be higher or lower than testamentary capacity? Why would that be the case?

3. *Judicial approach*: Because the test for testamentary capacity is rather soft and fact sensitive, it can be difficult to apply in certain factual settings. For the most part, the strong presumption of testamentary capacity coupled with the relatively low threshold for testamentary capacity has resulted in rather restrained use of the doctrine to invalidate a will.

One of the more well-known California cases in this area is *In re Wright's Estate*, 7 Cal. 2d 348 (1936). Decedent died at the age of 69. His wife predeceased him. His closest living relative was his only daughter. He owned two houses in Venice, California, land in Salt Lake City, Utah, and minimal personal property. He executed the document that was offered as his will just over one year before his death. In the will, he gave one house to his daughter, the other house to a "friend," 50-year-old Charlotte Josephine Hindmarch, the land in Utah to his granddaughter, and $1.00 to several of his other relatives. "The drawer of the will, a notary public and realtor, and the two subscribing witnesses ... [testified] that they were of the opinion that the testator was of unsound mind." Moreover, each of the several witnesses who testified at trial testified that they believed the testator was of unsound mind. The following is representative of the testimony given by the different witnesses:

> Mrs. Brem had known testator for sixteen years ... she was sure from the way he lived alone in his little shack, with all the dirt and junk he had, that he was not right; he once gave her a fish (he spent much time in fishing) which he said he had caught and she found it had been soaked in kerosene and when he asked her how she liked it he laughed and said he had put the kerosene on it before he brought it to her; ....

> Mrs. Daisy Smith, a cousin not named in the will, testified that she believed him to be unsound in mind. Her reasons were that he drank and was drunk much of the time since his wife died; that some years ago he suffered an injury to his head and several stitches were required to close the wound; that the injury seemed to change him; ... on one or more occasions he ran out of the house only partly dressed and they had to follow him and had difficulty in getting him back to bed; that he picked up silverware and other articles from the garbage cans and hid these things around the house; that he picked up paper flowers from the garbage cans, and waste, and pinned them on rose bushes in his yard and took the witness to look at his roses; ....

Hariett E. McClelland said she had known testator for a number of years. She believed him to be of unsound mind. She testified that she had been closely associated with him and that ... he told her about a number of houses that he had at Salt Lake City, his former home and where she had known testator, but she knew that he did not own them; he collected paper flowers from the garbage cans and pinned them on the bushes in his yard and laughingly said to her that he would fool the people as they would think the flowers were blooming; that one time he told the witness in the presence of her mother that she was his natural daughter. The mother became exceedingly angry at him and it does not appear that he ever repeated the statement. The witness related an ailment which the testator had while living at her house during which he would be prone, hold his breath and appear to be dead; that when she returned from her quest for help she would find him up and walking about; that he said he did this to scare his neighbors and make them think he was dead.

Nevertheless, after reviewing all the evidence, the California Supreme Court ruled there was not enough evidence to establish the testator lacked testamentary capacity:

Testamentary capacity cannot be destroyed by showing a few isolated acts, foibles, idiosyncrasies, moral or mental irregularities or departures from the normal unless they directly bear upon and have influenced the testamentary act. No medical testimony as to the extent of any injury the testator had received or its effect upon him either physically or mentally was introduced in the case. The burden was upon contestant throughout the case. Taking all the evidence adduced by contestant as true, it falls far below the requirements of the law as constituting satisfactory rebuttal of the inference of testamentary capacity.... He went alone to the scrivener's with a list of beneficiaries prepared by himself, giving his daughter one piece of improved real property and Charlotte Josephine Hindmarch, whom he designated as his friend, the other.... There is no evidence that he did not appreciate his relations and obligations to others, or that he was not mindful of the property which he possessed. The opinions or beliefs of those who testified that he was not of sound mind rest upon testimony of the most trivial character and do not establish testamentary incapacity at the time he executed his will.

4. *Attorney's duty to determine capacity:* What exactly is the attorney's role in determining a client's capacity? Should an attorney have an ethical duty to draft an instrument only for a client that the attorney believes has capacity to execute it? This is a complex question and an in-depth exploration of the subject is well beyond the scope of this course. Clearly, an attorney cannot draft a testamentary-related document when it is clear that, sadly, the client lacks any degree of understanding of their surroundings and what is transpiring. The majority of situations in which capacity may be at issue, however, can be more difficult; aberrant behavior being less pronounced or conspicuous. During the course of a typical client interview, the attorney usually gets some idea of the client's cognition vis-à-vis the three basic components enumer-

ated in California Probate Code Section 6100.5(a)(2): (1) the client's understanding of the nature of the testamentary act he or she is performing; (2) the client's understanding and recollection of the nature and situation of their property; and (3) the client's ability to remember and understand their relations to living descendants, spouse, parents and those whose interests are affected by the will.

While it is not uncommon for a client to have some lapses in memory or be a bit "hazy" with respect to some matters, this does not necessarily preclude the drafting and execution of a will (or other testamentary document). Even where the attorney believes the client meets the threshold level of competency, if the dispositive provisions of the document are such that "eyebrows may be raised" and there is a risk that others may ultimately assert that the testator lacked capacity, measures may be taken to provide some degree of evidential support. The estate planning attorney's contact list often includes a psychiatrist or other medical professional who is familiar with testamentary thresholds for competency and who can provide, at the attorney's request (with consent of the client), a geriatric evaluation. Some estate planning attorneys routinely call upon someone in the medical profession (often a local psychiatrist or physician) to act as a witness in the execution of the testamentary document — in effect, providing an immediate, albeit limited, evaluation.

5. *Will versus will substitute capacity standards*: The three most common will substitutes are: (1) joint tenancies, (2) life insurance contracts, and (3) revocable living trusts (the latter being the closest to a will vis-à-vis function and content). One of the traditional explanations for why these will substitutes qualify as nonprobate transfers, and why they are subject to a different capacity requirement, is that technically they are *inter vivos* transfers, *not* testamentary transfers. A joint tenancy immediately conveys a present interest in the property to the other co-tenant. That interest is created and transferred the moment the joint tenancy is created *inter vivos*. A trust is a form of a gift. The trust beneficiaries who hold the future interest may not fully enjoy that interest until after the life tenant's death, but the future interest is a property interest. The future interest is created and transferred the moment the trust is created *inter vivos*. A life insurance contract is a *contract* that conveys a present benefit to the beneficiary of the contract — the rights under the contract. That interest is created and transferred the moment the contract is executed *inter vivos*.

Because all three of these nonprobate transfers involve the present transfer of a present interest, historically the assumption was that a higher standard of capacity should apply *because of the inter vivos consequences of the instrument*. In contrast, a will transfers no present property rights or interest to the will beneficiaries. Nothing passes until the testator dies. A will is purely testamentary in nature, hence the lower level of capacity: testamentary capacity. Consistent with that logic, California Probate Code section 852 sets forth the general capacity standard for the nonprobate instruments. That standard is often referred to as "contractual capacity."[6] Bottom line, the

---

6. Whether that is exactly the same as the contractual capacity you learned in your Contracts course is beyond the scope of this course. For purposes of this course, you can assume it is.

higher capacity requirement for the nonprobate instruments has guided some estate planners to draft a will for clients who meet the relatively low wills standard but whose capacity may be at issue for purposes of a revocable living trust or other non-probate instrument.

That bottom line, however, may have to be reassessed in light of the ruling in *Andersen v. Hunt*, 196 Cal. App. 4th 722 (2011). The court ruled that the lower standard, testamentary capacity, applied to the question of whether the settlor had the requisite capacity to execute amendments to a revocable living trust. That a court would apply testamentary capacity—and not contractual capacity—to a nonprobate trust amendment is potentially a landmark decision and has been the talk of the estate planning community. Some estate planners argue that the court's ruling appears to be based on the perceived complexity of the trust amendments: simple trust amendments require the lower wills standard (testamentary capacity), while more complex trust amendments require the higher nonprobate standard (contractual capacity). Other estate planners argue the distinguishing variable is whether the trust amendment has inter vivos significance (in which case the higher contractual capacity standard should apply) or whether the trust amendment has only testamentary significance (in which case the lower testamentary capacity standard should apply).

In 2014, in *Lintz v. Lintz*, 222 Cal. App. 4th 1346 (2014), the court agreed with the decision in *Andersen* and held that the distinguishing variable was the complexity of the trust and trust amendments—that a complexity-dependent "sliding contract scale" standard for capacity should be the default rule for trusts (and trust amendments).

Both the *Andersen* and *Lintz* cases have the estate planning community debating the future course of the law vis-à-vis testamentary capacity for all forms of testamentary documents. Legally and historically, the lower capacity standard for wills is not a sliding scale, unlike what appears to be the new sliding-scale contract-based capacity standard for trusts. If the distinguishing factor for applying lower or higher standards for capacity is the complexity of the underlying document, however, then it can be argued that the same sliding-scale standard of capacity should apply across the board to all testamentary documents. The notion that the general nature and complexity of a living trust (the typical will substitute) and its dispositive provisions are inherently more complex than that of a will is somewhat specious. The complexity spectrum of wills (from simple to exceptionally complex with embedded testamentary trusts, and a plethora of tax-sensitive provisions, including marital deduction clauses, "unified credit" trusts and "generation skipping transfer tax" clauses) is, for all intents and purposes, the same as for those in a living trust (the typical will substitute). Can differing standards for capacity for wills versus trusts be defensible? Should they be different?

6. *Aging population*: Historically the courts were rather restrained in their use of general testamentary capacity to invalidate a will. It remains to be seen, however, whether they will maintain this approach as life expectancies continue to increase. In 1900, the life expectancy for someone born that year was 46 years for men, 48 years for women. By 1950, life expectancies had jumped to 65 years and 71 years, re-

spectively; by 2007, to 75 and 80 years. Dementia, Alzheimer's, and other ailments of the mind are strongly correlated with age. Should the courts be more aggressive in analyzing whether an individual has testamentary capacity to help protect our increasingly aging population? Or would that wrongfully deprive the elderly of their testamentary freedom?

Problems

1. "On the morning of March 2, 1944, decedent Maude R. Rich, then 66 years of age, executed an holographic will by the terms of which her entire estate was bequeathed to Mrs. Clara Wills, who had been legally adopted when she was seven years of age, by decedent's mother. This holographic will was placed by decedent in her safety deposit box at the Bank of America at San Pedro, California, at 10 o'clock on the morning of the same day it was executed. Shortly thereafter the testatrix boarded a train at San Pedro, bound for Los Angeles, where at about noon of the same day she committed suicide by jumping out the 8th story window of an office building in downtown Los Angeles."

   What relevance, if any, should the fact that the testator committed suicide shortly after executing the will have on the issue of whether the testator had the requisite testamentary capacity? *See In re Rich's Estate*, 179 P.2d 373 (Cal. Ct. App. 1947); *In re Card's Will*, 8 N.Y.S. 297, 297 (1889) ("Suicide is competent evidence upon the issue of insanity, but only as a circumstance in connection with others, and is not presumptive evidence of it.").

2. Cases involving testamentary capacity are often messy, fact-sensitive cases that arguably could go either way. For example, Charles P. Galatis, unmarried and with no children, suffered from a number of ailments. His medical problems included diabetes, hyperkalemia (excess potassium in the blood), and major depression. His 12 medications included antidepressants and narcotics for pain relief. On January 15, 2000, he was diagnosed with stage IV lung cancer and admitted to the hospital. His dosages for both the antidepressants and the painkillers were "aggressively" increased. On February 8, he had an adverse reaction to one of his medications; and, as a result, developed facial droop, slurred speech, increased drowsiness, inability to pay attention, and required constant stimulation to be able to generate answers to questions. As a result of this incident, he was diagnosed with encephalopathy (a brain disorder) and prescribed yet more medications that helped with these new physical symptoms. The following day, February 9, several nurses and friends interacted with Galatis (all of whom gave differing accounts with respect to his mental condition). An attorney stopped by and had him execute a will (leaving most of his estate — real estate in Greece — to the town of Skiathos, Greece).

   He died February 25, 2000. Two of his cousins contested the will, claiming he lacked testamentary capacity. The trial court made 559 factual findings that totaled 71 pages. *See In re Estate of Galatis*, 36 N.E.3d 1247 (Mass. App. Ct. 2015). How would you rule on the issue of his testamentary capacity?

III. Defects in Testamentary Capacity

Even though a testator may have general testamentary capacity, a testator may suffer from a defect in capacity that may invalidate part or all of a will.

A. Insane Delusions

The first possible defect, insane delusion, is based on the premise that an individual can develop a delusion that is so strong, and held so passionately and stubbornly, that it overpowers the testator's ability to think rationally with respect to that particular belief or issue (i.e., the person is just "crazy" on that issue). If the delusion becomes that strong *and* it causes the testator to dispose of his or her property in a way that he or she would not have otherwise, for all practical purposes the testator lacks testamentary capacity to that limited extent. The testator may have general testamentary capacity, but he or she may suffer from a defect in capacity that may invalidate all or part of the will. At an abstract, academic level the doctrine makes sense.

On the other hand, a delusion is analogous to a mistake, and the traditional and still general rule is that courts should not correct mistakes. If courts were to correct mistakes, that would open the door to fraud and increase costs of administration. Where does the law draw the line — and how does it articulate the line — between a delusion/mistake and an *insane* delusion? Is that a defensible line, or does it permit the jury/court to strike down a gift or will that *the jury/court* thinks is indefensible? Is the doctrine of insane delusion compatible with testamentary freedom?

In re Honigman's Will

168 N.E.2d 676 (N.Y. 1960)

DYE, Judge.

Frank Honigman died May 4, 1956, survived by his wife, Florence. By a purported last will and testament, executed April 3, 1956, just one month before his death, he gave $5,000 to each of three named grandnieces, and cut off his wife with a life use of her minimum statutory share plus $2,500, with direction to pay the principal upon her death to his surviving brothers and sisters and to the descendants of any predeceased brother or sister, per stirpes. The remaining one half of his estate was bequeathed in equal shares to his surviving brothers and sisters and to the descendants of any predeceased brother or sister, per stirpes, some of whom resided in Germany.

When the will was offered for probate in Surrogate's Court, Queens County, the widow Florence filed objections. A trial was had on framed issues, only one of which survived for determination by the jury, namely: "At the time of the execution of the paper offered for probate was the said Frank Honigman of sound and disposing mind and memory?" The jury answered in the negative, and the Surrogate then made a decree denying probate to the will. [The New York Supreme Court, Appellate Division, held Mr. Honigman's belief was not an insane delusion, that there was not sufficient evidence to submit the question to the jury, and the court ordered the will admitted to probate.]

We read this record as containing more than enough competent proof to warrant submitting to the jury the issue of decedent's testamentary capacity. By the same token the proof amply supports the jury findings, implicit in the verdict, that the testator, at the time he made his will, was suffering from an unwarranted and insane delusion that his wife was unfaithful to him, which condition affected the disposition made in the will. The record is replete with testimony, supplied by a large number of disinterested persons, that for quite some time before his death the testator had publicly and repeatedly told friends and strangers alike that he believed his wife was unfaithful, often using obscene and abusive language. Such manifestations of suspicion were quite unaccountable, coming as they did after nearly 40 years of a childless yet, to all outward appearances, a congenial and harmonious marriage, which had begun in 1916. During the intervening time they had worked together in the successful management, operation and ownership of various restaurants, bars and grills and, by their joint efforts of thrift and industry, had accumulated the substantial fortune now at stake.

The decedent and his wife retired from business in 1945 because of decedent's failing health. In the few years that followed he underwent a number of operations, including a prostatectomy in 1951, and an operation for cancer of the large bowel in 1954, when decedent was approximately 70 years of age.

From about this time, he began volubly to express his belief that Mrs. Honigman was unfaithful to him. This suspicion became an obsession with him, although all of the witnesses agreed that the deceased was normal and rational in other respects. Seemingly aware of his mental state, he once mentioned that he was "sick in the head" ("Mich krank gelassen in den Kopf"), and that "I know there is something wrong with me" in response to a light reference to his mental condition. In December, 1955 he went to Europe, a trip Mrs. Honigman learned of in a letter sent from Idlewild Airport after he had departed, and while there he visited a doctor. Upon his return he went to a psychiatrist who Mr. Honigman said "could not help" him. Finally, he went to a chiropractor with whom he was extremely satisfied.

On March 21, 1956, shortly after his return from Europe, Mr. Honigman instructed his attorney to prepare the will in question. He never again joined Mrs. Honigman in the marital home.

To offset and contradict this showing of irrational obsession the proponents adduced proof which, it is said, furnished a reasonable basis for decedent's belief, and which, when taken with other factors, made his testamentary disposition understandable. Briefly, this proof related to four incidents. One concerned an anniversary card sent by Mr. Krauss, a mutual acquaintance and friend of many years, bearing a printed message of congratulation in sweetly sentimental phraseology. Because it was addressed to the wife alone and not received on the anniversary date, Mr. Honigman viewed it as confirmatory of his suspicion. Then there was the reference to a letter which it is claimed contained prejudicial matter but just what it was is not before us, because the letter was not produced in evidence and its contents were not established. There was also proof to show that whenever the house telephone rang Mrs. Honigman would answer it. From this Mr. Honigman drew added support for his suspicion that she was having an affair with Mr. Krauss. Mr. Honigman became so upset about it that for the last two years of their marriage he positively forbade her to answer the telephone. Another allegedly significant happening was an occasion when Mrs. Honigman asked the decedent as he was leaving the house what time she might expect him to return. This aroused his suspicion. He secreted himself at a vantage point in a nearby park and watched his home. He saw Mr. Krauss enter and, later, when he confronted his wife with knowledge of this incident, she allegedly asked him for a divorce. This incident was taken entirely from a statement made by Mr. Honigman to one of the witnesses. Mrs. Honigman flatly denied all of it. Their verdict shows that the jury evidently believed the objectant. Under the circumstances, we cannot say that this was wrong. The jury had the right to disregard the proponents' proof, or to go so far as to hold that such trivia afforded even additional grounds for decedent's irrational and unwarranted belief. The issue we must bear in mind is not whether Mrs. Honigman was unfaithful, but whether Mr. Honigman had any reasonable basis for believing that she was.

In a very early case we defined the applicable test as follows: "If a person persistently believes supposed facts, which have no real existence except in his perverted imagination, and against all evidence and probability, and conducts himself, however logically, upon the assumption of their existence, he is, so far as they are concerned, under a morbid delusion; and delusion in that sense is insanity. Such a person is essentially mad or insane on those subjects, though on other subjects he may reason, act and speak like a sensible man." (*American Seamen's Friend Soc. v. Hopper*, 33 N.Y. 619, 624–625.)

… When, in the light of all the circumstances surrounding a long and happy marriage such as this, the husband publicly and repeatedly expresses suspicions of his wife's unfaithfulness; of misbehaving herself in a most unseemly fashion, by hiding male callers in the cellar of her own home, in various closets, and under the bed; of hauling men from the street up to her second-story bedroom by use of bed sheets; of making contacts over the household telephone; and of passing a clandestine note through the fence on her brother's property and when he claims to have heard noises which he believed to be men running about his home, but which he had not investigated, and which he could not verify the courts should have no hesitation in placing the issue of sanity in the jury's hands. To hold to the contrary would be to take from the jury its traditional function of passing on the facts.…

The proponents argue that, even if decedent was indeed laboring under a delusion, the existence of other reasons for the disposition he chose is enough to support the validity of the instrument as a will. The other reasons are, first, the size of Mrs. Honigman's independent fortune, and, second, the financial need of his residuary legatees. These reasons, as well as his belief in his wife's infidelity, decedent expressed to his own attorney. We dispelled a similar contention in *American Seamen's Friend Soc. v. Hopper, supra*, 33 N.Y. at page 625, where we held that a will was bad when its "dispository provisions were or *might have been* caused or affected by the delusion" (emphasis supplied).…

The order appealed from should be reversed and a new trial granted, with costs to abide the event.

FULD, Judge (dissenting).

I am willing to assume that the proof demonstrates that the testator's belief that his wife was unfaithful was completely groundless and unjust. However, that is not enough; it does not follow from this fact that the testator suffered from such a delusion as to stamp him mentally defective or as lacking in capacity to make a will. "To sustain the allegation," this court wrote in the Clapp case, 34 N.Y. 190, 197, "it is not sufficient to show that his suspicion in this respect was not well founded. It is quite apparent, from the evidence, that his distrust of the fidelity of his wife was really groundless and unjust; but it does not follow that his doubts evince a condition of lunacy. The right of a testator to dispose of his estate, depends neither on the justice of his prejudices nor the soundness of his reasoning. He may do what he will with his own; and if there be no defect of testamentary capacity, and no undue influence or fraud, the law gives effect to his will, though its provisions are unreasonable and unjust." . . .

Moreover, I share the Appellate Division's view that other and sound reasons, quite apart from the alleged decision, existed for the disposition made by the testator. Indeed, he himself had declared that his wife had enough money and he wanted to take care of his brothers and sisters living in Europe.

In short, the evidence adduced utterly failed to prove that the testator was suffering from an insane delusion or lacked testamentary capacity. The Appellate Division was eminently correct in concluding that there was no issue of fact for the jury's consideration and in directing the entry of a decree admitting the will to probate. Its order should be affirmed.

Notes

1. *Doctrinal split*: Jurisdictions are split over how best to articulate a workable standard for the insane delusion doctrine. One school of thought borrows from the torts notion of "the average reasonable person" but with a testamentary spin on the fictional legal character:

> An insane delusion, in the legal sense, is "a belief in things impossible, or a belief in things possible, but so improbable under the surrounding circumstances that *no man of sound mind* could give them credence," . . . [citation omitted], otherwise defined, an insane delusion is "a false belief, for which there is *no reasonable foundation,* and which would be incredible under similar circumstances to the same person *if he were of sound mind,* and concerning which his mind is not open to permanent correction through argument or evidence," . . . [citation omitted]. *Benjamin v. Woodring,* 268 Md. 593, 601 (1973) (emphasis added).

A second approach to the doctrine focuses on the evidentiary support for the testator's belief/conclusion in question:

> *If there are any facts, however little evidential force they may possess, upon which the testator may in reason have based his belief, it will not be an insane delusion*, though on a consideration of other facts themselves his belief may seem illogical or foundationless to the court; for a will, it is obvious, is not to be overturned [merely] because the testator has not reasoned correctly. *In re Solomon's Estate*, 334 Mich. 17, 27–28 (1952) (*quoting* 1 UNDERHILL ON WILLS § 94).

Which approach is better: the "no person of sound mind could have reached that conclusion" approach or the "no factual basis to support the belief" approach? Which approach is more protective of a testator's intent (i.e., under which approach is it more difficult for a jury to substitute its belief/conclusion in place of the testator's belief/conclusion)?

Which approach did the court apply in *Honigman*? Did Mr. Honigman suffer from an insane delusion or just a delusion—a mistake? Or might Mrs. Honigman simply have been the second coming of the Wife of Bath from Chaucer's Canterbury Tales (five times widowed, she admits to a voracious sexual appetite that her older husbands could not satisfy)?

2. *California approach*: Unfortunately, the California courts have been a bit too loose in their phrasing of what constitutes an insane delusion to definitely state the California approach. One court held:

> "One cannot be said to act under an insane delusion if his condition of mind results from a belief or inference, however irrational or unfounded, drawn from facts which are shown to exist." *Estate of Scott*, 128 Cal. 57, 62, 60 P. 527, 529; *Estate of Shay*, 196 Cal. 355, 237 P. 1079; *Estate of Perkins*, 195 Cal. 699, 235 P. 45; *Estate of Powell*, 113 Cal.App. 670, 299 P. 108...." If the belief or opinion has no basis in reason or probability, and is without any evidence in its support, but exists without any process of reasoning, or is the spontaneous offspring of a perverted imagination, and is adhered to against all evidence and argument, the delusion may be truly called insane; but if there is any evidence, however slight or inconclusive, which might have a tendency to create the belief, it cannot be said to be a delusion." * * * "It must be a delusion of such character that no evidence or argument will have the slightest effect to remove." ... If there is any evidence, however slight or inconclusive, which might have a tendency to create a belief such belief is not a delusion. (57 Am.Jur. 92, sec. 82.)

In re Alegria's Estate, 87 Cal. App. 2d 645, 654 (Ct. App. 1948). Based on that quote, California seems rather solidly in the camp that if there is any factual basis to support the belief, it is not an insane delusion. But then, in *In re Watson's Estate*, the court, in dicta, had the following to say about the *In re Alegria's Estate* approach: "We agree fully with the definition of insane delusion there given, requiring that such a delusion be the product of a disordered mind, and that it be one which cannot be accounted for upon any *reasonable* hypothesis." *In re Watson's Estate*, 195 Cal. App. 2d 740, 743

(Ct. App. 1961) (emphasis added). Reconciling these two descriptions of the insane delusion doctrine in California is tough. On balance, however, it would appear that if there is any evidence to support the belief, it is not an insane delusion.

3. *Unnatural dispositions*: While testamentary freedom is one of the hallmarks of the American legal system, that claim is a bit of an overstatement. In non-community property states, it is impossible to disinherit one's spouse. A surviving spouse has a statutory right to come into probate court and force the testator's estate to give him or her a statutory share of the estate (typically one-third of the estate). In *Honigman*, note the court's statement in the opening paragraph that the will "cut off his wife with a life use of her *minimum statutory share plus $2,500*" (emphasis added). For all practical purposes Mr. Honigman was doing his best, to the extent permitted by law, to disinherit his wife of nearly 40 years. Is that right? Is that natural? If you were on the jury in the case, would Mrs. Honigman's equitable claim that she deserved more trump Mr. Honigman's testamentary freedom?

Where family members are disinherited (either completely, for all practical purposes, or to the extent permitted by law), they usually challenge the will on one or more of the capacity grounds. Studies have repeatedly found that where family members are disinherited and the will is challenged on capacity grounds, juries disproportionately find for the disinherited family members, only to have the court of appeals reverse in more than 50 percent of the cases. Note, *Will Contests on Trial*, 6 Stan. L. Rev. 91, 92 (1953) (a study of California cases between 1892 and 1953 where a will was challenged on capacity grounds found that 77 percent of the trial court proceedings ended in favor of the contestant; but of those appealed, 62 percent were reversed). In light of the high costs of administration inherent in such a scheme, can we do better, or is this simply the cost of having a capacity requirement? In response to what some viewed as a jury's decision often being based on "fairness" as opposed to the proper application of the law, California was among a number of states that eventually eliminated the right to a jury trial in most probate and probate-related matters.[7] Do you think trial judges are more likely to "get it right"?

In many countries, it is virtually impossible to disinherit family members. The courts often have broad powers to override the terms of the will to ensure that the probate process adequately provides for family members. Spouses and children (dependent or not) are given substantial rights in the decedent's estate, leaving relatively little for the testator to dispose of as he or she wishes. Many scholars argue that if the United States granted greater protection to family members there would be less abuse and manipulation of the capacity material—that the latter is our indirect way of trying to protect family members where we think the testator has wronged his or her family. *See* Melanie Leslie, *The Myth of Testamentary Freedom*, 38 Ariz. L. Rev.

---

7. *See* CPC § 8252. Enacted in 1988 and effective in 1989, jury trials for probate code matters (other than certain unrelated conservatorship matters) were eliminated. Oddly, and with no explanation, the 2009 will contest case of Monier Kilgore v. Flores (Cal. App. 3d Dist.) was decided by a jury.

235 (1996). Do you agree? Should we grant greater protection to family members to ensure that they receive a fair and equitable share of the testator's estate?

Problems

1. Heath and Winnie are married and expecting their first child, Charlotte. Tragically, Winnie dies during childbirth and Heath is traumatized by the loss of the love of his life. He hires a nanny to raise Charlotte and sends her away to boarding school.

    As a child, Charlotte developed a condition similar to eczema (itchy, dry, red skin). When someone mentioned the condition was "gross," Heath went on a tirade, insisting on several different occasions that the daughter was "gross" in every way. By the time his daughter was eight or nine years old, Heath "spoke of her only as wicked, having vices not possible of a girl that young, depraved in spirit, vile, of unequaled depravity, deceitful, and violent in temper. He told others that she was a child of the devil and a 'special property of Satan.'"

    Although everyone else considered Charlotte well-behaved, sweet and docile, when she moved back home as a grown daughter, Heath treated her as a servant and physically tortured her at home, while boasting to others that he lavished her with love and gifts when nothing could have been further from the truth.

    A few years before he died, while his behavior was usual in all other respects, Heath executed a will that disinherited Charlotte. Following his death, Charlotte challenged his will.

    Does Heath have general testamentary capacity? Is Heath suffering from an insane delusion? Should the will be declared invalid? *See Dougherty v. Rubenstein*, 914 A.2d 184, 186 (Md. App. 2007) (discussing *Dew v. Clark*, 162 Eng. Rep. 410 (Prerog. 1826) (this latter case is generally recognized as the first case to recognize the insane delusion doctrine)).

2. Louisa F. Strittmater was born in 1896. She never married. She lived with her parents until they died in 1928. She died testate in 1944, with a will that left all her property to the National Women's Party—an organization for which she had worked as a volunteer one day a week from 1939 to 1941.

    At the time of her parents' deaths, all indications were that Louisa and her parents had a normal, loving relationship. Starting in 1935 she began to write comments and memorandum evidencing a change in her attitude. In 1938, she wrote: "My father was a corrupt, vicious, and unintelligent savage, a typical specimen of the majority of his sex. Blast his wormstinking carcass and his whole damn breed." Her cousins, whom she saw very little of during the last few years of her life, challenged her will.

    The New Jersey Appeals court had the following to say about her:

    > The Master who heard the case in the court below, found that the proofs demonstrated 'incontrovertably her morbid aversion to men' and 'feminism to a neurotic extreme.' This characterization seems to me not strong enough. She regarded men as a class with an insane hatred. She looked forward to

the day when women would bear children without the aid of men, and all males would be put to death at birth. Decedent's inward life, disclosed by what she wrote, found an occasional outlet such as the incident of the smashing of the clock, the killing of the pet kitten, vile language, etc. On the other hand — and I suppose this is the split personality — Miss Strittmater, in her dealings with her lawyer, Mr. Semel, over a period of several years, and with her bank, to cite only two examples, was entirely reasonable and normal.

Does Louisa have general testamentary capacity? Is Louisa suffering from an insane delusion — or is she just a feminist ahead of her time, and the court cannot accept her political views? Should the will be declared invalid? *See In re Strittmater's Estate*, 53 A.2d 205 (N.J. 1947) (it should be noted that the court's opinion has been heavily criticized — why?).

B. Undue Influence

Undue influence is a tough doctrine. At the conceptual level it is fairly easy to state and understand. Undue influence occurs when a party unduly influences the testator to substitute the undue influencer's intent for the testator's intent. It makes sense that a party who used undue influence to secure a testamentary gift should not benefit from his or her wrongdoing. The doctrine of undue influence goes hand in hand with testamentary freedom in that it protects testamentary freedom — it protects the testator's intent from others who wish to substitute their intent for the testator's intent.

At the doctrinal level, however, it is difficult to articulate what constitutes undue influence in a way that does not open the door to the trier of fact, in the name of protecting the testator's intent, from substituting its intent for the decedent's intent. Not surprising, legal scholars disagree on how the law should approach the doctrine of undue influence. At one end of the spectrum are scholars who argue that undue influence is coercion, and that absent coercion a trier of fact should not substitute its view of what is right for the decedent's expressed testamentary intent. At the other end of the spectrum are scholars who argue that undue influence is simply inappropriate influence. Although the underlying theme for both ends of the spectrum is inappropriate persuasion, there are subtle, but important, distinctions between the two. Notice the different thresholds a will contestant would have to meet under the conflicting views of the doctrine: coercion versus inappropriate influence. If you were invoking the doctrine in an attempt to invalidate a will, which approach to undue influence would you prefer the jurisdiction held? Under which approach is it easier for a party contesting a will to show undue influence?

Finally, undue influence typically occurs behind closed doors. Rarely is there direct evidence of the misconduct. Instead, undue influence typically is inferred from circumstantial evidence. Because a properly executed will gives rise to a presumption of validity, the party claiming undue influence has the burden of proof. CPC § 8252. What type of circumstantial evidence will permit inferring undue influence varies from jurisdiction to jurisdiction. The RESTATEMENT THIRD OF PROPERTY (Wills & Donative Transfers) sets forth the most generally accepted statement:

> In the absence of direct evidence of undue influence, circumstantial evidence is sufficient to raise an inference of undue influence if the contestant proves that (1) the donor was susceptible to undue influence, (2) the alleged wrongdoer had an opportunity to exert undue influence, (3) the alleged wrongdoer had a disposition to exert undue influence, and (4) there was a result appearing to be the effect of the undue influence.

In addition to this "indicia of undue influence" approach where the contestant bears the burden of proof, almost all jurisdictions also have a "presumption of undue influence" approach where, if the contestant can meet the elements of the presumption approach, a presumption of undue influence arises and the burden shifts to the accused party to rebut the presumption.

The California approaches to the indicia of undue influence doctrine, and to the presumption of undue influence doctrine, are a bit different from the general approaches. Both of the California doctrines are set forth and discussed in the case below. Note that because undue influence is a rather fact-sensitive doctrine, it tends to result in fact-intensive opinions.

In re Estate of Henault

G025278, 2002 WL 1335602 (Cal. Ct. App. June 19, 2002)

FYBEL, J.

FACTS

The Parties

Decedent [Eric W. Henault] died July 20, 1996, at the age of 48 of liver failure. He was HIV positive and an alcoholic. He left no surviving spouse, issue, or parents. For many years before his death, Decedent had close personal relationships with the Castagnas. Decedent had been a hairdresser for and friend of Lori Castagna since approximately 1972. [Charles Castagna II ("Castagna")] had known Decedent since the early 1980's and had been a general handyman for Decedent since approximately 1990. During the last months of Decedent's life, the Castagnas spent a significant amount of time with him, and more time than any other person. Castagna is the proponent of the will at issue.

Decedent's siblings and his friend Jan Atkinson jointly contested the will....

Decedent's Will, Estate Plan, and Other Transfers of Property

On May 29, 1996, Decedent executed a partly printed and partly typewritten, two-sided, single-page will, witnessed by two impartial witnesses (a third witness, Lori Castagna, is Castagna's wife and therefore not an impartial witness). The will execution took place at the Castagnas' home; Castagna had picked Decedent up and brought him to his home that day for a barbecue. Whether Castagna was physically present when Decedent signed the will was disputed. The witnesses testified Decedent knew he was signing his will, was in control of his faculties, and generally knew what he was doing.

Decedent's name is spelled correctly in the title and three times in the typewritten portions of the will, but is twice spelled incorrectly in the typewritten portions, and Jan Atkinson's married name is spelled incorrectly. (Atkinson testified, however, that she still used her maiden name and that Decedent knew her by her maiden name.)

The will is entitled "Last Will and Testament of Ernest William Henault." On the front page, Castagna is named as executor, and the following paragraphs are typewritten:

> "I Ernest W. Henault being of sound mind, give my property located at 4201 Dana Road, in the City of Newport Beach, to Charles L. Castagna, who has been a dear and trusted friend for so many years. He has for years helped me care for and maintain the property and I want him to have it.
>
> "I Ernist [sic] W. Henault being of sound mind request that the remainder of my personal belongings, financial assets, and any additional items of value be divided as follows between:
>
> "1) Charles Castagna of Huntington Beach.   50%
>
> 2) Jan Hensin [sic] of Foster City California.   10%
>
> 3) James Henault of Massachusetts.   40%
>
> "I Ernest W. Henault being of sound mind leave any of the remaining members of my immediate family the sum of $1.00 (one dollar). Although I have always love [sic] my family, I have been deeply hurt by the way they have shunned me because I chose to live an alternate lifestyle. I wish them well."

The back page of the will contains the dated signatures of Decedent and the witnesses.

The day after the will was executed, Decedent executed a durable power of attorney prepared by Castagna, naming Castagna as his attorney-in-fact. On June 13, 1996, Decedent signed a durable power of attorney for health care, giving Castagna the ability to make his health care decisions. Castagna was present at the hospital when Decedent signed the power of attorney for health care.

On June 7, 1996, Decedent executed a grant deed transferring title to the real property in Newport Beach from Decedent as sole owner to Decedent and Castagna as joint tenants. That was the same property that had been bequeathed to Castagna in Decedent's will only 10 days earlier and was also the subject of a purported written agreement between Decedent and Castagna in 1993, in which Decedent allegedly agreed to give the property to Castagna.

At some time during this period, Decedent also designated Castagna as the beneficiary of his IRA.

Decedent's Life and Lifestyle

As would be expected in a will contest case, a significant portion of the testimony at trial focused on Decedent's personality, habits, and lifestyle. Much of the testimony was conflicting, requiring the trial court to weigh the evidence and make determinations as to the witnesses' credibility....

DISCUSSION

...

B. The will was not the product of undue influence.

The trial court also found Decedent's will was the product of the undue influence of Castagna. As the will contestants, the Henaults had the burden of proof of undue influence. (Prob.Code § 8252, subd. (a).) A strong showing is necessary to establish undue influence to invalidate a properly executed will. "Clear and convincing proof is required." "In an action to set aside a will of a deceased person on the ground of undue influence, it is necessary to show that the influence was such as, in effect, to destroy the testator's free agency and substitute for his own another person's will. Evidence must be produced that pressure was brought to bear directly upon the testamentary act. Mere general influence, however strong and controlling, not brought to bear upon the testamentary act, is not enough; it must be influence used directly to procure the will, and must amount to coercion destroying free agency on the part of the testator. It is further held that mere opportunity to influence the mind of the testator, even coupled with an interest or a motive to do so, is not sufficient." ([O]riginal italics.) "The unbroken rule in this state is that the courts must refuse to set aside the solemnly executed will of a deceased person upon the ground of undue influence unless there be proof of 'a pressure which overpowered the mind and bore down the volition of the testator at the very time the will was made.'"

"[U]ndue influence can be established by circumstantial evidence so long as the evidence raises more than a mere suspicion that undue influence was used; the circumstances proven must be inconsistent with the claim that the will was the spontaneous act of the testator."

Undue influence can be established in two ways. First, "When a confidential relationship exists between the decedent and the beneficiary, and the beneficiary both actively participates in procuring the execution of the will and unduly profits by it, a presumption of undue influence arises and places on the beneficiary the burden to show that the will was freely made." Second, when no presumption arises, sufficient indicia of undue influence may still be proven....

1. The evidence does not support a finding of a presumption of undue influence.

For the presumption to arise, all three elements—confidential relationship, active participation in will procurement, and undue benefit—must be present. The absence of any one element prevents the court from applying the presumption, no matter how strong the evidence of the others may be.

We begin by considering whether there was substantial evidence of a confidential relationship between Decedent and Castagna. As noted above, Castagna did not become Decedent's fiduciary until after the will was executed, and the trial court therefore erred by presuming that a confidential relationship existed.

A confidential relationship arises when one party places his confidence in the integrity of another, and that person voluntarily accepts that confidence. Whether such a relationship exists is a highly fact-driven determination.... We look to the factual underpinnings of the cases that have considered the existence of a confidential relationship (or lack thereof) to guide our analysis.

A close friendship, even one that extends over many years, in which one party provides physical and emotional care for another, does not create a confidential relationship without something more.... What constitutes that something more differs from case to case.

One fact that frequently appears in the cases finding a confidential relationship is the beneficiary's handling of the decedent's business affairs....

Other determining factors include whether the beneficiary actually drafted the will [citation omitted] and whether the beneficiary exercised physical control over the decedent and prevented him or her from communicating or interacting with others.

In light of the facts of the foregoing cases, where along the spectrum does the present case fall? With respect to the issue of undue influence, the evidence at trial established the following: Decedent and the Castagnas had been friends for many years; Castagna provided services as a handyman for Decedent without remuneration since the early 1990's; neither of the Castagnas provided health care or nursing services to Decedent, although Lori Castagna spent time with Decedent and cared for his home during the last two or three months of his life; and Decedent was able to care for himself, go shopping, cut his customers' hair in his home, and do some gardening until a couple of weeks before his death. There was no testimony Decedent ever lived with the Castagnas. Friends and hospice workers visited Decedent, both before and after the will was executed, and Decedent had a full-time, live-in caregiver the last few weeks of his life.

Castagna became a fiduciary by means of a power of attorney and started paying Decedent's bills after the durable power of attorney was executed on May 30, 1996. There was no testimony Castagna had anything to do with Decedent's finances or business affairs at any time before the will was executed, other than performing work as a handyman on Decedent's property and purportedly entering into the questionable 1993 contract regarding the property.

Lori Castagna testified Decedent depended on Castagna and placed his trust in him; no testimony was elicited as to when or how Decedent placed his trust in Castagna, and no other witness was questioned on the subject.

As to the issue of Castagna's influence over the execution of the will, testimony was adduced as follows: Castagna took Decedent to Staples, where Decedent typed up his will; Castagna brought Decedent to the Castagnas' home the day the will was signed; Castagna's wife obtained the witnesses to the will execution and those witnesses knew Decedent prior to that date; the witnesses testified Decedent knew what he was doing when he executed his will; and Castagna may or may not have been in the room at the time Decedent executed the will.

Based on all the evidence at trial, there was not substantial evidence to support a finding that a confidential relationship existed between Decedent and Castagna on May 29, 1996. True, Decedent considered Castagna a friend and Castagna and his wife took care of Decedent and his property. But the evidence does not support a finding Castagna was Decedent's fiduciary before the will was executed, prevented Decedent from having visitors or communicating with friends, or exercised physical or mental control over Decedent. The testimony that Decedent trusted Castagna, without any indication as to when he placed his trust in Castagna, or whether Castagna accepted Decedent's trust, cannot, standing alone, meet the high standard of proof by clear and convincing evidence. On this record, we find no confidential relationship between Castagna and Decedent as of May 29, 1996.... The Henaults were not entitled to a presumption of undue influence to assist them in contesting the will.

2. The evidence does not support a finding of undue influence by Castagna sufficient to subvert the testamentary capacity of Decedent.

Even when no presumption arises, undue influence may still be found. There are several nonexclusive questions to be considered in determining whether the beneficiary exercised undue influence in the procurement of a will: "1. Does the will cut off the natural objects of the decedent's bounty, and unduly benefit the proponent? [¶]2. Is there a variance between the terms of the will and the expressed intentions of the testatrix? [¶]3. Was there an opportunity afforded by the legatee's relationship to the decedent to influence the testatrix? [¶]4. Was the decedent's mental and physical condition such as to permit a subversion of her freedom of will? [¶]5. Was the beneficiary active in procuring the execution of the will?" [Citation omitted.] These factors must be considered in combination. (12 Witkin, Summary of Cal. Law (9th ed. 1990) Wills and Probate, § 189.)

Although the trial court did not make any findings as to the existence or nonexistence of any of the foregoing factors, we have reviewed the record and have determined there was not substantial evidence to support a finding of undue influence. While Castagna was benefited in the sense that he would receive the largest share of Decedent's estate under the will, the siblings who were cut off by the will were not the "'natural ... objects of [decedent's] bounty.'" [siblings, nieces and nephews are not the natural objects of one's bounty, as are spouses, children and parents].) ...

No party offered evidence of any previous wills, which would be indicative of a change in the Decedent's expressed intentions as to the disposition of his estate.... No testimony was offered to indicate that Decedent tried to change the will, or even stated that he disavowed the will or wanted to bequeath his property to anyone else during the almost two months between the date the will was signed and the date of his death. On the whole, we do not find the foregoing is sufficient evidence that the terms of the will were contrary to Decedent's expressed intentions.

The record provides substantial evidence that the relationship between Decedent and Castagna afforded Castagna at best the opportunity to influence Decedent. Without more, however, the mere opportunity to exercise undue influence cannot support a finding Castagna did in fact do so.

While there was substantial evidence Decedent was very ill at the time he executed his will, the testimony showed that on the day the will was executed, Decedent was not too ill to understand what he was doing.

Next, we consider whether there was substantial evidence Castagna actively procured the will. Several witnesses testified Castagna stated he took Decedent to Staples to have the will typed up. This testimony alone does not establish Castagna actively procured the will. The activity we are concerned with is activity " 'in the ... preparation of the will.' " ... see *Estate of Mann, supra,* 184 Cal.App.3d 593, 608, 229 Cal.Rptr. 225 [urging decedent to make a will, taking her to an attorney, and being present when will was executed does not constitute procurement]; *Estate of Evans, supra,* 274 Cal.App.2d 203 at pp. 211–212, 79 Cal.Rptr. 1 [procurement found when beneficiary had will typed and brought it to decedent's hospital room, where he read it to her, obtained witnesses, and remained while will was executed].) There was no testimony Castagna himself drafted or typed up the will.

When all is said and done, the evidence before the trial court did not support a finding of undue influence by Castagna in the execution of Decedent's will.

Notes

1. *Indicia versus presumption of undue influence:* In California, there is a real tendency for the case law to rely more on the presumption of undue influence doctrine than the indicia of undue influence doctrine. Because of the way California has articulated each doctrine, there is a heavier than usual overlap between the two doctrines, so much so that if one can show the indicia of undue influence one typically can show the elements of the presumption of undue influence. Accordingly, it is rare to find a California case that leads with the indicia of undue influence. Lead with the presumption doctrine.

2. *Burden of proof:* There appears to be some confusion in the California case law as to the proper burden of proof for a claim of undue influence. Some courts, like the court in the *Henault,* require clear and convincing evidence of undue influence. Other courts require only a preponderance of the evidence. *See Estate of Gelonese,* 36 Cal. App. 3d 854, 111 Cal. Rptr. 833 (1974). A majority of the courts appear to adopt the latter position, an approach implicitly supported by Section 8252 of the California Probate Code. Section 8252 provides as follows:

> (a) At the trial, the proponents of the will have the burden of proof of due execution. The contestants of the will have the burden of proof of lack of testamentary intent or capacity, undue influence, fraud, duress, mistake, or revocation.

The failure of Section 8252 to require clear and convincing evidence supports the view that the default burden of proof, preponderance of the evidence, should apply.

3. *Unduly benefits:* The final requirement of the presumption of undue influence doctrine is that the will contestant must show that the alleged undue influencer "unduly benefits" under the terms of the instrument. In assessing what constitutes undue influence, should the courts take more of a quantitative approach to the element (how much would the beneficiary take if the instrument were not valid) or should the courts take more of a qualitative approach (assess the gift in light of the relationship between the parties)? *See Estate of Sarabia,* 221 Cal. App. 3d 599, 604 (1990).

4. *Nuanced nature of undue influence:* Undue influence is one of the toughest, most fact-sensitive doctrines in the law. In *In re Estate of Rosasco,* 927 N.Y.S.2d 819 (Sur. 2011), Judge Kristin Booth Glen of the New York Surrogate's Court had this to say about the doctrine:

> Courts have long wrestled with the concept of undue influence. In the nineteenth century, the Court of Appeals noted:
>
>> It is impossible to define or describe with precision and exactness what is undue influence; what the quality and the extent of the power of one mind over another must be to make it *undue,* in the sense of the law, when exerted in making a will. Like the question of insanity, it is to some degree open and vague, and must be decided by the application of sound principles and good sense to the facts of each given case. [Citation omitted.] But the influence exercised over a testator which the law regards as undue or illegal, must be such as to destroy his free agency; but no matter how little the influence, if the free agency is destroyed it vitiates the act which is the result of it. In 1 Jarman on Wills, 36, it is said: "That the amount of undue influences which will be sufficient to invalidate a will must of course vary with the strength or weakness of the mind of the testator; and the influence which would subdue and control a mind naturally weak, or one which had become impaired by age, sickness, disease, intemperance, or any other cause, might have no effect to overcome or mislead a mind naturally strong and unimpaired."
>
>> The undue influence is not often the subject of direct proof. It can be shown by all the facts and circumstances surrounding the testator, the nature of the will, his family relations, the condition of his health and mind, his dependency upon and subjection to the control of the person supposed to have wielded the influences, the opportunity and disposition of the person to wield it, and the acts and declarations of such person. [Citations omitted.] *Rollwagen v. Rollwagen,* 63 N.Y. 504, 519 (1876).

Note that the court acknowledges that the amount of influence necessary to overcome a testator's free will varies with the testator's mental strength or weakness. Accordingly, where there are issues concerning a testator's general testamentary capacity, it is not uncommon for there to be issues—or at least claims—of undue influence.

5. *No contest clauses in testamentary instruments:* If Eric W. Henault had gone to an attorney to have his will prepared, no doubt the attorney would have considered

including a no contest clause. Virtually every testamentary document (e.g., a will or will substitute) contains a no contest clause (also known as an "In Terrorem" clause). The idea is to create a disincentive for will beneficiaries to contest the document, say by claiming that the testator lacked the requisite mental capacity or was subject to undue influence. The typical no contest clause is simple: if a beneficiary brings suit contesting the document or the estate plan reflected in the document, then he or she runs the risk of losing his or her right to take under the instrument. (Note that for a no-contest clause to be effective, the person must be a beneficiary under the instrument so he or she has something to lose if he or she sues.) It is as if the testator/settlor/transferor is saying "If you want to challenge this, then be prepared to forfeit what is being given to you under this will." Of course, if there is a challenge, and it is successful, and the document is deemed invalid (say by reason of undue influence or lack of capacity), then the clause typically has no relevance because the testamentary document is gone and disposition of the decedent's property falls back to the statutory intestate succession scheme.[8] But if the challenger is unsuccessful, the testamentary document stands and, pursuant to the no contest clause, the challenger should forfeit what he or she would have otherwise received.

Enforcement of such clauses has been the source of much controversy over the years. A no contest clause presents an interesting dilemma for courts. On the one hand, no contest clauses are good because they help to protect the testator's intent and reduce the risk of spurious litigation. On the other hand, no contest clauses are contrary to public policy because they may deter interested parties from bringing appropriate challenges out of fear of losing their gifts, thereby shielding a wrongdoer's actions.

Courts have responded to these conflicting public policy considerations by: (1) adopting the general rule that no contest clauses are valid; (2) construing no contest clauses narrowly; and (3) recognizing exceptions to enforcement of no contest clauses where the challenge in question is deemed meritorious. What constitutes a meritorious challenge varies from jurisdiction to jurisdiction.

In 2010, California statutorily overhauled its approach to the validity and enforcement of no contest clauses. Prior law generally recognized no contest clauses as valid, but a plethora of exceptions to their enforcement existed (and procedurally, one could file a petition seeking the court's determination of whether the contemplated challenge would violate the no contest clause). A beneficiary who was considering filing a claim would typically petition the court for guidance with respect to whether the claim would trigger the no contest clause, leading to increased litigation. While the new statutory approach continues to recognize the validity of no contest clauses, it addresses more clearly and directly which challenges fall within the scope of a standard no

---

8. Where there is a claim of defect in capacity, the remedy typically is to strike as much of the instrument as was affected by the defect. That may be all of the will, in which case the probate estate likely will fall to intestacy (unless there is a prior will that would now dispose of the property)—or it may mean that only part of the will is invalidated (say a specific or general gift), and so long as the will's residuary clause is still valid, the property will not pass via intestacy. See Chapter 7 for further discussion of the effect of a failed gift without a will.

contest clause, and it explicitly abolishes a beneficiary's ability to petition the court for guidance as to whether a claim would violate the no contest clause.

CPC § 21311. Enforcement of Clause

(a) A no contest clause shall only be enforced against the following types of contests:

    (1) A direct contest that is brought without probable cause.

    (2) A pleading to challenge a transfer of property on the grounds that it was not the transferor's property at the time of the transfer. A no contest clause shall only be enforced under this paragraph if the no contest clause expressly provides for that application.

    (3) The filing of a creditor's claim or prosecution of an action based on it. A no contest clause shall only be enforced under this paragraph if the no contest clause expressly provides for that application.

(b) For the purposes of this section, probable cause exists if, at the time of filing a contest, the facts known to the contestant would cause a reasonable person to believe that there is a reasonable likelihood that the requested relief will be granted after an opportunity for further investigation or discovery.

California Probate Code Section 21311(a)(1) provides that a no contest clause applies to a "direct contest" brought without probable cause. California Probate Code Section 21310 defines a "direct contest" to include, among other items, actions alleging lack of capacity, undue influence, and fraud. Of important note in the new no contest enforcement statute is the use of the "probable cause" standard to articulate the scope of the exception to the enforcement of a no contest clause. This approach applies to anyone who challenges the validity of a document on, for example, the grounds of lack of capacity or undue influence (a direct contest). Of course, the new statute changes nothing if the challenge is successful and the testamentary document is deemed invalid (which, in the typical setting, will result in the property passing through the intestate succession scheme). If, however, a challenger's direct contest fails (i.e., the court does not find there to be a lack of capacity, undue influence, etc.), the no contest clause would still be unenforceable if the challenger could prove that he or she had "probable cause" to bring the claim—i.e., that at the time the challenge was filed, the facts known to the contestant "would cause a reasonable person to believe that there was a reasonable likelihood" that the contestant would prevail following further investigation. If the court finds probable cause existed to support the challenge, then the no contest clause would not be enforceable and the challenger would not forfeit gifts or property to be received under the document. If, however, the court does not find that probable cause exists to support the claim, then the no contest clause would apply, and the challenger would take nothing.

6. *Relevance of "nontraditional" relationships*: Do certain relationships, typically those outside of one's family, provide fertile ground for the seeds of undue influence? The more "nontraditional" the relationship the more likely the claim of undue influence? Is it appropriate to take the "nontraditional" nature of the relationship into consideration when analyzing whether a party exercised undue influence, or does

that reflect a weakness in the system? Another scenario that has proved a fertile source of undue influence claims has been gifts to the decedent's attorney. If the attorney who drafted the will is a primary beneficiary thereof, does this pass the "smell" test?

In re Moses' Will

227 So. 2d 829 (Miss. 1969)

SMITH, Justice:

Mrs. Fannie Traylor Moses died on February 6, 1967. An instrument, dated December 23, 1957 and purporting to be her last will and testament, was duly admitted to probate in common form in the Chancery Court of the First Judicial District of Hinds County. Thereafter, on February 14, 1967, appellant, Clarence H. Holland, an attorney at law, not related to Mrs. Moses, filed a petition in that court tendering for probate in solemn form, as the true last will and testament of Mrs. Moses, a document dated May 26, 1964, under the terms of which he would take virtually her entire estate. This document contained a clause revoking former wills and Holland's petition prayed that the earlier probate of the 1957 will be set aside.

The beneficiaries under the 1957 will (the principal beneficiary was an elder sister of Mrs. Moses) responded to Holland's petition, denied that the document tendered by him was Mrs. Moses' will, and asserted, among other things, that it was (1) the product of Holland's undue influence upon her, (2) that at the time of its signing, Mrs. Moses lacked testamentary capacity, and, (3) that the 1957 will was Mrs. Moses' true last will and testament and its probate should be confirmed. By cross bill, respondents prayed that Holland's apparent ownership of an interest in certain real estate had been procured by undue influence and that it should be cancelled as a cloud upon the title of Mrs. Moses, the true owner.

By agreement, the case was heard by the chancellor without a jury.

After hearing and considering a great deal of evidence, oral and documentary, together with briefs of counsel, the chancellor, in a carefully considered opinion, found that (1) the 1964 document, tendered for probate by Holland, was the product of undue influence and was not entitled to be admitted to probate, (2) the earlier probate of the 1957 will should be confirmed and, (3) Mrs. Moses had been the true owner of the interest claimed by Holland in the real estate and his claim of ownership should be cancelled as a cloud upon the title of Mrs. Moses.

Holland's appeal is from the decree entered denying probate to the 1964 document and cancelling his claim to an undivided one-half interest in the real estate....

A brief summary of facts found by the chancellor and upon which he based his conclusion that the presumption was not overcome, follows:

Mrs. Moses died at the age of 57 years, leaving an estate valued at $125,000. She had lost three husbands in less than 20 years. Throughout the latter years of her life her health became seriously impaired. She suffered from serious heart trouble and cancer had required the surgical removal of one of her breasts. For 6 or 7 years preceding her death she was an alcoholic.

On several occasions Mrs. Moses had declared her intention of making an elder sister her testamentary beneficiary. She had once lived with this sister and was grateful for the many kindnesses shown her. Mrs. Moses' will of December 23, 1957 did, in fact, bequeath the bulk of her estate to this sister.

The exact date on which Holland entered Mrs. Moses' life is unclear. There is a suggestion that she had met him as early as 1951. Their personal relationship became what the chancellor, somewhat inaccurately, characterized, as one of 'dubious' morality. The record, however, leaves no doubt as to its nature. Soon after the death of Mrs. Moses' last husband, Holland, although 15 years her junior, began seeing Mrs. Moses with marked regularity, there having been testimony to the effect that he attended her almost daily. Holland was an attorney and in that capacity represented Mrs. Moses. She declared that he was not only her attorney but her 'boyfriend' as well. On August 22, 1961, a date during the period in which the evidence shows that Holland was Mrs. Moses' attorney, she executed a document purporting to be her will. This instrument was drawn by an attorney with whom Holland was then associated and shared offices, and was typed by a secretary who served them both. It was witnessed by Holland's associate and their secretary. In addition to other testamentary dispositions, this document undertook to bequeath to Holland 'my wedding ring, my diamond solitaire ring and my three gold bracelets containing twenty-five (25) pearls each.' In it Holland is referred to as 'my good friend.' The validity of this document is not an issue in the present case.

After Mrs. Moses died, the 1964 will was brought forward by another attorney, also an associate of Holland, who said that it had been entrusted to him by Mrs. Moses, together with other papers, for safekeeping. He distinguished his relation with Holland from that of a partner, saying that he and Holland only occupied offices together and shared facilities and expenses in the practice of law. He also stated that he saw Mrs. Moses on an 'average' of once a week, most often in the company of Holland.

Throughout this period, Mrs. Moses was a frequent visitor at Holland's office, and there is ample evidence to support the chancellor's finding that there existed a continuing fiduciary relationship between Mrs. Moses and Holland, as her attorney.

In May, 1962, Holland and the husband of Holland's first cousin, one Gibson, had contracted to buy 480 acres of land for $36,000. Mrs. Moses was not, it appears, originally a party to the contract.... At the time, Mrs. Moses had annuity contracts with a total maturity value of some $40,000 on which she obtained $31,341.11. This sum was deposited in a bank account called 'Cedar Hills Ranch.' She gave Holland authority to check on this account, as well as upon her personal account.... At closing, the persons present, in addition to the grantors and their agents and attorney, were Mrs. Moses and Holland, her attorney. Mrs. Moses had no other counsel. Holland issued a check on the Cedar Hills Ranch account (in which only Mrs. Moses had any money) for the $31,000 balance. Although none of the consideration was paid by Holland, the deed from the owners purported to convey the land to Holland and Mrs. Moses in equal shares, as tenants in common. On the day following, Holland issued another check on the Cedar Hills Ranch account (in which he still had deposited no money) for $835.00 purportedly in payment for a tractor. This check was issued by Holland to his brother. Eight days later Holland drew another check on this account for $2,100.00 purportedly for an undisclosed number of cattle. This check was issued to Holland's father.

The evidence supports the chancellor's finding that the confidential or fiduciary relationship which existed between Mrs. Moses and Holland, her attorney, was a subsisting and continuing relationship, having begun before the making by Mrs. Moses of the will of August 22, 1961, under the terms of which her jewelry had been bequeathed to Holland, and having ended only with Mrs. Moses' death. Moreover, its effect was enhanced by the fact that throughout this period, Holland was in almost daily attendance upon Mrs. Moses on terms of the utmost intimacy. There was strong evidence that this aging woman, seriously ill, disfigured by surgery, and hopelessly addicted to alcoholic excesses, was completely bemused by the constant and amorous attentions of Holland, a man 15 years her junior. There was testimony too indicating that she entertained the pathetic hope that he might marry her. Although the evidence was not without conflict and was, in some of its aspects, circumstantial, it was sufficient to support the finding that the relationship existed on May 26, 1964, the date of the will tendered for probate by Holland.

… Moreover, he [the chancellor] was correct in his conclusion of law that such relationship gave rise to a presumption of undue influence which could be overcome only by evidence that, in making the 1964 will, Mrs. Moses had acted upon the independent advice and counsel of one entirely devoted to her interest.

Appellant takes the position that there was undisputed evidence that Mrs. Moses, in making the 1964 will, did, in fact, have such advice and counsel. He relies upon the testimony of the attorney in whose office that document was prepared to support his assertion.

This attorney was and is a reputable and respected member of the bar, who had no prior connection with Holland and no knowledge of Mrs. Moses' relationship with him. He had never seen nor represented Mrs. Moses previously and never represented her afterward. He was acquainted with Holland and was aware that Holland was a lawyer.

A brief summary of his testimony, with respect to the writing of the will, follows:

Mrs. Moses had telephoned him for an appointment and had come alone to his office on March 31, 1964. She was not intoxicated and in his opinion knew what she was doing. He asked her about her property and 'marital background.' He did this in order, he said, to advise her as to possible renunciation by a husband. She was also asked if she had children in order to determine whether she wished to 'pretermit them.' As she had neither husband nor children this subject was pursued no further. He asked as to the values of various items of property in order to consider possible tax problems. He told her it would be better if she had more accurate descriptions of the several items of real and personal property comprising her estate. No further 'advice or counsel' was given her.

On some later date, Mrs. Moses sent in (the attorney did not think she came personally and in any event he did not see her), some tax receipts for purposes of supplying property descriptions. He prepared the will and mailed a draft to her.... On the one occasion when he saw Mrs. Moses, there were no questions and no discussion of any kind as to Holland being preferred to the exclusion of her blood relatives. Nor was there any inquiry or discussion as to a possible client-attorney relationship with Holland. The attorney-draftsman wrote the will according to Mrs. Moses' instructions and said that he had 'no interest in' how she disposed of her property. He testified 'I try to draw the will to suit their purposes and if she (Mrs. Moses) wanted to leave him (Holland) everything she had, that was her business as far as I was concerned. I was trying to represent her in putting on paper in her will her desires, and it didn't matter to me to whom she left it ... I couldn't have cared less.'

When Mrs. Moses returned to the office to execute the will, the attorney was not there and it was witnessed by two secretaries. One of these secretaries, coincidentally, had written and witnessed the 1961 will when working for Holland and his associate.

The attorney's testimony supports the chancellor's finding that nowhere in the conversations with Mrs. Moses was there touched upon in any way the proposed testamentary disposition whereby preference was to be given a nonrelative to the exclusion of her blood relatives. There was no discussion of her relationship with Holland, nor as to who her legal heirs might be, nor as to their relationship to her, after it was discovered that she had neither a husband nor children.

It is clear from his own testimony that, in writing the will, the attorney-draftsman, did no more than write down, according to the forms of law, what Mrs. Moses told him. There was no meaningful independent advice or counsel touching upon the area in question and it is manifest that the role of the attorney in writing the will, as it relates to the present issue, was little more than that of scrivener. The chancellor was justified in holding that this did not meet the burden nor overcome the presumption.

In *Croft v. Alder*, 237 Miss. 713, 724, 115 So.2d 683, 686 (1959) there was an extensive review of the authorities relating to the question here under consideration. This Court said:

> *Meek v. Perry*, 1858, 36 Miss. 190, 243, 244, 252, 259, is perhaps the leading case. It involved a will by a ward leaving a substantial amount of her property to her guardian. The Court held that the presumption of invalidity applies to wills as well as deeds. It was said the law watches with the greatest jealously transactions between persons in confidential relations and will not permit them to stand, unless the circumstances demonstrate the fullest deliberation on the part of the testator and the most abundant good faith on the part of the beneficiary. Hence the law presumes the existence of undue influence, and such dealings are prima facie void, and will be so held 'unless the guardian show by clearest proof' that he took no advantage over the testator, and the cestui's act was a result of his own volition and upon the fullest deliberation....

... In *Jamison v. Jamison*, 1909, 96 Miss. 288, 298, 51 So. 130, 131, it was said: "The difficulty is also enhanced by the fact, universally recognized, that he who seeks to use undue influence does so in privacy. He seldom uses brute force or open threats to terrorize his intended victim, and if he does he is careful that no witnesses are about to take note of and testify to the fact. He observes, too, the same precautions if he seeks by cajolery, flattery, or other methods to obtain power and control over the will of another, and direct it improperly to the accomplishment of the purpose which he desires. Subscribing witnesses are called to attest the execution of wills, and testify as to the testamentary capacity of the testator, and the circumstances attending the immediate execution of the instrument; but they are not called upon to testify as to the antecedent agencies by which the execution of the paper was secured, even if they had any knowledge of them, which they seldom have." *In re Coins' Will (Fortner v. Coins)*, 1959, (237 Miss. 322) 114 So.2d 759.

We do not think that the testimony of the attorney who attested the will, as to his observations at that particular time, can suffice to rebut the already existing presumption. As stated in *Jamison*, he naturally would have had no knowledge of any precedent activities ...

...

Holland, of course, did not personally participate in the actual preparation or execution of the will. If he had, under the circumstances in evidence, unquestionably the will could not stand. It may be assumed that Holland, as a lawyer, knew this.

In *Croft, supra*, this Court said that the presumption of undue influence in the production of a will may arise from 'antecedent circumstances' about which its draftsman and the witnesses knew nothing. The rule, as stated in that case, is that undue influence will be presumed where the beneficiary 'has been actively concerned in some way with the preparation or execution of the will, or where the relationship is coupled with some suspicious circumstances, such as mental infirmity of the testator.' (emphasis added).

Undue influence operates upon the will as well as upon the mind. It is not dependent upon a lack of testamentary capacity.

The chancellor's finding that the will was the product of Holland's undue influence is not inconsistent with his conclusion that 'Her (Mrs. Moses) mind was capable of understanding the essential matters necessary to the execution of her will on May 26, 1964, at the time of such execution.' A weak or infirm mind may, of course, be more easily over persuaded. In the case under review, Mrs. Moses was in ill health, she was an alcoholic, and was an aging woman infatuated with a young lover, 15 years her junior, who was also her lawyer. If this combination of circumstances cannot be said to support the view that Mrs. Moses suffered from a 'weakness or infirmity' of mind, vis-a-vis Holland, it was hardly calculated to enhance her power of will where he was concerned. Circumstances in evidence, both antecedent and subsequent to the making of the will, tend to accord with that conclusion.

The sexual morality of the personal relationship is not an issue. However, the intimate nature of this relationship is relevant to the present inquiry to the extent that its existence, under the circumstances, warranted an inference of undue influence, extending and augmenting that which flowed from the attorney-client relationship. Particularly is this true when viewed in the light of evidence indicating its employment for the personal aggrandizement of Holland. For that purpose, it was properly taken into consideration by the chancellor....

As stated in *Croft, supra*, the rule that a presumption of undue influence arises when a fiduciary relationship is established applies with even greater stringency in cases of transactions inter vivos. In the land transaction, Holland attended as Mrs. Moses' attorney. She had no other advice or counsel. The chancellor correctly held that, under the circumstances, Holland, as her attorney, could take no interest adverse to Mrs. Moses in the land purchased by her. He took title to the half interest in the land as trustee for Mrs. Moses and not otherwise. His apparent claim of ownership of a half interest was properly cancelled and removed as a cloud upon the title of Mrs. Moses to the complete fee. *Johnson v. Outlaw*, 56 Miss. 541 (1879) and *Cameron v. Lewis*, 56 Miss. 601 (1879). See also *Sojourner v. Sojourner*, 247 Miss. 342, 153 So.2d 803, 156 So.2d 579 (1963) and *Smith v. Dean*, 240 S.W.2d 789 (Tex. Civ. App.) (1951).

For the foregoing reasons, the petition for rehearing is sustained, the original majority opinion is withdrawn, this opinion will be that of the Court, and the decree of the chancery court will be affirmed.

Petition for rehearing sustained, original opinion withdrawn, and decree of chancery court affirmed.

ROBERTSON, Justice (dissenting):

I am unable to agree with the majority of the Court that Mrs. Moses should not be allowed to dispose of her property as she so clearly intended....

Mrs. Fannie T. Moses was 54 years of age when she executed her last will and testament on May 26, 1964, leaving most of her considerable estate to Clarence H. Holland, her good friend, but a man fifteen years her junior. She had been married three times, and each of these marriages was dissolved by the death of her husband. Holland's friendship with Mrs. Moses dated back to the days of her second husband, Robert L. Dickson. He was also a friend of her third husband, Walter Moses.

She was the active manager of commercial property in the heart of Jackson, four apartment buildings containing ten rental units, and a 480-acre farm until the day of her death. All of the witnesses conceded that she was a good businesswoman, maintaining and repairing her properties with promptness and dispatch, and paying her bills promptly so that she would get the cash discount. She was a strong personality and pursued her own course, even though her manner of living did at times embarrass her sisters and estranged her from them....

There is no proof in this voluminous record that Holland ever did or said anything to Mrs. Moses about devising her property to anybody, much less him. It is conceded that in the absence of the presumption of undue influence that there is no basis to support a finding that Holland exercised undue influence over Mrs. Moses. This being true, the first question to be decided is whether the presumption of undue influence arises under the circumstances of this case.

It is my opinion that the presumption did not arise. The fact, alone, that a confidential relationship existed between Holland and Mrs. Moses is not sufficient to give rise to the presumption of undue influence in a will case....

It was not contended in this case that Holland was in any way actively concerned with the preparation or execution of the will. Appellees rely solely upon the finding of the chancellor that there were suspicious circumstances. However, the suspicious circumstances listed by the chancellor in his opinion had nothing whatsoever to do with the preparation or execution of the will. These were remote antecedent circumstances having to do with the meretricious relationship of the parties, and the fact that at times Mrs. Moses drank to excess and could be termed an alcoholic, but there is no proof in this long record that her use of alcohol affected her will power or her ability to look after her extensive real estate holdings. It is common knowledge that many persons who could be termed alcoholics, own, operate and manage large business enterprises with success. The fact that she chose to leave most of her property to the man she loved in preference to her sisters and brother is not such an unnatural disposition of her property as to render it invalid.

In this case, there were no suspicious circumstances surrounding the preparation or execution of the will, and in my opinion the chancellor was wrong in so holding. However, even if it be conceded that the presumption of undue influence did arise, this presumption was overcome by clear and convincing evidence of good faith, full knowledge and independent consent and advice.

Notes

1. *Gifts from a client to his or her attorney—the California approach*: Notice that while gifts to one's attorney do not pass most people's "smell" test, these gifts are not per se invalid under either the indicia of undue influence doctrine or the presumption of undue influence doctrine. As recently as 1992 California did *not* have a rule prohibiting an attorney from accepting gifts from his or her client—that is, until the questionable nature of a particular attorney's practice came to the attention of the media and, ultimately, the legislature.

The attorney in question opened his office next to Leisure World, a gated retirement community in Orange County. By 1992, with more than 21,000 retired residents, Leisure World had grown into the country's largest gated retirement community. The attorney's practice grew with Leisure World, and by 1992 he was involved in the drafting of thousands of wills and trusts in which he was also often a beneficiary. One of the more egregious gifts was a will and trust that the attorney arranged to have drafted and executed for a 98-year-old blind and bedridden client just six weeks before he died. The documents reportedly: (1) left the attorney $3.5 million in assets; (2) made the other beneficiaries under the instruments liable for the $2 million in estate taxes on his gifts; and (3) included a no contest clause to deter the other beneficiaries from suing.

Over the course of three decades the attorney in question received millions of dollars in questionable "gifts" until the Los Angeles Times wrote an expose about his practice.[9] The public outcry was heard all the way up in Sacramento, where the legislature responded by enacting the California Interested Drafter statutes. The legislative history behind the California Interested Drafter statutes includes the following description of the attorney's practice:

> Reportedly, [the attorney in question] has engaged in a series of highly questionable, if not, arguably, illegal acts, which may be characterized in the following manner:
>
> - Drafting wills which name [the attorney in question] as a major (or exclusive) beneficiary of large estates, to the exclusion of more natural beneficiaries, including immediate family members.
>
> - Drafting trust documents, in which [the attorney in question] is named the exclusive trustee of large, discretionary estates.
>
> - As trustee, authorizing payment of large sums of money to his law partners for legal services.
>
> - As trustee, expending money in a manner contrary to the instructions of the settlor and in a manner that benefited businesses or charities in which [the attorney in question] had significant and, perhaps, controlling, interest.
>
> - Having himself named as conservator of a client and, subsequently, authorizing payment of large sums of money to his law partners for legal services ... [or] drafting wills naming [the attorney in question] as a primary, if not exclusive, beneficiary.
>
> - Investing trust assets in financial institutions owned, or controlled, by [the attorney in question].
>
> - Currently, [the attorney in question] is the subject of an investigation by the State Bar. The Orange County Sheriff has established a hotline in its fraud unit to collect information about possible criminal conduct by [the attorney in question]. Additionally, the chief probate judge of Orange County has initiated a review of all matters handled by [the attorney in question].

---

9. The full article is well worth reading: http://articles.latimes.com/1992-11-22/news/mn-2315_1_leisure-world.

California Bill Analysis, Assembly Committee, 1993–1994 Regular Session, Assembly Bill 21 (February 10, 1993).

California's statutory response to the issue of undue influence in "suspect" relationships was Probate Code Sections 21350 through 21356, which were later repealed and replaced in 2010 with the following sections. The principal response of the former sections is carried over to the new provisions, with relatively minor changes.

CPC § 21380. Prohibited transferees; definitions

(a) A provision of an instrument making a donative transfer to any of the following persons is presumed to be the product of fraud or undue influence:

   (1) The person who drafted the instrument.

   (2) A person in a fiduciary relationship with the transferor who transcribed the instrument or caused it to be transcribed.

   (3) A care custodian of a transferor who is a dependent adult, but only if the instrument was executed during the period in which the care custodian provided services to the transferor, or within 90 days before or after that period.

   (4) A person who is related by blood or affinity, within the third degree, to any person described in paragraphs (1) to (3), inclusive.

   (5) A cohabitant or employee of any person described in paragraphs (1) to (3), inclusive.

   (6) A partner, shareholder, or employee of a law firm in which a person described in paragraph (1) or (2) has an ownership interest.

(b) The presumption created by this section is a presumption affecting the burden of proof. The presumption may be rebutted by proving, by clear and convincing evidence, that the donative transfer was not the product of fraud or undue influence.

(c) Notwithstanding subdivision (b), with respect to a donative transfer to the person who drafted the donative instrument, or to a person who is related to, or associated with, the drafter as described in paragraph (4), (5), or (6) of subdivision (a), the presumption created by this section is conclusive.

(d) If a beneficiary is unsuccessful in rebutting the presumption, the beneficiary shall bear all costs of the proceeding, including reasonable attorney's fees.

CPC § 21382. Exclusions from presumption

Section 21380 does not apply to any of the following instruments or transfers:

(a) A donative transfer to a person who is related by blood or affinity, within the fourth degree, to the transferor or is the cohabitant of the transferor.

(b) An instrument that is drafted or transcribed by a person who is related by blood or affinity, within the fourth degree, to the transferor or is the cohabitant of the transferor.

   ...

(d) A donative transfer to a federal, state, or local public entity, an entity that qualifies for an exemption from taxation under Section 501(c)(3) or 501(c)(19) of the Internal Revenue Code, or a trust holding the transferred property for the entity.

(e) A donative transfer of property valued at five thousand dollars ($5,000) or less, if the total value of the transferor's estate equals or exceeds the amount stated in Section 13100 [$150,000].

(f) An instrument executed outside of California by a transferor who was not a resident of California when the instrument was executed.

CPC § 21384. Certificate of independent review

(a) A gift is not subject to Section 21380 if the instrument is reviewed by an independent attorney who counsels the transferor, out of the presence of any heir or proposed beneficiary, about the nature and consequences of the intended transfer, including the effect of the intended transfer on the transferor's heirs and on any beneficiary of a prior donative instrument, attempts to determine if the intended transfer is the result of fraud or undue influence, and signs and delivers to the transferor an original certificate in substantially the following form:

CERTIFICATE OF INDEPENDENT REVIEW

I, _____, have reviewed
(attorney's name)

_____ and have counseled the transferor
(name of instrument)

_____, on the nature and consequences of any
(name of transferor)

Transfers of property to _____
(name of person described in Section 21380 of the Probate Code)
that would be made by the instrument.

I am an "independent attorney" as defined in Section 21370 of the Probate Code and am in a position to advise the transferor independently, impartially, and confidentially as to the consequences of the transfer.

On the basis of this counsel, I conclude that the transfers to

_____ that would be made by
(name of person described in Section 21380 of the Probate Code)
the instrument are not the product of fraud or undue influence

_____   _____
(name of attorney)   (date)

...

CPC § 21386. Treatment of gifts that failed under this part

If a gift fails under this part, the instrument making the gift shall operate as if the beneficiary had predeceased the transferor without spouse, domestic partner, or issue.

CPC § 21390. Contrary provision in instrument; application of part

This part applies notwithstanding a contrary provision in an instrument.

2. *Epilogue*: The attorney whose questionable practice contributed to the adoption of California's prohibited transferee statutes above resigned from the practice of law

and surrendered his license in 1994 with ethical charges pending against him. There is no record of how much, if any, of the "gifted" property he received from his clients was returned. How would his questionable actvities be analyzed today in California? How would the *Moses* case be analyzed in California today?

3. *Caused to be transcribed*: In *Rice v. Clark*, 47 P.3d 300 (Cal. 2002), the California Supreme Court was called upon to construe the then-current statutory provision (similar to the provision in the current statutes, above) that the interested drafter doctrine applies to "[a] person in a fiduciary relationship with the transferor who transcribed the instrument *or caused it to be transcribed*" (emphasis added). In *Rice*, Cecilia Clare's husband died in 1988 when she was 76 years old. They had no children. She hired Richard Clark, a handyman, to make some repairs to her house and some income-producing property she owned. By 1994, Clark was handling almost every aspect of the property management of the properties, as well as helping Clare with an increasing number of personal chores, such as taking her to the store and the bank several times a week.

Between 1992 and 1995 Clare executed a number of donative and testamentary instruments that increasingly gave her property to Clark. Clark encouraged Clare to see an attorney to deal with the testamentary instruments. In fact, he drove her to the meetings, sometimes he sat in on the meetings, and sometimes he provided a list of relevant assets to the attorneys. At least once he talked her into executing a set of instruments that she initially expressed misgivings about, arguing that it would only cost her more money to have another attorney re-do them. A beneficiary under one of Clare's prior testamentary instruments sued, asserting that Clark constituted an interested drafter under Section 21380 because he was "[a] person in a fiduciary relationship with the transferor who ... caused it [the testamentary instrument in question] to be transcribed." The pertinent part of the court's opinion is set forth below:

> Here, the lower courts construed "cause to be transcribed" as limited to direct involvement in the instrument's transcription, as by ordering another person to transcribe a document. This was in accord with the *Swetmann* court, which concluded that "a person who causes the document to be transcribed is one who directs the drafted document to be written out in its final form and, like the transcriber, is in a position to subvert the true intent of the testator." (*Swetmann, supra,* 85 Cal.App.4th at pp. 819–820, 102 Cal.Rptr.2d 457.) Rice, on the other hand, argues that a person causes an instrument's transcription if he "makes use of other persons to draft and transcribe the instruments, and ... then persuades the testator to execute them." In short, Rice argues, *Swetmann*'s interpretation was too narrow: the presumption of disqualification should apply to any fiduciary "whose conduct is a substantial factor in the creation or execution of the donative instruments."
>
> ...
>
> Because of the ambiguity inherent in the term "causes," neither party's construction of the statute can be absolutely excluded by the plain language.

Our interpretation must in addition be guided by an understanding of the legislative purposes and history. (*Swetmann, supra,* 85 Cal.App.4th at p. 818, 102 Cal.Rptr.2d 457.)

In light of those purposes and that history, we agree with the *Swetmann* court's analysis of section 21350 [now, in essence CPC § 21380].

...

Clark did not direct or oversee, or otherwise participate directly in, the will's or trust's transcription. Both instruments were transcribed by Hardy's secretary at Hardy's direction. Clark facilitated the instruments' preparation and execution by giving Hardy's office a list of Clare's assets that were to be placed in the trust, and by arranging appointments for Clare and driving her to them. He urged Hardy's secretary to prepare the documents promptly after the May 4, 1995, meeting. He encouraged Clare to execute the will and trust after she initially balked at doing so on June 14, 1995. Clark was present at meetings where the disposition of Clare's estate was discussed, but he did not direct Hardy, or anyone else, to include any particular gifts or other provisions in the instruments. In short, Clark materially assisted Clare to dictate the contents of her will and trust to an attorney and to execute the instruments drafted by the attorney, but did not himself directly participate in transcribing the instruments. For this reason, as the lower courts concluded, he did not "cause[ ] [the instruments] to be transcribed" within the meaning of section 21350, subdivision (a)(4).

The judgment of the Court of Appeal was affirmed.

4. *The care custodian doctrine*: Subsection (a)(3) of Probate Code Section 21380 creates a rebuttable presumption of wrongful conduct when an instrument makes a donative transfer to a "care custodian of a transferor who is a dependent adult, ..." Section 21366 elaborates on who qualifies as a dependent adult:

"Dependent adult" means a person who, at the time of executing the instrument at issue under this part, was a person described in either of the following:

(a) The person was 65 years of age or older and satisfied one or both of the following criteria:

(1) The person was unable to provide properly for his or her personal needs for physical health, food, clothing, or shelter.

(2) Due to one or more deficits in the mental functions listed in paragraphs (1) to (4), inclusive, of subdivision (a) of Section 811, the person had difficulty managing his or her own financial resources or resisting fraud or undue influence.

(b) The person was 18 years of age or older and satisfied one or both of the following criteria:

(1) The person was unable to provide properly for his or her personal needs for physical health, food, clothing, or shelter.

(2) Due to one or more deficits in the mental functions ... the person had substantial difficulty managing his or her own financial resources or resisting fraud or undue influence.

Section 21362 elaborates on the term "care custodian" as follows:

(a) "Care custodian" means a person who provides health or social services to a dependent adult, except that "care custodian" does not include a person who provided services without remuneration if the person had a personal relationship with the dependent adult (1) at least 90 days before providing those services, (2) at least six months before the dependent adult's death, and (3) before the dependant adult was admitted to hospice care, if the dependent adult was admitted to hospice care. As used in this subdivision, "remuneration" does not include the donative transfer at issue under this chapter or the reimbursement of expenses.

(b) For the purposes of this section, "health and social services" means services provided to a dependent adult because of the person's dependent condition, including, but not limited to, the administration of medicine, medical testing, wound care, assistance with hygiene, companionship, housekeeping, shopping, cooking, and assistance with finances.

The courts have struggled with how apply the relevant terms, finding that the decedent had to qualify as a dependent adult before a defendant can be a care custodian. *See Estate of Shinkle*, 97 Cal. App. 4th 990 (Ct. App. 2002) (where the court found that a long-term-care ombudsman at the facility where the settlor resided for a period of time qualified as a care custodian because of the personal and financial information the ombudsman acquired concerning the resident); *Conservatorship of Davidson*, 113 Cal. App. 4th 1035 (Ct. App. 2003) (neighbor who stepped in to help testator and took care of her *not* care custodian); and *Bernard v. Foley*, 139 P.3d 1196 (Cal. 2006) (where the California Supreme Court held neighbors who took settlor in and cared for her for the two months "provided substantial, ongoing health services to decedent while, at the end of her life, she was residing in their home" and therefore *were* care custodians for purposes of trust amendments made three days before she died that made donative transfers to them).

5. *Certificate of Independent Review*: The above statutory scheme provides the mechanism for a "certificate of independent review" to address otherwise prohibited transfers. As an attorney being asked to prepare such a certificate, would you prepare one? Why would most established estate planning attorneys probably answer: "No, I would never prepare a certificate of independent review!" Why not? What are his or her concerns?

C. Fraud

Fraud is a concept that appears in many areas of law and, as a student, you have probably encountered it before in at least one of your law school courses. The classic statement is easy to formulate—an intentional misrepresentation made with the intent to affect someone's actions, and causing such actions—and is easy to apply to a testator. Although fraud and undue influence can sometimes appear to overlap, the law prefers to think of them as distinct and separate wrongful acts.

In re Bottger's Estate

14 Wash. 2d 676, 685, 129 P.2d 518 (1942)

STEINERT, Justice.

...

[Ida Bottger was married to John Bottger, a farmer, and they had nine children. After her husband died their son Jesse, who owned and occupied a farm not too far from his mother's house, took on the job of helping his mother. He took good care of her, and although she loved all of her children and grandchildren, they acknowledged that Jesse was her favorite. In 1922, Jesse hired an unmarried woman, Charlotte, to work for him in his "traveling cookhouse" which he used during harvesting season. When not working for Jesse, he had her help out with domestic chores for mother Ida. Although Charlotte worked primary for Jesse and Ida, she got to know the rest of the family, and in 1938 she married Jesse's brother Harry.

Tragically, Jesse died intestate in 1939. His brothers and sisters thought they would inherit Jesse's property, but when one of the children consulted an attorney, Clyde Belknap, he informed them that Ida was Jesse's sole heir. Ida was 92 years old at the time of Jesse's death. The day after Jesse's death Ida asked Charlotte to move in with her to help her, which Charlotte did, and Charlotte lived with Ida until her death. Charlotte never received any pay for helping Ida, but Ida conveyed her farmland and the farmland she inherited from Jesse to Charlotte's husband, Harry, to the exclusion of the other kids. (The attorney, Mr. Belknap advised Ida to wait until her death to transfer the farmland to Harry, but she insisted on transferring it to him immediately.)

A few months later, on February 5, 1940, Ida executed a will bequeathing $10 to each of her children other than Harry, and leaving all the rest of her property to Harry. Unbeknownst to Ida, three days before she executed the will, all of the other children signed a petition to have a guardian of her estate appointed on the grounds that she was no longer competent to manage her own property. She was served with notice of the petition February 17, 1940. At the time the children were executing and filing the petition to have a guardian appointed for Ida, they did not know she was drafting and executing the will.

When Ida learned of the petition for appointment of a guardian for her she was livid and initially vowed to fight it. As the date for the trial on the petition drew closer, however, Ida became more and more distressed about the situation. The day before the hearing, she instructed Mr. Belknap to settle the matter, telling him: "I would rather die than go in there and go through with this proceeding, to have my own children in there trying to make out that I am crazy." Although the attorney tried to explain to her what it meant to be declared incompetent to manage her estate, her response was 'incompetent is just a lawyer's word for crazy.' After some negotiations among the parties concerned, the matter was settled and Mr. Belknap and the attorney for the children were appointed to act jointly the guardian. Ida died a little less than year later, on January 2, 1941. The children who for all practical purposes were disinherited under the will challenged the validity of the will on the basis of lack of capacity, in particular due to undue influence and fraud by Harry and his wife Charlotte.]

The respondents' second ground of attack upon the will was that it was executed as the result of undue influence exerted upon the testatrix by Harry Bottger and Charlotte Bottger, his wife.... [R]espondents alleged that Harry and Charlotte, by blandishments and promises, obtained controlling influence over the testatrix, at a time when she was weakened in body and mind, and were thereby enabled to dictate to her what she should do with respect to her property. They further charged that Harry and Charlotte, by entreaty, undue persuasion, blandishment, promises, threats, and untrue and improper statements poisoning Mrs. Bottger's mind against her other heirs, prevailed upon her to such an extent that against her true wishes she executed, in form but really at their dictation, the will here in question, which she never would have done had it not been for the domination and control exercised by Harry and his wife....

It will be noted that these allegations include charges of both undue influence and fraud. While some of our decisions have referred to both these elements as though they were merely different aspects of the same thing, and while, of course, they are closely related, there is nevertheless a distinction between them which we think should be recognized.

It is the universal rule that a will procured by undue influence is invalid, but the courts have always recognized that a will cannot be overthrown upon this ground unless the influence complained of was, in fact, undue influence....

... [T]he person accused of ... [undue influence] must have imposed his wishes upon the ... [testator], not by persuasion directed to his intellect or by appeal to sentiment, but by coercion of his mind by threats, force, or unbearable insistence, so that the testament, though in form that of the testator, is in fact that of another who has established ascendency over the mind of the former.

On the other hand, a will can also be invalidated, either in whole or in part, on the ground of fraud, whether it be fraud in the execution or fraud in the inducement. In this case, there is no claim of fraud in the execution of the will, so we are concerned only with the doctrine that a will can be avoided for fraud in its inducement.

In a case where a will is attacked because allegedly induced by fraud, it may be avoided, not because the testator's mind was coerced, but because his mind was deceived. The will is actually the free and voluntary act of the testator and expresses his wishes at the time, but it is subject to attack on the ground that his disposition of his estate was based upon false data as the result of fraudulent representations made by, or on behalf of, the person or persons benefiting from his will as made. There is thus a real distinction between fraud and undue influence. Atkinson, Wills (1937) 218, §97; 68 C.J. 740, Wills, §433; Note (1934) 28 A.L.R. 787, 792. In 1 Page, Wills, Lifetime Ed.1941, 353, §179, this type of fraud is defined as follows:

"Fraud in the inducement consists of wilfully false statements of fact other than those relating to the nature of contents of the instrument, made by a beneficiary under the will which is thus induced, which are intended to deceive testator, which do deceive him, which induce him to make a will, and without which he would not have made such will."

Expressed otherwise, the representations must be with reference to extrinsic facts, and must be made to the testator by, or on behalf of, a person benefiting under the will; the statements must be false and must be known to be so by the person making them (although in some circumstances mere suppression of the facts may be sufficient to constitute fraud); and the facts misrepresented must be material and must induce the making of the will in question See Atkinson, Wills (1937) 221, §99....

We have already expressed our conviction that Ida Bottger's mind was not overcome nor her volition impaired at the time she executed her will. It remains to be determined whether she was induced to make that will by fraudulent misrepresentations as to any pertinent extrinsic fact.

Her principal reason for leaving all her property to Harry seems to have been that he and Charlotte were good to her, while her other children and her grandchildren neglected and quarreled with her. These are all facts clearly established by the record in this proceeding, and of course Mrs. Bottger was aware of them without being told. There is no evidence that Harry or Charlotte ever made any effort to prevent the others from seeing the testatrix, and Mr. Belknap actually tried to persuade Herman and Bill to visit their mother. There can be no doubt but that Mrs. Bottger was deeply hurt by the attitude of respondents.

In the second place, the testatrix was incensed by the fact that some of the children were planning to institute proceedings for the appointment of a guardian of her estate or person.... There is nothing to indicate that Harry or Charlotte ever told Mrs. Bottger anything about a contemplated guardianship, but even if they had done so, their statement would have been true, and therefore not fraudulent.

A guardianship proceeding was subsequently instituted, as related above, and Mrs. Bottger felt very bitter about it....

In cases of this sort, the suspicion of fraud is sometimes difficult to overcome entirely. We are convinced, however, that respondents have failed to sustain the burden of proof on this issue, as they were required to do, and that appellant more than met any presumption of fraud or undue influence which may have arisen because she and Harry had the opportunity of influencing the testatrix and because the latter actually left the bulk of her estate to Harry.

We believe that Ida Bottger actually wished to dispose of her property exactly as provided in her will and that her reasons for doing so were not the result of fraudulent misrepresentations. It is not our function to assess the soundness of those reasons, for the law permits one to dispose of his property by will in any lawful manner he may wish, and it would be without precedent or reason to hold that a will may be invalidated simply because it is unusual or even unjust. In re Patterson's Estate, supra. On all the facts in this case, we conclude that Ida Bottger executed her will freely and voluntarily, and not through fraud or undue influence....

The judgment is reversed with direction to dismiss the contest proceeding.

———

Notes

1. *Fraud in the inducement versus fraud in the execution*: As the court in *Bottger* noted, there are two types of fraud: fraud in the inducement and fraud in the execution. The allegation in *Bottger* involved fraud in the inducement. What is fraud in the execution? What is the classic example of fraud in the execution?

2. *Fraud versus undue influence*: Some courts have stated that fraud, at a theoretical level, is a form of undue influence. How so? Other courts have argued that such a characterization is not helpful (so if conceptually that statement does not help you, do not force it — a number of judges agree with you).

Problem

1. H is married to W. Nevertheless, H tells F that he is not married, never has been married, and that he loves her. H proposes, F accepts, and they go through a marriage ceremony that is legally invalid (because H is still married to W). In good faith, F believes the marriage is valid. A month after the wedding, F executes a will devising a number of small gifts to friends and family members, and the rest of her estate, the bulk of her estate, to "my husband, H." One year later, F dies. F's heirs contest the validity of the will on the basis of H's alleged fraud.

    Which type of fraud will they invoke? What arguments would you make if you represented F's heirs? What arguments, if any, would you make if you represented H? Assuming, *arguendo*, the court finds there was fraud, what is the appropriate remedy? *See In re Carson's Estate*, 184 Cal. 437, 194 P. 5 (1920).

D. Duress

Some jurisdictions recognize duress as a distinct defect in capacity that can be pleaded and proved to invalidate a will. Other jurisdictions tend to see it more as a subset of undue influence (undue influence with a physical component or a threat of force component). The case law in California reflects that while claims of "duress, threat and menace" are often thrown in a case as part of a party's pleading along with undue influence and/or fraud, rarely is there separate analysis of the duress claim. Instead, it is probably best to think of it as a subset of undue influence (substituted intent) via a physical component (or threat of a physical component).

E. Elder Abuse

Unfortunately, with advancing age often comes increased vulnerability to some form of elder abuse. According to the National Institute of Justice (the U.S. Department of Justice's research, development, and evaluation agency), one in ten older Americans is believed to experience some form of abuse each year. Obviously, this is an important topic that deserves attention for a number of legal, ethical, and policy reasons. Addressing some of the more salient legal issues, the State Bar of California has produced an excellent pamphlet addressing the logistical aspects of elder abuse: what it is, what to do if one suspects a loved one is the victim of elder abuse, reporting guidelines and instructions, etc. It is available at: http://www.calbar.ca.gov/Public/Pamphlets/ElderAbuse.aspx#2.

While elder abuse is an issue of great import to our loved ones and to society as a whole, we turn our attention to the aspect of elder abuse that most directly relates to wills and trusts: where elder abuse is used to secure a testamentary gift, should the abuser be permitted to take. Phrased that way, the issue is similar to the slayer material covered in Chapter 4. Organizationally, we could have included this material in that chapter, but elder abuse overlaps so heavily with the doctrines of capacity, undue influence, and/or fraud, we thought it best to place it with those doctrines. The California legislature relatively recently adopted California Probate Code Section 259 to address the problem.

CPC § 259. Elder Abuse

(a)   Any person shall be deemed to have predeceased a decedent to the extent provided in subdivision (c) where all of the following apply:

   (1)   It has been proven by clear and convincing evidence that the person is liable for physical abuse, neglect, or fiduciary abuse of the decedent, who was an elder or dependent adult.

   (2)   The person is found to have acted in bad faith.

   (3)   The person has been found to have been reckless, oppressive, fraudulent, or malicious in the commission of any of these acts upon the decedent.

   (4)   The decedent, at the time those acts occurred and thereafter until the time of his or her death, has been found to have been substantially unable to manage his or her financial resources or to resist fraud or undue influence.

      . . .

(d)   For purposes of this section, the following definitions apply:

      [Physical abuse, neglect, financial abuse as defined in sections of the Welfare and Institutions Code, and false imprisonment as defined in the Penal Code]

      . . .

A detailed analysis of the problem of elder abuse, and the statutory response, is best left to an elder law course. But we would be remiss if we did not take a quick look at the potential significance of the doctrine here. To the extent this is a relatively new doctrine, how would you proceed if, as a practicing attorney, a client complained to you that another had committed elder abuse against someone close to your client. Would you proceed on the more traditional doctrines of undue influence and/or fraud, or would you proceed on the newer doctrine of elder abuse? In reading the *Lowrie* case below, pay particular attention to the remedy the court awarded.

In re Estate of Lowrie

118 Cal. App. 4th 220, 12 Cal. Rptr. 3d 828 (2004)

ALDRICH, J.

INTRODUCTION

In this case, a granddaughter accuses her uncle of financial abuse, isolation, and neglect constituting elder abuse of her grandmother....

Laura Marie Lowrie (decedent) had three children, all of whom are still living: Norma Goodreau, Alan Lowrie, and appellant Sheldon Lawrence Lowrie (Sheldon). Decedent had six grandchildren, including respondent Lynelle L. Goodreau (Lynelle) who is the eldest daughter of Norma Goodreau.

Decedent's husband died in 1986, leaving to decedent gold coins, cash in bank accounts, a number of pieces of commercial property, and two single family residences located in Burbank, California. Decedent's husband also left to decedent an airplane parts business, SAL Instruments (SAL), located in Burbank. Decedent lived in the residence located on Kenwood Street. The second residence, on Edison Boulevard, was the house where Lynelle had lived with her grandparents when Lynelle was an infant. During this time, Lynelle and decedent developed a special bond.

After his father died, Sheldon started to run SAL. Alan assisted by doing the bookkeeping.

Decedent executed a will in 1988 and a revised will in January 1989. On March 20, 1989, decedent reformulated her estate plan and executed a will (pour over) and a trust, the effect of which placed most of her real and personal property in trust. On March 19, 1992, decedent, amended the trust.

In the March 1989, estate documents, Sheldon was named as the executor, Lynelle was designated as the successor executor, decedent was designated as the trustee, Sheldon was designated as the first successor trustee, and Lynelle was designated as the second successor trustee. Additionally, Alan Lowrie and Norma Goodreau each were bequeathed the sum of $10,000 and Lynelle was to receive the Edison Boulevard residence. Sheldon was bequeathed the remainder of the estate (which would be the bulk of the property), and if Sheldon did not survive decedent, Lynelle was to receive the remainder. The 1992 trust amendment was a one-page document which deleted the bequest to Lynelle of the house and replaced it with a monetary bequest of $10,000.

Unbeknown to others, decedent transferred the Edison Boulevard residence and the Kenwood Street residence to Sheldon in 1993 and 1995, respectively. In 1993, decedent transferred all of her personal property to Sheldon.

In August 1997, decedent resigned as trustee of her trust and Sheldon became trustee.

Decedent died on August 13, 1999, at the age of 89. At the time of her death, decedent's estate was worth approximately $1 million....

On November 1, 2000, Lynelle filed a multiple-part petition (No. BP064664) challenging the March 19, 1992, trust amendment, seeking findings and damages for elder abuse, and requesting an order pursuant to Probate Code section 259 disinheriting Sheldon. Lynelle contended, among other allegations, that Sheldon exploited his relationship with decedent, and through manipulation, fraud and undue influence enticed decedent to gift him property and to change her estate plan so Sheldon would receive substantially all of decedent's assets. Further, Sheldon abused decedent physically and financially, and intentionally isolated decedent. Lynelle alleged that over the years, "Sheldon isolated Decedent from her two other children, her five grandchildren and from most of the outside world. Sheldon intentionally prevented Decedent from seeing or speaking with family members and other people and denied family members and others access to Decedent's house by among others: duct taping her telephones so that she could not receive or make telephone calls; by locking her metal security door from the outside so that decedent could not open her front door to leave the house and so that she could not allow in visitors such as family members; and by affixing a sign to her door which stated: 'DAY SLEEPER, DO NOT DISTURB!! NO SOCIAL WORKERS. NO PEDDLERS. WILL NOT ANSWER DOOR.'" The complaint also alleged that Sheldon denied and delayed medical care to decedent and failed to assist her with personal hygiene.

Among other relief, Lynelle sought to void the 1992 trust amendment, to set aside the transfer of real property, compensatory and punitive damages, a finding pursuant to Probate Code section 259 that Sheldon was deemed to have predeceased decedent and thus was not entitled to inherit the remainder of decedent's estate, imposition of a constructive trust, attorney fees, and costs....

Prior to trial, the trial court rejected Sheldon's argument that Lynelle had no standing to bring this case for elder abuse.

A bifurcated trial was held before the court. At the end of the first phase of the trial, the court found, by clear and convincing evidence, that Sheldon was guilty of elder abuse by reason of neglect, isolation, and financial abuse. In that Sheldon was found to be liable for elder abuse, the trial court found that Sheldon was disinherited from decedent's estate (Prob.Code § 259). The trial court made a specific finding that Sheldon acted with recklessness, oppression, fraud and malice, entitling Lynelle to attorney fees and punitive damages. (Welf. & Inst.Code § 15657; Civ.Code § 3294.) Damages were awarded to Lynelle as follows: $250,000 for pain and suffering; $665,623 for financial abuse; attorney fees to be determined upon written motion; and punitive damages to be based upon proof of Sheldon's net worth.

Thereafter, a hearing before the court was held on the issues of attorney fees, costs, and punitive damages. The trial court found that "during the pendency of this action,

[Sheldon] intentionally and systematically liquidated virtually all of his assets and the assets of the trust (of which [Sheldon] was the sole beneficiary) prior to completion of this trial ... so that his assets would be unavailable for execution by [Lynelle] as a potential judgment creditor of [Sheldon]." The trial court awarded Lynelle $392,621.20 in attorney fees, $32,406.37, in costs, and $50,000 for punitive damages.

A judgment was entered awarding $665,623 for financial abuse, $250,000 for pain and suffering, $392,621.20 in attorney fees, $32,406.37 in costs, and $50,000 for punitive damages, disinheriting Sheldon from decedent's trust (Prob.Code, § 259), and other relief. Sheldon appeals....

The purpose of Probate Code section 259 was to deter the abuse of elders by prohibiting abusers from benefiting from the abuse. (Note, Extinguishing Inheritance Rights: California Breaks New Ground in the Fight Against Elder Abuse But Fails to Build an Effective Foundation (2001) 52 Hastings L.J. 537, 569; Civ.Code § 3517 ["No one can take advantage of his own wrong."]; cf. Prob.Code, § 250 [killer of decedent not entitled to benefit under decedent's will or trust].) Probate Code section 259 was enacted, like other forfeiture statutes, to produce a fair and just result. By enacting this statute, the Legislature hoped that the threat of extinguishing inheritance rights, and the financial incentive to others to report abuse, would deter abuse. (Moskowitz, Golden Age in the Golden State: Contemporary Legal Developments in Elder Abuse and Neglect, supra, 36 Loyola L.A. L.Rev. at pp. 653–656; Note, supra, 2 Hastings L.J. at pp. 572–573.)

DISPOSITION

The judgment is affirmed. Sheldon Lowrie is to pay all costs on appeal.

F. Tortious/Intentional Interference with an Expectancy

About half of the states recognize a tort doctrine known as tortious interference with an expectancy. The RESTATEMENT SECOND OF TORTS describes the doctrine as follows: "One who by fraud, duress or other tortious means intentionally prevents another from receiving from a third person an inheritance or gift that he would otherwise have received is subject to liability to the other for loss of the inheritance or gift." RESTATEMENT (SECOND) OF TORTS, § 774B.

Recently a California court made the following observations about the doctrine:

> In general, most states recognizing the tort adopt it with the following elements: (1) an expectation of receiving an inheritance; (2) intentional interference with that expectancy by a third party; (3) the interference was independently wrongful or tortious; (4) there was a reasonable certainty that, but for the interference, the plaintiff would have received the inheritance; and (5) damages. (*See, e.g., Fell v. Rambo* (Tenn.Ct.App.2000) 36 S.W.3d 837, 849.) Most states prohibit an interference action when the plaintiff already

has an adequate probate remedy. (*See, e.g., Minton v. Sackett* (Ind.Ct.App.1996) 671 N.E.2d 160, 162–163 (*Minton*).

Beckwith v. Dahl, 205 Cal. App. 4th 1039, 1050 (Ct. App. 2012).

Inasmuch as the doctrine overlaps heavily with the traditional probate doctrines of fraud, duress and/or undue influence, opponents of the doctrine argue that the doctrine should not be recognized because such claims should be brought in probate as part of the probate process. Even states that recognize the doctrine typically prohibit the claim if the party already has adequate relief in probate. Nevertheless, the doctrine's proponents argue that it should be recognized because there are wrongs where the probate system does not offer an adequate remedy.

The tort claim of tortious interference with an expectancy is widely considered to have a number of benefits over a claim in probate: (1) as a tort claim it is not subject to the shorter statute of limitations usually associated with probate; (2) as a tort claim a prevailing party is entitled to greater damages, including potentially punitive damages; and (3) as a tort claim it would not trigger a no contest clause if the instrument in question has one.

Twice within the last five years the same California Court of Appeal has had the opportunity to consider whether California should recognize the tort doctrine. In *Munn v. Briggs*, the Court of Appeal for the Fourth District, Division 1, quoted extensively from the opinion in *Wilson v. Fritschy*, 132 N.M. 785 (2002) in considering the issue:

> Noting that inheritance laws are "purely a creature of statute" (as is true in California (see *In re Darling* (1916) 173 Cal. 221, 223, 159 P. 606)), the court in *Wilson* refused to allow niece and nephew to circumvent the probate code by "calling a will contest an action in tort." *Wilson* explained: "We feel compelled to protect the jurisdictional space carved out by our legislature when it enacted the Probate Code and created remedies, such as a will contest, designed exclusively for probate. We note that a will contest in probate requires a greater burden of persuasion than an independent action in tort. A presumption of due execution normally attaches to a testamentary instrument administered in probate, but not necessarily in tort. If we were to permit, much less encourage, dual litigation tracks for disgruntled heirs, we would risk destabilizing the law of probate and creating uncertainty and inconsistency in its place. We would risk undermining the legislative intent inherent in creating the Probate Code as the preferable, if not exclusive, remedy for disputes over testamentary documents." (*Ibid.*)

Based in large part on these arguments, and in light of the fact that: (1) the legislature had just recently overhauled California's approach to no contest clauses, and (2) the legislature had not recognized the tort, the court in *Munn* declined to recognize the tort doctrine.

Just two years later, in *Beckwith v. Dahl*, 205 Cal. App. 4th 1039 (Ct. App. 2012) the Court of Appeal for the Fourth District, Division 3, declined to follow the reasoning in *Munn*. The court *in Beckwith* recognized the cause of action. The facts of the *Beckwith* case are particularly compelling:

1. Marc Christian MacGinnis

[Brent] Beckwith and his partner, Marc Christian MacGinnis (MacGinnis), were in a long-term, committed relationship for almost 10 years.... MacGinnis had no children and his parents were deceased. His sister, Susan Dahl, with whom he had an estranged relationship, was his only other living family. At some point during their relationship, MacGinnis showed Beckwith a will he had saved on his computer. The will stated that upon MacGinnis's death, his estate was to be divided equally between Beckwith and Dahl. MacGinnis never printed or signed the will.

In May 2009, MacGinnis's health began to decline. On May 25, 2009, MacGinnis was in the hospital awaiting surgery to repair holes in his lungs. He asked Beckwith to locate and print the will so he could sign it. Beckwith went to their home and looked for the will, but he could not find it. When Beckwith told MacGinnis that he could not locate the will, MacGinnis asked Beckwith to create a new will so he could sign it the next day. That night, Beckwith created a new will for MacGinnis using forms downloaded from the Internet. The will stated: "'I [MacGinnis] give all the rest, residue and remainder of my property and estate, both real and personal, of whatever kind and wherever located, that I own or to which I shall be in any manner entitled at the time of my death (collectively referred to as my "residuary estate"), as follows: (a) If Brent Beckwith and Susan Dahl survive me, to those named in clause (a) who survive me in equal shares.'"

Before Beckwith presented the will to MacGinnis, he called Dahl to tell her about the will and e-mailed her a copy. Later that night, Dahl responded to Beckwith's e-mail stating: "'I really think we should look into a Trust for [MacGinnis]. There are far less regulations and it does not go through probate. The house and all property would be in our names and if something should happen to [MacGinnis] we could make decisions without it going to probate and the taxes are less on a trust rather than the normal inheritance tax. I have [two] very good friends [who] are attorneys and I will call them tonight.' [Emphasis added.]" After receiving the e-mail, Beckwith called Dahl to discuss the details of the living trust. Dahl told Beckwith not to present the will to MacGinnis for signature because one of her friends would prepare the trust documents for MacGinnis to sign "in the next couple [of] days." Beckwith did not present the will to MacGinnis.

Two days later, on May 27, MacGinnis had surgery on his lungs. Although the doctors informed Dahl there was a chance MacGinnis would not survive the surgery, the doctors could not discuss the matter with Beckwith since he was not a family member under the law. Nor did Dahl tell Beckwith about the risks associated with the surgery. Dahl never gave MacGinnis any trust documents to sign. After the surgery, MacGinnis was placed on a ventilator and his prognosis worsened. Six days later, Dahl, following the doctors' recommendations, removed MacGinnis from the ventilator. On June 2, 2009, MacGinnis died intestate. He left an estate worth over $1 million.

2. The Probate Proceedings

Following MacGinnis's death, Beckwith and Dahl met to discuss the disposition of MacGinnis's personal property. After Beckwith suggested they find the will that MacGinnis prepared, Dahl told Beckwith "we don't need a will." Two weeks after MacGinnis' death, on June 17, 2009, Dahl opened probate in Los Angeles Superior Court. Dahl verbally informed Beckwith that she had opened probate, but she did not send him any copies of the probate filings. In the filing, she did not identify Beckwith as an interested party. Dahl also applied to become the administrator of the estate.

In September 2009, Beckwith began to ask Dahl for details of the probate case. Dahl informed Beckwith that she had not had any contact with the probate attorney so she did not know anything. [Beckwith e-mailed Dahl several times over the course of the next two years with questions about the probate process and offers to help, but Dahl never responded.] ... Beckwith e-mailed Dahl again on December 18, 2009, asking about the probate proceedings. This time Dahl responded by e-mail, stating: " 'Because [MacGinnis] died without a will, and the estate went into probate, I was made executor of his estate. The court then declared that his assets would go to his only surviving family member which is me.' " A few weeks later, in January 2010, Dahl filed a petition with the probate court for final distribution of the estate. Beckwith filed an opposition to Dahl's petition in March 2010. After a hearing, at which Beckwith was present in pro se, the probate judge found that Beckwith had no standing because he was "not a creditor of the estate" and he had "no intestate rights" with regard to MacGinnis's estate.

3. The Civil Action and Demurrer

On July 30, 2010, while the probate case was still pending, Beckwith filed the instant civil action against Dahl alleging IIEI, deceit by false promise, and negligence. In the complaint, Beckwith asserted Dahl interfered with his expected inheritance of one half of MacGinnis's estate by lying to him about her intention to prepare a living trust for MacGinnis to sign. Beckwith further alleged Dahl made these false promises in order to "caus[e] a sufficient delay to prevent [MacGinnis] from signing his will before his surgery" because she knew that if MacGinnis died without a will, she would inherit the entire estate. Finally, Beckwith claimed that as a result of his reliance on Dahl's promises, "he was deprived of his ... share of [MacGinnis's] estate," and because he had no standing in probate court, a civil action against Dahl was his only remedy.

Dahl demurred to all three causes of action. As to the IIEI cause of action, she argued the "claim fails on its face" because "California does not recognize a cause of action for 'interference with inheritance.'" ...

At the hearing on the demurrer, the trial court stated, it was not "in a position to recognize" a new tort for IIEI because "that really is an appellate decision." ... Beckwith timely appealed the order sustaining the demurrer....

The court was moved by the allegations:

The tort of IIEI [Intentional Interference with an Expected Inheritance — the California term for the doctrine] developed under the "general principle of law that whenever the law prohibits an injury it will also afford a remedy." (Citations omitted.) Similarly, it is a maxim of California jurisprudence that, "[f]or every wrong there is a remedy." (Civ.Code, § 3523.) In addition, in California, "[e]very person is bound, without contract, to abstain from injuring the person or property of another, or infringing upon any of his or her rights." (Civ.Code, § 1708.) "[W]e cannot let the difficulties of adjudication frustrate the principle that there be a remedy for every substantial wrong." (*Dillon v. Legg* (1968) 68 Cal.2d 728, 739, 69 Cal.Rptr. 72, 441 P.2d 912 (*Dillon*); see also *Lucas v. Hamm* (1961) 56 Cal.2d 583, 589, 15 Cal.Rptr. 821, 364 P.2d 685 [holding that intended beneficiaries of wills can recover in tort against a negligent draftsman even though there was a lack of privity because if such plaintiffs were precluded from bringing a tort claim, "no one would be able to do so and the policy of preventing future harm would be impaired"].) Recognition of the IIEI tort in California is consistent with and advances these basic principles.

Although the court recognized the claim, the court noted that Beckwith's complaint still had hurdles to clear:

Having decided we can recognize a cause of action for IIEI, we turn to whether Beckwith sufficiently stated the cause of action in his complaint....

... [A]n IIEI defendant must direct the independently tortious conduct at someone other than the plaintiff. The cases firmly indicate a requirement that "[t]he fraud, duress, undue influence, or other independent tortious conduct required for this tort is directed at the testator. *The beneficiary is not directly defrauded* or unduly influenced; the testator is." (*Whalen v. Prosser* (Fla.Dist.Ct.App 1998) 719 So.2d 2, 6, (*Whalen*), italics added.) In other words, the defendant's tortious conduct must have induced or caused the testator to take some action that deprives the plaintiff of his expected inheritance. (Citations omitted.) ...

Here, Beckwith alleged he had an expectancy in MacGinnis's estate that would have been realized but for Dahl's intentional interference. However, Beckwith did not allege Dahl directed any independently tortious conduct at MacGinnis. The only wrongful conduct alleged in Beckwith's complaint was Dahl's false promise to him. Accordingly, Beckwith's complaint failed to sufficiently allege the IIEI tort.

The court remanded the matter back to the trial court level to see if Beckwith could amend his petition to state a claim.

Notes

1. *Tort committed against whom?* What if Dahl's conversation with Beckwith in which she stated "I have [two] very good friends [who] are attorneys and I will call them tonight" had been with her brother instead of with Beckwith. Assuming Dahl did not follow up on that statement (and did not intend to do so when she made the statement), who would have a claim then, and for what? What is the classic remedy for that claim? What other remedy, if any, might the court apply in such a case?

2. *Probate remedy?* If Dahl's conversation had been with her brother before he died, would Beckwith have a remedy in probate? Would this moot the question of intentional interference with an expected inheritance? If the probate court finds that this conversation actually occurred and gave effect to it, would the court de facto be giving effect to the draft will on Dahl's computer that he never executed? Is that appropriate? Are you comfortable with courts giving effect to wills that were never signed?

3. In *Latham v. Father Divine*, 81 N.Y.S.2d 681 (1948), the decedent's first cousins — who were not the heirs who would take under decedent's intestate distribution — alleged that the decedent wanted to revoke her will and execute a new will leaving them the property, but that she was prevented from doing so because of the wrongful acts of Father Divine's followers. The court ruled that if the first cousins could prove their allegations, it had the equitable power to impose a constructive trust in their favor. Would giving effect to the unexecuted draft of the brother's will on the computer be that different from the court giving effect to the unexecuted will in the *Father Divine* case?

Chapter 6

Wills Act Formalities

I. Introduction

A testator's will is a document or instrument for directed disposition of one's assets at death. A will, by its nature, is an ambulatory document[1] that takes effect upon the decedent's death. The will, of course, must be properly executed during the decedent's lifetime. Whether a will has been properly executed depends on which type of will it is. Historically, and generally speaking, there are two types of wills: *attested wills* and *holographic wills*. An attested will typically appears in typed or "drafted" form[2] and is also referred to as a "traditional will," "formal will" or "witnessed will." A holographic will, legal in California (but not in all states), typically refers to a document that is in the testator's handwriting and is generally not signed by any witnesses. If a person refers to a "will," without specifying which type of will, the assumption is he or she is referring to a traditional attested will.

The statutory requirements or "execution formalities" necessary to properly execute a valid will are set forth in a state's Wills Act. The Wills Act formalities vary from state to state, and the requirements also depend on which type of will it is: a traditional attested will or a holographic will. The "Wills Act formalities" evolved initially, for the most part, out of the Statute of Frauds, though some states copied more from England's original Wills Act of 1837. Over the years, however, the American Wills Act has developed into a doctrine with a life of its own that bears little resemblance to the parent doctrines.

II. Attested Wills

The Wills Act formalities have evolved over time, and they are still evolving. Having a sense of that evolution is important to understanding the current approach—and the debate about the current approach. The English case of *In re Groffman* typifies the traditional approach to whether a document constituted a validly executed will under the jurisdiction's Wills Act.

---

1. A document executed at one point in time but not effective until a later point in time.
2. Attested wills need not be drafted uniquely for a testator. They also can include pre-printed wills, those generated from will-drafting software and, most notably, the California Statutory Will from California Probate Code Section 6240.

A. The Traditional Approach

In re Groffman

1 W.L.R. 733 (Probate Div. 1969)

SIR JOCELYN SIMON P.

In this case the executors of a will dated September 1, 1964, propound it in solemn form of law. The will is of the late Mr. Charles Groffman, who died on April 11, 1967. The first plaintiff, being the first executor named, is the son of the deceased testator. The second plaintiff, Mr. Block, is the second executor named and is the solicitor who prepared the will.... The estate consists partly of what was the matrimonial home (as to just over half the total estate). That house belonged to the deceased. There was also a building society account held by the deceased; ...

The defendant was the second wife of the deceased. They married about 1948, the deceased being a widower and the defendant a widow. The marriage was childless; but the deceased had two children, the first plaintiff and a daughter who is in America....

Most of the relevant events took place in 1964; and I do not think any witness can really be expected to remember the details, even Mr. Block the solicitor who prepared the will. Indeed. I think that many of the witnesses now think that they can remember more than they actually can. But the rough outline of events was this.

Sometime in the summer of 1964, the deceased went to Mr. Block, the solicitor. He was senior partner in the firm of Maxwell and Lawson. The deceased was not a regular client of his, but had been recommended to him by another client. He gave instructions for a will and the instructions were put into a draft, ... That appointed the executors and trustees; it devises the house to the trustees on trust to allow the defendant to have the use and enjoyment of this during her lifetime. It also bequeaths all chattels to her for use during her life. Then the residue—what was not disposed by the dispositions I have referred to—was disposed of in this way. It was to be divided between the first plaintiff, the daughter in America, and the stepdaughter, Miss Berenson.... That draft was handed ... to the deceased, who took it away to discuss it with his son, the first plaintiff. As a result of that discussion, ... some nine corrections were made.... The document as amended was then typed out, engrossed ready for execution.

The second plaintiff told the deceased very generally what was the right method of execution; but realising that the deceased was an intelligent man relied in the main on the attestation clause to be a guide to the deceased. That was in the usual form, and it seems to me to have been a perfectly reasonable course for the second plaintiff to have taken.

The deceased and his wife were close family friends of a Mr. and Mrs. David Block and a Mr. and Mrs. Julius Leigh. They spent at least the summer holidays of 1964 together, and it was their custom to meet alternately at their respective houses, generally on a Tuesday night. This was because Mr. Leigh was a taxi driver and the Tuesday was his free evening. On a number of occasions after the engrossed document was handed to the deceased, he mentioned the matter to Mr. David Block, saying that he would like Mr. Block and Mr. Leigh to be witnesses to his will. Mr. Block, in a very usual reaction, said: "There's no hurry about that; there's plenty of time to be thinking about that sort of thing"—or words to that effect.

The parties met on a Tuesday evening in September, 1964. That may have been September 1, which is the date that the will bears. They met at the house of Mr. and Mrs. David Block, and the will purports to have been executed that evening in circumstances to which I shall have to refer. It is sufficient to say that, as I have already indicated, the attestation clause is the normal one, and Mr. Block and Mr. Leigh signed as attesting witnesses. The document also bears what is admittedly the signature of the deceased, and the date, September 1, 1964.

I am perfectly satisfied that that document was intended by the deceased to be executed as his will and that its contents represent his testamentary intentions.

After he had obtained the signatures of his friends, he took the will and handed it to his son, the first plaintiff. He appears to have referred to it to Mr. Block on a number of occasions thereafter; but nothing turns on that, since the only question that arises in this suit is as to the execution of the document.

The deceased died, as I have said, on April 11, 1967. The funeral was on April 13, and thereafter the widow and the first plaintiff observed a period of ritual mourning, during which there was no discussion of any testamentary instrument or disposition....

Some time shortly thereafter there was another meeting, as I have indicated, and the defendant showed considerable dissatisfaction with the dispositions in the purported will. She used the words, "My Charlie wouldn't have done that to me."...

As I have said, the only question that arises for the determination of the court is whether this will was duly executed. That takes me back to the occasion in September, 1964, which may have been September 1—the episode at the house of Mr. and Mrs. David Block....

I think that what happened on the evening in question was this. I have already said that the deceased had previously indicated to Mr. David Block that he would like him and Mr. Leigh to witness his will. On the evening in question, which was in all probability a Tuesday and possibly September 1, 1964, the deceased and the defendant, Mr. and Mrs. David Block and Mr. and Mrs. Julius Leigh, were all together in the lounge of the Blocks' house. Mr. Block's son, Stewart, was also in the house, though not in the lounge at the commencement of the transaction to which I refer.

During the course of the evening, when the coffee table, the only available table, was laden with coffee cups and cakes, the deceased said words to this effect, which he addressed to Mr. David Block and Mr. Julius Leigh: "I should like you now to witness my will." I think he may well have gestured towards his coat. The will in question as engrossed was of the usual double foolscap folded in two and then in four, so as to be a convenient size for putting in an inside pocket of a coat. That is where it was on this occasion. However, it was not taken out by the deceased in the lounge. At the most, he gestured towards the pocket where it was. There seems to me to be an overwhelming inference that his signature was on the document at that time. There being no convenient space for the execution in the lounge, Mr. Block led the deceased into the adjacent dining room. That was just across a small hall. There the deceased took the document from his pocket, unfolded it, and asked Mr. Block to sign, giving his occupation and address. The signature, as I have already said, was on the document at the time and was visible to Mr. Block at the time; indeed, he noted this. Mr. Leigh, who seems to have been somewhat cumbrous in his movements, was left behind. He was not there when Mr. Block signed his name. Mr. Block then returned to the lounge, leaving the deceased in the dining room. He said to Mr. Leigh words to this effect: "It is your turn now, don't keep him waiting, it's cold in there." Mr. Leigh then went into the dining room and, according to his statement, and as is indeed borne out by the form of the document that we now have, signed his name beneath that of Mr. David Block. In the meantime Mr. Block had remained in the lounge.

In other words, we are left with this situation — that the signature of the deceased was on the document before he asked either Mr. Block or Mr. Leigh to act as his witnesses; that Mr. Block signed his name in the presence of the deceased but not in the presence of Mr. Leigh; and that Mr. Leigh signed his name in the presence of the deceased but not in the presence of Mr. Block. The deceased did not sign in the presence of either of them; and the question is whether he acknowledged his signature in the presence of both of them.

As must appear from the fact that I have been satisfied that the document does represent the testamentary intentions of the deceased, I would very gladly find in its favour; but I am bound to apply the statute, which has been enacted by Parliament for good reason. The provision with which I am concerned is section 9 of the Wills Act, 1837. That reads:

> "... no will shall be valid unless it shall be in writing and executed in manner hereinafter mentioned; (that is to say,) it shall be signed at the foot or end thereof by the testator, or by some other person in his presence and by his direction; and such signature shall be made or acknowledged by the testator in the presence of two or more witnesses present at the same time, and such witnesses shall attest and shall subscribe the will in the presence of the testator, but no form of attestation shall be necessary."

The question, as I have indicated, is whether the testator acknowledged his signature in the presence of Mr. Block and Mr. Leigh, those two witnesses being present at the same time. The matter has been considered by a number of eminent judges, starting with Dr. Lushington, and followed by the members of the Court of Appeal in *Blake v. Blake* (1882) 7 P.D. 102 and *Daintree v. Butcher and Fasulo* (1888) 13 P.D. 102. It seems presumptious to say that I agree with their construction of the statute; but it appears to me to be clear. In any event I am bound by what was decided by the Court of Appeal, even if I were to disagree with it, which I do not. It seems to me that the authorities establish that the signature of the testator must be on the document at the time of acknowledgment (as I think it was), and that the witnesses saw or had an opportunity of seeing the signature at that time, in other words, at the time of acknowledgment....

... In my view, *Daintree v. Butcher and Fasulo*, 13 P.D. 102, bears out what I have described from *Blake v. Blake*, 7 P.D. 102, namely, that if there is to be an acknowledgment within the statute the attesting witnesses must either see or be capable of seeing the signature; or at the very least must see or be capable of seeing a will on which there is a signature. In the present case, none of those conditions was satisfied.

...

There is, however, one final argument. Having submitted originally that there was a sufficient acknowledgment to satisfy the statute in what happened in the lounge, when admittedly both attesting witnesses were present, Mr. Craig puts his argument alternatively in this way. He says that what happened was all part of one res gestae— there was no break in the continuity of the transaction. Both attesting witnesses had an opportunity of seeing the signature at the time they signed the will, which was within a matter of seconds of each other and within a matter of seconds of being asked to witness it. On that argument the acknowledgment started in the lounge but ended in the dining room. Now, it seems to me that there is one fatal flaw in that argument; namely, that if the acknowledgment was not completed until the dining room, then there was no completed acknowledgment in the presence of both attesting witnesses being present at the same time.

In the end, therefore, although I would gladly accede to the arguments for the plaintiffs if I could consistently with my judicial duty, in my view there was no acknowledgment or signature by the testator in the presence of two or more witnesses present at the same time; and I am bound to pronounce against this will.

The defendant has succeeded in this action, but the plaintiffs are executors of a will which is apparently valid on the face of it. They acted reasonably in my view in propounding it in solemn form once a caveat had been entered. The fact that there has been litigation is due to the unfortunate error in execution committed by the deceased, and in the exercise of my discretion I order that the costs of all parties should come out of the estate.

Notes

1. *Functions underlying the Wills Act*: Most scholars acknowledge that the traditional Wills Act formalities serve a number of important functions:

> a. *Evidentiary*: The Wills Act formalities serve an evidentiary function by ensuring that the document offered for probate truly reflects the testator's last wishes as to who should take his or her property.

> b. *Protective*: The Wills Act formalities serve a protective function by making it more difficult to bring fraudulent claims and by protecting the testator's intent as expressed in the properly executed will.

> c. *Ritualistic*: The Wills Act formalities serve a ritualistic function by impressing upon the testator the importance and finality of the act being performed.

d. *Channeling*: The cumulative effect of the Wills Act formalities serve a channeling function by encouraging individuals to consult an attorney to draft and supervise the execution of their wills, thereby facilitating the probating of the will and decreasing administrative costs.

The core requirements for an attested will are that it must be in writing, signed, and witnessed. To some degree each of these core requirements serves all of the functions, yet one can argue that each requirement *primarily* serves one of the functions. Which function is primarily served by each of the requirements?

2. *Modern trend*: Take a closer look at the Wills Act involved in the *Groffman* case. What happened to the three core requirements in the attested Wills Act? How many requirements are there in the statute? If you do not think the outcome in *Groffman* is defensible, what could the law do to remedy the situation?

3. *Degree of compliance with Wills Act formalities*: Judge Simon wrote "I am perfectly satisfied that that document was intended by the deceased to be executed as his will and that its contents represent his testamentary intentions." Then why did he invalidate the will? We opened the course by saying that the prevailing answer to the question "who gets your property when you die?" is "whomever you wish"—what happened to decedent's intent? Is the court looking for a way to uphold it or to invalidate it? Does that make any sense? How would you describe how the court applied the Wills Act formalities? What degree of compliance did it insist on? If you do not think the outcome in *Groffman* is defensible, what could you do to remedy the situation?

4. *Malpractice liability*: Should the attorney in *Groffman* be liable for failing to supervise the will execution ceremony? Should an attorney be liable to the named beneficiaries where an attorney properly drafts a will, gives it to the client for review, but fails to follow up to see if the client executes or wants to execute the draft? *See Radovich v. Locke-Paddon*, 35 Cal. 4th 946 (1995).

B. Response to Traditional Approach

As the Wills Act in *Groffman* evidences, historically a Wills Act typically required a good number of formalities to properly execute a will, including, but not limited to, the following:

1. A writing;

2. Signed by the testator (or signed for the testator by another person at the testator's direction and in the testator's presence);

3. With the testator's signature at the end or foot of the document;

4. Signed in the presence of all attesting witnesses;

5. "Published" by the testator (he or she declares or otherwise communicates to the witnesses that they are witnessing the testator's will and not some other legal document);

6. That there are two (or more) attesting witnesses;

7. That the testator requested the witnesses to sign as witnesses; and

8. Signed by the witnesses at the end of the will, in the testator's presence, as well as in the presence of each other, all at the same time — at the same sitting.

Moreover, as the *Groffman* case shows, traditionally, not only were there a myriad of statutory requirements, but courts required strict, i.e., "absolute," compliance. Any deficiency in the execution procedure resulted in an invalid will. Improper execution meant no will, regardless of how confident the court was that the document reflected the testator's intent.

With time scholarly criticism grew that this traditional approach was needlessly formalistic, exulting formalism at the expense of the testator's intent. The first attempt at ameliorating the effects of this traditional approach was to re-examine each of the Wills Act formalities, asking if there might not be some that could be eliminated, thereby reducing the risk that a testator might accidentally trip up on a formality. The 1969 Uniform Probate Code adopted this approach. The 1969 UPC Wills Act requires only the following formalities:

1. A writing

2. Signed by the testator (or signed for the testator by another person at the testator's direction and in the testator's presence);

3. Signed in the presence of all attesting witnesses;

4. That there are two (or more) attesting witnesses; and

5. That the witnesses sign the will.

California was a bit slow in following the UPC lead, not revising its Wills Act until 1984. Compared to the Wills Act in the *Groffman* case, the 1984 California Wills Act is significantly more streamlined:

1984 Version of CPC § 6110. Requirements for valid will

(a) Except as provided in this part, a will shall be in writing and satisfy the requirements of this section.

(b) The will shall be signed by one of the following:

(1) By the testator.

(2) In the testator's name by some other person in the testator's presence and by the testator's direction.

(3) By a conservator pursuant to a court order to make a will under Section 2580.

(c) The will shall be witnessed by being signed by at least two persons each of whom (1) being present at the same time, witnessed either the signing of the will or the testator's acknowledgment of the signature or of the will and (2) understand that the instrument they sign is the testator's will.

Other than the additional express requirement that the witnesses understand that the instrument is the testator's will, does the 1984 version of the California Wills Act reduce the number of requirements to the 1969 UPC list set forth above?

Even with the "leaner" Wills Acts, scholarly criticism continued to grow with respect to whether the judicial approach was still needlessly formalistic. In 1975 Professor John Langbein, one of the acknowledged leaders in the field, openly called for the courts to abandon strict compliance and to adopt substantial compliance: even if a will was not properly executed it could nevertheless be probated as long as there was: (1) clear and convincing evidence the decedent intended the document to be his or her will, and (2) clear and convincing evidence the decedent substantially complied with the Wills Act formalities. The state of Queensland, Australia, essentially adopted Professor Langbein's substantial compliance proposal, but the state of South Australia adopted a dispensing power approach that authorized the courts to dispense with the defective Wills Act formalities as long as the court was "satisfied that there can be no reasonable doubt that the deceased intended the document to constitute his will."[3] After studying how the courts interpreted and applied the two approaches, Professor Langbein concluded that the dispensing power approach was better. He modified the doctrine slightly to better fit the American legal system and re-named it the harmless error doctrine.

In 1990 the Uniform Probate Code adopted the harmless error approach:

UPC § 2-503. Harmless error doctrine

Although a document or writing added upon a document was not executed in compliance with Section 2-502 [the UPC provision that sets forth the requirements for a validly executed will — attested or holographic], the document or writing is treated as if it had been executed in compliance with that section if the proponent of the document or writing establishes by clear and convincing evidence that the decedent intended the document or writing to constitute (i) the decedent's will, (ii) a partial or complete revocation of the will, (iii) an addition to or an alteration of the will, or (iv) a partial or complete revival of his [or her] formerly revoked will or of a formerly revoked portion of the will.

The harmless error proposal has been met with mixed results. Some states have adopted it as is, some states have adopted a more "limited" version of the doctrine, and a majority of the states have declined to adopt it. California was in the latter camp until 2008 when the legislature amended the Wills Act to include its "limited" harmless error doctrine:

CPC § 6110. Necessity of writing; other requirements (2008 Revised Version)

(a)   Except as provided in this part, a will shall be in writing and satisfy the requirements of this section.

---

3. Section 12(2) of the new, local Wills Act, Wills Act Amendment Act (No. 2) of 1975, § 9 amending Wills Act of 1936, § 12(2), 8 S. Austl. Stat. 665.

(b) The will shall be signed by one of the following:

   (1)   By the testator.

   (2)   In the testator's name by some other person in the testator's presence and by the testator's direction.

   (3)   By a conservator pursuant to a court order to make a will under Section 2580.

(c) (1)   Except as provided in paragraph (2), the will shall be witnessed by being signed, during the testator's lifetime, by at least two persons each of whom (A) being present at the same time, witnessed either the signing of the will or the testator's acknowledgment of the signature or of the will and (B) understand that the instrument they sign is the testator's will.

   (2)   If a will was not executed in compliance with paragraph (1), the will shall be treated as if it was executed in compliance with that paragraph if the proponent of the will establishes by clear and convincing evidence that, at the time the testator signed the will, the testator intended the will to constitute the testator's will.

Notes and Problems

1.   *California versus UPC harmless error doctrine*: Has California adopted the "harmless error" approach championed by the UPC? How would you describe the California approach? Does California still follow strict compliance? Does it apply substantial compliance? Does it apply harmless error? Does it apply some hybrid version of the above?

2.   *Witnesses must sign during testator's lifetime*: Note that subsection (c)(2) is not the only revision to section 6110. The legislature also revised section (c)(1) to require that the witnesses sign the will "during the testator's lifetime." In light of subsection(c)(2), how important is that amendment?

3.   *Requirement versus "strongly recommended"*: Circling back for a moment to the discussion of the reduced number of Wills Act formalities under the 1969 UPC approach, after California adopted its limited "harmless error" doctrine, how many items on that list are still "requirements" and how many are de facto "recommendations" that can be waived under the harmless error doctrine?

4.   *Evidentiary burden*: What constitutes "clear and convincing evidence that, at the time the testator signed the will, the testator intended the will to constitute the testator's will"?

5.   *Practitioner's perspective*: Notwithstanding the UPC's version of the "harmless error" doctrine, or the more limited California version, in practice, the doctrine is never viewed as default law or one on which a practitioner would rely for drafting purposes. Why is this the case? Why would a practitioner not factor in the harmless error doctrine to his or her approach to his or her will execution ceremony? Perhaps the word "harmless" is not the most accurate description of the doctrine. In the practitioner's world, any idea of equating "harmless error" to something akin to "no harm, no foul," is absurd. An attorney drafting a testamentary document who is somehow relying on "harmless error" to validate it is

not only inviting a will contest (never the goal of an estate planner) but is also opening up the door to a malpractice lawsuit. A tarnished or ruined career is strong incentive to avoid any necessity of reliance on "harmless error." It is no surprise that estate planning attorneys continue to comply with the "old-fashioned," traditional requirements for executing a will (*see, infra* page 189).

Estate of Stoker

193 Cal. App. 4th 236 (Ct. App. 2011)

GILBERT, P.J.

At one time the Probate Code appeared to refute the dictum, "Nothing endures but change." Not anymore.

. . .

Destiny Gularte, Donald Karotick and Robert Rodriguez (appellants) appeal a judgment that denied a petition to probate a 1997 will and a trust of Steven Wayne Stoker (decedent), and granted the petition of Danine Pradia and Darrin Stoker (respondents) to probate decedent's 2005 will....

FACTS

On May 22, 1997, decedent executed a will and nominated Gularte to be the executor of his estate. In Article Two of the will, he listed Karotick and Gularte as the beneficiaries of gifts of personal property. In Article Three, he stated, "I give the residue of my estate to the trustee of the 1997 Steven Wayne Stoker Revocable Trust, created under the declaration of trust executed on the same date as, but immediately before, the execution of this will...." Gularte was listed as the successor trustee of that trust. Decedent died on February 27, 2008.

. . .

On April 28, respondents filed a petition to probate a handwritten will signed by their father on August 28, 2005. The will provides, "To Whom It May Concern: I, Steve Stoker revoke my 1997 trust as of August 28, 2005. Destiny Gularte and Judy Stoker to get nothing. Everything is to go to my kids Darin [sic] and Danene [sic] Stoker. Darin [sic] and Danene [sic] are to have power of attorney over everything I own." The will contained no witnesses' signatures.

At trial, Anne Marie Meier testified that she was a very close friend of decedent. One night in 2005, decedent was discussing "estate planning," and he asked Meier to "get a piece of paper and a pen." He then dictated the terms of the 2005 will. Meier wrote that document in her handwriting "word for word" from decedent's dictation. She handed it to him, "he looked at it and he signed it." Decedent told Meier that this was his last will and testament. Moreover, in front of the witnesses, he urinated on the original copy of the 1997 will and then burned it.

Homer Johns, a friend of decedent's, testified that he saw decedent sign the 2005 will.

The trial court found that respondents "established that the 2005 document was created at Decedent Stoker's direction and that he signed it," and that there was clear and convincing evidence that the 2005 will "evinces Decedent Stoker's intent." The court ruled that "[s]ince the 2005 will has been accepted for probate by this Court, the 1997 will has been revoked by operation of law."

DISCUSSION

. . .

The Validity of the 2005 Will

Appellants claim that the will does not meet the requirements for a "[f]ormal [w]itnessed [w]ill," and therefore the trial court erred by admitting it to probate. A will must be signed by the testator and at least two witnesses. (§ 6110, subds. (b)(1) & (c)(1).) (Here the 2005 will is signed by decedent, but it contains no witnesses' signatures. Two witnesses, however, saw decedent sign it, and they testified in court to verify that this will was genuine.

Respondents note that the Probate Code contains a provision that allows wills that are defective in form to be admitted to probate if they are consistent with the testator's intent. Section 6110, subdivision (c)(2) provides, "If a will was not executed in compliance with paragraph (1), the will shall be treated as if it was executed in compliance with that paragraph if the proponent of the will establishes by clear and convincing evidence that, at the time the testator signed the will, the testator intended the will to constitute the testator's will." Here the trial court found that the 2005 document constituted decedent's last will.

Appellants argue that the Legislature never intended this provision to apply to cases involving handwritten documents. We disagree. ""It is a prime rule of construction that the legislative intent underlying a statute ... must be ascertained from its language; if the language is clear, there can be no room for interpretation, and effect must be given to its plain meaning."" (citations omitted). Where the statute is inclusive, containing no limiting or qualifying language to exclude persons from its scope, the words the legislators used should control.

Here the statutory language is clear and broad, and there is no language to support the limitation appellants propose. This statute applies to wills that are "in writing" and signed by the testator. (§ 6110, subd. (a); id., subd. (b)(1).) The 2005 document is a written will signed by decedent. The statute contains no language to indicate that the wills covered by this section are limited to typewritten wills. Consequently, handwritten non-holographic wills are not excluded from the scope of this statute.

Moreover, statutes "should be given a construction consistent with the legislative purpose...." (citations omitted.) Remedial statutes should be broadly and liberally construed to promote the underlying legislative goals. (citations omitted.) The broad and remedial goal of this provision is to give preference to the testator's intent instead of invalidating wills because of procedural deficiencies or mistakes. Including the 2005 will within the purview of this statute is consistent with that purpose.

Retroactivity

[The new subdivision (c)(2) of CPC § 6110 effective January 1, 2009 was held to be retroactive in application — here to a document made prior to the effective date of the statute.]

...

Substantial Evidence

Appellants contend there is no evidence to show that the 2005 document was intended to be decedent's will. They claim it does not contain "testamentary language," does not use the word will or make reference to death.

The document is certainly not a model will. But "[n]o particular words are necessary to show a testamentary intent" as long as the record demonstrates that the decedent intended the document to be his or her last will and testament (citation omitted).

Here decedent's testamentary intent is evident. The document provides that all of decedent's property will go to his children — the respondents, that the 1997 trust is revoked, that Gularte will receive "nothing," and that his children will have power of attorney "over everything."

Moreover, even if the document is ambiguous, the trial court properly admitted extrinsic evidence. (citation omitted.) That evidence confirmed decedent's testamentary intent. Meier testified that decedent told her the document was "my last will and testament," and "[t]hese are my wishes." Johns testified that decedent told him that the will represented "his final wishes."

...

The judgment is affirmed. Costs on appeal are awarded in favor of respondents.

Estate of Ben-Ali

216 Cal. App. 4th 1026 (2013)

Margulies, Acting P.J.

The intestate heirs of decedent Taruk Joseph Ben-Ali appeal from a judgment admitting the decedent's will to probate. Appellants contend there was insufficient evidence of due execution under Probate Code section 6110....

A. *The Parties*

Taruk, born in 1968, was the only biological child of Hassan Ben-Ali and Ann Jackson.... According to Hassan's attorney, respondent Ivan Golde, Hassan was a very shrewd and savvy real estate investor who had owned a lot of properties over the years and had also gone through financial problems, including tax problems. One of Hassan's properties was an apartment building at 2235 Ashby Avenue in Berkeley (hereafter Ashby property or Ashby building), which Hassan had transferred to Taruk in approximately 1993, perhaps to avoid losing the property to the IRS.

In 1995, Jackson moved into an apartment in the Ashby building. Hassan lived in the building on and off during that time period and, according to Jackson, continued to handle all aspects of managing the property despite title being in their son's name. On August 3, 2002, Taruk married appellant Wendelyn Wilburn. According to Wilburn, Hassan opposed the marriage, believed Wilburn just wanted to obtain a portion of the Ashby property, and persisted in trying to talk Taruk out of marrying her down to the day of their wedding.... Wilburn was aware when she married Taruk that he had spent time in prison and had a history of drug problems. According to Wilburn, drugs were not an issue for Taruk during their relationship and marriage until sometime in early 2004, when he relapsed into using drugs.

B. *Decedent's Disappearance and Death*

Wilburn was on a business trip in Las Vegas on June 8, 2004, when she communicated with Taruk by telephone for the last time. Over the next two days, Wilburn repeatedly tried to call Taruk from Las Vegas, but got no answer. When she returned from her trip, she called Hassan to find out if he knew where Taruk was. Hassan told her Taruk had decided to leave her and start a new life somewhere else. He told similar stories to Jackson and others who inquired about Taruk's whereabouts. Wilburn testified she did not believe Hassan, and made attempts to locate Taruk, but neither Wilburn nor anyone else reported Taruk's disappearance to the police. Between June 2004 and December 2008, Hassan continued to manage Taruk's apartment building in Taruk's name, collected rents, forged Taruk's name on checks drawn against Taruk's bank accounts, and refinanced the property in the amount of $600,000 by forging Taruk's signature and the signature of a notary.

In November 2008, Hassan called Golde and asked to meet with him. Hassan informed Golde that Taruk had in fact died in 2004. Hassan explained he had found Taruk dead of a drug overdose in a hotel room. Not wanting to report the death for fear of losing the Ashby property, he had taken Taruk's body to the property and hidden it in the wall of a storage area of the building. Hassan further informed Golde that a person who had assisted him in the removal and concealment of Taruk's body was extorting substantial sums of money from him by threatening to reveal what had happened.

Hassan committed suicide on December 15, 2008, while Berkeley police officers were visiting the property. Two days later, Taruk's body was discovered on the premises. Police believed Taruk had died four and half years earlier, in June 2004. Hassan left a will, not contested in this proceeding, in which he named his former spouse, Ann Jackson, as the sole beneficiary of his estate.

C. *Decedent's Will*

Among Hassan's possessions, police found a purported will of Taruk, bearing the apparent signatures of Taruk and two attesting witnesses. The typewritten document was dated August 16, 2002, two weeks after Taruk and Wilburn were married, and the day before they were to leave town for a honeymoon in Hawaii. It recited that Taruk had one living child, Brittany Desmond. The document provided Taruk's "wife," who was the only person not referred to by name in it, was to receive all of Taruk's personal property, and his father, Hassan Ben-Ali, was to receive all other assets. It further stated Desmond "has been provided for by a life insurance policy on my life, which is held in trust for her by my father, Hassan Ben-Ali." Hassan was identified as executor of the estate in the document, and "Attorney Ivan Gold" was named as the alternate executor.

The purported will contained an attestation clause stating it was signed by Taruk in the presence of two witnesses who also signed in the presence of each other and that Taruk declared to them the document was his "Last Will and Testament." One of the witness signatures was of "Wendy Ben-Ali" with an address of "2235 Ashby # 201 Berkeley, Ca." The handwritten name and address of the second purported witness were illegible, and the identity of that person has never been determined.

D. *Probate Court Proceedings*

[Both sides hired forensic document experts who testified as to the authenticity of the signatures on the will. Respondent's expert testified that he believed with a "high degree of certainty" that Taruk's signature was authentic and that Wilburn's signature was "probably" genuine. Appellants' expert opined that it was "highly probable" both signatures were not genuine. The Probate Court accepted the testimony of Respondent's expert and held the regular and complete attestation clause on the signature page of the will constituted prima facie evidence of the validity of the unknown witness signature and of the will's due execution.

The appellate court agreed that "proof of the signatures of the decedent and the witness*es* makes out a prima facie case of due execution." (Emphasis added.) "Proof of the signature of the decedent and of *only one* of the witnesses does not." (Emphasis added.) The appellate court went on to find that "No ... [authenticating] evidence was produced in this case regarding the signature of the unidentified purported witness." Accordingly, the appellate court ruled the will could not be admitted to probate as a validly executed will under section 6110, subdivision (c)(1).]

   ...

C. *Evidence of Testator's Intent*

A will not executed in compliance with section 6110, subdivision (c)(1) may nonetheless be admitted to probate if the proponent establishes by clear and convincing evidence the testator intended the instrument to constitute his will at the time he signed it. (§ 6110, subd. (c)(2).) The clear and convincing standard " 'requires a finding of high probability....' 'so clear as to leave no substantial doubt'; 'sufficiently strong to command the unhesitating assent of every reasonable mind.' " " (*Lackner v. North* (2006) 135 Cal.App.4th 1188, 1211–1212, 37 Cal.Rptr.3d 863.) In our view, no reasonable trier of fact could find that standard has been reached on the record before us.

Taruk was only 34 years old when he allegedly executed his will. No witness in this case knew anything about the will or the circumstances of its execution. There was no evidence Taruk had spoken about his testamentary intentions with anyone, or that Wilburn ever mentioned the will to anyone between 2002 and its discovery in 2008 — despite the fact that her husband's decision not to provide for her in his will would presumably have been a topic of some interest to her. There was also no testimony as to how the typewritten will had been prepared, who had drafted it, or who Taruk might have consulted about its terms or phrasing. Significantly, no original or copy of the will was found at Taruk's residence or among his belongings. The will was found among the belongings of Taruk's father, Hassan. The evidence showed Hassan was a man willing to go to extremes of fraud and dishonesty in order to protect his financial interests and, in particular, to retain control of the Ashby property — which was both his residence and a major source of his income. Before taking his own life, Hassan had hidden his son's body behind a wall, perpetrated a callous fraud on Taruk's mother, spouse, and friends about Taruk's fate, and had impersonated Taruk and forged his name to multiple documents, all apparently for financial reasons connected to the property. At the same time, no convincing theory was offered to explain how Hassan's decision to conceal the death for financial reasons was consistent with the existence of a valid will passing Taruk's property to him. There was vague testimony about possible tax concerns, but no competent evidence of Hassan's tax situation in 2004 was admitted. On the other hand, Hassan would have had an obvious financial motive for concealing Taruk's death if a will leaving the building to Hassan did not in fact exist when Taruk died. The will document itself was far from self-authenticating. In the will, Taruk referred to Wilburn as "my wife" rather than mentioning her by name, even though they had just been married two weeks earlier. Whoever signed Wilburn's name used the Ashby property as her address even though Wilburn had never lived there. Both the signature and address of the second witness were completely indecipherable. The life insurance policy for Brittany Desmond referenced in the will has never been found, and no evidence was produced of any premiums paid for such a policy. Taruk's signature on the will — the only real evidence of Taruk's intent to make a will — was primarily authenticated by the proponents' document examiner who was not told about or shown any of the known documents on which Hassan had forged Taruk's signature.

By highlighting circumstances casting doubt on the will's provenance, we do not discount the other circumstances and evidence that persuaded the trial court Taruk did in fact sign the document in issue, and intend it as his will. But in light of the many unusual events surrounding the document, and the paucity of evidence Taruk had discussed his testamentary intent with others, we do not believe a reasonable fact finder could conclude those facts were proven by clear and convincing evidence.

Accordingly, we reverse the judgment and remand for further proceedings consistent with the views expressed herein....

III. DISPOSITION

The judgment is reversed and the matter is remanded to the probate court for the entry of a new judgment upholding appellants' contest of the will based on insufficient evidence of due execution, denying admission of the will to probate, and providing for the administration of the estate in a manner consistent with those determinations.

C. Continuing and Evolving Issues

Notwithstanding that California, like most states, has modified its Wills Act, for attested wills the three core requirements still remain: the will must be in writing, it must be signed, and it must be witnessed (*maybe*). As the material above reflects, what constitutes compliance with these components is evolving, with different jurisdictions taking different approaches. What follows is an attempt at delineating these three core requirements, but such an attempt often ends up raising more questions than providing answers.

1. The Writing Requirement

This "writing" requirement sounds rather simple and, in practice, it is usually not the source of problems. While this section of the book is focused on attested wills, we shall see that a holographic will also requires a writing. Does this writing requirement preclude oral wills? Some states do allow oral wills (officially known as "nuncupative" wills), but where valid, their use is typically severely limited (for example, permitted only in emergency situations or where dealing with property of limited value). At one time, California accorded limited validity to nuncupative wills, but that era is long gone and, while interesting, has no significance today.

So what qualifies as a writing? Wills that are typed, computer printed, or preprinted[4] obviously qualify. Handwritten wills (either by the testator or transcribed by another[5]) also meet this requirement. Must a writing be on paper? Paper is, by far, the most common and recommended medium of compliance, but a testator can use parchment, canvas (written in "paint"), and the like. The more traditional and tangible the medium, the more likely it is to be accepted as a writing even if it is not on paper.

Problems

1. A Farmer is out riding his tractor when he gets down off the tractor to adjust something on it. Tragically, the tractor shifts into reverse, pinning him beneath it. Unable to free himself and bleeding badly, he uses his pocketknife to scratch the following into the tractor's fender: "In case I die in this mess, I leave all to the wife. Cecil Geo Harris." Sadly, he dies from the injuries he sustained. Assuming the other Wills Act formalities are satisfied, if the fender was removed from the tractor and submitted for probate, does the scratching on the fender constitute "a writing" for purposes of the Wills Act formalities? Should it? *See* Jim D. Sarlis, *From Tractor Fenders to Iphones, Holographic Wills*, 86 N.Y. St. B.J. 10 (2014).

---

4. As previously indicated, the California Statutory Will (CPC § 6240) is a common example.

5. *See Stoker, supra* page 170. The testator dictated his will to his friend who wrote it down, "word for word," in her handwriting. This meets the requirements of a writing.

2. The decedent was found dead on his couch, his testamentary wishes written on his shirt. Assuming the other Wills Act formalities are satisfied, does the shirt constitute "a writing" for purposes of the Wills Act formalities? Should it? *See* Jim D. Sarlis, *From Tractor Fenders to Iphones, Holographic Wills*, 86 N.Y. St. B.J. 10 (2014).

3. Maggie Nothe enjoyed cooking. She has a recipe book in which she writes out her favorite recipes. One day she makes the following entry in her own handwriting:

   > *4 quarts of ripe tomatoes, 4 small onions, 4 green peppers, 2 teacups of sugar, 2 quarts of cider vinegar, 2 ounces ground allspice, 2 ounces cloves, 2 ounces cinnamon, 12 teaspoonfuls salt. Chop tomatoes, onions and peppers fine, add the rest mixed together and bottle cold. Measure tomatoes when peeled. In case I die before my husband I leave everything to him. Maggie Nothe*

   Assuming the other Wills Act formalities are satisfied, does the entry in the recipe book constitute "a writing" for purposes of the Wills Act formalities? Should it? *See* Robert Menchin, Where There's a Will 81 (1980).

4. Beth Bear is blind. She picks up a pen, handwrites out who should get what when she dies, using language that clearly expresses her testamentary intent, signs the document, folds it up and puts it in an envelope. Sadly, because she is devoid of sight, Beth did not realize that the pen she was using was out of ink. Following her death, a handwriting expert testifies she can make out the words on the blank pages from the indentations made by the pen. Assuming the other Wills Act formalities are satisfied, do the "blank pages" constitute "a writing" for purposes of the Wills Act formalities? Should they? *Id.*

5. Andrew Komlody and his wife have a volatile relationship. He often gets jealous and upset at her, sometimes so much so that she has to call the police. Andrew, who eventually is incarcerated, is so distraught that he hangs himself with strips of material torn from his prison blanket. When they find him, they also find that he had used a pencil to write out and signed his final wishes on his prison wall. Assuming the other Wills Act formalities are satisfied, does the writing on the prison wall constitute "a writing" for purposes of the Wills Act formalities? Should it? *Id.*

6. Robert Reed tape-recorded his final wishes, put the tape in an envelope, sealed it, and then wrote on the outside of the envelope: "Robert Reed To be played in the event of my death only! [signed] Robert G. Reed." Assuming the other Wills Act formalities are satisfied, does the tape recording's "magnetic voice print" constitute "a writing" for purposes of the Wills Act? Should it? *See In re Estate of Reed*, 672 P.2d 829 (Wyo. 1983); *see also* Unif. Probate Code § 2-502 & cmt. (a).

   California is home to Hollywood: what about videotaped wills? You can imagine a testator deciding "I'm going to make a video will! When I die, my lawyer will gather everyone together to see my last, great, theatrical performance: a soliloquy of my testamentary dispositions and thoughts on life and love." A video will is not a video of the will execution ceremony that was discussed in Chapter Five in connection with issues of capacity (that would still involve a traditional, written will). Rather, a video will is one where the will itself is in video format.

Other than in the handful of states that allow nuncupative wills where the video may be deemed the equivalent, the overwhelming majority view is that a video does not constitute a writing and thus does not create a valid will. (Can one argue in good faith that the California harmless error doctrine changes California's view on that?)

With the advancement of technology, electronic documents, replete with digital signatures, are at the forefront of many legal issues, particularly in the world of contracts. Would an electronic will (with a digital signature, stored on a computer drive, thumb drive, DVD, tablet, etc.) constitute a writing? *Should* an electronic writing constitute a will?[6] To date, only Nevada has statutorily recognized such "documents" as meeting the writing requirement for a will.[7] Nevada's allowance of electronic wills, however, is strictly circumscribed by detailed statutes governing their validity.

2. The Signature Requirement

Virtually all Wills Acts require that the testator sign the document. That obviously gives rise to the question: what constitutes a valid signature? Must the decedent sign his or her legal signature? What if the testator uses a short form of his or her name? What about a nickname? Does signing with an "X" count as a valid signature? What if the testator requires assistance in signing — for example, if he or she suffers from a neurological disease and his or her hand is guided or steadied by another? May someone sign on behalf of the testator?

Most courts take an intent-based approach to analyzing what constitutes a valid signature: whatever the decedent intended as his or her signature qualifies as his or her signature — i.e., "with the intention by so writing it to authenticate the document."[8] The problem is, because the decedent is dead, it is difficult to determine the decedent's intent. Thus, the general assumption is that, as long as he or she stops voluntarily, whatever the decedent wrote is what he or she intended as his or her signature. If, however, the decedent is interrupted during the signature process and does not come back and complete whatever he or she was writing, the assumption is that the decedent

---

6. For an interesting presentation of the case in support of electronic wills, *see* Joseph Karl Grant, *Shattering and Moving Beyond the Gutenburg Paradigm: The Dawn of the Electronic Will*, 42 U. MICH. J.L. REFORM 105 (2008).

7. Nev. Rev. Stat. Ann. § 133.085 (West 2013); *but see* In re Estate of Javier Castro, No. 2013ES00140 (Lorain Cnty. Ohio Ct. Com. Pl. June 19, 2013) (upholding a will drafted on a Samsung Tablet), and Re: Yu [2013] QSC 322. Karter Yu typed out his testamentary wishes on the Notes app of his iPhone and then typed his name at the end. The Supreme Court of Queensland, Australia, ruled that this "instrument" constituted a valid will.

8. In re Bauman's Estate, 114 Cal. App 551, 556 (1931).

intended to write more and so the incomplete writing is *not* a valid signature. This view is consistent with the traditional strict compliance approach but arguably not with the more modern trend intent-based approach.

How would you characterize the court's analysis of the issue in *In re Moore's Estate*, 92 Cal. App. 2d 120, 123–24 (1949):

> While in some cases it has been said that an instrument is deemed signed although the signature is typed, lithographed, rubber-stamped, printed or photographed, even assuming that such a signature might, under some circumstances, be held sufficient to render an instrument enforceable, we think that in the case of a will the statute requires a handwritten signature, ... To hold that the mere typed name of a testator is sufficient to satisfy the requirements of section 50 of the Probate Code[9] would open the door to an easy form of fraud, when the purported signer was dead. We are in accord with the statement of Mr. Justice Beatty, in *Re Estate of Seaman, supra*, when he said, 146 Cal. at page 465, 80 P. at page 704, 106 Am.St.Rep. 53, 2 Ann.Cas. 726:
>
>> He [appellant] insists that section 1276 of the Civil Code [now section 50, Probate Code], like the rest of its provisions, must be liberally construed, "with a view to effect its objects and promote justice." Civ.Code, § 4. I fully agree with him on this proposition; but I apply it differently. His argument is, in effect, that we should give a liberal construction to wills which deviate from the statute in the mode of their execution, for the purpose of sustaining them, whereas a proper application of the principle requires us to give a liberal construction and full effect to every provision of the statute designed to prevent the probate of spurious wills, although in so doing we may in a particular instance defeat an honest attempt on the part of a decedent to make a testamentary disposition of his estate. The evil of occasionally defeating such an attempt is far less serious than the establishment of a precedent which would open the door to the frauds which the statute was designed to prevent. Every statute of frauds is designed to promote justice by requiring wills and contracts to be executed with such formalities and indicia of genuineness as to make simulated and fraudulent writings of the classes defined impossible, or at least very difficult. Such statutes, in the long run, promote justice—which is their sole object—by shutting out opportunities of fraud. Where they defeat one honest purpose, they prevent unnumbered frauds which in their absence would be feasible and measurably safe....

In contrast, in *Estate of McCabe*, 224 Cal. App. 3d 330 (Ct. App. 1990), the decedent executed his will 15 days before he died and was too weak to sign his name. Instead he wrote an "X" directly above his typewritten name on the line designated for his

---

9. Now Section 6110 of the Probate Code.

signature. A witness (other than the attesting witnesses) acknowledged the decedent's mark, signed her name and wrote the date, her address, and the word "witness" near the mark. The court held the will was validly signed: "Where, as here, the mark was witnessed separately by someone other than the attesting witnesses, the opportunity for fraud is minimal. Thus, strict compliance with the statutory requirements in order to remove that opportunity was unnecessary." (The court was referring to California's Civil Code provision for when a mark may qualify as a signature.)

Look back at California Probate Code section 6110. Does it allow for someone to sign on behalf of the testator? When?

Under the traditional strict compliance approach, any scenario that potentially opened the door for fraud would be held invalid—to avoid even the potential for fraud. In light of that view, how would you analyze a "rubber-stamped" signature? Or an electronic "signature" that is made by the testator changing fonts on the computer so that his or her printed-out "signature" appears in a cursive font to mimic an actual signature? *See Taylor v. Holt*, 134 S.W.3d 830 (Tenn. App. 2003). While there is judicial precedent for holding this latter technique to be valid (comparing it to the contract law's progression in the area of the Statute of Frauds), the vast majority of states, including California, have held that these would not constitute a valid signature for purposes of a will.

Traditionally, states' Wills Acts[10] required that the testator's signature be at the end, or the foot, of the instrument. A close look at California's statute reveals that this is no longer the case. Yet, as discussed later in this chapter, estate planning attorneys continue to utilize the traditional requirements, including that the testator sign at the end of the will. Can you see why? If the signature is not at the end of the instrument, what questions inherently arise?

Problems

1. Testator had a will that left all of his estate to his three children. Years later, he remarried. Thereafter, he had an attorney draft a new will that left all of his estate to his new wife. At the time of the will's execution, testator was wheelchair-bound and legally blind to the point that he was unable to read the document. When it came time to sign the will, his hands were so shaky that his wife came to his aid and guided his hand in order to sign the will. After his death, his children challenged the validity of the will. Was the will properly signed? *See Muhlbauer v. Muhlbauer*, 686 S.W.2d 366 (Tex. App. 1985).

2. What if in Problem 1, when the attorney handed the pen to the testator to sign the will, testator had said his hands were "shaky" and that he would need help. His wife then came over and wrote his name while the testator rested his hand on her arm. Was the will properly signed? *See In re Kehl's Estate*, 73 N.E.2d 437 (Ill. 1947).

---

10. Including those in California. *See* former California Probate Code section 50 (the precursor to Probate Code section 6110).

3. What if in Problem 1, instead of signing the document, the testator asked his wife to use a rubber stamp of his signature, which he often used because of his physical ailments, to "sign" the will. Should the rubber stamped "signature" qualify as a valid signature? *See Phillips v. Najar*, 901 S.W.2d 561 (Tex. App. 1995).

3. The Witness Requirement

Traditional Wills Act statutes had two "presence" requirements: (1) the testator had to sign the will in the "presence" of at least two witnesses, present at the same time; and (2) the witnesses had to sign the will in the presence of the testator and each other. Together, the two requirements de facto required "simultaneous signing." The 1969 UPC "leaner" Wills Act eliminated the requirement of simultaneous signatures: the witnesses no longer need to sign the will in the presence of the testator or in the presence of each other. When California revised its Wills Act in 1984, did it follow the UPC lead, or did it retain the two "presence" requirements? Notwithstanding California's recent adoption of the "harmless error rule," in subsection 6110(c)(2), what is "required" in California under subsections 6110(c)(1)–(2)(a)?[11]

Problem

The following facts are from *In re Estate of Peters*, 526 A.2d 1005 (N.J. 1987). How would the case come out in California the first time through your analysis? Would you have to resort to the harmless error rule?

> On December 30, 1983, Sophia Gall came to the testator's [Conrad Peter's] hospital room with her husband and Marie Peters. Ms. Gall read the provisions of the will to Mr. Peters; he then assented to it, and signed it. Although Ms. Gall, her husband, and Mrs. Peters were present at the time, none of these individuals signed the will as witnesses. It was the apparent intention of Ms. Gall, who was an insurance agent and notary, to wait for the arrival of two employees from her office, who were to serve as witnesses.
>
> When those two employees, Mary Elizabeth Gall and Kristen Spock, arrived at the hospital, Sophia Gall reviewed the will briefly with the testator, who, in the presence of the two women, again indicated his approval, and acknowledged his signature. Ms. Gall then signed the will as a notary, but neither of the two intended witnesses placed her signature on the will. Ms. Gall folded the will and handed it to Mrs. Peters. Conrad Peters died fifteen months later, on March 28, 1985. At the time of his death the will was still not signed by either of the witnesses.
>
> At the Probate Court proceeding, Ms. Gall testified as to why the two intended witnesses never signed the will:

---

11. California's Statutory Will (California Probate Code Section 6240) is another version of an attested will. Do the California Statutory Will provisions require more than California's primary Wills Act (California Probate Code Section 6110)?

"As I say, just because of the emotional aspect of the whole situation, my sister-in-law was there, my husband, her brother was there, myself and the two girls. There were six of us. The other patients had visitors. It got to be kind of—I don't know how to explain it, just the situation, and the girls were in a hurry to get back to the office, because they had to leave the office.

I honestly think in their minds, when they saw me sign the will, they thought that is why they were there. And we folded up the will, gave it [to] my sister-in-law. It was just that type of situation."

In an affidavit executed on June 28, 1985, Ms. Gall explained that her failure to obtain the signatures of the two witnesses was the result of her being "affected emotionally by [the testator's] appearance."

According to Sophia and Charles Gall, Conrad Peters signed the instrument in their presence but before the arrival of the intended witnesses. However, an affidavit submitted to the court by Mary Elizabeth Gall on July 29, 1985, alleges that Mary Elizabeth Gall was present while Conrad Peters signed his will, and that she actually observed him as he executed the document. Plaintiff's only explanation for this discrepancy is that the affidavit was executed approximately eighteen months after the ceremony at the hospital. The State, however, does not argue that the contradictory versions raise the possibility of fraud with respect to Conrad Peters' will.

To the extent that California's Wills Act statute (CPC § 6110) requires that the witnesses be in "the presence of each other" when they witness the testator sign or acknowledge, what does it mean to be in each other's presence? Traditionally, this required that the witnesses are physically present, typically together at the table when the signing takes place. The first articulation of this requirement was known as the "line of sight" test: the party in whose presence the act had to be performed had to be able to see the other party's performance if the party were to look. They technically did not have to look (though it was expected he or she would)—the party just had to have a clear "line of sight" so that, if the party did look, he or she would see the performance in question. The modern trend approach to the presence requirement is known as the "conscious presence" test: as long as the party can tell, from a totality of the circumstances (sight, hearing, awareness of what was going on, etc.) that the other party is performing, the presence test is satisfied.[12]

Which approach does California apply?

---

12. A word of caution with respect to the witness requirements for the California Statutory Will— they are more strict than those adopted by California case law. *See* California Probate Code section 6240.

In re Tracy's Estate

182 P.2d 336 (Cal. Ct. App. 1947)

McCOMB, Justice.

[Nell B. Tracy validly executed a valid will on July 18, 1945. On September 30, 1945, Nell B. Tracy executed a second will that purported to revoke her will. She died October 14, 1945. The issue on appeal was whether the second will was validly executed and, in particular, whether the witnesses had signed the will in the presence of the testator. The trial court had ruled that the witnesses had. Note that California law has dispensed with the requirement at issue in this case. California no longer requires that both attesting witnesses sign in the "presence" of the testator. The court's analysis of the "presence" requirement, however, applies to the continuing California requirement that both witnesses be "present," at the same time, to witness the testator's signature or acknowledgment.]

… The evidence discloses that at the time decedent signed the revocation she was suffering from cancer and confined to her home in a small bedroom about 9 by 12 feet in size. She stated to her nurse, Reba Thornton, and a neighbor, Leora B. Blot, that she desired to revoke her will and requested Miss Thornton and Mrs. Blot to sign as witnesses. They received the instrument from her after witnessing decedent sign the same, and hearing her declare that it was her signature and that she desired to revoke her former will. Since there was no place in the room where the witnesses could conveniently sign the revocation, decedent directed them to take it into the adjoining dining room and sign on the table there. In accordance with these instructions the witnesses walked some twenty feet to the dining room table and affixed their signatures to the revocation. The testatrix could see into the dining room and hear the witnesses in conversation, but could not actually see the act of signing. After they had signed the document Mrs. Blot returned to the bedroom where decedent expressed her satisfaction at having revoked her will.

Section 74 of the Probate Code provides that a will may be revoked by a writing executed with the same formalities as are required for the execution of a will. Section 50 of the Probate Code provides as one of the requirements for the execution of a will that it be signed by at least two witnesses in the testator's "presence." "Presence" is defined in Webster's New International Dictionary, 2dEd., 1939, page 1955 thus: "The part of space within one's ken, call, influence, etc.; immediate nearness or vicinity of one; proximity."

In a number of decisions where the meaning of the word "presence" has arisen in connection with the execution of wills, the courts have adopted what is known as the 'conscious presence rule' which means that the testator need not actually view the act of signing by the witnesses, but that these elements must be present: (1) the witnesses must sign within the testator's hearing, (2) the testator must know what is being done, and (3) the signing by the witnesses and the testator must constitute one continuous transaction. …

All of these elements were present in the instant case. The witnesses signed within the decedent's hearing, she knew what was being done, and the signing by the witnesses and decedent constituted one continuous transaction. It is our opinion that the finding of the trial court that the revocation was signed by the witnesses in decedent's presence is, under the foregoing rule, sustained by the evidence.

––––––––––

Problems

1. "The will of Ozias Walker, deceased, was written by C. G. Warren, the attorney at law of the testator, and was executed in the presence of H. C. White and C. G. Warren, who were requested by the testator to attest, as witnesses, its execution. The requirements of the statute were complied with in all respects saving that the witness C. G. Warren, in signing his name as a witness at the end of the will, inadvertently wrote the name 'C. G. Walker,' thus employing his own initials but the testator's surname." Has the will been properly executed? *See In re Walker's Estate*, 42 P. 815 (Cal. 1895). If not, can the document be saved under California's new harmless error doctrine?

2. Testatrix was ill, so ill that she was bedridden. Not wanting anyone to see her in this condition, she refused to let the witnesses who were there to witness her sign the will come into her bedroom. Her attorney set up a video monitor downstairs in the living room. The witnesses were downstairs in the living room when the testator executed her will in her bedroom upstairs. Then the attorney took the will downstairs, and the witnesses signed the will. Has the will been validly executed? *See Whitacre v. Crowe*, 972 N.E.2d 659 (Ohio Ct. Ap. 2012). If not, can it be saved under the California harmless error doctrine?

3. The following facts are from the *In re Weber's Estate*, 387 P.2d 165 (Kan. 1963). How would the case come out in California the first time through your analysis? Would you have to resort to the harmless error rule?

    Henry Weber went to the home of Ben Heer in Riley. Mr. Heer was not at home but his wife was, and Mr. Weber advised Mrs. Heer he was ill and needed help to get into the hospital. He stated he wished to go to the Riley County Hospital in Manhattan. Mrs. Heer telephoned the hospital and made arrangements to have Mr. Weber admitted.

    After arrangements were completed Mrs. Heer offered to put Mr. Weber's clothes in a suitcase and otherwise help him prepare to go to the hospital. Next, she called a neighbor who in turn went to where Mr. Heer was working, which was about four miles from Riley, and told Mr. Heer that Henry Weber was at Heer's home and wanted to see him. Heer went immediately to his home. When he arrived Weber advised Heer of his illness and of his desire to make a will leaving one-half of his estate to his wife and one-half to his niece, Lillian Price. Heer and Weber then decided to go to see Harold Holmes, president of the Riley State Bank, to have the will prepared.

The distance from the Heer residence to the bank was three or four blocks. The two men drove to the bank, each in his own automobile. Mr. Weber parked his car at an angle against the curb of the street and beneath a window on the north side of the bank and asked Mr. Heer, who had parked on the east side and had come over to the Weber car, to see if Mr. Holmes would come out to the car and talk to him. Weber remained in his car and Heer went into the bank and talked to Holmes who then came out and got into the front seat of Weber's car. At Weber's request Heer got into the back seat of the automobile. It was a chilly November day and the car windows were kept closed. Weber explained to Holmes how he desired to dispose of his property, one-half to be left to his wife and one-half to his niece, and that he wanted Heer to be his executor. Holmes took notes as Weber talked. After Holmes concluded taking notes he went back into the bank and prepared the purported will on a printed form captioned 'Last Will and Testament' by filling in a portion of the blank spaces thereof with the information contained in the notes he had made, except that he failed to mention Weber's wife in the purported will.

The third paragraph of the will reads:

'Third. I give, devise and bequeath to *My Niece, Lillian Price of Junction City, Kansas My share of land situated in the Eureka Valley in Ogden and Manhattan Townships also My share of all Real estate located in Madison Township, Riley County Kansas* and I do devise and bequeath all the rest and residue of my estate both real, personal and mixed to *My Niece Lillian Price, any and all, money, stocks or Bonds, any and all personal property which I may possess at my death, whatsoever.'*

The italicized portion of the above quotation was that part typed from Holmes' notes onto the printed will form.

While Holmes was inside the bank he directed three bank employees, Mr. and Mrs. Chamberlain and Mrs. Carlson, to go to and stand in front of a closed window in the bank in order that they could serve as witnesses to the signing of the will. The window was approximately eight to ten feet from where Weber was sitting in his closed automobile.

About fifteen minutes later Holmes returned to Weber's automobile with a clipboard to which the purported will was fastened. Holmes re-entered Weber's automobile and handed the document to him. Weber read the document, Holmes and Heer being in the automobile at this time.

Holmes and Weber having previously discussed the need for witnesses, Holmes directed Weber's attention to the window of the bank where the above-named bank employees were standing. By waving to them, Weber indicated he saw them, and they in turn waved back to him. After looking the purported will over, Weber placed the clipboard on the steering wheel of his automobile where it could be seen through the closed windows by the witnesses, and signed the document.

Holmes then returned to the bank with the document, and there, standing before the bank window as heretofore described, the witnesses signed their names. The table upon which the signing occurred was against the window but the table top was a foot to a foot and a half beneath the window sill. Hence Weber could see the witnesses in the window as they signed but could not see the pen or the purported will on the table at the time of signing. Only that portion of the body of each witness in the window could be seen by him.

After the three witnesses signed the purported will Holmes took it back out to Weber's automobile, showed it to him, Weber looked it over, and at Weber's request Holmes retained the document at the bank.

The record disclosed that all three witnesses were acquainted with Weber prior to November 16, 1960, and knew his signature when they saw it. They recognized Weber's signature on the purported will. However, none of the witnesses could read any of the writing or printing on the document while it was being signed by Weber in his automobile.

It is noted from the record that at no time was there any type of communication between Weber and the witnesses other than their waving to one another; no verbal communication whatsoever. Weber never entered the bank building during this period of time and heard nothing of what was said inside the building; and even more important, the witnesses never left the building, so they couldn't possibly have heard any of the conversation that occurred in Weber's automobile.

The transaction at the bank took approximately one to one and a half hours to complete. Weber then proceeded to drive his automobile, unaccompanied, approximately twenty miles to the Riley County Hospital where the earlier admittance arrangements had been made, and it was there on November 21, 1960, just five days later, he died.

D. The "Interested" Witness

The witnessing requirement is concomitant with the "protective" and "evidentiary" functions of the Wills Act. Where a witness has a "stake" in the will (is to benefit from the will) that he or she has witnessed, such an interest in the will creates a conflict of interest that arguably undermines the reasons for requiring witnesses for attested wills. The witness requirement inherently presumes a "disinterested" witness. What should be the legal consequences if one, or both, of the witnesses are "interested" witnesses?

At common law, the failure to have the requisite number of non-interested witnesses would cause the entire will to be invalidated. The most modern approach, exemplified by the UPC but adopted by only a few jurisdictions, goes to the opposite end of the spectrum and abolishes the entire interested witness doctrine, leaving challenges to the validity of the will within the confines of other remedies such as undue influence, fraud, etc. In the middle are varying approaches where the will remains valid, but: (1) any gifts to an interested witnesses are voided, (2) the interested witness is purged of their "excess interest" under the will (the interested witness receives the lesser of their share under the will or what they would take if the will were not valid), or (3) a rebuttable presumption of misconduct arises, and if the interested witness rebuts the presumption, he or she takes the share under the will but if not, apply the purging approach.

Which approach has California adopted?

CPC § 6112. Witnesses; interested witnesses

(a) Any person generally competent to be a witness may act as a witness to a will.

(b) A will or any provision thereof is not invalid because the will is signed by an interested witness.

(c) Unless there are at least two other subscribing witnesses to the will who are disinterested witnesses, the fact that the will makes a devise to a subscribing witness creates a presumption that the witness procured the devise by duress, menace, fraud, or undue influence. This presumption is a presumption affecting the burden of proof. This presumption does not apply where the witness is a person to whom the devise is made solely in a fiduciary capacity.

(d) If a devise made by the will to an interested witness fails because the presumption established by subdivision (c) applies to the devise and the witness fails to rebut the presumption, the interested witness shall take such proportion of the devise made to the witness in the will as does not exceed the share of the estate which would be distributed to the witness if the will were not established. Nothing in this subdivision affects the law that applies where it is established that the witness procured a devise by duress, menace, fraud, or undue influence.

Notes

1. *Interested witness doctrine versus harmless error*: In light of California's new "harmless error" doctrine, has the legislature de facto abolished the interested witness doctrine? As long as there is clear and convincing evidence that at the time the decedent signed the will he or she intended it to be his or her will, does it matter if one or more of the witnesses are interested witnesses?

2. *Practitioner's perspective*: From the practitioner's perspective, California's adoption of the "harmless error" doctrine is, for all intents and purposes, irrelevant for drafting purposes relating to "interested witnesses" (and otherwise). *See supra*, page 169 and *infra*, page 189.

Problem

D dies testate survived by her three children, X, Y and Z. D's will, witnessed by X and Y, leaves $10,000 to child X, $3,000 to child Y, and the residue (which amounted to $2,000) to child Z (assume D is survived by no other heirs). Following D's death, how should D's estate be distributed, and why?

E. "Swapped-Wills"

Mirror wills (also known as "mutual wills") occur where two persons (almost always spouses or similarly situated individuals) have wills prepared that are "mirror images" of each other: "All to my spouse, _____, if he/she survives me; if not, to the children equally." The dispositive provisions are, for all practical purposes, the same, with the logical exception that the names of the spouses are different. The two have the same lawyer draft the wills and go together to execute them. You can see what is coming—the two "execute" the wills at the same time (signatures and witnesses) but accidentally sign the wrong will (the other's will). We clearly have a problem. Should a court declare the will (or wills) valid notwithstanding that they were not signed by the person for whom they were intended?

Under the traditional strict compliance approach the answer clearly is no. These are, simply put, not validly executed wills; end of analysis.

There have been a few cases, however, in strict compliance jurisdictions, where the court has stretched the "misdescription" doctrine to probate the will the decedent signed. Misdescription is a will construction doctrine that typically applies *after* a will is determined to be a validly executed will. It is used to help courts construe drafting mistakes. Mechanically, if the court applies the doctrine, it strikes out the "misdescriptions" in the will and then checks to see if there is enough information left with respect to the gift in question that the court feels comfortable it can ascertain and give effect to the testator's intent. We will examine the "misdescription" doctrine as a construction doctrine in Chapter 9. As applied to the "swapped wills" scenario, the courts apply the doctrine as a curative doctrine in an attempt to cure the defect in execution. The courts strike all the "misdescriptions" in the will, including the name on the front page of the will, and then see if there is enough information left in the will to give effect to it as the will of the party who signed it. Strict compliance purists oppose using the construction doctrine in an attempt to cure the execution defect. Even if the court is open to using the doctrine as a curative doctrine, whether the language of the will factually permits it is very fact sensitive. It depends on the phrasing in the instrument.

In the 1981 New York case of *In re Snide*, 418 N.E.2d 656, the court adopted a new and interesting approach. In *Snide*, decedent Harvey Snide and his wife, Rose Snide, intended to execute mirror wills at a common execution ceremony, but each accidentally executed the will prepared for the other. Rose offered the instrument Harvey actually signed for probate. A guardian ad litem representing a minor child objected to the probate of the will, asserting that it lacked testamentary intent. The court acknowledged that a valid will requires testamentary intent but declined to accept the view that this intent attaches only to the prepared document and not the testamentary scheme that it reflects. The court emphasized the obvious nature of the mistake and noted that the two wills were reciprocal elements of a unified testamentary scheme that were executed as part of one unified execution ceremony. The court ruled that the will was properly admitted to probate.

In *Snide*, did the court essentially apply substantial compliance without expressly admitting it because it feared the administrative costs and potential for fraud that could occur if the doctrine were applied to all execution defects?

There are no reported California cases addressing the swapped-wills scenario. Which approach do you think a California court would apply, and why? Does California's harmless error doctrine help the California courts with this scenario?

F. Real Life — Practice versus What Is Permitted by Statutes and Courts

It is common practice for estate planning attorneys to draft a will and conduct an organized "will execution" ceremony that appears to be a throwback to the old Wills Act requirements in *Groffman* (and then some). The ceremony begins with the lawyer: (1) gathering the parties—the testator, *three* attesting witnesses, and the lawyer, (2) taking them all into a small conference room, (3) closing the door, and (4) letting the witnesses interact with the testator for a few minutes. Then the lawyer takes control of the meeting, asking the testator: (1) if the document before them is the testator's will, (2) if he or she has read it, (3) if it disposes of his or her property as he or she wishes, and (4) if he or she would like the witnesses to witness the will. The questions are designed to ensure that the testator makes the appropriate declarations in the presence of the witnesses. Then, with all of the signatories there at the same time and in each other's presence (typically with the testator on one side of the conference table and the witnesses on the other side, sitting directly across from the testator), the testator signs the will first (signing at the foot/end of the will), and the witnesses signing immediately after the testator (and immediately below the testator's signature). Why do estate planners typically go to such trouble? By law, much of this is no longer necessary. So if this is the norm for estate planning attorneys, why is there such a push for removing or relaxing the requirements of a validly executed will?

If estate planners continue to comply with the old-fashioned Wills Act requirements, what is the objective of those supporting the UPC to dispense with most of the formalities (along with less stringent compliance standard with what remains)?

III. Holographic Wills

The primary factor that distinguishes holographic wills from attested wills is that holographic wills do not have to be witnessed. To offset the lack of witnesses, however, historically holographic wills had to be in the testator's handwriting. Accordingly, holographic wills are also often referred to as "handwritten" wills. Many states do not recognize the validity of holographic wills (only about half do). Their concerns include (and are not limited to) questions about whether the testator had capacity at the time the document was written, the increased potential for undue influence and fraud, and whether the testator truly intended for this writing to serve as his or her will.

California has long recognized the validity of holographic wills and, not surprisingly, the requirements for a valid holographic will have changed over the years. It is fair to say that in general, and consistent with attested wills, there has been some relaxation of the requirements. Prior California statutes required that a holographic will be "entirely written, dated and signed by the hand of the testator himself." (Former CPC § 53). As with attested wills, traditionally courts required strict compliance with these requirements.

Estate of Billings

64 Cal. 427 (1884)

MYRICK, J.

The body of the script proposed as an olographic will[13] was entirely written, and was signed by the hand of the deceased. The date reads thus: "Sacramento, April 1, 1880." The words "April 1st" were written by the deceased; the balance was printed, the deceased having evidently taken a sheet of paper with a letter-head, stating the business and location of his firm, the name of the place, "Sacramento," and the year "1880," printed, and filled in the month and day, "April 1st."

We had occasion to consider the principle underlying the facts of this case, in *Estate of Martin*, 58 Cal. 580, and *Estate of Rand*, 61 Cal. 468. Section 1277, Civil Code, requires that a paper, to constitute an olographic will, must be entirely written, dated, and signed by the hand of the testator. It must be entirely written, it must be entirely dated, and it must be entirely signed by him. If it be partly written by him and partly written by another, or printed; if it be partly dated or signed by him and partly by another — it is not a compliance with the statute. The words "April 1st" do not constitute a date — do not show on what April 1st, the paper was written — there being, as was suggested on the argument, many days "April 1st" in the life of any man; it was requisite that the whole date, April 1, 1880, should have been written by him in order to comply with the statute.

Order affirmed.

––––––––––

Just as with attested wills, the original holographic will statutes contained numerous detailed formalities and the courts required strict compliance with these formalities. Countless holographic wills were deemed invalid because they were not dated, or because the will contained some typed or pre-printed portions that prevented the document from being entirely written.

Just as with attested wills, over time scholars and even some California courts indicated their displeasure with the harsh outcomes that occurred when the burdensome statutory requirements were strictly enforced. The California legislature

––––––––––

13. That is not a typographical error — holographic wills were originally known as olographic wills.

responded by amending the statutory scheme to make the requirements less stringent. The following are the current versions of California's primary statutes relating to holographic wills:

CPC § 6111. Holographic wills; requirements

(a) A will that does not comply with Section 6110 is valid as a holographic will, whether or not witnessed, if the signature and the material provisions are in the handwriting of the testator.

(b) If a holographic will does not contain a statement as to the date of its execution and:

(1) If the omission results in doubt as to whether its provisions or the inconsistent provisions of another will are controlling, the holographic will is invalid to the extent of the inconsistency unless the time of its execution is established to be after the date of execution of the other will.

(2) If it is established that the testator lacked testamentary capacity at any time during which the will might have been executed, the will is invalid unless it is established that it was executed at a time when the testator had testamentary capacity.

(c) Any statement of testamentary intent contained in a holographic will may be set forth either in the testator's own handwriting or as part of a commercially printed form will.

CPC § 6111.5. Extrinsic evidence; admissibility

Extrinsic evidence is admissible to determine whether a document constitutes a will pursuant to Section 6110 or 6111, or to determine the meaning of a will or a portion of a will if the meaning is unclear.

Those are the statutory provisions in the abstract; what about in application? Assume the following facts: after the decedent's death, a two page, handwritten document is found in the decedent's desk drawer. The only other important document in the drawer is a checkbook. The document is written on the front and back page of the first page of a note pad. It is in the decedent's handwriting, and the entire text is in block-style capital letters. At the top of the first page are the words "Last Will, Etc. or What? Of Homer Eugene Williams." The document goes on to name two family members his executors, to give his collectibles to his nephew, to state that in the event of illness he did not want to be kept alive by life support means, to list his "House" and "Bank Account" as his "Estate", and finally it states: "I would like my step daughter, Debra Cox to be able to live in the house as long as she wants before putting it up for sale." The next two sheets of the note pad are blank, and the next page contains a list of movies in the same block printing. The only place on the note pad where the decedent's name appears is in the heading at the top of the first page. An electronic image of the document is set forth at the top of the next page. Does the document qualify as a holographic will? Is it signed? Does it have testamentary intent?

ATTACHMENT 4e(2)

Last Will etc. or What?
of
HOMER EUGENE WILLIAMS
1945 SERGE AVE.
SAN JOSE, CA 95130-1850

EXECUTORS:
STEP   DEBORAH COX
DAUGHTER 1945 SERGE AVE. SJ.

SISTER   LORNA WILLIAMS
IN LAW   6731 Mt. LENEVE DR. SJ

POWER OF ATTORNEY: NOW
DEBORAH COX

ALL MY COLLECTABLES: EVERYTHING
INCLUDING TWO PISTOLS & TWO
RIFLES, NONE FIRED: TO NEPHEW
KIRK BELL
2504 No. 56 th St. Apt #7
LINCOLN, NE 68504

ATTACHMENT 4e(2)

IN THE EVENT OF A SERIOUS SICK-
NESS OR ACCIDENT: I DO NOT WANT
TO BE KEPT ALIVE BY LIFE SUPPORT
MEANS. AND I NAME MY EXECUTORS
TO SEE TO MY WISHES ARE CARRIED
OUT.

MY ESTATE:

HOUSE. PRESENT MARKET VALUE
$225,000 TO $350,000.00
BANK ACCOUNT: CHECKING
AND SAVINGS.

I WOULD LIKE MY STEP
DAUGHTER, DEBRA COX TO BE
ABLE TO LIVE IN THE HOUSE
AS LONG AS SHE WANTS BEFORE
PUTTING IT UP FOR SALE.

In re Estate of Williams

155 Cal. App. 4th 197 (2007)

BAMATTRE-MANOUKIAN, Acting P.J.

In this probate case, Eric Williams Towle, the biological son of the decedent, Homer Eugene Williams, appeals from orders admitting to probate a holographic will offered by the decedent's stepdaughter, Deborah Ann Cox, and appointing Cox executor. Appellant's principal argument is that the document is not a valid holographic will under Probate Code section 6111 because it is not signed by the decedent. Appellant also argues that the document is not a valid will because it does not completely dispose of the decedent's assets and because it lacks language demonstrating testamentary intent....

BACKGROUND

Procedural History

Homer Eugene Williams died on December 7, 2005. On February 21, 2006, his son, Eric Williams Towle (Towle), filed a petition to administer his father's estate, alleging that his father had died intestate. The petition was granted on March 22, 2006.

On May 10, 2006, the decedent's stepdaughter, Deborah Ann Cox (Cox), filed a petition for suspension of Towle's powers as personal representative of the estate. Concurrently, she filed a petition to admit a holographic will into probate, and a petition to be named the executor of the estate, as specified in the will. Towle objected to Cox's petition for probate of the holographic will and to her appointment as the executor of the estate.

On May 23, 2006, following a hearing on May 19, 2006, the court ordered Towle's powers as personal representative suspended, pending a decision on the purported holographic will.

A hearing was held [and] … the court granted Cox's petitions and issued orders entering the holographic will into probate and naming Cox as executor of the decedent's will.

Towle … appeals the order admitting the holographic will to probate and the order appointing Cox as executor.

Evidence

Cox, Towle, and Virginia Towle, the decedent's first wife, testified at the hearing. Testimony centered around the circumstances in which the will was found, the decedent's customary way of signing and completing documents, the relationship the decedent had with his children and stepchildren, and his expressions of his testamentary wishes.

After the decedent's death, Towle was unable to locate a will in the decedent's belongings and thus began probate proceedings based on the understanding that no will existed. About a week after the decedent's death, Cox found what appeared to be a holographic will in "the center drawer of [decedent's] desk" and later brought this to the attention of Towle's attorney. The desk contained other important documents such as bank statements and tax returns. The center drawer did not appear to contain any important documents other than a checkbook.

The document found by Cox was handwritten on the front and back of the first page of a note pad. The entire text was written in block-style capital letters. The next two sheets of the note pad were blank. After the blank pages, the next page of the note pad contained what appeared to be a list of movies, in the same block printing. The remaining pages were blank.

The words "Last Will, Etc. or What? Of Homer Eugene Williams" appear at the top of the document, followed by the decedent's address. The document then names Deborah Cox and Lorna Williams as executors, states their relationships to the decedent (stepdaughter and sister-in-law respectively), and includes their addresses. It then states, "Power of Attorney: Now Deborah Cox." This is followed by a disposition of the decedent's collectibles. The document says, "All My Collictables: Everything including two pistols and two rifles, none fired: to Nephew Kirk Bell." Kirk Bell's address is included. Next is a paragraph stating, "In the event of a serious sickness or accident: I do not want to be kept alive by life support means. I name my executors to see to my wishes are carried out." Then there is a heading entitled "My Estate." This is followed by two items — "House" and "Bank Account." The present market value of the house is stated to be "$225,000 to $350,000." The bank accounts include "Checking and Savings," but no balances are stated. The final paragraph states, "I would like my step daughter, Debra Cox to be able to live in the house as long as she wants before putting it up for sale."

Cox testified that the name written at the top of this document appeared to be written by the decedent. She explained that the decedent often left her notes to do things for him that were in block letters, with his name also written in block letters, similar to that on the holographic will. Cox had never seen the decedent write in cursive, although she had come across checks where he had signed his name. Cox explained that her stepfather was aware of the value of properties in the neighborhood because he would talk to people on the block when properties were for sale. Therefore, she believed that his estimate of the value of the house at $225,000 to $350,000 likely reflected values at the time he wrote the document. Cox estimated that the current value of the house is approximately $700,000, which she believed indicated that the document was written some years ago. Where she found the notepad, in the decedent's desk drawer, he would have had easy access to it.

Cox testified that the decedent had told her that "he put [her and his sister-in law] both down as the executor for his will." He was aware that Cox had previously been the executor for her grandmother's estate and he knew that the probate had gone smoothly. Cox testified that she is "the general cashier in charge of the cash" at the Marriott Hotel in Santa Clara. In this position, she handles forty-nine thousand dollars in cash each day. Prior to being the general cashier, Cox was "the accounts payable" person and was in charge of "paying bills." Cox also testified that "on two occasions" her stepfather had promised her the house. He had told her "if I stayed there with him, I would get the house if he died, and then also when the house was paid off and he showed me the paper from the bank and says now, you don't have anything to worry about." The decedent had two life insurance policies. One was payable to Cox, and her niece was the beneficiary of the other one.

The decedent and Virginia Towle divorced when their two children, Eric and Gayle, were three and seven respectively. Virginia Towle remarried four years later and subsequently began using Towle as her last name and the last name for her children. The decedent also remarried and began living with his second wife and her children, including Cox. In the 1970's, they moved as a family to 1945 Serge Avenue, San Jose, where the decedent lived until his death in 2005. Cox left home while in college, but moved back into the home at 1945 Serge Avenue for good in 1988, at her stepfather's request after her mother had died. She provided companionship and care for her stepfather for the last 17 years of his life. She did things such as fixing his dinner, cleaning, shopping, doing laundry, running errands, picking up medications, and taking him to the doctor. When he became ill, she continued to take care of him. The night before he died, she went to the hospital with him and stayed with him until he died. The Towle family decided not to have a funeral because the family had plans for Virginia Towle's birthday. Cox later learned that the cremation had taken place and that the ashes had been sent back to Nebraska. She and her niece were very upset by this.

Cox testified that she and her stepfather had a close, loving, familial relationship. She called him "dad." He had mentioned to her that he wanted to adopt her. In contrast, she testified that the decedent had a "distant" relationship with his biological children. She said that Eric Towle only visited his father "five times" in thirty years, although he lived in Scotts Valley and worked in San Jose. His father's home was only approximately 15 minutes off of the route Towle would take back and forth to work. Cox thought Towle called his father "two or three times a year." Cox remembered four occasions when the decedent's daughter visited him in thirty years. She did not remember the decedent's daughter calling. Cox felt that the families were completely separate after the divorce and that the decedent essentially became part of his second wife's family. She said her stepfather had been "very upset" when he found out that his biological children were no longer using his name.

Towle and Virginia Towle provided testimony that conflicted with Cox's testimony regarding family relationships and the way the decedent wrote documents. Virginia Towle testified that the decedent loved his biological children and that she and her children socialized with the decedent "constantly." "He was invited to everything and anything that had to do with graduation, special performances in school.... There was constantly baptisms and weddings.... [We] were always there together." Virginia Towle explained that Cox "never" attended those events and that the decedent never discussed Cox. Virginia Towle continues her relationship with the decedent's remaining siblings. She testified that the funeral was not held for the decedent because "no one was interested and it seemed why, there was no one to go to it."

Virginia Towle testified that she had never seen the decedent print anything and that "any letters, documents and things were always written" rather than being printed. Additionally, Virginia Towle had asked the decedent about making a will at "a party about ten years ago." She explained, "I said, have you done anything about the will and the property? He said I'll do it, I'll do it. I go, you have to. What about the house? He said it goes to Gail and Eric."

Towle testified that he "had a very good relationship with [his] father." He did not see him regularly because "I was in a very busy phase of my life, and he basically, like many elderly people, became much more bound to his routines, and the list of things he would do got shorter and shorter." According to Towle, the relationship was not "estranged" and the decedent sent Towle and his sister "birthday and Christmas cards every year." The cards to Towle were signed, "love, dad." He also sent his grandchildren "cards and gifts." Towle testified that Cox's relationship with the decedent was not close. "He never talked about her and she seemed to be living a separate life.... [T]here was nothing they ever did together." Pictures introduced during Towle's testimony depicted the decedent with his biological children and their families at family events such as a wedding and a christening.

Towle testified that he had never seen his father write any documents in block letters similar to that in the purported holographic will. He introduced credit cards, checks, and identification cards, all of which the decedent had signed in cursive. Towle identified the signatures on those documents as his father's.

ANALYSIS

The Holographic Will Statute

... The primary purpose of the holographic will statute is to prevent fraud by requiring that the material provisions be in the testator's writing. (*Estate of Southworth* (1996) 51 Cal.App.4th 564, 59 Cal.Rptr.2d 272.) "Whether a document should be admitted to probate as a holographic will depends on proof of its authorship and authenticity, and whether the words establish that it was intended to be the author's last will and testament at the time she [or he] wrote it." (*Id.* at p. 571, 59 Cal.Rptr.2d 272.) "Courts are to use common sense in evaluating whether a document constitutes a holographic will." (*Id.* at p. 570, 59 Cal.Rptr.2d 272; *Estate of Black, supra,* 30 Cal.3d at pp. 885–886, 181 Cal.Rptr. 222, 641 P.2d 754.)

As the Supreme Court observed in *Estate of Black, supra,* 30 Cal.3d 880, 181 Cal.Rptr. 222, 641 P.2d 754, "'[t]he policy of the law is toward "a construction favoring validity, in determining whether a will has been executed in conformity with statutory requirements." [citations].'" (*Id.* at p. 883, 181 Cal.Rptr. 222, 641 P.2d 754.) The high court affirmed "'"the tendency of both the courts and the Legislature ... toward greater liberality in accepting a writing as an holographic will...."'" [Citation.] "'*Substantial compliance with the statute, and not absolute precision is all that is required....*'" [Citation.]" (*Ibid.,* original italics; see also *Estate of Baker* (1963) 59 Cal.2d 680, 683, 31 Cal.Rptr. 33, 381 P.2d 913.)

The Signature Requirement

Appellant's primary argument is that the will was not a holographic will because it did not contain a valid signature. Since the trial court admitted the holographic will to probate, we must presume that the court found it complied with the statute requiring that "the signature and the material provisions are in the handwriting of the testator." (§ 6111.) Two components of the signature requirement are relevant here: the location of the name in the document, and whether the testator's use of block letters constituted his signature.

A. Location of the Signature

There is no requirement that the signature on a holographic will must be at the end of the document, so long as it appears from the document itself that the signature was intended to authenticate the document. "It is settled in California that the signature need not be located at the end but may appear in another part of the document, provided the testator wrote his name there with the intention of authenticating or executing the instrument as his will." (*Estate of Bloch* (1952) 39 Cal.2d 570, 572–573, 248 P.2d 21.) ...

In the holographic will before us, ... the testator did not include his name at the end of the document. However, the evidence on the face of the document as a whole supports a finding that the name was placed with the intention of authenticating the document. The phrase "Last Will ... of Homer Eugene Williams" located at the top of the document is almost identical to the title of the holographic will in Morgan. In addition, there are other factors indicating that the document was complete. Cases have shown that completeness is highly relevant in determining if the name was written with an intent to authenticate the document.

"From the earliest consideration of the question, completeness of the testamentary declaration has been deemed sufficient evidence of the 'signing' of the writing, even though the declarant's name was written by him at a place other than the end." (*Estate of Kinney, supra,* 16 Cal.2d at p. 56, 104 P.2d 782 (*Kinney*).) In *Kinney,* the name of the decedent is included in only one location, after the date at the top of the page. The first sentence states, "I Anna Leona Graves Kinney, do bequeath all my possessions to my four sisters who were living in 1923." (*Id.* at p. 52, 104 P.2d 782.) The court noted that two characteristics indicated the document was complete. First, "[i]t was written with studied care, indicated by the fact that the decedent copied into her will the names and addresses of her sisters who were living at the time stated...." (*Id.* at p. 55, 104 P.2d 782.) Second, "[t]he fact that sufficient space remained on the paper to include additional writing if the decedent intended any further declaration is also some evidence of finality and completeness." (*Ibid.*) The court concluded: "The writing here involved appears to be a complete testamentary declaration." (*Ibid.*)

The document before us has similar indicia of completeness. First, the decedent took the time, "with studied care," to list the addresses of those people included in the will: Cox, his sister-in-law, and his nephew. (*Kinney, supra,* 16 Cal.2d at p. 55, 104 P.2d 782.) He also wrote down his own address. Second, as in *Kinney,* there was sufficient room at the end of the document for the decedent to write more if he had wanted to do so. Another characteristic indicating completeness was the age of the document. Here the inference could be drawn from the property values stated in the document that it was written a number of years ago. Cox testified that she found it in the decedent's center desk drawer, where it was readily available had he wanted to change or add to it. All of this evidence reasonably supports the conclusion that "the writer *had done everything* that he intended to do." (*Estate of Brooks, supra,* 214 Cal. at p. 140, 4 P.2d 148, italics in original.)

The case before us differs from *Estate of Bernard* (1925) 197 Cal. 36, 239 P. 404, in which the document clearly appeared to be unfinished. There the court wrote: "The abrupt termination of the document near the middle of the last page is a strong indication of decedent's intent to do something more in order to make it a complete will." (*Id.* at p. 40, 239 P. 404.) In contrast, here the decedent appointed an executor, disposed of his collectables, listed assets for reference, and then indicated his intention for the house. Unlike the will in *Brooks, supra,* the document ended with a period. (See also *Estate of Bloch, supra,* 39 Cal.2d at p. 575, 248 P.2d 21 (*Bloch*) [court noted that the document appeared to have a period at the end when determining if it was complete].)

From an evaluation of the whole document in the case before us, it appears that the name at the top of the document was intended as a mark of execution....

Under the foregoing cases, the document before us provides sufficient indicia of completeness from which to conclude that the name at the top was intended to be a mark of authentication. "'When the name is used to identify the decedent as the author of the alleged will … or to identify the instrument as decedent's will … and in addition the instrument appears to be a complete testamentary document, it may reasonably be inferred that the name was placed where it was with the intention of executing the instrument. In such cases the name is linked to the alleged testamentary act and the probabilities that it was intended as a signature are strong.'" (*Estate of Rowe* (1964) 230 Cal.App.2d 442, 447, 41 Cal.Rptr. 52.)

B. Form of the Signature

Appellant contends that the decedent's name at the top of the document is written in block letters, and therefore, cannot be considered a signature. This argument is based upon the decision in *Estate of Twohig* (1986) 178 Cal.App.3d 555, 223 Cal.Rptr. 352 (*Twohig*). *Twohig* concerned a handwritten codicil to an executed formal will. However, the testator failed to sign the codicil....

Our case is distinguishable from *Twohig*. In *Twohig*, the codicil did not include the testator's name at all. There was therefore no authenticating mark from which an intent to execute the document could be inferred. Further, it appeared that the testator had intended to sign it because he wrote "signed" on a particular date. Thus, unlike our case, the document on its face tended to show that there was something else the testator intended to add before the document was complete, namely his signature. Finally, there was no issue in our case that the document attempted to modify a valid will. The holographic will in our case was the testator's only expression of his testamentary wishes. Finally, there was no issue in our case that the document attempted to modify a valid will. The holographic will in our case was the testator's only expression of his testamentary wishes.

Appellant asserts that the block letters at the top of the document are not in the form the decedent used to sign legal documents and, therefore, it must be found that the document was not properly executed. However, several cases illustrate that the way a testator signs a holographic will does not need to be identical to a signature used to sign other legal documents. In *Estate of Morris* (1969) 268 Cal.App.2d 638, 640, 74 Cal.Rptr. 32 (*Morris*), the court found that "[t]he use of the initials as a signature was an effective signing of the will. [Citations.]" The words, "Love from 'Muddy,'" signed at the end of a holographic will in the form of a letter, were also considered a valid signature. (*Estate of Button* (1930) 209 Cal. 325, 328, 334, 287 P. 964 (*Button*).) And similarly, in *Estate of Henderson* (1925) 196 Cal. 623, 634, 238 P. 938 (*Henderson*), the court found the phrase "Your loving mother" constituted a valid signature.

    . . .

Other Evidence of Testamentary Intent

"Before an instrument may be admitted to probate as a will, it must appear from its terms, viewed in the light of the surrounding circumstances, that it was executed with testamentary intent. [Citations.]" (*Estate of Geffene* (1969) 1 Cal.App.3d 506, 512, 81 Cal.Rptr. 833.) Therefore, we must evaluate whether there was substantial evidence supporting a finding that the holographic document was intended to be a testamentary document. It is established that "'"[n]o particular words are necessary to show a testamentary intent. It must appear only that the maker intended by it to dispose of property after his death, and parol evidence as to the attending circumstances is admissible." [Citation.]'" (*Estate of Spitzer* (1925) 196 Cal. 301, 307, 237 P. 739 (*Spitzer*).)

Appellant contends that three characteristics of the will undermine the conclusion that the document is testamentary. First, he asserts that the title "Last Will Etc. or What?" creates an ambiguity and implies that the decedent was unaware of what he was writing. Second, he contends the failure of the document to dispose of all of the decedent's property indicates it is not testamentary in nature. Third, appellant asserts that the statement "I would like ..." in the provision regarding the house (italics added) is ambiguous and does not clearly demonstrate an intent on the part of the decedent to dispose of his property. We address each of these contentions separately.

... "In determining whether the instrument propounded was intended to be testamentary, reference will be had to the surrounding circumstances, and the language will be construed in the light of these circumstances. If it shall then appear that the instrument was intended to be testamentary, the court will give effect to the intention, if it can be done consistently with the language of the instrument and the particular form of the instrument is immaterial." (*Id.* at pp. 799–800, 222 P.2d 692.)

"'"The true test of the character of an instrument is not the testator's realization that it is a will, but his intention to create a revocable disposition of his property to accrue and take effect only upon his death and passing no present interest." [Citation.]'" (*Spitzer, supra,* 196 Cal. at pp. 307–308, 237 P. 739.) In the instant case, the text of the document indicates that the intent of the decedent was to dispose of his property upon his death. As in Smilie the parts of the text that are confusing or extraneous, such as the words "Etc. or What?" can be ignored as surplusage in order to uphold the intent of the decedent. Intent is demonstrated on the face of the document by the use of the words "Last Will" in the title, the naming of an executor, and the disposal of identified property. The decedent clearly contemplated that the identified property would be disposed of after his death.

Similarly, the inclusion of instructions regarding the decedent's wishes upon a serious illness, and the mention of Deborah Cox as having his power of attorney, which would normally be provisions that would be made effective during the person's lifetime, could also have been properly ignored by the trial court. In *Estate of Sargavak* (1950) 35 Cal.2d 93, 216 P.2d 850, the decedent wrote a letter shortly before her death that included testamentary and non-testamentary provisions. The court held that the decedent "decided to leave her property to two men she had known for more than forty years and for whom she had demonstrated a warm personal affection. This purpose is clearly expressed by the terms of the instrument. It is not negatived by evidence that she had an additional purpose, expressed in the letter and corroborated by the testimony upon which contestants rely.... The inclusion of nontestamentary provisions with those of a testamentary nature does not make the instrument inoperative as a will." (*Id.* at p. 101, 216 P.2d 850.) In our case as well, the non-testamentary provisions, and the decedent's uncertainty about the proper title, do not serve to make the instrument inoperative as a will.

Appellant's second contention is that the will is invalid because it does not dispose of all of the decedent's property. However, in *Estate of Rowe, supra,* 230 Cal.App.2d 442, 41 Cal.Rptr. 52, the court found a holographic will to be valid that did not dispose of all of the decedent's property....

In the case before us, the failure of the decedent to dispose of all of his property similarly does not compel a conclusion that the will is invalid or that the document lacks indicia of testamentary intent. Decedent specifically expressed a testamentary intent and disposed of some of his property. In particular, the phrase, "All my collectables: everything including two pistols and two rifles, none fired: to nephew Kirk Bell ..." in combination with the title, "Last Will ..." indicates that the decedent had a testamentary intent.

Appellant next contends that the words "I would like," with regard to the house, do not show testamentary intent, but are rather a suggestion or recommendation. Whether these words are construed as an expression of testamentary intent or a suggestion depends on whether they indicate an intended disposition of property after the testator's death, or whether they are directed to a beneficiary to make some further division or disposition of property.

... [T]he language in the holographic will before us does not express a suggestion or wish to a legatee or devisee regarding the future disposition of property being devised. Rather it is an expression of the testator's intent as to the house he and his stepdaughter are living in, in the event of his death. It provides: "I would like my step daughter, Debra Cox, to be able to live in the house as long as she wants before putting it up for sale." There is no one else named in the will as a devisee of this property. It is reasonable to conclude that the phrase, "I would like," in this context is addressed to the executors of the estate, who had been previously identified in the document. Therefore, under the cases cited above, this phrase can be construed as an expression of testamentary intent, rather than a suggestion.

Finally, we note that the evidence presented at trial supported the finding that the document in this case was written with testamentary intent. Declarations of the testator are admissible to demonstrate a testamentary intent. (*Estate of Spies* (1948) 86 Cal.App.2d 87, 194 P.2d 83 (*Spies*).) ...

In the case before us, Cox's testimony as to the decedent's express wishes upon his death provided evidence, similar to that in *Spies,* that the holographic document, which was consistent with those wishes, was "testamentary in character." (*Spies, supra,* 86 Cal.App.2d at p. 91, 194 P.2d 83.) Cox testified that the decedent had told her that he would make provision for her regarding the house if he died. She also testified that he asked her to be executor and that he told her he had "put us both [Cox and his sister-in-law] down as the executor for his will." As in *Spies,* testimony regarding the decedent's statements about his will and future intentions were admissible to demonstrate testamentary intent. This testimony, in addition to the title of the document as a "Last Will," the "studied care" with which the decedent set forth the names and addresses of those identified in the will (*Estate of Kinney, supra,* 16 Cal.2d at p. 55, 104 P.2d 782), the indicia of completeness of the document, and the express terms disposing of some of the decedent's property, all support a finding that the document was written with testamentary intent.

DISPOSITION

The orders are affirmed.

Notes

1. *Judicial approach*: How far have the California courts come since *Estate of Billings*? To the extent they have adopted substantial compliance with respect to the holographic statutory requirements, should they adopt substantial compliance with respect to the attested statutory requirements?

2. *Paradigm scenarios*: The *Estate of Billings* case is fairly representative of the traditional holographic will: one that is essentially entirely handwritten by the testator. While the *Estate of Williams* case is hardly representative of a typical holographic will vis-à-vis style and presentation, it too is traditional in nature in that the document is entirely in the testator's "handwriting."

When the legislature changed the law to no longer require the entire document to be in the testator's handwriting, but only the "material provisions," it led to testators going down to their local business supply store and purchasing a pre-printed form will, filling in the blanks in their handwriting, and then signing it. Should such a document qualify as a valid holographic will? Are the "material provisions" in the testator's handwriting? What constitutes the "material provisions"?

In re Estate of Johnson

630 P.2d 1039 (Ariz. 1981)

WREN, Chief Judge.

This appeal involves the question of whether the handwritten portions on a printed will form, submitted to the trial court as a holographic will, were sufficient to satisfy the requirements of A.R.S. § 14-2503 that the material provisions of such a will must be entirely in the handwriting of the testator.

Arnold H. Johnson, the decedent, died on January 28, 1978 at the age of 79....

The document claimed by appellants to be decedent's last will and testament was a printed will form available in various office supply and stationery stores. It bore certain printed provisions followed by blanks where the testator could insert any provisions he might desire. The entire contents of the instrument in question are set forth below, with the portions ... [*italicized and bolded* being the portions that] are in the decedent's handwriting.

THE LAST WILL AND TESTAMENT

I *Arnold H. Johnson* a resident of *Mesa Arizona* of *Maricopa* County, State of Arizona, being of sound and disposing mind and memory, do make, publish and declare this my last WILL AND TESTAMENT, hereby revoking and making null and void any and all other last Wills and Testments heretofore by me made.

FIRST — My will is that all my just debts and funeral expenses and any Estate or Inheritance taxes shall be paid out of my Estate, as soon after my decease as shall be found convenient.

SECOND — I give devise and bequeath to *My six living children as follows:*

To *John M. Johnson*   *1/8 of my Estate*
Helen Marchese   *1/8*
Sharon Clements   *1/8*
Mirriam Jennings   *1/8*
Mary D. Korman   *1/8*
A. David Johnson   *1/8*

To W. V. Grant, Souls Harbor Church
3200 W. Davis Dallas Texas   *1/8*

To Barton Lee McLain
and Marie Gansels
Address   *901 E. Broadway* ~~*Phoenix*~~
~~*Az*~~   *Mesa*   *1/8*

I nominate and appoint *Mirriam Jennings my Daughter* of *Nashville Tenn.* as execut*ress* of this my Last Will and Testament *Adress 1247 Saxon Drive Nashville Tenn.*

IN TESTIMONY WHEREOF, I have set my hand to this. My Last Will and Testament, at _____ this *22* day of *March*, in the year of our Lord, One Thousand Nine Hundred *77*

The foregoing instrument was signed by said *Arnold H. Johnson* in our presence, and by _____ published and declared as and for _____ Last Will and Testament, and at _____ request, and in _____ presence, and in presence of each other, we hereunto subscribe our Names as Attesting Witnesses, at _____ This *22* day of *March*, 1977

My Commission expires

Jan. 16, 1981   Ann C. McGonagill
                (Notary public seal)

Initially it is to be noted that Arizona has adopted the Uniform Probate Code, the holographic will provisions being contained in § 2-503, and found in A.R.S. § 14-2503:

> A will which does not comply with § 14-2502 is valid as a holographic will, whether or not witnessed, if the signature and the material provisions are in the handwriting of the testator.

The statutory requirement that the material provisions be drawn in the testator's own handwriting requires that the handwritten portion clearly express a testamentary intent. *Estate of Morrison*, 55 Ariz. 504, 103 P.2d 669 (1940). Appellants argue that the purported will here should thus be admitted to probate, since all the key dispositive provisions essential to its validity as a will are in the decedent's own handwriting; and further, when all the printed provisions are excised, the requisite intent to make a will is still evidenced. We do not agree. In our opinion, the only words which establish this requisite testamentary intent on the part of the decedent are found in the printed portion of the form.

The official comment to § 2-503 of the Uniform Probate Code (U.L.A.) sheds some light upon the situation where, as here, a printed will form is used:

> By requiring only the "material provisions" to be in the testator's handwriting (rather than requiring, as some existing statutes do, that the will be "entirely" in the testator's handwriting) a holograph may be valid even though immaterial parts such as date or introductory wording be printed or stamped. A valid holograph might even be executed on some printed will forms if the printed portion could be eliminated and the handwritten portion could evidence the testator's will. For persons unable to obtain legal assistance, the holographic will may be adequate....

This court, in *In re Estate of Mulkins*, 17 Ariz.App. 179, 180, 496 P.2d 605, 606 (1972) traced earlier Arizona decisions and determined that the "important thing is that the testamentary part of the will be wholly written by the testator and of course signed by him" (citing *Estate of Morrison, supra*) (emphasis in original). Mulkins also found that the printed words of the will, set forth below were not essential to the meaning of the handwritten words and could not be held to defeat the intention of the deceased otherwise clearly expressed.

It is thus clear that, under the terminology of the statute and the comment thereto, an instrument may not be probated as a holographic will where it contains words not in the handwriting of the testator if such words are essential to the testamentary disposition. However, the mere fact that the testator used a blank form, whether of a will or some other document, does not invalidate what would otherwise be a valid will if the printed words may be entirely rejected as surplusage.

In support of their position appellants rely on *Estate of Blake v. Benza*, 120 Ariz. 552, 587 P.2d 271 (App.1978). In *Blake* this court upheld the trial court's admission to probate, as a valid holograph the postscript to a personal letter:

> P.S. You can have my entire estate.

> /x/ Harry J. Blake (SAVE THIS).

There having been no contention that the letter was not written and signed by the decedent, it was held that the postscript was more than a mere casual statement, and was deemed sufficient to demonstrate a testamentary intent. Analogizing to *Blake* which held that the use of the word "estate" by the decedent inferred that he was making a disposition of his property to take effect upon his death, appellants point to that portion of the document here which states:

TO (the name of the respective person) 1/8 of my estate.

as being sufficient to likewise establish the requisite intent. Again, we do not agree.

Blake did not rely solely upon the use of the word "estate" to determine that the testator had a testamentary intent. The opinion focused upon the emphasized words "SAVE THIS" to support the position that the letter was to have a future significance. The fact that the formal signature following the dispositive clause bore the testator's name in full as opposed to simply "Your Uncle Harry", as in previous letters, was also supportive of a testamentary intent. Finally, the dispositive clause itself in Blake contained the phrase "you can have," which clearly imported a future connotation.

Contrasting the *Blake* will to the handwritten segments of the purported will before us, we find a marked difference. Though the decedent here used the word "estate", this word alone is insufficient to indicate an animus testandi.

In Webster's New Collegiate Dictionary, G & C Merriam & Company, Springfield, 1975 at 391, one of the definitions of the word, "estate" is, "the assets and liabilities left by a person at death." However, the same word is also defined as:

the degree, quality, nature, and extent of one's interest in land or other property. POSSESSIONS, PROPERTY esp : a person's property in land and tenements.

Clearly then the word "estate" is not the sine qua non of an intent to draft a will. Likewise, the word "TO", by itself, has neither a present nor a future meaning. We are thus unable to determine from the handwritten portions of the will form whether it was meant by decedent to have a testamentary significance and thus hold that the trial court did not err in refusing to admit it to probate.

Admittedly, as pointed out in the special concurrence, our decision here might well do violence to the intent of the decedent, Arnold H. Johnson. However, as was stated by our Supreme Court in *Estate of Tyrrell*, 17 Ariz. 418, 153 P. 767 (1915):

If the statute requires the testator to sign the instrument and he omits to sign it, although he intended to do so, such omission may not be cured by his intention. The omission is fatal to the validity of the will. The omission of any of the requirements of the statute will not be overlooked on the ground that it is beyond question that the paper was executed by the decedent as his will while he possessed abundant testamentary capacity, and was free from fraud, constraint or undue influence, and there is no question of his testamentary purpose, and no obstacle to carrying it into effect had his will been executed in the manner prescribed by the statute. (Citations omitted) 17 Ariz. at 422, 153 P. at 768.

Further, quoting from *In re Walker's Estate*, 110 Cal. 387, 42 P. 815, 52 Am.St.Rep. 104, 30 L.R.A. 460, 42 P. 815, Tyrrell went on to state:

When a will is proved every exertion of the court is directed to giving effect to the wishes of the testator therein expressed, but in the proving of the instrument the sole consideration before the court is whether or not the legislative mandates have been complied with. id. (emphasis added).

We thus have stringent requirements for finding that a document, which might appear in a thousand different forms, is a valid and authentic holographic will.

This document having failed as a will, we dismiss appellants' argument that we may look to extrinsic evidence to determine the testator's intent. Appellants' motion to strike an instrument attached to the estate's reply memorandum and response to cross motion for summary judgment, purportedly written by the deceased, is therefore granted.

Judgment affirmed.

CONTRERAS, Judge, specially concurring.

I find myself compelled to concur in this decision because established legal principles clearly indicate that the trial court did not err in refusing to admit the document to probate....

... But it is an illogical result which defeats the intent of the decedent and fails to uphold the proffered will. In addition, it ignores the practical consideration of a lay person who desires to dispose of his small estate without the assistance of an attorney.

Notes and Problems

1. Is testamentary intent a material provision? Following the *Johnson* decision and its progeny, the California legislature amended section 6111 to add subsection (c). How would the *Johnson* printed form will type of case be decided in California today? Was the legislature a bit too focused in its amendment? What if a decedent takes out his or her lawyer-prepared, validly executed, typed will, and on the bottom of the last page, under the signature, handwrites "And I also give $50,000 to my good friend Franco." The testator then initials and dates it. Is that a valid holographic codicil? (The legislature also added Probate Code Section 6111.5 in 1990 in response to the *Johnson* case and its progeny).

2. *Intent versus formalities*: In light of the court's analysis and decision in *In re Estate of Williams*, and in light of the legislative action in amending Probate Code Sections 6111 and 6111.5, at least with respect to holographic wills, would you say California takes a formalistic approach or a more intent-based approach?

3. *Internet-based form wills*: What if, in *Johnson*, instead of purchasing a pre-printed form will, the testator went to his computer, downloaded a form will from the Internet, typed in the provisions, printed it out, signed it in his study, and then died later that night? Is it a valid holographic will? Does California's harmless error doctrine apply? If so, should a court probate it?

4. Testatrix, Eileen Foxley, is an independent woman who is used to handling her own affairs. She had raised six daughters and two sons. She validly executed an

irrevocable trust and will that left her estate to her daughters equally (each daughter was named). She took the will—along with a photocopy of it—home with her after executing it. Thereafter, her daughter Jane died, survived by her son Hogan (who then would take Jane's share under Foxley's trust and will). Foxley did not like Hogan; she believed he had abused his mother. After Jane's death, Foxley tried to amend the trust to remove Hogan, but her attorney explained to her that it was impossible. Foxley was so adamant that he not participate in the trust she instructed the attorney to "buy him out." When the attorney offered to help with the will, she told him "take care of it." The attorney interpreted her response as her telling him "to butt out." After Foxley's death, the will and photocopy were found. The will had no marks on it, but on the photocopy, in the clause leaving her estate to her daughters, she had drawn a line through her daughter Jane's name. Moreover, in the margin, she had written, signed, and dated the following: *"her share to be divided between five daughters."* Does the writing qualify as a valid holographic codicil? Which, if any, elements are at issue? How so? *See In re Estate of Foxley,* 575 N.W.2d 150 (Neb. 1998).

5. *The modern trend judicial approach*: As you may have sensed, holographic will cases are often fact sensitive. Courts appear rather willing to stretch the law to uphold what appears to be a holographic will. Assume the following handwritten index card is found among Tai-Kin Wong's belongings following his death. Is there enough on the card to be a valid holographic will?

> *All Tai-Kin Wong's → Xi Zhao, my best half*
> *TKW 12-31-92.*

Estate of Wong

40 Cal. App. 4th 1198 (Ct. App. 1995)

WUNDERLICH, Associate Justice.

In this case we review the trial court's decision that a document containing eight words, seven of them proper names and an appellation, constituted a holographic will.

Tai-Kin Wong (Tai) was a successful 44-year-old businessman who until just before death had a history of good health. He was living with his girlfriend Xi Zhao (Xi), and he enjoyed a close and loving relationship with his large family. On New Year's Eve in 1992, he took ill and died in a hospital emergency room of unexplained causes. Sometime after his death, found in his office was a sealed envelope, decorated with stickers and containing a handwritten note which read "All Tai-Kin Wong's → Xi Zhao, my best half TKW 12-31-92." This document—containing no subject, no verb, no description of property, and no indication of its subject matter or purpose—was found by the trial court to be a holographic will, passing Tai's entire estate to Xi. Tai's father, Kok-Cheong Wong (appellant) brought this appeal....

FACTS/PROCEDURAL HISTORY

At the time of his death, Tai was 44 years old. He had never married and he had no children. For the previous three years, he and Xi had lived together in Saratoga. Tai and Xi had met in 1987 at a scientific conference. They fell in love and began to live together in 1989 after Xi received her doctorate in cell biology. They lived together until the time of Tai's death on New Year's Eve.

When Xi relocated to California to be with Tai, she turned down several job offers that were more attractive than the one she accepted at Stanford University. Previously she had visited Tai in California and they had kept in close touch. She immediately moved into his house in Saratoga and worked at her full-time job at Stanford. Tai, meanwhile, was engaged in running a company he founded with his brother, Danny Wong (Danny) called Baekon, Inc. Xi helped Tai run Baekon, working for Baekon in the evenings and on weekends. In 1990 Tai and Xi founded a new company, Transgenic Technologies, Inc. (TTI) which they owned equally. Tai worked every day at TTI in Fremont, developing the new business. Baekon was wound down; Danny transferred his interest in the business to Tai.

Tai and Xi thus lived together and worked together for the last three years of Tai's life. Whether their love relationship was flourishing or floundering was disputed at trial. Though supposedly lovers, on the day of Tai's death, New Year's Eve, they had arranged to dine separately—Tai with his close friend, Dr. Jianmin Liu and his girlfriend, and Xi with a man she describes as then a casual social acquaintance, Brien Wilson, a local attorney.

The evidence Xi introduced tended to show that she was close to Tai's family, indeed, practically accepted as a member of it. After Mr. Wong came home from the hospital following a stroke, Tai and Xi took care of him four nights a week, Monday through Thursday. Mr. Wong viewed Xi as his son's companion, and presented her with gifts of money, traditionally given only to family members in Chinese families.

When Tai died on December 31, 1992, it was in the throes of an illness which was similar in its symptoms to sicknesses that had afflicted him two or three times earlier that month. On December 11, 1992, he felt very ill while dining in a restaurant. Xi told him to see a doctor. On December 20, 1992, Tai collapsed at home but recovered and told Xi he would be fine. On December 21st he called Xi at her Stanford office and told her he was sick again. Xi told Tai to call "911"; he was taken to Washington Hospital in Fremont by ambulance. He spent three days in the intensive care unit. Doctors were unable to diagnose his illness, but wished to do a test which Tai declined. On December 31st, he again became ill, was taken to the hospital by ambulance, and died with the same symptoms.

The onset of the final episode was unclear. During the day on New Year's Eve, Tai was working at his office in Fremont. He had business meetings that afternoon until about 4:30, which Xi and others attended. Although not 100 percent healthy, he appeared to be well and to be functioning well. He called Dr. Liu two or three times to finalize dinner arrangements for the evening. Another employee who was working at the office waved good-bye to Tai at 6 p.m. and he appeared to be just fine. At 7 p.m. Dr. Liu received a call from Tai saying that he was feeling very ill. Dr. Liu's girlfriend advised him to call "911" which Tai did. His friends agreed to come to the Fremont office from Berkeley. When they reached the office the ambulance had already taken Tai to the hospital. The ambulance attendants found Tai conscious upon their arrival at the office building, but he lost consciousness in the ambulance, never regained it, and died at the hospital before midnight.

By the time Dr. Liu and his girlfriend Jennifer Zhang arrived at the hospital, Tai was in a coma. When the doctors told Dr. Liu that Tai was dying, he tried to reach members of Tai's family. Because he did not have their telephone numbers, he called Tai's Saratoga house trying to reach Xi. There was no answer. Meanwhile, Xi was having dinner with Brien Wilson at a fancy French restaurant in Los Gatos. She had concealed from Tai the fact that she was dining on New Year's Eve with Brien Wilson, a man she moved in with two and one-half months after Tai's death. After dinner, she returned to the Saratoga house, and shortly after her arrival she received a call from Dr. Liu informing her that Tai was in the hospital. (Dr. Liu testified he never did reach Xi on the telephone. Rather, she called him at the hospital after Tai's death.) According to Xi, when she arrived at the hospital, close to midnight, Tai was already dead. While Tai had some symptoms similar to those that characterized his illness 10 days earlier, the cause of death was mysterious and has never been determined.

The questioned document or purported will was discovered in the following way: Xi made no effort to find a will at the residence she shared with Tai. Instead, on January 18, 1993, two weeks after Tai's funeral, Xi, Roy Tottingham (then a business consultant to TTI and now vice-president), Dr. Gin Wu (a TTI employee) and Heston Chau (an old friend of Tai's) searched Tai's office. Xi had asked Danny Wong to help go through Tai's papers, but he refused to do it. These four people, then, including Xi, divided the papers into business documents and personal papers and placed them in separate boxes.

During this search they found a sealed envelope in one of Tai's desk drawers, but Xi could not remember which one nor who saw it first. The upper left hand corner contained Tai's address label, the center of the envelope bore two stickers: a rainbow with the words "You're Special," and a rainbow with the words "Love You." This sealed envelope was placed in the box of Tai's personal papers which itself was sealed. Later the sealed box was placed in Xi's office where it remained unopened.

Dr. Victor Vurpillat, (the co-CEO of TTI when Tai was alive), opened the box in Xi's office sometime later. The only item he removed from the box was the envelope with the stickers. Vurpillat took the envelope and the following day he and Roy Tottingham met with TTI's attorney, together with a probate attorney, John Willoughby, who opened the envelope.

After Tai's death, Xi and Tottingham and Vurpillat incorporated a new company called Transcell Therapeutic Infusion, Incorporated. (TTI, Inc.) Obviously the initials are the same as for Transgenic Technologies, Inc. The new business involves intracellular therapy. Its product is one that delivers ribozyme (a specific molecule) into cells to achieve intracellular therapy for patients infected with viruses. Xi claims to have invented the technology used in TTI, Inc. but could not recall when. She was also certain that TTI, Inc.'s processes did not require the use of any TTI or Baekon technology.

Xi filed a petition for probate of the purported will. Xi was first appointed personal representative and Tottingham was appointed special administrator for the purpose of handling Tai's real estate and voting his shares of stock. Mr. Wong, from whom the family had kept word of Tai's death for some six weeks because of Mr. Wong's poor health, filed the will contest on May 14, 1993.

CONTENTIONS OF PARTIES

Appellants contend: the document admitted to probate is not a valid will, because as a matter of law, the words in the document cannot constitute a will and because there is not sufficient evidence of testamentary intent. Appellants also contend that the trial court erroneously excluded decedent's statements regarding his feelings toward respondent and also erred in granting respondent's motion to quash certain deposition subpoenas. Respondent Xi disputes each contention.

DISCUSSION

The document the trial court found to be a will reads as follows: "All Tai Kin Wong's → Xi Zhao, my best half." Beneath are the initials "TKW" and the date "12-31-92." The document is completely handwritten.

. . .

A holographic will is one entirely in the writing of the testator. The requirements are that it be signed, dated, and that it evidence testamentary intent. (See Prob.Code, §6111.) The trial court resolved the issue of whether the will was in the writing of the testator in favor of proponent Xi. Clearly the document is dated at the bottom. Regarding the third requirement, Witkin says "[I]t must appear that decedent intended to make a testamentary disposition by that particular paper, and if this cannot be shown it is immaterial that his testamentary intentions were [or would have been] in conformity with it." (12 Witkin, Summary of Cal.Law (9th ed. 1990) Wills & Probate, §213, p. 251, italics in original.)

No particular words are required to create a will. "Thus, a letter or other informal document will be sufficient if it discloses the necessary testamentary intent, i.e., if it appears that the decedent intended to direct the final disposition of his property after his death. The surrounding circumstances may be considered in reaching a conclusion on this issue. [Citations.]" (12 Witkin, Summary of Cal.Law, supra, §209, p. 248, italics added.) In other words, if it is not completely clear that the document evidences testamentary intent, it is possible to resort to extrinsic evidence of the surrounding circumstances in order to provide it.

...

We can see that the instant case ... differs from even the existing similar cases. In most ... cases..., we find descriptions of property and words expressing donative intent. In the cases in which it is a little bit doubtful whether the proffered document is a will, we often have the express statement of the decedent, made shortly before death, that decedent has written his or her will and provided for decedent's loved ones in a certain letter or in a certain document. Clearly such direct extrinsic evidence is extremely probative on the question of whether a document is a will. In the instant case, we have no such helpful extrinsic evidence.

Appellants contend the document admitted to probate cannot, as a matter of law, constitute a will. We agree.

We consider this document which is offered as a holograph to be unique. The document consists of eight handwritten words—five of them constituting two proper names and three of them constituting an appellation, one arrow, a date and initials at the bottom. This series of words contains no recognizable subject, no verb and no object. The trial court below found these words constituted a valid holographic will under California law, the import of which was to bequeath all of decedent's estate to Xi. We conclude that it simply does not contain words sufficient to constitute a valid will.

No particular words are required to create a will. (*Estate of Weber* (1926) 76 Cal.App. 723, 725, 245 P. 776.) But every will must contain operative words legally sufficient to create a devise of property. (*Estate of Young* (1899) 123 Cal. 337, 343, 55 P. 1011.) In this case, the words are either absent or are so ambiguous in meaning that it is impossible to tell what, if anything, is meant to be given, much less that it is intended to be a transfer of property upon death.

First, no words describe the property allegedly meant to be bequeathed, or even that it is property which is the subject of the note. In attempting to determine the meaning of this first phrase the question is, all of Tai-Kin Wong's what? The trial court found that the absence of a "what" meant all of Tai's property but there is nothing in the document that supports that speculation.

Nor does the document contain any donative words—not "give," "bequeath," "will," or even "want Xi Zhao to have." Instead of a word that indicates a gift or transfer of some sort, Xi contends that the arrow is meant to transfer Tai's entire estate to her upon his death. However, an arrow is not a word at all. It is a symbol with no fixed meaning, either in the general community or as used by the decedent himself. As such, it does not have one meaning which allows it to be used in place of a word, nor can it be used to supply any meaning to the words around it.

Appellants did not find, nor have we, a single case in which a symbol has been used in place of words indicating donative intent in a will. In fact, we have not found a case in which a symbol of no fixed meaning has been used in any material clause of a will. The Probate Code itself assumes that words will be used to create a will. (See, e.g., § 6162.) The entire purpose of a will is to express the decedent's wishes for disposition of his or her property after death. If there are insufficient words in the document to do that, or if there are no words at all but ambiguous symbols, the decedent has failed in his or her purpose even if decedent did intend to write a will. The document in this case falls into that category; it simply does not contain operative words legally sufficient to accomplish a transfer of property upon death. Because this first issue is dispositive, we need not address appellants' other assignments of error.

DISPOSITION

Because the questioned document cannot constitute a will as a matter of law, the judgment is reversed and the trial court is directed to enter judgment in appellants' favor. Costs to appellants.

Notes and Problems

1. *Testamentary intent versus probable intent*? The court made a point of noting that on the evening Wong died: "Xi was having dinner with Brien Wilson at a fancy French restaurant in Los Gatos. She had concealed from Tai the fact that she was dining on New Year's Eve with Brien Wilson, a man she moved in with two and one-half months after Tai's death." Does the court seem to think that is relevant? Is there any evidence that Wong knew she was out having dinner with Wilson that night? Is the court seeking to determine and give effect to Wong's intent at the time he created the index card or his probable intent in light of all the facts (even some he did not know)? Did the court in *In re Estate of Williams* really apply probable intent (was that document *really* a will or was it just a document that the court was convinced more likely expressed his probable intent than the intestate scheme)? Should the courts be more open to probable intent in the context of holographic wills given that they are homemade wills?

2. Testatrix executed a valid holographic will. Paragraph 12 of the will gave her "books and diploma" to her niece, Doris. Thereafter testatrix fell ill and was hospitalized for several weeks. When she was finally well enough, her nephew Fred and his wife took testatrix home. She asked him to retrieve a box from a dining room closet. Inside the box was the holographic will. She instructed Fred to draw a line through Doris's name in paragraph 12 of the will, and to insert, in Fred's handwriting, the following "Fred Bieber daughters." Testatrix died without doing anything else to the will. Does the will qualify as a valid holographic will? The books and diploma in question are of minimal market value. *See In re Estate of Krueger*, 529 N.W.2d 151 (N.D. 1995).

3. The following facts are from a recent California case, *Estate of Southworth*, 59 Cal. Rptr. 2d 272, 274–75 (Ct. App. 1996). Is there a valid holographic will?

   Decedent [Dorothy Southworth] never married and had no children. On March 4, 1986, in response to decedent's request for information, NSAL sent a letter to her describing its lifetime pet care program and explaining how to register for it. NSAL asked that she return its enclosed pet care registration card, contact her attorney to include her bequest to NSAL in her estate and send a copy of the bequest to NSAL. NSAL informed her that "[e]ven if you don't currently have a will, we'll accept your Registration on good faith and maintain an Active file on your pet while you're arranging the Bequest." Decedent never returned the registration card to NSAL.

On September 4, 1987, decedent requested registration with The Neptune Society for cremation of her body upon her death. On the registration form, she stated that she never married and that Neptune should contact the Ventura County Coroner to make arrangements. On the same date, decedent sent a letter to NSAL asking whether or not it destroys animals.

Her letter to NSAL states, "I have been terribly upset since I heard [that NSAL destroys animals] because I have always truly believed that you did not destroy animals and this was the determining factor in my selection of you as the beneficiary of my entire estate as I have no relatives and do not want the State of California, courts, or attorneys to benefit from my hard earned labor.

"I should appreciate greatly if you would clarify this point about the destruction of animals at your shelter and tell me honestly and truly what your policy is [and] not hedge because I have mentioned leaving my estate to your organization."

On September 9, 1987, NSAL wrote to assure her that it would not destroy any pet. NSAL included a brochure regarding estate planning. The brochure explained that a letter or a verbal promise will not effectuate a testamentary gift; that a proper written will is required. The mailing urged members to consult an estate planning attorney to avoid the possibility that the estate might end up with "distant relatives whom you didn't even know." Decedent never prepared a formal will.

NSAL sent a donor card to the decedent. It stated: "Your newest gift to the North Shore Animal League will help get more homeless dogs and cats out of cages and into new homes." The donor card thanked her "for your interest in making a bequest to the League." It explained that she could change her life insurance policy or provide for animals in her will by calling her attorney. It sought gifts and legacies and asked her to complete and return the donor card.

On April 19, 1989, she returned the donor card to NSAL. The card provided three options: a. naming NSAL as a beneficiary of a life insurance policy, b. changing one's will to leave securities or cash to NSAL, or c. not taking immediate action, but stating her intentions.

On the card, the decedent circled printed option (c) which states: "I am not taking action now, but my intention is [in the blank space provided she wrote] My entire estate is to be left to North Shore Animal League."

The donor card also included a printed statement which reads, "The total amount that the animal shelter will someday receive is [she wrote in the blank space] $500,000." The card then stated, "I would like the money used for:

"Food and shelter for the animals

"Adoption Fund to advertise for new owners

"Spaying and Neutering Program

"Unrestricted use[.]"

Decedent placed an "x" next to the food and spaying options listed. She signed and dated the donor card.

On May 10, 1989, NSAL sent a thank you letter to decedent for "letting us know that you will remember the North Shore Animal League in your will." The letter requested that decedent "have your attorney send us a copy of your will[.]"

The Neptune Society asked for additional information to complete the death certificate, pursuant to amendments to the Probate Code. Decedent returned Neptune's supplemental form and stated that there are "[n]o living relatives" and to "[p]lease notify North Shore Animal League." She included NSAL's address, telephone numbers and the name of the executive director of NSAL. She signed the supplemental form and dated it October 20, 1989.

On September 2, 1992, NSAL sent a letter to decedent acknowledging that in March 1989 she wrote NSAL to state that she intended to take action leading to its becoming one of the beneficiaries of her estate. NSAL requested a meeting with decedent, thanking her for her "kind thoughts and generous support." She never responded to this request.

On January 14, 1994, Dorothy Southworth died....

Did Dorothy die testate or intestate?

Chapter 7

Will Revocation

I. Introduction

A will is an ambulatory document: a document that does not take immediate effect upon execution; it becomes effective at some point in the future (i.e., when the testator dies). A will is also revocable. Between the time of execution and the testator's death, the testator can revoke the will at any time (and make a new one if he or she wishes). The fact that a will is revocable gives rise to an obvious question: what is required to properly revoke a will?

In many respects, revoking a will is the inverse of executing a will. Revocation is a testamentary act that requires the same testamentary capacity as is necessary to execute a will. Similar to execution, the most common forms of revocation require intent and an act: more specifically, the intent to revoke and a corresponding act (we will see that the "corresponding act" depends on how the testator is attempting to revoke his or her will). In the will execution material, we examined the tension about which variable should be given more weight in the analytical process—the intent or the act. Historically, strict compliance emphasized the *formalities* associated with the act requirement. In contrast, the modern trend approach (most notably the "substantial compliance/ harmless error" movement) shifts the focus to the intent component.

As you read the revocation material, you might want to keep in mind this historical approach to the two variables. With respect to the law of revocation, have courts historically focused likewise on the formalities surrounding the revocation act? Has there been a modern trend shift to the intent component?

A. The Traditional Approach

Thompson v. Royall
163 Va. 492 (1934)

HUDGINS, Justice.

The only question presented by this record, is whether the will of Mrs. M. Lou Bowen Kroll had been revoked shortly before her death.

The uncontroverted facts are as follows: On the 4th day of September, 1932, Mrs. Kroll signed a will, typewritten on five sheets of legal cap paper; the signature appeared on the last page duly attested by three subscribing witnesses. H. P. Brittain, the executor named in the will, was given possession of the instrument for safe-keeping. A codicil typed on the top third of one sheet of paper dated September 15, 1932, was signed by the testatrix in the presence of two subscribing witnesses. Possession of this instrument was given to Judge S. M. B. Coulling, the attorney who prepared both documents.

On September 19, 1932, at the request of Mrs. Kroll, Judge Coulling, and Mr. Brittain took the will and the codicil to her home where she told her attorney, in the presence of Mr. Brittain and another, to destroy both. But instead of destroying the papers, at the suggestion of Judge Coulling, she decided to retain them as memoranda, to be used as such in the event she decided to execute a new will. Upon the back of the manuscript cover, which was fastened to the five sheets by metal clasps, in the handwriting of Judge Coulling, signed by Mrs. Kroll, there is the following notation:

> "This will null and void and to be only held by H. P. Brittain, instead of being destroyed, as a memorandum for another will if I desire to make same. This 19 Sept 1932
>
>   "M. Lou Bowen Kroll."

The same notation was made upon the back of the sheet on which the codicil was written, except that the name, S. M. B. Coulling, was substituted for H. P. Brittain; this was likewise signed by Mrs. Kroll.

Mrs. Kroll died October 2, 1932, leaving numerous nephews and nieces, some of whom were not mentioned in her will, and an estate valued at approximately $200,000. On motion of some of the beneficiaries, the will and codicil were offered for probate. All the interested parties including the heirs at law were convened, and on the issue, devisavit vel non, the jury found that the instruments dated September 4th and 15, 1932, were the last will and testament of Mrs. M. Lou Bowen Kroll. From an order sustaining the verdict and probating the will this writ of error was allowed.

For more than one hundred years, the means by which a duly executed will may be revoked, have been prescribed by statute. These requirements are found in section 5233 of the 1919 Code, the pertinent parts of which read thus: "No will or codicil, or any part thereof, shall be revoked, unless * * * by a subsequent will or codicil, or by some writing declaring an intention to revoke the same, and executed in the manner in which a will is required to be executed, or by the testator, or some person in his presence and by his direction, cutting, tearing, burning, obliterating, canceling, or destroying the same, or the signature thereto, with the intent to revoke."[1]

The notations, dated September 19, 1932, are not wholly in the handwriting of the testatrix, nor are her signatures thereto attached attested by subscribing witnesses; hence under the statute they are ineffectual as "some writing declaring an intention to revoke." The faces of the two instruments bear no physical evidence of any cutting,

---

1. This method of revoking a will is similar to and based upon the English Wills Act of 1837.

tearing, burning, obliterating, canceling, or destroying. The only contention made by appellants is, that the notation written in the presence, and with the approval, of Mrs. Kroll, on the back of the manuscript cover in the one instance, and on the back of the sheet containing the codicil in the other, constitute 'canceling' within the meaning of the statute.

Both parties concede that to effect revocation of a duly executed will, in any of the methods prescribed by statute, two things are necessary: (1) The doing of one of the acts specified, (2) accompanied by the intent to revoke — the animo revocandi. Proof of either, without proof of the other, is insufficient. [Citation omitted.]

The proof established the intention to revoke. The entire controversy is confined to the acts used in carrying out that purpose. The testatrix adopted the suggestion of her attorney to revoke her will by written memoranda, admittedly ineffectual as revocations by subsequent writings, but appellants contend the memoranda, in the handwriting of another, and testatrix's signatures, are sufficient to effect revocation by cancellation. To support this contention appellants cite a number of authorities which hold that the modern definition of cancellation includes, "any act which would destroy, revoke, recall, do away with, overrule, render null and void, the instrument."

Most of the authorities cited, that approve the above, or a similar meaning of the word, were dealing with the cancellation of simple contracts, or other instruments that require little or no formality in execution. However there is one line of cases which apply this extended meaning of 'canceling' to the revocation of wills. The leading case so holding is *Warner v. Warner's Estate*, 37 Vt. 356. In this case proof of the intent and the act were a notation on the same page with, and below the signature of the testator, reading: 'This will is hereby cancelled and annulled. In full this the 15th day of March in the year 1859,' and written lengthwise on the back of the fourth page of the foolscap paper, upon which no part of the written will appeared, were these words, 'Cancelled and is null and void. (Signed) I. Warner.' It was held this was sufficient to revoke the will under a statute similar to the one here under consideration.

. . .

The construction of the statute in *Warner v. Warner's Estate, supra,* has been criticized by eminent textwriters on wills, and the courts in the majority of the states in construing similar statutes have refused to follow the reasoning in that case. [Citations omitted.]

The above, and other authorities that might be cited, hold that revocation of a will by cancellation within the meaning of the statute, contemplates marks or lines across the written parts of the instrument, or a physical defacement, or some mutilation of the writing itself, with the intent to revoke. If written words are used for the purpose, they must be so placed as to physically affect the written portion of the will, not merely on blank parts of the paper on which the will is written. If the writing intended to be the act of cancelling, does not mutilate, or erase, or deface, or otherwise physically come in contact with any part of written words of the will, it cannot be given any greater weight than a similar writing on a separate sheet of paper, which identifies the will referred to, just as definitely, as does the writing on the back. If a will may be revoked by writing on the back, separable from the will, it may be done by a writing not on the will. This the statute forbids.

The learned trial judge, A. C. Buchanan, in his written opinion, pertinently said:

"The statute prescribes certain ways of executing a will, and it must be so executed in order to be valid, regardless of how clear and specific the intent. It also provides certain ways of revoking and it must be done so in order to a valid revocation, regardless of intent....

"The same reasoning led the Illinois court to the same conclusion in *Dowling v. Gilliland*, * * * [122 N.E. 70, 72 (Ill. Sup. Ct.)], where it is said:

" 'The great weight of authority is to the effect that the mere writing upon a will which does not in any wise physically obliterate or cancel the same is insufficient to work a destruction of a will by cancellation, even though the writing may express an intention to revoke and cancel. This appears to be the better rule. To hold otherwise would be to give to words written in pencil, and not attested to by witnesses nor executed in the manner provided by the statute, the same effect as if they had been so attested."

. . .

The attempted revocation is ineffectual, because testatrix intended to revoke her will by subsequent writings not executed as required by statute, and because it does not in any wise physically obliterate, mutilate, deface, or cancel any written parts of the will.

For the reasons stated, the judgment of the trial court is affirmed.

Affirmed.

Notes

1. *Judicial approach*: How would you characterize the court's application of the statutory revocation requirements in *Thompson*: strict compliance, substantial compliance, or harmless error?

2. *California approach*: In *Thompson*, the court discussed the two principal methods of revocation: revocation by writing that qualifies as a new will, and revocation by destructive act. Chapter 6 covered what is necessary to create a new will in California. California's statute on revocation by writing and revocation by act is on the next page. After you read it, circle back to the *Thompson* case. How would the *Thompson* case come out in California? Why?

II. Express Revocation

A. Introduction

The different methods of revocation fall into two logical groupings: express revocation and implied revocation. The express revocation category includes those methods of revocation where the testator's intent to revoke is either express, or it is associated with an act where the presumed evidence of testator's intent is so strong it is deemed de facto express intent. Express revocation includes: (1) revocation by writing a new will (that either expressly or by inconsistency revokes the old will), or (2) revocation by destructive act. Typically, express revocation involves some affirmative, or semi-affirmative, act by the testator. The *Thompson* case is an example of an attempted express revocation.

Implied revocation, on the other hand, typically occurs where there is no direct, express evidence of testator's intent to revoke, yet under the circumstances a presumption of revocation arises. For example, if a will was last in the testator's possession, and the will cannot be found following the testator's death, what are the two most logical explanations for why it cannot be found? Inasmuch as the will is a very important document, which is the more likely explanation? Similarly, if testator's will provides for his or her spouse, but at the time of the testator's death the marriage has been dissolved and the couple are no longer married, what are the two most logical explanations for why the testator did not change his or her will? Knowing human nature, which is the more likely explanation? Even though there is not direct, express evidence of the testator's intent to revoke his or her will, in certain circumstances a presumption of revocation will arise by operation of law.

We will begin our examination of revocation with the preferred method of revocation: express revocation. California Probate Code Section 6120 sets forth the two ways one can expressly revoke a will in California: (1) by a subsequent writing that qualifies as a will (commonly referred to as "revocation by writing"), or (2) by a destructive act (commonly referred to as "revocation by act").

CPC § 6120. Express revocation of a will

A will or any part thereof is revoked by any of the following:

(a) A subsequent will which revokes the prior will or part expressly or by inconsistency.

(b) Being burned, torn, canceled, obliterated, or destroyed, with the intent and for the purpose of revoking it, by either (1) the testator or (2) another person in the testator's presence and by the testator's direction.

B. Revocation by Writing

1. Codicil versus Will

Notwithstanding its brevity, California Probate Code Section 6120 contains a significant amount of information. Subsection (a) sets forth the first method a testator can use to affirmatively revoke a will: a testator can revoke a will by properly executing a subsequent will. But note that the introductory clause to the section provides that this subsequent will may revoke the underlying will in whole or in part. Where a subsequent will validly revokes a prior will in whole (so there is no reason for the probate court to resort to the prior will), the subsequent will controls and the revoked will no longer has any testamentary life or legal significance. From a drafting perspective, a commonly used phrase is "this will revokes all prior wills." That phrase, in a validly executed will, adequately expresses the intent to revoke all prior wills and will validly revoke all prior wills.

Where, however, a subsequent will only *partially* revokes or amends a prior will (i.e., there is still reason for the probate court to refer to the underlying will to determine and give effect to testator's intent), the subsequent will is "a codicil" to the prior will. Both the codicil and the underlying will have testamentary life and significance.

The most common codicil is one that amends an existing will (as opposed to another codicil). For example, assume the testator has a will that makes 100 different gifts. The testator wants to change just one gift—the gift in paragraph 23 of the will. Rather than re-typing the entire will (which in the old days would have involved quite a bit of time, labor, and cost), the lawyer could draft a short document for the testator's execution that expressly revoked paragraph 23 of the old will, sets forth the new paragraph 23 with the new gift, and otherwise expressly re-affirms and re-publishes the underlying will. When the testator properly executes that document, the new document will be a codicil to his or her will, and the codicil will have the legal effect of re-executing and re-dating the underlying will as of the date of the codicil—all now properly revised to reflect the testator's intent.

While codicils still exist as a legal option, they are generally not the first choice of estate planning attorneys to amend an existing will. Today, most attorney-prepared wills are stored in electronic format on a computer. Rather than having the client execute a codicil, with all the risks inherent in multiple documents, most estate planning attorneys prefer to integrate the client's changes into the existing will that is stored in electronic format. The new, amended will is then printed out and executed with, of course, clear and express language revoking all prior wills (and any codicils). Nonetheless, codicils (and concepts that, in substance, implicate codicils) have continued relevance in the study of wills.

A testator can have as many codicils as he or she wishes. First and foremost, though, a codicil has to be a validly executed will. It is a will that only partially amends or revokes an existing will. Technically there cannot be a codicil unless there is a valid will at the time the codicil is executed. Legally, the codicil and the will have an interesting relationship. Revocation of a will revokes all codicils thereto, but revocation of a codicil only affects the codicil—it does not revoke the underlying will.

Problems

1. Testator validly executes Will #1, which leaves all of his property to his alma mater, The University of Nirvana. Thereafter, Testator hears that Nirvana has appointed a new President, whom Testator does not like. Testator takes out a piece of paper on which he handwrites, dates, and signs the following: "*I hereby revoke my last will and testament.*" Is that a valid revocation? Is that a valid will?

2. Testator validly executes Will #1. It makes more than 100 different gifts to family members, friends, and charities. Thereafter, Testator decides she wants to change one gift. Testator validly executes Will #2, which changes one gift from beneficiary

A to beneficiary X. The heading at the top of the document says "*Will #2*"—but all it does is change one gift. Is *Will #2* a will or a codicil?

3. Testator validly executes Will #1. It makes more than 100 different gifts to family members, friends, and charities. Thereafter, Testator decides she wants to change one gift. Testator's attorney pulls up the document on the computer, changes the one gift, re-prints the entire document, and Testator validly executes the new document. Is the new document a will or a codicil?

2. Revocation by Writing: Expressly versus by Inconsistency

California Probate Code Section 6120(a) also provides that where the revocation is by a subsequent will, the writing can *either* "expressly or by inconsistency" revoke the underlying will. Express revocation occurs where a clause is included in the subsequent will that expressly revokes the prior will in whole or in part. A standard express revocation clause often says the following: "I hereby revoke any and all prior wills and codicils." No magic language is required; it is a question of intent. That intent can be expressed in either an attested will or a holographic will (regardless of the whether the underlying will is an attested will or a holographic will). For all intents and purposes, express revocation is the sole method of revocation used by estate planning attorneys. It is almost inconceivable that a professionally drafted attested will would fail to contain, typically near the beginning of the will, an express revocation clause setting forth both the intent to revoke and the scope of the revocation (i.e., whether it revokes the prior will in whole or in part).[2]

California Probate Code Section 6120(a) also authorizes a subsequent will (or codicil because the term "will" includes codicils) to revoke a prior will "by inconsistency." This can be more problematic because of the different types of gifts that can be made in a will. While the different fact patterns can run the full gamut, here is the basic set-up: Testator has a validly executed and dated will—Will #1. Thereafter, Testator validly executes Will #2. The dispositive provisions of Will 2 are different from those in Will #1. There would be no problem if Will #2 contained an express revocation clause stating this new will "revoked all prior wills." Will #1 would clearly and expressly be revoked; end of story. Assuming, however, Will #2 has no such clause, and we have two validly executed wills, albeit one more recent than the other. Should the law assume that by making Will #2 the testator intended to revoke Will #1?

The above hypothetical is a classic example where the second part of CPC Section 6120(a) applies. While Will #2 is a writing, this situation is often referred to as implied revocation by inconsistency. While Will #2 did not expressly revoke Will #1, the statute provides that Will #2 will revoke Will #1, but only to the extent that Will

---

2. The very simple California Statutory Will (the pre-printed, "fill in the blank" will that is found in CPC § 6240) has, as the first enumerated item, the following: "*1. Will. This is my Will. I revoke all prior Wills and codicils.*" This is a classic example of a valid express revocation of all prior wills and codicils, and it is boilerplate language that is included in most well-drafted wills.

#2's provisions are inconsistent with the provisions in Will #1. This could play out one of two ways: (a) the entirety of Will #1 being revoked if the dispositive provisions of Will #2 are wholly inconsistent; or (b) Will #2 could be only a partial revocation (hence a codicil) where some inconsistencies between the two wills exist, but some gifts in Will #1 still stand. Again, there are countless fact patterns that could yield very different results.

Problems

Assume a validly executed Will #1 followed, at a later date, by a validly executed Will #2. Will #2 does not contain language specifically revoking Will #1. Who takes the testator's property in the following variations?

1. Testator Tricia's Will #1 leaves all of her property to her granddaughter, Grace. Will #2 leaves all of Tricia's property to her grandson, Gary.

2. The dispositive provisions of Testator Tricia's Will #1 gives her car to her daughter, Dalia, her gold watch to her other daughter, Deborah, her Malibu home to her son, Steven, and the balance of her property to her grandson, Gary. Will #2, however, leaves the same car to her nephew, Ned, the same watch to her niece, Nancy, her Malibu home to her sister, Sally, and the balance of her property to her granddaughter, Grace.

3. Testator Tricia's Will #1 leaves all of her property to her granddaughter, Grace. Will #2 leaves her car to her daughter, Dalia, her gold watch to her other Daughter, Deborah, and her Malibu home to her son, Steven.

4. Same as Question #2, above, except that Will #2 leaves her car to her daughter Dalia, her gold watch to her sister, Sally, and her Malibu home to her son, Steven.

C. Revocation by Act

In addition to revocation by writing, most states also permit revocation by act if a destructive act is performed to the will, and the testator has the intent to revoke. California recognizes revocation by act. CPC §6120(b). You may recall the *Estate of Stoker* case in the previous chapter. The case involved California's limited new harmless error doctrine with respect to the *witness* attestation requirement. The precise issue in the case was whether testator had executed a valid will where he had a friend hand-write the will provisions as he dictated them, and then he signed the document but the witnesses did not. After creating what he assumed was a new will, the testator told his friends who were present that he no longer wanted his original will to be valid and performed a series of rather unique and expressive destructive acts to the original 1977 will:

> Gretchen Landry, a friend of decedent's, testified that in 2001 decedent took his original copy of the 1997 will, urinated on it and then burned it. We hesitate to speculate how he accomplished the second act after the first. In any

event, decedent's actions lead to the compelling conclusion he intended to revoke the 1997 will.

Estate of Stoker, 193 Cal. App. 4th at 245. The court had no trouble finding that Steven Stoker's actions constituted a valid revocation by act.

1. The Physical Act

The revocation by act method of revoking a will has two components: (1) the intent to revoke, and (2) the destructive act. While the two elements are distinct, they also overlap. Sometimes the nature of the destructive act is so obvious that the courts will infer the intent to revoke. Conversely, where the intent to revoke is clear, one could argue that the courts should take a more flexible view of the act requirement. Not everyone, however, agrees on that point.

This second scenario—where the intent to revoke is clear but the compliance with the act requirement is not—was at issue in the *Thompson* case. The less than perfect act required the court to explore the underlying latent issue in the revocation by act doctrine. What does it mean to say that the destructive act must be done to the will? What constitutes the will? Does the piece of paper on which the words are written constitute the will, or must the destructive act affect the actual printed words of the will? What if the testator's handwritten notations or markings are on the will (for example, in the margin), but they do not physically touch the written words of the will?

The Uniform Probate Code expressly addresses the issue and takes more of a modern trend, intent-based approach: "A burning, tearing, or canceling is a 'revocatory act on the will,' whether or not the burn, tear, or cancellation touched any of the words on the will." UPC § 2-507(a)(2). The statutory provision in the *Thompson* case did not expressly address the issue. The court applied the traditional, majority approach. What is that approach? How would you describe that approach from a strict compliance versus substantial compliance versus harmless error perspective?

Look back at the California statutory revocation material. Does it expressly address the issue of whether the destructive act must affect the printed words of the will? In other words, must the crossing out or written words indicating revocation actually touch the will's printed words? Is it sufficient if words or the like expressing the intent to revoke are written in the margins? Should it make any difference if, instead of words, a destructive act is performed on the margin? In *Thompson* (not a California case), the writings in the margins of the will were not sufficient. Surprisingly, no California court has analyzed the issue, though a few older opinions have language that implies California follows the traditional majority approach.

As for what constitutes a destructive act, this is usually not at issue in the typical revocation by act scenario: when the testator, with the accompanying requisite intent, totally destroys a will with the intent to revoke by tearing it up, burning it, crossing out all of the pages of the will while writing "null and void" on the face of every page, sending it through a shredder, and so on. But what if only parts of the will are crossed out? What if the destructive act is performed across only one paragraph or one section of the will? What if that section is the signatory block? Revocation by act is yet another example of a doctrine where a layperson may not necessarily know what he or she is doing or, more accurately, he or she may not know the ramifications of what he or she is doing.

Problems

1. Testatrix validly executed her will and took it home with her. Following her death, initially the will could not be found. After a more extensive search, however, her will was found—completely intact and with no markings on it—inside a paper bag with other items of trash in a hallway closet area that the testatrix referred to as "trash alley." Has the will been validly revoked? *See SouthTrust Bank of Alabama, N.A. v. Winter,* 689 So. 2d 69 (Ala. Civ. App. 1996).

2. Tommy Smith, who was separated but not divorced from his wife, validly executed a typed will that was only three paragraphs long. Paragraph (a) authorized the payments of his just debts. Paragraph (b) left all of his property to his brother, Bob Smith. Paragraph (c) appointed his brother Bob executor. Thereafter, Tommy and Bob had a falling out. Tommy took out the will and in the margin next to paragraphs (b) and (c) wrote the following: "*Bob Smith, Jr., this 31st day of 2010.*" Bob Smith, Jr. is his nephew (his brother's son). In addition, in paragraphs (b) and (c) of the typed will where it mentions Bob Smith, Tommy inserted, in his own handwriting, the word "*Jr.*" after each reference. Thereafter, Tommy died. Is the handwriting on the typed will sufficient to constitute a codicil? Is the handwriting on the typed will sufficient to constitute a revocation by act? *See Wiley v. Wiley,* 184 So. 2d 854 (Miss. 1966).

III. Implied Revocation

A. Implied Revocation by Act

Many scholars complain that the threshold for creating a valid will is too high (hence the substantial compliance and harmless error movement). To the extent that revoking a will is the flip side of executing a will, should the threshold for revoking a will be similar? Or, because the testator is "coming back home" to the state's intestate scheme, should the threshold for revoking a will be lower? Moreover, when might it be appropriate for a court to infer from the facts that the testator revoked a will even in the absence of any direct evidence that the testator (or another person) performed a destructive act to the will? If a will was last in the testator's possession, and the will cannot be found following the testator's death, is there a valid revocation?

Estate of Obernolte

91 Cal. App. 3d 124 (Ct. App. 1979)

COBEY, Acting Presiding Justice.

Dona Wilson appeals from an order denying her petition for revocation of the probate of a will of Jennie Vessels Obernolte, deceased, executed some two months before her death on December 21, 1974....

On October 17, 1974, the decedent, being of sound mind, duly executed in the office of her attorney, Mr. Forde, an original and a duplicate original of a will under which she left her estate, share and share alike, to her only child, the just-mentioned petitioner, Dona Wilson, Mrs. Wilson's two children, and the decedent's sister and two brothers. She apparently took the original of the will home to her apartment and placed it in a cedar chest in her bedroom. She kept this chest locked and she and her sister had the only two keys to it.

The only person living with the decedent, off and on, was her handyman, Mr. Vance Mayers, who helped her in her personal wants and maintained the apartment complex which she owned and managed. She was a lonely and fearful woman, whose contact with the just-mentioned members of her family was almost entirely by telephone. She was apparently unhappy with practically all of the members of her family, including Mrs. Wilson. She complained that they never visited her and she was frequently depressed. Consequently she told at least two people in November of 1974 that she was tearing up her will, so "that she wasn't leaving anyone a 'd' thing, [and that] if they got anything, they would have to fight for it."

On the other hand, during the approximately two months that intervened between the making of her last will and her death, she expressed concern about the security in her apartment of the original of the will and suggested that she might move it from the locked cedar chest to a cupboard in her kitchen. Furthermore, although she visited her attorney's office, which was only a block and a half from her apartment, eleven days before her death to try to consult with him about a business matter, and although she chatted with his secretary at length at least seven times about how lonely and unhappy she was and her fears for her safety, she never mentioned to either of these people anything about destroying her will or having it redone.

Within hours of her death on December 21st, one of her tenants informed her daughter of her demise. Mrs. Wilson came over immediately and, according to her testimony, searched the apartment unsuccessfully for the original of the will for a couple of days. According to her, she found the empty envelope from the cedar chest in which the will had apparently been kept, but she could never locate the original instrument itself. Her further extensive search for a possible safe deposit box was also unsuccessful.

The day after the decedent's funeral, Mr. Forde informed Mrs. Wilson by telephone that he had at his office the duplicate original of the will and generally of its provisions. A few days later Mrs. Wilson came to the office and according to Mr. Forde "she was most unhappy and distressed" when she actually saw the duplicate original of the instrument.

The trial court found, among other things, that persons other than the decedent had access to the original copy of the will at her place of residence prior to her death and that, as already noted, it is "equally probable" that if the decedent's copy of the will was destroyed, it was destroyed by someone other than the decedent.

DISCUSSION

I. *The Rebuttable Presumption of Revocation Came Into Play in This Case*

Such a presumption arises when it is shown that (1) the decedent had the will in her possession prior to her death; (2) she was competent until that time; (3) the will could not be found after her death. (*Estate of Ross* (1926) 199 Cal. 641, 646, 648 [250 P. 676) *Sparks v. Lauritzen* (1967) 248 Cal.App.2d 269, 274–275 [56 Cal.Rptr. 370].)

This Presumption Is a Rebuttable Presumption Affecting the Burden of Producing Evidence Rather Than the Burden of Proof

Evidence Code 600 defines a presumption as "an assumption of fact that the law requires to be made from another fact or group of facts found or otherwise established in the action." ... Evidence Code section 604 provides that the effect of this kind of presumption is to require the trier of fact to assume the existence of the presumed fact until evidence is introduced which would support a finding of its nonexistence. On the other hand, according to Evidence Code section 606, the effect of a presumption affecting the burden of proof is to impose upon the party against whom it operates the burden of proving the nonexistence of the presumed fact....

[In] *Estate of Bristol,...*, 23 Cal.2d at pages 224–225[,] ... the court said that this presumption could be rebutted by evidence showing that "it is *equally probable* (1) that the will was destroyed by another person than the decedent, or (2) that the act was not done with an intention to revoke the instrument." (Italics in original.) Equal probability does not satisfy a burden of proof; it does, however, satisfy a burden of producing evidence. (See Evid. Code, §§ 115, 550, subd. (a).) In other words, the effect of the rebuttable presumption of revocation of a will is prima facie only; it exists only until rebutted by substantial evidence. (See *Betts v. Jackson* (N.Y. 1830) 6 Wend. 173, 182–183.)

III. *There Is Substantial Evidence in Support of the Challenged Key Finding of Equal Probability*

In the approximately two months that intervened between the preparation of the decedent's last will and her death, she talked quite a bit about destroying the will. But talking about her will, particularly to its beneficiaries, appears to have been a habit of hers. We entertain no doubt that she was quite unhappy with practically all of the will's beneficiaries and apparently was unaware of what would happen to her property if she died without a will. But, on the other hand, she did express definite concern about the security of her will and, although she visited the office of her attorney, who had drawn three wills for her, eleven days before her death and chatted at length several times with his secretary, who seems to have been something of a confidante for this lonely woman, she never mentioned to either of these people anything about destroying or redoing her will.

We regard this last-mentioned evidence as substantial evidence rebutting the presumption of revocation and supporting the key finding of equal probability. This finding is a carefully drawn finding. It is conditional in form because an equal probability did exist that if the decedent's will was destroyed, this act was done by someone other than the decedent; namely, either Mr. Vance Mayers, the handyman who was not a beneficiary under the will and who could possibly have had access to it before her death, or the petitioner, who stood to inherit all of her mother's estate without a will (see Prob. Code, §222) but only one-sixth under the will.

DISPOSITION

The order of denial of revocation of the probate of the decedent's last will is affirmed.

Notes

1. *The presumption of revocation*: The presumption of revocation is a fairly "soft" presumption. It shifts the burden of producing evidence to the will proponent. If, however, the will proponent brings forth evidence offering an alternative explanation for why the will cannot be found, the question of whether the will was validly revoked becomes a question of fact for the fact-finder. And as the court held in *Obernolte*, so long as the alternative explanation is equally plausible, the presumption has been rebutted.

The presumption of revocation is basically a subset of which type of express revocation (revocation by writing or revocation by act)? How so? What is the logic underlying the presumption of revocation doctrine?

2. *Duplicate originals*: The decedent in *Obernolte* executed both "an original and a duplicate original" of her will. What is a "duplicate original"? In applying the presumption of revocation, should it matter whether the testator executed a duplicate original? How does the presence of a duplicate original affect the logic underlying the presumption of revocation doctrine? Did the presence of a duplicate original affect the court's analysis of the doctrine in the *Obernolte* case? Subsequent to the court's opinion in *Obernolte*, the California legislature codified the presumption of revocation doctrine. Would the *Obernolte* case come out the same way today?

CPC §6124. Presumption of revocation

> If the testator's will was last in the testator's possession, the testator was competent until death, and neither the will nor a duplicate original of the will can be found after the testator's death, it is presumed that the testator destroyed the will with intent to revoke it. This presumption is a presumption affecting the burden of producing evidence.

In legal practice, "duplicate original" wills are an anomaly—pretty much nonexistent if the will is drafted by an estate planning attorney. A duplicate will is *not a* photocopy of an original will. As used in CPC Section 6124, duplicate original wills represent two identical copies of the same will, each of which is properly executed at the same time. Basically, they are two identical, fully executed versions of the same will. Again, in practice estate planning attorneys rarely do this because there is no reason for a testator to have duplicate original wills. Nonetheless, duplicate original wills can exist and CPC Section 6124 addresses the legal consequences duplicate original wills when they overlap with the revocation by presumption doctrine.

3. *Will found post-death with a destructive mark on it*: Should the logic underlying the presumption of revocation doctrine apply if the testator's will is found following his or her death, but with a destructive act across all or part of the will? In a 1906 California Supreme Court case, *Wikman's Estate*, 148 Cal. 642 (1906), the will was last in the testator's possession, the testator had capacity until death, and the will was found after his death with a line drawn through the executor's name. Should the presumption arise that it was the testator who made the destructive act to the will with the intent to revoke?

> [T]he will was in the possession of the testator from the time of its execution until his death; that immediately after his death it was found among his effects in his trunk; and that when so found the ink-lines were over and through ... [the name of the executor]. ... "From these circumstances alone arise the presumptions: (1) That the cancellations were the act of the testator; and (2) that they were performed with the intent and purpose of revoking the instrument." The general authorities are to the same effect.

4. *The lost will doctrine*: Assume that a will cannot be found following the testator's death, but either (a) the will was not last in the testator's possession, or (b) if the presumption arises, it is rebutted. Can the court probate a will that cannot be found? How? The general rule is that the terms of a lost will must be proved by clear and convincing evidence. California used to require that the will provisions be "clearly and distinctly proved by at least two credible witnesses." CPC § 350. But in 1982 the statutory provision was repealed. California now requires only that the terms of the lost will be proved by a preponderance of the evidence, with no minimum number of witnesses.

Problems

1. Assume the probate court found the following facts. Does the presumption of revocation arise? If so, is it rebutted?

    Decedent prepared an original will plus a fully conformed copy (a conformed copy is not a duplicate original; her attorney kept the conformed copy of the will). Decedent informed various individuals that she had made a will leaving everything to her granddaughter (to the exclusion of her daughter) and that decedent and her granddaughter were very close. Decedent kept all her valuable documents in a brown handbag. Decedent told witnesses that she had her will with her several days before her death. Decedent's handbag was on her bed when she died. Several persons had access to the brown handbag after she died. Various individuals searched for the will to no avail. Decedent had not indicated to anyone that she had destroyed her will.

See In re Estate of Richard, 556 A.2d 1091 (Me. 1989).

2. Testatrix validly executed her typed will. When the will was being typed up, the typist generated a carbon copy of the will.[3] The testatrix signed the carbon copy (in addition to the actual typed will), but the witnesses signed only the typed will (and not the carbon copy). Testatrix took both documents home with her. Following her death, a sealed envelope was found among her personal papers. On the outside of the envelope, in the Testatrix's handwriting, were the following notes: "Copy of Deed to Lutheran Cemetery," "Copy of Last Will and Testament" and the signature "A. C. Engelken." On the back of the envelope, written across the flap, was the signature "A. C. Engelken." The envelope contained a deed to a cemetery plot and the carbon copy of the will. On the back side of the last page of the carbon copy of the will, in the Testatrix's handwriting, were the following handwritten words: "Copy of Last Will and Testament of Anna C. Engelken" and "Original in Safe Deposit Box in Jam. Savings Bank." At the time of her death, Testatrix no longer had a safe deposit box at Jamaica Savings Bank; and while she had a safe deposit box at National Bank, the will was not there. Does the presumption of revocation arise? If so, is it rebutted? *See Will of Engelken*, 426 N.Y.S.2d 894 (1980).

B. Implied Revocation by Operation of Law

Because a will is an ambulatory document (executed at one point in time, but not effective for most purposes until death), there is a risk that the circumstances surrounding the testator may change between the will's execution and the testator's death — and that those changes may affect the average testator's intent. Can you think of any milestones or events in one's life that are so significant that even in the absence of a testator expressing the intent to revoke, the law will presume that the will is revoked (at least in part) upon that event's occurrence?

CPC §6122. Provisions in will in favor of spouse; effect of dissolution or annulment of marriage

(a) Unless the will expressly provides otherwise, if after executing a will the testator's marriage is dissolved or annulled, the dissolution or annulment revokes all of the following:

(1) Any disposition or appointment of property made by the will to the former spouse.

(2) Any provision of the will conferring a general or special power of appointment on the former spouse.

---

3. The term "carbon copy," as used here, is an "old school" concept of a second, under-copy duplicate with the use of carbon paper between the original typed sheet and a second "copy" sheet. The pressure of typewritten letters make an impression, via the carbon paper, on the under-copy sheet. True carbon copies usually predate the wide-scale use of photocopiers.

(3)   Any provision of the will nominating the former spouse as executor, trustee, con-servator, or guardian.

(b)   If any disposition or other provision of a will is revoked solely by this section, it is revived by the testator's remarriage to the former spouse.

(c)   In case of revocation by dissolution or annulment:

(1)   Property prevented from passing to a former spouse because of the revocation passes as if the former spouse failed to survive the testator....

(2)   Other provisions of the will conferring some power or office on the former spouse shall be interpreted as if the former spouse failed to survive the testator....

Historically the revocation by operation of law doctrine applied only to probate testate property (do you see why it does not apply to probate intestate property?). To the extent the doctrine is based on the assumption that upon a dissolution of marriage (more commonly referred to as a divorce), a testator no longer wishes to give any property to his or her former spouse, does it make sense to limit the doctrine to pro-bate testate property as opposed to non-probate property? Nevertheless, that was the situation in most states, including California, until relatively recently. In 2002 the California legislature adopted the following statutory provision.

CPC § 5600. Provisions in nonprobate instrument in favor of spouse; failure of provision due to dissolution or annulment of marriage

(a)   Except as provided in subdivision (b), a nonprobate transfer to the transferor's former spouse, in an instrument executed by the transferor before or during the marriage, fails if, at the time of the transferor's death, the former spouse is not the transferor's surviving spouse as defined in Section 78, as a result of the dissolution or annulment of the marriage....

(b)   Subdivision (a) does not cause a nonprobate transfer to fail in any of the following cases:

(1)   The nonprobate transfer is not subject to revocation by the transferor at the time of the transferor's death.

(2)   There is clear and convincing evidence that the transferor intended to preserve the nonprobate transfer to the former spouse.

(3)   A court order that the nonprobate transfer be maintained on behalf of the former spouse is in effect at the time of the transferor's death.

(c)   Where a nonprobate transfer fails by operation of this section, the instrument making the nonprobate transfer shall be treated as it would if the former spouse failed to survive the transferor.

...

(e)   As used in this section, "nonprobate transfer" means a provision, other than a provision of a life insurance policy, of either of the following types:

(1)   A provision of a type described in Section 5000.

(2)   A provision in an instrument that operates on death, other than a will, conferring a power of appointment or naming a trustee.

Is CPC Section 5600 essentially the same as the probate testate version of the doctrine, CPC Section 6122?

The revocation by operation of law doctrine also applies to property held in joint tenancy:

CPC § 5042. Joint tenancy severed if former spouse not decedent's surviving spouse; exceptions

(a) Except as provided in subdivision (b), a joint tenancy between the decedent and the decedent's former spouse, created before or during the marriage, is severed as to the decedent's interest if, at the time of the decedent's death, the former spouse is not the decedent's surviving spouse as defined in Section 78, as a result of the dissolution or annulment of the marriage. A judgment of legal separation that does not terminate the status of husband and wife is not a dissolution for purposes of this section.

(b) Subdivision (a) does not sever a joint tenancy in either of the following cases:

   (1) The joint tenancy is not subject to severance by the decedent at the time of the decedent's death.

   (2) There is clear and convincing evidence that the decedent intended to preserve the joint tenancy in favor of the former spouse.

(c) Nothing in this section affects the rights of a subsequent purchaser or encumbrancer for value in good faith who relies on an apparent severance under this section or who lacks knowledge of a severance under this section.

(d) For purposes of this section, property held in "joint tenancy" includes property held as community property with right of survivorship, as described in Section 682.1 of the Civil Code.

1. Same-Sex Couples

As previously discussed in Chapter 3, a domestic partner is, for all intents and purposes, a spouse. Accordingly, it follows that the same provisions regarding revocation of a spouse's interest in a will or non-probate instrument should apply equally to same-sex couples that terminate their domestic partnership. While that arguably is the case, it is not as clear-cut as one might assume it should be.

While same-sex couples are now permitted to marry in California, which means the operation by law provisions set forth above would apply equally to same-sex couples who divorce, there was a period of time when same-sex couples were not permitted to marry but were permitted to register as domestic partners. Same-sex relationships are much like heterosexual relationships in that not all of them last "until death do us part." Because registered domestic partners were not married, they could not divorce. Instead, they could "terminate" the domestic partnership.

California Probate Code Section 6122.1 applies the revocation by operation of law doctrine to *the wills* of registered domestic partners who terminate their partnership.[4]

---

4. The termination of a California domestic partnership is, for all intents and purposes, the same process as that for a dissolution of a marriage (a divorce). An adjudicated matter, the termination of

It is virtually identical to CPC Section 6122, other than the necessary changes in phrasing to reflect that it applies to domestic partners when their partnership is terminated. At first blush you might be surprised to learn that there are no corresponding statutory provisions explicitly applying revocation by operation to *non-probate instruments* held by domestic partners who officially terminate their partnership. Recall that while at one time California adopted a piecemeal approach to granting spousal rights to registered domestic partners, in Family Law Code Section 297.5 California granted "across the board" spousal rights to registered domestic partners, thereby mooting the need to adopt parallel statutory provisions every time there is a statute dealing with spousal rights and/or duties. California Family Code Section 297.5 expressly provides, in part, that "[r]egistered domestic partners have the same rights, protections, and benefits, ... as are granted to and imposed upon spouses." Numerous provisions in the California Probate Code historically were amended to make express reference to domestic partners/partnerships, but most of these specific references have now been removed as they are redundant (with domestic partners being equivalent to spouses). Perhaps the failure to remove CPC Section 6122.1 is merely an oversight. Whatever the reason for CPC Section 6122.1, revocation by operation of law should apply to non-probate property held by registered domestic partners who terminate their relationship just as the doctrine applies to non-probate property of spouses who get divorced.

Note

The family protection doctrines: Chapter 10 will cover what are commonly referred to as the *family protection doctrines*. These doctrines, in certain circumstances, grant family members who have been left out of a decedent's estate planning instruments a statutory right to share in the decedent's property despite not being named a beneficiary. The omitted family members are *granted* gifts by operation of law. That being the case, the family protection doctrines have the indirect effect of *revoking*, at least in part, other gifts in the instrument to other beneficiaries. Accordingly, the doctrines could be covered here as additional examples of revocation by operation of law, but because their primary purpose is to grant a new gift, and not to revoke a gift per se, these doctrines will be covered as part of the family protection material.

Problem

T executes duplicate wills that leave all her property to Hastings Law School. T takes one copy home with her and leaves the other copy with her attorney. After T's death, the will that T brought home with her cannot be found, but a handwritten, signed but undated instrument is found, which provides as follows: "I give everything I own to Santa Clara Law School." Assuming no other evidence

---

a California domestic partnership effectuates the proper classification and distribution of "marital" property (e.g., community property, separate property, etc.).

is brought forward concerning T's intent or actions, what arguments will the respective law schools make? Under the California Probate Code, what is the most likely outcome, and why?

IV. Revival of Revoked Wills

Once a will has been revoked, is it a "dead" legal instrument? Are there any circumstances, short of re-executing the instrument, where the instrument might nevertheless be probated as a valid will? The next two sections of the material address two doctrines that permit a court to probate a validly revoked will: (1) revival, and (2) dependent relative revocation. While these doctrines are similar in some respects, they are separate doctrines that operate differently. Dependent relative revocation is a particularly challenging doctrine that will require your best effort to master.

The concept and doctrine of revival is probably best introduced by a simple real-world example that typifies the context in which the issue arises. Assume a testator has a valid will (Will #1), and thereafter testator validly executes Will #2, which either expressly or implicitly revokes Will #1. Thereafter the testator changes his or her mind and validly revokes Will #2. The question that naturally arises is what effect, if any, should revocation of Will #2 have on Will #1. Should Will #1 be automatically revived, or should the testator have to take affirmative steps to restore testamentary life to Will #1? Should the testator have to re-execute the document with all the Wills Act formalities, or should the law establish a different threshold for "revival" of a revoked will?

English common law reasoned that because a will is an ambulatory document that does not take effect until the testator's death, Will #1 was treated as never having been revoked. Under the English approach, Will #2 only revoked Will #1 if Will #2 still existed at the testator's death. If Will #2 is revoked, Will #2 merely "came and went" before the testator's death, so it never had any effect for any purpose. Accordingly, Will #1 not need be revived because it was never revoked. Only a handful of states apply some vestiges of the English approach.

Under what is often referred to as the "American approach," Will #2 is deemed effective immediately for revocation purposes (i.e., it immediately revokes Will #1 — an exception to the general rule that a will is an ambulatory document that has no legal effect until the testator's death). Therefore, if Will #2 is revoked, does revocation of Will #2 automatically revive Will #1, or must the testator do something to revive Will #1? The overwhelming majority of states reject the aforementioned English approach, under which revocation of Will #2 would automatically revive Will #1. Instead, under the majority American approach, the testator must do something to revive Will #1. What that "something" is depends on the jurisdictional approach. The more traditional, strict compliance, formalities-based end of the spectrum requires the testator to re-execute Will #1 with all necessary "Wills Act" formalities. The other end of the spectrum takes more of an intent-based approach (and this is the approach a majority of the states have adopted). The California approach is set forth below:

CPC § 6123. Second will revoking first will; revocation of second will and possible revival of first

(a) If a second will which, had it remained effective at death, would have revoked the first will in whole or in part, is thereafter revoked by acts under Section 6120 or 6121, the first will is revoked in whole or in part unless it is evident from the circumstances of the revocation of the second will or from the testator's contemporary or subsequent declarations that the testator intended the first will to take effect as executed.

(b) If a second will which, had it remained effective at death, would have revoked the first will in whole or in part, is thereafter revoked by a third will, the first will is revoked in whole or in part, except to the extent it appears from the terms of the third will that the testator intended the first will to take effect.

Which approach has California adopted?

The following is not a California case, but it presents a typical revival factual scenario and serves as a good example of how the doctrine can be applied. While the South Dakota approach to revival is not identical to the California approach, it is close enough to be a good teaching case.

The case also serves as a good reminder of the role family dynamics can play in estate planning and in a testator's statements and actions.

In re Estate of Heibult

653 N.W.2d 101 (S.D. 2002)

GILBERTSON, Chief Justice.

[¶ 1.] Anna K. Heibult executed a will in 1990 devising a larger portion of her property to Ronald Heibult, the youngest of her four children. In 1991, on a visit to California to see the three older siblings, Anna executed a second will and trust dividing the property equally. Neither the original nor a signed copy of the second will was ever found. When Anna died in February 2000, the three older siblings petitioned for adjudication of intestacy. The circuit court, however, granted Ronald's petition to probate the 1990 South Dakota will....

FACTS AND PROCEDURE

[¶ 2.] Anna and George Heibult were married for over fifty years. During these years, they lived on their farm near Parker, South Dakota, and raised four children: Calvin, Georgiann, Melba, and Ronald. Ronald was the only sibling to remain in South Dakota. He farmed with his father until George's death in 1989. Ronald then took over the operation of the farm and cared for his mother.

[¶ 3.] After her husband's death, Anna wished to draft a new will and sought the advice of Attorney John E. Burke. Burke had represented the couple since the 1950's. Burke testified at trial:

> She came, Anna came in and asked me to draw a new will. And she told me
> that both before and after her husband's death Ron had always been there

when she needed him. Everybody else had moved to California and she wanted to give him a little, some more than she was giving the rest of the children, his brother and sisters.

In accordance with Anna's instructions, Burke drafted a will that left an undivided one-half interest in the "home place" and another quarter section of the Heibult farm entirely to Ronald. The will also provided that Ronald could purchase the other half by paying the appraised value to the other three siblings over a period of twenty years. The rest of Anna's estate, including the remaining eighty acres of the farm, was divided equally among all four siblings. After execution ["the 1990 South Dakota will"], the will remained in Burke's possession until Anna's death in February 2000.

[¶ 4.] In June 1991, Anna traveled to California to visit Calvin, Georgiann, and Melba. During her visit, the subject of Anna's will was discussed. Ethel Wolleson, Georgiann's neighbor and good friend, testified that she had shown Anna a copy of her own will, which divided her estate equally among her children. According to Ethel, Anna had immediately exclaimed that she wanted the same thing. The next morning, Ethel took Anna to see Ethel's attorney, accompanied by Anna's three children. There, Anna paid $850 to attorney Charles Blek to draw up a new will and a trust, which divided her property equally among the four Heibult siblings and revoked all previous wills. The following morning, Anna, Ethel and the three siblings returned to Blek's office to execute the will.

[¶ 5.] The day after the California will was executed, Anna flew home to South Dakota. Instead of returning alone as she had planned, Georgiann and Ethel accompanied her. Immediately upon arrival, Georgiann and Ethel took Anna to the bank to ensure that Anna put the new will in her safe deposit box. Next, Georgiann and Ethel drove Anna to the county courthouse to convey the deeds to the farm property into the trust drawn up by Blek. Anna refused, however, to allow Georgiann or Ethel to come in with her. When she returned to the car, she told Georgiann and Ethel that she had transferred the deeds and she showed them a receipt. That evening, the three started a fire in the backyard, purportedly to "celebrate" by burning the 1990 South Dakota will.

[¶ 6.] It appears however, that Anna fooled them all. While she did burn several papers in the fire, none was the 1990 South Dakota will, as she led Georgiann and Ethel to believe. Instead, the original 1990 South Dakota will remained, as it always had been, in Burke's possession. In addition, neither the original nor any signed copy of the 1991 California will was ever found in Anna's safe deposit box or elsewhere. The trust was found in the safe deposit box, but no property had been placed in the trust to fund it. Instead of considering the possibility that Anna herself had removed and destroyed the 1991 California will, or possibly never had placed it there to begin with, Ronald's siblings claim Ronald had ample opportunity to remove and destroy it. Both Calvin, who moved back to South Dakota in 1993, and Ronald had keys to the safe deposit box. But the bank's safe deposit admission record for box 338 shows the only two people to have accessed the box since 1991 were Anna and Calvin. Finally, when Anna had visited the courthouse seemingly to transfer the deeds to her farm into the trust, she had instead paid $5 and received two copies of her husband's death certificate.

[¶7.] On December 29, 1993, Anna again met with Burke regarding her estate. Burke testified at trial that Anna had relayed the events surrounding the execution of the 1991 California will. According to Burke, Anna told him that she had deliberately misled Georgiann and Ethel into thinking she was burning the 1990 South Dakota will, when in fact, she had burned the 1991 California will. Then Anna gave Burke the unrecorded deeds and explained how she had also misled Georgiann and Ethel at the courthouse. Burke testified Anna had asked what she needed to do to ensure the 1990 South Dakota will would remain in effect. Burke advised her that because the 1991 California will had been burned with intent to revoke it, and the 1990 South Dakota will was still in his possession, she needed to do nothing further.

[¶8.] Anna died on February 29, 2000. Georgiann, Melba, and Calvin filed a petition for adjudication of intestacy, determination of heirs, and appointment of a personal representative. Ronald resisted the petition for intestacy and filed a petition for formal probate of the 1990 South Dakota will. None of the parties dispute that Anna was of sound mind and acted of her own free will during the times in question. No allegations of undue influence were made.

... [The court of appeals agreed with the trial court that the California will had been validly revoked by act.]

[¶19.] **3. Whether there was sufficient evidence to establish the revival of the 1990 South Dakota will.**

[¶20.] There is no dispute that the 1990 South Dakota will was revoked upon execution of the 1991 California will. *See* SDCL 29A-2-507(a)(1). Therefore, we must ascertain whether, the 1990 South Dakota will was revived upon revocation of the subsequent will.

[¶21.] Under common law, the destruction of a will containing a revocatory clause revived the former will, so long as it was preserved uncanceled. 79 Am.Jur.2d *Wills* §689 n. 35 (1975). South Dakota law, however, provides:

> If a subsequent will that wholly revoked a previous will is thereafter revoked by a revocatory act under §29A-2-507(a)(2), the previous will is revived only if it is evident from the circumstances of the revocation of the subsequent will or from the testator's contemporary or subsequent statements that the testator intended the previous will to take effect as executed.

SDCL 29A-2-509(a). As noted above, Ronald's siblings were unable to successfully rebut the presumption that Anna had destroyed the 1991 California will with the intent to revoke it. There is also a presumption in favor of finding testacy over intestacy. *Estate of Martin*, 2001 SD 123, ¶19, 635 N.W.2d 473, 476 (citing 79 Am.Jur.2d *Wills* §745 (1975)). As a result, the circuit court determined that Anna had intended the 1990 South Dakota will to be revived.

[¶22.] It is evident from the circumstances surrounding the 1991 California will's revocation, as well as from Anna's subsequent statements, that she intended the 1990

South Dakota will to take effect as executed. Anna intentionally misled Georgiann and Ethel regarding both wills. Whether Anna actually burned the 1991 California will in place of the 1990 South Dakota will, as testified by Burke, is less significant than Anna's deception regarding the issue. The 1990 South Dakota will was never burned, the 1991 California will was never found, the deeds were never transferred, and the trust was never funded. All of this was in direct contradiction to Anna's representations to Georgiann, Ethel, Melba, and Calvin.

[¶ 23.] Ronald's siblings argue that it makes little sense for Anna to pay $850 for a will she did not intend to keep. Yet, $850 may be a small price to pay for a decade of family accord. Ronald was a natural object of Anna's bounty, given he was the only child to remain in South Dakota, actively farm with his father, and care for his parents. *See Rowett v. McFarland,* 394 N.W.2d 298, 305 (S.D.1986). In any event, it seems clear that Anna knew exactly what she was doing; neither party has alleged she was not of sound mind. *See Estate of Klauzer,* 2000 SD 7, ¶ 9, 604 N.W.2d 474, 477 (stating intent of the testator is ultimate factor in settling will contest). Therefore, given the entirety of the evidence, this Court is not left with a definite and firm conviction that a mistake has been committed. We deem the 1990 South Dakota will revived and affirm the trial court's admission of it to probate.

Notes

1. *California's revival approach*: California's revival statute, CPC Section 6123, contains two subsections. Why? What are the two possible revival scenarios? Do you see how they match up with the different requirements for revival? How would you rewrite the statute to make it more obvious what is required for revival as it relates to the two different ways a testator can revoke Will #2? In which scenario is extrinsic evidence of testator's intent admissible, and in which scenario is the extrinsic evidence not admissible?

2. *Practitioner's perspective*: One of the themes in the course focuses on the fact that many of the "problem issues" covered in the material can be avoided with proper drafting or by utilizing a qualified estate planning attorney. To what extent could proper drafting or proper estate planning advice make revival a "non-issue"? When could revival be an issue, notwithstanding a professionally drafted will?

Problem

The following facts are from *Shinn v. Phillips,* 220 N.E.2d 674 (Ohio Ct. App. 1964):

The testator, Danna T. Burns, died on September 28, 1962. During his lifetime he executed two wills, one dated March 15, 1961, to which a codicil was attached dated October 25, 1961, and a second will dated February 15, 1962. The later will contained a provision specifically revoking all prior wills. Upon the testator's death, his later executed will could not be found, but a carbon copy of his first will was found, with a typewritten statement attached 'The original draft of my last will is in the hands of Attorney Morris Phillips.

I have destroyed the will recently drawn by Attorney J. Elmer Narnum.' This paper writing was signed by the testator and dated but was not witnessed.

If this were a California case, how would it be analyzed?

V. Dependent Relative Revocation ("DRR")

Dependent Relative Revocation (DRR) is one of the more challenging doctrines in the law of wills. It is an equitable doctrine that is an ancillary component to the world of will revocation. Part of the difficulty with the doctrine stems from its name: at first blush, it is not self-defining at all. Conceptually, it might help to think about the doctrine as "the conditional revocation doctrine." There is no doubt that a revocation can be conditional so long as that intent is express in the instrument ("I give my daughter Carolyn $10,000, but if she marries Matt, her gift is revoked"). Is it appropriate for a court to *infer* that a testator's valid revocation was conditional?

One way to think about DRR is that it is a judicially created doctrine where the courts may *infer* that the testator's revocation was conditional (even though that condition was not expressed). Where the testator's revocation appears to be based on an underlying assumption, and that assumption was incorrect (i.e., the assumption was *a mistake*), the court *may* decide the revocation was conditioned upon the assumption and thus should not be given effect.[5] The challenge then becomes identifying when is it appropriate for a court to infer that a valid revocation was conditional upon an unexpressed condition, and to articulate the doctrine for practical application.

Kroll v. Nehmer
705 A.2d 716 (Md. 1997)

WILNER, Judge.

Margaret Binco died on December 19, 1994, leaving four wills — one dated July 24, 1980, a second dated April 12, 1985, a third dated June 28, 1990, and a fourth dated October 27, 1994. We are concerned here only with the second will — the 1985 will.

The 1980 will, it appears, had been altered, and, although it was at one time offered for probate, no one now contends that it has any validity. When Ms. Binco drew the 1990 will, she wrote on the back of her 1985 will "VOID-NEW WILL DRAWN UP 6-28-90." The 1990 and 1994 wills, all parties agree, are ineffective because they lack the signatures of attesting witnesses, as required by Maryland Code, Estates and Trusts Article, § 4-102. Accordingly, if the 1985 will was effectively revoked by Ms. Binco, she would have died intestate, in which event appellant, her brother and closest surviving relative, who was not named as a beneficiary under the 1985, 1990, or 1994

---

5. Is the court "ignoring the revocation" or "*reviving* the revoked material" on the testator's presumed intent? While DRR technically is not a subset of revival because DRR can apply even in the absence of a second will, there is no doubt that *conceptually* some of the revival doctrine has made its way into the DRR jurisprudence.

wills, would inherit. The dispute now before us is therefore between appellant, urging that the 1985 will had been revoked, and appellee, the person who offered that will for probate and who was appointed as personal representative to administer the estate under the will, who contends that the 1985 will had not been effectively revoked.

Over appellant's objection, the Orphans' Court for Baltimore County, apparently applying the doctrine of dependent relative revocation, admitted the 1985 will to probate, notwithstanding its apparent revocation by Ms. Binco. The Circuit Court for Baltimore County affirmed that decision. We granted *certiorari* on our own initiative before any proceedings in the Court of Special Appeals to consider whether the lower courts erred in applying the doctrine and finding the 1985 will to be valid....

Dependent Relative Revocation

Section 4-105 of the Estates and Trusts Article permits a will to be revoked by "cancelling ... the same, by the testator himself...." It is clear, and neither party now suggests otherwise, that, by writing on the 1985 will "VOID-NEW WILL DRAWN UP 6-28-90" and retaining the will, so marked, among her papers, Ms. Binco intended to revoke that will and that, unless saved by the doctrine of dependent relative revocation, that will was effectively revoked.

As we indicated in *Arrowsmith v. Mercantile-Safe Deposit*, 313 Md. 334, 343, 545 A.2d 674, 679 (1988), no reported Maryland appellate decision has ever applied that doctrine. The doctrine, in its most general form, is described in 2 William J. Bowe & Douglas H. Parker, Page on the Law of Wills § 21.57 at 446 (rev. ed.1960):

> "In general the doctrine of dependent relative revocation applies to invalidate the revocation of a will where it is shown that the revocation was conditioned on the occurrence of certain facts which never came to pass or upon the existence or nonexistence of circumstances which were either absent or present contrary to the condition."

As most commentators, including the revisors of Page's opus, point out, in applying the doctrine, courts often speak in terms of a *conditional* revocation, regarding the revocation as conditioned on the existence of a set of facts or circumstances that the testator assumes to exist, when, in reality, the revocation is itself unconditional but is rather based on a mistaken frame of mind—a mistake of either fact or law. They give as an example of a mistake of fact the circumstance in which a testator physically destroys his will believing that the document he is destroying is not his will but some other instrument. In that circumstance, they suggest, the necessary intention to revoke the will is clearly lacking, and a "mistake of this sort prevents revocation, although all the other elements are present." *Id.* at 448. There is no need in that situation to construe the revocation as a "conditional" one—the presumed condition being that the document being destroyed is not the testator's will—for a mistake of that kind suffices on its own to justify granting relief.

The more troublesome branch of the doctrine is where the mistake is not in the act of revocation itself but in the inducement for the act, arising from facts or circumstances extrinsic to the instrument revoked. This often takes the form of a mistake of law or of legal consequences. The most common instance of this form is "where a testator revokes a later will in the belief that he can thus put a prior will into effect, or where he revokes a prior instrument thinking that a later instrument has been executed in due form and that no other facts exist which will prevent such instrument from operating as a later will." *Id.* at 448. *See also* Joseph Warren, *Dependent Relative Revocation,* 33 Harv. L.Rev. 337, 342 (1920).

It is possible, of course, for a testator to make clear that his revocation of an existing will is conditioned on the legal validity or effectiveness of some other instrument, but, as the Page authors note, in most instances the testator has simply assumed that state of affairs and has articulated no such condition. In such cases, the revocation is really less of a conditional one than one based on a mistake of law which, if regarded in that manner, would not normally suffice to avoid an otherwise deliberate act. Some courts, in an effort to effectuate what they presume would have been the testator's intent had he known the true circumstances, have thus constructed the fiction of a conditional, or dependent relative, revocation, as a more plausible theory upon which to provide relief. *See* George E. Palmer, *Dependent Relative Revocation and its Relation to Relief for Mistake,* 69 Mich. L.Rev. 989–90 (1970–71):

> "The one part of the law of wills in which courts often do give relief for mistake is in connection with revocation by holding that an apparent revocation was ineffective because of mistake in underlying assumptions. Rarely, if ever, however, does a modern court rest its decision squarely on its power to relieve for mistake. Instead, the testator's intent to revoke is regarded as conditioned upon the truth of the matter in question; since the condition has not been met the conclusion is reached that there was no revocation for lack of the requisite intent. This is the doctrine of dependent relative revocation. *It rests upon an analysis that, with few exceptions, is found nowhere else in the law relating to mistake in underlying assumptions.*"

(Emphasis added.)

... As Page, and increasingly many courts, have warned, however, the testator's true intentions in a mistake of law-implied condition context are often ambiguous—harder to discern with real clarity and authority—and, before applying legal fictions based on undocumented presumptions to accept as valid a will that has otherwise been facially revoked in accordance with all legal prerequisites, courts need to examine the circumstances with great care and caution. We shall turn now to those circumstances, as they appear in this case....

Neither the 1990 will nor the 1994 will make any reference to any earlier will, and, as noted, neither contains the signatures of any attesting witnesses, although the 1990 will has a place designated for witnesses.

... The sole question presented to the circuit court was whether the orphans' court erred in applying the doctrine of dependent relative revocation and admitting the 1985 will to probate, notwithstanding its apparent revocation. After a brief evidentiary hearing, the court entered an order affirming the admission of the 1985 will to probate.

The basis of its ruling was that "the revocation of the April 12, 1985 Will was so related to the making of the June 28, 1990 Will as to be dependent on it. Therefore, since the June 28, 1990 Will was invalid, the April 12, 1985 Will, whose contents can be ascertained, should be given effect."

Application of Dependent Relative Revocation

At issue here is the branch of the dependent relative revocation doctrine that, in effect, disregards conduct otherwise qualifying as a revocation of a will when that conduct, in the court's view, was based on an assumption by the testator that the will being revoked would be immediately replaced by a valid new will. It is the "mistake of law" branch of the doctrine. Two overlapping and confluent assumptions underlie the theory. One was expressed in a 1929 Annotation, A.G.S., *Effect of Testator's Attempted Physical Alteration of Will After Execution*, 62 A.L.R. 1367, 1401 (1929):

> "It is based upon the presumption that the testator performed the act of revocation with a view and for the purpose of making some other disposition of his property in place of that which was canceled, and that there is, therefore, no reason to suppose that he would have made the change if he had been aware that it would have been wholly futile, but that his wishes with regard to his property, as expressed in his original will, would have remained unchanged, in the absence of any known and sufficient reason for changing them."

See also the 1952 update of that Annotation, L.S. Tellier, *Effect of Testator's Attempted Physical Alteration of Will After Execution*, 24 A.L.R.2d 514, 554 (1952).

A second, or perhaps simply a different articulation of the same, theory offered in support of the doctrine comes into play when, as is often the case, the effect of not disregarding the revocation is for the decedent's estate, or some part of it, to pass intestate. *See In re Macomber's Will*, 274 A.D. 724, 87 N.Y.S.2d 308, 312 (1949): "The rule seeks to avoid intestacy where a will has once been duly executed and the acts of the testator in relation to its revocation seem conditional or equivocal." *See also Goriczynski v. Poston*, 248 Va. 271, 448 S.E.2d 423, 425 (1994). The law disfavors intestacies and requires that, whenever reasonably possible, wills be construed to avoid that result. *Crawford v. Crawford*, 266 Md. 711, 719, 296 A.2d 388, 392 (1972). Courts have made it clear, however, that the law's preference for a testate disposition is always subordinate to the intention of the testator, whether ascertained or presumed. *See Charleston Library Soc. v. Citizens & Southern Nat. B.*, 200 S.C. 96, 20 S.E.2d 623, 632 (1942).

Although, as noted, this Court has never applied the doctrine, we have discussed aspects of it in three cases. In *Semmes v. Semmes*, 7 H. & J. 388 (Md.1826), the testator had a will leaving his entire estate to his wife, in trust for herself and his infant son until the child reached 21, at which point one-half of the personal property was to go to her absolutely. When his wife predeceased him, the testator used a pen to obliterate his signature and those of the attesting witnesses and to write on the bottom of the will, "In consequence of the death of my wife, it is become necessary to make another will." *Id.* at 389. Unfortunately, he died before making another will. The orphans' court refused to probate the existing will, and this Court affirmed that judgment. Our predecessors discussed the doctrine of dependent relative revocation as it had been applied in some English cases, notably *Onions v. Tyrer,* 1 P. Williams, 343 (1717), characterizing the doctrine as based on a mistake principle:

> "The cancelling of a will is said to be an equivocal act, and not to effect a revocation, unless it is done *animo revocandi.* And where it is a dependent relative act, done with reference to another, which is meant and supposed to be good and effectual, it may be a revocation or not, as to that to which it relates is efficacious or not. As where a man having duly executed one will, afterwards causes another to be prepared, and supposing the second to be duly executed, under that impression alone cancels the first. In such case it has been held, that on the second turning out not to have been duly executed, the cancelling the first, being done by mistake and misapprehension, would not operate as a revocation."

7 H. & J. at 390–91.

Having so characterized the doctrine, the Court made clear that the doctrine would never apply "where a man has deliberately and intentionally cancelled his will, as in this case, in the entire absence of all accident or mistake, notwithstanding he may, at the time, have intended to make another will." *Id.* at 391. We accepted, from the evidence, that the testator did not intend to die intestate but held that "however that may be, we cannot make a will for him." *Id.* On its facts, *Semmes* was similar to the situation in *In re Emernecker's Estate, supra,* 218 Pa. 369, 67 A. 701, where the revocation also was not actually accompanied by the preparation of a new, albeit ineffective will....

This case presents for the first time a situation in which the doctrine *might* be applied and in which other courts have applied it. It is not a situation, however, in which we believe it appropriate to apply the doctrine.

It is important to keep in mind that, in the context now before us, the doctrine rests on a fiction that is, in turn, supported only by an assumption as to what Ms. Binco would have done had she known that her 1990 will was invalid. As Professor Warren observed in his law review article, "[t]he inquiry should always be: What would the testator have desired had he been informed of the true situation?" Joseph Warren, *Dependent Relative Revocation, supra,* 33 Harv. L.Rev. at 345. The most rational and obvious answer to that question, of course, is that the testator would have desired to make the new instrument effective, and, if presumed intent were to control, the court would simply overlook the statutory deficiency and probate the new will, rather than overlook the legal effect of an otherwise deliberate revocation and probate the old one. That is an option the law does not permit, however. We thus must look for secondary, fictional intentions never actually possessed by Ms. Binco. The real question is what Ms. Binco would have wanted to do if she had been told that she was unable to make a new will: would she have preferred her estate to pass under the existing (1985) will to persons she had decided to remove as beneficiaries, or would she have preferred that her estate pass intestate to her brother?

In attempting to arrive at a reasonable answer to that kind of question, courts have considered all of the relevant circumstances surrounding the revocation — the manner in which the existing will was revoked, whether a new will was actually made and, if so, how contemporaneous the revocation and the making of the new will were, parol evidence regarding the testator's intentions, and the differences and similarities between the old and new wills. The courts recognize that the question is always one of presumed intent. In many cases, because the other evidence is either inconclusive or nonexistent, the principal focus is on the differences and similarities between the two instruments. In that regard, the courts have generally refused to apply the doctrine unless the two instruments reflect a common dispositive scheme. (Citations omitted.)

Conversely, courts that have applied the doctrine have looked to the similarity of the new and old dispositive schemes as a basis for concluding that the testator indeed intended the revocation to be conditional and that he would have preferred to have his estate pass under the old will rather than through an intestacy. (Citations omitted.)

In the case before us, Ms. Binco indicated a clear intent to revoke her 1985 will by writing VOID on the back of it. Unlike the situation in *Safe Dep. & Trust Co., supra,* 117 Md. 154, 83 A. 45, there is nothing ambiguous about her intent to revoke that will. Also unlike that case and *Semmes,* however, she did contemporaneously handwrite a new will, thereby indicating with some clarity that her act of revocation was based on her mistaken belief that the new will was valid and would replace the old one. The confluent inference, that she intended to revoke the 1985 will based on her belief that it would be superseded by the 1990 will, does not alone justify application of the doctrine of dependent relative revocation. We must still search for that fictional presumed intent of what she would have done had she been informed that she could not make a new will. There was some evidence that Ms. Binco did not have a good relationship with her brother and would not have desired that he take any part of her estate. That evidence was contradicted, however, by testimony that appellant and his sister did have a cordial relationship.

We turn, then, to a comparison of the 1985 and 1990 wills and, as noted, we find two very different dispositive schemes. Apart from the fact that the 1990 will did not contain a residuary clause and may not have effected an entirely testate disposition, the fact is that, with the possible exception of the First Church of God, whose status under the 1990 will is, at best, unclear, none of the beneficiaries under the 1985 will were named in the 1990 will. The 1990 will replaced them all, indicating that Ms. Binco did not wish any of them (again with the possible exception of the First Church of God) to be benefitted. The effect of applying the doctrine and disregarding her revocation, however, is precisely to do what she clearly did not want done — to leave her estate to people she had intended to disinherit. We cannot fairly presume such an intent on her part; nor should the lower courts have done so.

We need not decide in this case whether the doctrine of dependent relative revocation, as articulated above, is part of Maryland law and, if it is, the circumstances under which it may properly be applied. It cannot be applied under the circumstances of this case.

Notes

1. *DRR—conceptually and doctrinally*: As difficult as the court's opinion may appear to one reading about DRR for the first time, the court actually does an excellent job of explaining: (1) the conceptual logic behind the doctrine, and (2) the doctrinal challenges inherent in articulating a workable formulation of the doctrine.

First, DRR is not at issue unless there is a valid revocation. If an attempted revocation is not valid, a party need not invoke DRR to ask the court to ignore the revocation; an invalid revocation is no revocation. Thus, the first requirement for DRR is a valid revocation. Look back at the court's opinion in *Kroll*. The first paragraph under the DRR heading establishes that the testatrix validly revoked her 1985 will.

Second, the revocation must have been based upon a mistake (a mistake of either fact or law). The court does an excellent job of noting that while many authorities and courts talk in terms of an incorrect assumption, the general rule is that the flawed assumption must rise to the level of a *mistake at the time of the revocation*. The court makes that point not only in its generic discussion of DRR (in the remaining paragraphs under the DRR heading in the court's opinion), but also in its discussion of the *Semmes* case. In *Semmes*, the testator revoked his will, intending to execute a new will. He *assumed* he would get around to executing a new will before he died. But as the court pointed out, "[u]nfortunately, he died before making another will." The court correctly noted that this would not be an appropriate scenario for DRR. There was no *mistake* at the time of revocation that caused, or at least contributed to, the testator's decision to revoke the will. Things did not turn out as the testator assumed (i.e., he did not execute a new will before he died), but that was an assumption that did not turn out as he thought it would. It technically was not a mistake of law or fact at the time he revoked the will.

In *Kroll*, the court found that there was sufficient connection between the revocation of the 1985 will and the attempted execution of the 1990 will to rise to the level of a mistake at the time of revocation: "Unlike ... *Semmes*, however, she [the testatrix] did contemporaneously handwrite a new will, thereby indicating with some clarity that her act of revocation was based on her mistaken belief that the new will was valid and would replace the old one." This conclusion is also supported by the note handwritten by the testatrix on the back of the 1985 will: "VOID-NEW WILL DRAWN UP 6-28-90". Testatrix apparently believed the 1990 document was a "new will" when in reality it was not a valid new will. The testatrix revoked her 1985 will because of a mistake of law.

Third, the court does an excellent job of pointing out that even assuming, *arguendo*, that the testator revoked his or her will based upon a mistake, the doctrine should not apply unless it can be established that the testator's probable intent would be to have the revocation ignored:

> We thus must look for secondary, fictional intentions never actually possessed by Ms. Binco. The real question is what Ms. Binco would have wanted to do

if she had been told that she was unable to make a new will: would she have preferred her estate to pass under the existing (1985) will to persons she had decided to remove as beneficiaries, or would she have preferred that her estate pass intestate to her brother?"

The court acknowledges this can be a rather open-ended inquiry into the decedent's probable intent: "In attempting to arrive at a reasonable answer to that kind of question, courts have considered all of the relevant circumstances surrounding the revocation . . . ."

Courts, however, are rather uncomfortable with such an open-ended inquiry. Whenever possible they appear to favor a "spectrum" type of an analysis. As the court noted, it has only two options: the court can either: (1) apply DRR and ignore the revocation (i.e., give effect to the revoked instrument/gift), or (2) decline to apply DRR and give effect to the revocation. Those are the two ends of the spectrum. The testator's failed testamentary scheme is his or her true intent, but the court cannot give effect to that because the testator failed to execute it properly. To the extent, however, that that appears to be the testator's *true* intent, invariably the courts ask where on the spectrum between the court's only two options does the testator's true intent fall? If the failed true intent is more like the revoked instrument/gift end of the spectrum, the court should apply DRR and ignore the revocation. If, however, the testator's true intent is more like the outcome if the revocation is given effect, the court should decline to apply DRR. (Note that the burden of proof is on the party invoking DRR, so if the court cannot discern which outcome the decedent would have preferred, the court should decline to apply DRR).

Note that in *Kroll* the court de facto applied the spectrum analysis. The court compared her *true* intent at the time of revocation (the provisions of the 1990 will) to the provisions of the 1985 will and found them to be nothing alike (which de facto gives rise to the presumption that the testator would not want DRR to apply):

> We turn, then, to a comparison of the 1985 and 1990 wills and, as noted, we find two very different dispositive schemes. Apart from the fact that the 1990 will did not contain a residuary clause and may not have effected an entirely testate disposition, the fact is that, with the possible exception of the First Church of God, whose status under the 1990 will is, at best, unclear, none of the beneficiaries under the 1985 will were named in the 1990 will. The 1990 will replaced them all, indicating that Ms. Binco did not wish any of them (again with the possible exception of the First Church of God) to be benefitted. The effect of applying the doctrine and disregarding her revocation, however, is precisely to do what she clearly did not want done — to leave her estate to people she had intended to disinherit. We cannot fairly presume such an intent on her part; nor should the lower courts have done so.

Applying the spectrum analysis, the court concluded that it was more probable that if the testatrix knew she had only two options, the 1985 will or intestacy, she probably would have preferred intestacy.

2. *The revival overlap:* At this point, DRR may not look so complicated. All it appears to require is a valid revocation, based upon a mistake, and the testator would not have revoked but for the mistake. That statement of the doctrine, however, overlooks a latent limitation inherent in the doctrine. If that were all that was required, what would stop someone from coming in to court anytime there is a revocation (in whole or in part) and arguing DRR in an attempt to get a share of the estate? To rein in the doctrine, the courts have incorporated some of the evidentiary restrictions inherent in the revival doctrine into the DRR doctrine.

The modern trend approach to revival focuses on the testator's intent. Assume Will #1 and Will #2, and then the testator revokes Will #2. Will #1 is revived if the testator intends to revive Will #1. The testator need not re-execute the will (Will #1) to revive it. The key then, whenever the testator revokes Will #2, is whether the testator *intended* to revive Will #1. The testator's intent controls. From an evidentiary perspective, the question then becomes: what evidence of the testator's intent to revive will the courts accept? Note that the revival statute very carefully addresses that issue. What evidence is admissible depends on how Will #2 was revoked. If Will #2 is revoked by writing (Will #3), the intent to revive must be set forth in Will #3. If, however, Will #2 is revoked by act, the statute permits extrinsic evidence as to the testator's intent.

Just as the revival statute restricts the evidence that is admissible to show testator's intent, the courts have developed similar (but not identical) restrictions on the evidence that is admissible with respect to the mistake requirement in DRR. The material above established the traditional articulation of DRR: DRR applies anytime there is a valid revocation, based upon a mistake, and the testator would not have revoked but for the mistake. The key to DRR is the testator's *conditional* intent, which is inferred from the testator's mistake. The issue then becomes: what evidence of the mistake (the basis for inferring the testator's conditional intent) will the courts accept? Like revival, the answer depends on how the revocation in question was achieved (the revocation the court is being asked to ignore). If the revocation was in writing (i.e., Will #2), the mistake must be set forth or reflected in the writing (Will #2). If, however, the revocation was by act, the courts invariably require evidence of a failed attempt at a new testamentary disposition — typically a new will, though it need not be, as it just needs to be a failed attempt at a new testamentary disposition that involves a writing (thus making it difficult to fabricate such evidence).[6] This evidentiary restriction is implicit in the court's discussion of DRR in *Kroll* though it is not stated as expressly as are the doctrine's other requirements:

> The most common instance of this form [of DRR—DRR where the revocation is by act] is "where a testator revokes a later will in the belief that he can thus put a prior will into effect, or where he revokes a prior instrument thinking that a later instrument has been executed in due form and that no other facts exist which will prevent such instrument from operating as a later will." (Quot-

---

6. In *Kroll*, the failed attempt at a new testamentary disposition was the June 28, 1990 Will.

ing from Joseph Warren, *Dependent Relative Revocation*, 33 Harv. L. Rev. 337, 342 (1920), one of the leading law review articles on the doctrine).

In discussing DRR by act, the court (and the article) implicitly set forth the need for a failed attempt at a new testamentary disposition. In the first scenario discussed, the failed attempt at a new testamentary disposition is a failed attempt at reviving a prior will—an evidentiary restriction that helps rein in the scope of the doctrine. In the second scenario discussed in the quoted material, the failed attempt at a new testamentary disposition is a failed attempt at executing a new will.

The court implicitly applies and uses the evidentiary restriction in its application of DRR to the *Kroll* case. How did the testatrix revoke the 1985 will in *Kroll*? She revoked it by act. The court carefully pointed out that "by writing *on the 1985 will*" (emphasis added) she revoked the 1985 will (the writing on the will was not signed, thus providing additional support for the conclusion that it constituted revocation by act—the act of canceling the will). Inasmuch as the revocation in question was by act, the party invoking DRR must prove the mistake (the basis for the revocation) by proving a failed attempt at a new testamentary disposition. In *Kroll*, the failed attempt at a new testamentary disposition is the failed 1990 will. The mistake is a mistake of law (the testatrix believed the 1990 will was valid when it was not). The key, however, is the latent evidentiary restriction that courts invariably apply to DRR. Where the revocation is by act, the party invoking DRR is limited in the evidence the party can offer to prove the mistake. Admissible evidence is limited to showing a failed attempt at a new testamentary disposition. Where the revocation is in writing (Will #2), the mistake must be set forth in or reflected in the writing (Will #2).

Problems

1. Testator's validly executed will (Will #1) leaves all of his property to his friend, Fred, and lists Elise as the executor. Testator decides to make a new Will #2, which retains Fred as the sole beneficiary but replaces Elise with Edward as executor. Testator validly revokes Will #1 by physical act (e.g., he crosses out the face of each page and writes "revoked" across the face of each page). Assume, however, that Will #2 was not validly executed (e.g., it was not properly signed).

   Testator dies and his relatives assert that they are entitled to all of Testator's property via intestate succession, claiming that Testator died without a valid will. Can Fred successfully invoke DRR, and if so, how much would he get?

2. Assume Testatrix has a valid typed will that provides, in pertinent part, as follows: "I give $10,000 to my daughter Carolyn." Thereafter Testatrix decides she wants to increase the gift to Carolyn to $15,000. Testatrix takes out the will, draws a line through the "$10,000" amount typed in the will and handwrites "*$15,000*" above it. The Testatrix then puts the will back in her desk. No one knows what she has done until it is found after her death. How much, if anything, does Carolyn get?

   Originally Carolyn was to receive $10,000. When Testatrix drew a line through that gift, however, that act constituted a valid revocation by act. At that point

Carolyn would receive nothing. Then Testatrix handwrote $15,000 on the will. The question is whether that is a valid codicil to her typed will. It does not qualify as an attested will because there are no witnesses and it is not signed. It does not qualify as a holographic will because not all of the material provisions are in her handwriting and it is not signed. It does not qualify as a will under the harmless error doctrine because it is not signed. Accordingly, at this point Carolyn would receive nothing.

Can Carolyn successfully invoke DRR? If so, how much would she get?

3. Assume the same scenario as in Problem 2, only this time assume Testatrix handwrites in $1,000. Inasmuch as the handwritten interlineation is not a valid codicil, can Carolyn successfully invoke DRR? If so, how much would she get?

4. In 1955, Testatrix executed a valid will in Milwaukee (none of her heirs are named as beneficiaries). In 1959, Testatrix executed a valid will in Kankakee (only one heir is named as a beneficiary). The bulk of her estate under both wills was devised to three of her close friends (the same friends under both wills). Testatrix subsequently destroyed the Kankakee will (but her attorney had a photocopy of it) with the intent to revoke it. She told several witnesses that she wanted the Milwaukee will to stand. Thereafter Testatrix died.

   If the controlling law requires a revoked will to be re-executed to be revived, did testatrix validly revive Will #1 (the Milwaukee will)? If not, can the beneficiaries under either will (or both wills) invoke DRR? What would be your analysis if the beneficiaries asked the court to apply DRR? *See In re Estate of Alburn,* 118 N.W.2d 919 (Wis. 1963).

5. Assume Testator has a validly executed will that bequeaths $5,000 to his good friend Paul. Thereafter Paul goes to Africa to work with an NGO (a non-governmental organization doing good in Africa). Thereafter Testator receives word that the village Paul was working in was attacked, and everyone was killed. Testator validly executes a codicil that provides, in pertinent part, as follows: "I hereby revoke my gift to Paul because he is dead." Testator dies in a car crash later that day, and a week later Paul turns up alive in another remote village in Africa. Is Paul entitled to take from Testator's estate?

6. Assume the same scenario as in Problem 5, only this time the codicil says: "I hereby revoke the gift to Paul." Testator told several witnesses that the reason he revoked the gift was because he had heard Paul was dead. What is the most likely result?

7. Assume the same scenario as above in Problem 5, only this time the codicil changes Paul's gift from an outright gift to a gift in trust (and it is a significantly larger gift). Unbeknownst to Testator the new gift to Paul violates the Rule Against Perpetuities and thus is void. The problem is not discovered until after Testator's death. To what, if anything, is Paul entitled?

8. Testator, a resident of New York, validly executed Will #1, which contained a gift to a Loyola High School (a private, Jesuit high school). Later, Testator moves to

California and validly executes an identical Will #2 (expressly revoking Will #1), and dies within days of making Will #2. Under an old law (no longer valid in most jurisdictions) gifts to charities made by a will within a certain period after a testator's death were null and void. If the law still applied in the jurisdiction, Will #2 in effect would contain no gift to Loyola. If Loyola invokes DRR, what would be your analysis?

9. X had a will devising all of her property to her brother, B. Subsequently, X's mental state deteriorated and a conservator, C, was appointed for X. Thereafter C mistakenly told X that B had died in a car crash, and X executed a new will that expressly provided: "I hereby revoke my prior will and devise all of my property to Santa Clara Law School." Absent additional evidence, upon X's death, what is the most likely result under the California Probate Code, and why?

10. In 1968, testatrix executed and brought home with her a will leaving the bulk of her estate to her son, Donald (to the exclusion of her other son, Robert). In 1970, testatrix executed and brought home with her a new will that expressly revoked the 1968 will and left her estate "to Donald and Robert, share and share alike." At her death, the 1970 will could not be found. How should testatrix's property be distributed, and why?

Chapter 8

Components of a Will

I. Introduction

As circular as it may sound initially, a will can consist of more than just the will. A will can have several components. This chapter explores the doctrines that permit the probate court to expand on the scope of a will—to give effect to the testator's intent even when that intent is expressed outside of what the layperson would consider the pages of the testator's will.

II. Integration

Whenever the law discusses a document that can have multiple pages, at some point the law must define what constitutes the pages of that document. Most law students encounter this issue during the first year of law school when examining the issue of what constitutes a valid contract under the Statute of Frauds. No doubt included in that material was a discussion of what is required for various separate "papers" or "writings" to be considered an integrated written contract. A similar issue can arise with respect to a will: what constitutes the pages of a testator's will? The doctrine of integration addresses that question.

A. Attested Will

In the typical attested will execution scenario, the doctrine of integration is as logical and straightforward as one might expect. The pieces of paper that are physically present at the time of execution and that the testator intends to be part of the will constitute the pages of the will. Rarely is integration an issue for attested wills because of the role of the drafting and supervising attorney. Virtually all attested wills are drafted by an attorney, and the will execution ceremony is invariably supervised by the attorney. All of the pages of the will are successively numbered, in the same type font, and securely fastened together. Such preparation should leave no doubt that the multiple pieces of paper physically present and fastened together when the execution ceremony begins are intended by the testator to constitute the pages of his or her will. That is why in real life there are very few attested will cases where integration is an issue. There are none to date in California. Holographic wills, however, are another story.

B. Holographic Will

The threshold question for integration as applied to holographic wills is whether the courts should modify the doctrine in light of the fact that holographic wills are homemade wills by laypeople. In the case of *In re Estate of McCarty*, 211 Cal. App. 2d 23, 27–28 (Ct. App. 1962), the court had the following to say about the doctrine of integration as it applies to holographic instruments:

> 'In the law of wills, integration ... occurs when there is no reference to a distinctly extraneous document, but it is clear that two or more separate writings are intended by the testator to be his will.' (*Estate of Wunderle, supra*, 30 Cal.2d at p. 281, 181 P.2d at p. 878.) Thus several writings which are connected by sequence of thought (*Estate of Swendsen* (1941) 43 Cal.App.2d 551, 111 P.2d 408), folded together (*Estate of Merryfield* (1914) 167 Cal. 729, 141 P. 259), or physically forming one document (*Estate of Clisby* (1904) 145 Cal. 407, 78 P. 964), have been admitted to probate as constituting a holographic will. It is also clear that a holographic will need not be signed at the end (*Estate of Morgan* (1927) 200 Cal. 400, 253 P. 702), and that the testator may make alterations to a holographic will on a date subsequent to the date on which it was signed. (*Estate of Finkler* (1935) 3 Cal.2d 584, 599–602, 46 P.2d 149.) Such alterations, when made in the testator's handwriting, operate to adopt the old date and signatures. (See *Estate of Dumas* (1949) 34 Cal.2d 406, 410–411, 210 P.2d 697, and authorities therein cited.) 'If the papers are all holographic and there is a dating and signing somewhere among them, it is immaterial when or where the dating or signing was done so long as it may be reasonably inferred that the testator meant all the papers together to constitute his will and that the signature was written with the intent that it should there serve as a token of execution.' (*Estate of Moody, supra*, 118 Cal.App.2d at p. 308, 257 P.2d at p. 713.)

Notes

1. *Integration—holographic versus attested will*: Is the law of integration the same for holographic wills as it is for attested wills? How would you articulate the doctrine of integration as it applies to holographic writings?

2. *Holographic codicils to holographic wills*: The general rule is that a codicil must be executed with the same Wills Act formalities as are required for a valid will. This applies to attested codicils to attested wills, and to holographic codicils to attested wills, but in light of the court's statement above, does it apply to holographic codicils to holographic wills? What is the rule for holographic codicils to holographic wills?

Problem

Following Frank Blain's death, seven separate sheets of paper, each wholly in his handwriting and signed by him, were found in his safe deposit box, folded together and enclosed in a sealed envelope, on which was written in the decedent's handwriting

"Last Will F. B." Three of the sheets of paper were dated June 1, 1949, and the other four were dated April 9, 1952. Six of the sheets of paper dealt with separate devises or bequests to separate beneficiaries, and the seventh authorized the sale of a parcel of real property to cover the inheritance taxes and probate expenses. In addition, the same safe deposit box contained a small piece of paper with five words written in the decedent's handwriting "to Sonia Lambert Frank Blain." Sonia is Frank's granddaughter. The small piece of paper was wrapped around a small ring box that contained a dinner ring worth $120. Should the seven sheets of paper be considered seven distinct wills or, rather, one will under integration? Can the small piece of paper be integrated with the other sheets of paper? *See In re Blain's Estate*, 140 Cal. App. 2d 917 (1956).

III. Republication by Codicil

The basics of a codicil were covered in the last chapter. A codicil is a will that amends or revises an existing will. Because a codicil "amends or revises an existing will," it obviously can have the effect of expanding the scope of the will by permitting the court to give effect to the testator's intent expressed not only in the will but also in the codicil. But to the extent the two documents are wills, one can argue that a codicil does not really expand the scope of the will—it just becomes a component of the will. However it is viewed, a codicil obviously affects the scope of a will.

A codicil is an interesting legal instrument because it has a unique relationship with the underlying will—a relationship that is difficult to articulate. Not only does a codicil revise and/or amend a will, the general rule is that a codicil *republishes* the will. Republishing the will means, as a general rule, that a codicil re-executes and re-dates the will to the date of the codicil. Both of these ancillary codicil rules are simple to state in isolation, but that simplicity can be misleading because these ancillary rules can overlap, and interact with, a plethora of other rules, thereby giving rise to a whole host of interesting crossover issues.

For example, re-executing the will can clean up possible execution issues involving the original will execution ceremony. Assume a beneficiary under the testator's original will is one of the two attesting witnesses to the will execution ceremony (which would give rise to the interested witness doctrine), but that interested witness is not a witness to the codicil. Most courts hold that the codicil would cure the potential interested witness scenario (assuming there is no interested witness involved in the codicil execution ceremony) because the codicil republishes (re-executes) the underlying will.

In addition, re-dating the will can interact with other date-sensitive doctrines, thereby creating another set of interesting overlap issues. For example, historically, if a person executed a will while single and thereafter married, the marriage automatically voided the will.[1] The logic behind the doctrine was to make sure the new

---

1. Do not worry about the details of this doctrine, the pretermitted spouse doctrine, at this point. It is covered in Chapter 10 (and the current California approach is much different from this traditional

spouse was not accidentally omitted. Voiding the will would force the testator's property through intestacy where the new spouse would receive a share. But what if, after his or her marriage, the testator executed a codicil that changed only the executor of his or her estate? Should the codicil be deemed to re-date the will to after the date of the wedding, thereby knocking out the protection for the new spouse under the omitted spouse doctrine?

There are too many potential overlaps between the republication by codicil doctrine and other doctrines to examine them all, but it is helpful to get a sense of how the courts deal with the overlaps.

In re McCauley's Estate

71 P. 512 (Cal. 1903)

CHIPMAN, C.

Jennie C. McCauley duly executed a will on February 12, 1900, in which she, among others, made several bequests to charitable institutions. On March 16, 1900, she duly executed a codicil to this will. She died April 14, 1900, 28 days after the execution of the codicil. The state, by the attorney general, filed objections and contest to the petition for final distribution, so far as concerned the charitable bequests, and prayed that they be adjudged void, and that they be distributed to the state for the support of the common schools. The trial court adjudged the said bequests to be valid, and decreed distribution accordingly. The state appeals from the decree.

The codicil did not attempt to change any of the charitable bequests, or any of the general provisions of the will, but related solely to specific bequests and devises to certain individual legatees. It stated that 'the foregoing codicil * * * was, at the date hereof, * * * signed, sealed, and published as, and declared to be, together with the will set forth on the preceding pages, to be her last will and testament,' etc. Section 1313, Civ. Code, provides as follows: 'No estate, real or personal, shall be bequeathed or devised to any charitable or benevolent society or corporation, or to any person or persons in trust for charitable uses, except the same be done by will duly executed at least thirty days before the decease of the testator.'[2] Section 1287 of the same Code reads as follows: 'The execution of a codicil, referring to a previous will, has the effect to republish the will, as modified by the codicil.' The testatrix left 'no relatives or next of kin,' as she declared in her will, and, as seems to be conceded by respondents, the bequests in question will escheat if, as to such bequests, the will is invalid.

Appellant's contention is 'that the effect of the republication of the will by the codicil of March 16, 1900, and the testatrix dying in less than 30 days thereafter, is

_____

approach). We are using the doctrine here just to help you appreciate the potential overlapping consequences of the republication by codicil doctrine.

2. Such statutes limiting a testator's right or ability to devise his or her estate to a charitable organization were commonly referred to as mortmain statutes and were derived from the traditional English statutes. Most states have abolished their mortmain statutes. California abolished the mortmain restrictions at issue in *McCauley* in 1971.

to invalidate all the bequests to charity contained in the will.' Appellant cites numerous cases to the effect that the codicil brings the will to it, and makes it the will from the date of the codicil. Some of the cases speak of the codicil as a republication of the whole will at the date of the codicil. Still others hold that the codicil operates as a republication of the will, the effect of which is to bring down the will to the date of the codicil, so that both instruments are to be considered as speaking at the same date, and taking effect at the same time. *Payne v. Payne,* 18 Cal. 292, at page 302, and *In re Ladd,* 94 Cal. 670, 30 Pac. 99, are cited as in line with the authorities elsewhere holding as above stated. In the *Ladd* Case it was said that 'the execution of the codicil had the effect 'to republish the will as modified by the codicil' (Civ. Code, § 1287) as of the date of the codicil (*Payne v. Payne,* 18 Cal. 302).' Again: 'The effect of its execution was to republish the entire will, and not merely the clause so modified, "as if the testator had inserted in the codicil all the words of the will." *Doe v. Walker,* 12 Mees. & W. 597. In giving construction to the will it was said that 'the whole of the original will and the codicil are to be construed as a single instrument executed at the date of the codicil, and of which all the parts are to be construed, "so as, if possible, to form one consistent whole." Civ. Code, § 1321. But it was also said: 'A codicil is never construed to disturb the dispositions of the will further than is absolutely necessary for the purpose of giving effect to the codicil. 1 Jarman on Wills, 176. 'The dispositions made by a will are not to be disturbed by a codicil further than is absolutely necessary in order to give it effect, and a clear disposition made by the will is not revoked by a doubtful expression or inconsistent disposition in a codicil.' *Kane v. Astor's Exors.,* 5 Sandf. 533. "The different parts of a will, or of a will and codicil, shall be reconciled if possible; and, where a bequest has once been made, it shall not be revoked, unless no other construction can fairly be put upon the language used by the testator *Colt v. Colt,* 32 Conn. 446. See, also, *Wetmore v. Parker,* 52 N. Y. 462; *Johns Hopkins University v. Pinckney,* 55 Md. 365." No one for a moment can suppose that the codicil in the present will was intended to disturb the bequests made in the original will in aid of the charities named. These bequests were not only left untouched by the codicil, but the testatrix declared that 'the foregoing codicil * * * was * * * published as, and declared to be, together with the will set forth on the preceding pages, to be her last will.' That the testatrix intended her bequests first made in the will to stand unaffected by the codicil can admit of no doubt, and yet we are asked to give such construction to section 1287 as shall destroy a large number of her bequests, and practically nullify the testatrix's clearly expressed intention with respect to them. We have seen that no such construction can be given to the codicil itself. Can we—or, rather, are we compelled to—so construe the statute as to destroy these bequests, and thus thwart the design of the testator? ... In construing section 1287, we must keep in view the various sections relation to the subject of wills, and must so construe that section as to preserve the letter and spirit of all the provisions of the statute so far as possible. The section should have such construction, if it is possible in reason to do so, as will carry out the known intention of the testator. Section 1313 invalidates the charitable bequest unless the will is 'duly executed at least thirty days before the decease of the testator.' When the will is once 'duly executed,' it remains the will of the testator until revoked. This may be done as prescribed in section 1292. A codicil does not disturb the will except so far as it is inconsistent with it, or in terms or by necessary intendament (sic) revokes it. As was said in the *Ladd* Case: 'Where a bequest has once been made, it shall not be revoked unless no other construction can fairly be put upon the language used by the testator.' For some purposes, no doubt, the will speaks from the date of the codicil, but this is true only so far as the codicil requires that it should so speak. It is entirely consistent with the statute and the codicil now before us that the contested bequests should stand as made of the date of the will. The testatrix declared the will as first executed to be her will, except as to the changes made in the codicil, and the statute (section 1287) says that the effect of the codicil is 'to republish the will, as modified by the codicil,' and not otherwise. To construe the statute, as is contended for by appellant, is to leave a large part of the estate undisposed of, as well as to defeat the object of the testatrix. We do not think it should be given any such construction.

Notes

1. *Republication by codicil and testator's intent*: As the court's analysis in *McCauley* demonstrates, there is often tension when the republication by codicil overlap creates an outcome that appears to be inconsistent with the testator's intent. A competing consideration—that the court did not pay much attention to in the *McCauley* case—is the public policy behind the overlapping doctrine. The principal public policy consideration behind most mortmain statutes was to discourage hasty decisions by testators who assumed they were about to die and who arguably were trying to "buy their way into the afterlife" at the exclusion of persons who would ordinarily be the objects of their bounty. Assuming, *arguendo*, those were the public policy considerations behind the mortmain provisions in *McCauley*, the court's decision not to apply republication by codicil to void the gifts in question appears even more defensible. The original gifts were executed well outside the restricted timeframe.

2. *Republication by codicil—rule of law or rule of construction?* As a general rule, where the overlap appears to facilitate giving effect to the testator's apparent intent, the courts liberally recite and apply the overlapping rules to avoid or cure any potential problem. Where, however, the overlap appears to impede or conflict with the testator's apparent intent, many courts state that the republication by codicil rule is a rule of construction and not a rule of law per se, thereby permitting the court to decline to apply the doctrine if it concludes that application would be inconsistent with testator's overall intent.

3. *Express republication clause*: The republication by codicil doctrine applies regardless of whether there is an express republication clause in the codicil or not. Where the republication conflicts with the testator's intent, the *McCauley* case shows that the courts are, in fact, open to not applying the republication by codicil doctrine. What if the codicil *expressly* states that it republishes and redates the underlying will?

Should that affect the court's analysis of whether it can/should decline to republish and redate the will?

4. *Analytical approach*: Because it is impossible to examine all the possible overlaps between republication by codicil and other will-related doctrines, it is more important that you are sensitive to the possible tension in the overlapping scenarios and that you know the different arguments the affected parties would make. Lead with the general rule that the codicil republishes the underlying will, but be open to exceptions where republication appears inconsistent with the testator's overall intent.

Problems

1. In most states, under the pretermitted child doctrine (also known as the omitted child doctrine in some states), a child who is born to the testator after execution of the will is entitled to a share of the testator's estate — on the assumption that the testator intended to provide for the child but forgot to modify his or her will. The details of the doctrine vary from state to state, and this book covers the doctrine in detail in Chapter 10. Based upon that fairly simple statement of the doctrine, should the child in the following fact pattern be entitled to invoke the doctrine?

    Testator executed a valid will that created a testamentary trust for his spouse for life, remainder to his then-living children. Thereafter testator had another child, Patricia. Thereafter testator contacted his attorney and asked her to prepare a new will that would include Patricia. After reviewing the proposed new will, testator and his attorney had a disagreement about the worth of testator's assets and how that affected the provisions of the proposed new will. The attorney advised testator to execute a codicil to the old will to address a concern with the marital trust for his spouse and to revisit the issue of providing for Patricia after they resolved the asset issue. Testator executed the codicil to the old will. The codicil expressly republished the underlying will. Tragically, testator died four months later from a heart attack at the age of 38. Can Patricia successfully invoke the pretermitted child doctrine? *See Azcunce v. Estate of Azcunce*, 586 So. 2d 1216 (Fla. Dist. Ct. Ap. 1991).

2. Testatrix executed a will and two codicils. Michael O'Connell was both a witness and a beneficiary under the will. Joan Baller was a witness to the first codicil, but not the will or the second codicil. Assuming the jurisdiction has an interested witness statute that voids gifts to an interested witness, can either witness take their gift? *See King v. Smith*, 302 A.2d 144 (N.J. Super. 1973).

IV. Incorporation by Reference

What if a document is not physically present when the testator executes his or her will, but the testator has expressed the intent that the probate court recognize and give effect to the intent expressed in the "other" document. As a general rule, can the court give effect to that intent if the intent is not part of the will — if it was not executed with Wills Act formalities? Can the testator "expand" the scope of the will to give effect to intent expressed outside the will (i.e., can a testator incorporate by reference an extrinsic document into the will)? Under what conditions, if any, might you think it appropriate for a testator to incorporate another document into a will?

A. Classic Incorporation by Reference

Must testamentary intent—an individual's wishes with respect to what he or she wants done with his or her property at time of death—*always* be expressed in a document that qualifies as a will? Can the testator express his or her testamentary wishes in another document, a document other than the will (and a document that does *not* qualify as a nonprobate instrument) and still have the court give effect to the testamentary wishes expressed in that document? If so, when? And under what conditions? To what extent does permitting a court to give effect to the testamentary wishes expressed in a document other than a will create a loophole that undermines the Wills Act formalities?

Testator Bob validly executes a will dated January 1, 2015, and the will contains various dispositive provisions, standard clauses regarding executors, etc. One of the dispositive clauses, however, states that $50,000 as well as his Ferrari are to be distributed to the individual who is identified in a letter that is being held by the executor of Bob's estate. Bob dies and his executor produces the referenced letter. The letter is dated December 1, 2014, and states that the $50,000 and the Ferrari are to be distributed to his pal, Pete. Bob's will does not provide for the disposition of either the $50,000 or the car, but the residue of his estate goes to charity. Who gets the car and the $50,000? Why?

Simon v. Grayson
102 P.2d 1081 (Cal. 1940)

WASTE, C. J.

The question presented for determination upon this appeal involves the construction and effect to be given a provision in a will purporting to incorporate a letter by reference. Respondent's claim to certain of the estate's funds is based upon the terms of the letter. The appellants, who are residuary legatees under the will, contend that the attempted incorporation by reference was ineffectual. The facts, which were presented to the trial court upon agreed statement, are as follows:

S. M. Seeligsohn died in 1935. His safe deposit box was found to contain, among other things, a will and codicil and a letter addressed to his executors. The will, which was dated March 25, 1932, contained a provision in paragraph four, leaving $6,000 to his executors "to be paid by them in certain amounts to certain persons as shall be directed by me in a letter that will be found in my effects and which said letter will be addressed to Martin E. Simon and Arthur W. Green (the executors) and will be dated March 25, 1932." Paragraph four also provided that any one having an interest in the will "shall not inquire into the application of said moneys" and that the executors "shall not be accountable to any person whomsoever for the payment and/or application of said sum ... this provision ... is in no sense a trust".

The letter found in the testator's safe deposit box was dated July 3, 1933, and stated: "In paragraph VIII of my will I have left you $6,000—to be paid to the persons named in a letter and this letter is also mentioned in said paragraph. I direct that after my death you shall pay said $6,000 as follows: To Mrs. Esther Cohn, 1755 Van Ness Ave. San Francisco, Calif. the sum of $4,000— ... If any of the said persons cannot be found by you within six months after my death, or if any of the said persons shall predecease me, the sum directed to be paid to such persons ... shall be paid by you to my heirs as described in paragraph IX of my said Will...." This letter was written, dated and signed entirely in the handwriting of the testator. No letter dated March 25, 1932, was found among his effects.

The codicil to the will was executed November 25, 1933. It made no changes in paragraph IV of the will and contained no reference to the letter, but recited, "Except as expressly modified by this Codicil, my Will of March 25th 1932 shall remain in full force and effect."

Esther Cohn's whereabouts was known to the testator's executors immediately following his death, but she herself died a week later. Respondent, as her executrix, claimed the $4,000 mentioned in the letter. This claim was challenged by appellants, residuary legatees under Seeligsohn's will, and his executors brought suit interpleading the disputants. From the agreed facts the trial court drew conclusions of law and rendered judgment in favor of the respondent. The chief question is whether the letter was effectually incorporated by reference into the will.

It is settled law in this state that a testator may incorporate an extrinsic document into his will, provided the document is in existence at the time and provided, further, that the reference to it in the will clearly identifies it, or renders it capable of identification by extrinsic proof. *Estate of Plumel*, 151 Cal. 77, 90 P. 192, 121 Am.St.Rep. 100; *Garde v. Goldsmith*, 204 Cal. 166, 267 P. 104; *Estate of Martin*, 31 Cal.App.2d 501, 88 P.2d 234; 16 Cal.L.Rev. 154. An attempt to incorporate a future document is ineffectual, because a testator cannot be permitted to create for himself the power to dispose of his property without complying with the formalities required in making a will. *Keeler v. Merchant's Loan & Trust*, 253 Ill. 528, 97 N.E. 1061.

In the case at bar the letter presumably was not in existence when the will was executed, for the letter bore a date subsequent to the date of the will. Code Civ.Proc., sec. 1963, subd. 23. However, the letter was in existence at the time the codicil to the will was executed. The respondent points out that under the law the execution of a codicil has the effect of republishing the will which it modifies (Prob.Code, sec. 25), and argues from this that Seeligsohn's letter was an 'existing document' within the incorporation rule. The only authorities cited by the parties on this point are several English decisions. These cases hold that although an informal document is not in existence when the will referring to it is executed, a later republication of the will by codicil will satisfy the 'existing document' rule and will incorporate it by reference provided the testamentary instruments sufficiently identify it. *In re Goods of Lady Truro* [1866] L.R. 1 P. & D. 201; compare *In re Goods of Smart* [1902], L.R.Prob.Div. 238; 4 Calif.L.Rev. 356. The principle of republication thus applied is unquestionably sound. In revising his scheme of testamentary disposition by codicil a testator presumably reviews and reaffirms those portions of his will which remain unaffected. In substance, the will is re-executed as of that time. Therefore, the testator's execution of the codicil in the present case must be taken as confirming the incorporation of the letter then in existence, provided the letter can be satisfactorily identified as the one referred to in the will. And this is true, notwithstanding the codicil made no reference to the letter and recited that the will should remain in full force 'except as expressly modified by this codicil', for the letter, if properly incorporated, would be an integral part of the republished will.

We are also of the opinion that the trial court did not err in concluding that the letter found with the will was the letter referred to in the will. Conceding the contrary force of the discrepancy in dates, the evidence of identity was, nevertheless, sufficient to overcome the effect of that factor. The controlling authorities in this state do not require that the informal document be identified with exact precision; it is enough that the descriptive words and extrinsic circumstances combine to produce a reasonable certainty that the document in question is the one referred to by the testator in his will. *Estate of Miller*, 128 Cal.App. 176, 17 P.2d 181; *Estate of Martin*, supra; *In re Plumel's Estate*, supra. Here the letter was found in the safe deposit box with the will. It was addressed to the executors, as the will stated it would be. No other letter was found. Moreover, the letter is conceded to have been written by the testator, and its terms conform unmistakably to the letter described in the will. It identifies itself as the letter mentioned in the will and deals with the identical subject matter referred to in that portion of the will. All these circumstances leave no doubt that the letter of July 3, 1933, is the one that the testator intended to incorporate in paragraph four of his will.

...

The judgment is affirmed.

———

Not all states recognize the doctrine of incorporation by reference. California does, and it has codified the doctrine:

CPC § 6130. Incorporation by reference

A writing in existence when a will is executed may be incorporated by reference if the language of the will manifests this intent and describes the writing sufficiently to permit its identification.

The doctrine is straightforward. So long as the will references a document that is outside the will, describes it so that the court can identify it with reasonable certainty, and the proponents of the intent in the document can prove that the document was in existence at the time the will was executed, the courts typically presume that by referring to the document the testator intended to incorporate the document into his or her will. Historically the element the courts were strictest on was proof that the document was in existence at the time the will was executed. Why?

Notes

1. *Independent doctrine*: Incorporation by reference is its own free-standing doctrine and need not overlap with republication by codicil. That being said, the *Simon* case has the added benefit of demonstrating how republication by codicil can overlap with other wills doctrines, this time incorporation by reference. What if the testator in *Simon* had not executed the codicil? Could the court have still used incorporation by reference to give effect to the intent expressed in the letter? Notice how by using incorporation by reference the court was able to de facto expand the scope of the will to give effect to testamentary intent expressed outside of the will.

2. *Incorporation by reference versus republication by codicil*: In states that do not recognize incorporation by reference, courts will sometimes stretch republication by codicil to cover wills that were defectively executed (and arguably have no testamentary life). In California there is no real need to do that. Technically a codicil is only a codicil if it amends and/or revises an *existing will* — a will that currently has testamentary life (at the time the codicil is executed). An existing will implies a will that, at the time the codicil is executed, has some testamentary life. If the underlying document has a defect that causes it to have *no* testamentary life, typically it can still be given effect but through incorporation by reference, not republication by codicil. If you are concerned about whether the underlying will has any testamentary life at the time the "codicil" is executed, argue both doctrines in the alternative and let the court sort it out.

The principal difference between incorporation by reference and republication by codicil is whether the underlying document qualifies as a will with some testamentary life at the time the codicil is executed. If you return to the opening sentence in the above quote from the *McCarty* case (the indented material on the second page of this chapter), the omitted material from that sentence identified one of the principal differences between incorporation by reference and integration. Now that you have a better understanding of incorporation by reference, here is that full, often repeated statement: "In the law of wills, integration, as distinguished from incorporation by reference, occurs when there is *no reference to a distinctly extraneous document*, but it is clear that two or more separate writings are intended by the testator to be his will." (emphasis added; quoting from *Estate of Wunderle*, 30 Cal. 2d 274, 281 (1947)).

3. *Strict compliance?* In *Simon*, the testator's will described the document to be incorporated as "... a letter that will be found in my effects and which said letter will be addressed to Martin E. Simon and Arthur W. Green (the executors) and will be dated March 25, 1932." In fact, the letter was dated July 3, 1933. Is the court fudging on the requirement that the will "describes the writing sufficiently to permit its identification"? Should the court apply the same lax approach to the other requirements

(that the language of the will expresses the intent to incorporate the document and that the document to be incorporated is "in existence when a will is executed …")?

B. Modern Trend — Tangible Personal Property List (Relaxation of Incorporation by Reference)

Traditionally, the courts were rather strict in applying the requirement that the document to be incorporated be in existence at the time the will was executed. Moreover, the document could be incorporated only as it existed at the time the will was executed. Any subsequent changes to the document to be incorporated could not be given effect, as it would de facto permit a testator to revise or amend his or her testamentary intent without executing a new will or codicil.

The drafters of Uniform Probate Code (UPC) decided that the element of incorporation by reference requiring an existing writing should be relaxed when it comes to disposing of less valuable property. Not to stereotype, but anyone who has spent time with an elderly relative knows that it is not uncommon for such relative to constantly change their mind with respect to who should get which items of tangible personal property. It is also not too uncommon to find "sticky" notes on some of their tangible personal property, and the sticky notes often change with each family member's visit! If the law of wills were strictly enforced against such an individual, every time the individual changed his or her mind with respect to who should get what, the person would have to execute a new will or at least a codicil. But often the cost, and accompanying inconvenience, of doing so is greater than the value of the item in question (the item often has great sentimental value, but not significant market value).

The drafters of the UPC decided that in the typical scenario (as described above), the benefits of requiring the person to execute a new will or codicil each time he or she changed his or her mind did not offset the cost of the new will or codicil. Accordingly, under the UPC's "tangible personal property list" doctrine (UPC § 2-513), a testator is permitted to dispose of his or her tangible personal property via a list *not* executed with Wills Act formalities, even if the list was created *after* the testator executed his or her will, as long as the will expressly states the intent to create such list. The doctrine is essentially incorporation by reference but without the "existing writing" requirement for the list disposing of the tangible personal property. The idea here is that the testator can make changes, from time to time, to the testamentary disposition of his or her "small stuff" without incurring the costs and hassles of executing a new will or codicil.

In 2007, California adopted its own version of the tangible personal property list doctrine.

CPC § 6132. Tangible personal property list

    (a) Notwithstanding any other provision, a will may refer to a writing that directs disposition of tangible personal property not otherwise specifically disposed of by the will, except for money that is common coin or currency and property used primarily in a trade or business. A writing directing disposition of a testator's tangible personal property is effective if all of the following conditions are satisfied:

(1) An unrevoked will refers to the writing.

(2) The writing is dated and is either in the handwriting of, or signed by, the testator.

(3) The writing describes the items and the recipients of the property with reasonable certainty.

(b) The failure of a writing to conform to the conditions described in paragraph (2) of subdivision (a) does not preclude the introduction of evidence of the existence of the testator's intent regarding the disposition of tangible personal property as authorized by this section.

(c) The writing may be written or signed before or after the execution of the will and need not have significance apart from its effect upon the dispositions of property made by the will. A writing that meets the requirements of this section shall be given effect as if it were actually contained in the will itself, except that if any person designated to receive property in the writing dies before the testator, the property shall pass as further directed in the writing and, in the absence of any further directions, the disposition shall lapse.

(d) The testator may make subsequent handwritten or signed changes to any writing. If there is an inconsistent disposition of tangible personal property as between writings, the most recent writing controls.

(e) (1) If the writing directing disposition of tangible personal property omits a statement as to the date of its execution, and if the omission results in doubt whether its provisions or the provisions of another writing inconsistent with it are controlling, then the writing omitting the statement is invalid to the extent of its inconsistency unless the time of its execution is established to be after the date of execution of the other writing.

(2) If the writing directing disposition of tangible personal property omits a statement as to the date of its execution, and it is established that the testator lacked testamentary capacity at any time during which the writing may have been executed, the writing is invalid unless it is established that it was executed at a time when the testator had testamentary capacity.

        …

(g) The total value of tangible personal property identified and disposed of in the writing shall not exceed twenty-five thousand dollars ($25,000). If the value of an item of tangible personal property described in the writing exceeds five thousand dollars ($5,000), that item shall not be subject to this section and that item shall be disposed of pursuant to the remainder clause of the will. The value of an item of tangible personal property that is disposed of pursuant to the remainder clause of the will shall not be counted towards the twenty-five thousand dollar ($25,000) limit described in this subdivision.

(h) As used in this section, the following definitions shall apply:

(1) "Tangible personal property" means articles of personal or household use or ornament, including, but not limited to, furniture, furnishings, automobiles, boats,

and jewelry, as well as precious metals in any tangible form, such as bullion or coins and articles held for investment purposes. The term "tangible personal property" does not mean real property, a mobilehome as defined in Section 798.3 of the Civil Code, intangible property, such as evidences of indebtedness, bank accounts and other monetary deposits, documents of title, or securities.

(2) "Common coin or currency" means the coins and currency of the United States that are legal tender for the payment of public and private debts, but does not include coins or currency kept or acquired for their historical, artistic, collectable, or investment value apart from their normal use as legal tender for payment.

Problems

1. What was the legislature trying to accomplish with subsection (b) of CPC Section 6132? What would you argue it means?

2. Testator Bob validly executes a will dated January 1, 2015, and the will contains various dispositive provisions, standard clauses regarding executors, etc. One of the dispositive clauses, however, states that $50,000 as well as his Ferrari are to be distributed to the individual who is identified in a letter that is being held by the executor of Bob's estate. Bob dies and his executor produces the referenced letter. The letter is dated December 1, 2014, and states that the $50,000 and the Ferrari are to be distributed to his pal, Pete. Bob's will does not provide for the disposition of either the $50,000 or the car, but the residue of his estate goes to charity. Who gets the Ferrari and the $50,000?

3. Testator Tricia validly executes Will #1. Subsequently Tricia validly executes Will #2 that expressly revokes Will #1. Tricia then physically destroys Will #2. At some later date, Tricia executes a "codicil" (conforming to required formalities) that states, in part, "This is a codicil to Will #1 and by this codicil, I leave my Porsche to my friend, Fumiko." Assuming that Fumiko was not named as a beneficiary in either of Tricia's wills, is she entitled to receive the Porsche at Tricia's death?

4. Assume the same facts as Problem 2 but assume that the letter produced by the executor is dated February 1, 2015. Is Pete entitled to receive $50,000 and Bob's Ferrari? What if, instead of a Ferrari, the car Bob was gifting to Pete is an old, beat-up VW vanagon in need of lots of work (and the reference in the will was to the VW vanagon, not the Ferrari). Might that make a difference?

V. Acts of Independent Significance

Acts of independent significance[3] is yet another doctrine that can de facto expand the scope of the will and permit the probate court to give testamentary effect to acts or events that occur outside the four corners of the document. Acts of independent

---

3. Some jurisdictions and authorities refer to it as *facts* of independent significance. Either way, it is the same doctrine.

significance is somewhat similar to dependent relative revocation in that at first blush the name of the doctrine does not appear to be very helpful: what acts, and significance independent of what? The typical articulation of the doctrine can also be rather abstract. Leading with an example might be helpful.

Assume the testator, a professor, has a validly executed will that provides in pertinent part as follows: "I give $1,000 to whomever is my research assistant at the time of my death." The will tells the probate court how much the beneficiary is to take, but it does not identify the beneficiary by name. Instead, the beneficiary is described generically, and more important, the wording used inherently reflects the possibility that the identity of the beneficiary may change in the future. Each year the professor hires a third-year law student, who then graduates in the spring, requiring the professor to hire a new research assistant each year. The identity of the beneficiary changes with each new research assistant. Normally, if a testator is changing a beneficiary in her will, strict compliance would seem to require that the testator execute a new will or a codicil for the change to be valid.

The doctrine of acts of independent significance permits a change in the beneficiary, or a change in the gift, without a need for a codicil—so long as the reason for the change comes within the scope of the doctrine. As long as the referenced act in the will (i.e., here the referenced act is the change in who is the professor's research assistant) is performed or occurs for reasons *independent* of its effect on testator's probate estate, then the referenced act is not really a testamentary act despite its testamentary consequences. As long as the referenced act is being performed primarily for reasons other than its effect on who takes what when the testator dies, it can be given effect under acts of independent significance. Here, the logical assumption is that when the professor hires a new research assistant, it is because he or she needs research assistance with his or her writing projects. The professor is not hiring a new research assistant primarily for the purpose of making a testamentary gift—though that may be a testamentary consequence of the hiring decision. Accordingly, the testator need not execute a new will or codicil every time she changes her research assistant.

Although the doctrine of acts of independent significance was originally a judicial doctrine, California has codified it:

CPC § 6131. References to extrinsic acts and events

A will may dispose of property by reference to acts and events that have significance apart from their effect upon the dispositions made by the will, whether the acts and events occur before or after the execution of the will or before or after the testator's death. The execution or revocation of a will of another person is such an event.

While the doctrine permits reference to acts and events that can occur either "before or after" the will's execution, the doctrine poses its greatest analytical issues when it is referring to acts or events that occur in the future. Analytically, the keys to the doctrine are: (1) identify the act or event referenced in the will that is to occur outside the will, and then (2) analyze whether that act or event has significance (i.e., meaning or consequences) independent of its effect upon the testator's probate estate. Typically, the independent significance will mean that the referenced act has to be performed for some *inter vivos* reason, though the doctrine can apply even if the referenced act has only testamentary significance so long as the testamentary significance affects something other than just the testator's probate estate.

In the hypothetical above, the referenced act in the will is the professor changing her research assistant. Is she performing that act to affect who takes under her will, or is she performing that referenced act for independent, *inter vivos* reasons? She is changing research assistants because they graduate each year, and she needs someone to help her with her research and writing. Even without the will she would need a research assistant. The referenced act clearly has its own *inter vivos* significance, independent of its effect upon who takes what under her will. Whoever is her research assistant at her death will be able to claim the gift under her will.

Acts of independent significance typically applies to *who* takes under the will (as the example above demonstrates); it can, however, also apply to cases involving *what* a beneficiary takes. Assume the testator validly executes a will that provides in pertinent part as follows: "I give all the funds in my checking account to my brother, Shehad." Thereafter, the testator deposits and withdraws funds from his checking account. Should he have to execute a new will or codicil each time? No, because the testator is making withdrawals and deposits for valid *inter vivos* reasons (no doubt to pay his bills) and is not doing so to affect the gift to his brother. Shehad should receive whatever funds are in the checking account when the testator dies.

In re Tipler

10 S.W.3d 244 (Tenn. App. 1998)

HOLLY KIRBY LILLARD, Judge.

. . .

Mrs. Gladys S. Tipler ("Testatrix") executed a formal will on April 2, 1982. This will left the bulk of her estate to her husband, James Tipler ("Husband"), upon the contingency that he survive her. The will did not address the distribution of the estate in the event that Husband predeceased Testatrix. Two days later, Testatrix executed a holographic codicil to the formal will. The codicil reads as follows:

> Should my husband predecesse [sic] me I hereby declair [sic] that his last Will and testament upon his death is our agreement here to four [sic] made between us in Section III of my Will. With the exception Mr. Tipler or myself can elect to make any changes as we desire depending upon which one predeceasest [sic] the other. If no changes are made by either of us this will be our last will and testament.

Thus, the codicil indicated that if Husband predeceased Testatrix, his last will and testament would control the disposition of her estate. At the time the codicil was executed, Husband had not yet executed a will. Husband died in 1990. His will, executed six months prior to his death, created a trust for Testatrix, and directed that upon her death the property be distributed to his relatives. Testatrix died in 1994.

The beneficiaries under Husband's will sought enforcement of Testatrix's codicil in Shelby County Probate Court. This action was challenged by Testatrix' heirs, who would otherwise take under the Tennessee intestacy statute. The Testratix' heirs asserted that the holographic codicil should not be enforced because it referred to a document not yet in existence, i.e. Husband's will. They argued that Tennessee law requires that for a holographic will to be enforceable, "all its material provisions must be in the handwriting of the testator...." Tenn.Code Ann. § 32-1-105 (1984). Since Testatrix' holograph referred to Husband's will, Testatrix' heirs maintained that material provisions were not in Testatrix' handwriting.

At the trial, the beneficiaries under Husband's will introduced evidence regarding Testatrix' intent. The testimony indicated that Testatrix was not close to her family. One witness stated that Testatrix described her sisters as "greedy," indicating that "if anything happened to her [Testatrix]," her sisters would be like "a bunch of vultures" or "a bunch of barracudas...." Evidence indicated that Testatrix "thought of Mr. Tipler's family as her family." Witnesses testified that Testatrix loved her husband dearly and frequently said, "whatever Tippy [Husband] wants is what I want."

After the bench trial, the trial court issued a Memorandum Opinion. The trial court found that the issue of incorporation by reference was not applicable because Husband's will was not in existence at the time Testatrix' codicil was written. The trial court then stated:

> The relevant inquiry is whether the doctrine of facts of independent significance applies in the case at bar. Tennessee recognizes the doctrine of independent significance. *Smith v. Weitzel*, [47 Tenn.App. 375,] 338 S.W.2d 628, 637 (Tenn.[App.]1960) ("As to the proposition of independent significance ... we call attention to Sec. 54.2 of Scott on Trusts).

Scott on Trusts, 4th Edition, Section 54.2, page 9, states:

> Section 54.2: Where disposition is determined by facts of independent significance. There is another doctrine of the law of wills that is sometimes confused with the doctrine of incorporation by reference. Even though a disposition cannot be fully ascertained from the terms of the will, it is not invalid if it can be ascertained from the facts that have a significance apart from their effect upon the disposition in the will. Indeed, it is frequently necessary to resort to extrinsic evidence to identify the persons who are to take or the subject matter of the disposition.

Therefore, under the doctrine of independent significance, a court may refer to extrinsic evidence to identify the persons who are to take under the will. In the case at bar, Mrs. Tipler left her residuary estate in Section III to her husband. However, in her holographic codicil, she stated, in her handwriting, that if her husband predeceased her, her residuary estate would pass according to their agreement as indicated in his will.

* * *

A testator may [have] intended for his property to go the same persons who are named in another person's will, and the gift of the testator's property by his will can be upheld on the ground of independent significance. This doctrine of independent significance is an escape mechanism from the strict requirements of incorporation by reference. 2 Bowe-Parker: Page on Wills, Section 19.34, page 119.

* * *

In the case bar, Mrs. Tipler left her residuary estate to Mr. Tipler in her Last Will and Testament, on April 2, 1982. Like the *Klein* case, she modified that provision in her holographic codicil two days later in order to give Mr. Tipler the privilege of naming the persons who would take his part of her estate should he die first. The doctrine of independent significance is satisfied because Mr. Tipler's will had an independent significance of distributing his estate and was not written with the intention of distributing Mrs. Tipler's estate.

. . .

The trial court then ordered that Testatrix' residuary estate be distributed in accordance with Husband's will, concluding as follows:

> The Court finds and holds that Mrs. Tipler's codicil contained all of the material provisions necessary to determine how her residuary estate would be distributed. Her estate is to be distributed according to an agreement which she identifies in her own handwriting. The identity of the beneficiaries agreed upon can be determined from the facts of independent significance contained in Mr. Tipler's Will as well as from the testimony of Ms. Meredith and Mr. May. The Court further rules that Mrs. Tipler intended to dispose of her residuary estate to her husband; if her husband predeceased her, she intended to dispose of her estate to Mr. Tipler's relatives in the manner in which Mr. Tipler distributed his estate in his will. Therefore, this Court further finds and so holds that Mrs. Tipler's handwritten document dated on April 4, 1982 was a valid holographic codicil. This Court further finds and holds that the identity of the beneficiaries and the percentage of their shares under Mrs. Tipler's estate are found in Article V of Mr. Tipler's Last Will and Testament. This Court finds and holds that this extrinsic evidence found in Mr. Tipler's Will is incorporated into Mrs. Tipler's will under the Tennessee recognized doctrine of independent significance.

Testatrix' heirs, who would receive Testatrix' residuary estate if the codicil were invalid, now appeal the decision of the trial court.

. . .

In sum, then, the doctrine of facts of independent significance is applicable in this case to permit Testatrix' codicil to refer to Husband's will, provided the document is a valid holographic codicil. To determine whether the holograph contains all material provisions in Testatrix' handwriting, the trial court properly considered Testatrix' intent. Evidence preponderates in favor of the trial court's finding that Testatrix was estranged from her family and wanted her estate to go to Husband's family. Since Testatrix wanted her estate to go to whomever Husband wished, the codicil contained all material provisions in Testatrix' handwriting, even though it stated only that her estate should go to the beneficiaries under Husband's will and did not specifically name beneficiaries. Therefore, the trial court did not err in distributing Testatrix' estate to the beneficiaries under Husband's will.

For the above reasons, we affirm the decision of the trial court. Costs of appeal are assessed against the Appellants, for which execution shall issue, if necessary.

———————

Problems

1. Testator's will states: "I leave the contents of my safe deposit box to my brother, Bill." Following testator's death, what, if anything, does Bill receive?

2. Testator's will has a provision making a $10,000 gift to "each of the persons I will identify in a letter that I will leave with my executor." Assume a letter — with names identifying the beneficiaries — is left for and found by the executor. The letter is dated after the date of the will. What, if anything, do the beneficiaries receive?

3. Testator's will leaves "all of my household furniture to my daughter, Diane, and the rest/residue of my property (my estate) to my grandson, Grant." Thereafter, Testator changes out some of the household furniture (e.g., the testator buys a beanbag chair for the TV room). What, if anything, is Diane entitled to pursuant to Testator's will?

4. For purposes of this question only, assume the jurisdiction does *not* recognize holographic wills.

   X writes in her own handwriting an instrument that is dated, states that it is her "last will and testament," and she alone signs. The instrument devises the residue of her estate to UCLA. A year later, X's attorney drafts an instrument that states that it is a "codicil" to the first instrument. The "codicil" bequeaths $50,000 to USC. The "codicil" refers to X's "will" and states that the "codicil" otherwise affirms the terms of the "will." The "codicil" is duly signed and witnessed in compliance with all the Wills Act formalities. A year later, X writes in her own handwriting an instrument that is dated, states that it is her "second codicil to her last will and testament," and she alone signs. The second codicil bequeaths $100,000 to USC. The "second codicil" refers to X's "will and first codicil" and states that the "second codicil" otherwise affirms the terms of the "will and first codicil." Six months later X dies. Assuming the jurisdiction does *not* recognize holographic wills, and assuming there is no other relevant evidence, what is the most likely disposition of X's property? What instruments, if any, control the disposition of X's property, and why?

5. Testator's will provided in pertinent part as follows:

   "I give and bequeath unto my wife the sum of $50,000, for the purposes set forth in a sealed letter that will be found with this will."

   An undated letter directing testator's wife to pay $50,000 to X was found with the will in decedent's desk drawer. What is the most likely result, and why, with respect to the $50,000?

VI. Contracts Concerning Wills

A promise to make a will is never admissible as a will. This is the case even if the contract is in writing, witnessed, or made with other execution formalities. For example, assume an aging grandfather wants his grandson to move in with him and help run the family business (or the family farm) and makes the grandson an offer: move in with me and help me run the business, and I promise to leave you the business in my will when I die. Grandson fulfills his end of the bargain, grandfather dies, but his will leaves nothing to the grandson. What, if anything, does the grandson get?

This is a contracts question, not a wills issue. The contract between the grandfather and his grandson does not serve as a will. Under contract principles, however, the grandson has a potential claim against his grandfather's estate and would file such as a creditor of the estate. If the grandson is successful in making his contract claim, the contract will be enforced against the estate and he will receive property from the grandfather. To that extent, a contract concerning a will can affect (and disrupt) a testator's intent.

While there is not time to delve too deeply into the contracts relating to wills material, a core question is: should the issue of whether there is an enforceable contract be governed solely by contract principles, or should the law of wills principles apply to some degree? In particular, should oral contracts and/or doctrines like equitable estoppel apply or should all such claims have to be in writing, similar to a will?

The Uniform Probate Code has decided that all contract claims relating to a will should have to be in, or at least evidenced by, some type of a writing that was signed by the decedent:

UPC § 2-701. Contracts concerning succession

A contract to make a will or devise, or not to revoke a will or devise, or to die intestate, ... can be established only by (1) provisions of a will stating material provisions of the contract; (2) an express reference in a will to a contract and extrinsic evidence proving the terms of the contract; or (3) a writing signed by the decedent evidencing the contract. The execution of a joint will or mutual wills does not create a presumption of a contract not to revoke the will or wills.

California essentially adopted UPC Section 2-701 in 1983 when it enacted California Probate Code Section 150. One would have thought this would have settled the issue of whether oral claims of promises to make a will, or not to revoke a will, would be valid in California. A California Court of Appeals described the legislative history behind California Probate Code Section 150 as follows:

> In proposing the statutory language in section 150, the California Law Revision Commission ("Commission") recognized that under Civil Code section 1624, former subdivision 6., the courts frequently enforced "oral promise[s] to make or not to revoke a will in order to avoid the harshness

that would be caused by a strict application of the Statute of Frauds." (16 Cal.Law Revision Com.Rep. (December 1982) p. 2348.) The Commission, however, criticized this practice explaining "[w]here an oral agreement to make or not to revoke a will is alleged after promisor is deceased and unable to testify, there is an opportunity for the fabrication of testimony concerning the existence of the agreement. Sound policy requires some form of written evidence that such an agreement actually exists." (*Id.* at pp. 2348–2349) ... The Commission concluded "[t]he proposed law ... will provide a clearer, more detailed statutory statement than the present Statute of Frauds and will limit the opportunity for fraud by fabricated proof of an oral agreement."5 (16 Cal.Law Revision Com.Rep., *supra,* at p. 2350.)

Juran v. Epstein, 23 Cal.App.4th 882, 893–94 (1994).

Nevertheless, litigants continued to press their claims of oral promises concerning wills, and even after the legislature adopted the Uniform Probate Code language, the same California Court of Appeal concluded that such oral claims should still be enforceable if equity demanded it:

> Examining section 150's statutory language and legislative history, we do not believe the Legislature intended to eliminate a court's authority to apply equitable principles in the area of contracts to make (or not to revoke) a will. It is a firmly rooted legal principle in this state that "... the statute of frauds, having been enacted for the purpose of preventing fraud, shall not be made the instrument of shielding, protecting or aiding the party who relies upon it in the perpetration of a fraud...." (citations omitted).

Id.

The California legislature revisited the issue in 2000 when they expanded the doctrine to include non-probate instruments. The legislature also added subsections (a)(4) and (a)(5). Who ended up winning the battle of whether oral contracts concerning wills or other instruments are valid—the legislature or the courts?

CPC § 21700. Contracts to make will, trust or transfer; establishment; joint or mutual wills

(a) A contract to make a will or devise or other instrument, or not to revoke a will or devise or other instrument, or to die intestate, ... can be established only by one of the following:

    (1) Provisions of a will or other instrument stating the material provisions of the contract.

    (2) An expressed reference in a will or other instrument to a contract and extrinsic evidence proving the terms of the contract.

    (3) A writing signed by the decedent evidencing the contract.

    (4) Clear and convincing evidence of an agreement between the decedent and the claimant or a promise by the decedent to the claimant that is enforceable in equity.

(5) Clear and convincing evidence of an agreement between the decedent and another person for the benefit of the claimant or a promise by the decedent to another person for the benefit of the claimant that is enforceable in equity.

(b) The execution of a joint will or mutual wills does not create a presumption of a contract not to revoke the will or wills.

Note

Joint or mutual will: A "joint will" or "mutual will" is a single will validly executed by two people (typically husband and wife). The intent is that the two parties agree on how they want their property to be disposed, regardless of which one dies first, so they decide to execute just one will for both of them. Assuming it is not revoked, it is probated twice—following the death of each of them as it applies to their respective estates upon death.

As a general rule, joint wills are *not* a good idea and the overwhelming majority of estate planners would not use one. A couple can achieve the same legal arrangement with mirror wills (two wills, one for each party, with "mirror" dispositive provisions: i.e., one simple but common example is where each will says "all to my surviving spouse, if I have one, otherwise to our children equally").

The issues that arise most often with respect to joint wills are beyond the scope of this class, except one. If a couple executes a joint will, should that give rise to a contract not to revoke—or at least a presumption of a contract not to revoke? Assuming the joint will has an express contract not to revoke, does that mean neither spouse can change their mind and revoke the will? Can one spouse de facto "waive" their right to revoke their will?

Chapter 9

Construing Time of Death Gifts

I. Introduction

Assuming there is what appears to be a validly executed will, when, if ever, should a court admit extrinsic evidence with respect to the will? In one of the following cases, the court admits the extrinsic evidence (oral statements of the testator with respect to his testamentary intent), while in the other case the court refuses to admit the extrinsic evidence (testatrix's oral and written statements with respect to "her testamentary intention"). Are the cases reconcilable?

Mahoney v. Grainger

186 N.E. 86 (Mass. 1933)

RUGG, Chief Justice.

This is an appeal from a decree of a probate court denying a petition for distribution of a legacy under the will of Helen A. Sullivan among her first cousins who are contended to be her heirs at law. The residuary clause was as follows: "All the rest and residue of my estate, both real and personal property, I give, demise and bequeath to my heirs at law living at the time of my decease, absolutely; to be divided among them equally, share and share alike; ..."

... About ten days before her death the testatrix sent for an attorney who found her sick but intelligent about the subjects of their conversation. She told the attorney she wanted to make a will. She gave him instructions as to general pecuniary legacies. In response to the questions "Whom do you want to leave the rest of your property to? Who are your nearest relations?" she replied "I've got about twenty-five first cousins * * * let them share it equally." The attorney then drafted the will and read it to the testatrix and it was executed by her.

The trial judge ruled ... "that the words heirs at law were words in common use, susceptible of application to one or many; that when applied to the special circumstances of this case that the testatrix had but one heir, notwithstanding the added words 'to be divided among them equally, share and share alike,' there was no latent ambiguity or equivocation in the will itself which would permit the introduction of the statements of the testatrix to prove her testamentary intention." Certain first cousins have appealed....

There is no doubt as to the meaning of the words "heirs at law living at the time of my decease" as used in the will. Confessedly they refer alone to the aunt of the testatrix and do not include her cousins. *Gilman v. Congregational Home Missionary Society*, 276 Mass. 580, 177 N. E. 621; *Calder v. Bryant* (Mass.) 184 N. E. 440.

A will duly executed and allowed by the court must under the statute of wills (G. L. [Ter. Ed.] c. 191, §1 et seq.) be accepted as the final expression of the intent of the person executing it. The fact that it was not in conformity to the instructions given to the draftsman who prepared it or that he made a mistake does not authorize a court to reform or alter it or remold it by amendments. The will must be construed as it came from the hands of the testatrix. *Polsey v. Newton*, 199 Mass. 450, 85 N. E. 574, 15 Ann. Cas. 139. Mistakes in the drafting of the will may be of significance in some circumstances in a trial as to the due execution and allowance of the alleged testamentary instrument. *Richardson v. Richards*, 226 Mass. 240, 115 N. E. 307. Proof that the legatee actually designated was not the particular person intended by the one executing the will cannot be received to aid in the interpretation of a will. *Tucker v. Seaman's Aid Society*, 7 Metc. 188, 210. See *National Society for the Prevention of Cruelty to Children v. Scottish National Society for the Prevention of Cruelty to Children*, [1915] A. C. 207....

It is only where testamentary language is not clear in its application to facts that evidence may be introduced as to the circumstances under which the testator used that language in order to throw light upon its meaning. Where no doubt exists as to the property bequeathed or the identity of the beneficiary there is no room for extrinsic evidence; the will must stand as written. *Barker v. Comins*, 110 Mass. 477, 488; *Best v. Berry*, 189 Mass. 510, 512, 75 N. E. 743, 109 Am. St. Rep. 651.

In the case at bar there is no doubt as to the heirs at law of the testatrix. The aunt alone falls within that description. The cousins are excluded. The circumstance that the plural word "heirs" was used does not prevent one individual from taking the entire gift. *Calder v. Bryant* (Mass.) 184 N. E. 440.

Decree affirmed.

Fleming v. Morrison

72 N.E. 499 (Mass. 1904)

LORING, J.

All the rulings asked for at the hearing have been waived, and the only contention now insisted upon by the contestants is that, on the finding made at the hearing, the proponent of the will has failed to prove the necessary animus testandi. We are of the opinion that this contention must prevail. The finding that, before Butterfield and Goodrich 'parted,' Butterfield told Goodrich that the instrument which had been signed by Butterfield as and for his last will and testament, and declared by him to be such in the presence of Goodrich, and attested and subscribed by Goodrich as a witness, 'was a fake, made for a purpose,' is fatal to the proponent's case. This must be taken to mean that what had been done was a sham.... The whole finding, taken together, amounts to a finding that Butterfield had not intended the transaction which had just taken place to be in fact what it imported to be; that is to say, a finding that when Butterfield signed the instrument, and asked Goodrich to attest and subscribe it as his will, he did not, in fact, then intend it to be his last will and testament, but intended to have Mary Fleming think that he had made a will in her favor to induce her to let him sleep with her.

We are of opinion that it is competent to contradict by parol [evidence] the solemn statements contained in an instrument that it is a will; ... For similar cases as to wills, see *In the Goods of Hunt*, L. R. 3 P. & D. 250, where it was held that it could be shown by parol that the instrument executed was executed by mistake, ... 'The momentous consequences of permitting parol evidence thus to outweigh the sanction of a solemn act are obvious. It has a tendency to place all wills at the mercy of a parol story that the testator did not mean what he said,' in the words of Sir J. P. Wilde in *Lister v. Smith*, 3 Sw. & Tr. 282, 288.... The punctum temporis in case of a will is when it is signed, or, having been previously signed, when the signature is acknowledged in the presence of three or more witnesses. And where that is done before each witness separately, as it may be done in this commonwealth (*Chase v. Kittredge*, 11 Allen, 49, 87 Am. Dec. 687), the animus testandi must exist when it is signed or acknowledged before, and attested and subscribed by, each of the necessary three witnesses. If this is not done, the statutory requirements have not been complied with. Assuming that the acknowledgment animo testandi of a signature not originally made with that animus is enough, the will in the case at bar would have been duly executed had Butterfield subsequently acknowledged the instrument before three in place of two additional witnesses. But he did not do so. The instrument, having been acknowledged and attested and subscribed by two witnesses only, is not a valid will, within Rev. Laws, c. 135, § 1.

...

Decree to be entered reversing decree of probate court, and disallowing the instrument as the will of Butterfield.

Note

Why is the extrinsic evidence being offered in *Mahoney*? Why is the extrinsic evidence being offered in *Fleming*? The first key to analyzing whether extrinsic evidence is admissible is to determine *why* it is being offered.

II. Extrinsic Evidence to Help Construe a Will

To the extent that a will constitutes the testator's expression of his or her testamentary intent, why would a court need extrinsic evidence to help construe that intent? Is not the testator's last will and testament the best evidence of the testator's intent? In an ideal world, a testator's will *would be* the best evidence of his or her testamentary wishes, but we do not live in an ideal world. The assertion that "the testator's will is the best evidence of testator's intent" overlooks two realities: (1) humans make mistakes, and (2) the circumstances surrounding a testator typically change between the time of execution of the will and the time of the testator's death—and those changes can create ambiguities as to what is to happen in light of the changed circumstances.

If a will is properly drafted, then generally there should be nothing for a court to construe—and in the vast majority of wills probated in California, that is the case: the will is "clean," and it effectively disposes of the testator's property. While in theory extrinsic evidence should not be needed to help construe a well-drafted will, not all wills are well drafted. Not all attorneys are equal, and some non-estate planning attorneys think they can dabble in will drafting. In addition, California recognizes holographic wills. Few laypeople know how to write a will to make sure it properly expresses their intent. Estate planners have a saying: "You can pay me now (for drafting a well-written will), or your estate can pay me later (for litigating issues associated with probating a poorly written will)."

Drafting mistakes constitute the first category of ambiguities for which different parties surrounding the testator at time of death would like to offer extrinsic evidence to help the court "construe/re-write" the ambiguity. How open to that extrinsic evidence should the court be? Are the parties offering the court the extrinsic evidence to help "construe" the will, or are they hoping the court will "re-write" the will? Should the courts be open to "re-writing" the will? If not, what is the difference between "construing" a will and "re-writing" a will? If the courts should be open to re-writing a will, *when* should they re-write a will? What should a party have to show before a court will re-write a will?

Second, even assuming, *arguendo*, a well-drafted will, construction issues can arise because of changed conditions. A well-drafted will tells the world *who* gets *what*— but not until the testator dies. Because a will is an ambulatory document, the circumstances surrounding the testator can change between time of execution of the will and time of the testator's death. For example, a beneficiary can predecease the testator, or property being gifted to a beneficiary can be stolen. Such changes in a beneficiary's status or the testator's property between time of execution and time of death can create unexpected construction issues.[1] Should extrinsic evidence be admissible to help resolve such construction questions, and if so, when?

Note that, unlike drafting mistakes, construction issues that arise because of changed conditions are fairly common and foreseeable. Two points follow from that difference. In theory, a well-drafted will should address all possible changes that are reasonably foreseeable. Change-in-circumstance construction issues can often be avoided by taking the time to think through all possible scenarios and to provide for them in the will. But assuming a will does not, because the possible change-in-circumstance scenarios are fairly typical and generic in nature (for example, a beneficiary may predecease the

---

1. A sophisticated estate planner might argue that *all* possible scenarios should be covered in a well-drafted will, but at some point the benefits of covering all possible scenarios exceed the costs— at least for most testators.

testator, or a testator may sell property that is listed as being given away in the will), the law has developed a set of default construction rules for what should happen in these scenarios. To the extent the law has developed the default construction rules, the issue becomes whether extrinsic evidence should still be admissible to help the court determine the testator's intent, or should the testator have to accept the outcome under the default rule if he or she does not draft around it?

In contrast, drafting ambiguities are so fact sensitive and unique that it is difficult, if not impossible, to have a set of default rules for them. The courts either are open to extrinsic evidence to help construe the particular drafting mistake, or they are not. To put it mildly, the courts have struggled with the issue, and the struggle continues.

Look back at the *Mahoney* case: did it involve a drafting mistake or an ambiguity that arose because of a change in circumstances surrounding the testator between time of execution of the will and time of death? Was the court open to extrinsic evidence or not? Should it have been? When probating a will, should the court's goal be to ascertain and give effect to the testator's intent, or to ascertain and give effect to the testator's intent *as expressed in the will*? What is the difference in those two statements? You might want to keep them in mind as you move through the material in this chapter.

A. Drafting Mistakes

1. Common Law Approach

Consistent with its strict compliance mentality, the common law was not amenable to admitting extrinsic evidence to help construe a will. The common law approach, as evidenced by the *Mahoney* case, applied a two-step process. First, the common law would admit extrinsic evidence if the will contained a latent ambiguity (but not if the ambiguity was a patent ambiguity). In addition, in determining whether the will contained an ambiguity, the court applied the plain meaning rule. The plain meaning rule provides that the words in the will should be given their plain and ordinary meaning. If such a reading reveals no ambiguity, no extrinsic evidence should be admissible. The court's concern is the testator's intent as *expressed in the will*, not the testator's true intent. As the court stated in *In re Beldon's Estate*, 71 P.2d 326, 327 (Cal. Ct. App. 1937):

> [I]t is a cardinal rule of construction that, where no ambiguity in phraseology exists, the intention of the testator is to be discovered in the express language which he used. *Ryan's Estate*, 191 Cal. 307, 216 P. 366. As was said in *Estate of Ogden*, 78 Cal.App. 412, at page 414, 248 P. 680, 681, "the question for the court to determine is not what she intended to declare in her will, but what she intended by what she did declare therein." Employment by a testator of language that is clear and certain affords no justification for wresting an unnatural meaning therefrom to save a will from condemnation, however beneficial the testator's unexpressed intention may have been. *Doane's Estate*, 190 Cal. 412, 213 P. 53. Indulgence in speculation and conjecture as to what a testator's intention was affords no proper basis for a decree of distribution

[*Estate of Zilke*, 115 Cal.App. 63, 1 P.(2d) 475], and a court is not permitted to adopt a construction founded on conjecture or to supply an omission by rewriting a will in order to avoid a conclusion of partial intestacy [*Estate of Hisey*, 106 Cal.App. 678, 289 P. 889].

Moreover, as the court in *Mahoney* emphasized when discussing the relationship between a latent ambiguity and the admissibility of extrinsic evidence to help construe a will: "[it is] only where testamentary language is not clear *in its application to facts* that evidence may be introduced as to the circumstances under which the testator used that language in order to throw light upon its meaning" (emphasis added). Accordingly, a latent ambiguity arises only if, when the personal representative goes to give effect to the express words in the will, it is unclear: (1) who qualifies as the beneficiary, or (2) what property is to be devised or bequeathed.

Two quick examples of two of the more common latent ambiguities may help. The first is the misdescription scenario. Assume the testator has a validly executed will that provides in pertinent part as follows: "I devise my house, at 433 Tuxedo Bld., to my good friend, Tanya." On its face the will appears to be fine. But after the testator dies and the executor goes to give effect to the gift, the executor learns that the testator lived at 432 Tuxedo Blvd. The testator cannot give away a house she does not own. This is a classic example of a latent ambiguity. On the face of the will the gift appears fine; it is only when the executor went to *apply the language in the will to the facts outside of the will* that the ambiguity became apparent. Extrinsic evidence is necessary to show the court that there is a problem with the language in the will. Having opened the door to the extrinsic evidence to show that there is a problem with the language in the will, the court is open to admitting extrinsic evidence to resolve the problem.

Under the common law approach, however, while the court is open to construing the will, it is *never* to re-write a will. This logic underlies the misdescription doctrine: if the court concludes that the will contains a misdescription, rather than correcting the misdescription (rewriting the "433" to read "432"), the court would strike the language in the will that creates the misdescription and then analyze whether the remaining language in the will provides enough information for the court to give effect to the gift. Here, the court would strike the number in the address and then re-read what is left in the will to see if there is enough left so that, when applied to the facts *now*, it is clear who gets what. Assuming the testator owned only one home on Tuxedo Blvd., the court would give effect to the gift as modified under the misdescription doctrine.

The second well-recognized latent ambiguity under the common law approach is the equivocation scenario. Assume the testator has a validly executed will that provides in pertinent part: "I give $1,000 to my favorite 2011 Spring semester student Taurean." Again, on the face of the will the gift appears fine. But after the testator dies, and the executor goes to give effect to the gift, it turns out the testator had two students in his Spring 2011 class named Taurean. The fact that there are two (or more) individuals who match the description in the will creates an equivocation. To which "Taurean" was the professor referring? The ambiguity is not apparent on the face of the will (it is not a patent ambiguity); the ambiguity becomes apparent only when the executor attempts to apply the language in the will to the facts outside of the will (it is a latent ambiguity). Assume that additional extrinsic evidence shows that one of the two Taureans was the professor's research assistant, that the professor had served as a reference for the student, and that the two had kept in contact even after the student had graduated. There is no evidence that the professor had any meaningful relationship with the other student named Taurean. The most likely result is that the court would admit the extrinsic evidence in question and give the gift to the student named Taurean who was the professor's research assistant.

An equivocation can also apply to property in the sense that the will devises an item of property and there are two or more items of property that arguably match the express language of the will.

As should be apparent by now, a patent ambiguity is one that is apparent on the face of the will—one that arises from the four corners of the document, before and independent of any attempt to apply the language to the facts outside of the will. Under the traditional common law approach, inasmuch as extrinsic evidence was not necessary to prove the existence of the patent ambiguity, extrinsic evidence was not admissible to help resolve the patent ambiguity.

Finally, even assuming, *arguendo*, extrinsic evidence is admissible, to minimize the potential for fraud, the courts favored admitting extrinsic evidence that was hard to fabricate—not evidence that would be easy to fabricate. Accordingly, the courts would admit extrinsic evidence of the circumstances surrounding the testator at the time he or she executed the will, but not extrinsic evidence of alleged oral statements made by the testator.

Thus, under the common law approach, with respect to extrinsic evidence that a party seeks to admit to help the court construe a will: (1) the extrinsic evidence was admissible only if there was a latent ambiguity (but not a patent ambiguity); (2) in determining whether there is an ambiguity in the will, the court applies the plain meaning rule; and (3) even where the court is open to extrinsic evidence to help it construe an ambiguity in a will, the court will not re-write a will.

2. Modern Trend Approach

The modern trend takes a very different approach to the admissibility of extrinsic evidence to help a court construe a validly executed will. Consistent with the modern trend's intent-based approach (as evidenced by the substantial compliance and harmless error doctrines), the modern trend takes a much more open view of admitting extrinsic evidence. The modern trend abolishes the plain meaning rule: extrinsic evidence is admissible to help establish that there is an ambiguity in the will. The modern trend abolishes the distinction between patent and latent ambiguities: extrinsic evidence is admissible anytime there is an ambiguity in the will. The modern trend abolishes the distinction between the different types of extrinsic evidence: whether it appears to be hard to fabricate or easy to fabricate. All of the relevant extrinsic evidence is admissible to help construe the will, and it is up to the trier of fact to determine its credibility. And finally, even in the absence of an ambiguity, the modern trend authorizes the admissibility of extrinsic evidence to help a court "reform" (i.e., rewrite?) a will:

> to conform the text to the donor's intention if it is established by clear and convincing evidence (1) that a mistake of fact or law, whether in expression or inducement, affected specific terms of the document; and (2) what the donor's intention was. In determining whether these elements have been established by clear and convincing evidence, direct evidence of intention contradicting the plain meaning of the text as well as other evidence of intention may be considered.

RESTATEMENT (THIRD) OF PROP.: WILLS & DONATIVE TRANSFERS § 12.1 *Reforming Donative Instruments To Correct Mistakes* (2003).

Most states are somewhere in between the traditional common law approach and the cutting-edge modern trend; they have done away with most of the rigid formalistic rules that comprised the common law approach, but most jurisdictions are reluctant to abolish the distinction between construing a will and rewriting a will.

3. The California Approach

Estate of Taff

63 Cal. App. 3d 319 (Ct. App. 1976)

FRANSON, Associate Justice.

. . .

FACTS

Pearl Phyllis Taff signed her will on February 28, 1961. Prior to her signing, she had instructed her attorney, T. N. Petersen, who prepared the will, that the residue of her estate was to go to her sister, Margaret M. Aulman; in the event Margaret M. Aulman did not survive her, then Pearl Taff wanted the residue "to go to her own family, her own blood relatives." As part of her instructions, she told Petersen that "she felt she was making adequate provision for Harry's (her predeceased husband's) family in the two specific gifts to Harry's sisters which she was providing in her will and she felt no obligation to the other members of Harry's blood relations and was making no gifts to them."

On February 22, 1961, six days before signing her will, Pearl Taff wrote to her sister, Margaret Aulman. In the letter Pearl Taff stated that the residue of her estate was to pass "to my dear sister, Margaret M. Aulman—or if she predeceases me in death—then to her heirs."

In the will as prepared, the residue of the estate is bequeathed to decedent's sister, Margaret M. Aulman, but in the event Margaret M. Aulman does not survive the decedent:

"... the residum (sic) of my estate, after payment of debts and taxes and specific bequests as set forth, is to pass to my heirs in accordance with the laws of intestate succession, in effect at my death in the State of California, or in effect in such other state or such other place as I may be a resident at the time of my death."

The decedent's sister, Margaret M. Aulman, predeceased the decedent on January 9, 1966.

Pearl Taff died childless on January 27, 1975. Her will was admitted to probate on February 18, 1975.

Appellants are related to the decedent's predeceased husband, Harry C. Taff, as sister, nieces, nephew and grandnephews. Respondents are related to the decedent as blood nephews and nieces. Three of the respondents are children of decedent's predeceased sister, Margaret M. Aulman; one is the daughter of decedent's predeceased sister, Stella Susan Wickert. Appellants claim they are entitled to a portion of the residue of decedent's estate pursuant to the California laws of intestate succession, specifically Probate Code sections 228 and 229. Their claim is predicated upon the residuary provision in decedent's will quoted above.

DISCUSSION

The sole issue is whether the trial court erred in admitting extrinsic evidence to prove that the decedent intended her residuary estate to go in a manner contrary to the seemingly clear and unambiguous language used in her will....

The trial court heard testimony of decedent's attorney, T. N. Petersen, to the effect that decedent had told him that she wanted to leave the residue of her estate to her sister, Margaret Aulman, or in the event that Margaret Aulman predeceased her, then to the members of decedent's own family, "her own blood relatives." This declaration, of course, is contrary to the residuary clause as it appears in decedent's will which was written by T. N. Petersen.

The trial court also received into evidence and considered a letter written by the decedent to her sister six days before the decedent signed her will and apparently after she had visited Petersen and instructed him as to her wishes in drawing the will. This letter recited that the residue of the decedent's estate was to pass to her sister, Margaret M. Aulman—or if Margaret Aulman predeceased the decedent—then to Margaret Aulman's heirs. This declaration also is contrary to the residuary clause as it appears in the decedent's will.

Appellants rely on *Estate of Watts* (1918) 179 Cal. 20, 175 P. 415 (1921) 186 Cal. 102, 198 P. 1036, for the proposition that when the language of intent in the testatrix's will is clear and unambiguous, "it 'must be interpreted according to its ordinary meaning and legal import, and the intention of the testator ascertained thereby.'" (179 Cal. at 23, 175 P. at 417; see also Prob.Code § 106; *Estate of Willson* (1915) 171 Cal. 449, 456, 153 P. 927.) In *Watts, supra,* the Supreme Court excluded evidence of oral declarations by the testatrix to the draftsman of her will that when she used the words 'my heirs' she intended to refer only to her own kin. (186 Cal. at 104–105, 198 P. 1036.)

Under *Watts, supra,* if the words chosen by the testator had a common, general and unambiguous meaning, evidence of a special meaning which the testator actually attached to such words was inadmissible. (See Prob.Code § 106; *Estate of Willson, supra,* 171 Cal. at 456, 153 P. 927; *Estate of Loescher* (1955) 133 Cal.App.2d 589, 594, 284 P.2d 902.)

However, in *Estate of Russell* (1968) 69 Cal.2d 200, 70 Cal.Rptr. 561, 444 P.2d 353, our Supreme Court substantially abrogated the "plain meaning" rule. (See 7 Witkin, Summary of Cal. Law, Wills and Probate § 162 pp. 5678–5679; 22 Hastings Law Journal (1971) pp. 1350–1355.) ... In approving the consideration of the extrinsic evidence, the Supreme Court stated:

> "... extrinsic evidence of the circumstances under which a will is made (except evidence expressly excluded by statute) may be considered by the court in ascertaining what the testator meant by the words used in the will. If in light of such extrinsic evidence, the provisions of the will are reasonably susceptible of two or more meanings claimed to have been intended by the testator, 'an uncertainty arises upon the face of a will' (s 105) and extrinsic evidence relevant to prove any of such meanings is admissible (see § 106)...." (69 Cal.2d at 212, 70 Cal.Rptr. at 569, 444 P.2d at 361.)

Under *Russell, supra,* extrinsic evidence is admissible both to show that a latent ambiguity exists and to resolve the latent ambiguity. (*Estate of Flint* (1972) 25 Cal.App.3d 945, 954, 102 Cal.Rptr. 345.) "Extrinsic evidence is now admissible to show that the apparently clear and unambiguous language of the will is in fact ambiguous ... If ... the extrinsic evidence does reveal a reasonable second interpretation, the will is deemed to be ambiguous, and (Prob.Code) section 105 will permit the admission of extrinsic evidence to discover the testator's intent." (22 Hastings Law Journal (1971) pp. 1353–1354.)

Although *Russell, supra,* did not expressly overrule *Watts, supra,* it clearly ended the vitality of *Watts* insofar as the plain meaning rule is concerned by permitting the trial court to consider extrinsic evidence to prove a reasonable second meaning of the language used in the will. Extrinsic evidence contradicting the express terms of a will will be excluded today only where no reasonable ambiguity is made to appear by the extrinsic evidence. (69 Cal.2d 208–212, 70 Cal.Rptr. 561, 444 P.2d 353.)

In the present case the declarations of the decedent to her attorney and her sister exposed a latent ambiguity, i.e., that when the testatrix used the term "my heirs" in her will, she intended to exclude the relatives of her predeceased husband, Harry. Under *Russell, supra,* the extrinsic evidence was properly received both to create the ambiguity in the word "heirs" and to resolve the ambiguity. (*Estate of Flint, supra,* 25 Cal.App.3d at 954, 102 Cal.Rptr. 345.)

Appellants argue that Probate Code section 105 precludes the consideration of a testator's oral declarations as to his intent. Section 105 provides:

> "When there is an imperfect description, or no person or property exactly answers the description, mistakes and omissions must be corrected, if the

error appears from the context of the will or from extrinsic evidence, *Excluding the oral declarations of the testator as to his intentions*; ... (Emphasis added.[2])

However, it has long been held that oral declarations made by a testator to the scrivener of the will are admissible to resolve a latent ambiguity. In *Estate of Dominici* (1907) 151 Cal. 181, 90 P. 448, our Supreme Court noted that the statute prohibiting admission of oral declarations was contrary to the prevailing American and English law and declared:

> "(The prohibition) will not be extended, therefore, beyond its actual language, and will be held to apply to the mere incidental fugitive utterances or declarations of intent, as distinguished from specific instructions as to testamentary disposition which it may be proved were given." ... [Citations omitted.]

Appellants next argue that Probate Code section 106 and case law require a trial court to interpret technical words used in a will drawn by an attorney in their technical sense. Probate Code section 106 provides:

> "... technical words in a will are to be taken in their technical sense, unless the context clearly indicates a contrary intention, or unless it satisfactorily appears that the will was drawn solely by the testator, and that he was unacquainted with such technical sense."

The presumption of technical meaning established by section 106, however, is subordinate to the dominant purpose of finding and effecting the intent of the testator; the presumption is an aid to be used in ascertaining that intent, not a tool by which the court frustrates the testator's objectives.... [Citations omitted.]

   ...

Because the extrinsic evidence is not in conflict as to the decedent's intention to exclude the relatives of Harry C. Taff from taking any part of the residuary estate, and because the term "my heirs" as used in the will is reasonably susceptible to mean that decedent's heirs other than the relatives of Harry Taff, the trial court properly decided as a matter of law that appellants have no right to any portion of the residuary estate.

   ...

The judgment is affirmed.

Notes

1. *Estate of Russell*: As the court in *Taff* notes, the *Estate of Russell* case was the seminal 'modern trend' California case on the admissibility of extrinsic evidence to help construe a will. In addition to the language quoted in the *Taff* opinion, in *Estate of Russell*, the Court made another statement that might be of interest:

---

2. [Editors' footnote] Emphasis added by the court writing this opinion.

When the language of a will is ambiguous or uncertain resort may be had
to extrinsic evidence in order to ascertain the intention of the testator. We
have said that extrinsic evidence is admissible "to explain *any ambiguity* arising on the face of a will, or to resolve a latent ambiguity which does not so
appear"

In re Estate of Russell, 444 P.2d 353, 357 (Cal. 1968) (emphasis added).

In *Estate of Russell*, the testatrix (Thelma Russell) had an "index card will" that
provided in pertinent part (the front side of the card) as follows:

I leave everything
I own Real &
Personal to Chester
H. Quinn & Roxy Russell
Thelma L. Russell'

Thelma's heirs (Augusta and Georgia) wanted to admit extrinsic evidence to show
that Roxy Russell was a dog (gifts to animals are void, and so if the gift to Roxy failed
it would fall to intestacy and Thelma's heirs would take). Should the court admit
their extrinsic evidence?

In response to Augusta and Georgia's extrinsic evidence, Chester wanted to admit:
(1) "an address book of testatrix upon which she had written: 'Chester, Don't let Augusta and Georgia have one penny of my place if it takes it all to fight it in Court.
Thelma,'" and (2):

certain documentary evidence consisting of testatrix' address book and a certain quitclaim deed 'for the purpose of demonstrating the intention on the
part of the deceased that she not die intestate.' Of all this extrinsic evidence
only the following infinitesimal portion of Quinn's testimony relates to care
of the dog: 'Q (Counsel for Quinn) Prior to the first Roxy's death did you
ever discuss with Miss Russell taking care of Roxy if anything should ever
happen to her? A Yes.' Plaintiff carefully preserved an objection running to
all of the above line of testimony and at the conclusion of the hearing moved
to strike such evidence. Her motion was denied.

Chester argued the evidence helped establish that Thelma intended "to make an absolute and outright gift of the entire residue of her estate to Quinn who was 'to use
whatever portion thereof as might be necessary to care for and maintain the dog.'"
Should the court admit the extrinsic evidence?

The California Supreme Court ruled that "since ... the terms of the will are not
reasonably susceptible of the meaning claimed by Quinn to have been intended by
testatrix, the extrinsic evidence offered to show such an intention should have been
excluded by the trial court." *See Estate of Russell*, 444 P.2d at 363. While the California
Supreme Court clearly indicated that it was open to extrinsic evidence to help it construe an ambiguity in the will, the court appears to have concluded that the construction Chester was asking it to adopt went too far, in essence asking the court to rewrite
the will.

2. *Construing a will versus rewriting a will:* An issue implicitly raised by the California Supreme Court's opinion in *Estate of Russell*—but not addressed—is when does a court cross the line between construing a will and rewriting a will. Following the Court's opinion in *Estate of Russell*, that line was important because: (1) extrinsic evidence was admissible only if there was express language *in the will* that was ambiguous and that required construing, and (2) after admitting the extrinsic evidence, the court's construction of the ambiguity had to be consistent with one of the possible reasonable interpretations of the express language in the will that was ambiguous. Over time, the California courts stretched the concepts of: (1) what constituted an express ambiguity in the will, and (2) what constituted a *reasonable* interpretation of that ambiguity, but the courts held firm to that approach, declining to embrace the Restatement (Third) of Property, Donative Transfers, position authorizing courts to reform a will "if it is established by clear and convincing evidence (1) that a mistake of fact or law, whether in expression or inducement, affected specific terms of the document; and (2) what the donor's intention was."

The California Supreme Court was presented with an opportunity to revisit that position recently when it decided the case of *In re Estate of Duke*.

In re Estate of Duke

61 Cal. 4th 871 (2015)

CANTIL-SAKAUYE, C.J.

. . .

I. FACTS

In 1984, when Irving Duke was 72 years of age, he prepared a holographic will in which he left all of his property to "my beloved wife, Mrs. Beatrice Schecter Duke," who was then 58 years of age. He left to his brother, Harry Duke, "the sum of One dollar." He provided that "[s]hould my wife … and I die at the same moment, my estate is to be equally divided—[¶] One-half is to be donated to the City of Hope in the name and loving memory of my sister, Mrs. Rose Duke Radin. [¶] One-half is to be donated to the Jewish National Fund to plant trees in Israel in the names and loving memory of my mother and father—[¶] Bessie and Isaac Duke."

Irving further provided in his will that "I have intentionally omitted all other persons, whether heirs or otherwise, who are not specifically mentioned herein, and I hereby specifically disinherit all persons whomsoever claiming to be, or who may lawfully be determined to be my heirs at law, except as otherwise mentioned in this will. If any heir, devisee or legatee, or any other person or persons, shall either directly or indirectly, seek to invalidate this will, or any part thereof, then I hereby give and bequeath to such person or persons the sum of one dollar ($1.00) and no more, in lieu of any other share or interest in my estate."

The will appointed Beatrice the executrix of the estate. The only change Irving ever made to his will was the addition, in 1997, of the statement that "[w]e hereby agree that all of our assets are community property." Beatrice died in July 2002, but the will was not changed to select a new executor.

Irving died in November 2007, leaving no spouse or children. In February 2008, a deputy public administrator for the County of Los Angeles obtained the will from Irving's safe deposit box. In March 2008, two charities, the City of Hope (COH) and the Jewish National Fund (JNF), petitioned for probate and for letters of administration. In October 2008, Robert and Seymour Radin (the Radins) filed a petition for determination of entitlement to estate distribution. The Radins are the sons of Irving's sister, Rose Duke Radin, who predeceased Irving. Their petition alleged that they are entitled to the distribution of Irving's estate as Irving's sole intestate heirs.

The Radins moved for summary judgment. They did not challenge the validity of the will. Instead, they asserted that the estate must pass to Irving's closest surviving intestate heirs, the Radins, because Irving did not predecease Beatrice, nor did Irving and Beatrice "die at the same moment," and there is no provision in the will for disposition of the estate in the event Irving survived Beatrice. In opposition to the motion, COH and JNF offered extrinsic evidence to prove that Irving intended the will to provide that in the event Beatrice was not alive to inherit Irving's estate when Irving died, the estate would be distributed to COH and JNF. The probate court concluded that the will was not ambiguous, and on that ground, it declined to consider extrinsic evidence of Irving's intent, and granted summary judgment for the Radins.

The Court of Appeal affirmed, ...

II. DISCUSSION

California law allows the admission of extrinsic evidence to establish that a will is ambiguous and to clarify ambiguities in a will.... As COH and JNF acknowledge, however, California law does not currently authorize the admission of extrinsic evidence to correct a mistake in a will when the will is unambiguous.... To evaluate whether there are circumstances in which this court should authorize the admission of extrinsic evidence to correct a mistake in an unambiguous will, we first consider whether the Legislature's actions in this field preclude this court from altering the rule.

A. Statutory and judicial development of the law concerning the admission of extrinsic evidence regarding wills

[Starting with the original Statute of Wills in 1950 and proceeding up to the present, the Court traced the slow but steady movement towards increasing the admissibility of extrinsic evidence with respect to the construction of wills. The Court noted that the movement has been the result of the interaction of both judicial and legislative action. In particular, the Court discussed in detail its decision in *Estate of Russell*, noting how the opinion significantly changed the law with respect to the admissibility of extrinsic evidence in California to help construe a will. As the Court noted, "although the Legislature had codified the historical grounds on which courts had authorized the admission of extrinsic evidence, we did not perceive its provisions to be a limitation on the continued development of the common law." The Court went on to conclude:]

This history of statutory provisions concerning the admissibility of evidence of a testator's intent reflects that the Legislature has codified legal principles developed by the courts, and has taken steps to ensure that its enactments do not restrict the admissibility of extrinsic evidence beyond the principles established by the courts. Nothing in this history suggests that the Legislature intended to foreclose further judicial developments of the law concerning the admissibility of evidence to discern the testator's intent, and "we see no reason to interpret the legislation as establishing a bar to judicial innovation." (*American Motorcycle Assn. v. Superior Court* (1978) 20 Cal.3d 578, 601, 146 Cal.Rptr. 182, 578 P.2d 899.... Moreover, it does not appear that the Legislature has addressed the issue of reformation of wills. Therefore, as we did in *Estate of Russell, supra,* 69 Cal.2d 200, 70 Cal.Rptr. 561, 444 P.2d 353, we may continue to develop the law concerning the admissibility of evidence to assist in the determination of the testator's intent when the language of the document is clear on its face.

B. No sound basis exists to forbid the reformation of unambiguous wills in appropriate circumstances

. . .

In California, extrinsic evidence is generally admissible to correct errors in documents, including donative documents other than wills....

In addition, California courts have admitted extrinsic evidence to apply to the *construction* of a will to accomplish what is arguably or has the effect of reforming a will. For example, ... *Estate of Karkeet* (1961) 56 Cal.2d 277, 281–283, 14 Cal.Rptr. 664, 363 P.2d 896 [extrinsic evidence was admissible to establish that a will that named the testatrix's good friend as executrix, but made no testamentary disposition, was intended to leave the estate to the good friend]; *Estate of Akeley* (1950) 35 Cal.2d 26, 30, 215 P.2d 921 [evidence that testatrix was unmarried, had no relatives, and drafted her will herself was cited in support of ruling that three charities that were each given one-quarter of the residue of the estate would each receive one-third].)

Principles allowing the admission of extrinsic evidence to identify and resolve ambiguities in wills have also been invoked to correct attorneys' drafting errors and thereby to reform wills. For example, in *Estate of Taff* (1976) 63 Cal.App.3d 319, 133 Cal.Rptr. 737, the testatrix directed her attorney to provide that if the testatrix's sister did not survive her, the residue of the estate would go to her sister's children. Her will, however, stated that if her sister predeceased her, the residue would go to "'my heirs in accordance with the laws of intestate succession.'" (*Id.* at p. 322, 133 Cal.Rptr. 737.) The court found that the extrinsic evidence of the testatrix's instructions to her attorney and statements to her sister "exposed a latent ambiguity, i.e., that when the testatrix used the term 'my heirs' in her will, she intended to exclude the relatives of her predeceased husband, Harry." (*Id.* at p. 325, 133 Cal.Rptr. 737.) ...

Extrinsic evidence is admissible not only to aid in the construction of a will, but also to determine whether a document was intended to be a will. (*Halldin v. Usher* (1958) 49 Cal.2d 749, 752, 321 P.2d 746 [parol evidence is admissible to prove a document was intended as a will rather than a contract]; *Estate of Sargavak* (1950) 35 Cal.2d 93, 96, 216 P.2d 850 [evidence is admissible to prove a will was executed in jest, as a threat to induce action, under the mistaken belief it was a mortgage, to induce illicit relations, or in response to annoyance from one who seeks to inherit].) In addition, courts have long recognized that extrinsic evidence is admissible to prove that a will has been lost or destroyed, and to prove its contents....

Thus, extrinsic evidence is admitted to correct donative documents other than wills after the donor's death. Moreover, myriad circumstances exist in which California courts appropriately admit evidence to establish a testator's intentions. Because extrinsic evidence is not inherently more reliable when admitted for these various purposes than when admitted to correct an error in a will, Professors John Langbein and Lawrence Waggoner, leading advocates of an extension of the doctrine of reformation to unambiguous wills, conclude that evidentiary concerns do not explain or justify the bar on reformation of wills. In their view, a greater obstacle to reformation has been concern with the formalities required in the execution of a will by the statute of wills. (Langbein & Waggoner, *Reformation of Wills on the Ground of Mistake: Change of Direction in American Law?* (1982) 130 U.Pa. L.Rev. 521, 524–529 (hereafter Langbein and Waggoner).) ...

Applying the analysis developed with respect to the statute of frauds, Langbein and Waggoner observe, "Whereas an oral will instances total noncompliance with the Wills Act formalities, a duly executed will with a mistakenly rendered term involves high levels of compliance with both the letter and the purpose of the Wills Act formalities. To the extent that a mistake case risks impairing any policy of the Wills Act, it is the *evidentiary* policy that is in question." (Langbein & Waggoner, *supra,* 130 U.Pa. L.Rev. at p. 569, italics added.) With respect to evidentiary concerns, the authors advocate that reformation be allowed only in cases of clear and convincing evidence of the alleged mistake and the testator's intent. (*Ibid.*) As noted, we have previously imposed a clear and convincing evidence standard to support a claim of inheritance based on equitable adoption. (*Estate of Ford, supra,* 32 Cal.4th 160, 172, 8 Cal.Rptr.3d 541, 82 P.3d 747.)

In cases in which clear and convincing evidence establishes both a mistake in the drafting of the will and the testator's actual and specific intent at the time the will was drafted, it is plain that denying reformation would defeat the testator's intent and result in unjust enrichment of unintended beneficiaries. Given that the paramount concern in construing a will is to determine the subjective intent of the testator (*Estate of Russell, supra,* 69 Cal.2d at p. 205; 70 Cal.Rptr. 561, 444 P.2d 353 4 Page on Wills (Bowe-Parker rev.2004) § 30.1, p. 2), only significant countervailing considerations can justify a rule categorically denying reformation.

The Radins cite various factors in support of their contention that reformation of wills should never be allowed, some of which we have addressed above. First, they distinguish wills from other written instruments, noting that probate of a will always occurs after the testator's death, whereas contract litigation typically occurs when the parties to the contract are alive, and trust administration "frequently" begins before the testator's death. In addition, anyone may claim to be an intended beneficiary of a will, but the parties to a contract typically are few. We are not persuaded by these arguments in favor of a categorical bar on reformation.... Categorically denying reformation may result in unjust enrichment if there is a mistake of expression in the will, and imposing a burden of clear and convincing evidence of both the existence of the mistake and of the testator's actual and specific intent at the time the will was drafted helps safeguard against baseless allegations....

Second, the Radins express concern that reformation overrides the formalities required to execute a will. The fact that reformation is an available remedy does not relieve a testator of the requirements imposed by the Statute of Wills. (See Prob.Code, §6111.) Therefore, the formalities continue to serve various functions associated with the rituals of will execution, such as warning the testator of the seriousness of the act and clearly identifying the document as a will. (See fn. 12, *ante.*) To the extent reformation is inconsistent with the formalities' evidentiary purpose of establishing the testator's intent in a writing, the inconsistency is no different from the tension between reformation and the statute of frauds. As explained above, the evidentiary concern is addressed by requiring clear and convincing evidence of a mistake in expression and the testator's actual and specific intent. We should not allow stringent adherence to formalities to obscure the ultimate purpose of the statute of wills, which is to transfer an estate in accordance with the testator's intent.

Third, the Radins assert that allowing reformation in circumstances in which the estate would otherwise pass pursuant to the laws of intestacy constitutes an attack on the laws of intestacy. We disagree. The purpose of reformation is to carry out the wishes of the testator, and the remedy reflects no judgment other than a preference for disposition pursuant to the wishes of the testator. This preference is consistent with the statutory scheme. (See Prob.Code, §§6110 [a will that is not properly executed is enforceable if clear and convincing evidence establishes it was intended to constitute the testator's will], 21120 ["Preference is to be given to an interpretation of an instrument that will prevent intestacy or failure of a transfer, rather than one that will result in an intestacy or failure of a transfer"].)

Fourth, the Radins assert that allowing reformation will result in a significant increase in probate litigation and expenses. Claimants have long been entitled, however, to present extrinsic evidence to establish that a will is ambiguous despite the fact that it appears to be unambiguous. (*Estate of Russell, supra,* 69 Cal.2d at pp. 206–213, 70 Cal.Rptr. 561, 444 P.2d 353.) Therefore, probate courts already receive extrinsic evidence of testator intent from claimants attempting to reform a will through the doctrine of ambiguity.... The task of deciding whether the evidence establishes by clear and convincing evidence that a mistake was made in the drafting of the will is a relatively small additional burden, because the court is already evaluating the evidence's probative value to determine the existence of an ambiguity. To the extent additional claims are made that are based on a theory of mistake rather than a theory of ambiguity, the heightened evidentiary standard will help the probate court to filter out weak claims. Finally, fear of additional judicial burdens is not an adequate reason to deny relief that would serve the paramount purpose of distributing property in accordance with the testator's intent....

Fifth, the Radins discount justifications for allowing reformation in appropriate circumstances. They assert that Probate Code section 6110, subdivision (c)(2), which allows the probate of a will that was not executed in compliance with statutory attestation requirements if clear and convincing evidence establishes that the testator intended the writing to be a will, was not intended to lessen required formalities. Although section 6110 does not reduce the formalities of attestation, it reflects a judgment that the formalities should not be allowed to defeat the testator's intent when clear and convincing evidence satisfies the evidentiary concerns underlying the formalities of the statute of wills. The Radins also reject as a factor in support of a reformation remedy the avoidance of unjust enrichment. They state that no one has a right to inherit, and they recite various facts that they believe reflect that it is more just for Irving's relatives to inherit his estate than for the charities to receive it. If, however, a testator did not intend to devise property to a particular party, that party's receipt of the property as a result of a mistake constitutes unjust enrichment.

In sum, the Radins identify no countervailing considerations that would justify denying reformation if clear and convincing evidence establishes a mistake in the testator's expression of intent and the testator's actual and specific intent at the time the will was drafted.

. . .

D. The charities have articulated a valid theory that will support reformation if established by clear and convincing evidence

COH and JNF contend that Irving actually intended at the time he wrote his will to provide that his estate would pass to COH and JNF in the event Beatrice was not alive to inherit his estate when he died, but that his intent was inartfully expressed in his will and thus there is a mistake in the will that should be reformed to reflect his intent when the will was drafted. Their contention, if proved by clear and convincing evidence, would support reformation of the will to reflect Irving's actual intent.

First, the alleged mistake concerns Irving's actual intent at the time he wrote the will. As explained above, reformation of a document that is subject to the statute of frauds or the statute of wills entails the enforcement of the written document in a manner that reflects what was intended when the document was prepared. If Irving's only intent at the time he wrote his will was to address the disposition of his estate in the circumstances in which he died before Beatrice or they died simultaneously, his will accurately reflects his intent. In that circumstance, his mistake, if any, would be in failing subsequently to modify the will after Beatrice died, and that mistake would not be related to the will he wrote and that COH and JNF seek to have reformed. (See generally 1 Witkin, Summary of Cal. Law, *supra*, Contracts, § 278, p. 308.)

Second, the alleged mistake and intent are sufficiently specific. The allegations are precise with respect to the error and the remedy: the charities assert Irving specifically intended when he wrote his will to provide that his estate would pass to COH and JNF not only upon the simultaneous death of Irving and Beatrice, as the will expressly states, but also in the event Beatrice was not alive to inherit the estate at the time of his death. Although COH and JNF do not allege that the error was merely clerical, but instead assert that Irving's intent was inartfully expressed, their theory alleges "a mistake in the rendering of terms that the testator has authored or approved. The remedy in such a case has exactly the dimensions of the mistake. The term that the testator intended is restored." (Langbein & Waggoner, *supra*, 130 U.Pa. L.Rev. at pp. 583–584.)

The charities' theory, which sets forth a specific disposition of assets Irving allegedly intended when he wrote his will, distinguishes this case from circumstances in which it is alleged that the testator had a more general intent regarding the disposition of the estate which was not accomplished by the will as written. An example of an error involving general intent would be a case in which a testator intended in his or her will to provide adequate resources to one of the will's beneficiaries to support that beneficiary for a lifetime, but the specific gift set forth in the will proves to be inadequate for that purpose. Thus, that will accurately sets forth the testator's specific intent with respect to the distribution of assets, but due to a mistake with respect to the value of those assets or the needs of the beneficiary, the will fails to effect the testator's intent to provide adequate assets to support the beneficiary. In contrast to cases in which the alleged error is in the rendering of the specific terms intended by the testator, cases in which the alleged error is in failing to accomplish a general intent of the testator would require a court to determine the testator's putative intent: if the testator had known of the mistake, how would the testator have changed the will? The case before us presents only the issue of whether a will may be reformed when extrinsic evidence establishes that the will fails to set forth the actual specific intent of the testator at the time the will was executed, and we express no opinion on the availability of reformation in cases involving claims of general and putative intent.

Finally, for the reasons discussed above, evidence of the testator's intent must be clear and convincing. Among the evidence to be considered is the will itself, but when reformation rather than construction of a will is at issue, the rules of construction, which set forth principles for determining disposition of estate assets where the testator's intention is not reflected in the will (Prob.Code, § 21102), do not apply where extrinsic evidence supplies the missing terms. (Langbein and Waggoner, *supra*, 130 U.Pa. L.Rev. at pp. 579–580.) Other doctrines of interpretation are also supplanted by the remedy of reformation. For example, although the terms of a will may be inadequate alone to establish a dominant dispositive plan that would warrant a gift by implication..., those aspects of the will that tend to reflect an intent to make a particular gift should be considered together with the extrinsic evidence of intent to determine whether there is clear and convincing evidence of an intent to make a gift. Similarly, although a disinheritance clause cannot prevent heirs from inheriting pursuant to the statutory rules of intestacy (*Estate of Barnes, supra,* at pp. 582–583, 47 Cal.Rptr. 480, 407 P.2d 656), any intent reflected in such a clause may be relevant when reformation is sought.

III. CONCLUSION

We hold that an unambiguous will may be reformed to conform to the testator's intent if clear and convincing evidence establishes that the will contains a mistake in the testator's expression of intent at the time the will was drafted, and also establishes the testator's actual specific intent at the time the will was drafted. We reverse the judgment of the Court of Appeal and remand the matter to the Court of Appeal with directions to remand the case to the trial court for its consideration of extrinsic evidence as authorized by our opinion.

Notes

1. *Construing versus rewriting:* What does the California Supreme Court's opinion in *Estate of Duke* do to the traditional line between construing an express ambiguity in a will and rewriting a will? To the extent the opinion abolishes that line that authorizes a court to admit extrinsic evidence in either case, does that mean that the distinction between construing an express ambiguity in a will and rewriting the will is abolished and has no legal significance?

2. *Estate of Taff:* Notice the Court's characterization in *Estate of Duke* of the Appellate Court's opinion in *Estate of Taff.* Would the Appellate Court in *Estate of Taff* agree with the Supreme Court's characterization of its opinion? To the extent the Supreme Court is saying that the Appellate Court in *Estate of Taff* stretched the law to reach a decision it thought was fair and just, is that not always a risk with any law? In the future, might lower courts reform a will to give effect to what the court thinks is the decedent's "probable intent" even if there is no clear and convincing evidence of the intent at the time the will was executed? Is that really where the intent movement (the movement the California Supreme Court described, including the harmless error doctrine and the increasing admissibility of extrinsic evidence concerning the decedent's intent) is headed? Would it be good to acknowledge that many probate and appellate courts are *de facto* applying a "probable intent" standard? Is that all they are doing? Is that good as a matter of public policy?

3. *Burden of proof:* What must the charities show on remand before the probate court should reform the will? What if the only evidence the charities have is: (1) the checks Irving gave to a senior gift planning officer totaling $300,000 on three different occasions over a six-month period from August 2003 to January 2004; and (2) alleged oral statements Irving made to the senior gift planning officer for one of the charities that he was "leaving his estate" to the charities? What constitutes clear and convincing

evidence? Should it matter if the evidence is offered by only one of the interested parties?

What is the temporal focus of the test the Court articulated in *Estate of Duke*? Is evidence of the decedent's intent before that point in time and/or after that point in time relevant to his or her state of mind at that point in time?

How would you rule if you were the probate court judge hearing the case on remand, and why?

The *Estate of Duke* case should give you a better feel for the complexity of the issue of whether courts should reform wills and, if so, under what conditions. For an interesting judicial discussion of these issues, *see Estate of Irvine v. Oaas*, 372 Mont. 49 (2013) (where the Montana Supreme Court adopted the RESTATEMENT (THIRD) approach but then held that it would be inappropriate to apply it to the facts of that case).

Problems

1. Dirk knew he was ill and drove to his attorney's office to have his will prepared. When he arrived, Dirk remained in his car and his attorney came out to him. Dirk told his attorney that he wanted his property to go half to his wife, and half to his niece. The attorney returned to her office, drew up the will, but failed to include the devise to Dirk's wife.

   After drawing up the will, the attorney took the will out to Dirk's car. Two of the attorney's employees served as witnesses by standing at the office window and waving to Dirk while they watched him read and sign the will while he remained in the car. There were no verbal communications between Dirk and the witnesses. The will was then returned to the attorney's office, where the employees signed it while standing at the window. The witnesses knew Dirk and his signature.

   a. Should Dirk's will be admitted to probate?

   b. Assuming, *arguendo*, Dirk's will is admitted to probate, if Dirk's wife wishes to present extrinsic evidence to prove that she is entitled to take under the will, is the evidence admissible? What is the burden of proof she would have to satisfy for the court to permit her to take? Has she met that burden?

2. Testatrix Thelma Russell handwrites and signs a valid holographic will that provides as follows:

   I leave everything
   I own Real &
   Personal to Chester
   H. Quinn & Roxy Russell.
   Thelma L. Russell

   Assume (1) Roxy is a dog, and (2) California still applied the traditional common law rule that if part of the residue fails, it falls to intestacy. Chester wishes to admit extrinsic evidence to show that Thelma's intent was for him to receive all of the property and to use some of it to care for Roxy. Is the evidence admissible? What is the burden of proof he would have to satisfy for the court to permit him to take? Has he met that burden?

3. Testatrix tells her attorney that she wishes her estate to go to her 25 first cousins. The attorney drafts and has testatrix execute a will that states that her estate will pass "to my heirs at law." It turns out that testatrix is survived by an aunt. The 25 first cousins seek to admit extrinsic evidence that shows that testatrix's intent was for them to take. Is the evidence admissible? What is the burden of proof they would have to satisfy for the court to permit them to take? Have they met that burden?

4. Consider the following fact pattern from the Massachusetts case of *Flannery v. McNamara*, 738 N.E.2d 739 (Mass. 2000):

On September 30, 1995, the decedent died in Arlington. The decedent's will, dated January 20, 1973, left his entire estate to his wife, Katherine M. White (Katherine). The relevant part of the will provides that:

"I give, devise, and bequeath all of the property of which I die possessed real, personal, and mixed of nature and wheresoever located to my beloved wife, Katherine M. White."

The decedent's will failed to name a contingent beneficiary and it did not contain a residuary clause.

Katherine died October 14, 1993, survived by the decedent and her two sisters, the Flannerys. The couple had no children. McNamara, the decedent's attorney, repeatedly advised the decedent to let him review the will, but the decedent never showed the will to McNamara. The decedent died survived by his intestate heirs who were discovered through a genealogical search. The heirs are the decedent's first cousins, once removed.

The Flannerys make the following allegations. For almost five decades, they had a close relationship with the decedent. Moreover, after Katherine's death, the decedent relied heavily on the Flannerys for advice and assistance with daily matters. After the decedent died, he was buried in the Flannerys' family plot. On several occasions, the decedent told members of the Flannerys' family that his Arlington residence and its contents "will be [theirs] some day." Additionally, the decedent informed McNamara that he understood that, if Katherine were to predecease him, his will provided for his property to go to the Flannerys. In contrast, the decedent did not have a close relationship with the heirs.

Assuming, *arguendo*, that the fact pattern arose in California, should the Flannerys' extrinsic evidence be admissible to show that the testator's intent was that they were to take in the event Katherine predeceased him? What is the burden of proof they would have to satisfy for the court to permit them to take? Have they met that burden?

III. Types of Testamentary Gifts; Failure

A will answers the question "Who gets a testator's property when he or she dies?" A will expresses the testator's intent to make an at-death gift of the property to the identified beneficiaries. Knowing the different types of gifts that can be made in a will is important because different rules apply to different types of at-death gifts.

A. Types of Testamentary Gifts

California has formally identified six types of "time-of-death" transfers, four of which are relevant to our examination:

CPC § 21117. Categories of 'at-death' transfers

At-death transfers are classified as follows:

(a) A specific gift is a transfer of specifically identifiable property.

(b) A general gift is a transfer from the general assets of the transferor that does not give specific property.

(c) A demonstrative gift is a general gift that specifies the fund or property from which the transfer is primarily to be made.

…

(f) A residuary gift is a transfer of property that remains after all specific and general gifts have been satisfied.

While a gift's categorization is ultimately a question of the testator's intent, the language in the will is the starting point for analyzing his or her intent. Thus, the key to analyzing the type of gift in a testator's will is to look to the description in the will of the property being gifted.

Assume the testator owns a 1987 Volkswagen Vanagon. His will includes the following clause: "I give my best friend Bob my most treasured item: my 1987 VW Vanagon. I know how much he has always envied it and desired it." The will specifically identifies a particular asset the testator owns and that the testator wants to give to the beneficiary. There is only one item in the world that matches the description: "*my* 1987 VW Vanagon." No other item can satisfy the gift. This is a classic example of a specific gift.

In contrast, a gift of an asset of a general description to be made out of testator's general assets is a general gift. The testator does *not* have in mind a specifically identified asset. Thus, the gift can be satisfied by any asset that matches the general description of the gift. The classic example of a general gift is a gift of money: "I give $10,000 to Remi." The testator has not specified which dollar bills in particular are to be given to Remi, any $10,000 will do. The gift can come from the testator's savings account, her checking account, or from selling other assets. Any of the testator's general assets (assets not specifically gifted) can be used to satisfy the gift. While gifts of money are the classic example of a general gift, a general gift can be of any nature. If the will provides "I give 1,000 shares of IBM stock to Bert," is that a general gift or a specific gift? The gift is of stock in a particular company, but there are millions of shares of IBM stock outstanding. Did the testator specify which 1,000 shares are to be given to Bert?

A legal rule that follows from classifying a gift as a general gift is that if, at time of death, the testator does not own an asset that matches the general gift, the personal representative has a legal duty to go out and purchase the asset and give it to the beneficiary.[3] If the gift of IBM stock above is a general gift, and the testator does not own 1,000 shares of IBM stock at time of death, the personal representative has a duty to go out and purchase 1,000 shares of IBM stock to give to the beneficiary. What if the testator's will provides as follows: "I give a 2015 Tesla S to my love, Gerri." Specific or general gift? What if the testator does not currently own a Tesla?

A residuary gift is a catch-all gift. It is the gift that gives away all of the testator's property that has not already been given away as a specific or general gift. Again, whether a gift is a residuary gift is a question of intent. The classic language for a residuary clause gift is "I give the rest, residue, and remainder of my property to Lulu." The intro clause ("I give *the rest* ...") implies that the testator is giving away the rest of his or her property after making the specific and general gifts in the will. But what type of gift a testator is making is a question of intent, and thus no special language is necessary. If the will simply says, "I give all my property to Lulu," the gift is a residuary gift: it gives away *all* of the testator's property. There are no specific or general gifts in such a simple will, but because the clause is giving away all of the testator's property, it is a residuary gift.

The fourth type of gift, the demonstrative gift, is a hybrid of the first two types. It is a general gift from a specific source: "I give Bert $10,000 from my checking account at Bank of America." The first half of the gift makes it look like a general gift, but the second half makes it look like a specific gift. If the testator intended the charge to be against the specific fund *only*, the gift is a specific gift. If, however, the testator intended the charge to be against the general assets of his or her estate in the event the specific fund failed, the gift is a demonstrative gift. Legally, demonstrative gifts are treated as a subset of general gifts. If the funds are no longer available from the specifically referenced source, that is not a problem. Because demonstrative gifts are a subset of the general gifts category, the funds would simply be taken from the testator's general funds (i.e., from the property that would otherwise pass through the residuary clause).

Problems

1. Testatrix's will provides in pertinent part as follows: "I give all my jewelry to my daughter Kristin." How would you classify the gift? *See Haslam v. Alvarez*, 38 A.2d 158, 161–62 (R.I. 1944).

2. Testatrix's will provides in pertinent part as follows: "I give all the shares of Amgen stock I inherited from my mother to my daughter Carolyn." How would you classify the gift? *See Haslam v. Alvarez*, 38 A.2d 158, 162 (R.I. 1944).

---

3. There are exceptions to this rule, but they will be covered later.

3. Testatrix's will provides in pertinent part as follows: "I give my nephew $5,000 to be paid from the money, as and when received, from my former husband in connection with our divorce, whereby he is obligated to pay me $25,000.00." It turns out testatrix's husband was not obligated to pay her $25,000.00 under the divorce decree and never paid this money. How would you classify the gift to the nephew? Is he entitled to receive $5,000 from testatrix's general assets?

4. Testator's will provides in pertinent part as follows: "I give my grandson $12,000, contained in the bond that is in my safe deposit box." How would you classify the gift? If there is no bond in the safe deposit box, is the grandson entitled to $12,000 out of the testator's general assets? *See In re Smallman's Will*, 247 N.Y.S. 593, 609 (1931). What if the will had provided "I give my grandson the bond that is in my safe deposit box." Same case or different case? How would you classify the gift?

5. Testator's holographic will provided in pertinent part as follows: "I give all my property to Lulu." How would you classify the gift?

6. Testator's holographic will provides in pertinent part as follows: "I give all my baseball cards to my brother, Bob." How would you classify the gift?

7. The testator's lawyer drafted a will that provides in pertinent part as follows: "I give 100 shares of Acadia Pharmaceuticals to my brother, Siqi." At the time of execution testator owns 100 shares of Acadia Pharmaceuticals. How would you classify the gift? What difference, if any, would it make if the will were a holographic will? *See In re Blackmun's Estate*, 98 Cal. App. 2d 314 (1950).

B. Failure of Testamentary Gift

A testamentary gift can fail for any number of reasons: for example, the gift was the result of an insane delusion, it was the result of undue influence, it was the result of fraud, the beneficiary disclaimed the gift, or the beneficiary failed to meet the survival requirement. If a gift fails, what happens to the gift? On the one hand, it can be argued that a failed gift creates an ambiguity in the will, and the court should take extrinsic evidence to determine what testator's intent would be if he or she had known that the gift would fail. On the other hand, the courts can create default rules with respect to what happens if a gift fails, and if a testator does not like the default rule, he or she can draft around it.

Which approach is the better approach? Why? The modern trend with respect to the will execution doctrines (substantial compliance and harmless error) is to admit extrinsic evidence in the interest of trying to determine and give effect to testator's intent. Should the modern trend approach extend to construction issues? Should the court take extrinsic evidence to determine the testator's probable intent and give effect to it?

In re Estate of McFarland

167 S.W.3d 299 (Tenn. 2005)

WILLIAM M. BARKER, J.

. . .

On November 14, 1994, Ms. Merle Jeffers McFarland executed a holographic will. . . . The will . . . directed that the remainder of her estate was to be divided among eighteen named individuals and entities. . . .

. . .

On October 12, 2001, seven years after making the will, Ms. McFarland passed away at the age of eighty-four. . . . [T]hree of the residuary beneficiaries named in the will, Minnis Rankin Jeffers, Willie Lee Jeffers, and Mary Louise McFarland, had predeceased the testatrix, Ms. McFarland. Also, none of these predeceased beneficiaries had left a surviving spouse or issue. It was therefore uncertain as to how these individuals' shares were to be distributed.

. . .

. . . The issue presented is whether the lapsed residuary gifts pass to the testatrix's heirs at law or to the remaining residuary beneficiaries. The estate administrator, along with the remaining residuary beneficiaries, argue that the lapsed gifts should be divided among the remaining residuary beneficiaries in proportion to their interests granted in the will. In opposition, the surviving heirs argue that the lapsed gifts pass by intestate succession.

. . .

Analysis

. . .

A gift or devise in a will which fails because the beneficiary predeceases the testator is said to lapse. *White v. Kane,* 178 Tenn. 469, 159 S.W.2d 92, 94 (1942). To avoid this problem, Tennessee, like many other states, has enacted an "anti-lapse" statute which works to save lapsed gifts for the representatives of the predeceased beneficiary. . . .

This statute attempts to further the presumed intent of the testator in the absence of any contrary intent expressed through the will. *Weiss v. Broadway Nat'l Bank,* 204 Tenn. 563, 322 S.W.2d 427, 432 (1959). However, the anti-lapse statute saves the gift only if the predeceased beneficiary has left issue surviving the testator; otherwise, the statute has no application, and the gift lapses. *See Cox v. Sullins,* 181 Tenn. 601, 183 S.W.2d 865, 866 (1944).

Another manner of disposing of lapsed gifts is through a will's residuary clause. If the will contains specific gifts or devises of property which lapse, these are deemed to fall into the residue and are disposed of through the provisions of the residuary clause, unless the testator has manifested a contrary intention. *Milligan v. Greeneville Coll.,* 156 Tenn. 495, 2 S.W.2d 90, 93 (1928). Yet a particular problem arises when, as in the present case, the anti-lapse statute is inapplicable, and the gift which has lapsed is already a part of the residue. Under such circumstances, the traditional rule, derived from the English common law, is that the lapsed gift falls out of the terms of the will and passes by intestate succession to the testator's heirs at law....

Despite its stability in our state, this rule has been much criticized in other jurisdictions and by legal commentators, with the main argument being that the rule defeats the most probable intent of the testator in this situation. Due in part to this criticism, the Uniform Probate Code adopts an alternative rule, often called the "modern" rule, which directs that "if the residue is devised to two or more persons and the share of one of the residuary devisees fails for any reason, his share passes to the other residuary devisee, or to other residuary devisees in proportion to their interests in the residue." Unif. Probate Code § 2-606 (1974). The UPC rule has gained widespread support, having been adopted, either by statute or through case law, in the vast majority of other states. By contrast, the common-law or *Ford* rule remains in effect in only a minority of states, including Tennessee.

Nevertheless, although widely abandoned in other jurisdictions, the *Ford* rule cannot fairly be termed either incorrect or illogical. The reasons supporting the modern UPC rule are generally that it more closely comports with the probable intent of the testator and that it avoids partial intestacy. *See In re Slack's Trust*, 220 A.2d at 473–74; *Corbett*, 207 P. at 822. However, in our view, it is just as likely that a person would consider the implications of the traditional or *Ford* rule when executing his or her will and thus implicitly intend that lapsed gifts should pass to the heirs, rather than to the remaining residuary beneficiaries. Therefore, neither of the rules is more logically correct than the other. The two divergent rules simply represent two competing schools of thought as to what a testator would most probably desire to happen when a residuary gift lapses.

. . .

Conclusion

In summary, we hold that the lapsed residuary gifts at issue in this case are not to be divided among the remaining residuary beneficiaries. Rather, the lapsed gifts result in a partial intestacy and therefore pass under the laws of intestate succession to the testatrix's heirs at law....

Note

Partial failure of residuary clause: Look back at the brief description of the *Estate of Russell* case a few pages back. What type of gift was the gift to Roxy and Chester? In light of the rule that an animal is not an eligible taker under a will, the gift to Roxy failed. Which approach did California apply at the time? Like Tennessee, California revisited the issue statutorily (see below). Did California join the majority, modern trend approach or did California stick with the common law approach? How would the *McFarland* case come out in California?

CPC § 21111. Testamentary transfers that fail

(a) Except as provided in subdivision (b) and subject to Section 21110, if a transfer fails for any reason, the property is transferred as follows:

    (1) If the transferring instrument provides for an alternative disposition in the event the transfer fails, the property is transferred according to the terms of the instrument.

    (2) If the transferring instrument does not provide for an alternative disposition but does provide for the transfer of a residue, the property becomes a part of the residue transferred under the instrument.

    (3) If the transferring instrument does not provide for an alternative disposition and does not provide for the transfer of a residue, or if the transfer is itself a residuary gift, the property is transferred to the decedent's estate.

(b) Subject to Section 21110, if a residuary gift or a future interest is transferred to two or more persons and the share of a transferee fails for any reason, and no alternative disposition is provided, the share passes to the other transferees in proportion to their other interest in the residuary gift or the future interest.

(c) A transfer of "all my estate" or words of similar import is a residuary gift for purposes of this section.

Notice that CPC Section 21111 creates a default approach that applies in the absence of express intent in the document. If the decedent expressly states what he or she wants to happen if a gift fails, the decedent's express intent controls. *See* CPC § 21111(a)(1).

Historically the construction issues that arise because of a will's ambulatory nature were governed by a set of judicially created default presumptions that were collectively known as the "wills-related" construction rules. The wills-related construction rules govern the ambiguities that arise because of the changes that can occur between the time a will is executed and the time the testator dies that can affect the gifts in the will: for example, a beneficiary may predecease the decedent, or a specific gift of property may no longer be in the testator's estate at time of death.

The rest of this chapter examines the more common wills-related construction rules, starting with how the law treats failed gifts. It should be noted, however, that under the modern trend an issue has arisen with respect to the scope of the wills-related construction rules. To the extent the nonprobate instruments function very much like a will, they are, in many respects, ambulatory documents similar to a will. A person executes the nonprobate instrument at one point in time, and for all practical purposes the gift under the instrument does not take effect until some future date. Changes can occur between time of execution and time of death that can create ambiguities with respect to what should happen to the gift. To the extent the same basic issues can arise under a nonprobate instrument, should the wills-related construction rules apply only to wills, or should they apply to the nonprobate instruments as well?

Look back at the terminology used in California Probate Code Section 21111. How does it refer to the instrument in question? Look at the section number. The general California probate intestate and probate testate sections are in the 6400 series. The failed gifts section is in the 21000 series. The 21100 series was adopted in 2003 and is titled "Construction of Wills, Trusts and Other Instruments." Section 21101 specifically provides as follows: "Unless the provision or context otherwise requires, this part applies to a will, trust, deed, and any other instrument."

In California, are the wills-related construction rules limited to wills, or do they now apply, as a general rule, to nonprobate instruments as well? Note that Section 21104 creates something of an exception: "As used in this part, 'at-death transfer' means a transfer that is revocable during the lifetime of the transferor, but does not include a joint tenancy or joint account with right of survivorship."

Because, historically, these doctrines applied only to wills, most of the cases and hypotheticals in this section will involve a will. Nevertheless, you should keep in mind that California has adopted the modern trend and now applies these construction rules to wills, trusts, and other instruments (unless the provision or context otherwise requires).

Problem

The terms of Settlor's trust provide that upon her death, all remaining trust assets should be distributed in two equal shares. One share is to go to her friend, Fran; but if Fran predeceases Settlor her share is to go to Fran's surviving issue, by right of representation. The other share is to go to her niece, Nina; but if Nina predeceases Settlor, that share is to go to Settlor's friend Fran. Both Fran and Nina predecease Settlor. Who gets the share that was to go to Fran? Who gets the share that was to go to Nina? Who are the parties that are fighting over the share that was to go to Nina? Who should prevail with respect to each share, and why? *See Dilworth v. Gray Tiernan*, No. A139476, 2014 WL 3353249 (Cal. Ct. App. July 9, 2014).

IV. Change in Beneficiary — Default Construction Rules

Near the start of this chapter, the material pointed out that there are essentially two categories of will construction scenarios: (1) those that arise from drafting mistakes, and (2) those that arise from a change in circumstances surrounding the testator. Because testamentary instruments are by their nature ambulatory documents, changes can occur between time of execution and time of death. The most common change that can occur with respect to a beneficiary/transferee is that he or she predeceases the decedent.

A. Lapse

As the court noted in *McFarland*, where a gift fails because a beneficiary predeceases the testator, the gift is said to lapse.[4] The logic underlying the lapse doctrine is rather

---

4. A gift may lapse — or fail — for a variety of reasons (i.e., the beneficiary may not accept the gift, or an express condition precedent that is tied to the gift may not occur, etc.). The most common

self-evident. The testator intended the person to benefit from the gift. If the prede-ceased beneficiary were still entitled to the gift, it would go into the predeceased ben-eficiary's estate and end up going to someone else, possibly someone the testator never met. Moreover, passing it through the predeceased beneficiary's estate would subject the gift to double probate. Thus, the lapse doctrine presumes that where the beneficiary predeceases the testator, the testator would prefer that the gift fail rather than go to the beneficiary's estate.

B. Anti-Lapse

But, as the court in *McFarland* also noted, the anti-lapse doctrine presumes that under certain circumstances the testator might still want the gift to go forward even if the beneficiary predeceased the testator. What are those circumstances? California's anti-lapse statute, immediately below, is fairly representative of most states' approach to anti-lapse. Although written in classic legalese, which will make the task harder than it needs to be, see if you can extract from the statute the basic requirements and the logic behind the anti-lapse doctrine.

CPC § 21110. Transferee's death; taking by representation; contrary intent in instrument

(a) Subject to subdivision (b), if a transferee is dead when the instrument is executed or fails or is treated as failing to survive the transferor or until a future time required by the instrument, the issue of the deceased transferee take in the transferee's place in the manner provided in Section 240. A transferee under a class gift shall be a transferee for the purpose of the subdivision unless the transferee's death occurred before the execution of the instrument and that fact was known to the transferor when the in-strument was executed.

(b) The issue of a deceased transferee do not take in the transferee's place if the instru-ment expresses a contrary intention or a substitute disposition. A requirement that the initial transferee survive the transferor or survive for a specified period of time after the death of the transferor constitutes a contrary intention. A requirement that the initial transferee survive until a future time that is related to the probate of the transferor's will or administration of the estate of the transferor constitutes a contrary intention.

(c) As used in this section, "transferee" means a person who is kindred of the transferor or kindred of a surviving, deceased, or former spouse of the transferor.

---

reason, and the focus of our examination, is that the designated beneficiary predeceased the testa-tor/transferor. The full scope of the lapse doctrine is beyond the scope of the introductory class.

Estate of Lensch

177 Cal. App. 4th 667 (Ct. App. 2009)

HAERLE, Acting P.J.

I. INTRODUCTION

…

II. FACTUAL AND PROCEDURAL BACKGROUND

On March 12, 2008, at 2:30 a.m. Gladys Lensch died in a San Mateo County nursing home. She was 98 years old. She left the following three-sentence holographic will: "I Gladys Lensch do hereby declare, being of sound mind, that my estate be equally divided between my daughter Claudia and my son Jay. [¶] Claudia being married has 2 daughters, and my son by a previous marriage has 2 sons. They will provide for the well being of my grandchildren in the event of my death or serious incapacity due to lengthy illness. [¶] God Bless the Family. [¶] Gladys Clausen Lensch May 10, 1993."

Eleven hours after Gladys died, Jay, Gladys's son, was found dead in his home in Trinity County. He had shot himself with a 12-gauge shotgun. The time of death on Jay's death certificate was recorded as the time his body was found: 1:15 p.m. on March 12, 2008. Jay's body was cremated without an autopsy and his remains were buried five days later.

In a 10-page handwritten will, with a four-page addendum, Jay made small cash gifts to friends, and left another friend an undeveloped parcel of land. The residue of his estate was left in equal shares to the Unitarian Universalist Service Committee and Direct Relief International. He left nothing in his will to his two sons, appellants Jason and Ean Lensch.

On June 25, 2008, Jason and Ean Lensch filed a "Petition to Determine Survival and to Determine Persons Entitled to Distribution." This petition was verified by petitioner's attorney because petitioners reside "out of this county and state."

The petition asked the court to find that "it cannot be determined by clear and convincing evidence who died first, Gladys Mildred Lensch or her son, Petitioner's father, Jay Alfred Lensch. Because it cannot be determined who died first, Jay Lensch should not take under Gladys Lensch's will and his issue, Petitioners, should take in his place."

The petition stated that "Shortly after noon [on the same day Gladys Lensch died] the body of her son, Jay Lensch was found. Jay Lensch died in his Trinity County home of a self-inflicted gunshot wound. Petitioners and their attorney spoke to the Trinity County Deputy Coroner who investigated Jay Lensch's death and the Deputy Coroner said that he could not determine the precise time of Jay Lensch's death. To Ean Lensch, the Deputy Coroner said that Jay Lensch had been dead at least 24 hours before his body was found and that death might have occurred two or more days earlier. To Petitioner's attorney, the Deputy Coroner said that Jay Lensch had last spoken to another person two days before his body was discovered and that death could have occurred any time between that conversation and the time of discovery. On the death certificate, the Deputy Coroner used the time of discovery as the time of death, as is customary in cases like this. The Deputy Coroner is certain that Jay died earlier than the time stated on the death certificate, 1:15 p.m., but explained to Petitioner's counsel that there is no way to tell what was the actual time of death." Petitioners asked the court to find that "it cannot be determined by clear and convincing evidence who died fist, Gladys Clausen Lensch or Jay Alfred Lensch," and that the court deem Gladys to have survived Jay for the purpose of the transfers created by Gladys's will and that the court rule that the transfer made to Jay in Gladys's will fails.

On July 25, 2008, Jay's executor, respondent Darin Wright, filed an opposition to Jason and Ean's petition to determine survival. He argued that Jason and Ean had the burden of proving that Jay did not survive Gladys. He also argued that survival was not required by the terms of Gladys's will. Relying on the death certificate of both decedents, respondent argued that because death certificates are proof of time of death, and claimant's petition was based on "inadmissible opinions, speculation, and hearsay," the only evidence of time of death was the death certificate.

. . .

The court denied the petition to determine survival. The court held that "the evidence offered shows that decedent's will did not require survival, but nevertheless, that Jay Lensch survived decedent Gladys Mildred Lensch, and that no further evidentiary hearing is required."

This timely appeal followed.

III. DISCUSSION

A. *Survivorship*

Jason and Ean contend the trial court erred in denying their petition on the basis that Gladys's will did not require that Jay survive her in order to take under her will. We exercise de novo review in interpreting the terms of Gladys's will (*Estate of Edwards* (1988) 203 Cal.App.3d 1366, 1371, 250 Cal.Rptr. 779) and conclude that, although the trial court was correct in finding that Gladys's will contains no survivorship requirement, it erred in denying appellants' petition on this basis, apparently because it did not understand the legal consequences of the lack of a survivorship requirement in Gladys's will.

Gladys's will does not express any intent with regard to survivorship. Nor does it contain any provision for an alternate disposition in the event Jay predeceased her. In this situation, we look to section 21109 and the anti-lapse statute, section 21110, for guidance. Section 21109, subdivision (a), provides that "A transferee who fails to survive the transferor of an at-death transfer or until any future time required by the instrument does not take under the instrument." Section 21110, subdivision (a), provides that "Subject to subdivision (b), if a transferee is dead when the instrument is executed, or fails or is treated as failing to survive the transferor or until a future time required by the instrument, the issue of the deceased transferee take in the transferee's place in the manner provided in Section 240." Subdivision (b) provides, however, that "[t]he issue of a deceased transferee do not take in the transferee's place if the instrument expresses a contrary intention or a substitute disposition. A requirement that the initial transferee survive the transferor or survive for a specified period of time after the death of the transferor constitutes a contrary intention. A requirement that the initial transferee survive until a future time that is related to the probate of the transferor's will or administration of the estate of the transferor constitutes a contrary intention."

Therefore, in the absence of any requirement of survivorship, "a transfer that is to occur on the transferor's death lapses if the transferee dies first." (*Burkett v. Capovilla* (2003) 112 Cal.App.4th 1444, 1449, 5 Cal.Rptr.3d 817.) As the court explained in *Estate of Mooney* (2008) 169 Cal.App.4th 654, 657, 87 Cal.Rptr.3d 115, "[u]nder ... the antilapse statute, if a bequest is made to kindred, and is not conditioned on survivorship and is not subject to an alternate disposition, and the beneficiary predeceases the transferor, the bequest passes to the predeceased beneficiary's issue."

Here, as the probate court found, Gladys's bequest was not conditioned on Jay's survival. Nor did she make an alternate disposition. Therefore, under sections 21109 and 21110, if Jay died before Gladys, then Gladys's bequest to Jay fails under section 21109 and passes to Jay's children, appellants, under section 21110. Put simply, the court's finding that Gladys's will contained no survival requirement was the beginning of the story, not the end.

Respondent, who seems to understand at this point in the proceedings the significance of the fact that Gladys's will contained neither a survival requirement nor an alternate disposition, argues that Jay's will, in which Jay complains about his sons' conduct toward him, constitutes extrinsic evidence from which the probate court "could reasonably infer ... that Gladys knew and disapproved of [Jason and Ean]'s conduct, and for that reason intended in her will to give Jay complete discretion over his bequest whether he survived her or not. In other words, respondent contends that the trial court should have construed Gladys's will as containing a provision that Jay was not required to survive her based on language contained in Jay's will, which was written well after Gladys's. We disagree.

The rules for construing the meaning of a will are well established. "'The paramount rule in the construction of wills, to which all other rules must yield, is that a will is to be construed according to the intention of the testator as expressed therein, and this intention must be given effect as far as possible.' [Citation.] The rule is imbedded in the Probate Code. [Citation.] Its objective is to ascertain what the testator meant by the language he used." (*Estate of Russell* (1968) 69 Cal.2d 200, 205–206, 70 Cal.Rptr. 561, 444 P.2d 353 (*Russell*).)

"[E]xtrinsic evidence of the circumstances under which a will is made (except evidence expressly excluded by statute) may be considered by the court in ascertaining what the testator meant by the words used in the will. If in the light of such extrinsic evidence, the provisions of the will are reasonably susceptible of two or more meanings claimed to have been intended by the testator, 'an uncertainty arises upon the face of a will' (§ 105) and extrinsic evidence relevant to prove any of such meanings is admissible (see § 106) subject to the restrictions imposed by statute (§ 105). If, on the other hand, in the light of such extrinsic evidence, the provisions of the will are not reasonably susceptible of two or more meanings, there is no uncertainty arising upon the face of the will (§ 105; [citations]) and any proffered evidence attempting to show an intention *different* from that expressed by the words therein, giving them the only meaning to which they are reasonably susceptible, is inadmissible. In the latter case the provisions of the will are to be interpreted according to such meaning." (*Russell, supra,* 69 Cal.2d at p. 212, 70 Cal.Rptr. 561, 444 P.2d 353, fns. omitted.)

Finally, "it is 'solely a judicial function to interpret a written instrument unless the interpretation turns upon the credibility of extrinsic evidence.' ... Accordingly, 'an appellate court is not bound by a construction of a document based solely upon the terms of the written instrument without the aid of extrinsic evidence, where there is no conflict in the evidence, or a determination has been made upon incompetent evidence. [Citations.]' [Citations.]" (*Russell, supra,* 69 Cal.2d at p. 213, 70 Cal.Rptr. 561, 444 P.2d 353.)

Applying these principles to the case before us, we conclude that the language in Jay's will expressing his disappointment in his sons does not, as respondents contend, indicate that Gladys intended that, should Jay predecease her, his children would not share in her estate. Jay's will demonstrates only that Jay appears to have disapproved of his sons when he wrote *his* will. There is no evidence that Gladys was even aware of her son's difficult relationship with his children or that she agreed with her son's assessment of his children's behavior. To the contrary, her will explicitly mentions her desire that Jay and his sister care for Gladys's grandchildren, which would include appellants Jason and Ean. If anything, Gladys's will indicates that it was her intent that her estate benefit her grandchildren as well as her children.

Having correctly concluded that Gladys's will contained no requirement that Jay survive her and in light of the fact that the will also contains no provision for an alternate disposition, the next step in the probate court's analysis was to consider the issue of whether Jay did, in fact, survive Gladys. It is this issue to which we next turn.

. . .

———————

Notes

1. *Degree of relationship*: The lapse doctrine presumes that if a beneficiary predeceases the testator/transferor, that the testator/transferor would prefer that the gift fail than that it go to the predeceased beneficiary's estate. Anti-lapse, however, creates a contrary presumption *if* the predeceased beneficiary has issue who survive the testator/transferor, and *if* the predeceased beneficiary meets *the degree of relationship* test. The degree of relationship test varies from jurisdiction to jurisdiction, depending on each state's approach to the anti-lapse doctrine.

California has one of the broadest scopes of coverage with respect to the degree of relationship test. What is it? Notice the coverage casts a rather large net around the testator/transferor, catching almost everyone even remotely connected by blood or marriage with the testator/transferor with one notable exception: who, somewhat surprisingly, is *not* included? (At least one professor likes to refer to the scope of California's anti-lapse coverage as a "donut" doctrine if that helps.) Does this exception make any sense? How so?

2. *Anti-lapse — express contrary intent*: In *Lensch* the court discusses the implications of the lack of a "survivorship" clause in Gladys's will and what this means for purposes of applying, or not applying, California's anti-lapse statute. This is separate from the issue of "survivorship" for purposes of determining whether a beneficiary survived the testator. As most drafted wills contain some form of "survivorship clause," what effect, if any, should a survivorship clause have on the application of anti-lapse?

Anti-lapse is based on the testator/transferor's *presumed* intent. The logic is if the will expresses a contrary intent (an intent that is inconsistent with the application of anti-lapse), the will's express contrary intent should trump the anti-lapse doctrine's presumed intent. Historically there were two classic forms of express contrary intent: (1) an express gift over clause (a clause in the instrument that expressly states what should happen to the gift if the gift should fail), and (2) an express survival requirement. The logic for why each of these should constitute an express contrary intent to anti-lapse is rather straightforward. With respect to the express gift over clause, such a clause evidences that the testator has contemplated to whom he or she would like the gift to go if the beneficiary predeceases the testator/transferor. The court does not need to invoke the *presumed* intent of the testator/transferor via anti-lapse where the testator/transferor has indicated his or her *express* intent as to what should happen. Express intent should trump presumed intent.

As for an express survival requirement constituting an express contrary intent barring application of anti-lapse, the logic is not quite as direct, but historically it was nevertheless deemed compelling. The logic was where the will expressly conditioned the gift on the beneficiary surviving the testator, the testator had expressed his or her intent as to what should happen to the gift if the beneficiary should predecease the testator: the gift should not be made. In terms of constituting an express contrary intent to anti-lapse, a survival requirement is not as quite clear as an express gift over clause in that the latter follows through and indicates where the gift should go — a clear and direct express contrary intent. Nevertheless, a survival requirement arguably constitutes an express condition precedent to the gift being made in the first place. Testator's express intent with respect to under what circumstances the gift should even be made arguably should trump the presumed intent underlying the anti-lapse doctrine. Hence, the traditional and general rule that an express survival requirement in a will or nonprobate instrument constituted an express contrary intent barring application of anti-lapse.

That traditional and general rule presumes, however, that the testator/transferor actually talked with the drafting attorney about the issue, understood the legal significance of the survival issue, and then knowingly and deliberately used the survival language. In 1990, the Uniform Probate Code, in one of its more controversial provisions, adopted the position that an express survival requirement in a will or nonprobate instrument is more likely the result of the boilerplate language used by the drafter than an expression of the testator/transferor's knowing and deliberate intent. *See* UPC § 2-603(b)(3) ("words of survivorship, such as in a devise to an individual 'if he survives me,' or in a devise to 'my surviving children,' are not, in the absence of additional evidence, a sufficient indication of an intent contrary to the application of this section."). Some courts have judicially adopted that position. *See Ruotolo v. Tietjen*, 93 Conn. App. 432 (2006):

> The argument can reasonably be extended to urge that the use of words of survivorship indicates that the testator considered the possibility of the devisee dying first and intentionally decided not to provide a substitute gift to the devisee's descendants. The negative inference in this argument, however, is speculative. It may or may not accurately reflect reality and actual intention. It is equally plausible that the words of survivorship are in the testator's will merely because, with no such intention, the testator's lawyer used a will form containing words of survivorship.... Furthermore, words of survivorship "might very well be no more than a casual duplication of the survivorship requirement imposed by the rule of lapse, with no independent purpose. Thus, they are not necessarily included in the will with the intention of con-tradicting the objectives of the antilapse statute." *Id.*, 1109–10.... Put simply, the intent of the testator cannot definitely be discerned on the basis of words of survivorship alone.

Id. at 445–46 (quoting from E. Halbach, Jr. & L. Waggoner, *The UPC's New Survivorship and Antilapse Provisions*, 55 ALB. L. REV. 1091 (1992).). The policy argument is that anti-lapse is remedial in nature, designed to prevent accidental disinheritance of a familial line of descendants, and therefore anti-lapse should be construed and applied broadly to minimize accidental disinheritance.

Where does California fall on this issue? With this fuller backdrop and understanding of the issue, a careful re-reading of the California anti-lapse statute should bring greater meaning to the legalese. Do you agree with the California approach? Could a party, in good faith, make a *Ruotolo*-type argument and ask a California court to adopt the UPC approach judicially?

3. *Will language*: How much of the wording in a will is boilerplate language that is included in virtually every will a lawyer drafts? To what extent, if any, should that affect a court's construction of a will? Increasingly, testators are going to the Internet and downloading and completing form wills—should that affect a court's analysis of whether a survival requirement in the instrument constitutes an express contrary intent? Is it better to have one uniform and absolute default approach in the event of poor drafting or should the court take extrinsic evidence in each case?

4. *Practitioner perspective*: Virtually every estate planning attorney-drafted testamentary instrument will cover the possibility of a gift lapsing. Does that express language in the instrument necessarily mean the attorney covered the possibility with the client? How do you think the estate planning bar responded to the UPC provision

that an express survival requirement does not constitute express contrary intent for purposes of the anti-lapse statute? If you were in a jurisdiction that applied the UPC approach, how would you draft around it?

Can a will defeat the application of the anti-lapse doctrine by a clause such as the following?

> *Any failed gift shall lapse, and it is my intent that no provisions of any anti-lapse statute shall apply to this will. Currently, at the time of execution of this will, the anti-lapse statutory provisions are in California Probate Code Sections 21110(a)–(c).*

Problems

1. D's will specifically bequeathed $10,000 "to my brother A if A survives me, otherwise to my uncle B." The residue devised to A's domestic partner, C. A, B, and C all predecease D, and all are survived by issue. Who most likely takes the $10,000, and why?

2. H and W execute a joint will giving the survivor "all the estate of every description ... which either or both of us may own, ... and upon the death of the survivor, all of such estate shall be the property of" H's niece, N. H died, then N died survived by issue, then W executed a codicil to the joint will devising all of her estate to Santa Clara Law School. What are the arguments the respective parties will assert following W's death? Who is entitled to the property, and why?

3. Testatrix's will left the bulk of her estate to her two sisters, Gerri and Suzy. Both sisters predeceased her. Gerri is survived by four children; Suzy by three. What's the issue raised by the fact pattern? How should the property be distributed, and why? *See In re Estate of Mooney*, 169 Cal. App. 4th 654 (Ct. App. 2008).

4. Assume the following facts:

Testatrix's will gives $100 to her church and provides that the remainder of her estate should be distributed as follows: a one-third interest to her sister Susan Dennis; a one-third interest to her sister Kate Armstrong; a one-sixth interest to her niece Dora Kirby; and a one-sixth interest to her niece Marguerite O'Reilly.

Paragraph Four of her will provides as follows:

> I have purposely made no provision for any other person, whether claiming to be an heir of mine or not, and if any person, whether a beneficiary under this will or not, or mentioned herein, shall contest this will or object to any of the provisions hereof, I give to such person so contesting or objecting the sum of one ($1.00) Dollar and no more, in lieu of the provisions which I have made, or which I might have made, for such person so contesting or objecting. In connection with this paragraph I specifically have in mind all of my relatives not herein specifically mentioned,

and it is my will and wish that none of my said relatives other than those specifically herein mentioned receive anything from my estate.

The testatrix died on October 30, 1950, leaving no spouse and no issue. Both Susan Dennis and Kate Armstrong predeceased her. Kate Armstrong was survived by her daughters, Dora Kirby and Marguerite O'Reilly, both of whom were living when the testatrix died. The lineal descendants of Susan Dennis, who were living at the time of testatrix's death, include a son, five daughters, and four children of a deceased son.

The will was admitted to probate, and in due course Marguerite O'Reilly filed a petition to determine who was entitled to distribution. Marguerite alleged that, except for the gift to the church, she and Dora Kirby were entitled to all of the estate in equal shares. This claim was based on the argument that since the survivors of Susan Dennis were not mentioned in the will, they were excluded under Paragraph Four from receiving any part of the estate. Dora Hecht, a daughter of Susan Dennis, filed a claim on the ground that the lineal descendants of Susan Dennis were entitled to her one-third of the residue of the property of said estate.

How would you describe Marguerite and Dora's argument (*legally* that is, in terms of Paragraph Four of testatrix's will and how it relates to the lapse/anti-lapse doctrines)? How would you rule on the argument? Who is entitled to the two-thirds share that was gifted to the testatrix's sisters who were alive at time of execution, and why? *See In re Pfadenhauer's Estate,* 159 Cal. App. 2d 686 (Ct. App. 1958).

C. Class Gifts

Whenever there is a gift to more than one individual, there is a potential for the gift to be considered a class gift. There is legal significance to calling a gift a class gift, so it is good to have a sense of when a gift to multiple individuals is a class gift as opposed to merely a gift to multiple individuals.

Cain v. Dunn

241 So. 2d 650 (Miss. 1970)

ETHRIDGE, Chief Justice:

This case involves the question of whether a testamentary bequest is a gift to named individuals only or to a class....

William E. Harreld, age 62, died suddenly and unexpectedly on February 5, 1967, leaving a last will and testament dated July 25, 1961. Under the will a specific bequest was made to testator's surviving wife of approximately one-half of the total estate, and Article II(B) made the following residuary bequests:

The rest, residue and remainder of my estate I devise and bequeath, in equal share, to my son, William E. Harreld, Jr., and each of my grandchildren,

Malley Harreld, William E. Harreld, III, Wilson Harreld, Eastland Harreld and John Cowan Harreld as shall survive me, and in the event that my said son or any of my said grandchildren shall predecease me, then I give, devise and bequeath the share of said deceased son or grandchild in equal shares to my said son and/or grandchildren per capita.

Testator's son, William E. Harreld, Jr., was appointed executor of the will. He is the only surviving son of testator; one other child died in 1959 without having married. William E. Harreld, Jr., had been married to Ann Arrington Harreld for sixteen years. They had six children, four boys and two girls, with the children ranging in age at the time of trial from fifteen to seven years of age. The youngest child, Lee Ann, was born December 4, 1961, about four months after the will was executed. Lee Ann was born prematurely by about three months, and although the mother was pregnant when the will was signed, her condition was not apparent. Testator was not aware that his sixth grandchild was on the way. The evidence shows that Mr. Harreld was very close to and fond of all his grandchildren, including Lee Ann after her birth.

The attorney who drafted the 1961 will said that testator intended for him to draft a "temporary" will, and that after it was executed there were numerous conferences about a more elaborate will, but the details were never worked out to Mr. Harreld's satisfaction, so no "permanent" testament was ever executed.

. . .

The principal question is whether the sixth grandchild, Lee Ann Harreld, born after execution of the will, is entitled to participate in the residuary estate along with the testator's son and other grandchildren.... The intention of the testator is, of course, the controlling factor.

The rule with which we are here concerned is outlined in 5 American Law of Property section 22.4 (1952):

> The phrase "class gifts" is designed to suggest one fundamental idea, and once this is fully grasped the concept has some utility. That fundamental idea is simply this. A gift to a class is involved when the beneficiaries of a disposition form an entity or a unit and the gift is to that entity or unit rather than to the separate and distinct individuals who comprise the entity or unit. The idea may also be expressed in this way: whenever the transferor is group-minded with respect to his beneficiaries, rather than individual-minded, the gift is to them as a class.

When the beneficiaries of a will are specified by their individual names, it may be reasonably inferred, prima facie, that the transferor was thinking of them as separate and distinct individuals and not as a group or an entity. Accordingly, a "construction preference" is said to be that if transferees are specified by name the gift is one to individuals and not to a class. *Lee v. Foley*, 224 Miss. 684, 80 So.2d 765 (1955); 5 American Law of Property § 22.5 (1956). However, even though the testator has named his beneficiaries individually, additional evidence of a different intent may be present from the terms of the will and surrounding circumstances which would require a conclusion that the transferor was group-minded with respect to his beneficiaries even though he named them individually.

In *Shannon v. Riley*, 153 Miss. 815, 121 So. 808, 75 A.L.R. 768 (1929), ... [the Court] recognized that the definition of class donees is difficult, with a numberless variety in language and circumstances, and then stated "a general or approximate description":

> All we shall attempt, therefore, is an approximation or general description of what is meant by a gift to a class, which we shall state thus: When there is a gift or grant to a number of persons, although one or all of them may be named, if the naming of them was intended merely as a matter of identification, and these persons are united or connected by some common tie, and it is clear that the donor was looking to the body as a whole or as a group, rather than to the members constituting the body as individuals, and that he intended that the group might fluctuate in numbers, so that, to preserve the group, if one or more of that body died during the period in question, the survivors should take the gift between them, either in equal or in some other naturally related portions, the gift is to be construed as one given to them as a class. (153 Miss. at 826, 121 So. at 811).

The Court concluded that putting aside "labored technicalities," the donor's intent was to treat the beneficiaries "as a unified class." Significance was found in the provision that the survivors would take the share of a brother or sister dying without issue, "for the naturally interrelated fluctuations necessary * * * to preserve the unity of the group * * *" The similarities between the gifts in *Shannon* and those here, and the criteria described by Justice Griffith in *Shannon* are applicable, we think, to the instant case.

...

In favor of an interpretation that the instant gift is to the named individuals is the prima facie rule; this gift is made to individuals by name, testator's son and five of his grandchildren. 4 Page on Wills § 35.4 (Bowe-Parker Rev.1961). Also, the reference to "said grandchildren" relates to those named. On the other hand, this construction preference is offset by more significant factors appearing in the will and from surrounding circumstances. Harreld was not aware that a sixth grandchild was on the way when he made his "temporary" will. He was at least equally fond of Lee Ann as of his other grandchildren. There is no express statement in the will indicating an intent to exclude her, and there was no reason to set her apart for discriminatory treatment. Moreover, the testator could have made clearly a class gift or one to individuals, simply by using language expressing definitely that intention, and there would have been no room for construction. His dominant, manifest purpose was to leave the remaining one-half of his estate to his son and his grandchildren as a group or unit.

The context of a will may show that the names of the beneficiaries were added to the description of them as the members of a class for the purpose of greater certainty. Page on Wills § 35.4 (Bowe-Parker Rev.1961). We think that is what occurred here, and where such specific identities occur simply for the purpose of greater certainty, the gift should be treated as one to a class.

Further, the last part of the bequest states that, if testator's son or grandchildren predecease him, then he leaves the deceased's share equally to his son and/or grandchildren per capita. A gift to persons who are described as a class and who are also named, followed by a provision that the share of one who dies without issue shall go to the survivors of the group, has been held to be a gift to a class. It indicates that the class, here the son and grandchildren, are all to take in equal portions. 4 Page on Wills § 35.3, p. 465 (Bowe-Parker Rev.1961); 5 American Law of Property § 22.8, p. 264 (1952). This circumstance may justify, as here, a logical inference of an intent to give to the class and its survivors, i.e., a purpose to maintain the integrity of the class. [Citations omitted.] ...

The manifest objects of testator's bounty were his son and his son's children. A reading of this will in its entirety discloses that Harreld had worked out a general plan of distribution for his entire estate, in which the major objective was an equal distribution of his property, after providing for his wife, among a group consisting of his son and his son's children. The gift to the survivors, if one or more of this group predeceased testator, was for the preservation of his plan of equality of distribution. His intent, and his love for his grandchildren, are emphasized by the fact that he placed them on a par with his son in the distribution. The fulfillment of a general plan of distribution has often been held to be sufficient basis to justify the conclusion that the gift is a class gift rather than to the named individuals only. For all of these reasons, we conclude that the testator was group-minded with respect to his beneficiaries, rather than individual-minded, and that the gifts are to them as a class, the testator's son and all of his grandchildren. 5 American Law of Property § 22.8, pages 266–267 (1952); see also Annot., 75 A.L.R. 773 (1931).

Affirmed.

Notes

1. *Class gift intent—relevant variables*: As the court articulated in *Cain*, the question of whether a gift is a class gift or a gift to multiple individuals ultimately is a question of testator/transferor's intent. The problem is that too often the instrument fails to expressly indicate the testator's intent. Thus, courts are left to infer whether the gift is a class gift or a gift to multiple individuals. As in *Cain*, the California courts have noted that one of the central questions is whether the testator/transferor appears to be have been "group-minded" with respect to the beneficiaries: whether they were to constitute one entity. In analyzing that question, the courts tend to focus on four variables.

The first variable examines how the takers were described by the instrument: by name or by generic reference? If the instrument identifies the takers by name, that cuts against a finding of a class gift, so much so that some courts hold specifically identifying takers by name per se bars a finding of a class gift. The general rule, however, is consistent with the court's position in *Cain*: that while identifying the takers by name is an important variable, it is not a dispositive variable.

The second variable examines how the instrument described the gift. One of the legal consequences of finding a gift to be a class gift is that a party's interest in the class gift is not set upon execution of the instrument. Rather, a party's interest can fluctuate until the testator/transferor's death. New members can enter the class, and members can leave the class. A class gift is somewhat like a joint tenancy in that if one member of the class dies before the testator/transferor, one of the legal attributes of a class gift is that that share is simply redistributed among the other class members. Hence, a class member's share cannot be determined until the testator/transferor's death. A gift that specifies each beneficiary's fractional share or percentage cuts against a finding of a class gift.

The third variable examines whether the beneficiaries "are united or connected by some common tie." The notion of "group-mindedness" implicitly assumes that there should be something uniting or connecting the individuals; otherwise they are just a group of individuals and not a class. Even where there is something connecting the individuals, however, some courts look to see if there is anyone who shares the connection who was left out. If there is, some courts have found that this cuts against a finding of a class gift.

Finally, how does calling the gift a class gift — or not calling it a class gift — fit within testator's apparent overall testamentary scheme? When the class gift question arises in the contest of a predeceased beneficiary, often the court will examine who would take if the gift were called a class gift, who would take if the gift were not called a class gift, and which outcome appears more consistent with testator's overall intent. Courts will also look at how the testator described that gift or other gifts to see if the testator's description implies class gift-like significance. In *Cain*, the testator's express intent was that if one of the takers died without issue, his or her share would be distributed to the other takers. That express intent was consistent with a finding that the testator intended a class gift.

2. *Saving effect*: The class gift doctrine is another way of trying to save an otherwise failing gift. Under anti-lapse, an otherwise failing gift is saved in favor of whom? Under a class gift, an otherwise failing gift is saved in favor of whom?

3. *Class gift — anti-lapse overlap*: Assuming a member of a class meets the degree of relationship test under anti-lapse and is survived by issue, should anti-lapse apply to members of the class, or should the creation of a class gift constitute an express contrary intent to application of anti-lapse? For the California answer, see Probate Code Section 21110(a).

4. *Residue of the residue rule*: What if the testator's will provides, in pertinent part, as follows: "I leave my wife 70% of my estate, and I leave the rest, residue and remainder of my estate, equally, to my friend, Fran, my research assistant, Taurean, and my barber, Bob." Thereafter Bob dies. Who takes Bob's share? Circling back to

the question of what happens when part of a residuary clause fails, does the modern trend treat every residuary clause to multiple individuals as a de facto class gift regardless of testator's intent (as least for purposes of what should happen if part of the residuary clause fails)?

Problems

1. Testatrix's will created a testamentary trust in favor of her husband, for life. The will then went on to provide that upon the death of her husband, the trust shall terminate and the trust property shall be distributed as follows:

   "[I]n equal shares to my following brothers and sisters:

Name	Last Known Address
Rebecca Reef	Odessa, Russia
David Reef	London, England
Percy Reef	London, England
Lilly Reef	Odessa, Russia
Frank Reef	London, England
Jack Reef	London, England

   if they be living, or, if they be not living, in equal shares to the then living children and grandchildren of my husband's brothers, Vinton E. Newbert, Paul R. Newbert, Karl M. Newbert, and my husband's sister, Rose M. Newbert Peters."

   Assume Percy Reef was the only brother or sister to survive the testatrix and her husband. All of her other brothers and sisters died without issue. What claim will Percy assert? Who will oppose him? How would you rule, and why? *See Estate of Newbert*, 555 P.2d 1189 (Wash. Ct. App. 1976).

   What difference, if any, would it make if some of the testatrix's other brothers and sisters who predeceased her had surviving issue?

2. Testatrix inherited an undivided one-fifth interest in approximately 260 acres of farmland from her husband when he passed away. In her will, she provided as follows:

   [B]elieving as I do that those farm lands should go back to my late husband's side of the house, I therefore give; devise and bequeath my one-fifth (1/5) interest in said farm lands as follows: One-half (1/2) of my interest therein to Stewart Wilson, a nephew, now living in Birmingham, Michigan and One-half (1/2) of my interest to Gene Burtle, a nephew, now living in Mission, Kansas.

   Testatrix devised the residue of her estate to two close friends. Stewart Wilson and Gene Burtle were two of five nieces and nephews who survived her husband. Thereafter, Gene predeceased the decedent. Gene had no surviving issue.

   What's the issue when testatrix dies? What will Stewart claim? What will the residuary takers claim? What do you think the outcome should be, and why? *See Dawson v. Yucus*, 239 N.E.2d 305 (Ill. App. Ct. 1968).

V. Change in Testator/Transferor's Property — Default Construction Rules

Just as there can be changes in a beneficiary's status between when the instrument is executed and when it becomes effective, there also can be changes in the testator's/transferor's property. Such changes create ambiguities as to what should happen—what, if anything, should the beneficiary take? Some of the scenarios are so common the courts have developed a set of default rules to address them. Again, inasmuch as the modern trend is to take more of an intent-based approach, are the default rules consistent with that approach? Should the courts be more open to extrinsic evidence to ascertain and give effect to the testator's/transferor's *true* intent under the circumstances?

A. Ademption

Ademption extinguishes a gift. There are two types of ademption: (1) ademption by extinction (more commonly known as simply "ademption,") and (2) ademption by satisfaction (more commonly known as "satisfaction").

1. Ademption by Extinction ("Ademption")

Ademption by extinction is one of those doctrines that is easy to understand conceptually, but difficult to understand doctrinally. It is easy to understand the issue underlying the doctrine because it arises logically from a relatively simple scenario. Assume Testatrix executes a will in which she provides: "I hereby give the car I now own to my mom." Thereafter, Testatrix sells her car. Years later, Testatrix dies without revising the will. What, if anything, should her mom get? (Notice that ademption by extinction applies only if the gift is a specific gift; if the gift were deemed a general gift, the personal representative would go out and buy mom another car.)

At one end of the spectrum is the traditional approach to ademption. Not surprisingly, the traditional approach takes a strict, compliance-type approach. In a 1786 English case, *Ashburner v. MacGuire,* 2 Bro. C.C. 108, 29 Eng. Rep. 62 (Ch. 1786), Lord Thurlow articulated what has come to be known as the identity approach to ademption: (1) is the gift a specific gift, and (2) if so, can the particular item subject to the gift be identified in the testator's estate following his or her death (i.e., is the item still there—can it be identified?)? If the item is not in testator's estate (i.e., it is "extinct"), that gives rise to a presumption of revocation, and extrinsic evidence is not admissible to rebut the presumption. The gift is adeemed. Under the traditional identity approach to ademption, there is no analysis of testator's probable intent. There is no inquiry into *why* it is not in the testator's estate. The identity approach adopts a bright-line default rule that prioritizes efficiency over intent. Testators should draft around the rule if they do not like the result. Better to put the burden on the testator to clarify his or her intent than to have the courts try to ascertain the testator's probable intent.

At the other end of the spectrum is the approach advanced by the Uniform Probate Code. The UPC rejects the identity approach and its presumption of revocation and instead adopts the "intent approach," which includes a presumption *against* revocation. If the testator goes out and acquires a new item to replace the missing item that was the subject of the specific gift, the beneficiary is entitled to the replacement item. UPC § 2-606(a)(5). If the testator is owed any balance outstanding at the time of death as a result of the missing item being transferred, the beneficiary is entitled to the outstanding balance. UPC § 2-606(a)(1)–(a)(4). Moreover, if neither of the above provisions results in the beneficiary receiving a gift, the beneficiary is entitled to a general pecuniary gift that is equal in value to the gift *if* "it is established that ademption would be inconsistent with the testator's manifested plan of distribution or that ... the testator did not intend ademption of the devise." UPC § 2-606(a)(6) (note that the beneficiary bears the burden of proof).

Although the traditional approach to ademption is still the general rule, virtually all states have adopted a number of avoidance or softening doctrines. Some jurisdictions follow the traditional approach, but only where the presumption of revocation appears consistent with the circumstances and reasons surrounding the missing item no longer being in the testator's estate. Some courts decline to apply the doctrine where the testator did not have a reasonable opportunity prior to death to revise his or her will, to express his or her intent with respect to what should happen. Interestingly, the 1969 version of the UPC essentially accepted the traditional approach, albeit begrudgingly. The 1969 UPC provision, however, also codified a number of exceptions to the doctrine. The 1990 version of the UPC rejects the traditional "presumed revocation" approach in favor of a presumption against revocation. The jurisdictions cannot agree on which approach makes the most sense. As such, where a particular jurisdiction falls on the ademption spectrum typically requires close examination of the relevant caselaw and statutory provisions to determine the interplay between the traditional approach and that jurisdiction's particular exceptions and softening doctrines.

The most widely recognized judicial exception to ademption is the "change in form not substance" doctrine. This doctrine basically accepts the logic underlying the traditional approach to ademption but reasons that the item is really still there, it just looks a little different—it has changed in form, but not substance. If the executor looks hard enough, he or she will recognize it in its new form. A classic example of a change in form not substance scenario is where a will makes a specific gift of the testator's checking account at Bank of America, and after executing the will the testator moves her checking account to Chase Bank. Depending on how one construes the will's description of the item being gifted, one could argue that the item is still in the testator's estate. Is she gifting her checking account at Bank of America (in which case the gift is adeemed because *that* particular item is not longer part of her estate), or is she gifting her checking account (in which case the item being gifted is still part of her estate, but it has changed form from a checking account at Bank of America to a checking account at Chase Bank)?

One of the problems with the change in form doctrine is the courts run the spectrum on whether the doctrine should be applied narrowly or broadly. Courts that apply it narrowly have held that moving funds from a savings account to a certificate of deposit to get a higher interest rate is a change in substance, not form, and the gift is adeemed. In contrast, some courts that apply the doctrine broadly hold that where the testator's will specifically gifts a house, and thereafter the testator sells the house and deposits the proceeds in a checking account, that is merely a change in form, not substance, and the gift is not adeemed (the beneficiary receives the proceeds from the sale). Go figure.

California has not adopted the 1990 UPC ademption provision, but California has a number of intent-based doctrines. Based on the following case (and note material after it), where would you put California on the ademption spectrum: closer to the traditional common law approach or closer to the modern trend/UPC intent-based approach?

Estate of Austin

113 Cal. App. 3d 167 (Ct. App. 1980)

ANDREEN, Associate Justice.

The testatrix, Lucille Ann Austin, executed her will on March 9, 1977. Two specific bequests were made to a friend, Betty Guldberg, who is appellant herein. The first bequest was an oil portrait of the testatrix' mother and the other was as follows:

> "4(L) The promissory note which I own and hold, made by GARY GRENZ, together with the deed of trust or mortgage securing said promissory note, I give to my friend, BETTY GULDBERG; ..."

The will is somewhat unique, in that it contains nine separate legacies ranging from $2,000 to $15,000 to individuals and organizations. In addition, there are three bequests; the two mentioned above and a dog. The remainder of the estate is given to the respondent Shrine Hospital for Crippled Children, which is also the beneficiary of a $5,000 legacy.

The case is before us because the Grenz note given to Betty Guldberg was paid in full on July 1, 1977, about four months after the will was executed. The payoff was $17,065.88 and was made contemporaneous with the sale of the property which was the underlying security. The note did not include a due on sale clause.

Five days after the payoff, the note proceeds were placed in a savings account which at that time had a balance of $7,727.67 (plus a small amount of accrued but unposted interest).

Thereafter, on August 9, 1977, the testatrix withdrew $20,000 from the account and loaned it to the Inmans. She received in return a promissory note secured by a deed of trust. The note was due in six months.

On January 14, 1978, about 10 months after the will was executed, the testatrix died without having changed her will.

The Inman note was paid off in full shortly thereafter, and the proceeds rest in an estate savings account.

The short trial had no testimony as to extrinsic evidence of the testatrix' intent.

The court below held that the legacy was specific and adeemed, so that it fell into the residue of the estate and thus went to the respondent hospital.

...

The parties have cited numerous authorities which purport to assist one side or the other. We will discuss each of them.

The respondent hospital relies on *Estate of Calori* (1962) 209 Cal.App.2d 711, 26 Cal.Rptr. 281. The case is readily distinguishable. The testatrix bequeathed a promissory note secured by real property to appellant. There was no evidence as to the terms of the note, whether it was payable in installments or in a lump sum and whether the consent of the testatrix to its payment in full was required or given. There was no evidence identifying the cash as part of the estate at date of death. That is, the funds were not traceable into an account or another promissory note.

The trial court's finding of ademption was affirmed. The reviewing court found that there was nothing in the case to show that the bequest was general rather than specific. Of assistance to respondent here is the statement by the court that: "It is difficult to regard full payment of the note as a mere change in form...." (Id., at p. 713, 26 Cal.Rptr. 281.)

Estate of Calori has rested on the shelves since 1962 without benefit of citation, except in *Estate of Mason* (1965) 62 Cal.2d 213, 42 Cal.Rptr. 13, 397 P.2d 1005. In the latter no ademption was found.

Respondent cites *Estate of Peyton* (1956) 143 Cal.App.2d 379, 299 P.2d 897. However, that too is distinguishable. In *Peyton*, the testator voluntarily sold his fractional interest in the land which was the subject of a specific bequest to his sons. In the case at bench, there was no voluntary sale.

Finally, respondent cites *Estate of McLaughlin* (1929) 97 Cal.App. 481, 275 P. 874 for the fact that if proceeds are commingled there is an ademption. However, in the instant case there was but one deposit into and one withdrawal from the account, so tracing is easy. (*Hicks v. Hicks* (1962) 211 Cal.App.2d 144, 27 Cal.Rptr. 307.)

We turn to an examination of appellant's cases.

Estate of Mason, supra, 62 Cal.2d 213, 42 Cal.Rptr. 13, 397 P.2d 1005 is distinguishable. The testatrix devised her home to appellant. Several years later, she became mentally incompetent and a guardian was appointed of her estate which sold the home and used all but $556.66 of the proceeds thereof for her support. The trial court held that there was a partial ademption to the extent that the funds had been spent, so only the remainder of the proceeds, the $556.66, be distributed to appellant. The remainder of the estate, $6,808.08, was ordered distributed to the residuary legatees. The high court reversed and held that the residuary legatees must contribute in full to satisfy the appellant's specific gift. To hold otherwise would permit the guardian to frustrate its ward's testamentary plan. The court found an analogy in the statutory rules governing abatement of testamentary gifts to satisfy debts and expenses during probate or for family allowance.

The case is significant, however, in that it sets a course away from the strict rules of ademption, and draws a clear distinction between an extinction of a legacy by some act of the testator and the act of a third person. If the testator has disposed of a specific legacy, it may be presumed that he intended that the gift fail. Where it is done by act of a third person, in Mason a guardian, no such intent can be presumed.

Estate of Ehrenfels (1966) 241 Cal.App.2d 215, 50 Cal.Rptr. 358 adds nothing to appellant's position. In it, a guardian exchanged Standard Oil stock for stock in a mutual fund. The trial court held there was no ademption and that the beneficiaries should receive the stock in the mutual fund. This was affirmed on appeal.

In *Estate of Newsome* (1967) 248 Cal.App.2d 712, 56 Cal.Rptr. 874, certain real property was devised to the testator's wife and other real property devised to his daughter. He then sold one of the parcels of real property which had been devised to the wife. At time of death, the proceeds were in a savings account. The court held that there was no ademption because there was no residuary clause in the will, evidencing an intent by the testator to dispose of all of his estate through the specified devises and bequests and not to cause any thereof to fail by his voluntary transmutation of the property. In the instant case, of course, there is a residuary clause.

Estate of Creed (1967) 255 Cal.App.2d 80, 63 Cal.Rptr. 80 involved a will which devised real property in trust for the testator's grandchildren. For estate tax purposes, a corporation was formed to hold the property, and the testator made inter vivos transfers of the stock to the grandchildren to the maximum allowed by the exemptions and exclusions under the federal gift tax law. The trial court held and the appellate court affirmed that the intent of the testator to have no ademption was manifest. There was merely a change in form, whereby the real property was held through the device of a corporation formed to effectuate the transfer to the grandchildren with a minimum of estate taxes.

The above rather lengthy discussion of the authorities serves to prove the wisdom of Witkin at 7 Witkin, Summary of California Law (8th ed. 1975) Wills and Probate, section 159, pages 5675–5676 where the author states:

> "In cases dealing with interpretation of wills, as in other controversies, counsel and courts draw freely upon the enormous volume of reported decisions. But in ascertaining the intention of a particular testator decisions in other cases are seldom controlling. 'Of this class of questions it may be said, with more truth, perhaps, than of any other, that each case depends upon its own peculiar facts, and that precedents have comparatively small value.' (*Estate of Henderson* (1911) 161 C. (Cal.) 353, 357, 119 P. 496; see also *Estate of Wilson*, supra, 184 C. (Cal.) (63) 67 (193 P. 581); *Estate of Keller*, supra, 134 C.A. (Cal.App.) 2d (232) 238 (286 P.2d 889) ('no two wills are exactly alike and but few are sufficiently similar in the wording of dispository provisions

so that a decision interpreting one would be of any great help in interpreting another').)"

In discerning the intent of the testatrix, we look first at the will. It is remarkable for the number and diversity of the legacies and bequests. It demonstrates a mind that enjoyed giving to many beneficiaries. Although there is a residuary clause in the will, there is a manifest intention to particularize the disposition of assets.

There is nothing in the record to suggest that the testatrix did anything to initiate the payoff of the Grenz note. It was paid incident to the sale of the property which was the security of the note.

There is nothing to show that the testatrix had a change of mind as to the appellant being a proper beneficiary of her estate. The oil portrait of the testatrix' mother remained a bequest to appellant.

She did nothing with reference to the proceeds except deposit them in a manner which was easily traceable and invested them in an almost identical type of asset — a promissory note secured by a deed of trust.

In determining whether the change is in form only, California courts have lately tended to avoid strict rules of ademption; rather they look to the inferred or probable intent of the testator under the particular circumstances. The reasoning of these more modern cases was crystallized and confirmed by the following statement in *Estate of Mason, supra,* 62 Cal.2d at page 215, 42 Cal.Rptr. 13, 397 P.2d 1005:

> " "Ademption of a specific legacy is the extinction or withdrawal of a legacy in consequence of some act of the testator equivalent to its revocation, or clearly indicative of an intention to revoke. The ademption is effected by the extinction of the thing or fund bequeathed, or by a disposition of it subsequent to the will which prevents its passing by the will, from which an intention that the legacy should fail is presumed." [Citations.] A change in the form of property subject to a specific testamentary gift will not effect an ademption in the absence of proof that the testator intended that the gift fail. [Citations.] ..." (See also *Estate of Zahn* (1971) 16 Cal.App.3d 106, 113, 93 Cal.Rptr. 810.)

In absence of proof of an intent that the gift fail, there should be no ademption. (*Estate of Mason, supra,* 62 Cal.2d 213, 215, 42 Cal.Rptr. 13, 397 P.2d 1005; *Estate of Stevens* (1945) 27 Cal.2d 108, 116, 162 P.2d 918; *Estate of Holmes* (1965) 233 Cal.App.2d 464, 469, 43 Cal.Rptr. 693.)

We find that there is no indication of an intent by the testatrix to adeem, and that the judgment must be reversed.

We turn to appellant's contention that she is entitled to the amount of the Inman note, which was approximately $3,000 more than the payoff of the Grenz note.

In *Estate of Shubin* (1967) 252 Cal.App.2d 588, 60 Cal.Rptr. 678, the court held that there was no ademption and that the beneficiary of the specific devise should receive a more valuable piece of property. The will disposed of a piece of property which was subsequently condemned and the decedent took the proceeds, added approximately $2,000 to it and bought a new piece of property within nine days. The court was aided in determining the testator's intention because he had written the address of the new property in the will next to the dispositive provision.

And in *Estate of Cooper* (1951) 107 Cal.App.2d 592, 237 P.2d 699, the testator told his attorney simply "My car to Miss Hage." The attorney wrote "That certain Hudson Automobile, now owned by me." After the will was executed, the testator sold his car and a month later bought a new Hudson, which he owned at his death. The court had no difficulty in finding no ademption, citing a New York case which held that a bequest of a diamond brooch would not be adeemed where subsequent to the execution of the will the testatrix traded it in on a more expensive diamond brooch.

Shubin and *Cooper* are of no assistance to appellant. In each, once the court had found no ademption, it could do nothing other than order the beneficiary to take the property in its present form. The property was unique and there was no practical way to reduce its value to that of the property described in the will.

On the other hand, in this case the note has been converted to cash because it was paid off when due. Money is divisible, and the precise amount of the unpaid balance at the date of death is available.

The judgment is reversed and remanded. The trial court is directed to order that there is no ademption and that appellant take the amount of $17,065.88 by reason of subparagraph 4(L).

Notes

1. *Ambiguous language*: From a beneficiary's perspective, arguably the best way to avoid the ademption doctrine is to persuade the court that the gift is a general (or residuary) gift. Ademption by extinction applies to specific gifts only. Whether a gift is a specific or general/residuary gift is a question of the testator's intent, but where the gift is ambiguous some courts have acknowledged a preference for a general gift to avoid ademption. *Edmundson v. Morton*, 420 S.E.2d 106, 111 (N.C. 1992). The viability of this argument, however, depends on the express phrasing used in the will (or nonprobate instrument) to describe the gift.

2. *California approach*: Would you say that California leans more toward the traditional, identity-based approach to ademption or more toward the UPC "intent"-based approach? Would you say that California appears to apply the "change in form, not substance" doctrine narrowly or broadly?

3. *Construe at time of death versus replacement doctrine:* One of the cases discussed near the end of the court's opinion is *Estate of Cooper*. The general rule is that a will should be construed relative to the circumstances surrounding the testator at the time the will is executed. *In re Pierce's Estate*, 32 Cal. 2d 265, 268 (1948) ("It is fundamental in the interpretation of wills that the testator's intent be derived from the language of the will itself and, under Probate Code section 105, when an uncertainty appears

upon the face of the will, from the circumstances under which it was executed.") In *Cooper*, the testatrix owned a 1941 Hudson at the time she executed her will. She subsequently sold the car and bought a 1948 Hudson. As the court in *Austin* stated, "The court had no difficulty in finding no ademption...." Some have written that the court de facto adopted a "construe at time of death, not execution" doctrine to avoid application of ademption. Might this simply be an early judicial example of what the UPC calls the replacement doctrine?

4. *Outstanding balance doctrine*: The UPC has adopted the outstanding balance doctrine as part of its intent-based, ademption avoidance scheme. California has adopted its own outstanding balance doctrine — CPC Section 21133:

CPC § 21133. Specific gifts; recipient's rights to unpaid balance

A recipient of an at-death transfer of a specific gift has a right to the property specifically given, to the extent the property is owned by the transferor at the time the gift takes effect in possession or enjoyment, and all of the following:

(a) Any balance of the purchase price (together with any security interest) owing from a purchaser to the transferor at the time the gift takes effect in possession or enjoyment by reason of sale of the property.

(b) Any amount of an eminent domain award for the taking of the property unpaid at the time the gift takes effect in possession or enjoyment.

(c) Any proceeds unpaid at the time the gift takes effect in possession or enjoyment on fire or casualty insurance on or other recovery for injury to the property.

(d) Property owned by the transferor at the time the gift takes effect in possession or enjoyment and acquired as a result of foreclosure, or obtained in lieu of foreclosure, of the security interest for a specifically given obligation.

The "outstanding balance" doctrine applies regardless of who owes the decedent the funds (buyer or insurance company or public entity) and/or regardless of why the transfer occurred (voluntary transfer versus accidental loss versus condemned by the state). Ademption applies to the funds the decedent received while alive, but there is no ademption to any outstanding balance at time of death.

5. *Conservatorship/Durable power of attorney exception*: Consistent with the intent-based approach to ademption, a number of courts have declined to apply ademption where the transfer occurred after the testator became incapacitated (either because it is inappropriate to say it was the testator's intent and/or because the testator did not have the opportunity to revise his or her will to express his or her intent). California has adopted CPC Section 21134. To what extent is it consistent with these judicial concerns?

CPC § 21134. Specific gifts; transfers by conservator or agent acting under durable power of attorney; transferee's rights

(a) Except as otherwise provided in this section, if after the execution of the instrument of gift specifically given property is sold or mortgaged by a conservator or by an agent acting within the authority of a durable power of attorney for an incapacitated principal, the transferee of the specific gift has the right to a general pecuniary gift equal to the net sale price of, or the amount of the unpaid loan on, the property.

(b) Except as otherwise provided in this section, if an eminent domain award for the taking of specifically given property is paid to a conservator or to an agent acting within the authority of a durable power of attorney for an incapacitated principal, or if the proceeds on fire or casualty insurance on, or recovery for injury to, specifically gifted property are paid to a conservator or to an agent acting within the authority of a durable power of attorney for an incapacitated principal, the recipient of the specific gift has the right to a general pecuniary gift equal to the eminent domain award or the insurance proceeds or recovery.

(c) For the purpose of the references in this section to a conservator, this section does not apply if, after the sale, mortgage, condemnation, fire, or casualty, or recovery, the conservatorship is terminated and the transferor survives the termination by one year.

(d) For the purpose of the references in this section to an agent acting with the authority of a durable power of attorney for an incapacitated principal, (1) "incapacitated principal" means a principal who is an incapacitated person, (2) no adjudication of incapacity before death is necessary, and (3) the acts of an agent within the authority of a durable power of attorney are presumed to be for an incapacitated principal.

(e) The right of the transferee of the specific gift under this section shall be reduced by any right the transferee has under Section 21133.

Is it fair to say that the effect of the conservatorship exception to the ademption doctrine is, by operation of law, to turn all specific gifts in the incapacitated person's estate plan into general gifts? Note, however, that the conservatorship exception has a temporal limitation (*see* CPC § 21134(c)). What is the logic behind the limitation?

Review the section numbers and terminology used in the statutory provisions above. What is the scope of the ademption and ademption avoidance doctrines in California? Do they apply only to probate testate gifts or to nonprobate gifts as well?

6. *Exclusive remedy?* The *Austin* case above reflects the traditional California judicial approach. The statutory provisions above were adopted in 1994. One issue that naturally arises is how California's traditional judicial approach should be construed and applied in light of the new statutory provisions. To the extent there appears to be some conflict between the two, should the statutory provisions be construed as revising the traditional approach or as supplementing the traditional approach? California Probate Code Section 21139 addresses that issue:

CPC § 21139. Applicability of statutory sections

The rules stated in Sections 21133 to 21138, inclusive, are not exhaustive, and nothing in those sections is intended to increase the incidence of ademption under the law of this state.

Problems

1. Tess typed the following document:

   "I leave all of my estate to my sister and her children. I name my sister executor."

   The document was not dated or signed. Thereafter, Tess's sister gave birth to a child, Jessica. Tess handwrote the following on the bottom of the page that contained the above typed material:

   "February 1, 1990. I am deeply touched by the birth of my niece, Jessica. I hereby change my will to give Jessica the diamond ring which my mother left me."

   Tess signed the second writing at the end. One month later, Tess died.

   a. If both parts of the page are offered for probate, what is the best argument for admitting both parts of the page to probate, and why?

   b. Assuming, *arguendo*, both parts of the page are admitted to probate, if the diamond ring is not found in Tess's estate, what, if anything, does Jessica get?

2. Settlor created a valid inter vivos trust, the primary asset of which was a 95 percent ownership interest in a privately held company, Brown Electric. Settlor had two sons, Brown and Ross. Settlor's Tenth Amendment to the Trust provided that upon Settlor's death, 10 percent of the company's stock was to be distributed to Brown, 90 percent to Ross, and the rest of the trust's assets were to be distributed to Ross. Thereafter, a conservator was appointed for Settlor, and said conservator was also appointed as successor trustee. Thereafter, the conservator sold the business—as an asset sale, not a stock sale—for $24 million, with the payment ending up in the trust. Brown Electric was dissolved. Following Settlor's death, Ross claimed that ademption applies to the gift of stock. What is Brown's strongest argument? How would you rule? *See Brown v. Labow*, 157 Cal. App. 4th 795 (2007).

3. Testator owned several parcels of real property that were his separate property. His will devised certain parcels to his wife, and other parcels to his daughter. The will contained no residuary clause. Thereafter, testator sold one of the parcels devised to his wife. He deposited the proceeds in a savings account. Testator predeceased his wife. His daughter claimed the sale of the devised parcel "ademed the gift." Has the gift been ademed? *See Estate of Newsome*, 248 Cal. App. 2d 712 (1967).

2. Gifts of Stock

Historically, gifts of stock have given the courts fits because stock can inherently change in nature (companies can merge or be acquired) and because stock can change in quantity even if the party holding the stock does nothing (due to stock splits, stock dividends). If the stock changes nature, should ademption apply? If the number of shares of stock changes, should the beneficiary get the increased shares (or, less common but possible, the decreased shares)?

At common law, the controlling variable was whether the gift of stock was a specific gift or a general gift. If it was a specific gift, ademption applied and if the number of shares changed, the beneficiary received the benefit of the change. On the other hand, if the gift of stock were deemed a general gift, then ademption would not apply and the number of shares being gifted to the beneficiary would not change (just as a gift of $1,000 to a beneficiary does not change between time of execution and time of death because of any intervening inflation).

The modern trend is to apply ademption to gifts of stock where the change in the stock is initiated by the testator/transferor. Where, however, the change (in nature or quantity) is initiated by a corporate entity, the modern trend is to give the beneficiary the benefit of the change in stock regardless of whether the gift is specific or general. The logic is that it was the testator's intent to give the beneficiary a certain percentage interest in the company, and where there has been a change in the number of shares the testator has, the only way to fulfill the testator's original intent is if the beneficiary gets the benefit of the change in stock.

Not surprisingly, California has its own approach to gifts of stock. First, the California Supreme Court weighed in on the issue in its landmark opinion in *In re Buck's Estate*, 196 P.2d 769 (Cal. 1948). Frank Buck owned 40,000 shares of stock in Belridge Oil Company. He executed a will that bequeathed the stock as follows: 30,000 shares to his six children, 5,000 shares to Helen Peterson, and the residue of his estate to his wife. Thereafter he transferred 10,000 shares of the stock to his wife. Following his death, one of the issues was whether the gifts of stock were specific or general. The Court began its analysis by stating the general rules:

> In determining whether a bequest is specific or general, the fundamental and controlling factor is the intent of the testator at the time the will was drafted.

> Applying these rules to bequests of stocks, bonds and other securities, it has been held that a gift of a certain number of securities described by the name of the corporation, or by value or quantity, but not indicating any particular lot of such securities, will be construed as a general bequest if there is nothing on the face of the will or in evidence of the surrounding circumstances, where admissible, to indicate that the testator intended a gift only of the securities owned by him.... It has been held, however, that where there are bequests of shares of a closely held corporation the nonpublic character of the shares bequeathed is evidence of an intent to make a specific gift. [Citations omitted.]

Id. at 770–71. Extrinsic evidence showed that of the 1,000,000 shares of stock the Belridge Oil Company had issues, 61 percent was held in a voting trust that was controlled by only three families, and testator's. Furthermore, when gifting the stock in the will, in each gift the testator expressly referred to the stock as now "in my estate." The Court found that the gifts of stock were specific gifts.

In addition to the Court's guidance in *Buck's Estate*, the California legislature weighed in on the issue of how to treat changes in stock that occur after a will is executed and before the testator dies by adopting Probate Code Section 21132. What is the controlling variable as to whether the beneficiary gets the benefit of the change in stock under the California approach? Is that the same as under the traditional common law approach?

CPC § 21132. Gifts of securities

(a) If a transferor executes an instrument that makes an at-death transfer of securities and the transferor then owned securities that meet the description in the instrument, the transfer includes additional securities owned by the transferor at death to the extent the additional securities were acquired by the transferor after the instrument was executed as a result of the transferor's ownership of the described securities and are securities of any of the following types:

  (1) Securities of the same organization acquired by reason of action initiated by the organization or any successor, related, or acquiring organization, excluding any acquired by exercise of purchase options.

  (2) Securities of another organization acquired as a result of a merger, consolidation, reorganization, or other distribution by the organization or any successor, related, or acquiring organization.

  (3) Securities of the same organization acquired as a result of a plan of reinvestment.

(b) Distributions in cash before death with respect to a described security are not part of the transfer.

Note that the statutory provision applies only if the change in the stock is initiated by the corporate entity. If the change is initiated by the testator/transferor, perform the usual California ademption analysis.

Problems

1. Testatrix owned 1,212 shares of Standard Oil common stock. Her will bequeathed varying amounts of the stock (often coupled with gifts of her jewelry) to various beneficiaries, totaling 446 shares. Thereafter, Standard Oil declared a three-for-one stock split, causing testatrix's holdings to increase to 3,636 shares. Thereafter, testatrix was declared incompetent and a guardian was appointed for her. To diversify testatrix's investments, the guardian exchanged the Standard Oil stock for 9,502 shares of Diversification Fund — a mutual fund. Testatrix died without regaining competency. Testatrix's will further provided as follows: "The bequests of shares of stock of Standard Oil Company of New Jersey are intended to be said shares as presently constituted." In the same paragraph, another provision provided that if, prior to her death, said shares were changed by "splitting or otherwise" the legacies were to be "satisfied with the changed shares representing and being the equivalent of the presently outstanding shares."

   With respect to the gifts of Standard Oil stock: (a) what stock, if any, would the beneficiaries be entitled to following the three-for-one stock split; (b) what stock, if any, would the beneficiaries be entitled to following testatrix's death; and (c) what stock, if any, would the beneficiaries be entitled to if no guardian had been appointed and testatrix had exchanged the Standard Oil stock for the shares of stock in the Diversification Fund? *See In re Estate of Ehrenfel*, 241 Cal. App. 2d 215 (Cal. Ct. App. 1966).

2. T's will provides: "I leave 100 shares of ABC Corp. to A, and I leave $25,000 to B, payable out of the proceeds of the sale of my 100 shares of ABC Corp." Applying general rules of will construction, who gets what?

3. Ademption by Satisfaction ("Satisfaction")

Ademption by satisfaction, commonly referred to simply as "satisfaction," complements ademption by extinction. Ademption by extinction applies only to specific gifts, while ademption by satisfaction applies primarily to general gifts. Like ademption, it is easy to understand the issue underlying satisfaction because it arises logically from a relatively simple scenario. Assume Testatrix executes a will in which she provides: "I hereby give my mom *a* car." Thereafter the testatrix buys her mom a car. Should the inter vivos gift of the car be presumed to be in place of the testamentary gift in the will?

Phrased that way, one can see why satisfaction is a sibling doctrine to the doctrine of advancement. Advancement addresses the issue of whether an *inter vivos* gift should count against an heir's share of the estate if the decedent dies intestate. Satisfaction addresses the same basic issue if the decedent dies testate: should an *inter vivos* gift from a testator to a beneficiary in the will count against the donee/beneficiary's share of the testator's estate? Like advancement, the common law created a presumption in favor of satisfaction (or partial satisfaction as the case may be) where the *inter vivos* gift was of the same nature as the testamentary gift. In contrast, the modern trend UPC creates a presumption against satisfaction (or partial satisfaction, as the case may be) unless there is a writing expressing the intent for the *inter vivos* gift to count against the time of death gift.

Which approach does California apply? Does it follow the common law approach or the UPC approach?

CPC § 21135. Lifetime gift counts as satisfaction of testamentary gift; conditions justifying

(a) Property given by a transferor during his or her lifetime to a person is treated as a satisfaction of an at-death transfer to that person in whole or in part only if one of the following conditions is satisfied:

  (1) The instrument provides for deduction of the lifetime gift from the at-death transfer.

  (2) The transferor declares in a contemporaneous writing that the gift is in satisfaction of the at-death transfer or that its value is to be deducted from the value of the at-death transfer

  (3) The transferee acknowledges in writing that the gift is in satisfaction of the at-death transfer or that its value is to be deducted from the value of the at-death transfer.

(4) The property given is the same property that is the subject of a specific gift to that person.

(b) Subject to subdivision (c), for the purpose of partial satisfaction, property given during lifetime is valued as of the time the transferee came into possession or enjoyment of the property or as of the time of death of the transferor, whichever occurs first.

(c) If the value of the gift is expressed in the contemporaneous writing of the transferor, or in an acknowledgment of the transferee made contemporaneously with the gift, that value is conclusive in the division and distribution of the estate.

(d) If the transferee fails to survive the transferor, the gift is treated as a full or partial satisfaction of the gift, as the case may be, in applying Sections 21110 and 21111 unless the transferor's contemporaneous writing provides otherwise.

To the extent the California satisfaction doctrine appears to parallel the California advancement doctrine, how do the two doctrines treat a scenario where the donee predeceases the donor? Does the *inter vivos* gift still count against the share of the person who will take in the donee's place?

To date, there are no reported opinions applying or analyzing California's new statutory approach to satisfaction. It parallels the UPC approach in many respects, except for subsection (a)(4).

Notes and Problems

1. Testator Tina executes a will and it leaves $100,000 to each of her two sons, A and B, her Cartier watch to her daughter C, and the balance of her estate to her grandchildren. Assume that later, Tina makes a gift of $60,000 to her son A, and gives her Cartier watch to C. Tina then dies. Assume that Tina's assets, at her death, are comprised of $500,000 cash, and a parcel of real estate (with a value of $1 million). Thereafter Tina dies. Who would get what at Tina's death?

   Does subsection (a)(1) of the above statute have any relevance to this problem? If not, what would be an example of its application?

2. Same fact pattern as Problem 1, only this time assume that there is a valid writing by either Tina or A pursuant to subsections (a)(2) and (a)(3), respectively. If this were the case, how would Tina's property be distributed?

3. What does subsection (d) mean? When does it apply? It has no relevance to our fact pattern, but how could you change the facts to make it relevant? Whatever this subsection means, does California's advancement doctrine, set forth in CPC Section 6409 (discussed in Chapter 4), have a comparable provision? If so, are they consistent with one another?

4. Parent gave child X $10,000 during Parent's lifetime. Parent thereafter executed a will leaving her estate valued at $110,000 to her brother, B. Unbeknownst to Parent, B died before Parent executed her will. Parent is survived by three children, X, Y, and Z, and B is survived by issue I. Who takes how much of Parent's estate, and why?

B. Exoneration

The doctrine of exoneration (also known as "exoneration of liens") addresses the issue that arises when a testator/transferor makes a testamentary transfer (either by will or will substitute such as an revocable living trust) of an asset that is encumbered with debt. For example, testator devises a house that is subject to a mortgage, or a car that is subject to a car loan. Should the default rule be that the devisee takes the asset free and clear of the debt, or should the devisee take the asset subject to the debt? If the devisee takes the gift free and clear of any debt, where will the money come from to pay off the debt?

A well-drafted testamentary document (will or will substitute) can address this issue and should clearly indicate the decedent's wishes with respect to the debt. If he or she wants the asset to go to the beneficiary free and clear, the testamentary document can specifically provide that it goes without debt, instructing the executor/trustee to pay the debt from the decedent's other assets (typically the residue of the estate). Alternatively, the document can specify that the loan goes with the asset (the beneficiary taking the asset subject to the loan).

This is all fine, but what if the testamentary document (will or will substitute) is *not* well drafted and it says nothing specific about the debt attached to the asset? What should be the default rule? Traditional common law provided that unless otherwise specified, the beneficiary would take the property free and clear of any debt. The proper terminology is to say that the beneficiary is *exonerated* from the accompanying debt. The doctrine of exoneration is also known as "*exoneration of liens.*"

The common law approach was heavily criticized as being unfair to the decedent's residuary beneficiaries (they would be saddled with paying the debt on property going to other beneficiaries — those beneficiaries being exonerated of the debts). This led to what is now the modern trend and general rule. The modern trend reverses the default presumption. The prevailing approach is that unless otherwise specifically indicated, a specific devise/bequest (it only makes sense with specific gifts) with accompanying debt passes to the beneficiary subject to such debt. The loan goes with the property unless the testator/transferor adequately expresses a contrary intent.

Which approach does California apply?

CPC § 21131. Specific gifts; right of exoneration

A specific gift passes the property transferred subject to any mortgage, deed of trust, or other lien existing at the date of death, without right of exoneration, regardless of a general directive to pay debts contained in the instrument.

Problems

1. Testator's will provides that he devises his house to his daughter, Daisy, and the remainder of his property to his son, Sam. When he dies, he still owes $300,000 on the purchase money loan he used to acquire the house. He dies with two prin-

cipal assets: his house, worth approximately $500,000, and a bank account with $500,000 in it. Who gets what?

2. Tammie's validly executed will contains, in pertinent part, the following provisions:

"I bequeath $1,000 to each of the following:

(a) any son- or daughter-in-law of mine at my death;

(b) my housekeeper at my death; and

(c) each of the persons listed on the paper I shall place with this will.

I bequeath to my friend Fred:

(d) all of my household furnishings in my house at my death;

(e) the funds in my personal checking accounts; and

(f) all of my securities in my safe-deposit box."

a. Tammie's spouse, Wendy, challenges the validity of each provision, claiming each provision permits Tammie to affect her testamentary disposition without complying with the Wills Act formalities. Putting aside any community property issue, which provisions, if any, are invalid in California, and why?

b. At Tammie's death, there are no securities in Tammie's safe-deposit box, but there are securities in Tammie's desk at home. Who is most likely entitled to the securities, and why?

C. Abatement

Assume the testator has a will (or will substitute such as a revocable living trust) with various devises and/or bequests—some specific and some general in classification. The testator dies. The estate will most likely incur a variety of administration fees (probate, lawyer, executor, trustee, appraisal, recording, etc.) and, possibly, estate taxes. Now, for whatever reason, assume that the property in the decedent's estate is *not* sufficient to fulfill all of the testator's devises and/or bequests. Estate fees must be paid, but what happens if there is not enough left to cover all of the testamentary gifts? Sometimes a decedent has a reversal of fortune between executing a will and dying, such that his or her will attempts to devise more property than he or she has at the time of death.

After estate fees are covered, the doctrine of abatement sets forth a default approach with respect to which of the testator's gifts will be "short-changed" or *abated* if there is not enough property to "make good" on all of the gifts. Should all of the testamentary gifts be reduced proportionally (in proportion based on their relative amount of the total of all gifts), or should some of the gifts get knocked-out (abated) first?

Because abatement is a default doctrine, it is very common for a professionally drafted will (or will substitute) to contain an "abatement" clause that clearly spells out the method of abatement should it be necessary to do so (of course, if there are sufficient assets, there is no abatement problem). But what if the will (or will substitute) contains no abatement clause—what is the default approach? California's default approach is set forth in California Probate Code Sections 21400, 21402:

CPC § 21400. Scope of abatement doctrine

Notwithstanding any other provision of this part, if the instrument provides for abatement, or if the transferor's plan or if the purpose of the transfer would be defeated by abatement as provided in this part, the shares of beneficiaries abate as is necessary to effectuate the instrument, plan, or purpose.

CPC § 21402. Order of abatement

(a) Shares of beneficiaries abate in the following order:

   (1) Property not disposed of by the instrument.

   (2) Residuary gifts.

   (3) General gifts to persons other than the transferor's relatives.

   (4) General gifts to the transferor's relatives.

   (5) Specific gifts to persons other than the transferor's relatives.

   (6) Specific gifts to the transferor's relatives.

(b) For purposes of this section, a "relative" of the transferor is a person to whom property would pass from the transferor under Section 6401 or 6402 (intestate succession) if the transferor died intestate and there were no other person having priority.

Abatement is a fairly mechanical doctrine that has much more significance in probate and estate administration (and courses related thereto).

Problem

Testator wins $50,000,000 in the lottery (after taxes), and feeling rather generous, validly executes a will that provides that he gives each student in his current Wills, Trusts, and Estates class that year $100,000. The rest, residue and remainder of his estate goes to his lovely wife, Gerri. Thereafter, Testator goes to Las Vegas and blows most of his wealth. Devastated, he commits suicide. At the time of his death his estate had shrunk to $5,000,000. Assuming he had 100 students in his class, who takes what? Whose gift should be reduced first, and why?

Chapter 10

Family Protection

I. Introduction

To the extent the issue in this course is "who *should* get your property when you die," answering that question arguably is easier for a single individual than a married individual. All of a single person's property is his or her separate property. No one has a claim to the property while the person is alive, so no one has a claim to the property when he or she dies. But what if the decedent is married? Should the fact that the decedent is married make any difference? Should the surviving spouse have a right to some of the decedent's property regardless of the decedent's intent?

A. Marital Property and Spousal Protection at Time of Death

Marriage is an interesting social and legal arrangement. Marriage inherently involves two people blending their lives together. How the parties blend their lives, and to what extent that blending includes property rights, varies by couple. Inevitably, however, all marriages end and an issue that naturally arises at the end of the marriage is how to divide the couple's property. Should that question be left exclusively to the parties to work out, or should the state get involved to ensure the property is split "fairly"? When a couple gets married, the assumption is they love each other. If they love each other, one would expect each spouse to leave most, if not all, of his or her property to the surviving spouse. But while a marriage may begin full of love, some marriages are running on fumes by the time the marriage ends. For some couples, the assumption that they *still* love each other, and that each spouse will leave a fair share of his or her property to the surviving spouse, is a sham. Should the state step in to protect the surviving spouse? If so, how? When? To what extent?

The equities behind the question of spousal protection are even more compelling when one considers the historical notion of the "ideal" nuclear family. Historically, it was not uncommon for a married couple to decide to start a family and for one spouse to stay home and focus on raising the children. In the event a couple opted for this traditional scenario, one spouse opted for the role of being the financial provider for the family, and the other spouse opted for the role of being the homemaker for the family. The risk of opting into the role of homemaker, if there is no spousal protection doctrine, is that in the typical marriage it potentially leaves that spouse economically dominated and vulnerable. In this traditional scenario, absent some form of spousal protection, all of the couple's wealth would be in one spouse's name. Absent some type of spousal protection, the working spouse could completely disinherit the non-working spouse.

The modern trend focuses less on the possible inequities of the stay-at-home spouse being disinherited and more on the partnership model of marriage. Partners should *share* in the property acquired as a result of the partnership. Each partner has a right to a fair share of the property acquired by the partnership.

No matter how the institution of marriage is viewed theoretically, a surviving spouse arguably has a right to some of the property acquired during the marriage. Every state has some form of a spousal protection/marital property sharing doctrine to ensure that a surviving spouse is adequately provided for at the time of death.

Nationally there are two basic default schemes with respect to how marriage affects property rights between spouses: community property and the common law separate property approach. As covered in Chapter 2, California has adopted the community property approach to marital property. The California community property statutory scheme creates a general presumption that any property acquired during marriage by either spouse, other than by gift, devise, or inheritance, is community property that is owned by the community and held in equal shares (50-50) by the parties.[1] To the extent that community property is a form of spousal protection, that protection kicks in and applies the moment the property is acquired by either spouse. Because community property rights attach the moment the property is acquired, the question in community property jurisdictions is whether a surviving spouse is entitled to any more protection at the time of death?

While California has adopted the community property scheme, the overwhelming majority of the states apply the common law, separate property approach to marital property. Under that approach, marriage has no immediate effect on a couple's property rights. Just as a party's property acquired before marriage is his or her separate property, property acquired after marriage is his or her separate property. But while the common law marital property approach has no *immediate* property consequences, at the time of death the marriage gives rise to a property right in the surviving spouse: the elective share (or the forced share as it is called in some jurisdictions). The elective share assumes that spouses will do the right thing at time of death: that the first spouse to die will leave a fair share of his or her property to the surviving spouse. But just in case the first spouse to die does not leave the surviving spouse a fair share,

---

1. This general presumption can be rebutted, however, by a number of other doctrines and special presumptions. A common example of this is the doctrine of tracing. Under tracing, the general presumption of community property can be rebutted if the funds used to acquire the asset were separate property funds. The details of tracing, and the other doctrines and special presumptions that can rebut the general presumption of community property, are best left to the Community Property class.

the surviving spouse had the right[2] to come into probate court and claim one-third of the deceased spouse's probate property regardless of the terms of the deceased spouse's will.[3]

California, again, is a community property jurisdiction. There is no elective share or forced share in California. Community property rights attach the moment either spouse acquires community property. Community property is then divided

---

2. The elective share is a discretionary right in that the surviving spouse has to claim the right. It is at his or her discretion that the doctrine applies — or not. If the surviving spouse does not receive one-third of the deceased spouse's estate, but the surviving spouse decides not to claim the elective share, the deceased spouse's property passes as provided in his or her will.

3. The elective share doctrine has evolved over time, and (to put it mildly) its evolution has been convoluted and complex. The elective share doctrine sets a floor for how the first spouse to die should treat the surviving spouse. It sets a minimum amount that the surviving spouse is entitled to, and if the surviving spouse does not receive that amount, he or she can elect to claim his or her statutory share and come into court to force the decedent's estate to give him or her his or her statutory share. At common law, the surviving spouse was entitled to one-third of the deceased spouse's *probate* estate (based on the common law dower/curtesy concept), regardless of how long they had been married, regardless of when the deceased spouse acquired the property (before marriage or during the marriage), and regardless of how it was acquired (by gift or earned). Over time, devious spouses began to realize they could avoid the elective share doctrine by putting their property in non-probate arrangements. Initially states responded by adopting a variety of doctrines that attempted to analyze whether the nonprobate transfers were inappropriate attempts to avoid the elective share (in which case the property was subject to the elective share despite being a nonprobate transfer) or whether the nonprobate transfer was a valid nonprobate transfer (in which case the property in question was not subject to the elective share).

To foreclose this avoidance technique, and to eliminate the costs of administration associated with the judicial approaches that attempted to distinguish the appropriate from the inappropriate nonprobate transfers, the UPC expanded the scope of the property subject to the elective share doctrine from the decedent's probate estate to the decedent's "augmented estate." As initially enacted, the augmented estate included the decedent's probate property, the decedent's nonprobate transfers, and even some of the decedent's *inter vivos* transfers. As initially enacted, the UPC still granted the surviving spouse a one-third interest in the decedent's augmented estate, regardless of the length of the marriage or when or how the property was acquired.

In a rather interesting development, the 1990 version of the UPC elective share doctrine decided to apply a community property conceptual approach to the non-community property elective share doctrine. The drafters of the UPC decided that the share of the deceased spouse's estate the surviving spouse should be able to claim under the elective share should approximate the amount of property the surviving spouse would be entitled to if the surviving spouse were entitled to half of the marital property the couple had acquired (i.e., the amount the surviving spouse would have received under a community property approach). The drafters of the 1990 UPC elective share doctrine then reverse engineered a complicated formula where the property subject to the elective share includes all assets owned by either spouse. The percentage of the property the surviving spouse is entitled to claim depends on how long the couple has been married (starting at 3% if the couple has been married between one and two years) and capping out at 50% (for couples married fifteen years or longer). The resulting share of the couple's augmented estate is intended to approximate half of the marital property that a typical couple married for that number of years would have accumulated. Because California is a community property jurisdiction, we will spare you the details and mechanics of the new UPC elective share doctrine.

at the time of death, with the surviving spouse automatically receiving 50 percent of the community property outright, and the deceased spouse's half passing into his or her probate estate. Knowing the basics of the traditional elective share doctrine is helpful, however, to understanding the quasi-community property doctrine, a doctrine created to solve the community property problem created by migrating couples.

B. Migrating Couples

A migrating couple is a couple that spends some of their marital years in a community property state and some of their marital years in a non-community property state. Their migration from one jurisdictional approach to the other highlights the latent temporal differences between the two approaches. Property is characterized as separate or community the moment the property is acquired based upon the law of the state where the couple is domiciled at the time of acquisition. The time of death spousal protection/marital asset division doctrine (community property or the elective share) that applies to a couple depends on the domicile of the couple at the time of death of the first spouse to die. Historically, this temporal difference created some interesting problems for migrating couples.

The historical problems created by migrating couples can be easily demonstrated by a few hypotheticals. Assume a traditional married couple, where one spouse stays at home and works very hard raising the children and caring for the home but who never holds a job that brings in any money. The other spouse works outside the home, earns all of the money acquired by the couple during the marriage, and deposits that money in a bank account in his or her name only:

1. If the couple lived their entire working careers in a non-community property state, and the wage-earning spouse accumulated $1,000,000 in a bank account (after family expenses are covered), how would you characterize the money in the bank account? Assume thereafter the couple retires and moves to a community property state, establishes domicile, and one week later the wage-earning spouse dies with a will leaving all of his or her property to his or her alma mater, Midwest U. Which spousal protection approach applies to the couple? Assuming no migrating couple doctrine applies, just the applicable spouse protection doctrines, to how much of the $1,000,000 is the surviving spouse entitled?

2. Reverse the migration. If the same married couple lived their entire working careers in a community property state, how would you characterize the $1,000,000 bank account? The couple retires and moves to a non-community property state, establishes domicile, and a week later the wage-earning spouse dies with a will leaving all of his or her property to his or her alma mater. Which spousal protection approach applies to the couple? Assuming no migrating couple doctrine applies (just the applicable spouse protection doctrines) to how much of the $1,000,000 is the surviving spouse entitled?

C. Quasi-Community Property

To address the issues created by a migrating couple who moves from a non-community property state to a community property state, most community property states have adopted a doctrine known as quasi-community property.

California Family Code § 125. Quasi-community property[2]

"Quasi-community property" means all real or personal property, wherever situated, acquired before or after the operative date of this code in any of the following ways:

(a) By either spouse while domiciled elsewhere which would have been community property if the spouse who acquired the property had been domiciled in this state at the time of its acquisition.

   …

The California legislature first attempted to deal with the problem created by couples migrating from a non-community property state to California (a community property state), by adopting legislation that applied quasi-community property principles the moment a couple moved into the state. In *Estate of Thornton*, 1 Cal. 2d 1 (1934), the California Supreme Court declared such a statutory scheme unconstitutional on the grounds that the limitation of the vested rights of one spouse in his or her separate property was a denial of due process and an abridgement of the privileges and immunities clause of the Constitution. The Court concluded that just because the couple had moved into the state, the state did not have a sufficient interest to justify changing the property from one spouse's separate property to quasi-community property. Justice Langdon, however, in his dissent, argued that while moving into the state did not provide a sufficient state interest, if the spouse had subsequently died in California, the state's interest in regulating succession of a deceased spouse's property would provide sufficient state interest to justify imposing quasi-community property status on the deceased spouse's separate property.

The legislature responded to Justice Langdon's dissent by adopting Section 201.5 of the Probate Code, which read as follows:

Upon the death of either husband or wife one-half of all property, wherever situated, heretofore or hereafter acquired after marriage by either husband or wife, or both, while domiciled elsewhere, which would not have been the separate property of either if acquired while domiciled in this state, shall be-

---

2. The Family Code provision for quasi-community property is commonly used as the general definition of quasi-community property. The Family Code, however, applies where the marriage ends in dissolution (divorce). There is an almost identical definition in the California Probate Code at Section 66. The slight variance is, in reality, a non-definitive limitation respecting California's lack of *in rem* jurisdiction with respect to real property located outside of California (application to real property located "in this state" versus the Family Code more expansive real property "located anywhere"). This subtle difference can sometimes, but not always, lead to rather complex "choice of law" issues. As we will see in the trust-specific chapters later in the book, this typically becomes irrelevant if a decedent's testamentary document is the classic will substitute—a revocable living trust.

long to the surviving spouse; the other half is subject to the testamentary disposition of the decedent, and in the absence thereof goes to the surviving spouse, subject to the debts of the decedent and to administration and disposal under the provisions of Division 3 of this code.

In *Paley v. Bank of America*, 159 Cal. App. 2d 500, 510 (Ct. App. 1958), Mrs. Paley's estate argued that the revised quasi-community property legislation applied to Mr. Paley's separate property, thereby entitling her to devise half of the separate property he brought into the state as quasi-community property. Mr. Paley objected on the grounds that the legislature did not intend the statute to apply to the separate property of the living spouse, and if the legislature did, such application would be unconstitutional as the state did not have adequate state interest to apply it to the separate property of the surviving spouse.

The Paleys were married in Illinois in 1906. After living back east in Illinois and Pennsylvania (two non-community property states), they moved to California in 1936.

Lillian died testate on January 2, 1954, survived by the plaintiff. On her death she owned real and personal property valued in excess of $1,750,000. At the time of Lillian's death, plaintiff was the owner of property having a value of about $8,000,000, none of which was community property, all having been acquired as aforesaid, as his sole and separate property. At the trial, defendant contended that under section 201.5 of the Probate Code, Lillian had a right to and did, by will, devise and bequeath to her beneficiaries (who did not include plaintiff) not only her own property but one-half of plaintiff's sole and separate property.

In analyzing the scope and constitutionality of the revised quasi-community property statute, the California Supreme Court began by quoting from its earlier opinion in *In re Miller*, 31 Cal. 2d 191, 196, and from a Court of Appeal decision that had commented on the legislation:

From the authorities cited it is clear that from the beginning section 201.5 of the Probate Code was interpreted by our courts strictly as a succession statute governing the devolution, on death, of the property of a decedent and that it was not intended to operate in such a way as to dispose of the property of a living person which, in effect, would rearrange the property rights of the spouses during their lifetimes. ...

We conclude from its history, its language and from prior judicial interpretation, that section 201.5 of the Probate Code is strictly a statute of succession which does not extend, nor purport to give, to one spouse the testamentary power to dispose of the surviving spouse's separate property, in which she has no interest, during the latter's lifetime. Otherwise construed and applied to the facts in the instant case, its operation would be unconstitutional.[4]

Current California Probate Code Section 101 does a better job of clarifying that quasi-community property principles apply only to the deceased spouse's property:

> Upon the death of a married person domiciled in this state, one-half of the *decedent's* quasi-community property belongs to the surviving spouse and the other half belongs to the decedent.

(*Emphasis added.*)

Problems

1. In 2003, Hagop and Wamil married in Nebraska (a common-law/non-community property state). In 2010, they moved to and became domiciled in California. This year, Hagop died with a valid will giving all of his property to his friend, Fiona. One item in contention is a painting that was purchased in 2014.

   a. Without any additional information, what is the character of the painting and how should it (or its value) be distributed?

   b. Assume the same facts, but for this question only, we have additional information that the money used to buy the painting came from funds Wamil saved from *her 2013 wages*. What result?

   c. Assume the same facts, but for this question only, we have additional information that the money used to buy the painting came from funds Hagop saved from *his 2013 wages*. What result?

   d. Assume the same facts, but for this question only, we have additional information that the money used to buy the painting came from funds Hagop saved from *his post-marriage Nebraska wages*. What result?

   e. Assume the same facts, but for this question only, we have additional information that the money used to buy the painting came from funds Hagop saved from *his pre-marriage Nebraska wages*. What result?

---

4. For couples who acquire property in a community property state and then move to a non-community property state and one spouse dies, the Uniform Law Commission has adopted the Uniform Disposition of Community Property Rights at Death Act to address the potential for a surviving spouse to "double dip" in the two time-of-death spousal protection doctrines. The Act addresses the rights of the respective spouses in any community property brought into the non-community property state:

§ 3. Disposition of Community Property Upon Death
Upon death of a married person, one-half of the property to which this Act applies is the property of the surviving spouse and is not subject to testamentary disposition by the decedent or distribution under the laws of succession of this State. One-half of that property is the property of the decedent and is subject to testamentary disposition or distribution under the laws of succession of this State. With respect to property to which this Act applies, the one-half of the property which is the property of the decedent is not subject to the surviving spouse's right to elect against the will.

2. How would your answers to Problem 1 and its subparts change if, rather than Hagop dying, Wamil is the decedent (with a valid will leaving all of her property to her sister, Setha)?

3. In addition to the painting in Problems 1 and 2, prior to moving to and becoming domiciled in California, Hagop purchased a parcel of raw land in Malibu, California, titling it solely in his name. Who gets this land at Hagop's death, assuming that he is the first to die (with his same will leaving everything to his friend, Fiona)? Alternatively, what happens if Wamil is the first to die (with her same will, leaving everything to her sister, Setha)? Do your answers depend on when Hagop bought the land or what funds were used to purchase it?

4. Edmund and Treva Fredericks were twice married. While domiciled in Pennsylvania, they married in 1953 and divorced in 1972. Edmund began receiving his military pension in 1973. They then remarried in Pennsylvania in 1975, moved to California in 1977, and divorced in 1981. Is Edmund's military pension his separate property or quasi-community property? *See Fredericks v. Fredericks*, 226 Cal. App. 3d 875 (Ct. App. 1991).

II. Pretermitted Spouse

In Chapter Seven, we discussed revocation by operation of law when a married testator (or one who is in a registered domestic partnership) has a will (or will substitute) that provides for a spouse (or domestic partner), and then the marriage (or domestic partnership) dissolves, but the testator dies before any changes were made to the will (or will substitute). You may recall that generally, the law steps in to automatically revoke any such testamentary disposition to whomever is, at the testator's death, a former spouse. The pretermitted spouse doctrine is, generally, the flip side of this. It is also, in a way, a form of revocation by operation of law — but most scholars and attorneys prefer to think of it in a more positive light, as do we, hence its coverage in this part of the material.

Estate of Shannon
224 Cal. App. 3d 1148 (Ct. App. 1990)

HUFFMAN, Acting Presiding Justice.

. . .

FACTUAL AND PROCEDURAL BACKGROUND

On January 25, 1974, Russell, an unmarried widower, executed his last will and testament, naming his daughter, Beatrice Marie Saleski, executrix and sole beneficiary. The will also provided his grandson, Donald Saleski, would inherit his estate in the event Beatrice did not survive him for "thirty (30) days" and contained a disinheritance clause which provided as follows:

"SEVENTH: I have intentionally omitted all other living persons and relatives. If any devises, legatee, beneficiary under this Will, or any legal heir of mine, person or persons claiming under any of them, or other person or persons shall contest this Will or attack or seek to impair or invalidate any of its provisions or conspire with or voluntarily assist anyone attempting to do any of those things mentioned, in that event, I specifically disinherit such person or persons. [¶] If any Court finds that such person or persons are lawful heirs and entitled to participate in my estate, then in that event I bequeath each of them the sum of one ($1.00) dollar and no more."

On April 27, 1986, Russell married Lila. On February 22, 1988, Russell died. He did not make any changes in his will after his marriage to Lila and before his death. His 1974 will was admitted to probate May 9, 1988, and Beatrice was named executrix of his estate.

. . .

On March 24, 1989, the probate court issued its order denying Lila's petition to determine heirship. She timely appealed only from this latter order.

During the pendency of this appeal, Lila died and her son Brown was named executor of her estate and substituted in her place as appellant. He has objected to the distribution of Russell's estate until after this appeal is decided.

DISCUSSION

On appeal, Lila contends she was a pretermitted spouse within the meaning of section 6560 and does not fall under any of the exceptions under section 6561 which would preclude her from sharing in Russell's estate as an omitted spouse....

Section 6560, added to the Probate Code in 1983, amended in 1984 and applicable to estates of decedents who died on or after January 1, 1985 (Stats.1983, ch. 842, § 55; Stats.1984, ch. 892, § 45), states:

"Except as provided in Section 6561, if a testator fails to provide by will for his or her surviving spouse who married the testator after the execution of the will, the omitted spouse shall receive a share in the estate consisting of the following property in the estate: [¶] (a) The one-half of the community property that belongs to the testator.... [¶] (b) The one-half of the quasi-community property that belongs to the testator.... [¶] (c) A share of the separate property of the testator equal in value to that which the spouse would have received if the testator had died intestate, but in no event is the share to be more than one-half the value of the separate property in the estate."

Section 6561 states:

"The spouse does not receive a share of the estate under Section 6560 if any of the following is established: [¶] (a) The testator's failure to provide for the spouse in the will was intentional and that intention appears from the will. [¶] (b) The testator provided for the spouse by transfer outside the will and the intention that the transfer be in lieu of a testamentary provision is shown by statements of the testator or from the amount of the transfer or by other evidence. [¶] (c) The spouse made a valid agreement waiving the right to share in the testator's estate."

...

It is well established section 6560 reflects a strong statutory presumption of revocation of the will as to the omitted spouse based upon public policy. (*Estate of Duke* (1953) 41 Cal.2d 509, 261 P.2d 235.) Such presumption is rebutted only if circumstances are such as to fall within the literal terms of one of the exceptions listed in section 6561. (See *Estate of Sheldon* (1977) 75 Cal.App.3d 364, 142 Cal.Rptr. 119.) The burden of proving the presumption is rebutted is on the proponents of the will. (See *Estate of Paul* (1972) 29 Cal.App.3d 690, 697, 105 Cal.Rptr. 742.)

Here, Russell failed to provide for Lila in his will. Under the language of section 6560, she is thus an omitted spouse and the crucial inquiry becomes whether Beatrice met the burden of rebutting this presumption. Specifically, the issues are whether the will shows a specific intent to exclude Lila pursuant to section 6561(a) and whether Beatrice presented sufficient evidence to show Russell had intended to otherwise provide for Lila outside of his will in lieu of her taking under it pursuant to section 6561(b), or to show Lila waived her rights to share in his estate under section 6561(c).

The will on its face does not evidence an intent on Russell's part to disinherit Lila. As the presumption under section 6560 is only rebutted by a clear manifestation of such intent on the face of the will, "regardless of what may have been the wishes of the [decedent]" (*Estate of Basore* (1971) 19 Cal.App.3d 623, 627–628, 96 Cal.Rptr. 874; see also *Estate of Duke, supra,* 41 Cal.2d 509, 261 P.2d 235 and *Estate of Paul, supra,* 29 Cal.App.3d 690, 105 Cal.Rptr. 742), the section 6561(a) exception has not been established.

Contrary to Beatrice's reliance on *Estate of Kurtz* (1922) 190 Cal. 146, 210 P. 959 to argue the language "any legal heir of mine" in the disinheritance clause contained in Russell's will somehow shows his intent to disinherit Lila, whom he married 12 years after executing the will, that case has been effectively overruled by subsequent case law. (See *Estate of Axcelrod* (1944) 23 Cal.2d 761, 769–770, 147 P.2d 1 (conc. opn. of Carter, J.).) *Estate of Axcelrod, supra,* 23 Cal.2d at pp. 765–769, 147 P.2d 1 distinguished the *Kurtz* case and held a general provision in a will that the testator "intentionally omitted all of my heirs who are not specifically mentioned herein, intending thereby to disinherit them", may not be construed as mentioning a subsequently acquired spouse in such a way as to show an intention not to make provision for the spouse, where the testator at the time the will was executed had no spouse who could become "an heir." (*Id.* at p. 767, 147 P.2d 1.)

Case law has also held exclusionary clauses in wills which fail to indicate the testator contemplated the possibility of a future marriage are insufficient to avoid the statutory presumption. (*Estate of Poisl* (1955) 44 Cal.2d 147, 149–150, 280 P.2d 789; *Estate of Paul, supra,* 29 Cal.App.3d 690, 105 Cal.Rptr. 742.) Even testamentary clauses specifically disinheriting a named individual whom the testator planned to marry and a clause stating "any other person not specifically mentioned in this Will, whether related by marriage or not" have been held insufficient to disclose the explicit intention of a testator to omit provision for another woman the testator married after executing the will either as a member of the designated disinherited class or as a contemplated spouse. (*Estate of Green* (1981) 120 Cal.App.3d 589, 593, 174 Cal.Rptr. 654.) As there is no mention of Lila or the fact of a future marriage in the disinheritance clause of the will, it does not manifest Russell's intent to specifically disinherit Lila as his surviving spouse.

Nor have the circumstances of section 6561(b) or (c) been established. Beatrice asserts a retired California Highway Patrolmen Widow's and Orphan's Fund from which $2,000 was paid to Lila as Russell's beneficiary, coupled with a declaration of Russell's attorney "[t]hat in the twelve months immediately preceding [Russell's death, he] informed this declarant that he had remarried and that his wife was independently wealthy and that she had more than he had and that he wanted his daughter to have his estate upon his death ...", evidence Russell's intent to provide for Lila outside the will in lieu of a testamentary provision and satisfy the requirements of section 6561(b). In support of this argument she cites a New Mexico case, *Matter of Taggart* (1980) 95 N.M. 117, 619 P.2d 562, which held the omission of an after-acquired spouse in a will can be shown to be intentional by a transfer outside the will such as life insurance or other joint arrangement based on evidence of the testator's statements, the amount of the transaction, or other evidence. She claims Russell's intent she take his entire estate is paramount and the presumption under section 6560 must yield to that intent. (See *Estate of Smith* (1985) 167 Cal.App.3d 208, 212, 212 Cal.Rptr. 923.)

However, as Lila notes, the evidence of the widow's and orphan's trust fund benefits and Beatrice's attorney's declaration were excluded from evidence at the court hearing on the probate heirship matter making it impossible for the court to base its determination on such claimed transfer.

Even assuming the evidence were properly before the probate court at the time of the hearing, such was insufficient to rebut the presumption of section 6560 because it does not show Russell provided the trust fund benefits for Lila in lieu of sharing in his estate.

Moreover, the facts presented at the probate hearing that Russell and Lila kept their property separate during the course of their marriage is not sufficient to show "a valid agreement waiving the right to share" in each other's estate pursuant to section 6561(c). (See *Estate of Butler* (1988) 205 Cal.App.3d 311, 318, 252 Cal.Rptr. 210.)

Beatrice has simply not met her burden of proving Russell's intent to disinherit Lila and rebut the presumption of revocation under section 6560. The probate court therefore erred in denying Lila's petition to determine heirship.

DISPOSITION

The order denying Lila's petition for heirship is reversed and remanded for further proceedings consistent with this opinion.

Notes

1. *Presumed intent versus spousal protection*: Is the pretermitted spouse doctrine a corrective doctrine based on presumed intent (correcting decedent's mistake of not revising his or her will after getting married to provide for his or her new spouse), or is it a spousal protection doctrine, a doctrine intended to ensure that a surviving spouse is adequately provided for? Which view of the doctrine does the court in *Estate of Shannon* appear to favor?

2. *Scope*: California's pretermitted spouse doctrine was moved from the 6560s to the 21600s. What does that tell you about the scope of the current pretermitted spouse doctrine in California? Read Section 21601 in particular to gauge the scope of the revised doctrine:

CPC § 21601. "Testamentary instruments," "estate"

(a) For purposes of this part, "decedent's testamentary instruments" means the decedent's will or revocable trust.

(b) "Estate" as used in this part shall include a decedent's probate estate and all property held in any revocable trust that becomes irrevocable on the death of the decedent.

CPC § 21610. Share of omitted spouse

Except as provided in Section 21611, if a decedent fails to provide in a testamentary instrument for the decedent's surviving spouse who married the decedent after the execution of all of the decedent's testamentary instruments, the omitted spouse shall receive a share in the decedent's estate, consisting of the following property in said estate:

(a) The one-half of the community property that belongs to the decedent under Section 100.

(b) The one-half of the quasi-community property that belongs to the decedent under Section 101.

(c) A share of the separate property of the decedent equal in value to that which the spouse would have received if the decedent had died without having executed a testamentary instrument, but in no event is the share to be more than one-half the value of the separate property in the estate.

CPC § 21611. Spouse not to receive share; circumstances

The spouse shall not receive a share of the estate under Section 21610 if any of the following is established:

(a) The decedent's failure to provide for the spouse in the decedent's testamentary instruments was intentional and that intention appears from the testamentary instruments.

(b) The decedent provided for the spouse by transfer outside of the estate passing by the decedent's testamentary instruments and the intention that the transfer be in lieu of a provision in said instruments is shown by statements of the decedent or from the amount of the transfer or by other evidence.

(c) The spouse made a valid agreement waiving the right to share in the decedent's estate.

CPC § 21612. Manner of satisfying share of omitted spouse; intention of decedent

   (a) Except as provided in subdivision (b), in satisfying a share provided by this chapter:

   (1) The share will first be taken from the decedent's estate not disposed of by will or trust, if any.

   (2) If that is not sufficient, so much as may be necessary to satisfy the share shall be taken from all beneficiaries of decedent's testamentary instruments in proportion to the value they may respectively receive. The proportion of each beneficiary's share that may be taken pursuant to this subdivision shall be determined based on values as of the date of the decedent's death.

   (b) If the obvious intention of the decedent in relation to some specific gift or devise or other provision of a testamentary instrument would be defeated by the application of subdivision (a), the specific devise or gift or provision may be exempted from the apportionment under subdivision (a), and a different apportionment, consistent with the intention of the decedent, may be adopted.

Notes and Problems

1. What if the following fact pattern, from *Ganier's Estate v. Ganier's Estate*, 418 So. 2d 256 (Fla. 1982), had occurred in California?

   [Emma Kennedy and Frederic Ganier] met in 1973, when she was 79 years old and he was 76 years old. They became close friends and eventually shared a joint bank account from which they paid their living expenses. In January 1977, Mrs. Kennedy executed a will that included a provision bequeathing two of her personal bank accounts to Fred Ganier. Mrs. Kennedy and Mr. Ganier were married approximately eighteen months after this will was executed, in July 1978. Shortly after the marriage, Emma Ganier suffered a stroke. She was declared incompetent in November 1978; and, on December 16, 1978, Mr. Ganier was appointed her guardian. In October, 1978, before she was found incompetent, Mrs. Ganier closed one of the bank accounts she had bequeathed to Mr. Ganier. After he became his wife's guardian, Mr. Ganier had the second account she had bequeathed to him transferred to Mrs. Ganier's guardianship account. Mr. Ganier expended almost all the funds from the guardianship account prior to Mrs. Ganier's death on January 7, 1979.

   Following Emma's death, Frederick claimed that he was a pretermitted spouse. How would his claim most likely come out in California?

2. Testator, Todd, executed his will when he was single. It has all of his probate property going to his parents and siblings (in varying percentages). Thereafter Todd executed and funded a revocable trust, granting himself a life estate interest and his alma mater, UC-Nirvana, the remainder outright. Then Todd purchased a life insurance policy, with a one-time purchase payment, and designated his friend Fran the beneficiary. Thereafter Todd married Pauline. He did not change his will, his trust, or the beneficiary of his life insurance policy after marrying Pauline. Assume that the couple has community property and that Todd has substantial separate property.

How much, if anything, will Pauline be entitled to receive following Todd's death? What property is subject to the statutory share?

3. The share of assets to which a pretermitted spouse is entitled pursuant to CPC Section 21610 is often referred to as a "statutory share." Carelessly, it is sometimes referred to as an "intestate share." What is the distinction? How would you change the fact pattern in Problem 2, above, to show the difference between the statutory share and the intestate share?

4. California Probate Code Section 21611(a) provides that an otherwise qualifying pretermitted spouse cannot successfully invoke the doctrine if the deceased spouse intentionally omitted the surviving spouse "and that intention appears from the testamentary instruments." In *Shannon*, Russell's will contained a standard disinheritance clause that provides in pertinent part as follows: "I have intentionally omitted all other living persons and relatives." Nevertheless, the Court held that the clause did not constitute an adequate expression of Russell's intent to disinherit Lila.

    What would Russell's will have had to say to constitute an adequate expression of Russell's intent to disinherit Lila? Would Pauline be entitled to a statutory share if Todd's will contained one of the following alternative clauses?

    a. I have intentionally omitted all heirs not specifically mentioned and disinherit any such omitted heir.

    b. I am thinking about marrying Pauline [properly identified with full name]. It is my intent not to make any gift, bequest, devise, etc. to her in this will [or trust] notwithstanding any future marriage to her. Therefore, I intend for this provision to act as evidence of my contrary intent so as to defeat the application of California Probate Code Section 21610 to my estate, probate or nonprobate as the case may be.

    c. I am presently not married, but if I ever marry, I have purposefully intended to omit my spouse.

    d. I am presently not married, but if I ever marry, I give my spouse $10,000.00.

5. Assuming a spouse qualifies as a pretermitted spouse and is entitled to his or her statutory share, how is it funded? Inasmuch as property will inevitably have to be taken from other takers, are the gifts to the other takers under the instrument(s) abated or taken pro rata?

III. Pretermitted Child/Accidentally Omitted Child

There is a parallel doctrine to the pretermitted spouse doctrine, the pretermitted child doctrine. While the logic underlying the doctrines and the basic approach to the doctrines are very similar, there are a handful of differences between the two doctrines to reflect the differences between a spouse and a child.

Estate of Mowry

107 Cal. App. 4th 338 (Ct. App. 2003)

HASTINGS, J.

Toni Mowry MacDonald, the adopted daughter of decedent Paul Randall Mowry Jr., was omitted from his holographic will. Pursuant to Probate Code section 11700, she filed a petition to determine entitlement to distribution of decedent's estate as an omitted heir....

FACTS

The facts are not in dispute. Appellant was adopted by decedent, Paul Mowry, Jr., in 1974. Appellant's mother, Joanna Ruth Mowry, was married to decedent at the time. Decedent subsequently married Mildren Mowry, who passed away in 1989 leaving no issue.

On December 7, 1990, decedent executed a handwritten will. The entire testamentary portion of the will states: "I Paul Randall Mowry Jr. declare this to be my last will and testament, revoking all former wills and codicils. [¶] I hereby give all my estate real and personal to my brother, Joe Allen Mowry. [¶] I hereby appoint my brother Joe Allen Mowry to be the executor of my estate. No bond shall be required of my executor."

Decedent died on September 25, 2000....

Before the hearing scheduled for the first and final report and petition for distribution, appellant filed her petition to determine entitlement to distribution. Her petition established that she was decedent's only child and that decedent had failed to provide for her in his will or in any other testamentary instrument. She filed a declaration in support of her petition stating that her omission from her father's will must have been unintentional given their close relationship from the time decedent married appellant's mother up to his death.

Appellant's petition was denied.... The court granted respondent's petition for final distribution of decedent's estate. A timely appeal was noticed.

DISCUSSION

...

The probate court relied upon section 21620 in denying appellant's petition. That section states: "Except as provided in Section 21621, if a decedent fails to provide in a testamentary instrument for a child of decedent born or adopted *after* the execution of all of the decedent's testamentary instruments, the omitted child shall receive a share in the decedent's estate equal in value to that which the child would have received if the decedent had died without having executed any testamentary instrument." (Italics added.)

Recognizing that this section, by itself, precludes a determination that she is an omitted heir, appellant argues that section 21620 must be read in conjunction with section 21621, subdivision (a), which states: "A child shall not receive a share of the estate under Section 21620 if any of the following is established: [¶] (a) The decedent's failure to provide for the child in the decedent's testamentary instruments was intentional and that intention appears from the testamentary instruments."

Citing to *Estate of Torregano* (1960) 54 Cal.2d 234, 248, 5 Cal.Rptr. 137, 352 P.2d 505, and *Smith v. Crook* (1984) 160 Cal.App.3d 245, 249, 206 Cal.Rptr. 524, appellant points to the prior public policy against unintentional omission of a child from a parent's will. Relying on this policy, appellant urges that the only way subdivision (a) of section 21621 makes sense in the context of section 21620 is to apply section 21620 to children, like her, who are living at the time the testator executes his will. We cannot agree.

Because section 21621 follows directly after section 21620, and is referenced within that section, it is manifest that section 21621 is meant to apply only when section 21620 is applicable: where a child is born or adopted *after* execution of the testamentary document.

Appellant's reliance on the longstanding policy of this state to protect omitted heirs is misplaced. That policy was recognized in connection with prior section 90 and was legislatively repealed by enactment of sections 6570 and 6571. Those sections were themselves repealed in 1997 and replaced by sections 21620 and 21621, respectively. Except for the section numbers referenced in the statutes, the language of the two statutes remains the same. This change in policy was discussed in *Estate of Della Sala* (1999) 73 Cal.App.4th 463, 86 Cal.Rptr.2d 569 (*Della Sala*).

Della Sala dealt with an heir who claimed to qualify as an omitted heir under section 6572, now section 21622. That section provided: "If at the time of execution of the will the testator fails to provide in the will for a living child solely because the testator believes the child to be dead or is unaware of the birth of the child, the child shall receive a share in the estate equal in value to that which the child would have received if the testator had died intestate." (*Della Sala, supra,* 73 Cal.App.4th at p. 467, 86 Cal.Rptr.2d 569.) The petitioner in *Della Sala* contended that his father believed he was deceased when his father's will was executed. The trial court ruled that he had failed to prove his case and denied his petition. On appeal, as here, the son cited and relied upon authorities predating enactment of sections 6570 and 6572. The Court of Appeal explained the change in public policy effected by the Legislature:

> "It has been declared both legislatively and judicially that the paramount concern in the construction of wills is to ascertain and give effect to the intent of the testator, as far as possible. [Citations.] Although testamentary intent is not always easy to ascertain [citation], there is a strong assumption that a parent would not wish to inadvertently or mistakenly disinherit his or her progeny. [Citation.] In our omitted children statutes, the Legislature has attempted to balance the possibility of inadvertent disinheritance against the freedom of testamentary disposition of property with respect to the paramount concern of carrying out the testator's intent.

> "Most of the authorities upon which petitioner relies involved the former omitted child statute, section 90, which was enacted upon codification of

the Probate Code in 1931. [Citation.] Former section 90 provided: 'When a testator omits to provide in his will for any of his children, or for the issue of any deceased child, whether born before or after the making of the will or before or after the death of the testator, and such child or issue are unprovided for by any settlement, and have not had an equal proportion of the testator's property bestowed on them by way of advancement, unless is appears from the will that such omission was intentional, such child or such issue succeeds to the same share in the estate of the testator as if he had died intestate.'

"This broadly worded statute made no distinction between children with respect to their time of birth or the testator's awareness of their existence, and required affirmative indications in the will of an intent to disinherit.

"Over the years, section 90 provided difficult and inconsistent in application and came under criticism. In 1943, Professor Evans, who served as a draftsman for the Probate Code, asserted that the statute did at least as much harm as good and suggested that, if the statute serves to frustrate the testator's wishes, it should be repealed. [Citation.] Similar criticism was iterated in Niles, *Probate Reform in California* (1979) 31 Hastings L.J. 185, 197, in suggesting that a statutory scheme based upon Uniform Probate Code section 2-302, which distinguishes between after born or adopted children and children living when a will is executed, would be preferable.

"The Legislature took notice of these criticisms and enacted sections 6570 to 6572, which are based upon Uniform Probate Code section 2-302. With respect to the statutory treatment of a living child under section 6572, the Law Revision Commission explained: 'When the omission is not based upon such a mistaken belief, it is more likely than not that the omission was intentional.' [Citation.]

"Petitioner nonetheless would have us return to the standard applicable under former section 90, by requiring a proponent of the will to prove that, at the time of executing his will, the testator had his living child in mind and intentionally disinherited him. [Citation.] This we may not do. We must presume that, by repealing section 90 and replacing it with the current statutory scheme, the Legislature intended to change the law. [Citations.] The legislative history we have recounted confirms an intent to change the law." (*Della Sala, supra,* 73 Cal.App.4th at pp. 468–469, [86 Cal.Rptr.2d 569], fns. omitted.)

Accordingly, a child living at the time of a parent's execution of his or her will has the burden of proof regarding the parent's intent in omitting the child from the will. (*Della Sala, supra,* 73 Cal.App.4th at p. 467, 86 Cal.Rptr.2d 569.) Appellant failed to do so here, instead relying on the former presumption created by section 90.

Citing *Estate of Katleman* (1993) 13 Cal. App. 4th 51, 16 Cal. Rptr. 2d 468, appellant urges that the former presumption against unintentional omission of children remains. That case concerned an omitted spouse claim made by decedent's wife. A year after decedent divorced her, he executed a will with a no-contest clause, that is, a provision disinheriting anyone who contested the will. Four years later, decedent *remarried* his wife. (*Id.* at pp. 56–57, 16 Cal.Rptr.2d 468.) Quoting *Estate of Torregano, Katleman* stated that the policy underlying pretermission statutes "guards against the omission of surviving spouses and children by reason of oversight, accident, mistake, or unexpected change of condition." (*Id.* at p. 65, 16 Cal.Rptr.2d 468.) This general statement is correct, but it was applied in *Katleman* because the will at issue was drafted before Katleman's remarriage to his wife. The Court of Appeal explained: "[A] testator's intention to disinherit his 'heirs' or 'legal heirs' is determined as of the date of execution of the will. A person who was not then an heir or legal heir, and whose subsequent relationship was not yet known or contemplated, could not then have been considered by the testator to be such." (*Estate of Katleman, supra,* 13 Cal.App.4th at p. 60, 16 Cal.Rptr.2d 468.) This is consistent with our current statutes involving omitted children who are born or adopted *after* execution of the testamentary document.

Because appellant was adopted before execution of decedent's will, and failed to prove mistaken omission, she does not qualify for treatment as an omitted heir.

Notes

1. *Terminology*: Historically, like the traditional doctrine that protected one who became a spouse after execution of the will, the doctrine that protected a child born after execution of the will was known as the pretermitted child statute. In the interest of eliminating needless legalese, in states that recognize only one child protection doctrine, that doctrine has been re-named the omitted child doctrine. As the court's opinion in *Mowry* acknowledges, however, California has two different doctrines that protect against a child being accidentally omitted from a parent's testamentary instruments. Because California has the two different doctrines, to facilitate distinguishing between them it might be helpful to retain the traditional "pretermitted child doctrine" terminology for the traditional doctrine, and use the term "accidentally omitted child doctrine" for the other doctrine. Our material has adopted that approach in the interest of trying to minimize the confusion between the two doctrines.

2. *Property subject to claim*: California Probate Code Section 21610, set forth above with the pretermitted spouse statutory material, provides the definition for the term "decedent's testamentary instruments" as it applies to the pretermitted and omitted child doctrines as well.

3. *Pretermitted versus accidentally omitted child*: What is the difference between the pretermitted child and the accidentally omitted child doctrines? Carefully read Sections 21620 and 21622 below for the differences between the doctrines.

CPC § 21620. Pretermitted child (subsequently born or adopted)

Except as provided in Section 21621, if a decedent fails to provide in a testamentary instrument for a child of decedent born or adopted after the execution of all of the decedent's testamentary instruments, the omitted child shall receive a share in the decedent's estate equal in value to that which the child would have received if the decedent had died without having executed any testamentary instrument.

CPC § 21621. Exceptions to pretermitted child doctrine

A child shall not receive a share of the estate under Section 21620 if any of the following is established:

(a) The decedent's failure to provide for the child in the decedent's testamentary instruments was intentional and that intention appears from the testamentary instruments.

(b) The decedent had one or more children and devised or otherwise directed the disposition of substantially all the estate to the other parent of the omitted child.

(c) The decedent provided for the child by transfer outside of the estate passing by the decedent's testamentary instruments and the intention that the transfer be in lieu of a provision in said instruments is show by statements of the decedent or from the amount of the transfer or by other evidence.

CPC § 21622. Accidentally omitted living child

If, at the time of the execution of all of decedent's testamentary instruments effective at the time of decedent's death, the decedent failed to provide for a living child solely because the decedent believed the child to be dead or was unaware of the birth of the child, the child shall receive a share in the estate equal in value to that which the child would have received if the decedent had died without having executed any testamentary instruments.

4. *Presumption—rebuttable or irrebuttable*? Both the pretermitted child and the accidentally omitted child statutory schemes create a *de facto* presumption that if the conditions are present, the child was unintentionally omitted and therefore is entitled to his or her statutory share. Is the presumption rebuttable or irrebuttable? (That question is a good exercise in statutory construction—read carefully.)

If the presumption is rebuttable, look back at the problem above for the pretermitted spouse and try to determine what language—if any—in a decedent's will (or will substitute) would be sufficient to prevent the application of the child protection doctrine. Would a boilerplate clause such as "*I have intentionally omitted all heirs not specifically mentioned and disinherit any such omitted heir*" be sufficient to defeat the doctrine? How about something like: "*I have no children, but even if I ever do have any children, I purposefully intend that they are not to receive any of my property at my death.*" Where, on the spectrum of clauses that may defeat a claim that the child was accidentally omitted, would you put the following clause? "*I currently have [no or x number of children] and have [or have not] provided for them in this testamentary instrument. Should I have any children [additional children], including any adopted children, I purposefully intend to not provide for said children. By this provision I purposely intend to prevent the application of California Probate Code Sections 21620 or 21622 to my estate, probate or nonprobate as the case may be.*" An estate planning attorney can never be too cautious in his or her drafting efforts at expressing the decedent's intent that the child protection doctrines not apply, but there is no case law in California to date on what would qualify as an adequate expression of intent to defeat a claim that the child was accidentally omitted.

5. *Omitted child's share*: Assuming a child qualifies under one of the two child protection doctrines, what is the statutory share to which the child is entitled? What if the decedent had one or more children when he or she exercised the testamentary instruments, and each child who was alive at the time the testamentary instruments were executed are receiving the same, small token gift. Does that/should that affect the statutory share the protected child is entitled to? Do you think that might affect how a court applies the doctrine—making it more or less likely that the court would find that the doctrine applies? How is the statutory share funded?

CPC § 21623. How share of pretermitted/accidentally omitted child is funded

(a) Except as provided in subdivision (b), in satisfying a share provided by this chapter: (1) The share will first be taken from the decedent's estate not disposed of by will or trust, if any. (2) If that is not sufficient, so much as may be necessary to satisfy the share shall be taken from all beneficiaries of decedent's testamentary instruments in proportion to the value they may respectively receive. The proportion of each beneficiary's share that may be taken pursuant to this subdivision shall be determined based on values as of the date of the decedent's death.

(b) If the obvious intention of the decedent in relation to some specific gift or devise or other provision of a testamentary instrument would be defeated by the application of subdivision (a), the specific devise or gift or provision of a testamentary instrument may be exempted from the apportionment under subdivision (a), and a different apportionment, consistent with the intention of the decedent, may be adopt.

6. *The case of the DHL founder*: For a fascinating tale of the effects the child protection doctrines can have on a decedent's estate plan, consider the case of Larry Lee Hillblom, co-founder of the DHL Corp. courier service (he is the "H" in DHL). A graduate of UC-Berkeley law school, he came up with an ingeniously simple idea for transporting time-sensitive documents to delivery ports before the goods arrived, thereby saving cargo companies tens of thousands of dollars. In rather short order he became a self-made billionaire. He promptly moved to Saipan, a tropical island near Guam (and a U.S. Commonwealth), to enjoy his newfound wealth, where prostitution was legal and each taxpayer received a 95 percent rebate on his or her income taxes.

Hillblom's activities often pushed the envelope of what was legal, both professionally and personally. Although prostitution was legal, he reportedly had a preference for virgins, including underage ones. He allegedly boasted of having claimed the virginity of 132 women and of having spent more than $10 million on women. Another of his passions was flying vintage aircraft, often flying from one Micronesian island to another. In May 1995, he and two friends were reportedly flying a World War II-vintage Seabee plane when it crashed into the North Pacific Ocean. The bodies of the two passengers were found, but Hillblom's was not.

Hillblom died testate with an estate valued at close to $750 million. He devised his estate to a charitable trust he created, with instructions that it be used primarily to support research conducted at the University of California medical schools. Despite the size of his estate, his will was rather simple. It was only 11 pages long, and its primary focus appears to have been avoiding taxes (it contains 20 references to not paying taxes). What it did *not* contain was a disinheritance clause—and that is when the fun really began, at least from a legal perspective. Word got out about his rumored sexual exploits, and everyone knows no form of birth control is perfect. As a U.S. Commonwealth, Saipan had a standard pretermitted child statute. Hillblom was a life-long bachelor. With no surviving spouse, the intestate share of any issue would be enough to catch the eye of a number of professional heir finders and plaintiff's lawyers who scoured the bars in the Philippines, Vietnam, and Micronesia asking if anyone had spent time with him.

Eventually, eight children came forward and asserted claims to Hillblom's estate. At one time more than 200 lawyers were working on the case, more than 100 for the estate alone and close to 10 per child. Inasmuch as Hillblom was deceased, there were issues of paternity, but the claimants sued to obtain DNA samples from his siblings. In the end, the parties settled. The details of the settlement were never released, but if the leaks are accurate, four children received anywhere from $50 to $90 million each, with the remainder going to the charitable trust. And because of the children's claims, approximately $180 million ended up being paid to cover federal estate and income taxes—despite Hillblom's last wishes.

All for want of a well-drafted disinheritance clause.

For more details of the fascinating, bizarre, and sad life of Larry Lee Hillblom, *see* Susannah Cahalan, *One Man Is an Island*, NY Post (January 15, 2012) http://nypost.com/2012/01/15/one-man-is-an-island/; Mary Curtius, 4 *Children Get Part of DHL Founder's Estate*, LA Times (January 11, 1998), http://articles.latimes.com/1998/jan/11/news/mn-7237; and Mary Curtius, *Asian Children Finally Get Part of $550-Million Estate*, LA Times (May 20, 1999), http://articles.latimes.com/1999/may/20/news/mn-39088. For those interested in even more details, there is also a book by James D. Scurlock, titled King Larry: The Life and Ruins of a Billionaire Genius (2012); and a documentary film, *Shadow Billionaire*.

Still think wills and trusts issues are boring?

Problems

1. In 2000, Pete is married to Gerri. They have no children, and Pete has no will. In 2002, Pete has an affair with Lulu. In 2003, Lulu gives birth to a child, Sunshine. In 2005, Pete agrees to submit to a DNA test that shows there is a 99.9 percent chance that Sunshine is his daughter. Thereafter Pete executes a will that provides in pertinent part as follows: "I leave all my property to my loving—and long suffering—wife, Gerri. In the event she predeceases me, I leave my property to my heirs at law." In 2007, Lulu instituted legal proceedings seeking to have Pete declared Sunshine's father and seeking child support payments. Later that year, the court granted her petition. In 2009, Pete and Gerri separated, and Pete moved in with Mary Anne. In 2013, Mary Anne had a child, Fred. Pete dies, mysteriously,

in 2015. What claims do you expect would be asserted against his estate? Who should get his property, and why? *See Bailey v. Warren*, 319 S.W.3d 185 (Tex. Ct. App. 2010).

2. Pete and Gerri are married. They have four children: Carolyn, Paul, John, and Kristin. Pete dies, and Gerri marries Bob (Bob was then a happy man). Gerri executes a will that leaves all of her property to Bob. Thereafter, Gerri and Bob have a child, Sam. Thereafter, Gerri and Bob divorce. Then Gerri dies. Who, in good faith, can assert a claim of pretermitted child against her estate? How would you analyze the claim? *See Gray v. Gray*, 947 So. 2d 1045 (Ala. 2006).

Chapter 11

Nonprobate Transfers

I. Overview

Historically, there were four legally recognized nonprobate transfers: (1) life insurance contracts, (2) joint tenancies, (3) legal life estate and remainders, and (4) *inter vivos* trusts. If the instrument did not qualify as one of these four nonprobate arrangements, the attempted testamentary transfer would fail and fall into the decedent's probate estate, no matter how clear the decedent's intent.

The modern trend, intent-based approach seeks to facilitate nonprobate transfers by expanding the definition of an acceptable nonprobate transfer, thereby facilitating time-of-death transfers and honoring the decedent's intent. For each of the four traditional nonprobate transfers, keep an eye on whether there is a modern trend expansion of the exception and, if so, the scope of that expansion.

II. Life Insurance Contract Exception

A. Traditional Common Law Approach

Wilhoit v. Peoples Life Ins. Co.
218 F.2d 887 (7th Cir. 1955)

MAJOR, Circuit Judge.

The plaintiff, Robert Wilhoit, instituted this action against the defendants, Peoples Life Insurance Company (sometimes referred to as the company) and Thomas J. Owens, for the recovery of money held by the company. Roley Oscar Wilhoit was the insured and Sarah Louise Wilhoit, his wife, the beneficiary in a life insurance policy in the amount of $5,000, issued by Century Life Insurance Company and later reinsured in Peoples Life Insurance Company of Frankfort, Indiana. Mr. Wilhoit died prior to October 22, 1930 (the exact date not disclosed by the record), without having changed the beneficiary designated in the policy, and the proceeds thereof became due and payable to Mrs. Wilhoit. The amount due was paid to her and the policy surrendered, as is evidenced by the following receipt appearing on the back of the policy:

> "$4,749.00   Indianapolis, Ind.,
>   Oct. 22-1930.

Received from Century Life Insurance Company Forty Seven hundred forty nine Dollars in full for all claims under the within policy, terminated by death of Roley O. Wilhoit.

Sarah Louise Wilhoit."

The main body of the policy contained a provision entitled 'The Investment,' as follows:

"Upon the maturity of this policy, the amount payable hereunder, or any portion thereof, not less than One Thousand Dollars, may be left on deposit with the Company, and the Company will pay interest annually in advance upon the amount so left on deposit at such rate as the Company may declare on such funds so held by it, but never at a rate less than three per cent, so long as the amount shall remain on deposit with the Company. The said deposit may be withdrawn at the end of any interest year; or upon the death of the payee the amount of said deposit will be paid to the executors, administrators or assigns of said payee."

On November 14, 1930, Mrs. Wilhoit (twenty-three days after she had acknowledged receipt of the amount due her under the policy) from her home in Indiana signed and addressed a letter to the company in the same State, which in material parts reads as follows:

"I hereby acknowledge receipt of settlement in full under Policy No. C172 terminated by the death of Roley O. Wilhoit, the Insured, and I direct that the proceeds of $4,749.00 be held ... by the Peoples Life Insurance Company under the following conditions:

"(1) Said amount or any part thereof (not less than $100.00) to be subject to withdrawal on demand of the undersigned.

"(2) While on deposit, said amount or part thereof shall earn interest at the rate of 3 1/2%, compounded annually, plus any excess interest authorized by the Board of Directors of the Company. Interest may be withdrawn at the end of each six months period or whenever the principal of the fund is withdrawn or may be allowed to accumulate compounded annually. Interest on this ... fund shall begin as of October 9th, 1930.

"(3) In the event of my death, while any part of this ... fund is still in existence, the full amount, plus any accrued interest, shall be immediately payable to Robert G. Owens (Relationship) Brother."

The proposal contained in this letter was, on November 17, 1930, accepted by the company in the following form:

"The above agreement creating a ... fund is hereby accepted and we acknowledge receipt of the deposit of $4,749.00 under the above specified conditions."

Robert G. Owens, a brother of Mrs. Wilhoit and the person mentioned in her November 14 letter to the company, died January 23, 1932, and Mrs. Wilhoit died April

12, 1951, each leaving a last will and testament. The will of the former by a general clause devised all his property to Thomas J. Owens, a defendant, and was admitted to probate in Marion County, Indiana. The will of Mrs. Wilhoit was admitted to probate in Edgar County, Illinois, and contained the following provision:

> "I now have the sum of Four Thousand Seven Hundred Forty Nine Dollars ($4,749.00), or approximately that amount, which is the proceeds of an insurance policy on the life of my deceased husband, Oscar Wilhoit, on deposit with the insurance company, the Peoples Life Insurance Company of Frankfort, Indiana. This I give and bequeath to Robert Wilhoit, now of Seattle, Washington, who is another son of my said stepson, the same to be his property absolutely. * * *"

The fund in controversy, deposited with the company by Mrs. Wilhoit on November 17, 1930, remained with the company continuously until the date of her death, April 12, 1951. The company refused to recognize the claim to the fund made by the executor of her estate....

The company, after the institution of the action, paid the fund into court by interpleader and is no longer an active party to the litigation. The parties on both sides filed motions for a summary judgment.... The District Court, on March 11, 1954, without opinion sustained the motion of the plaintiff [Robert Wilhoit] for summary judgment and at the same time denied the motion of the defendant, Thomas J. Owens, and the intervenor, Emmelman. Thereupon, judgment was entered in favor of the plaintiff in the sum of $4,749.00, together with interest and costs. From this judgment the defendant, Thomas J. Owens, and the intervenor, Emmelman, appeal.

Defendants (this includes the intervenor-appellant) advance two theories in support of their argument for reversal, both of which are firmly grounded upon the premise that the agreement of November 17, 1930, between Mrs. Wilhoit and the company, was an insurance contract or a contract supplemental thereto. Thus premised, they argue (1) that the rights of the parties must be determined by the law of insurance and not by the statute of wills, and (2) that Mrs. Wilhoit as a primary beneficiary named Robert G. Owens as the successor beneficiary irrevocably, without right to revoke or change and without a 'pre-decease of beneficiary' provision, and that as a result the rights of such successor beneficiary upon his death prior to the death of the primary beneficiary did not lapse but passed on to the heirs and assigns of such successor beneficiary.

On the other hand, plaintiff argues, in support of the judgment, that the disposition of the fund is not controlled by the law of insurance because the agreement between Mrs. Wilhoit and the company was not an insurance contract or a supplement thereto but was nothing more than a contract of deposit, and that the provision in the agreement by which Robert G. Owens was to take the funds in the event of her death was an invalid testamentary disposition. Further, it is argued that in any event any interest acquired by Robert G. Owens was extinguished upon his death, which occurred prior to that of Mrs. Wilhoit.

. . .

Obviously, defendants' contention is without merit and the cases cited in support thereof are without application unless we accept the premise upon which the contention is made, that is, that the agreement between Mrs. Wilhoit and the company was an insurance contract or an agreement supplemental thereto. While there may be room for differences of opinion, we have reached the conclusion that the premise is not sound, that the arrangement between the parties was the result of a separate and independent agreement, unrelated to the terms of the policy....

The "investment" provision was an offer by the company by which Mrs. Wilhoit, on maturity of the policy, could have left the proceeds with the company on the terms and conditions therein stated. It is plain, however, that she did not take advantage of this offer. Instead, she accepted the proceeds, surrendered the policy and receipted the company in full 'for all claims under the within policy,' and presumably the proceeds were paid to her at that time. At any rate, it was not until twenty-three days later that she, by letter, made her own proposal to the company, which differed materially from that contained in the policy. The company proposed to pay interest annually in advance on the amount left on deposit, at a rate of interest not less than 3%. Her proposal provided for interest at the rate of 3 1/2%, compounded annually, with a right to withdraw interest at the end of any six-month period. The company proposal provided that Mrs. Wilhoit could withdraw the deposit only at the end of any interest year, it made no provision for the withdrawal of any amount less than the total on deposit, while the offer of Mrs. Wilhoit provided for the right to withdraw, on demand, any amount or part thereof (not less than $100). Undoubtedly the company was obligated, upon request by Mrs. Wilhoit, to comply with the terms of the investment provision and, upon refusal, could have been forced by her to do so. On the other hand, it was under no obligation to accept the proposal made by her and, upon its refusal, she would have been without remedy.

. . .

... Mrs. Wilhoit deposited her money with the company, which obligated itself to pay interest and return the principal to her on demand. Only "in the event of her death" was the deposit, if it still remained, payable to Robert G. Owens. If Mrs. Wilhoit had deposited her money with a bank rather than with the insurance company under the same form of agreement, we think that it would have constituted an ineffectual disposition because of failure to comply with the Indiana statute of wills.

In conclusion, we think it not immaterial to take into consideration what appears to have been the intention of the parties.... As already shown, Robert G. Owens, through whom defendants claim, died in 1932, and in his will made no mention of the funds in controversy. After the death of Mrs. Wilhoit almost twenty years later, the estate of Robert G. Owens was reopened for the express purpose of making claim to the fund. On the other hand, Mrs. Wilhoit in her will specifically devised the fund in controversy to plaintiff, Robert Wilhoit. It thus appears plain that Mrs. Wilhoit did not intend that the fund go to the successors of Robert G. Owens but that after his death she thought she had a right to dispose of the fund as she saw fit, as is evidenced by the specific bequest contained in her will. We recognize that the intention of the parties or the belief which they entertained relative to the fund is not controlling, but under the circumstances presented, we think it is entitled to some consideration.

The judgment of the District Court is

Affirmed.

––––––––––

The issue in *Wilhoit* is whether the November 1930 agreement between Mrs. Wilhoit and the life insurance company is (1) a life insurance contract (or a contract supplemental thereto), which would make it a valid will substitute, or (2) a deposit agreement, which would make the attempted disposition at death of the remaining funds in the account an invalid attempted testamentary transfer because it was not executed with Wills Act formalities. The court's analysis is very formal: in which category does the agreement fit—the life insurance category or the deposit agreement category? The court does not engage in an analysis of why it should matter. That rigid, formalistic analytical approach is typical of the common law courts. Either the instrument in question was one of the four valid nonprobate instruments or the attempted testamentary disposition was invalid and fell to probate.

A life insurance contract, however, is nothing more than a third-party beneficiary contract with a payment on death ("P.O.D.") clause. The insured and the insurance company enter into a contract for the benefit of a third party, the specified beneficiary, with the proceeds to be paid upon the insured's death. One could also argue that the deposit agreement in *Wilhoit* is nothing more than a third-party beneficiary contract with a P.O.D. clause. The deposit agreement was between Mrs. Wilhoit and the insurance company, and the P.O.D. clause was for the benefit of the specified beneficiary: Robert G. Owens. Any remaining funds in the account at Mrs. Wilhoit's death were to be paid to Robert G. Owens. Why should it matter if the contract is called a life insurance contract or a deposit agreement? Both are third party beneficiary contracts with a P.O.D. clause. Should *all* contracts with a P.O.D. clause be valid will substitutes? Would that be more consistent with the intent based modern trend, or would that create too much of an exception to the requirement that if property is going to be transferred at death it needs to go through probate and there needs to be a valid will?

B. Modern Trend Approach

The modern trend has been to expand the definition of what constitutes a valid nonprobate transfer, thereby promoting the nonprobate revolution. The case below, while not a California case, might as well be. California has adopted similar statutory provisions to those applied by the court. How far has the law come since the *Wilhoit* case?

In re Estate of Lahren

886 P.2d 412 (Mont. 1994)

NELSON, Justice.

This is an appeal from a Sixth Judicial District Court, Park County, order determining that the certificates of deposit at issue were held in joint tenancy with right of survivorship by Sylvester L. Lahren's (S.L. Lahren's) granddaughter, Signe Lahren (Signe). We affirm in part and reverse in part.

ISSUES

There are two issues on appeal:

I. Did the District Court err in determining that the bank certificates of deposit, which designate one depositor and one "P.O.D." beneficiary, are joint tenancy instruments?

II. Did the District Court err in determining that the P.O.D. designations on the bank certificates of deposit act to transfer the certificates outside of the probate estate at the time of the depositor's death as a non-testamentary transfer?

FACTUAL AND PROCEDURAL BACKGROUND

S.L. Lahren died testate on June 25, 1992. He bequeathed the residue of his estate, less items of personal property which he had specifically devised, to three of his four sons, namely Larry, Daniel and S.L. Lahren Jr. However, the bulk of S.L. Lahren's estate consisted of four bank certificates of deposit (CDs) at American Bank, formerly known as First Security Bank.

The four CDs include: Certificate Number 32989, issued on January 15, 1985, Certificate Number 33220, issued on June 15, 1989, Certificate Number 33493, issued on March 9, 1990, and Certificate Number 34197, issued on October 8, 1991. On three of the four CDs, the depositor was listed as S.L. Lahren P.O.D. Signe Lahren. The fourth CD named as depositor, S.L. or Signe Lahren. Signe is not only S.L. Lahren's granddaughter, but also the personal representative of S.L. Lahren's estate.

. . .

[The District Court concluded that the CDs were joint tenancy property.]

ISSUE I—JOINT TENANCY

Appellants argue that the District Court erred in determining that the three CDs at issue were joint property with right of survivorship. (The fourth CD which named the depositor as, S.L. Lahren or Signe Lahren, is not at issue on this appeal.) They contend that Signe did not have a present interest in the CDs and therefore, she had no joint tenancy or joint interest in the CDs.

In a fairly recent opinion, *Matter of Estate of Shaw* (1993), 259 Mont. 117, 855 P.2d 105, we provided some guiding principles for determining whether property is held in joint tenancy. In *Shaw*, we held that the creation of a joint interest or joint tenancy in property is by Montana statute. *Shaw*, 855 P.2d at 111. "Sections 70-1-

307 and 70-1-314, MCA, mandate that if parties want to create a joint tenancy (same as joint interest) in property, they must make *an express declaration* that they intend to create a joint tenancy or joint interest." *Shaw*, 855 P.2d at 111. (Emphasis added.) Absent an express declaration of intent that the ownership interest be held in joint tenancy or joint interest, then a tenancy in common or interest in common is created. *Shaw*, 855 P.2d at 111.

...

... We are left to determine whether S.L. Lahren made an express declaration that the property was to be held in joint tenancy or joint interest, thus creating a joint tenancy or joint interest in the property. The certificates state on the front in printed form:

> 'You' means the depositor(s) named above.... If more than one of you are named above, you will own this certificate as joint tenants with right of survivorship, (and not as tenants in common.) (You may change this ownership by written instructions.) We will treat any one of you as owner for purposes of endorsement payment of principal and interest, presentation (demanding payment of amounts due), transfer and any notice to or from you. Each of you appoints the other as your agent, for the purposes described above. We will use the address on our records for mailing notices to you. You cannot transfer or assign this certificate or any rights under it without our written consent.

Signe argues that this is the express declaration required under *Shaw* to create a joint tenancy or joint interest. However, also included on the face of the CDs is the written designation under depositors which states "S.L. Lahren P.O.D. Signe Lahren." The P.O.D. designation is not the same as a designation that the property is held in joint tenancy or joint interest. The dissimilarity in the two designations makes the document ambiguous. In *Shaw*, we stated unequivocally that in the absence of an *express and unambiguous* declaration, no joint tenancy or joint interest is created. Therefore, in the instant case, no joint tenancy or joint interest was created because there was no express and unambiguous declaration creating a joint interest on the documents.

Moreover, "the essential characteristic of a joint tenancy is the right of survivorship. The right of survivorship—the indispensable ingredient and characteristic of the estate, and not a mere expectancy or possibility, as for example, is the inchoate right of dower—accrues as a vested right when and as soon as the joint tenancy is created...." *Casagranda v. Donahue* (1978), 178 Mont. 479, 483, 585 P.2d 1286, 1288. (Citation omitted.) A joint interest or joint tenancy, then, assumes a present interest in the property.

A P.O.D. designation provides that the beneficiary receives an interest in the CD *only at the death of the depositor*. See Official Comments to §§ 72-6-211 and 213, MCA, Annotations. The P.O.D. certificate of deposit is akin to an insurance policy— the proceeds cannot be claimed by the beneficiary until death. At any time before the depositor's death, the depositor can change the beneficiary or withdraw the account and use the funds. However, the P.O.D. beneficiary has no such right. See Official Comments to §§ 72-6-211 and 213, MCA, Annotations. Therefore, a P.O.D. designation does not entitle the beneficiary to a *present* interest in the CDs and accordingly, the accounts cannot be held in joint tenancy or as a joint interest.

Finally, the face of the documents contain a pre-printed statement which provides that the CDs are owned in joint tenancy but the written designation of "S.L. Lahren P.O.D. Signe Lahren" indicates a different status of ownership. Sections 1-4-105 and 28-3-205, MCA, state that when an instrument contains partly written words and partly language in pre-printed form, the written words control the pre-printed form. In the instant case, the written words which designate a P.O.D. beneficiary would control over the pre-printed form purporting to create a joint tenancy or joint interest in the CDs.

We hold that, because there was no express and unambiguous declaration that the instrument be held in joint tenancy or joint interest, and because Signe Lahren held no present interest in the subject CDs while S.L. Lahren was alive, no joint tenancy or joint interest was created in the CDs. Signe Lahren is not entitled to the proceeds of the CDs at issue under a theory of joint interest or joint tenancy. Accordingly, we reverse the District Court on this issue.

ISSUE II — P.O.D. DESIGNATION

Appellants also argue that the P.O.D. designation on the three CDs was invalid ... [that] the P.O.D. designation is an invalid attempt at a non-testamentary transfer.

Signe counters that the non-testamentary transfer of the CDs by the P.O.D. designation was valid under § 72-1-110, MCA. She states that at the time the CDs were issued and S.L. Lahren died, and the estate was probated, § 72-1-110, MCA, controlled the disposition of the CD proceeds because the CDs were "deposit agreement[s]."

... The statute was revised by the 1993 Legislature and now reads:

> **Nonprobate transfers on death.** (1) A provision for a nonprobate transfer on death in an insurance policy, contract of employment, bond, mortgage, promissory note, certificated or uncertificated security, account agreement, custodial agreement, deposit agreement, compensation plan, pension plan, individual retirement plan, employee benefit plan, trust, conveyance, deed of gift, marital property agreement, or other written instrument of a similar nature is nontestamentary. This subsection includes a written provision that:
>
> (a) money or other benefits due to, controlled by, or owned by a decedent before death must be paid after the decedent's death to a person whom the decedent designates either in the instrument or in a separate writing, including a will, executed either before or at the same time as the instrument or later....

Section 72-6-111, MCA, (1993).

Essentially, the statute remains the same, and at all times applicable, provided the authority to conclude that the P.O.D. designation on the face of the CDs serves to create a valid non-testamentary transfer. As stated in the Official Comments to § 72-6-111, MCA,

> This section is a revised version of former Section 6-201 [72-1-110, repealed 1993] of the original Uniform Probate Code, which authorized a variety of contractual arrangements that had sometimes been treated as testamentary in prior law. For example, most courts treated as testamentary a provision in a promissory note that if the payee died before making a payment, the note should be paid to another named person; or a provision in a land contract that if the seller died before completing payment, the balance should be canceled and the property should belong to the vendee. These provisions often occurred in family arrangements. The result of holding such provisions testamentary was usually to invalidate them because not executed in accordance with the statute of wills. On the other hand, the same courts for years upheld beneficiary designations in life insurance contracts. The drafters of the original Uniform Probate Code declared in the Comment that they were unable to identify policy reasons for continuing to treat these varied arrangements as testamentary. The drafters said that the benign experience with such familiar will substitutes as the revocable inter vivos trust, the multiple-party bank account, and United States government bonds payable on death to named beneficiaries all demonstrated that the evils envisioned if the statute of wills were not rigidly enforced simply do not materialize. The Comment also observed that because these provisions often are part of a business transaction and are evidenced by a writing, the danger of fraud is largely eliminated.

> Because the modes of transfer authorized by an instrument under this section are declared to be nontestamentary, the instrument does not have to be executed in compliance with the formalities for wills prescribed under Section 2-502 [72-2-522]; nor does the instrument have to be probated, nor does the personal representative have any power or duty with respect to the assets.

> The sole purpose of this section is to prevent the transfers authorized here from being treated as testamentary.

Applying § 72-1-110, MCA, we conclude that the CDs at issue are "deposit agreement[s]," or "other written instrument[s] effective as a contract" and are a valid nontestamentary instrument. See, *Malek v. Patten* (1984), 208 Mont. 237, 244, 678 P.2d 201, 205. Moreover, "th[e] money ... controlled or owned by [the] decedent shall be paid after his death to [the] person designated by the decedent in ... the instrument ... executed at the same time as the instrument or subsequently." Section 72-1-110(1)(a), MCA. The three CDs naming Signe Lahren as the P.O.D. beneficiary, are valid non-testamentary transfers. Accordingly, the sums at issue belong to Signe Lahren as the P.O.D. beneficiary.

...

Notes

1. *Joint tenancy versus contract with P.O.D. clause*: By adopting Section 6-201, the Uniform Probate Code greatly expanded the scope of the first nonprobate exception to the Wills Act formalities, which went from including only contracts that qualified as a life insurance contract to all contracts with a P.O.D. clause. From a public policy perspective, is this a good development? What is the purpose and focus of a life insurance policy? When a party enters into any other type of contract, is their focus the payment on death provision, or is the P.O.D. clause more likely a throw-in clause just in case the party dies before the contract has been fully performed? Does the party signing the contract give the P.O.D. clause the same thought and attention as a party signing a life insurance contract? Does the party signing the contract give the P.O.D. clause the same thought and attention as a testator signing a will?

2. *California approach*: California has adopted the logic underlying UPC 6-201:

CPC § 5000. Written instruments with payment on death provision

(a) A provision for a nonprobate transfer on death in an insurance policy, contract of employment, bond, mortgage, promissory note, certificated or uncertificated security, account agreement, custodial agreement, deposit agreement, compensation plan, pension plan, individual retirement plan, employee benefit plan, trust, conveyance, deed of gift, marital property agreement, or other written instrument of a similar nature is not invalid because the instrument does not comply with the requirements for execution of a will, and this code does not invalidate the instrument.

(b) Included within subdivision (a) are the following:

(1) A written provision that money or other benefits due to, controlled by, or owned by a decedent before death shall be paid after the decedent's death to a person whom the decedent designates either in the instrument or in a separate writing, including a will, executed either before or at the same time as the instrument, or later.

(2) A written provision that money due or to become due under the instrument shall cease to be payable in event of the death of the promisee or the promisor before payment or demand.

(3) A written provision that any property controlled by or owned by the decedent before death that is the subject of the instrument shall pass to a person whom the decedent designates either in the instrument or in a separate writing, including a will, executed either before or at the same time as the instrument, or later.

(c) Nothing in this section limits the rights of creditors under any other law.

Problem

Assume Testatrix is unmarried. She owns real property and personal property, including a number of different types of financial accounts. Thereafter she adds a payment-on-death clause to the following assets she holds, gifting the asset in question to her old law school classmate Edrina:

a. Her checking account at Chase Bank.

b. Her savings account at Chase Bank.

c. Her pension account.

d. Her 401(k) account.

e. Her investment account with her brokerage company.

f. Her stock account at Merrill Lynch.

g. She lent $300,000 to a neighbor, Ned. She amends the promissory note to add her good friend, Edrina, as the beneficiary in the event there is any money still owed under the note when she dies.

h. She is a partner in an investment club. She amends her club agreement to insert a payment-on-death clause that provides that any benefits she is entitled to upon her death are to be paid to Edrina.

i. She validly executes a deed that purports to transfer the property to her niece, Katherine. She puts the deed in her safe deposit box where it is found after her death.

Which assets, if any, now constitute valid nonprobate transfers? Which assets, if any, do not constitute valid nonprobate transfers? *See Estate of O'Brien v. Robinson*, 749 P.2d 154 (Wash. 1988). Later in the chapter you will see that California recently adopted a transfer on death deed statute that sets forth rather detailed requirements regarding the validity of a deed that purports to transfer real property upon death of the grantor. Does that legislative action affect, in any way, your analysis of subpart (i) above?

III. Joint Tenancy

A. Introduction

The basic concurrent estates are covered in the first-year Property course. Arguably the two most common concurrent estates are joint tenancy and tenancy in common.[1] With both of these concurrent estates, the tenant owns the property in whole while also owning a fractional share. The key characteristic of joint tenancy is the right of survivorship. If one joint tenant dies, his or her interest is *extinguished* under the right of survivorship. The interest does not pass into probate. Technically no property interest passes at death. That is why property held in joint tenancy was deemed nonprobate property.

On the other hand, the key characteristic of tenancy in common is that there is *no* right of survivorship. When one tenant in common dies, his or her fractional

---

1. Technically community property is a concurrent estate as well. Most people tend not to think of it that way because it is marital property and thus not an option for all parties. Because community property typically is not included in the general discussion of the concurrent estates that are available to all parties, we will adopt that approach for now as well.

share passes into probate where it is subject to the probate process. If the tenant in common dies testate, he or she can devise his or her share of the property. If the tenant in common dies intestate, his or her share passes to his or her heirs.

From an estate planning perspective, a joint tenancy has been an important estate planning vehicle because, for all practical purposes, it transfers property at death while avoiding probate.[2] To properly use a joint tenancy as an estate planning vehicle, one needs to know how to create a joint tenancy. In most jurisdictions, including California, whether a joint tenancy has been created is primarily a question of intent, but what evidence of that intent is admissible depends on whether the property in question is real property or personal property (intangible property—checking accounts, savings accounts, and/or financial accounts).

B. Creation — Real Property

Historically, the type of asset most commonly held concurrently was real property; i.e., a farm. Common law presumed that it made more sense to keep the farm intact when one co-owner died (as opposed to breaking it up into smaller interests and pieces). Accordingly, at time of creation, common law favored a joint tenancy concurrent estate over a tenancy in common.[3] The modern trend presumes concurrent owners prefer to have the right to transfer their interest at death. Consistent with that presumption, the modern trend favors a tenancy in common. The modern trend and prevailing approach is that the default concurrent estate is the tenancy in common. A joint tenancy is not created unless the instrument creating the concurrent estate (typically a deed) adequately expresses the intent to create a joint tenancy.

In California, Section 683 of the Civil Code is the starting point for how to create a joint tenancy in real property. Does California require an express declaration that the real property be held in joint tenancy for a joint tenancy to arise?

Cal. Civil Code § 683. Joint tenancy; definition; creation

(a) A joint interest is one owned by two or more persons in equal shares, by a title created by a single will or transfer, when expressly declared in the will or transfer to be a joint

---

2. The risk with using joint tenancy as an estate planning vehicle, however, is that it does pass an irrevocable property interest the moment the joint tenancy is created. Assume O owns Greenacres, and O decides that O wants A to have Greenacres when O dies. If O puts Greenacres in joint tenancy with A, when O dies A will own Greenacres and it will avoid probate. But the moment O validly executes and delivers the deed to A, A becomes a joint tenant with O. A and O both own Greenacres in whole and in shares (A holds a 50 percent interest in the property) and, unlike a will, the joint tenancy is irrevocable. If O changes her mind, O's only option would be to sever the joint tenancy and turn it into a tenancy in common. O's share would then drop into O's probate estate when O died.

3. You may recall from first-year Property that, at common law, to create a joint tenancy all that was necessary was that the four unities of time, title, interest, and possession were intact at the time of the conveyance. The typical conveyance from O, an owner, to A and B, the grantees, meets the four unities, so a joint tenancy would be created unless the parties expressly opted out or they made sure the four unities were not present.

tenancy, or by transfer from a sole owner to himself or herself and others, or from tenants in common or joint tenants to themselves or some of them, or to themselves or any of them and others, or from a husband and wife, when holding title as community property or otherwise to themselves or to themselves and others or to one of them and to another or others, when expressly declared in the transfer to be a joint tenancy, or when granted or devised to executors or trustees as joint tenants. A joint tenancy in personal property may be created by a written transfer, instrument, or agreement.[4]

(b) Provisions of this section do not apply to a joint account in a financial institution if Part 2 (commencing with Section 5100) of Division 5 of the Probate Code applies to such account.

While historically the prototypical joint tenancy asset was a piece of real property, no doubt that was in large part because the principal form of wealth at common law was real property. As wealth has shifted from real property to personal property (stocks, bonds, checking accounts, savings accounts, and other financial instruments), increasingly the prototypical joint tenancy asset is a financial account of some sort. Should the same rules apply to both types of property? Jurisdictions disagree on that

---

4. Depending on the situation, knowing how to *sever* a joint tenancy may be just as important as knowing how to create a joint tenancy. Civil Code Section 683.2 governs severance of a joint tenancy:

(a) Subject to the limitations and requirements of this section, in addition to any other means by which a joint tenancy may be severed, a joint tenant may sever a joint tenancy in real property as to the joint tenant's interest without the joinder or consent of the other joint tenants by any of the following means:

    (1) Execution and delivery of a deed that conveys legal title to the joint tenant's interest to a third person, whether or not pursuant to an agreement that requires the third person to reconvey legal title to the joint tenant.

    (2) Execution of a written instrument that evidences the intent to sever the joint tenancy, including a deed that names the joint tenant as transferee, or of a written declaration that, as to the interest of the joint tenant, the joint tenancy is severed.

(b) Nothing in this section authorizes severance of a joint tenancy contrary to a written agreement of the joint tenants, but a severance contrary to a written agreement does not defeat the rights of a purchaser or encumbrancer for value in good faith and without knowledge of the written agreement.

(c) Severance of a joint tenancy of record by deed, written declaration, or other written instrument pursuant to subdivision (a) is not effective to terminate the right of survivorship of the other joint tenants as to the severing joint tenant's interest unless one of the following requirements is satisfied:

    (1) Before the death of the severing joint tenant, the deed, written declaration, or other written instrument effecting the severance is recorded in the county where the real property is located.

    (2) The deed, written declaration, or other written instrument effecting the severance is executed and acknowledged before a notary public by the severing joint tenant not earlier than three days before the death of that joint tenant and is recorded in the county where the real property is located not later than seven days after the death of the severing joint tenant.

(d) Nothing in subdivision (c) limits the manner or effect of:

    (1) A written instrument executed by all the joint tenants that severs the joint tenancy.

    (2) A severance made by or pursuant to a written agreement of all the joint tenants.

    (3) A deed from a joint tenant to another joint tenant....

question. How does California answer that question? (*See* subsection (b) of Civil Code Section 683, above.)

Problems

1. Consider the following facts from a recent, unpublished California opinion. Ernie ("Ernell") Velarde has two daughters, Laura Torres and Nancy Gonzales, and a son, Alfredo Velarde:

    a. On February 24, 1993, Rebecca C. Osborne, a widow, conveyed the Rome Street property to "Ernie A. Velarde, an unmarried man" by quitclaim deed.

    b. On April 1, 1999, Ernell executed a deed transferring a one-half interest in the Rome Street property to "Laura Velarde Torres ... in joint tenancy."

    c. On July 19, 2006, Ernell executed a deed transferring his "one half interest" in the property to Nancy Velarde Gonzales "as a co-owner."

    d. On July 22, 2007, Ernell, Laura, and Nancy executed a deed transferring the property to "Ernell A. Velarde + Laura Velarde." No language appeared next to or after their names designating the grantees as co-owners, tenants in common, joint tenants, or referring to a right of survivorship. The form deed was entitled "GRANT DEED." Underneath the title the following form language appears: "The undersigned grantor(s) declare(s): [¶] Documentary transfer tax is _____ [¶] ( ) computed on full value of property conveyed, or [¶] ( ) computed on full value less of liens and encumbrances remaining at time of sale. [¶] ( ) Unincorporated area: ( ) City of _____." In the blank space for writing in the amount of the documentary transfer tax, Ernell hand-printed the words "Joint Tenancy." The parties dispute whether Ernell wrote those words on the deed before or after Nancy signed it.

    Estate of Velarde, No. A133760, 2013 WL 364305 (Cal. Ct. App. 2013). Is the deed from Ernell to Nancy in 2006 sufficient to create a joint tenancy in the interest being conveyed? Is the deed from Ernell to Laura in 1999 sufficient to create a joint tenancy? Is the deed from Ernell, Laura, and Nancy to Ernell and Laura in 2007 sufficient to create a joint tenancy?

2. James and Vonda England, husband and wife, own Greenacres in true joint tenancy. Thereafter, James handwrites out and signs a document that provides in pertinent part as follows: "I hereby terminate my joint tenancy interest in Greenacres and devise my interest therein and contents to my son William J. England. I also give the residue of my estate to my son William." James signed the document. The document was neither notarized nor recorded. Is the document a valid will? Does the document validly sever the joint tenancy and devise his interest in Greenacres to his son? *See Estate of England*, 233 Cal. App. 3d 1 (Ct. App. 1991).

3. James and Vonda England, husband and wife, own Greenacres in true joint tenancy. Thereafter, James handwrites out and signs a document that provides in pertinent part as follows: "I hereby terminate my joint tenancy in Greenacres and

convey my interest therein to my son William J. England." The document is neither notarized nor recorded. Thereafter James dies with a will that leaves the rest of his estate to his wife, Vonda. Who is entitled to James's interest in Greenacres? *See Riddle v. Harmon*, 102 Cal. App. 3d 524 (Ct. App. 1980); Cal. Civ. Code Section 683.2 (footnote 4 above). What difference, if any, would it make if the instrument James handwrote purported to convey his interest in Greenacres to himself, and then, in his will, he specifically devised it to his son William?

C. Creation — Multiple-Party Financial Accounts

As wealth shifted from real property to personal property, people increasingly opened checking and savings accounts at their local banks or financial institutions. Just like real property, these accounts could be put in joint tenancy, but early on the courts acknowledged that the original owner of the account might have added the second party to the account for a variety of reasons:

1. The original owner might have wanted to create a true joint tenancy, thereby granting the newly added second party a half-interest in the account, with the right to withdraw and use the funds in the account as the newly added second party deemed appropriate, and with absolute ownership of any remaining funds upon death under the joint tenancy's right of survivorship;

2. The original owner might have wanted to create an agency account or convenience account, thereby granting the newly added second party no ownership interest in the account, only the right to withdraw and use the funds in the account for the benefit of the original party (i.e., to help pay bills), and the newly added party was to have no interest in the account when the original owner of the account died (i.e., all remaining funds at time of death would go into the original party's probate estate); or

3. The original owner might have added the second party solely as an attempt to avoid probate; i.e., an illegal attempt at a payment-on-death arrangement where the second party was to have no interest in the account while the original owner was alive, but upon the original owner's death, any and all funds remaining in the account should be paid to the second party (though at one point this would have been an illegal attempt at avoiding probate because payment-on-death accounts were not recognized early on).

While the original owner of the account might have different reasons for wanting to add a second party to his or her financial account, the bank or other financial institution typically offered the original party only one type of multiple-party account: a joint tenancy account. The bank or other financial institution favored this type of account because it protected the bank if it granted the second party full access to the funds both *inter vivos* and following death.

Early on, the courts realized that the boilerplate language in the bank's paperwork might not truly reflect the decedent's intent. In fact, the bank might have known that its paperwork did not reflect the party's intent but nevertheless insisted on the decedent signing the joint tenancy paperwork. Accordingly, the courts deemed the paperwork as creating only a presumption of a true joint tenancy account. If there was clear and convincing evidence that the depositor had a different intent in adding the second party to the account, the depositor's intent would control the disposition of the property[5] — not the bank's paperwork.

While this approach protected and promoted the decedent's intent, the courts quickly realized the high costs of administration associated with it. Opening the door to extrinsic evidence of the decedent's intent led to increased litigation and heightened the potential for fraudulent claims. Some jurisdictions decided that the cure was worse than the problem and accordingly have reverted to the rule that the bank's paperwork controls and no extrinsic evidence is admissible to counter it. Most jurisdictions have modified the situation by adopting a series of statutes that create new presumptions with respect to the parties' interests in situations with multiple party financial accounts (granting the parties different interests *inter vivos* versus at time of death).

Note that California Civil Code Section 683, above, expressly exempts joint accounts held by a financial institution from its requirements. Those types of multiple-party accounts are governed by Part 2 of the Probate Code, an implicit acknowledgement of their increasing importance in estate planning. Probate Code Section 5203 recognizes the different types of joint financial accounts that one can create in California:

CPC § 5203. Joint financial accounts; creation; wording; effect

(a) Words in substantially the following form in a signature card, passbook, contract, or instrument evidencing an account, or words to the same effect, … create the following accounts:

(1) Joint account: "This account or certificate is owned by the named parties. Upon the death of any of them, ownership passes to the survivor(s)."

(2) P.O.D. account with single party: "This account or certificate is owned by the named party. Upon the death of that party, ownership passes to the named pay-on-death payee(s)."

(3) P.O.D. account with multiple parties: "This account or certificate is owned by the named parties. Upon the death of any of them, ownership passes to the survivor(s). Upon the death of all of them, ownership passes to the named pay-on-death payee(s)."

(4) Joint account of husband and wife with right of survivorship: "This account or certificate is owned by the named parties, who are husband and wife, and is pre-

---

5. The depositor's intent should control assuming the intent was legal. If the depositor was intending an illegal POD account, the court would not give effect to the intent, but it would not give effect to the joint tenancy either, because that was not decedent's intent. The property in question would fall into probate as a result of the attempt at an illegal nontestamentary transfer.

sumed to be their community property. Upon the death of either of them, ownership passes to the survivor."

(5) Community property account of husband and wife: "This account or certificate is the community property of the named parties who are husband and wife. The ownership during lifetime and after the death of a spouse is determined by the law applicable to community property generally and may be affected by a will."

(6) Tenancy in common account: "This account or certificate is owned by the named parties as tenants in common. Upon the death of any party, the ownership interest of that party passes to the named pay-on-death payee(s) of that party or, if none, to the estate of that party."

(b) Use of the form language provided in this section is not necessary to create an account that is governed by this part. If the contract of deposit creates substantially the same relationship between the parties as an account created using the form language provided in this section, this part applies to the same extent as if the form language had been used.

While California Probate Code Section 5203 recognizes the different types of multiple-party accounts one can create in California, as well as the time of death consequences of each account, Probate Code Section 5301 addresses the *inter vivos* consequences of opening (or adding such language to) a financial account:

(a) An account belongs, during the lifetime of all parties, to the parties in proportion to the net contributions by each, unless there is clear and convincing evidence of a different intent.

...

(d) In the case of a P.O.D. account, the P.O.D. payee has no rights to the sums on deposit during the lifetime of any party, unless there is clear and convincing evidence of a different intent.

What was the common law default presumption (*inter vivos* and at time of death) if a second party's name was added to a bank account (or other similar financial account)? What is the default presumption (*inter vivos* and at time of death) under the current California statutory approach if a second party's name is added to a bank account (or other similar financial account)?

The threshold issue in *In re Estate of Lahren,* above, was whether the instruments in question might be construed as having created a joint tenancy and, if not, whether it could be construed as a valid P.O.D. account. How would the issues have been analyzed in California?

Problems

1. Anna Brezinski is an 87-year-old Polish immigrant with limited command of the English language. She has no car. When she was younger, she could walk the two miles into town to do her banking, but these days she is too old to walk to town. Accordingly, she puts Henry, one of her two sons, on the account so that he can

handle her banking. The bank has her complete the paperwork for a true joint tenancy bank account. Thereafter, Henry comes down with a mysterious illness. He pulls all the funds out of the joint account and puts them in a joint tenancy account that is in his name and his wife's name. Thereafter, Henry dies. Anna sues to recover the funds. What is the most likely result? *See Brezinski v. Brezinski*, 463 N.Y.S.2d 975 (1983).

2. Sadie Rust had a savings account at Farmer's Bank. Sadie: (1) directed the bank to add Mildred Howard to the account, (2) signed a signature card acknowledging that the account was a joint account, and (3) instructed the bank not to tell Mrs. Howard that she had been added to the account. Mrs. Howard never signed a signature card. Following Sadie's death, Sadie's executor argued that Sadie's intent was clearly to make a testamentary transfer and such transfer should fail because it fails to comply with the Wills Act formalities. How would you rule, and why? *See Farmer's Bank of State of Del. v. Howard*, 258 A.2d 299 (Del. Chan. 1969).

3. Henri, a California resident, is unmarried with no children. Over the years, he developed a close relationship with his niece, Marion, who lives in Texas. He came to depend on her to manage his affairs when he was unable to do so. In 1992, he opened a joint financial account with Dreyfus and transferred his prior existing account into it. Henri added her name to 34 of his stock certificates. Thereafter Henri suffered a heart attack. After two weeks in a hospital in San Francisco, Marion moved him to Texas. Understandably, Henri was unhappy in Texas. Despite Marion's loving care, Henri moved back to San Francisco roughly a month later. Henri then contacted the different entities holding his assets and asked that Marion's name be removed from the different accounts and stock certificates. Dreyfus and the different corporate entitles refused to do so absent Marion's consent. Marion refused to consent. Thereafter, Henri died. Henri's estate sued, claiming sole and complete ownership of all the assets in all the accounts. Who is entitled to the property, and why? *See In re Estate of Leleu*, No. A092532, 2002 WL 1839249 (Cal. Ct. App. 2002).

D. Marital Property: Taking Title as Community Property versus Joint Tenancy

In California, the default form of marital property is community property. The general presumption is that all property acquired during marriage is community property. Community property is a form of concurrent ownership that is limited to spouses (and registered domestic partners). If title to the property is taken as community property, *inter vivos* the spouses have equal ownership interests in the property. At time of the first spouse's death, his or her interest is considered a probate asset that may be devised to whomever the decedent wishes.

While community property is the default form of holding marital property in California, spouses may opt to hold property as joint tenancy. Joint tenancy between spouses is a bit complicated because it is both a form of concurrent ownership, and a form of separate property—separate in the sense that it is not community property. Joint tenancy between spouses is also a bit complicated because of a number of statutory presumptions that apply depending on how the marriage ends. If the marriage ends in dissolution, a special statutory presumption arises that, despite the form of title stating that the property was held in joint tenancy, the property is deemed and treated by the court as community property. On the other hand, if the marriage ends in death, the presumption is that the form of title controls (i.e., if the paperwork says the real property is held in joint tenancy, the property is presumed to be a true joint tenancy with right of survivorship).

Historically, married couples in California had a tough decision to make when they purchased their first home or condo. Should they take title to the property as community property or as joint tenants? Usually their real estate agent would recommend that they take title as joint tenants to avoid probate upon the death of the first spouse. But if they take title as community property, while the property is subject to probate (generally presumed to be a negative, but not always), community property status has certain tax advantages.

If a married couple purchases a house (or condo), their purchase price typically serves as their basis in the property (the basis is used to determine whether they make a profit when they sell it). Because they own the house 50-50 (whether they hold it as community property or as joint tenancy), each party's basis in the property is deemed his or her share of the purchase price. If the property appreciates, and then they sell the property, the couple typically will have to pay taxes on the gain realized by the sale (the sale price minus the purchase price—their basis). If, however, the couple holds on to the property until the death of the first spouse and the surviving spouse sells the property, significant tax differences can arise depending on whether they held the house as joint tenants or as community property.

Upon the death of the first spouse, if the property is held as community property, both spouses' interests in the property are stepped up to the fair market value at the time of the death of the first spouse. If the surviving spouse then sells the property the next day, because of the stepped-up basis, there would be no profit on the sale of the property. Because there was no profit, there would be no tax due on the sale. On the other hand, if the married couple took title to the property as joint tenants with right of survivorship, upon the death of the first spouse, only his or her basis in the property would receive a stepped-up basis. For tax purposes, the basis of his or her share in the property would be stepped up to his or her share of the fair market value at time of death, but the basis of the share of the surviving spouse would remain the same (his or her half of the purchase price). Assuming the surviving spouse sold the property the next day (the day after the other spouse died), if the property has appreciated between time of purchase and time of death of the first spouse, there would be gain following the sale, a gain which it is assumed would be subject to tax—a gain that could be avoided if the title had been held in community property.

E. Community Property with Right of Survivorship

In 2001, the California legislature decided to let the residents of California "have their cake and eat it too":

Cal. Civil Code § 682.1. Community property with right of survivorship

(a) Community property of a husband and wife, when expressly declared in the transfer document to be community property with right of survivorship, … shall, upon the death of one of the spouses, pass to the survivor, without administration, pursuant to the terms of the instrument, subject to the same procedures, as property held in joint tenancy. Prior to the death of either spouse, the right of survivorship may be terminated pursuant to the same procedures by which a joint tenancy may be severed….

(b) This section does not apply to a joint account in a financial institution to which Part 2 (commencing with Section 5100) of Division 5 of the Probate Code applies.

(c) This section shall become operative on July 1, 2001, and shall apply to instruments created on or after that date.

IV. Legal Life Estate and Remainders

A. Common Law Approach

Possessory estates and future interests typically are covered in the first-year Property course. Just as property can be divided physically, property can be divided temporally. If O owns Greenacres, a hundred-acre woods, O could divide the property and give 50 acres to Christopher and 50 acres to Winnie. Or O could give all 100 acres to Christopher for life, and when Christopher dies, it would go to Winnie. Christopher would have a life estate (the right to possess and enjoy the hundred-acre woods during his life), and upon Christopher's death, Winnie would own the property and would have the right to do whatever he pleased with it. Then, upon Winnie's death, his interest would be transmissible (inheritable and/or devisable).

Assuming the property is real property, the instrument O would most likely use is a deed. A deed transfers legal title to the property to the grantees. Assuming the deed is properly executed and delivered, Christopher would hold a *legal* life estate, and Winnie would hold a legal remainder interest in fee simple absolute.

England, the country that created possessory estates and future interests, does not permit *legal* possessory estates and future interests. Possessory estates and future interests can be created only in a trust, in which case the interests are called *equitable* possessory estates and future interests (more on this in the next chapter). America, however, is the land of the free. Accordingly, the United States permits *legal* life estates and future interests as created by a deed. But while they are permissible, it is generally not a good idea, for a number of reasons beyond the scope of this material, to create *legal* possessory estates and future interests. Such interests should be created in a trust.

Problem

Olivia owns Greenacres. She validly executes and records a deed that provides in pertinent part as follows: "I, Olivia Owner, do hereby convey Greenacres as follows: To Olivia Owner for life, then to my friend Edrina Nazaradeh and her heirs; but grantor hereby reserves the right to revoke this deed and/or to sell Greenacres during her life estate, and such sale shall revoke Edrina's remainder interest. If Grantor sells the property, Grantor has the right to use and/or devise the funds as she wishes." Several years later, Olivia dies with a will devising all her property to a different friend, Katherine Kilmer. Katherine sues Edrina, claiming: (1) that the power to revoke made the deed indistinguishable from a will (an attempted testamentary transfer), and (2) because the deed did not meet the requirements of the Wills Act formalities, it is invalid (it gets ugly between them). Who is entitled to Greenacres? *See Tennant v. John Tennant Memorial Home*, 167 Cal. 570 (1914).

Note

In first-year Property you learned that, in order for a deed to be effective, it not only has to be validly executed, but it also needs to be "delivered." What constitutes "delivery" is a term of art best left to that course. The paradigm example of delivery is when the when the physical piece of paper (the deed) is handed over to the grantee or recorded. In light of the modern trend approach to P.O.D. written instruments, which do not have to be delivered in order to be valid gifts, does that doctrine moot the common law delivery requirement for a deed to be valid, particularly if it grants a remainder interest to the grantee? Should California Probate Code Section 5000 (reproduced above), based on UPC 6-201, be deemed to have waived the delivery requirement for deeds, at least as applied to a deed creating a legal life estate and future interest? *See First Nat. Bank of Minot v. Bloom*, 264 N.W.2d 208 (N.D. 1978). Is this debate moot in light of California's new transfer-on-death deed statutory provisions?

B. Modern Trend Approach

1. Transfer-on-Death Deed

The modern trend approach to P.O.D. contracts as being nontestamentary transfers has been extremely successful in permitting decedents to transfer *personal property* at death with significant ease and minimal expense. Demand is growing for a comparable nonprobate means of transferring *real property* at the time of death. The proposed estate planning vehicle is something called a "Transfer on Death" deed ("TOD deed"). Conceptually, a transfer on death deed is a deed that essentially would not become effective until death. It would indicate who gets title to the real property when the owner dies, but it would not become effective *until* the owner dies—and it would be revocable. In that respect, functionally it would be similar to a will, but without the costs and hassles of a will—and it would be a nonprobate transfer. Another way to conceptualize the transfer on death deed is it would basically create a revocable life estate and remainder: the effect of executing the deed would be to grant the owner a life estate interest in the property and the "grantee" a remainder in fee simple (*but with no present rights*). The grantee would have the right to take possession and enjoy the property when the owner dies, as is the case with a life estate and remainder, but with a TOD deed it would be a revocable remainder.

In re Estate of Roloff

143 P.3d 406 (Kan. Ct. App., 2006)

GREEN, J.

[Henry Roloff planted a number of crops on his farm during the spring of 2004. Later that summer he properly executed a transfer on death deed (TOD deed) with respect to the farm, naming a long time employee, Charles Schletzbaum, as grantee beneficiary. The deed made no express reference to the crops. The deed was properly recorded in June, and less than a month later Roloff died intestate. Thereafter the crops were harvested and sold for a net profit of $67,424.65.

As a general rule, a conveyance of real property with no express reservations conveys all of the grantor's interest, including all growing crops. Where farmland is transferred as part of a decedent's probate estate, and the real property includes growing crops, Kansas statutory law provides that the growing crops pass as personalty to the decedent's administrator or executor and *not* to the heirs or devisees otherwise entitled to the real property. K.S.A. 59-1206. The statutory provision does not apply, however, where the taker is not an heir or devisee. The issue was whether the statutory provision should apply to a TOD deed scenario. In analyzing the question of first impression, the Kansas Court of Appeals included the following comments concerning TOD deeds:]

... [A] TOD deed creates basically the same interest that is created by the survivorship attribute of a joint tenancy deed—an interest with the right of survivorship:

> "Survivorship is the distinctive characteristic and the grand incidence of an estate in joint tenancy. On the death of a joint tenant the property descends to the survivor or survivors and the right of survivorship terminates only when the entire estate, without the tenants having disposed of their title or otherwise terminating the tenancy, comes into the hands of the last survivor." *Eastman, Administrator v. Mendrick,* 218 Kan. 78, 82, 542 P.2d 347 (1975) (quoting *Johnson v. Capitol Federal Savings & Loan Assoc.,* 215 Kan. 286, Syl. ¶ 3, 524 P.2d 1127 [1974]).

> "... [U]nder a joint tenancy agreement ... a surviving joint tenant ... does not take as a new acquisition from the deceased joint tenant under the laws of descent and distribution, but under the conveyance or contracts by which the joint tenancy was created, his estate merely being freed from the participation of the other. [Citations omitted.]" *In re Estate of Shields,* 1 Kan.App.2d at 692, 574 P.2d 229.

> "Property held by a decedent and another in joint tenancy passes to the survivor, and the property is not part of decedent's probate estate." [Citation

omitted.] *In re Estate of Harrison,* 25 Kan.App.2d 661, 669, 967 P.2d 1091 (1998), *rev. denied* 267 Kan. 885 (1999).

A TOD deed has many of the same survivorship characteristics as a joint tenancy deed. These characteristics are as follows: (a) that the record owner's interest automatically transfers to the grantee beneficiary upon the death of the record owner, K.S.A. 59-3501(a) and K.S.A. 59-3504(a); (b) that no other action or procedure is required to transfer full title to the grantee beneficiary, K.S.A. 59-3501(a) and K.S.A. 59-3504; (c) that any attempt by the record owner to revoke or convey the record owner's interest in real estate subject to a TOD deed by the record owner's will is invalid, K.S.A. 59-3503(c); (d) that because title in the real estate vests immediately in the grantee beneficiary upon the death of the record owner under K.S.A. 59-3501(a) and K.S.A. 59-3504(a), the real estate is not included in the record owner's probate estate; and (e) that the transfer of the real estate by a TOD deed is not testamentary in nature under K.S.A. 59-3507, and is not subject to the provisions of the probate code.

When a joint tenant dies, title to the property under the joint tenancy deed immediately vests in fee simple to the surviving joint tenants. *In re Estate of Mater,* 27 Kan.App.2d 700, 704–07, 8 P.3d 1274, *rev. denied* 270 Kan. 898 (2000). The deceased joint owner does not die seized of any heritable interest in the property under the joint tenancy deed that could be distributed under the terms of the deceased joint tenant's will. Upon the death of a joint tenant, no title passes to such joint tenant's heirs. Instead, fee simple title vests in the surviving joint tenants under the deed. As a result, a court does not have authority to distribute the joint tenancy property. 27 Kan.App.2d at 706–07, 8 P.3d 1274. The same result occurs with a TOD deed. A grantor of a TOD deed does not die seized of any heritable interest in the real estate that could be distributed under the terms of the grantor's will.... Moreover, no title to the real estate passes to the grantor's heirs; fee simple title vests in the grantee beneficiary upon the record owner's death, and a court has no authority to distribute the real estate....

[The Kansas Court of Appeals ruled that the grantee beneficiary under the transfer on death deed was entitled to the crops, not the decedent's estate.]

––––––––––

Conceptually the idea of a transfer on death deed is relatively simple: it basically takes the payment-on-death concept that has worked so well for personal property and applies it to real property. The problem, however, is that the law concerning the transfer of real property is much more complex. The challenge is how to fit the transfer on death deed concept into the existing legal framework. In addition, as is the case with most all non-probate arrangements, the arrangement may be treated more like a non-probate transfer for certain purposes, but more like a probate transfer for other purposes. For example, what should be the capacity requirement for executing a transfer on death deed? Should it be the default inter vivos standard of contractual capacity, or should it be the default testamentary capacity that is used for a will? What rights, if any, should creditors have in the property subject to a TOD deed? What rights does the transferor retain after executing a TOD deed? What rights, if any, does a transferee acquire after a TOD deed has been executed? Is that interest a property interest or more like an expectancy?

There are a plethora of overlapping legal doctrines that make the idea of transfer on death deeds more difficult than it appears at first blush. *Estate of Roloff* is just one example of such an overlap—note that the Kansas Court of Appeals decided the TOD deed was more like an inter vivos transfer for purposes of who is entitled to the crops growing on the land at the time of the transferor's death.

The following case is a good example of some of the more subtle complexities that can arise with respect to TOD deeds.

Sheils v. Wright

357 P.3d 294 (Kan. Ct. App. 2015)

LEGEN, J.

Kevin Wright appeals the district court's ruling that invalidated a transfer his uncle, Richard Sheils, made of an ownership interest in Richard's home. Shortly before Richard's death, he transferred his home to himself and Kevin as joint tenants with rights of survivorship. But when Richard died, his brother, Charles Sheils, claimed the property because Richard had previously signed a deed that would transfer the property to Charles upon Richard's death.

The district court held that because Richard had not revoked the transfer-on-death deed, the property became Charles' on Richard's death. [Kevin appealed, arguing that Richard was free to transfer the property during his lifetime, and that the joint transfer to himself and Kevin—with rights of survivorship—was therefore valid and meant that the property became Kevin's upon Richard's death.]

FACTUAL AND PROCEDURAL BACKGROUND

Richard signed a transfer-on-death deed to his house in 2010, providing that the house would become Charles' upon Richard's death. That deed was properly recorded in 2010.

Three years later, on July 12, 2013, Richard signed a quitclaim deed for the same property, transferring the property to himself and his nephew Kevin as joint tenants with the right of survivorship—a type of ownership in which the property passes to the surviving tenants when one tenant dies. The quitclaim deed wasn't recorded before Richard's death but was delivered to Richard's attorney, Chris Montgomery. Montgomery said after Richard's death that Richard had given him the quitclaim deed with instructions to record it with the register of deeds.

Richard died on September 6, 2013, and the quitclaim deed was recorded on September 20, 2013.

In March 2014, Charles and his wife, Sheryl, filed suit claiming title to the house. (They claimed title on behalf of a personal trust in which they held various assets.) They sued both Kevin and his wife, Nittaya; although the wives were not involved in the deeds, they were presumably included in the suit to resolve any potential interest they might have in the property. Kevin filed a counterclaim claiming he owned the property.

Both sides filed motions for summary judgment, and the district court ruled in Charles' favor. The court said that Richard had not revoked the transfer-on-death deed or recorded the quitclaim deed before his death. Based on those findings, the court held that Charles took the property under the transfer-on-death deed.

Kevin has appealed to this court.

ANALYSIS

A person may use one or more of several legal mechanisms to transfer property to an intended recipient upon the owner's death. Some use wills and trusts. Others use simpler methods, like the transfer-on-death deed or joint tenancy with rights of survivorship for real property. For personal property, similar methods include the transfer-on-death registration for vehicles or the payable-on-death designation for financial accounts. When a person uses more than one method — with conflicting directions — for the same piece of property, the matter often gets resolved in court. And so it is for Richard's home.

Either of the methods Richard used could have effectively transferred his home. Had only the transfer-on-death deed existed, the property would have transferred to Charles on Richard's death. Similarly, had there been only the deed transferring ownership jointly to Richard and Kevin with rights of survivorship, the property would have transferred to Kevin's sole ownership on Richard's death.

Charles asserts that he took ownership under the transfer-on-death deed, so let's begin by considering what that deed could have transferred here. The district court correctly ruled that the transfer-on-death deed had not been revoked. This is so even though Richard put a provision into the quitclaim deed saying that it revoked the transfer-on-death deed. Transfer-on-death deeds are authorized by statute, and they may be created — or terminated — only as provided by statute. The revocation of a transfer-on-death deed requires that the revocation be recorded with the register of deeds during the owner's lifetime. K.S.A. 59-3503(a). Since that wasn't done (the quitclaim deed wasn't recorded until after Richard's death), the transfer-on-death deed remained in effect at Richard's death.

But this doesn't answer the question that ultimately decides our case: Did any property remain to be transferred under the transfer-on-death deed at the time of Richard's death? If Richard retained the power to transfer the property out of his own ownership during his lifetime, then there might be nothing left to transfer to Charles at Richard's death.

This question is answered by statute too. K.S.A. 59-3504(b) provides that those receiving property through a transfer-on-death deed, called "grantee beneficiaries," take their interest subject to all conveyances the owner may yet make during his or her lifetime:

"Grantee beneficiaries of a transfer-on-death deed take the record owner's interest in the real estate at death subject to all conveyances, assignments, contracts, mortgages, liens and security pledges made by the record owner or to which the record owner was subject during the record owner's lifetime including, but not limited to, any executory contract of sale, option to purchase, lease, license, easement, mortgage, deed of trust or lien, claims of the state of Kansas for medical assistance..., and to any interest conveyed by the record owner that is less than all of the record owner's interest in the property." K.S.A. 59-3504(b).

So whatever Charles was to receive through the transfer-on-death deed could be diminished by Richard during his lifetime.

And that's just what Richard did—he conveyed the entire interest in the property to himself and Kevin as joint tenants with rights of survivorship. In a joint tenancy, the remaining joint tenant becomes owner of the full property interest upon the other's death. Since Richard conveyed all of the property away during Richard's lifetime, there was nothing to transfer on his death via the transfer-on-death deed.

The district court also noted that the quitclaim deed transferring the property to joint-tenancy ownership between Richard and Kevin wasn't recorded. But the lack of recording does not made that deed ineffective. As our court held in *Reicherter v. McCauley*, 47 Kan.App.2d 968, 974, 283 P.3d 219 (2012), a deed transfers title when it is effectively delivered during the grantor's life. In *Reicherter*, as in our case, the grantor delivered the signed deed to his attorney for recording. That made the deed effective between its parties—Richard and Kevin—even though it wasn't recorded.

An unrecorded deed isn't effective with respect to someone who takes action (like granting a mortgage or purchasing the property) after the unrecorded transfer without knowledge of it. See *Reicherter*, 47 Kan.App.2d at 974–75, 283 P.3d 219. But that rule does not apply to Charles, who took no action here—he was merely the beneficiary of an act undertaken by Richard. Charles certainly took no action after the signing and delivery of the quitclaim deed; he simply remained as the beneficiary of the transfer-on-death deed. That status did not entitle him to any notice of the quitclaim deed. The transfer-on-death-deed statutes do not require notice to the beneficiary when the grantor revokes the transfer-on-death deed altogether. K.S.A. 59-3503(a), (b). In addition, K.S.A. 59-3501(b) provides that "notice to a grantee beneficiary of a transfer-on-death deed shall not be required for any purpose during the lifetime of the record owner." (Emphasis added.) For these reasons, the failure to record this quitclaim deed did not make it ineffective.

The district court erred when it granted summary judgment to Charles and denied summary judgment to Kevin. The district court's judgment is reversed, and we remand with directions to grant Kevin's motion for summary judgment.

Notes

1. *Revocation versus ademption*: One way to think about the issue in the *Wright* case is whether the latter deed was an attempt to revoke the TOD deed or whether the latter deed was merely a transfer of the property interest, which meant the TOD

deed had no property interest upon which it could act—i.e., in "wills" terminology, whether the latter deed adeemed the property interest subject to the TOD deed. Because the TOD deed is purely a statutory creature, analysis of most all issues starts—and often ends—with the authorizing statutory language.

2. *The TOD deed movement*: To the extent TOD deeds are purely statutory creatures, the risk is that is that TOD deed validity and legal consequences may vary state by state based on the nuanced language employed by each legislature. The first TOD deed statute was adopted by Missouri in 1989. The second statutory adoption was not until 1997 when Kansas adopted the doctrine. Since then, the pace has picked up, but the progress has still been slow. Moreover, the nuances of the doctrine are in the details, which themselves tend to vary from state to state. To minimize such differences, in 2009 the Uniform Law Commission adopted and promulgated the Uniform Real Property Transfer on Death Act (URPTDA), but some states are still adopting the doctrine without adopting the URPTDA.

C. The California Approach

1. Background

In 2005, the California legislature passed a bill directing the California Law Revision Commission to study the pros and cons of the TOD deed. Between 2005 and 2015, several bills were brought to the floor of the California legislature proposing that California adopt some version of the TOD deed doctrine, but the bills were repeatedly sent back for further study. It was not until September 9, 2015, that the California legislature passed California Assembly Bill No. 139, adopting the TOD deed doctrine.[6] While the California TOD doctrine is consistent with the Uniform Real Property Transfer on Death Act in many respects, California *did not* adopt the uniform law. Moreover, the California legislature must still have some reservations about the TOD deed doctrine because one could argue that the current California approach is more of an experiment than a long-term provision. The bill the Governor signed authorizes the use of revocable TOD deeds only until January 1, 2021, at which time the doctrine is repealed unless the legislature acts again before that date (and the bill requires the California Law Revision Commission to study and make recommendations to the legislature by January 1, 2020). It is likely the TOD deed doctrine will become an important tool in the estate planning field and will be continued. Anyone working in the estate planning field should be familiar with the basics of the California approach.

2. Creation

California now officially recognizes a TOD deed as a valid nonprobate transfer even though the deed is not executed with Wills Act formalities. Cal. Prob. Code § 5000. The doctrine applies to a TOD deed executed by a transferor who dies on or after January 1, 2016, regardless of when the deed was executed. Cal. Prob. Code

---

6. Governor Brown signed it on September 21, 2015, to be effective starting January 1, 2016.

§ 5600(a). California prefers to call the instrument a "*revocable* transfer on death deed" and the grantee named in the deed a "beneficiary." Cal. Prob. Code §§ 5614, 5608. Although the revocable TOD deed is a nonprobate transfer, to be valid the transferor must have contractual capacity at the time he or she executes it (or revokes it). Cal. Prob. Code §§ 5620, 5630. The TOD deed is *not effective* unless (1) the deed identifies the beneficiary by name, Cal. Prob. Code § 5622; (2) the transferor signs and dates the deed and acknowledges the deed before a notary, Cal. Prob. Code § 5624; and (3) the deed is recorded within 60 days of its execution (traditional "delivery" and "acceptance" of the deed during the transferor's lifetime is not required), Cal. Prob. Code § 5626. If more than one revocable TOD deed is recorded with respect to the same property, the later executed and recorded deed controls. Cal. Prob. Code § 5628(a). If more than revocable TOD is recorded, and the *later* executed deed is revoked, the statute provides that the revocation "does not revive an instrument earlier revoked by recordation of that deed."[7] Cal. Prob. Code § 5628(b).

3. Consequences of Recording

After a revocable TOD deed has been executed and recorded, the transferor retains all the same ownership rights, duties, and benefits as if the revocable TOD deed had not been executed. Cal. Prob. Code § 5650. Conversely, following proper execution and recording of a revocable TOD deed, neither a beneficiary nor the creditors of a beneficiary acquire any rights, legal or equitable, in the property until the transferor dies. Cal. Prob. Code § 5650. Upon the transferor's death, all of the transferor's interest in the property (subject to any limitations—i.e., any liens, encumbrances, leases, easements, etc.) is transferred automatically and by operation of law, immediately subject to the beneficiary's right to disclaim. Cal. Prob. Code § 5652. Where there is more than one beneficiary, they hold the property as tenants in common. *Id.* There is an implied survivorship requirement for each beneficiary. Where the beneficiary fails to survive the transferor, the transfer lapses (and anti-lapse does not apply); but where there is more than one named beneficiary, the other beneficiaries share the lapsed share equally. *Id.*

As noted above, one of the more challenging issues concerning TOD deeds is how to fit the transfer on death deed concept into the existing legal framework. In particular, where there are multiple deeds and one or more of them is a revocable TOD deed, which one controls and why? That basically was the issue in the *Wright* case above. Like Kansas, California has a statute that indirectly addresses that issue. Section 5650 states that while the transferor is alive, executing and recording a revocable TOD deed does "not affect the ownership rights of the transferor, and the transferor or the transferor's agent or other fiduciary may convey, assign, contract, encumber, or otherwise deal with the property...." Cal. Prob. Code § 5650(a). The language in Section 5650, however, needs to be juxtaposed with the language in Section 5660:

---

7. It is a bit unclear, however, whether the statute absolutely and always bars revival or if it merely says that revival does not automatically apply absent the proponent of revival meeting the requirements of that doctrine.

**CPC § 5660. TOD deed and other instrument disposing of the same property —
controlling instrument**

If a revocable transfer on death deed recorded on or before 60 days after the date it was
executed and another instrument both purport to dispose of the same property:

(a) If the other instrument is not recorded before the transferor's death, the revocable
transfer on death deed is the operative instrument.

(b) If the other instrument is recorded before the transferor's death and makes a revocable
disposition of the property, the later executed of the revocable transfer on death deed
or the other instrument is the operative instrument.

(c) If the other instrument is recorded before the transferor's death and makes an irrevocable disposition of the property, the other instrument and not the revocable transfer
on death deed is the operative instrument.

You may recall from first-year Property that a validly executed deed is effective upon
delivery. The deed need not be recorded; but if it is not, the grantee's title is vulnerable
because a subsequent grantee may qualify for protection under the jurisdiction's
recording act (in which case, the subsequent party may trump the first-in-time
grantee). Most recording acts require the subsequent party to be a subsequent bona
fide purchaser without notice of the first-in-time party to qualify for protection under
the act. Does that traditional approach still apply if one of the instruments is a revocable TOD deed? How would the *Wright* case come out in California? Why? Does
it make a difference if the "other instrument" is executed and delivered before or after
the revocable TOD deed is recorded? Should it? What if the other instrument is a
deed transferring the property to a revocable trust?

4. TOD Deed's Effect on Concurrent Estate

One of the overlapping areas of law that generated significant discussion is what
if the property interest in question is part of a concurrent estate; i.e., the party interested in executing a TOD deed is a co-tenant in a joint tenancy, or a spouse holding
property as community property with right of survivorship, or a tenant in common?
What difference, if any, should that make? In particular, the traditional common
law view of the right of survivorship is that it becomes effective the moment the
party dies, and his or her interest is extinguished. If it is extinguished, there is
nothing to transfer (hence the logic for why joint tenancy and property held as community property with right of survivorship is non-probate). On the other hand, as
the court's discussion above in *Estate of Roloff* evidences, one way to think of a revocable TOD deed is that it also becomes effective immediately upon the transferor's
death and that is why it operates as a nonprobate transfer. If the transferor executes
a revocable TOD deed with respect to his or her interest in property held in joint
tenancy or as community property with right of survivorship, should the execution
and recording of the revocable TOD deed "sever" the property interest and thereby
destroy the right of survivorship? At death, should the original joint tenancy/
community property with right of survivorship control, or should the revocable
TOD deed?

CPC § 5664. Property held in joint tenancy or as community property with right of survivorship

> If, at the time of the transferor's death, title to the property described in the revocable transfer on death deed is held in joint tenancy or as community property with right of survivorship, the revocable transfer on death deed is void. The transferor's interest in the property is governed by the right of survivorship and not by the revocable transfer on death deed.

Is California Probate Code Section 5664 consistent with the general intent-based movement that dominates the modern trend? Is it defensible?

The general rules applicable to nonprobate transfers of community property apply to TOD deeds as well. Cal. Prob. Code § 5666. A spouse generally has the right to transfer his or her share of community property, whether that transfer is a probate or nonprobate transfer, without giving notice to the other spouse and/or without the other spouse's consent. Cal. Prob. Code § 5010 et seq.

5. Revocation

A transferor can unilaterally revoke a revocable TOD deed. The instrument revoking a revocable TOD deed must meet the same creation and recording requirements as apply to the creation of a revocable TOD deed.[8] Cal. Prob. Code § 5628(b).

6. Disqualification

The validity of a revocable TOD deed may be attacked on the same grounds as other instruments that effectuate an at-death transfer: lack of capacity, insane delusion, undue influence, and/or fraud. Cal. Prob. Code § 5696. Moreover, the statutory presumptions of undue influence and/or fraud apply to TOD deeds as well. Cal. Prob. Code § 5690.

7. Creditor's Rights

A particularly tricky area of TOD deeds is creditor's rights. While an important part of the law, it is not a focus of a Wills, Trusts, and Estates course. The most important creditor's rights provision in the California TOD deed statutes is Probate Code Section 5670. It unambiguously makes clear that a properly evidenced creditor of the transferor has priority over any and all creditors of the beneficiary:

> Notwithstanding any other statute governing priorities among creditors, a creditor of the transferor whose right is evidenced at the time of the transferor's death by an encumbrance or lien of record on property transferred by a revocable transfer on death deed has priority against the property over a creditor of the beneficiary, regardless of whether the beneficiary's obligation was created before or after the transferor's death and regardless of whether the obligation is secured or unsecured, voluntary or involuntary, recorded or unrecorded.

---

8. Interestingly, however, the statutory provision on revocation expressly says the revoking instrument must be recorded "before the transferor's death" while the creation statutory provision says only that the deed must be recorded within 60 days of being executed — it makes no reference to "before the transferor's death."

The subsequent statutory provisions go on to elaborate on the issue of creditors' rights, in particular on when a beneficiary is liable for the unsecured debts of the transferor, but the details of creditors' rights as they apply to revocable TOD deeds is beyond the scope of this material.

Problems

1. Testatrix owns Blackacres. She validly executes a transfer-on-death deed for Blackacres, designating her friend Pat as the beneficiary. She does not record the deed, but sends it to Pat instead (who does not record it). Thereafter, Testatrix executes a will devising all of her property to her alma mater, Nirvana University. Following testatrix's death, who is entitled to Blackacres? What arguments would each party make? *See In re Estate of Scott*, 842 N.E.2d 1071 (Ohio Ct. App. 2005).

2. Harold and Wilma are married. They own Greenacres as community property with right of survivorship. Thereafter Wilma found out that Harold was having an affair with his assistant, Lulu. Wilma moved out of the house. While divorce proceedings were underway, she learned that she had a terminal illness. Wanting to make sure that Harold did not take any more from her, she executed and recorded a transfer on death deed that specifically provided that it severed Greenacres and granted her interest in the property to her sister, Sally. Following Wilma's death, who owns Greenacres, and why?

V. *Inter Vivos* Trusts

An *inter vivos* trust is a trust that is created while the settlor (the party who creates the trust) is alive. It is a subset of the general law of trusts, which is such an important and complex area of law that it is the subject of the rest of this book. Only property transferred into the trust *inter vivos* avoids probate. What is necessary to transfer property to a trust is the subject of general trust law.

The modern trend is not so much to expand the scope of the *inter vivos* trust exception to the Wills Act formalities as it is to facilitate the creation of an *inter vivos* trust. By making it easier to create an *inter vivos* trust, the modern trend is de facto expanding its use by making it more accessible to more people. Historically, the trust was a specialized legal instrument used almost exclusively by the wealthy. Increasingly the trust is becoming the principal estate planning instrument for most people, including people of modest means. It is an indispensable tool in the estate planner's tool belt, one with which every estate planner must be very comfortable.

A. *Inter Vivos* Trust as a Will Substitute

An *inter vivos* trust is created during an individual's lifetime. Typically, the party who creates the trust makes it for his or her benefit during his or her lifetime, and at the individual's death, provides dispositive instructions with respect to the property in the trust. In this way, it functions similarly to a will. If the trust is revocable, it "feels" even more like a will. While all of the nonprobate instruments function, more or less, like a will (in that for all practical purposes they transfer property at death), the revocable "living" trust is the paradigm "will substitute." Like a will, a revocable living trust can be simple: "at my death, all of my property goes to X." Or it can be very complex (disposing of multiple property interests, to multiple takers, with some of the transfers outright and some in trusts to take effect at death, etc.). Accordingly, at one level, the primary purpose of both a will and a revocable living trust is the same: to transfer a party's property at death to the takers, and in the manner and form, that the party wishes. *How* the two estate planning vehicles transfer the property interests at death, however, is very different: property transferred via a will generally passes through probate, while property transferred via a revocable living trust does not.

In light of the similarities and differences between a will and revocable living trust, which legal arrangement is the "better" mechanism to use to transfer property at death? As with most questions in law school, the best answer is "it depends"—it depends on each individual's circumstance and what he or she wishes to achieve with his or her estate plan. While a full examination of this topic is beyond the scope of this course, a few words are in order. Historically the will was the primary vehicle for estate planning. Today, however, the revocable living trust is fast becoming the primary vehicle for estate planning. This is because of its perceived benefits, which include, among others: (1) costs, (2) time, (3) asset control, (4) privacy, (5) out-of-state real property, and (6) incapacity. These benefits stand in contrast to what are often perceived as the "horrors" of the probate process—the process through which wills must pass. A few words about each of the claimed benefits should give you a sense of the "will versus revocable living trust" debate.

B. Costs

There are threshold costs associated with properly drafting the necessary documents for wills and most all revocable living trusts. These costs are usually higher for a revocable living trust.[9] Moreover, a trust must be properly *funded*—a process that involves changing title to assets, which implicates various additional costs.[10] There are no comparable costs with the use of a will. The up-front costs associated with creating a simple trust typically are greater than the up-front costs of creating a simple will. The costs associated with the *creation* of a will versus a revocable living trust, however, typically are a relatively small part of the overall cost associated with the respective estate planning vehicles.

---

9. The simple trust document typically costs significantly more than a simple will—and, as discussed later, ancillary documents should also be prepared, such as a pour-over will.

10. Trust funding issues are covered in Chapter 12.

There are also costs associated with administering an estate, irrespective of whether one's assets are distributed via a will or a living trust. When someone dies with a will, the will is subject to probate and the estate incurs various probate costs—lawyer and executor fees,[11] state appraisal fees,[12] and court costs. These costs reduce the assets that will be available to be distributed to the decedent's beneficiaries. With a living trust, however, "all such probate costs are completely eliminated." That statement goes a long way toward explaining the widely held belief that for the typical individual with a simple estate, the costs associated with administering a revocable living trust are cheaper than are the costs associated with probating a will. Yet that statement, while true, can also be misleading if not kept in context.

The "administration" of a decedent's estate though a revocable living trust is *not* without costs. The executor's role in the probate setting is replaced by the trustee's role in the trust setting. While the fees paid to a trustee can be less than an executor's fees, they can also be greater (depending on the nature and complexity of the trust property). In addition, while typically a trustee is not required to seek legal assistance, the more complex the trust dispositions the more likely a prudent trustee will retain an attorney to ensure proper compliance with the trust provisions. Again, while the fees paid to the trust's attorney may be less than those paid to a probate attorney, they can be greater. Moreover, while there are no judicial filing fees with a revocable living trust, appraisal fees, title fees, and other logistical administrative costs are a part of administering an estate, regardless of whether the estate passes through a will or a revocable living trust. Thus, while the total cost of creating and administering a revocable living trust typically is lower for the average individual with a fairly simple estate and estate plan, one should not assume that this is always the case.

The topic of taxes deserves a quick word. One of the most enduring misunderstandings associated with revocable living trusts is that they result in tax savings. This is *not* the case. The use of a will or a revocable living trust has absolutely no relevance, nor does it create any difference, in income, estate, or gift taxes. The misconception likely arises because of an incorrect belief that because assets *avoid probate,* they also avoid inclusion in a decedent's estate for estate tax purposes. For estate tax purposes, the value of *all* assets in a decedent's revocable living trust are included in his or her gross estate. Avoiding probate has absolutely nothing to do with avoiding inclusion of assets in a decedent's gross estate for tax purposes. Either vehicle—a will or a revocable living trust—is equally compatible for creative, tax-sensitive estate planning.

---

11. In probate, executor and attorney fees are the two that are most prominent. In many jurisdictions, including California, these fees are set by statute and are a sliding scale based on the estate's value.

12. In California, a "probate referee" is assigned by the court for probate asset appraisals. Probate referee fees depend on the value of estate assets. It is probably fair to say that for larger estates, nonprobate appraisal fees charged by private appraisers can be substantially higher than those of a state probate referee.

Whether a decedent's assets do or do not go through probate, however, is irrelevant in determining what is included in a decedent's estate for estate tax purposes.

C. Time

Another important variable in the will versus revocable living trust debate is time: How long does it take following a decedent's death before the assets in question are distributed? Again, the best answer is "it depends": it depends on the decedent's circumstances and what he or she wishes to achieve with his or her estate plan. Nevertheless, some general observations can be made.

There is no denying that the probate process does take some time and can vary dramatically from state to state—and obviously it also depends on the complexity of a decedent's estate. The current trend of court delays due to budget constraints can exacerbate the situation. To properly assess the benefits of avoiding probate, however, one should keep in mind the primary purpose of the probate process. In probate, the court serves as a disinterested third party that ensures that the decedent's assets are distributed according to the testator's wishes. Probate was not designed as a form of state interference, but rather as a form of protection for the decedent. Part and parcel of this process is the orderly distribution of his or her estate: the estate must be inventoried, creditor claims against the decedent must be resolved, and remaining assets must be distributed—and the court must ensure that the executor/administrator is properly performing their duties. These core functions take some time.

If the decedent has a validly created revocable living trust, the general rule is that there is no judicial involvement in the trust administration. That does not necessarily mean, however, that the trustee will immediately distribute the trust property to the beneficiaries upon the settlor's death. While the trustee may have the power to make immediate distributions, most trustees will not act with such haste. The trustee's duties in administering a decedent's trust estate include most of the aforementioned components of the probate process, albeit without having to work through the judicial process and without court oversight.

Where a decedent's trust estate is fairly simple and his or her wishes fairly straightforward, a trustee typically can take advantage of the nonprobate process to distribute the trust property to the beneficiaries more quickly. Where, however, a decedent's trust estate is fairly complex, and/or his or her testamentary wishes are fairly complex, proper administration of the decedent's estate—even through a revocable living trust—takes time. A prudent trustee will be sensitive to the situation to avoid adverse results.

D. Control

In the probate versus non-probate/will versus revocable living trust debate, the issue of asset control, or loss thereof, often accompanies the discussion of "time." With a revocable living trust, a trustee carries out various duties during the administration of the trust pursuant to the instructions in the trust document, and, unless otherwise specified by the trust, the trustee acts without supervision, court or otherwise. If the trust document so permits, assets may be sold, debts incurred, etc., during this period without a court's permission (but always circumscribed by trustee fiduciary duties[13]). The trustee has control over the trust assets, subject only to the terms of the trust.

In the probate process, the executor/administrator of an estate, during its administration period, usually performs most functions without court approval, but may be required to petition the court for certain actions such as selling or encumbering estate assets. Most wills, however, authorize an executor to bypass court permission for most such actions pursuant to the Independent Administration of Estates Act (adopted in California and a number of states). Yet while the executor/administrator may be able to minimize court administrative approval, the executor/administrator cannot completely avoid probate court supervision.

While there is greater loss of control over the assets during the probate process, that loss of control is part and parcel of the protective function of probate. The probate court serves as a disinterested third party to oversee the disposition of the decedent's assets. This is an ex ante layer of safeguarding the proper distribution of a decedent's estate. While not perfect, and often a bit cumbersome, this protection generally does not exist with a revocable living trust. At best, the protection accorded the beneficiaries under a revocable living trust is an ex post claim of breach of trust. Depending on the situation, such ex post protection may be more in theory than reality. In no event, however, should the issue of *control* be equated to how a decedent's estate should be distributed. A probate court cannot override the wishes in a decedent's validly executed will, just as a trustee, acting within prescribed duties, cannot override the dispositive provisions in a revocable living trust.

Not surprisingly, the advice of a professional estate planner is helpful in: (1) assessing the risks of asset mismanagement and/or misconduct inherent in a party's personal situation and with respect to his or her testamentary wishes, and (2) determining when, in light of the party's personal situation and wishes, the party would be better served with ex ante probate protection versus ex post breach of trust protection.

E. Privacy

A will filed with a probate court is, in most instances, a "public document" and can usually be viewed by anyone. A visit to the county court probate clerk with a case number or the decedent's name and date of death is usually all that is required. In contrast, a revocable living trust remains private because it is not probated. For some individuals, the privacy issue is a great concern (especially for high-profile individuals) and he or she may not wish the world to see the dispositive details of his or her estate.

---

13. The fiduciary duties of a trustee are discussed in more detail in Chapter 14.

If privacy is a valid concern, then a revocable living trust is, at the time of death, superior to a will.

If privacy is an overriding concern, one needs to be sensitive to the *inter vivos* attributes of a revocable living trust. A revocable living trust requires "funding" during one's lifetime.[14] Funding involves transferring title of such assets, accounts, etc., while the individual is alive, from the individual to the trust. The trustee then has control over the assets. The institution in which such assets or accounts are held, however, will generally want documentation for their files showing that the trustee has the authority to manage such assets — i.e., a copy of the trust. If a copy of the entire trust is provided, the issue of privacy has been compromised. To prevent disclosure of the entire trust, most states require the inquiring institution to accept a shortened version of the trust. This shortened version of the trust is commonly called an abstract, certificate, or memorandum of trust. Key provisions of the trust, including the trustee's powers over the property, are included in such shortened versions, but dispositive and other sensitive provisions are not. In California, it is commonly called an *abstract of trust*, and if certain statutory requirements are met, institutions must accept it in lieu of the entire trust document.[15]

F. Out-of-State Real Property

An individual, domiciled in one state, may die owning real property located in another state. This raises *in rem jurisdiction*, an issue typically covered in first-year Civil Procedure. A California court, for example, typically does not have the jurisdiction to decide and effectuate the disposition of real property located outside of California. A revocable living trust has the clear-cut advantage over a will in this situation.

For a will, the lack of in rem jurisdiction will generally mean that a separate probate must be opened in the state in which the real property is located. This *ancillary probate* is in addition to the primary probate procedure in the decedent's home state. Not only does this create added expense and complexity (an attorney licensed in that state generally must be involved), but the state conducting the ancillary probate may use their state's laws in various dispositive matters, instead of the laws of the decedent's home state. This is a "choice of law" matter beyond the scope of the coverage in this introductory course. Needless to say, opening probate in every state in which the decedent owns real property is, at a minimum, costly and cumbersome.

A revocable living trust, if properly drafted and funded, circumvents the in rem jurisdiction problems associated with out-of-state real property. The trustee is the legal owner of all trust property and has the ability to manage and ultimately distribute the decedent's property in the manner prescribed by the trust document without the need to open ancillary probate. In addition, "choice of law" issues can be avoided be-

---

14. Funding, along with the other requirements to create a valid trust, are covered in detail in Chapter 12.

15. California Probate Code § 18100.5.

cause the trust will be administered using the laws of only one state (the trust document typically identifies the applicable state law and this is usually that of the state in which the decedent was domiciled).

G. Incapacity

1. Managing Assets

With Americans living longer and longer, the potential for incapacity has become a major estate planning issue. In the event that an individual becomes incapacitated and can no longer take care of his or her affairs, and if there has been no advanced planning, a court will appoint a conservator to manage and maintain his or her assets. Laws relating to conservatorship are quite involved and the appointment of a conservator is, in most instances, not the preferred solution to what is a difficult situation.

If an individual's primary testamentary document is a will, a durable power of attorney is typically also executed in order to prevent a conservatorship in the event of incapacity.[16] The maker of a durable power of attorney (also known as the "principal") appoints an agent (also known as the "attorney-in-fact"), to act on the maker's behalf, effectively stepping in to manage the maker's assets when he or she is unable, or unwilling, to do so.

The durable power of attorney for asset management comes in many forms, including, in California, a user-friendly "statutory" durable power of attorney.[17] The scope of financial matters for which the agent/attorney is legally authorized to act is governed by the document. Again, while a complete discussion of the subject is well beyond the scope of this course, a durable power of attorney for asset management can be an extremely important document and one that, generally, is relatively easy to create. It is important to remember that this document, like other documents discussed throughout this book, must be validly executed *before* the time when such a document becomes necessary. If an individual already lacks the capacity to make such a document, then it is too late to do so (and one must go to court for the appointment of a representative).

The durable power of attorney for asset management has, to an increasing degree, been supplanted with the ever-increasing use of revocable living trusts. Revocable living trusts not only work as a "will substitute" for disposition of one's property at his or her death, but they also double as a durable power of attorney-like instrument. The trustee of such a trust has the legal authority to handle and manage trust assets, and if the original maker/settlor (who often also serves as the initial trustee) is unable, or unwilling, to serve, a "successor" trustee steps in to assume such duties (the suc-

---

16. A durable power of attorney for asset management is sometimes called a "financial durable power of attorney."

17. *See* California Probate Code § 4401. The California Continuing Education of the Bar (CEB) publishes a great practitioner's book on the subject—CALIFORNIA POWERS OF ATTORNEY AND HEALTH CARE DIRECTIVES.

cessor trustee typically is named in the trust document). In effect, this third party has the authority, like an agent/attorney-in-fact in a durable power of attorney, to handle legal matters associated with trust assets. Nonetheless, it is prudent, for various reasons, to still have a durable power of attorney for asset management.

2. Health Care Decisions and End-of-Life Instructions

Incapacity can not only affect one's ability to make decisions concerning one's assets, but incapacity can also affect one's ability to make decisions relating to one's health care and end-of-life decisions. Increasingly, good estate planning covers such contingencies. Comprehensive coverage of the subject is beyond the scope of this course, but a quick look at the basics is warranted.

This area of practice deals with some of life's most difficult issues and, sadly, affects most families at some point. A loved one is in a serious state of decline, ravaged by the relentless progression of Alzheimer's disease or some other debilitating medical condition. A family member has been in a terrible accident and now, sadly, is in a persistent vegetative state with little hope of recovery. However difficult it is to even imagine such situations, let alone be touched by them in real life, this is a subject that requires planning. And this planning must be done *before* the debilitating illness or accident.

With respect to the issue of health care and end-of-life instructions, neither a revocable living trust nor a will is equipped to handle such matters. These issues include:

1. Who should make the necessary medical decisions for an individual who is unable to do so for himself or herself? Who should "give the OK" for proceeding with surgery or other medical procedures?

2. What are the individual's thoughts and wishes with respect to end-of-life or "ultimate health decisions"? Does he or she wish to be kept alive at all costs, or is it his or her desire not to prolong life?

Traditionally, the first issue above was handled with a document called a *durable power of attorney for health care.*[18] As with all durable powers of attorney, the maker (called the "principal") appoints an agent (called the "attorney-in-fact"), to act on the maker's behalf. In effect, the appointed representative (agent/attorney-in-fact) acts as a surrogate for the maker, stepping in to make medical decisions when the maker is unable to do so.

The durable power of attorney for health care has, at least in California, become somewhat of a relic—at least as a stand-alone document. With many states adopting the "Uniform Health Care Decision Act" (including California in July 2000), this form of durable power of attorney has been combined with a document typically used for end-of-life, or ultimate health care matters (issue two, above). Historically, one would have executed a durable power of attorney for health care (giving an agent/

---

18. A separate, distinct document from the previously discussed durable power of attorney for asset management.

attorney-in-fact the power to make health care decisions on behalf of the maker/ principal), and a separate document for *end-of-life matters*. The latter has gone by many names, including a "living will" (this does not address property dispositions and is not to be confused with a regular will or revocable living trust), a "directive to physicians," and a health "declaration."

Most states, including California, authorize the use of a document that is commonly known as an "Advanced Health Care Directive." The *advanced health care directive* combines into one form what was the traditional durable power of attorney for health care, and a declaration of one's end-of-life wishes. Thus, an individual can name an agent/attorney-in-fact *and* express his or her end-of-life wishes regarding prolongation (or not) of one's life in a single form.

An advanced health care directive form comes in numerous varieties and covers a wide spectrum, from attorney-prepared documents to ready-to-use pre-printed forms (statutory forms and forms from various organizations, usually related to the medical profession). It is advisable to use a pre-printed advanced health care directive form, preferably one with which doctors/hospitals will be familiar. The time when such a document needs to be used is usually in a time of crisis — typically when time is of the essence — so the last thing a family needs is to have medical personnel not accept the form because they need to have the document approved by their (or a hospital's) legal counsel. In California, the version most widely recognized by those in the medical profession is the *California Medical Association's (CMA) Advanced Health Care Directive*. It comes in "kit" form (instructions, wallet reference card, etc.), available from the California Medical Association. It is relatively easy for most individuals to complete. An attorney is generally unnecessary and, while it may mean some income loss for estate planning attorneys, it is common for them to have a shelf full of these forms that are given to clients at no cost. Clients enjoy getting free forms and legal help from an attorney and, more important, the form can play an invaluable role should the unfortunate situation arise when it needs to be used.

Chapter 12

Trusts: Creation and Revocability

I. Overview

The trust has been called the most flexible legal arrangement there is in the law. It can be used for a plethora of different purposes—so many, in fact, that its flexibility creates problems for many students. Most students start the course with a good conceptual understanding of a will. While they do not know the law of wills, they know that a will is a document that disposes of a decedent's property. Understanding the will's purpose makes it is easier to master the law of wills. In contrast, a trust is such an abstract and amorphous legal arrangement that it can be difficult for some students to wrap their minds around it.

Trusts can run the spectrum from the very simple to the very complex. The best way to get comfortable with the law of trusts, and what a trust is, is to start with a simple trust: a traditional gratuitous private trust (as opposed to a public or charitable trust). A traditional gratuitous private trust is nothing more than another way of making a gift. In fact, the law of trusts evolved out of the law of gifts.

A. Conceptual Understanding

1. Inter Vivos *Gift—Outright Gift*

The traditional paradigm private trust is nothing more than another way of making a gift. Envision the typical gift. One party (the donor) physically hands over an item to another party (the donee) with the intent to make a gift. The gift is completed quickly; upon delivery. The law of gifts reflects the paradigm gift scenario. A valid gift requires intent, delivery, and acceptance. The intent to make a gift is the present intent to relinquish all dominion and control over the property being gifted. Delivery depends on the item being gifted. At common law, if physical delivery was possible or practical, it was the only form of acceptable delivery. If physical delivery was impossible or impracticable, constructive or symbolic delivery was acceptable (no preference between the two).

Constructive delivery is physical delivery of something that would give control over the property being gifted. If the donor wants to gift a car, giving the keys to the car would be a classic example of constructive delivery. The keys give control over the item being gifted—the car.

Symbolic delivery is physical delivery of something that symbolizes the property being gifted. There is overlap between constructive delivery and symbolic delivery. For example, the keys to a car can also constitute symbolic delivery. The keys symbolize the car. The paradigm and most common form of symbolic delivery is a piece of paper. The paper symbolizes the item being gifted. A classic example of symbolic delivery is a deed. If a donor wants to gift Greenacres to a donee, the donor cannot pick up Greenacres and physically hand it over. And technically the donor is gifting title, an abstract bundle of rights that similarly cannot be physically delivered. At early common law, when most people were illiterate, the livery of seisin ceremony constituted symbolic delivery. The grantor would reach down and hand over a piece of dirt or twig from the property. Delivery of the piece of dirt, or the twig, constituted symbolic delivery. As people became more literate, it made more sense and became more common to use the deed as the form of symbolic delivery. But the law was very clear: a deed is not effective until it is delivered. Only delivery of the deed could transfer title.

The final requirement of the law of gifts is acceptance: the donee must accept the property being gifted. If, however, the property is of value, acceptance is presumed. Thus, for all practical purposes, acceptance is a non-issue unless there is reason to assume that a reasonable person would *not* accept the property.

2. Inter Vivos *Gift in Trust*

a. The Trust as a Bifurcated Gift

While most students are comfortable with the concept, and law, of gifts, they are uncomfortable with the concept, and law, of trusts. There are two key differences between a gift and a trust that are critical to mastering what a trust is and the law of trust. First, the typical trust is nothing more than a *bifurcated gift*; and second, the typical trust is nothing more than an *ongoing gift*.

In the gift scenario, there are two parties: the donor and the donee. A gift is a conveyance of a property interest. The donor delivers the property being gifted to the donee—and the gift is completed. Once delivered, the gift is the donee's property. The typical duration of an outright gift is, at most, however long it takes to complete the delivery.

A gift in trust is a bifurcated—or split—gift. First, a trust involves three parties: the settlor, the trustee, and the beneficiary. The settlor (or "trustor") is the donor—the law simply changes the party's name to reflect that this is a gift in trust as opposed to an outright gift. A gift in trust is a bifurcated gift in that the trustee takes legal title to the property being gifted, and the beneficiary takes equitable title to the property. The trust splits the legal and equitable interests in the property being gifted or conveyed.

But what, exactly, does it mean to say that the trustee takes legal title while the beneficiaries take equitable title? The bifurcated nature of a trust is rather abstract, so an example might help. Historically, a classic example of a private, gratuitous trust was a trust for widows or orphans. Back when wives often stayed home and raised the children, some husbands assumed that their wives were not capable of (or, in the alternative, some husbands did not want to burden their wives with task of) managing the husband's accumulated property. Rather than giving the property outright to his surviving spouse, the husband could create a trust. The trustee of the trust would take legal title of the property in question—along with the duty to hold and manage the trust property for the benefit of the beneficiaries: the surviving widow and children. The surviving widow and children would hold the equitable interest in the property—they would have the right to receive and enjoy the property in trust pursuant to the terms of the trust (i.e., the settlor's intent). Conceptually, the trust beneficiaries get all the benefits of the property in the trust with none of the hassles. It is the trustee's job, because he or she holds legal title, to tend to the hassles associated with the property. Thus, a trust is a bifurcated gift in that the donee is bifurcated (split) into the trustee (who holds legal title to the property) and the beneficiaries (who hold the equitable interest in the property).

Second, a gift in trust is a bifurcated gift in that the property being conveyed is bifurcated between the property initially gifted to the trust by the settlor (often referred to as the corpus or res), and the income generated by that property. The income generated by the property conveyed to the trust speaks to the second distinguishing characteristic of the typical gratuitous private trust: that it is an "ongoing" gift. The ongoing nature of a trust is also implicit in the description of the trustee's job: to *hold* and *manage* the trust property. The words "hold" and "manage" implicitly have a temporal component. Unlike the traditional outright gift, which is completed upon delivery, the gift in trust starts with the settlor's delivery of the property to the trustee, but because the trustee has a duty to hold and manage the property for the duration of the trust, the trust is an ongoing gift that continues until the trustee delivers all of the property in the trust to the beneficiaries. So long as there is property in the trust, the trustee has a fiduciary duty to hold and manage the property in the best interests of the beneficiaries. One of the sub-duties inherent in that fiduciary duty is to make the trust property profitable so that it grows (historically, so that it produced income and/ or generated interest). De facto, this meant that there are two types of property in a trust—the original property (called the corpus, res, or principal) and the income.

Third, a gift in trust is a bifurcated gift in that, at the equitable level (the beneficiaries' interest), the equitable interest invariably is split into some combination of possessory estates and future interests. Possessory estates and future interests typically are covered in the first-year Property course. At many law schools, however, Property has been reduced from two semesters to one, and coverage of possessory estates and future interests is one of the parts of the course that has been cut or significantly reduced. If that was the case at your law school, do not worry. All you need to know for this introductory coverage of trusts is the life estate and remainder combination. When we say that someone "owns" a piece of property, there is a temporal component to that ownership. When a person "owns" Greenacres, the law of possessory estates and future interests calls that type of ownership "fee simple absolute." From a temporal perspective, a party who holds property in fee simple absolute has the right to own it forever, but obviously he or she cannot live forever. Instead, holding fee simple absolute means that the party's death does not terminate his or her property interest. He or she can devise the property to whomever he or she wishes, and if there is no will, the party's fee simple absolute interest will pass to his or her heirs (who will then hold fee simple absolute).

The law of possessory estates and future interests governs how property interests can be split over time. That material is beyond the scope of this course, but a sense of it is important. The simplest and most common possessory estate and future interest is a life estate (the possessory estate) and a remainder (the future interest). A simple example will bring that combination to life. Assume a married couple (H and W) with two young children, C and D. Assume H learns that he has terminal cancer. His doctors tell him to get his financial affairs in order. He could execute a will leaving all of his property to his wife (a will typically devises the testator's fee simple absolute to the beneficiaries, each of whom takes a fee simple absolute). Or, the day after learning the news, H could create an *inter vivos* trust, funded with all of his property. At the equitable level, he could stipulate that the trust was for his benefit for the rest of his life (a life estate), then for his wife's benefit for the rest of her life (remainder in life estate), and then upon her death, any remaining property should be distributed outright to his surviving children (remainder in fee simple absolute). Because a trust is an ongoing gift that can last for years, if not decades, invariably the equitable interest is split between some combination of possessory estates and future interests.

Now you should have a better understanding of why some say that a trust is a bifurcated gift: (1) it splits the property being gifted between the trustee, who receives the legal title, and the beneficiaries, who receive the equitable interest; (2) it splits the property into the principal (the corpus or res) and the income generated by the principal over time (because a trust is also an ongoing gift); and (3) it splits the equitable interest into some combination of possessory estates and future interests (typically, a life estate and remainder). There are, however, other ways to conceptualize a trust. For example, a trust can be viewed as nothing more than a legal receptacle (i.e., a legal "bucket"). The trustee holds the bucket. The trustee puts the property in the bucket, but there really are two compartments in the bucket: one for the principal and one for the income. The terms of the trust (the settlor's intent) tell the trustee when he or she can or must reach into the bucket, grab some of the property, and give it to one or more of the beneficiaries. A beneficiary's interest in the trust can be either *mandatory* (if the terms of the trust *require* the trustee to give some of the property to the beneficiary at certain points in time), or *discretionary*. Finally, the beneficiary's interest can be in either the principal, or the income, or both.

With that conceptual understanding of a trust, it is easy to understand how the law of trusts (at least the law that governs the creation of a trust) evolved out of the law of gifts. To have a valid gift there must be intent, delivery, and acceptance—although because acceptance is presumed, one could argue that, for all practical purposes, there are only two requirements: intent and delivery. One can argue that the requirements for a valid trust are no more than the requirements for a valid gift, modified to reflect the fact that a trust is a bifurcated gift.

b. Requirements to Create a Trust

The first requirement to create a trust is intent. While similar to the intent to make an outright gift (in that there must be a present intent to relinquish dominion and control of the property in question), unlike the intent to make an outright gift, here the intent is to make a gift in trust: the intent to transfer the property to a trustee to hold and manage for the benefit of a third party—the beneficiaries. In light of the differences between an outright gift and a gift in trust (a bifurcated gift), the nuanced difference between the intent to make an outright gift and the intent to create a trust should now make sense.

The second requirement to create a trust is delivery. While similar to the delivery requirement for an outright gift in that a property interest must be conveyed, the law of trusts "bifurcates" the delivery into two requirements to reflect the bifurcated nature of the trust. One-half of the bifurcation (the second overall requirement for a valid trust) is that the trust must be funded (i.e., property must be delivered to the trustee). An empty bucket is not a trust. A trust is not created unless and until there is property in the trust for the trustee to hold and manage. So the first delivery requirement for a valid trust is that property must be delivered to the trust/trustee. The second half of the delivery bifurcation becomes the third trust requirement: ascertainable beneficiaries. Because of the bifurcated nature of a trust (i.e., inasmuch as the trustee takes only legal title), we need to know who holds the equitable interest—we need to know who has standing to enforce the terms of the trust against the trustee. The third requirement for a valid trust is that there must be ascertainable beneficiaries (i.e., the court must be able to name the parties that hold the beneficial interest).

Conceptually, one could argue that the requirements for a trust are the same as the requirements for a gift (intent and delivery). That being said, because a gift in trust is a bifurcated gift, the law bifurcates the delivery requirement: it requires delivery of the legal interest to the trustee (funding), and delivery of the equitable interest to the beneficiaries (ascertainable beneficiaries). Some commentators assert that there may be a fourth requirement for a valid trust: it may have to be in writing. A writing requirement, however, may also apply to outright gifts because some outright gifts have to be in writing to be valid. Whether an outright gift must be in writing depends on if it is an *inter vivos* gift (in which case the Statute of Frauds may require it to be in writing) or a testamentary gift (in which case the Wills Act formalities will require it to be in writing). Similarly, whether a trust has to be in writing to be validly created is not really a function of trust law; rather, it is a function of the trust as an *inter vivos* trust holding real property (in which case the Statute of Frauds will require it to be in writing) or a testamentary trust (in which case the Wills Act formalities will require it to be in writing).

Hermann v. Brighton German Bank Co.

16 Ohio N.P. (N.S.) 47 (1914)

OPPENHEIMER, J.

The plaintiff, who is an invalid, resided for some time prior to March 18, 1909, with his sister, Rose B. Boone. On that date Mrs. Boone went to the Brighton German Bank, in this city, and stated to the cashier of that institution that she desired to deposit some money for her brother, who was unable to come to the bank in person. Accordingly a deposit was made in the savings department in the name of "Rose B. Boone for L. P. Hermann," and a bank book was issued in the same name.

....

No money was ever withdrawn from the bank by Mrs. Boone, but additional deposits were made from time to time in the same account, and the interest upon the deposits was permitted to accumulate until, at the time of her death in 1912, the entire deposit aggregated $1,046.77. Upon her death the book was found in the safety deposit box heretofore mentioned, to which plaintiff had access as her deputy, and two other books covering deposits in her own name in other banks were likewise found.

Mrs. Boone left a will in which she made a number of bequests, including one of $1,000 to plaintiff. But her funeral expenses and the expenses incurred in connection with her last illness, together with other debts incurred by her in her lifetime, exceeded the residue of her estate.

....

We are now called upon to determine whether the deposit of the money by Mrs. Boone under the circumstances related operated either as a gift to Louis P. Hermann or as a valid, executed trust in his favor. If it did, then the fund must now be awarded to him; if not, it will pass to the executrix or administrator and become subject primarily to the payment of the debts of Mrs. Boone's estate.

... We shall therefore first consider the essentials of a gift *inter vivos*, and endeavor to ascertain whether, under the circumstances indicated by the testimony, such gift was made in this case.

A gift *inter vivos* is an immediate, voluntary and gratuitous transfer of property by one person to another. To constitute a valid gift, the intention of the donor to make the gift must be clearly and satisfactorily established. *Worthington v. Redkey*, 86 Ohio St. 128 [99 N. E. 211]. But mere intention, however clearly and positively it may be made to appear, is not sufficient. It must be consummated and carried into effect by such acts as are necessary to divest the donor of all right of property in the *res* which is the subject of the gift and to invest the donee therewith. *Worthington v. Redkey, supra; Martin v. Funk*, 75 N. Y., 134; *Wadd v. Hazelton*, 137 N. Y., 215 [33 N. E. 143]. A complete unconditional delivery is essential to the perfection of the gift, but the manner of delivery will, of course, depend upon the character of the thing which is given. The donor must part not merely with the possession, but also with the domination and control of the property, and they must thereafter vest exclusively in the donee. *Flanders v. Blandy*, 45 Ohio St. 108 [12 N. E. 321]; *Harrison Banking Co. v. Miller*, 190 Mo. 640 [89 S. W. 870; 1 L. R. A. (N. S.) 790]. It is not necessary, however, that the property be physically transferred from the possession of the donor to that of the donee. In some instances the property is already in the possession of the donee who holds it as agent for the donor, and in such case it is sufficient that the donor relinquish all domain over the property and recognize the possession of the donee as being in his own right. *Muir v. Gregory*, 158 Fed. 122; 168 Fed. 641; *Allen v. Cowen*, 23 N. Y., 502; *Newman v. Bost*, 122 N. C. 524 [295 S. E. 848]. In other instances the property will remain in the possession of the donor, it being sufficient that he cease to hold in his original character as owner and thereafter hold as representative of the donee. *Yonken v. Hicks*, 93 Ill. App., 667; *Martin v. Funk, supra.* There are still other cases where the delivery will be made, not to the donee himself but to a third person as agent or trustee, for the use of the donee, and under circumstances which unmistakably indicate an intention on the part of the donor to relinquish all right to the control of the property and to vest the present title in the donee.

Moreover the property may be of such a character as to make a manual delivery impossible. If such be the case, a constructive or symbolical delivery is sufficient. *Gano v. Fisk*, 43 Ohio St., 462 [3 N. E. 532; 54 Am. Rep. 819]; *Flanders v. Blandy,* supra. There are some cases which hold that, to perfect either a gift or a trust, the beneficiary must be informed of the donor's intention. *Gerrish v. New Bedford Inst. for Sav.*, 128 Mass., 159 [35 Am. Rep. 365]; *Bartlett v. Remington*, 59 N. H., 364. The weight of authority, however, favors the proposition that knowledge on the part of the beneficiary is not essential to the efficacy of the transfer, and that acceptance of the benefit of the trust will be presumed, because of the fact that ordinarily it is advantageous to him. Thus, it has been said in the case of *Harvey v. Gardner*, 41 Ohio St., 642, 649:

> "In general, any gift by deed, will, or otherwise, is supposed *prima facie*, unless the contrary appears, to be beneficial to the donee. Consequently the law presumes, until there is proof to the contrary, that every gift, whether in trust or not, is accepted by the person to whom it is expressed to be given."

There is a large class of cases which have to do with gifts of bank deposits. Where a donor deposits money in the name of the donee, and delivers to him or to a third person for him, a pass-book therefor, it is manifestly his intention to pass the legal title and control of the fund, and the gift is as complete as it would be if the money were manually transferred to the donee himself. But frequently the intention is not so apparent, and it is then necessary to examine the circumstances very carefully in order to ascertain, if possible, the purpose of the donor.

In the case at bar, plaintiff was, because of his physical afflictions, dependent upon Mrs. Boone. He lived with and was supported by her. She evidently realized that if anything were to happen to her, he would necessarily become a charge upon others, and so she determined to make some provision for him. There can be no doubt that she desired him to benefit by these deposits and that they were set apart for that purpose. The form in which they were made indicates this, as does the fact that she had several bank accounts in her own name in which she might have deposited this money, if she had been content that plaintiff should wait until her death to receive what she might leave him by will. The only doubt arises out of the fact that she retained control over the fund by keeping it in such form as to make it impossible for anyone except herself to draw the money and then placing the book in her own safety deposit box. It seems but natural, however, for her to arrange that only she might draw the money, for she knew that her brother was unable at all times to look after his own affairs. Moreover, she continued to make deposits in the same account, for which purpose it was necessary that she retain the book. Then, too, she may have desired to resume possession of the funds if he himself were to die. *Duffy, In re*, 127 App. Div. 74 [111 N. Y. S. 77], and the retention of the bank book was not in any event conclusive, even if she may be said to have retained it when she placed it in the box to which he had access as her deputy.

After much deliberation, we have reached the conclusion that even if the testimony does not show clearly and unequivocally that the transfer was effective as a gift *inter vivos*, it was nevertheless effective as a voluntary and irrevocable trust created by Mrs. Boone for the use and benefit of plaintiff. The distinction between such gift and trust may be said to be of a purely technical nature. In the case of a gift, the legal title passes to and vests in the donee; while in a trust, the equitable title vests in the *cestui que trust*,[1] while the naked legal title carrying with it the control of the property, rests in the trustee, *Bath Savings Inst. v. Hathorn, supra.* But though the distinction is technical, it is nevertheless recognized by our Supreme Court in the case of *Flanders v. Blandy, supra*, the court quoting (at pages 114–115) with approval from the opinion of the Court of Errors and Appeals of New York in the case of *Young v. Young*, 80 N.Y., 422, 430 [36 Am. Rep. 634], as follows:

> "The transaction is sought to be sustained in two aspects, first, as an actual executed gift, and secondly, as a declaration of trust. These positions are antagonistic to each other, for if a trust was created, the possession of the bonds and the legal title thereto remained in the trustee. In that case there was no delivery to the donee, and consequently no valid executed gift, while if there was a valid gift, the possession and legal title must have been transferred to the donee, and no trust was created."

The word "for" upon the deposit book and card is, in our opinion, equivalent to "trustee for." It unquestionably indicates a fiduciary relationship between the parties or a representation of one by the other. It also indicates beyond a doubt that Mrs. Boone intended, by making the deposit, to renounce her previous unqualified ownership of the money, and to retain the control in a purely representative capacity only.

This view is in accordance with the equitable principle that no particular form of words is necessary to create a trust.

> "It is not essential that a trust should be labeled a trust to make it such legally. The absence of that term is only a circumstance, and often one of very little

---

1. In some of the older opinions this was the Latin term used for the trust beneficiary.

value and influence. There is no stereotyped collection of words for the ed-ification of a trust. In equity there is no idolatry of words. Rights are the principals, remedies the accessories; the democracy of substance is preferred to the tyranny of form; the thing stated is more important than the statement of the thing." *Central Trust Co. v. Burke*, 2 Dec. 96 (1 N. P., 169.)

. . . .

In Hallowell *Sav. Inst. v. Titcomb*, 96 Me. 62 [51 Atl. 638], it is said:

> "The creation of a trust is but a gift of an equitable interest. An unequivocal declaration as effectually passes the equitable title to the *cestui que trust* as delivery does the legal title to the donee of a gift *inter vivos*. One may constitute himself trustee by a mere declaration."

. . . .

We are of the opinion that the fund in this case should be awarded to plaintiff, and a decree may be entered to that effect.

———————

Now that you have a conceptual understanding of a trust, and of the requirements for creating a valid trust, it is time to put the material under the microscope to gain a better appreciation of the issues that can arise with respect to the creation of a trust.

II. Trust Creation

A. Intent to Create a Trust

Inasmuch as the typical trust is a gratuitous trust, a trust is nothing more than an alternative way of making a gift. Not surprisingly, then, one needs to be careful to indicate whether one's intent is to make an outright gift or a gift in trust. If one's intent is unclear, it can lead to needless litigation.

In re Kearns' Estate
225 P.2d 218 (Cal. 1950)

GIBSON, C. J.

This appeal is taken by Marjorie Mallarino and Lois Graham from an order of the probate court which instructed respondent executrix with respect to the interpretation of the holographic will of George A. Kearns, the material portions of which are as follows:

> "1-I hereby bequeath to my beloved and devoted fiance Emma Traung Ham-mersmith of the City and County of San Francisco, California, all my real and personal property and belongings that I possess of are due me of what-soever nature.

"2-I hereby appoint my fiance Emma Traung Hammersmith sole executor of my Estate and to perform such duties without bond.

"3 I hereby bequeath to my brother, William L. Kearns $1.00 also to my niece Mrs. Marjorie Mallarino $1.00 and my niece Mrs. Lois Graham $1.00 and should any or either of them contest this will it shall avail them nothing.

"4 I hereby direct my Executor, Emma Traung Hammersmith to provide for my brother William L. Kearns, during his life and I depend entirely on her judgment, kindness, honesty and generosity to act as his provider in illness and in health.

"5-I hereby direct my Executor Emma Traung Hammersmith to provide for my nieces Mrs. Marjorie Mallarino and Mrs. Lois Graham as her judgment, kindness and honesty sees fit to do, and likewise to provide for any other kin or close friend which in her judgment warrants same."

At the hearing on the petition for instructions, after refusing to admit extrinsic evidence on the ground that the will is not ambiguous, the court instructed the executrix that clause 5 does not create any interest in favor of appellants.

Appellants contend that the provisions of clause 5 are mandatory rather than precatory and create a trust or equitable charge for appellants' benefit. They also argue that the court erred in refusing to admit extrinsic evidence to aid in construing the will. Respondent contends that the will, without ambiguity, shows a clear intent to make an absolute bequest to her and to repose in her an uncontrolled discretion to use the property for her own benefit or to assist others in accordance with the testator's recommendations.

In order to warrant a holding that either a trust or equitable charge was created it must appear that the testator intended to impose mandatory duties upon respondent. It is obvious that clause 1 of the will, standing alone, would operate to bequeath the property to respondent absolutely. On the other hand clause 5 directs respondent to provide for appellants as she sees fit, and the first question to be answered is whether the words used therein limit the estate created in clause 1 and impose enforceable duties on respondent, or whether they merely place her under a moral obligation to provide for appellants.

The authorities all agree that where, as here, an absolute estate has been conveyed in one clause of will, it will not be cut down or limited by subsequent words except such as indicate as clear an intention therefor as was shown by the words creating the estate. *Estate of Marti*, 132 Cal. 666, 672, 61 P. 964, 64 P. 1071. This rule is codified in section 104 of the Probate Code, which provides: "A clear and distinct devise or bequest cannot be affected by any reasons assigned therefor, or by any other words not equally clear and distinct, or by inference or argument from other parts of the will, or by an inaccurate recital of or reference to its contents in another part of the will."

There can be no question that the intention expressed by the testator in clause 5 is not on its face as clear and unequivocal as that shown by the absolute bequest in clause 1. Clause 5 contains language having both mandatory and precatory implications. The expression "I hereby direct" is ordinarily treated as mandatory, but it must not be read out of context, and if it appears from other provisions of a will that the testator intended by the use of the phrase to express only a wish, desire, or recommendation, those words will be treated as precatory rather than mandatory.

In determining whether the intent was to impose a legally enforceable duty or a mere moral obligation, the courts have taken into consideration whether the direction or request is given to an executor or legatee. Where the person addressed is the executor even language which might otherwise be considered as being merely precatory has been treated as being mandatory. On the other hand, under certain circumstances the expression "I direct" has been held to be merely precatory when addressed to a legatee. Where the person directed to carry out the wishes of the testator is both executor and legatee, the courts in construing the effect of the language have refused to follow the strict rule which imposes a mandatory duty on the executor and have apparently treated the words as being addressed to him in his capacity as legatee. In the present case, although clause 5 is directed to "my executor Emma Traung Hammersmith," she is both legatee and executrix, and the term "executor" may not have been used in its technical sense to designate the capacity in which she was to act in exercising her discretion. Words must be construed in conformity with the intention of the testator, and especially where, as here, the will is not drawn by an attorney, that intention should not be defeated by strict adherence to the technical sense of the words used. If the words are repugnant to the clear intention disclosed by the other parts of the instrument, they may be regarded as surplusage or restricted in application.

The question is also presented whether, looking at the whole of clause 5, any implication of a command arising from the opening words is weakened by the remainder of the clause under which respondent is to provide for appellants 'as her judgment, kindness and honesty sees fit to do.' Respondent argues that the broad discretion given to her in clause 5 is inconsistent with an intent to create a trust or equitable charge and in support of her position relies upon the early case of *Lawrence v. Cooke*, 1887, 104 N.Y. 632, 11 N.E. 144. In that case the testator gave the residue of his estate to his daughter and in a separately numbered clause stated: "I enjoin upon her to make such provision for (my) grandchild out of my residuary estate now in her hands, in such manner, at such times, and in such amounts as she may judge to be expedient and conducive to the welfare of said grandchild, and her own sense of justice and Christian duty shall dictate." It was held that no trust was created.

Appellant, on the other hand, relies on *Colton v. Colton*, 127 U.S. 300, 8 S.Ct. 1164, 32 L.Ed. 138, a diversity of citizenship case arising in California, where it was held that a trust was created although the legatee was given broad discretionary power and the words addressed to her were less imperative than those used in *Lawrence v. Cooke, supra*. In the *Colton* case a gift to the wife of all of the testator's property was immediately followed by the provision: "I recommend to her the care and protection of my mother and sister, and request her to make such gift and provision for them as in her judgment will be best." The interpretation of wills, of course, is not a question upon which the federal courts control the state courts, and some California cases have said that since the words addressed to the legatee in the *Colton* will were only recommendatory in character, that decision is out of harmony with the modern rule and does not represent the view of the courts in this state.... The case has also been distinguished upon the ground that, as stressed in the opinion, the bequest there involved was immediately followed by the words which were held to create a trust. *Estate of Marti*, 132 Cal. 666, 670–671, 61 P. 964, 64 P. 1071. An important factor, however, which has apparently been overlooked in cases which criticize the *Colton* decision, is that the court there had before it extrinsic evidence of the circumstances under which the will was made and relied upon such evidence in construing the instrument and holding that a trust was intended.

The cases sometimes reach contrary results in construing similar language, and it is difficult, if not impossible, to harmonize them, although they all agree that the primary object is to ascertain and give effect to the intention of the testator. The differences in result may in many instances be explained by the particular circumstances surrounding the execution of the will.

It appears to be settled in California that if the intention of the testator is to leave the whole subject as a matter of discretion to the good will and pleasure of the legatee, and if his directions are intended as mere moral suggestions to aid that discretion but not absolutely to control or govern it, the language cannot be held to create a trust.... The fact, however, that a legatee is given broad discretionary powers will not defeat a trust if it is clear that one is intended and the terms are sufficiently certain to permit their enforcement. (See *Estate of Davis*, 13 Cal.App.2d 64 [56 P.2d 584]; 25 Cal.Jur. 319.)

It is apparent from the foregoing discussion that clause 5 of the will is not on its face equally as clear as the provision in clause 1, and accordingly, in view of section 104 of the Probate Code, it cannot be said that a trust or equitable charge has been created which would limit the absolute bequest to respondent unless the intent of the testator to do so can be shown by extrinsic evidence. Section 104 must be read with section 105 of the Probate Code which provides that "when an uncertainty arises upon the face of a will, as to the application of any of its provisions, the testator's intention is to be ascertained from the words of the will, taking into view the circumstances under which it was made, excluding ... oral declarations" of the testator as to his intentions. As we have seen there is an uncertainty upon the face of the will as to the application of clause 5, which contains language having both mandatory and precatory implications, and evidence of the circumstances under which the will was made was therefore admissible. In cases involving a similar problem it has been said that the trier of fact may consider such matters as the size of the estate, the property involved in the gift, the circumstances of the parties, and their relation to each other and to the testator.

At the hearing on the petition for instructions the trial judge stated that the will was not ambiguous and that he did not wish to hear any extrinsic evidence. Accordingly, no witnesses were called, but a statement was made of the proof which appellants could produce if permitted to do so. Respondent asserts that some of the evidence which appellants state they could produce is not relevant and that some is incompetent under section 105 of the Probate Code. We need not, however, discuss in detail the different items of proof because it is apparent from the record that respondent objected to the admission of any extrinsic evidence and that it was the purpose of the court to exclude all such evidence. Although the statement made by appellants did not amount to a formal offer of proof, none was necessary since the trial court had declared the will was unambiguous and had clearly intimated that no extrinsic evidence would be received....

The order is reversed.

Notes

1. *Precatory language*: One way to think about the law of gifts is that at one end of the spectrum are outrights gifts, where the donee has no legal duty to use the property in question for the benefit of anyone else, and at the other end of the spectrum are gifts in trust, where the trustee has a legal duty to use the property in question for the benefit of a third party (the trust beneficiaries). While proper drafting can easily distinguish between the two, too often there is sloppy, precatory language included, which muddies the waters. Precatory language is language that expresses the wish or hope that the second party should use the property for the benefit of a third party, but it is unclear whether the language in question rises to the level of imposing a *legal* duty on the second party to use the property in question for the benefit of a third party — i.e., whether the language in question expresses the intent to create a trust as opposed to an outright gift.

2. *Terminology versus intent:* Where a grantor uses any of the official terminology associated with a trust (i.e., "trust," "trustee"), the courts will almost always assume the settlor know what he or she was doing and find an intent to create a trust. There are, however, a handful of exceptions where the court has found no trust even in the presence of trust terminology. *See In re Doescher's Estate*, 217 Cal. App. 2d 104 (1963). The more common terminology versus intent scenario, however, is where the party fails to use any of the traditional trust terminology but creates a scenario where a second party arguably is to hold the property for the benefit of a third party (as was the case in *Kearns' Estate*). Whether such language rises to the level of adequately expressing the intent to create a trust is extremely fact sensitive, and as the court's ruling in *Kearns' Estate* indicates, the courts are not limited to the settlor's language in trying to resolve the ambiguity.

Problems

1. Paragraph 5 of testator's valid will provides as follows:

   I intentionally give all of my property and estate to my said father, H.A. Bolinger, in the event that he shall survive me, and in the event he shall not survive me, I intentionally give all of my property and estate to my step-mother, Marian Bolinger, in the event she shall survive me, and in that event, I intentionally give nothing to my three children, namely: Harry Albert Bolinger, IV, Wyetta Bolinger and Travis Bolinger, or to any children of any child who shall not survive me. I make this provision for the reason that I feel confident that any property which either my father or my step-mother, Marian Bolinger, receive from my estate will be used in the best interests of my said children as my said beneficiaries may determine in their exclusive discretion.

After testator's death, testator's children sued claiming Paragraph 5 conveyed the testator's estate in trust for their benefit. Does Paragraph 5 express the intent to create a trust? *See Matter of Estate of Bolinger*, 943 P.2d 981 (Mont. 1997).

2. Alex Rugo started Rugo Construction Company. When he died, he devised the company to his three sons as follows: Joseph (40%), Guido (40%), and Leonard (20%). Joseph was the President of Rugo Construction, Guido was the Treasurer, and Leonard was the clerk. In 1929 the three brothers agreed to establish a fund "to help out the company" with Guido in charge of it.

    The court found that the brothers had agreed "the money in the fund was to be kept in cash, and controlled and managed by Guido; that ownership was to be 40 per cent each in Guido and Joseph, and 20 per cent in Leonard; that from 1929 on, the brothers made contributions to the fund, and loans were made to the company, which gave notes payable to Guido, that the money belonged to the brothers and not to the company; that from 1929 until November 1, 1945, the total contributions to the fund were $1,145,037, including the profit from stock transactions; and that the fund was controlled, managed, and held by Guido ... for the benefit of the three brothers in the above percentages."

    This arrangement worked well, and the company did well, until the early 1940s when the brothers began to feud. Their disputes included the characterization of the fund of money held by Guido. Joseph and Leonard argued the fund constituted a trust for the benefit of the three brothers in proportion to their ownership of the company. Guido argued that it was a "wage fund" for the company, that it could not be a trust because there was never any writing expressing an intent to form a trust, nor did the brothers ever orally refer to it as such, and that he was merely custodian of it.

    Does Guido hold the fund as trustee of a trust? *See Rugo v. Rugo*, 91 N.E.2d 826 (Mass. 1950).

3. Back in the 1930s and 1940s, it was a Polish tradition that when the minor children began to work and earn money, they would turn the money over to their mother, with such allowance as she wished to give them for spending money—with the understanding that upon marriage, the mother would gift some or all of the money, as she deemed appropriate, back to the child as a wedding gift.

Pelagia and Joseph Wojkowiak had eight children. As each of the children began to earn money, starting at the age of 12 or 13, he or she turned the money made over to their mother. When the first three of the children married, the Wojkowiaks made substantial wedding gifts to each. With the fourth and fifth children (Wallace and Genevieve), however, tensions arose. The sometimes-violent parent-child arguments became so bad that the two children moved out of the house. Subsequently, they sued Pelagia, claiming that when they were 12 and 13, they had entered into an agreement with their mother that if they obtained employment and turned their earnings over to her, she would deduct $5.00 a week for room and board and keep the remainder in trust for their benefit, to be turned over after they reached the age of majority and demanded said funds. Wallace claimed he had turned over $25,000 to his mother over the years; Genevieve claimed she had turned over $11,000. Pelagia denied any such agreement and refused to turn over any money the children had contributed to the family expenses.

Does Pelagia hold the funds transferred to her, in trust, for the benefit of the respective children? *See Wojtkowiak v. Wojtkowiak*, 85 N.Y.S.2d 198 (1947).

B. Trust Funding

Funding requires that the property interest in question be transferred to the trust/trustee. Assuming a gratuitous trust, funding means that the property is being gifted to the trust. Gifting requires the property to be delivered. What constitutes delivery depends on the type of property in question. Delivery is an interesting mix of intent, act, and formalities.

1. Third Party as Trustee

Uber v. Hoffmann

No. D037208, 2002 WL 199735 (Cal. Ct. App. Feb. 8, 2002)

McCONNELL, J.

This trust proceeding arises from defendant Horst W. Hoffmann's attempts to satisfy a judgment he obtained against Lloyd D. Uber in an underlying action. Hoffmann appeals a judgment for plaintiff Gordon T. Uber, trustee of the Alma Goettsche Uber Trust (the trust), and an order denying his motion for a new trial. Hoffmann contends the court erred by determining the trust is valid, all real and personal property of the trustor was transferred to the trust and Lloyd disclaimed his beneficial interest in the assets of the trust. We agree that stock certificates not endorsed by Alma, or by Lloyd as her attorney-in-fact during her lifetime, were not properly transferred to the trust. We reverse the judgment insofar as it concerns the stock certificates and affirm it in all other respects. We affirm the order denying the motion for a new trial.

FACTUAL AND PROCEDURAL BACKGROUND

On July 24, 1986, Alma executed a revocable living trust naming her sons, Gordon and Lloyd, as beneficiaries. The trust stated that its assets included real properties on Sterne Street and Tecumseh Way in San Diego County, as described in Exhibit A, and "any other property, real, personal or mixed" that Alma transferred to Lloyd as trustee. On Alma's death the trust assets were to be distributed as follows: a diamond and gold ring to Lloyd, the Tecumseh Way property to Gordon and the balance of assets in equal shares to Gordon and Lloyd. On the same date, Alma signed a will and a durable power of attorney designating Lloyd as her attorney-in-fact to manage her real and personal property.

On May 2, 1989, Lloyd was named conservator of Alma because of her incompetency. On May 29, 1989, he signed a document disclaiming "any interest" in the trust estate. On the same date, he signed deeds as Alma's attorney-in-fact, quitclaiming her interest in the Sterne Street and Tecumseh Way properties to him as trustee. The deeds were recorded on June 21, 1989.

Alma died in May 1995. Her will was not filed and no probate proceeding was commenced.

On July 2, 1996, Lloyd, as trustee, signed deeds quitclaiming the Sterne Street and Tecumseh Way properties to Gordon. The deeds were recorded on August 28, 1996.

In 1993 Hoffmann obtained a default judgment of $110,792.57 against Lloyd, a former attorney, in a malpractice action....

. . .

A trial was held in May 2000. Hoffmann's theory was that the trust was invalid because it was not properly funded....

The court determined the trust was valid, all of Alma's assets were transferred to the trust and Lloyd effectively disclaimed his interest in the trust. Judgment for Gordon was entered on September 14, 2000....

. . .

Validity of Trust and Trust Res

A

"An express trust is generally created in one of two ways: (1) a *declaration of trust,* by which the owner of property declares that he [or she] holds it as trustee for some beneficiary; (2) a *transfer in trust,* by which the owner transfers to another as trustee for some beneficiary, either by *deed* or other transfer *inter vivos,* or by will. [Citations.]" (11 Witkin, Summary of Cal. Law (9th ed. 1990) Trusts, §26, p. 911; Prob.Code, §15200.) The essential elements of a trust are the "intention of the settlor to create a trust, trust property, a lawful trust purpose, and an identifiable beneficiary. [Citations.]" (*Chang v. Redding Bank of Commerce* (1994) 29 Cal.App.4th 673, 684, 35 Cal.Rptr.2d 64; Prob.Code, §§15201–15205.) The term "'[p]roperty' means anything that may be the subject of ownership and includes both real and personal property and any interest therein."(Prob.Code, §62.)

When the trustee is a third party, rather than the settlor, as here, property must be transferred to the trustee to be considered trust property. (*Osswald v. Anderson* (1996) 49 Cal.App.4th 812, 820, 57 Cal.Rptr.2d 23.) "If a transfer to a trust is invalid, the legal title to the property remains in the grantor." (*Ibid.*) "[O]nly assets that have been transferred to the trust during the settlors' lifetimes will benefit from the advantages of a revocable trust, *e.g.*, probate avoidance." (Cohan, Drafting California Revocable Living Trusts (Cont.Ed.Bar 3d ed.1995), § 21.2, p. 581.)

...

Lloyd testified that he prepared the trust and at the time of its execution Alma intended to transfer "[e]verything that she had" to it. Lloyd also testified that "[s]hortly after the formation of the trust," or at the latest within 60 days of its execution, he took physical possession of Alma's diamond and gold ring, "household contents and personal effects," checking and savings accounts and two stock certificates for 100 shares each of The Price Company stock that Alma purchased in the mid-1980's. Lloyd also said that within 30 days of the trust's execution he opened a trust checking account. Further, he explained that immediately on the trust's execution he began receiving, as trustee, rent from Alma's properties. He used the funds to pay her health care and other living expenses, and beginning in 1989 the expenses of a series of in-house convalescent facilities. Lloyd had no written records to support his testimony, but it was uncontradicted.

Personal property can ordinarily be transferred by delivery, actual or constructive. (*Wheelon v. Patco, Inc.* (1968) 258 Cal.App.2d 71, 74, 65 Cal.Rptr. 533.) For instance, in *Logan v. Ryan* (1924) 68 Cal.App. 448, 454, 456–457, 229 P. 993, the court held that jewelry the settlor physically delivered to the trustee became property of the trust. Moreover, "a trust may be a valid instrument when funded by minimal sums (*e.g.*, $100)." (Cohan, Drafting California Revocable Living Trusts, *supra*, § 21.2, p. 581.)

... We conclude the trust was implemented by Alma's actual delivery of her diamond and gold ring and other tangible personal property to Lloyd as trustee.

B

Hoffmann contends the two certificates for The Price Company stock, which remained in Alma's name at her death, were not properly transferred to the trust and are thus not assets of the trust. He relies on California Uniform Commercial Code sections 8401 through 8407, which govern the transfer and registration of securities held in certificate form. (Cohan, Drafting California Revocable Living Trusts, *supra*, § 21.18, p. 609.) Section 8401 provides in part: "(a) If a certificated security in registered form is presented to an issuer with a request to register [a] transfer..., the issuer shall register the transfer as requested if the following conditions are met. [¶] ... [¶] (2) The endorsement ... is made by the *appropriate person* or by an agent who has actual authority to act on behalf of the appropriate person." (Italics added.) Stock certificates may also be transferred by an assignment separate from the certificate. (*Ibid;* § 8402, subd. (a)(1); *Martinez v. Dempsey-Tegeler & Co., Inc.* (1974) 37 Cal.App.3d 509, 511, 112 Cal.Rptr. 414.)

An "appropriate person" for endorsing a stock certificate is defined in section 8107. "The person's status as to appropriateness is determined as of the date the endorsement is made." (2 California Decedent Estate Practice (Cont.Ed.Bar 2001) § 21.5, p. 21-5; § 8107, subd. (e).) "For purposes of transferring securities after a death, the personal representative of the decedent or the decedent's successor taking under other law (e.g., surviving joint tenant) or an authorized agent of either is an appropriate person to endorse a security." (2 California Decedent Estate Practice, *supra*, § 21.5, p. 21-5; § 8107, subd. (a)(4).) "If securities are registered in the name of an individual and the individual dies, the law of decedent's estates determines who has the power to transfer the decedent's securities. That would ordinarily be the executor or administrator." (Ca. U. Com.Code com., 23C West's Ann. Ca. U. Com.Code (2002 supp.) foll. § 8107, p. 21.)

The trial court found the stock certificates were effectively transferred to the trust by mere physical delivery, because Lloyd had a durable power of attorney authorizing him to "buy, sell, endorse, transfer, hypothecate, and borrow against any shares of stock, bonds, or other securities defined as such under California law." We agree that Alma's intent to include the stock certificates in the trust is evidenced by their physical delivery to Lloyd in conjunction with the durable power of attorney. However, that does not resolve the issue of whether the stock certificates were properly transferred to the trust. As Gordon concedes, Lloyd's authority as attorney-in-fact terminated on Alma's death. (Prob.Code, § 4152, subd. (a)(4).)

In his respondent's brief, Gordon cites no authority for the proposition that stock certificates can be effectively transferred to a trust absent compliance with the California Uniform Commercial Code....

We decline to accept Gordon's unsupported position that compliance with the formalities of the California Uniform Commercial Code is not required to transfer stock certificates to a trust. We conclude that because no endorsement of the certificates was made during Alma's lifetime, the purported transfer to the trust was ineffective.

C

We reject Hoffmann's contention that the transfer of the Sterne Street and Tecumseh Way properties to the trust was ineffective because Lloyd did not execute quit claim deeds until after Alma was declared incompetent and placed under a conservatorship....

Under Probate Code section 15206, the applicable statute of frauds, "[a] trust in relation to real property is not valid unless evidenced by one of the following methods: [¶] (a) By a written instrument signed by the trustee, or by the trustee's agent if authorized in writing to do so. [¶] (b) By a written instrument conveying the trust property signed by the settlor, or the settlor's agent if authorized in writing to do so." Exhibit A to the trust expressly described the Sterne Street and Tecumseh Way properties, and Lloyd, as Alma's attorney-in-fact, quitclaimed her interest in the properties to himself as trustee. "All acts done by an attorney-in-fact pursuant to a durable power of attorney during any period of incapacity of the principal have the same effect ... as if the principal had capacity." (Prob.Code, § 4125.) Accordingly, an *inter vivos* transfer of the real properties to the trust was accomplished. (See *Reagh v. Kelley* (1970) 10 Cal.App.3d 1082, 1094, 89 Cal.Rptr. 425.)

...

DISPOSITION

The judgment is reversed insofar as it determines the two stock certificates for The Price Company stock are assets of the trust. In all other respects, the judgment is affirmed....

Note

Adequate property interest: The general rule is that a trust is not created until it is funded (i.e., until some property has been transferred to the trust/trustee). Virtually any property interest will qualify as an adequate property interest. As the court noted in *Uber*, "[t]he term '[p]roperty' means anything that may be the subject of ownership and includes both real and personal property and any interest therein." (Prob. Code § 62.) Virtually anything you can think of when you think of property qualifies as an adequate property interest such that if transferred to a trustee, it would fund the trust. The courts, however, have recognized two types of interests that are *not* property interests for purposes of funding a trust: (1) an expectancy, and (2) future profits. *See Brainard v. Comm'r of Internal Revenue*, 91 F.2d 880 (7th Cir. 1937) (holding that future profits did not constitute an adequate property interest for purposes of a gift in trust). *But see In re Pascal's Will*, 182 N.Y.S.2d 927 (1959) (holding that future profits constituted an adequate property interest for purposes of an outright gift).

2. Settlor as Trustee

Where the settlor and the trustee are two different people, what constitutes delivery is analogous to what constitutes delivery for purposes of an outright gift. Moreover, it is fairly easy to visualize what constitutes delivery where the two parties are different: either the item itself or something that legally qualifies as the item (symbolic or constructive delivery) must pass from one party to the other.

Where the settlor and the trustee are the same person, however, what constitutes delivery becomes a much more difficult issue. Does it make sense to require someone to transfer something from himself or herself to himself or herself? What constitutes a "transfer" where the same party is on both sides of the transfer? Should the party have to use a "straw party" to fulfill the transfer/delivery requirement? What if the person throws it up in the air and catches it? Has the item been "delivered"?

The courts have struggled with the issue over time. The following case is the seminal California decision on funding an *inter vivos* trust, and it is fairly representative of the modern trend approach (so should you expect more of a focus on formalities or intent?).

Estate of Heggstad

16 Cal. App. 4th 943 (1993)

PHELAN, Associate Justice.

...

On May 10, 1989, decedent Halvard L. Heggstad ... executed a valid revocable living trust, naming himself as the trustee and his son Glen, the successor trustee (hereafter the Heggstad Family Trust). All the trust property was identified in a document titled schedule A, which was attached to the trust document. The property at issue was listed as item No. 5 on schedule A, and was mislabeled as "Partnership interest in 100 Independence Drive, Menlo Park, California."

... This property remained in decedent's name, as an unmarried man, and there was no grant deed reconveying this property to himself as trustee of the revocable living trust. Both sides agree that decedent had formally transferred by separate deeds, all the other real property listed in Schedule A to himself as trustee of the Heggstad Family Trust.

About one month after executing these documents, the decedent married appellant Nancy Rhodes Heggstad. She was not provided for in either the will or the trust documents, and all parties agree that she is entitled to one-third of the decedent's estate (her intestate share) as an omitted spouse pursuant to Probate Code section 6560. She takes nothing under the terms of the trust and makes no claim thereto.

Decedent died on October 20, 1990, and his son was duly appointed executor of his estate and became successor trustee under the terms of the Heggstad Family Trust....

During the probate of the will, Glen, the successor trustee, petitioned the court for instructions regarding the disposition of the 100 Independence Drive property. The trustee claimed that the trust language was sufficient to create a trust in the subject property and that the property was not part of his father's estate.

In pertinent part, article 1 of the trust provided: "HALVARD L. HEGGSTAD, called the settlor or the trustee, depending on the context, declares that he has set aside and transfers to HALVARD L. HEGGSTAD in trust, as trustee, the property described in schedule A attached to this instrument."

...

To create an express trust there must be a competent trustor, trust intent, trust property, trust purpose, and a beneficiary. (Prob.Code, §§ 15201–15205; *Walton v. City of Red Bluff* (1991) 2 Cal.App.4th 117, 124, 3 Cal.Rptr.2d 275.) The settlor can manifest his intention to create a trust in his property either by: (a) declaring himself trustee of the property or (b) by transferring the property to another as trustee for some other person, by deed or other *inter vivos* transfer or by will. (11 Witkin, Summary Cal. Law (9th ed. 1990) Trusts, § 26, p. 911; see also *Getty v. Getty* (1972) 28 Cal.App.3d 996, 1003, 105 Cal.Rptr. 259 ["An *inter vivos* trust can be created either by agreement or by a unilateral declaration of the person who assumes to act as trustee." (Emphasis in original.)].)

These two methods for creating a trust are codified in Probate Code section 15200: "(a) A declaration by the owner of property that the owner holds the property as trustee," and "(b) A transfer of property by the owner during the owner's lifetime to another person as trustee." (§ 15200; see also Rest.2nd Trusts, § 17.)

Where the trust property is real estate, the statute of frauds requires that the declaration of trust must be in writing signed by the trustee. (§ 15206; accord Rest.2d, Trusts, § 40, com. b, at p. 105.) Here, the written document declaring a trust in the property described in Schedule A was signed by the decedent at the time he made the declaration and constitutes a proper manifestation of his intent to create a trust. Contrary to appellant's assertion, there is no requirement that the settlor/trustee execute a separate writing conveying the property to the trust. A review of pertinent sections of the Restatement Second of Trusts, illustrates our point. This consideration is particularly appropriate, since the Law Revision Commission Comment to section 15200 indicates: "This section is drawn from section 17 of the Restatement (Second) of Trusts (1957)." (Deering's 1991 Probate Code Special Pamphlet, p. 963.)

Section 17 of the Restatement provides that a trust may be created by "(a) a declaration by the owner of property that he holds it as trustee for another person; or [¶] (b) a transfer *inter vivos* by the owner of property to another person as trustee for the transferor or for a third person...." The comment to clause (a) states: "If the owner of property declares himself trustee of the property, a trust may be created without a transfer of title to the property." (*Ibid.*)

Illustration "1" of that same section is instructive. It reads: "A, the owner of a bond, declares himself trustee of the bond for designated beneficiaries. A is the trustee of the bond for the beneficiaries. [¶] So also, the owner of property can create a trust by executing an instrument conveying the property to himself as trustee. In such a case there is not in fact a transfer of legal title to the property, since he already has legal title to it, *but the instrument is as effective as if he had simply declared himself trustee.*" (Emphasis added.)

Section 28 of the Restatement announces the rule that no consideration is necessary to create a trust by declaration. This rule applies both to personal and real property, and it also supports our conclusion that a declaration of trust does not require a grant deed transfer of real property to the trust. Illustration "6" provides: "A, the owner of Blackacre, in an instrument signed by him, gratuitously and without a recital of consideration declares that he holds Blackacre in trust for B and his heirs. B is not related to A by blood or marriage. A is trustee of Blackacre for B."

More directly, comment m to section 32 (Conveyance *Inter vivos* in Trust for a Third Person) provides in pertinent part: "*Declaration of trust. If the owner of property declares himself trustee of the property a transfer of the property is neither necessary nor appropriate....*" (Second emphasis added.)

Additionally, comment b to section 40 (statute of frauds) establishes that a written declaration of trust, by itself, is sufficient to create a trust in the property. Comment b states: "*Methods of creation of trust.* The Statute of Frauds is applicable whether a trust of an interest in land is created *by the owner's declaring himself trustee,* or by a transfer by him to another in trust." (Second emphasis added.)

Finally, Bogert, in his treatise on trusts and trustees observes: "Declaration of Trust [¶] It is sometimes stated that the transfer by the settlor of a legal title to the trustee is an essential to the creation of an express trust. The statement is inaccurate in one respect. Obviously, if the trust is to be created by declaration there is no real transfer of any property interest to a trustee. The settlor holds a property interest before the trust declaration, and after the declaration he holds a bare legal interest in the same property interest with the equitable or beneficial interest in the beneficiary. No new property interest has passed to the trustee. The settlor has merely remained the owner of part of what he formerly owned." (Bogert, Trusts and Trustees (2d ed. rev. 1977) § 141, pp. 2–3, fn. omitted.)

These authorities provide abundant support for our conclusion that a written declaration of trust by the owner of real property, in which he names himself trustee, is sufficient to create a trust in that property, and that the law does not require a separate deed transferring the property to the trust.

. . .

The probate court's order declaring that the property identified as "100 Independence Way, Menlo Park, San Mateo County," is included in the living trust is affirmed.

Notes

1. *Real property formalities:* Although the court in *Heggstad* facilitated the funding of self-settled trusts, there are still some formalities with which the settlor should comply. In *Garatie-Symons v. Levenson*, No. B203156, 2009 WL 258102 (Cal. Ct. App. Aug. 24, 2009), the decedent hired an attorney to prepare an *inter vivos* trust, a will with a pour-over clause leaving the probate property to the trust, and a general assignment instrument assigning all of his property to the trust. His property included two pieces of real property he inherited when his mother died: the Canoga Park parcel and the California City parcel. The decedent signed the declaration of trust and the assignment but not the will.

Following his death, the decedent's widow filed a "*Heggstad* petition" to confirm that the two parcels of real property were part of the trust res based on the general assignment. The court, however, distinguished *Heggstad*, noting that in the case at bar, there was no asset schedule describing the Canoga Park and California City properties as part of the trust. The declaration of trust simply recited that it was being funded with $100 and left open additional funding by will or other instrument of transfer. While the general assignment constituted an instrument of transfer, it simply recited that it was assigning the husband's "property." No attempt was made to describe the property being transferred. Both the trial court and the court of appeals ruled that notwithstanding *Heggstad*, "the statute of frauds ... requires that an express trust of real property not only be in writing but describe the real property so that it can be identified with reasonable certainty."

While the opinion is unpublished, both the trial court and the court of appeal agreed that even where the settlor is the trustee, for real property to be transferred to the trust, either the declaration of trust or the general assignment must include a reasonable description of the real property the settlor intends to transfer to the trust. A generic reference to the settlor's property in a general assignment is not good enough. Moreover, the court declined to be swayed by appeals to the decedent's clear intent to include the parcels as evidenced by his overall testamentary intent. The court also rejected his widow's argument that parol evidence should be admissible to provide the missing description.

2. *Asset-specific formalities:* Using a general blanket assignment to transfer assets to an *inter vivos* trust can be risky. In *In re Brown*, No. O.C.NO.1435 IV, 2005 WL 3753142 (Pa. Com. Pl. Dec. 29, 2005), the decedent executed a blanket assignment that purported to transfer all of her extensive property holdings to her *inter vivos* trust: (1) tangible personal property (including the furnishings in her house and two cars); (2) intangible personal property (four bank accounts); (3) two real estate parcels; and (4) several nonprobate assets (three life insurance policies and three retirement accounts). After her death, her children (parties of interest under her estate) conceded that the blanket assignment validly transferred the decedent's household furnishings, but challenged the validity of all the other purported transfers.

The court ruled that the blanket assignment was valid with respect to the cars only if the certificate of title to each car was in her name alone (the state of the titles with respect to the cars was unclear). As to the bank accounts, those that were in joint names with her children were presumed to be joint accounts with right of survivorship and the general assignment was not deemed to overcome that presumption as neither the decedent nor the trustee made any attempt to change the joint accounts while she was still alive. As to the other accounts in her name alone, each banking institution had procedures that governed how accounts were to be changed. Inasmuch as neither the decedent nor the trustee made any attempt to change the accounts *inter vivos* in accordance with the bank's procedures, the court ruled the blanket assignment did not deliver the accounts in question to the trust *inter vivos*. As to her real property, the court ruled that the blanket assignment's express reference to "all of her right, title and interest in and to assets of every kind, including but not limited to real property...." was a sufficient description to constitute delivery of the real property she owned to the trust. With respect to the life insurance policies, again there was no evidence that either the decedent or the trustee made any attempt to contact the insurance companies *inter vivos* to initiate the process of executing the necessary change of beneficiary forms. The decedent's retirement accounts had similar provisions requiring change of beneficiary forms to be delivered to the company before any change of beneficiary would be valid, and again, the decedent's and the trustee's failure to even attempt to comply with the applicable change of beneficiary procedures *inter vivos* meant the assets had not been delivered *inter vivos* to the trust.

In *Kucher v. Kucher*, 192 Cal. App. 4th 90 (2011), the California Court of Appeal had an opportunity to analyze whether a general assignment should be deemed effective to transfer the settlor's real property and stock holdings. As to the real property, the court ruled: "The General Assignment was ineffective to transfer the Trustor's real property to the Trust. To satisfy the statute of frauds, the General Assignment was required to describe the real property so that it could be identified." *Id.* at 691–92. As to the stock, the court ruled: "The statute of frauds does not apply to such a transfer. (Civ.Code, § 1624.) There is no California authority invalidating a transfer of shares of stock to a trust because a general assignment of personal property did not identify the shares. Nor should there be." *Id.* at 692. *But see Ukkestad v. RBS Asset Finance, Inc.*, 235 Cal. App. 4th 156 (2015) (holding the express language in a revocation trust that the settlor was conveying "all his real and personal property" to himself, as trustee, notwithstanding the absence of any additional description of the two parcels of real estate which settlor owned and the absence of any separate writing conveying the parcels to the trust).

Problems

1. Mabee owns two parcels of real estate: (1) 1025 East Bobier Drive, in Vista, California; and (2) 80501 Avenue 48, Space 114, in Indio, California. Mabee validly executes in writing an *inter vivos* trust instrument that appoints him trustee and that declares that he transfers "all his personal and real property" to the trust. The trust otherwise makes no express reference to either parcel of real property nor does he execute any other instrument that purports to transfer either parcel to the trust. Has Mabee's personal property been properly transferred to the trust? Have the parcels of real estate been validly transferred to the trust? *See Ukkestad v. RBS Asset Finance, Inc.*, 235 Cal. App. 4th 156 (2015); *Kucher v. Kucher*, 192 Cal. App. 4th 90 (2011).

2. Gala Gerber validly executed a trust that appointed her son, Forest, trustee. Paragraphs II and V of the trust provide as follows:

    "II. FUNDING OF TRUST. This Trust shall be funded with assets transferred to this Trust by the Grantor at the time of creating this Trust, *or at any later time*....

    "V. DEATH OF THE GRANTOR. Upon the death of the Grantor, and after the payment of the Grantor's just debts, funeral expenses, and expenses of last illness, the following distributions shall be made: [¶] *A. Specific Distributions*. The following specific distributions shall be made from the assets of the Trust. [¶] 1. *4535 Bellflower Boulevard, Long Beach, CA. 90808. Tract Number, 19989 Lot Number 6* shall be distributed to Forest Randal Gerber and Thelma Sue Tutorow (nee Gerber)...."

    The trust makes no other reference to the real property. Thereafter Gala executed a deed that purported to transfer the Long Beach real property to her friend, Daisy. Thereafter Gala died testate, with a will devising all her property to the trustee of her trust, to hold and distribute pursuant to the terms of her trust.

Has the Long Beach real property been properly transferred to the trust? *See Tutorow v. Gerber*, No. B155752, 2002 WL 984777 (Cal. Ct. App. 2002).

C. Ascertainable Beneficiaries

It is often said that a trust is a bifurcated gift: legal title is transferred to the trustee, and the equitable interest is transferred to the beneficiaries. While at first blush that wording implies that some *thing* should be delivered to the beneficiaries to constitute symbolic or constructive delivery of their equitable interest, nothing could be further from the truth. Instead, the common law courts decided that so long as it could identify to whom the equitable interests had been transferred, that was sufficient.

No separate delivery of anything is needed; all that is needed is that the beneficiaries be ascertainable. That obviously begs the question: what constitutes ascertainable?

1. *"Ascertainable"*

Armington v. Meyer

236 A.2d 450 (R.I. 1967)

PAOLINO, Justice.

..

I. Pertinent Provisions of the Will

Simon W. Wardwell, hereinafter referred to as the "testator," died in Providence on February 19, 1921.... Under the Tenth paragraph of his will he left his entire estate to four persons named therein as trustees under the trust established therein for the benefit of certain persons or classes of persons, during their respective lives....

The testator provided for the distribution of up to $50,000 of the annual net income from the trust estate in specified amounts among (1) his wife and after her death to one of her brothers and three daughters of another brother; (2) testator's sisters and brother and after their respective deaths to their daughters and granddaughters; and (3) his trustees. Paragraph Tenth disposes of annual net income in excess of $50,000 according to the following provision:

> "That all net income in excess of fifty thousand dollars ($50,000.00) be administered in trust and distributed by my trustee (sic) aforesaid at their discretion and will for the benefit of all aforesaid persons and for any and all men and women among my employees and acquaintances known to my said trustees to have been loyal to me and my inventions during the hard, up-hill struggle to establish my Wardwell Braiding Machine business."

...

V. The Questions

...

We consider next the question whether the provision in clause Tenth providing for the distribution of income among the "employees and acquaintances" of the testator is void for indefiniteness and uncertainty. It appears from an affidavit executed on July 27, 1966, by Arthur A. Armington, the sole surviving original trustee, that he knew of only two former employees who were living in 1965 who were loyal to the testator and his inventions during the period in question, namely, Louis Shulver and Lucien Jules Geoffroy. The pertinent language of the clause in question reads as follows:

> "That all net income in excess of fifty thousand dollars ($50,000.00) be administered in trust and distributed by my trustee (sic) aforesaid at their discretion and will * * * for any and all men and women among my employees and acquaintances known to my said trustees to have been loyal to me and my inventions during the hard, up-hill struggle to establish my Wardwell Braiding Machine business."

The general rule is that in order to create a valid private trust, the instrument must set forth the person or class of persons who will be the beneficiaries thereunder, and in the absence of a definite and ascertainable beneficiary or class of beneficiaries, adequately described, the trust will be void for uncertainty. Bogert, Trusts (2d ed.), §§ 161, 162; 2 Scott, Trusts (2d ed.), §§ 112, 120, 122; 1 Restatement, Trusts 2d, §§ 112, 120, 122. See also *Gunn v. Wagner*, 242 Iowa 1001, 48 N.W.2d 292.

Employees and acquaintances known by the testator's trustees to have been loyal to him and his inventions do not constitute a definite and ascertainable class of beneficiaries capable of taking under the trust. 'Loyal' is a word of broad application. We have no way of determining what the testator meant when he used this word.

We conclude, therefore, that a sufficient criterion has not been furnished to the trustees or the court to govern the selection of individuals from amongst the testator's employees and acquaintances. See *Clark v. Campbell*, 82 N.H. 281, 133 A. 166, 45 A.L.R. 1433. In that case a gift by the testator to his trustees to be disposed of among "such of my friends as they * * * shall select" was declared void for this very reason. See also *Murdock v. Bridges*, 91 Me. 124, 39 A. 475, where the court refused to enforce a provision in a will which directed the testator's trustee to distribute his property to those people the trustee felt cared for the testator. Compare *Early v. Arnold*, 119 Va. 500, 89 S.E. 900. It follows that an attempted gift to employees and acquaintances under the clause in question is void for vagueness and indefiniteness.

...

Notes

1. *General rule:* The Court in *Armington* correctly states the general rule: for an express private trust there must be definite and ascertainable beneficiaries. As a practical matter that means the trust must either name the beneficiaries or contain a formula or class description that permits them to be objectively ascertainable ("made

capable of identification by the terms of the instrument creating the trust"). *Young v. Redmon's Trustee*, 300 Ky. 418, 421 (1945). As the court in *Meyer* states, gifts to "my employees and acquaintances known to my said trustees to have been loyal to me" and gifts to "my friends" are too subjective—they are not capable of identification from the terms of the instrument. What about gifts to "my heirs" or "my relatives"?

2. *Exceptions:* Despite the apparent absolute wording of the requirement, the courts have created exceptions to it. The first is for unborn children (or grandchildren). A settlor may create an *inter vivos* trust for his or her unborn children; a testator's will may create a testamentary trust for unborn grandchildren. As long as it is possible that a qualifying beneficiary may be born, the trust is valid and the courts will uphold the trust (for as long as permitted under the rule against perpetuities or until it is clear the possibility cannot materialize). If a qualifying beneficiary is not born, the courts will impose a resulting trust and order the property distributed back to the settlor's estate. A "not-yet-created" corporation is analogous to an unborn child in that a trust created for it would be upheld for a period of time as permitted under the rule against perpetuities. *See* RESTATEMENT (THIRD) OF TRUSTS § 44 (comment c) (2003).

Problems

1. Settlor executed a valid will that contains a testamentary trust. The dispositive provision of the trust provided as follows:

   > I direct my Trustee to distribute all of my estate according to my instructions which I may give to him from time to time in my own handwriting or otherwise, but nonetheless signed or initialed by me. In the event, by whatever circumstance, I fail to leave such instructions to my Trustee, then I direct my Trustee to distribute my estate according to his discretion, bearing in mind the many conversations we have had together in which I have named those who are the objects of my generosity.

   Assuming settlor gives the trustee no further instructions, are the beneficiaries ascertainable? *See In re Estate of Boyer*, 868 P.2d 1299 (N.M. Ct. App. 1994).

2. Settlor executed an *inter vivos* trust. The dispositive provision of the trust provided as follows:

   > A. During the lifetime of the Grantor, the Trustee shall manage the trust property and shall make distributions of income and principal in accord with the provisions of this Trust for the benefit of the Grantor. After Grantor's death, the Trustee shall manage the trust property and shall make distributions of income and principal in accord with the provisions of this Trust for the benefit of Grantor's children and the natural born children of Grantor's children, *and others as the Trustee in his discretion may deem appropriate.*

   Following the settlor's death, the takers under the residuary clause in settlor's will challenged the validity of the trust on the grounds that the trust beneficiaries are not ascertainable. Are they? *See Kunce v. Robinson*, 469 So. 2d 874 (Fla. Dist. Ct. App. 1985).

2. *Honorary Trusts—Noncharitable Purpose Trusts*
In re Voorhis' Estate
27 N.Y.S.2d 818 (1941)

DELEHANTY, Surrogate.

Deceased died in 1922 leaving a will which named Arthur J. Martin as executor and trustee. Mr. Martin died in November, 1924. Thereafter Samuel W. Maguire was appointed successor trustee. By separate order he was appointed to administer the trust created by the twenty-fourth paragraph of deceased's will. The text of this paragraph and that of the twenty-fifth paragraph, which is pertinent thereto, follows:

> "Twenty-fourth: I give and bequeath to my said trustee the sum of Ten thousand Dollars, to be used by him to place a memorial window, or some other memorials, to cost any sum in his discretion up to the sum of One thousand Dollars, in Christ Church Cathedral, at St. Louis, Mo., and to place monuments and markers in my family subdivision of the Clark and Glasgow plot in the Bellefontaine Cemetery, at St. Louis, Mo.

> "Twenty-fifth: I give and bequeath to Bellefontaine Cemetery Association of St. Louis, the sum of Four thousand Dollars, in trust, for the perpetual endowment care and maintenance of my family subdivision of the Clark and Glasgow plot in the Bellefontaine Cemetery, at St. Louis, Mo., according to the rules and regulations of said Association. Such interest as may be allowed on said bequest shall be applied to the care, maintenance, improvement and embellishment of my said plot and for the preservation, repair, restoration, or replacement of any monumental or other stone work on my said plot, should the occasion therefor arise."

... In the Bellefontaine Cemetery in St. Louis, Mo., the family of which deceased was a member owns a circular plot 92 feet in diameter. Its area is stated to be 6,647 square feet. Twenty-nine persons are there interred. In the plot are eighteen granite monuments and markers many of which are of substantial dimensions. The main and most imposing monument memorializes General William Clark of Lewis and Clark Expedition fame. Julia C. Voorhis was a granddaughter of General Clark. General Clark died in 1838 and the monument to his memory was unveiled in 1904. Its reproduction cost is $60,000. This monument is exposed to possible damage or destruction by smoke, falling trees and high winds. To provide against these and other contingencies Mr. Maguire from and after December, 1926, procured insurance on which to the date of the present account premiums aggregating $619.50 were paid. It is stipulated that neither the cemetery association nor the fund in the hands of Mr. Maguire under paragraph twenty-fourth of the will could replace the William Clark monument in the event of its destruction. It is also stipulated that since deceased's burial in 1922 one other member of the family has been interred in the family plot and that other members of the family may be buried there in the future.

...

In the absence of statute a bequest or devise to a trustee for erection of monuments and markers on private burial grounds is an anomalous gift. As a private trust it is defective because it has no specified beneficiary. As a public or charitable trust it is defective because it lacks even unascertained beneficiaries and is not for public purposes. Such a gift is analogous to the bequest considered in the leading case of *Morice v. Bishop of Durham*, 9 Ves.Jr. 399, 32 English Reprint 656, affirmed 10 Ves.Jr. 522, 32 English Reprint 947, where a gift was made to the Bishop accompanied by a direction that it should be applied to such objects of 'benevolence and liberality' as might be selected by him in his absolute discretion. Sir William Grant and Lord Eldon agreed that this gift produced a resulting trust with beneficial ownership in the *cestuis* thereof in no way limited by the power of disbursement which deceased purported to give to the Bishop. The circumstances that the Bishop was willing to carry out the intention of the deceased was deemed immaterial. Since there was no way of enforcing the Bishop's obligation (his duty resting on his honor rather than on someone's rights) the courts held that the testamentary scheme must fail.

Trust gifts wholly lacking in beneficiaries are treated by the law writers as honorary or incomplete trusts. Prof. Scott and Dean Ames are sharply critical of the doctrine of *Morice v. Bishop of Durham* in itself and as extended to gifts in trust to erect monuments and markers while Gray and Prof. Bogert are equally emphatic in supporting it (Scott: Control of Property by the Dead, 65 Pa.Law Rev. 527, 537, 538; 1 Scott on Trusts, section 124.2; Ames: The Failure of the Tilden Trust, 5 H.L.R. 389; Gray: Gifts for a Non-Charitable Purpose, 15 H.L.R. 510; 1 Bogert on Trusts and Trustees, sections 164–166). The actual point of disagreement between these scholars does not relate to whether a resulting trust is created by such gifts. The question they debate is whether the trustee of the resulting trust which is assumed to arise can divest the *cestui* of his interest in whole or in part by undertaking freely to discharge the honorary obligations of the trust. In this connection it is Scott's opinion that 'there is nothing illogical in allowing him to perform, although he cannot be compelled to do so; there is nothing unreasonable in holding that there is not an immediate and unconditional resulting trust for the next of kin (or residuary legatees), but that there is a resulting trust for them subject to a condition precedent of the failure of the (legatee) to perform'. 65 Pa.Law Rev. 527, 538. This seems to be a valid comment on the principle involved (Cf. Honorary Trusts and The Rule against Perpetuities, 30 Col.L.R. 60, 69) if the comment is understood to concede the immediate vesting of rights in the *cestuis* subject to defeat if the trustee acts within his powers.

...

Notes

1. *Cemeteries*: Cemeteries are not only where we take our loved ones to rest after their lives have come to an end, cemeteries also tell the history and stories of the people who lived in that village, town, or city. Typically the size of the monument or marker of an individual or family burial plot provides the threshold information

about the status of that individual or family and/or how important they were in their day. Only with the passing of time, however, can we determine whose lives truly left the greatest mark on history.

St. Louis, Missouri has two cemeteries in particular that tell the story of this fine city: Bellefontaine and Calvary. Bellefontaine is a non-profit, non-denominational cemetery, while Calvary is a Catholic cemetery run by the St. Louis Archdiocese. Both of these cemeteries were designed in the mid-1800s to meet the needs of a rapidly growing St. Louis population. Bellefontaine Cemetery was designed in 1849 and modeled after Pere Lachaise Cemetery in Paris. General William Clark, of the Lewis and Clark expedition, is buried in this cemetery, and a 35 feet high granite obelisk marks his grave. Perhaps the most notable St. Louis family buried here is the Busch family from the famous Anheuser-Busch brewery. Attached to the wrought iron front gate of the Busch Mausoleum are, interesting enough, beer bottle caps.

The slightly larger Calvary Cemetery is located right across the road from Bellefontaine Cemetery. While Calvary does not claim as many financially prominent residents as Bellefontaine, it does hold the remains of several St. Louisans who have left an indelible mark on U.S. history and the literary world. Dred Scott, who unsuccessfully sued for his and his family's freedom from slavery in the now famous Dred Scott Decision, was put to final rest in Calvary even though he was not Catholic. Scott passed away shortly after he was freed by his owner in 1857 and was buried in Calvary because it permitted the burial of non-Catholic slaves by their Catholic owners. Visitors to his gravesite often place Lincoln pennies on top of his tombstone for good luck. Calvary is also home to playwright Tennessee Williams and short story writer and novelist Kate Chopin, arguably America's first feminist author.

2. *Failed trust for lack of ascertainable beneficiary*: At first blush, the court's comment that as "a private trust it is defective because it has no specified beneficiary" might seem strange in that the trust clearly has a beneficiary: the family burial site. Why should that not qualify as a beneficiary? One of the reasons trust beneficiaries need to be ascertainable is because the court needs to know who has standing to come into court to sue to enforce the terms of the trust. In *Voorhis' Estate*, the trust *purpose* was to maintain the family burial grounds in Bellefontaine Cemetery, a specific and honorable purpose, but it is nevertheless an invalid purpose because it lacked an ascertainable beneficiary. The intended beneficiary, the family burial grounds, cannot come into court to seek enforcement of the terms of the trust if the trustee fails to honor the settlor's intent. Technically the trust fails, and therefore, by operation of law, a resulting trust should arise.

3. *Pet trusts — traditional view*: A similar problem arises with pet trusts — a trust created by the settlor for the settlor's pet. Many people consider their pets a member of the family. It should come as no surprise, then, that many people wish to leave property to their pets to ensure that they are provided for after they die. Obviously a settlor cannot give the property outright to the pet because an animal lacks legal capacity to hold property. Can a settlor leave his or her property in trust to care for his or her pets? Historically trusts for the care of one's pets were analogous to trusts

for the maintenance of one's burial plot. While intended for a specific and honorable purpose, a pet cannot come into court and enforce the terms of the trust against the trustee. Technically the trust fails, and a resulting trust arises unless the court recognizes the trust as an honorary trust.

4. *Failure as a charitable trust*: In *Voorhis' Estate*, after noting that the trust in question failed as an express private trust because it lacked a definite and ascertainable beneficiary, the court went on to note that "[a]s a public or charitable trust it is defective because it lacks even unascertained beneficiaries and is not for public purposes." Charitable trusts are covered in Chapter 15, but there are two key distinctions between private trusts and public/charitable trusts. The first is the purpose: a charitable trust must be for a charitable purpose. The second is that a charitable trust must *not* be for the benefit of a specific ascertainable beneficiary:

> The requisites of a valid private trust and one for a charitable use are materially different. In the former there must be not only a certain trustee who holds the legal title, but a certain specified cestui que trust [i.e., trust beneficiary], clearly identified, or made capable of identification by the terms of the instrument creating the trust, while it is an essential feature of the latter that the beneficiaries are uncertain, a class of persons described in some general language, often fluctuating, changing in their individual members, and partaking of a quasi-public character.

Young v. Redmon's Trustee, 300 Ky. 418, 420–21 (1945) (quoting from Am. Jur. Vol. 10, Section 6, page 589).

A trust to maintain cemeteries *generally* might qualify as a valid public/charitable trust, but that clearly was not the trust purpose or scope in *Voorhis' Estate*. As the court noted, the trust was for a specific purpose—the maintenance of a specific family burial plot—not for a general charitable purpose. Accordingly, the trust failed to qualify as a valid private trust because it did not have an ascertainable beneficiary who could come into court and enforce the terms of the trust; it also failed to qualify as a charitable trust because it had too specific of a purpose to be charitable and too specific of an intended benefit to be public in nature.

Similarly, a trust for the benefit of animals *generally* might qualify as a valid public/charitable trust, but a trust for the benefit of a decedent's pet(s) would not. The typical "pet trust" is for a specific purpose—the care of a specific pet, not for animals generally. Accordingly, historically pet trusts were held to be invalid: failing to qualify as a private trust because it did not have an ascertainable beneficiary who had standing to come into court and enforce the terms of the trust, and failing to qualify as a charitable trust because it had too specific of a purpose to be charitable and too specific of an intended benefit to be public in nature.

5. *Resulting trust*: A resulting trust is not really a trust at all—it is a judicial remedy. A resulting trust arises by operation of law anytime a trust fails, in whole or in part, at attempted creation or at any other point in time. The paradigm resulting trust scenario assumes that property has been delivered from the settlor to the trustee, but

then the trust fails. The issue that naturally arises is if the trust fails, should the trustee be permitted to keep the property, and if not, to whom should the property be delivered? The trustee holds legal title, but is it equitable to permit the trustee to keep the property if the trust fails? The resulting trust doctrine basically says "no," the trustee should have to give the property in question back to the settlor (or if the settlor is dead, to his or her estate). By operation of law the court will impose a resulting trust on the trustee in favor of the settlor/settlor's estate and order the property to be disbursed (i.e., returned) to the settlor/settlor's estate. Anytime a trust fails in whole or in part, a resulting trust should arise by operation of law to prevent the trustee from being unjustly enriched.

That last way to think about a resulting trust, to prevent the trustee from being unjustly enriched, overlaps with the rationale underlying the constructive trust (the other type of trust that arises by operation of law). Like resulting trusts, constructive trusts are not really trusts but rather are judicial remedies. In the *Mahoney* case (see Chapter 4), where the one spouse killed the other spouse and was convicted of manslaughter, the court ruled that a constructive trust should be imposed if it were determined that the one spouse voluntarily and intentionally killed the deceased spouse. A constructive trust is an equitable remedy that courts may use to prevent unjust enrichment. It is not a true trust that arises because of the settlor's intent; it is a judicial remedy the courts created to justify ordering the party who currently holds legal title to transfer the property to another party who holds a stronger equitable right to the property. Under the constructive trust, the wrongdoer is, by operation of law, de facto treated as if he or she is a "trustee" who holds legal title for the benefit of the party who has the stronger equitable claim to the property. The "trustee" is then ordered to disburse/transfer the property to the party with the stronger equitable claim, and the "trust" is terminated. The constructive trust doctrine analogizes to the trust model to justify ordering one party to transfer property to another party to prevent unjust enrichment. Whether a constructive trust should be imposed is a matter of judicial discretion, but it typically is imposed only where unjust enrichment would arise as a result of wrongful conduct.

6. *"Purpose" trusts*: Historically, trusts were broken into two types: private trusts (for individuals) and public trusts (for charitable purposes). Trusts, however, can also be categorized as trusts for charitable purposes and trusts for noncharitable purposes. A trust for a charitable purpose is just another way of saying a charitable trust (to be examined in greater detail in Chapter 15). Trusts for noncharitable purposes—i.e., private trusts—historically required ascertainable beneficiaries in order to be valid.

Phrased another way, historically there were two types of noncharitable purpose trusts: private trusts for ascertainable beneficiaries, which were permitted; and private trusts for noncharitable purposes, which lacked ascertainable beneficiaries and were therefore invalid. Should the law of trusts permit trusts for noncharitable purposes even in the absence of an ascertainable beneficiary?

One way to think about the *Voorhis* case is that it raises that precise issue: should the court recognize a private trust for noncharitable purposes even though it lacked ascertainable beneficiaries? In *Voorhis*, the trust was not for the benefit of an individual. Rather, the trust was for a purpose: to care for the settlor's family burial site. But because that purpose was noncharitable, it ran afoul of traditional trust law, which dictated the trust either had to be for charitable purposes or have ascertainable beneficiaries.

7. *Judicial relief—honorary trust*: People often want to create trust-like arrangements to achieve specific, good purposes (e.g., to maintain a burial plot or take care of one's pets). Technically, however, under traditional trust law, the arrangement typically would fail to meet the requirements of either a private trust (because it lacks ascertainable beneficiaries) or of a public/charitable trust (because it lacks a charitable purpose). Whenever a trust fails, a resulting trust arises. But early on, the common law decided that some trusts that failed for want of an ascertainable beneficiary, but that were for a specific and honorable purpose, should be permitted to continue so long as the trustee voluntarily agreed to honor and carry out the terms of the trust. The courts created the "honorary trust" doctrine to carry out that purpose.

An honorary trust is often defined as a noncharitable trust for a specific purpose that is neither illegal nor contrary to public policy. The classic examples of an honorary trust are trusts to maintain a gravesite, a trust for one's pet, or a trust for religious services for a period of time after one's death. Under strict application of traditional trust doctrine, an honorary trust is not really a trust at all. It is a judicial fiction where the court essentially agrees to look the other way and not declare a failed trust invalid so long as the trustee in question is willing to carry out the terms of the trust. If the trustee fails to honor the terms of the trust, or if the trustee is unable or unwilling to carry out the terms of the trust, the courts will not compel the trustee to comply, nor will the courts appoint a successor trustee. Instead, a resulting trust kicks in, and the honorary trust is terminated. The trust in *Voorhis' Estate* is a classic example of an honorary trust.

The development of the honorary trust was the first crack in the traditional way of thinking that private, noncharitable trusts are valid only if there is an ascertainable beneficiary. As the court noted: "Trust gifts wholly lacking in beneficiaries are treated by the law writers as honorary or incomplete trusts." In hindsight, we can see that the honorary trust was the law of trust's first step toward recognizing a private trust for noncharitable purposes even where there is no ascertainable beneficiary.

8. *Statutory relief—non-charitable private trust without an ascertainable beneficiary*: Although the honorary trust offered some relief for private trusts that lacked ascertainable beneficiaries, it was not a perfect solution because most jurisdictions held that honorary trusts were still subject to the dreaded Rule Against Perpetuities. In applying the Rule Against Perpetuities, the courts struggled with what constituted the "measuring life" for purposes of analyzing non-charitable private trusts. The resulting uncertainty effectively limited the development of the honorary trust doctrine. That failure, however, created pressure for the law to find another solution to permit such non-charitable trusts despite the absence of ascertainable beneficiaries.

The response was piecemeal and limited to specific purposes. In 1852, Kentucky became the first state to adopt legislation specifically permitting trusts to maintain a gravesite despite the fact that such trusts lacked an ascertainable beneficiary. Now almost all states have such a statute. More recently, states have increasingly adopted statutes that expressly recognize a pet trust as a valid purpose trust that is not subject to either the ascertainable beneficiary requirement or the Rule Against Perpetuities.

The Uniform Probate Code and Uniform Trust Code have adopted a broader approach. Both uniform laws expressly permit noncharitable purpose trusts for any and all lawful purposes even though the trust has no ascertainable beneficiary. Unif. Probate Code § 2-907; Unif. Trust Code § 409. Such trusts, however, may last for a maximum of only 21 years. This statutory movement clarifies the legality of noncharitable purpose trusts, eliminating the need for litigation over whether they qualify as honorary trusts and whether they are valid under the Rule Against Perpetuities. Moreover, while the trustee's duties were de facto "discretionary" under the honorary trust doctrine (in that honorary trusts last only so long as the trustee is willing to honor the terms of the trust), the trustee's duties are mandatory under the express noncharitable private trust doctrine, as they would be for any other type of trust (in that if the trustee is unwilling to honor the terms of the noncharitable purpose trust, the court will appoint a successor trustee to honor the terms).[2]

9. *The California approach*: Consistent with the national trend, California recognizes honorary trusts, but in addition the California legislature has provided statutory relief as well. California statutorily permits private trusts for the maintenance of one's gravesite. *See* Cal. Health & Safety Code § 8737. California statutorily permits private pet trusts. *See* CPC § 15212. And more generally, California permits trusts for noncharitable purposes:

CPC § 15211. Private trusts for noncharitable purposes

A trust for a noncharitable corporation or unincorporated society or for a lawful noncharitable purpose may be performed by the trustee for only 21 years, whether or not there is a beneficiary who can seek enforcement or termination of the trust and whether or not the terms of the trust contemplate a longer duration.

Problem

Testator gave his home, garage, contents, pets, and flower garden to his friend, Fran. Then he gave his residuary estate to his executrix in trust "for the maintenance of my pets [a dog and a parrot], which I leave to her kind care and judgment, and for their interment upon their respective deaths … Upon the death and interment of the last of my pets to survive, I give, devise and bequeath my entire residue estate so held in trust to Fran, absolutely and in fee." Has testator created a valid testamentary trust? *See In re Lyon's Estate*, 67 Pa. D. & C.2d 474 (1974).

---

2. For an excellent discussion of the history behind and the issues inherent in the "purpose" trust evolution, *see* Adam J. Hirsch, *Trusts for Purposes: Policy, Ambiguity, and Anomaly in the Uniform Laws*, 26 Fla. St. U. L. Rev. 913 (1999).

D. Writing Requirement

The final consideration for whether a trust has been validly created is whether the trust terms must be in writing. This variable is not really a function of the law of trusts. Rather it is a function of the either the Statute of Frauds or the Wills Act formalities, depending on whether the trust is an *inter vivos* trust or a testamentary trust. A trust is not created until it is funded. Accordingly, an *inter vivos* trust requires that property be transferred to the trustee while the settlor is alive. If the property being transferred includes real property, the general and traditional rule is that the Statute of Frauds required the trust terms be in writing. If the property being transferred to the trustee is purely personal property, the general and traditional rule is that the terms of the trust do not have to be in writing. Finally, if the trust were a testamentary trust, to be funded with probate property being distributed from the decedent's estate, the terms of the trust need to be in the testator's will. Inasmuch as the Wills Act requires wills to be in writing, testamentary trusts need to be in writing.

The writing requirement for a trust is simple enough. That is not the issue. The issue is what should happen if the settlor fails to meet the writing requirement, but there appears to be a transfer (or in the case of a will, an attempted transfer) of the property in question. Should the trustee be permitted to keep the property as a grantee/transferee/devisee?

1. *Failed* Inter Vivos *Trust*

Steinberger v. Steinberger

140 P.2d 31 (Cal. 1943)

PETERS, Presiding Justice.

...

The facts are as follows: In 1929, or prior thereto, Mary Louise Steinberger, grandmother of Earle and a relative of William Steinberger, deeded the property, ... to William, Earle and to Earle's brother. William was the uncle of Earle. Each of the grantees received an undivided one-third interest in the property. On September 12, 1930, Earle, at the request of William, executed a grant bargain and sale deed of his one-third interest to his uncle William. This deed was executed on the uncle's oral promise to reconvey upon the request of Earle. This promise was subsequently orally renewed and orally acknowledged. William died on February 8, 1940. Prior to that time there had been no request to reconvey. The administrator refused to recognize Earle's interest in the property. The present action was brought some time prior to June 10, 1941, the amended complaint having been filed on that date.

The court found that a confidential relationship existed between Earle and his uncle; that on the date of the deed Earle was about to leave San Francisco for Los Angeles for an indefinite period; that the uncle requested Earle to execute the deed in order to make it more convenient for William to take care of and manage the property; that the uncle promised that if Earle would execute the deed, he, the uncle, would take care of and manage the property for the benefit of Earle and of himself, and that he would reconvey Earle's one-third interest upon request; that in compliance with such request, and because the plaintiff reposed the utmost trust and confidence in his uncle, and because he believed and relied upon the promise to reconvey, Earle executed the deed in question; that the deed was executed without consideration; that from the date of the execution of the deed until the time of his death William continuously and on repeated occasions recognized that he was holding the one-third interest in trust for Earle; that William at no time repudiated the trust; that the defendant administrator has refused to reconvey upon demand of Earle.

On this appeal the administrator, while not denying that the evidence supports the finding of the oral agreement to reconvey and its subsequent acknowledgement, contends that all such evidence was inadmissible as being in violation of the parol evidence rule, and of the statute of frauds....

. . .

Under the parol evidence rule a party is prohibited from varying the terms of a written instrument by oral testimony. In the instant case plaintiff deeded the property to William by a grant bargain and sale deed. It is obvious, therefore, that the express trust, resting in parol, is unenforceable as an express trust, and that the oral evidence of such trust does tend to vary the terms of the deed. But this is not an action to enforce the oral express trust. It is an action to enforce a constructive trust which it is claimed arose by operation of law upon the repudiation of the promise to reconvey.

The law generally is unsettled on the question as to whether or not equity will enforce a constructive trust in real property upon breach of an oral contract to reconvey. The English cases hold that the transferee may set up the statute of frauds against enforcement of the oral express trust, and that no penalty will attach to him for so doing, but, if he sets up the statute, he is duty bound to restore the property received on the faith of his oral promise. If the transferee will not voluntarily make restitution, equity will compel such restitution through the medium of a constructive trust. The theory is that the constructive trust will be imposed to prevent the unjust enrichment of the transferee. Some few American cases have reached the same result by holding that the transferee's repudiation of his oral promise to reconvey is a fraud upon the transferor, which gives rise to the constructive trust.

The so-called majority American rule is that the repudiation of an oral promise to reconvey does not give rise to a constructive trust. The theory is that equity must respect and enforce the statute of frauds, and that to enforce a constructive trust is a violation of the spirit, if not the letter, of the statute. For discussion of the two rules, with many cases cited, see 3 Bogert, Trusts and Trustees, p. 1585, §495 et seq.; 1 Scott on Trusts, p. 246, §44 et seq.; 1 Perry on Trusts and Trustees, 7th Ed., p. 295, §181a et seq.

California has apparently aligned itself with the English and the so-called minority American view. In *Taylor v. Morris*, 163 Cal. 717, 127 P. 66, there was involved a similar problem to the one here presented. Without reference to the confidential relationship there existing, the court stated (page 722 of 163 Cal., page 68 of 127 P.):

"The statute of frauds is never permitted to become a shield for fraud, and fraud at once arises upon the repudiation by the trustee of any trust, even if that trust rests in parol. When it rests in parol, either parol evidence must be received to establish the trust, or the faithless trustee will always prevail. Certainly no elaboration of so plain a proposition is necessary....

...

Although the so-called majority American view is that no trust will arise upon a repudiation of the oral promise to reconvey, several important exceptions to that rule have been recognized. These exceptions are perhaps best stated in § 182 of the Restatement of the Law of Restitution and § 44 of the Restatement of the Law of Trusts, the two sections being substantially identical. Section 182 provides:

"Where the owner of an interest in lands transfers it *inter vivos* to another upon an oral trust in favor of the transferor or upon an oral agreement to reconvey the land to the transferor, and the trust or agreement is unenforceable because of the Statute of Frauds, and the transferee refuses to perform the trust or agreement, he holds the interest upon a constructive trust for the transferor, if

"(a) the transfer was procured by fraud, misrepresentation, duress, undue influence or mistake of such a character that the transferor is entitled to restitution, or

"(b) the transferee at the time of the transfer was in a confidential relation to the transferor, or

"(c) the transfer was made as security for an indebtedness of the transferor."

These exceptions, and particularly the one relating to confidential relations, are recognized in nearly every American state (see cases collected 3 Bogert on Trusts and Trustees, p. 1594, § 496; 1 Scott on Trusts, p. 253, § 44.2), and have clearly been adopted in California. (See California Annotations to the Restatement of the Law of Trusts (§ 44) and to the Restatement of the Law of Restitution (§ 182.) It is well settled in this state that breach of the oral promise to reconvey by the transferee or his administrator when the transferee was in a confidential relationship with the transferor at the time of the transfer constitutes sufficient "fraud" to create the constructive trust....

In the instant case the trial court found that Earle and his uncle William stood in a confidential relationship to each other. This finding is amply supported. There is not only the evidence of the status of uncle and nephew, and of cotenants, but there is ample evidence to show that a confidential relationship in fact existed. The respondent testified that he had trust and confidence in his uncle. The evidence shows that Earle and William lived in the house on the property here involved from the time of Earle's birth; that the uncle gave Earle money when he needed it, and that Earle reciprocated; that the uncle frequently expressed solicitude for his nephew Earle; that the uncle frequently stated he was keeping and holding the home for the boys. The evidence shows a friendly intimate relationship existed between Earle and his uncle. From this evidence it is apparent that the finding of confidential relationship is amply supported. It follows that whether California follows the English rule or the limited American rule, in the instant case a constructive trust arose upon the death of William and upon the repudiation of the trust by his administrator.

...

Notes

1. *Common law versus modern trend*: As the court in *Steinberger* acknowledges, American courts have struggled with the issue of what to do with an oral *inter vivos* trust for real property that fails for lack of a writing, but where the real property in question has been transferred to the "trustee." Older opinions believed that upholding the Statute of Frauds as it applied to the transfer deed was more important than the equitable principles underlying the constructive trust and/or resulting trust doctrines, hence what the court calls the majority American rule, which permits the "trustee" to keep the real property as a grantee.

Many commentators have argued that the modern trend American approach shows a greater willingness to impose either a constructive trust or a resulting trust and to order the property distributed back to the "settlor"/grantor. The court's opinion in *Scott v. Nelson*, 179 P.2d 116, 118 (Okla. 1947), evidnces this approach where, under similar facts, and with minimal discussion, the Oklahoma Supreme Court adopted the resulting trust approach:

> [T]he trust, if any, as shown by the evidence was an express trust and, since it rested in parol, it was invalid under the statute of frauds. The authorities cited sustain the contention that an *express* trust in relation to real property is invalid unless in writing. A *resulting* trust arises as an equitable doctrine where the legal estate is transferred and no trust or use is expressly declared, nor any circumstance, or evidence of intent, appears to direct the trust or use, which then *results* or comes back to the original grantor.
>
> From the terms of the disposition and the accompanying facts and circumstances, it appears here that the beneficial interest of the land was not intended to be enjoyed with the legal title. This trust is one implied. The trust results in favor of the grantor, deemed in equity to be the real owner. *Bobier v. Horn*, 95 Okl. 8, 222 P. 238.

In a recent unpublished California opinion, the court, quoting heavily from *Steinberger*, re-emphasized the constructive trust approach but de-emphasized the need for a confidential relationship. *See Armelin v. Armelin*, B161395, 2003 WL 22146528 (Cal. Ct. App. Sept. 18, 2003). *See also Martin v. Kehl*, 145 Cal. App. 3d 228, 237 (1983) ("'The essence of the constructive trust theory is to prevent unjust enrichment and to prevent a person from taking advantage of his own wrongdoing.' ... In such a trust based upon wrongdoing, an oral promise is sufficient and the existence or absence of a confidential relationship between the parties, in the strict sense, is not controlling.").

De-emphasizing the need to prove a confidential relationship is consistent with the overall modern trend preference for equitable relief rather than letting the "trustee" keep the property. Because the opinion is an unpublished opinion, however, it is unclear how much weight can be placed on the court's statement (though it is consistent with other opinions in other states).

2. *Unclean hands*: Both the constructive trust remedy and the resulting trust remedy are equitable remedies to the situation where an *inter vivos* trust fails for want of a proper writing. As such, both potential remedies are subject to equitable defenses. In fact, a number of courts have declined to impose either form of equitable relief where the grantor/settlor has been found to have "unclean hands" in the transfer process (i.e., if the settlor's initial motivation in conveying the property with no written record of the understanding between the settlor and the trustee was to put the property beyond the claims of possible creditors).

3. *Purchase money resulting trust*: Where one party puts forth all the purchase money but takes title in another person's name, an issue arises as to whether the second party is an intended donee or whether the second party was intended to hold it for the benefit of the purchaser. While that issue is a question of the purchaser's intent, the law has a set of rebuttable presumptions that may apply to the situation. Under the purchase money resulting trust doctrine, a rebuttable presumption arises that the purchaser did *not* intend a gift and is entitled to recover the property unless (a) the party in whose name title is taken is a natural object of the purchaser's bounty (in which case a rebuttable presumption of a gift arises), or (2) the property was put in the second party's name to accomplish an unlawful purpose. RESTATEMENT (THIRD) OF TRUSTS §9 (2003).

2. Failed Testamentary Trust

Pickelner v. Adler

229 S.W.3d 516 (Tex. App. 2007)

TIM TAFT, Justice.

. . .

Background

Shirley Alpha ("Shirley") executed a will in May 1997. Her long-time friend and attorney, Pickelner, drafted the will. The will made Pickelner the sole devisee:

> I give, devise and bequeath all the rest and remainder of my property of which I may die seized or possessed, or to which I may be in anywise entitled, whether real, personal or mixed, wherever situated and however acquired, to my long-time friend ROBERT S. PICKELNER, to be distributed in accordance with the specific instructions I have provided him.

The instructions to which the above-quoted provision refers were verbal, and Shirley did not reduce them to writing. The trial court received testimony of what Shirley's verbal instructions to Pickelner were. From that testimony, it is evident that Shirley's instructions to Pickelner did not cover all of the property that she bequeathed to him. Among her verbal instructions, Shirley required that Pickelner receive one of her homes and that Hurwitz, Shirley's close friend and portfolio manager, receive the other. Neither Pickelner nor Hurwitz was related to Shirley, and neither is her heir at law.

. . .

In April 2003, after a bench trial, the trial court rendered declaratory judgment that, for reasons that we set out further below, the bequest to Pickelner was void and that Shirley's heirs at law were to receive her property. Although the trial court indicated that it had considered the parol evidence concerning Shirley's distribution instructions to Pickelner, the court concluded that it could not give effect to those instructions....

. . .

Hurwitz's Appeal: Implicit Rejection of Request to Recognize a Constructive Trust

In his first issue, Hurwitz argues that the trial court "erred in failing to recognize a constructive trust over the property [Shirley] intended Hurwitz to receive." Specifically, Hurwitz contends that the will's distribution to Pickelner, with direction to distribute Shirley's property pursuant to verbal instructions that she had left him, required imposition of a constructive trust for Hurwitz's benefit.

. . .

B. Additional Facts

Pickelner, a long-time friend of Shirley's, drafted her will. The pertinent portion of the will, as quoted above, provided that all of Shirley's property was "devise[d] and bequeath[ed]" to Pickelner "to be distributed in accordance with the specific instructions which I have provided him." The undisputed testimony was that Shirley had given Pickelner verbal instructions that one of her homes was to be distributed to him, that another of her homes was to be distributed to Hurwitz, and that certain other property would be distributed to others; however, it was also undisputed that the verbal instructions that she gave Pickelner did not concern all of her property that passed to him under the will. It was further undisputed that Shirley did not give Pickelner the distribution instructions in writing.

. . .

C. Types of Trusts Generally

Generally speaking, Texas law recognizes three types of trusts:

"From the viewpoint of the creative force bringing them into existence, trusts may be classed as 'express trusts' and 'trusts by operation of law,' the latter being either resulting or constructive trusts. An express trust can come into existence only by the execution of an intention to create it by the one having legal and equitable dominion over the property made subject to it. A trust by operation of law, frequently called an 'implied trust,' comes into existence either through an implication of intention to create a trust as a matter of law or through the imposition of the trust irrespective of, and even contrary to any, such intention. *In other words, a trust intentional in fact is an express trust; one intentional in law is a resulting trust; and one imposed irrespective of intention is a constructive trust.*"

Mills v. Gray, 147 Tex. 33, 37, 210 S.W.2d 985, 987 (1948) (quoting 54 Am. Jur. 22, §5) (emphasis added).

1. Express Trusts Generally

... "To create a trust by a written instrument, the beneficiary, the *res,* and the trust purpose must be identified." *Perfect Union Lodge No. 10, A.F. & A.M., of San Antonio,* 748 S.W.2d at 220. This Court has referred to these requirements as "essential elements" of an express trust....

"The missing terms of an express trust may not be established by parol evidence." *Brelsford,* 564 S.W.2d at 406. That is, when an essential term is altogether missing from an attempted express trust, or is not at least reasonably certain, that term cannot be supplied by parol evidence, and the trust will fail.... ("[T]he language must be reasonably certain as to the material terms of the trust.... If the language is so vague, general, or equivocal that any of these necessary elements of the trust is left in real uncertainty, the trust will fail.") ...

2. Resulting Trusts Generally

A resulting trust is an equitable remedy that is implied by operation of law and that a trial court may impose to prevent unjust enrichment. *See, e.g., Hubbard v. Shankle,* 138 S.W.3d 474, 486 (Tex.App.-Fort Worth 2004, pet. denied). "When an express trust fails, the law implies a resulting trust with the beneficial title vested in the trustor or, in the case of the trustor's death, in her estate and devisees." *Brelsford,* 564 S.W.2d at 406; *see Nolana Dev. Ass'n v. Corsi,* 682 S.W.2d 246, 250 (Tex.1984) ("A resulting trust is implied in law ... when an express trust fails."). "The doctrine of resulting trust is invoked to prevent unjust enrichment, and equitable title will rest with the party furnishing the ... trust property when an express trust fails." *Corsi,* 682 S.W.2d at 250.

3. Constructive Trusts Generally

Like a resulting trust, a constructive trust is also an equitable remedy that is implied by operation of law and that a trial court may impose to prevent unjust enrichment. *See, e.g., Hubbard,* 138 S.W.3d at 485. "'[A] constructive trust generally involves primarily a presence of fraud, in view of which equitable title or interest should be recognized in some person other than the taker or holder of the legal title.'" *Mills,* 147 Tex. at 38, 210 S.W.2d at 988 (quoting 54 Am. Jur. 147, §188); *see Pope v. Garrett,* 147 Tex. 18, 21, 211 S.W.2d 559, 560 (1948) ("The case is a typical one for the intervention of equity to prevent a *wrongdoer,* who by his *fraudulent* or *otherwise wrongful* act has acquired title to property, from retaining and enjoying the beneficial interest therein, by impressing a constructive trust on the property in favor of the one who is truly and equitably entitled to the same.") (emphasis added). Because "[a] constructive trust escapes the unquestioned general rule that land titles must not rest in parol, … there must be strict proof of a prior confidential relationship and unfair conduct or unjust enrichment on the part of the wrongdoer." *Rankin v. Naftalis,* 557 S.W.2d 940, 944 (Tex.1977). Additionally, the remedy of imposing a constructive trust "must be used with caution, especially where … proof of the wrongful act rests in parol, in order that it may not defeat the purposes of the statute of wills, the statute of descent and distribution, or the statute of frauds." *Pope,* 147 Tex. at 25, 211 S.W.2d at 562.

D. Certain Trusts in the Context of Testamentary Conveyances

1. Secret Trusts and Constructive Trusts

In the context of a testamentary conveyance, a constructive trust can be imposed as a remedy when a testator conveys her property to another with the understanding that the devisee will deliver the property to a third person, but the will conveys the property outright to the devisee, without evidencing any intent to create a trust. *See generally* Gerry Breyer, 10 Texas Practice Series § 45.1 (3rd ed. 2002). The agreement between the testator and devisee in this scenario is sometimes referred to as a "secret trust" because it does not appear in the will. *See Temple v. City of Coleman,* 245 S.W. 264, 267–68 (Tex.Civ.App.-Austin 1922, writ dism'd) ("[I]f the testator is induced either to make a will or not to change one after it is made, by a promise, express or implied, on the part of a legatee that he will devote his legacy to a certain lawful purpose, a *secret trust* is created, and equity will compel him to apply property thus obtained in accordance with his promise.") (emphasis added) (quoting *Trustees of Amherst College v. Ritch,* 151 N.Y. 282, 45 N.E. 876, 37 L.R.A. 305 (1897)). In this situation, the remedy of a constructive trust may be imposed in favor of the intended third person if the devisee wrongfully refuses to convey the property to him or her; that is, a constructive trust may be employed to enforce the secret trust. *See Pope,* 147 Tex. at 21–22, 211 S.W.2d at 560. The constructive trust is imposed as a remedy not because the devise fails (the devise, in fact, succeeds), but because equity will not allow the wrongdoing devisee to enjoy the beneficial interest of the devise, *i.e.,* it will not allow him to be unjustly enriched in contravention of the secret trust. *See Pope,* 147 Tex. at 21, 211 S.W.2d at 560.

Concerning secret trusts, the Texas Supreme Court has explained:

> … "Where a trust not declared in the will is established by a court of chancery against the devisee, it is by reason of the obligation resting upon the conscience of the devisee, and not as a valid testamentary disposition by the deceased…. *Where the bequest is outright upon its face, the setting up of a trust, while it diminishes the right of the devisee, does not impair any right of the heirs or next of kin, in any aspect of the case; for, if the trust were not set up, the whole*

property would go to the devisee by force of the devise. If the trust set up is a lawful one, it inures to the benefit of the cestui que trust.... *Olliffe v. Welis.*

Heidenheimer v. Bauman, 84 Tex. 174, 183, 19 S.W. 382, 385 (1892) (emphasis added).

2. Semi-Secret Trusts and Resulting Trusts

The remedy of a resulting trust can be employed if the will on its face shows that the testator intended to give her property to the devisee to hold in trust, but the intended testamentary trust fails for lack of specificity. *See Ray,* 144 S.W.2d at 668–69. The devise attempting (but failing) to leave property in trust is sometimes referred to as a "semi-secret trust" because the intent to make a trust appears in the will, but the trust's essential terms do not. *See* Restatement (Third) of Trusts § 18 (2003), cmt. a. A semi-secret trust is, in essence, a failed express testamentary trust. As when any express testamentary trust fails, the remedy of a resulting trust arises by operation of law in favor of the testator's heirs, even if parol evidence would have shown that the heirs were not the intended beneficiaries of the failed trust. *See Heidenheimer,* 84 Tex. at 182–83, 19 S.W. at 384 ("The will upon its face showing that the devisee takes the legal title only, and not the beneficial interest, and the trust not being sufficiently defined by the will to take effect, the equitable intent goes, by way of resulting trust, to the heirs or next of kin as property of the deceased, not disposed of by his will.") (quoting *Olliffe v. Wells,* 130 Mass. 221, 225–26 (1881)); *Ray,* 144 S.W.2d at 669 ("We hold that, under the will in question, the defendant [devisee] did not take the legal and beneficial title to the property. The legal title only was vested in him. The trust attempted to be created is void for uncertainty. This being true, the beneficial title to the estate vested in the heirs. If this holding be correct as to the beneficial title to the property, the testatrix died intestate. In legal effect it is tantamount to a provision by the testatrix that after the debts are paid her estate should go to her legal heirs."); *see also Lowry v. Gallagher,* 190 S.W.2d 165, 168 (Tex.Civ.App.1945, writ ref'd w.o.m.); *Kramer v. Sommers,* 93 S.W.2d 460, 466 (Tex.Civ.App.-Fort Worth 1936, writ dism'd). The remedy of the resulting trust arises not because of any wrongdoing on the part of the devisee, but because the intended express trust (*i.e.,* the semi-secret trust) fails, and the will evidenced an intent that the devisee was to receive legal title only, not beneficial title. *See, generally, Heidenheimer,* 84 Tex. at 181–85, 19 S.W. at 384–85.

Concerning semi-secret trusts, the Texas Supreme Court has explained:

"[I]f ... trusts of a testamentary character might be declared by the testator by mere oral declarations, or by writing not executed with the same formalities required in the execution of wills, men's final dispositions would, in many cases, be made up largely of such acts and declarations as the cupidity of claimants and the recklessness or indifference of witnesses might dictate." 3 Redf. Wills, 579...."*If a testator should devise real or personal property to A. in trust, and state no trust on which A. is to hold, no paper not referred to in the will, and not duly executed, could be received in evidence to prove the trusts, nor could A. hold the beneficial interest because he is stamped with the character*

*of a trustee, but he would hold only the legal title, while the beneficial interest
would descend or result to the testator's heirs at law."* 1 Perry, Trusts, 93.

[The court affirmed the trial court's order imposing a resulting trust and granting
the property to the decedent's heirs.]

Note

Secret versus semi-secret trust—latent versus patent ambiguity: Another way to think
about the difference between a secret trust and a semi-secret trust is that the distinction
relates to the traditional common law rules concerning the admissibility of extrinsic
evidence. Under the traditional common law approach, extrinsic evidence was admissible only if there was a latent ambiguity in the will, not if there was a patent ambiguity. A secret trust is a latent ambiguity; a semi-secret trust is a patent ambiguity.
In the case of a semi-secret trust, without the benefit of extrinsic evidence to determine
the intended beneficiaries, the court has no option but to order a resulting trust and
give the property back to the settlor. In the case of a secret trust, extrinsic evidence
is necessary to prove that the named beneficiary was intended to take only legal title
and that equitable title was intended to vest in a third party. Knowing the identity
of the intended trust beneficiaries permits the court to order a constructive trust and
go forward with the testator's intent.

The modern trend is to admit extrinsic evidence any time there is an ambiguity
in a will, whether it is latent or patent. Is it merely a coincidence that the modern
trend is for courts to apply a constructive trust to both secret and semi-secret trusts?
(Though obviously not all jurisdictions follow the modern trend, as the court's holding
in *Adler* evidences.)

Problems

1. Fred and Mary have both experienced a prior marriage and divorce. Fred has
    two sons from his first marriage. Mary has a daughter from her first marriage.
    When the two finally found each other, they had almost given up on love, but
    they were convinced that their love was truly, "true love." After a few years of
    blissful marriage, Fred is diagnosed with cancer. While thinking about his final
    wishes, Mary promises that if Fred leaves his property to her, she will, when the
    time comes, devise whatever property she gets from him to his two boys. Fred
    executes a will leaving all of his property to his wife, Mary. After his death, Mary
    executes a will leaving all of her property to her daughter. Fred had told his sons
    about his understanding with Mary. They sue, seeking to enforce the under-
    standing. How would you rule, and why?

2. Decedent, who dies intestate, owns Greenacres. Decedent has two children, a
    son and a daughter, and a granddaughter by the daughter. The son disclaims his
    interest, vesting it in his sister. The granddaughter needs a place to live. She ap-
    proaches her mother and suggests that the mother disclaim her interest in the
    decedent's estate. She promises her mother that if she (the mother) ever needs

the property, she'll transfer it back to her. She also promises that she won't sell it while her mother is alive. Mother assigns her interest in Greenacres to her daughter. The probate court approves it, ordering the property to be distributed to the granddaughter.

Ten years later, the granddaughter puts Greenacres up for sale. Mother sues, claiming breach of trust. How would you analyze the situation? *See Armelin v. Armelin*, No. B161395, 2003 WL 22146528 (Cal. Ct. App. Sept. 18, 2003).

III. Trust Creation and Pour-Over Clauses

A. Introduction: *Inter Vivos* versus Testamentary Trusts

The two most important and most dominant estate planning instruments over the years have been the will and the trust. The will is an instrument that directs who will receive the testator's probate property when he or she dies. Bequests and/or devises in a will are nothing more than an outright gift made by the testator at the time of death. The classic trust is an *inter vivos* trust that avoids probate. Property transferred to the trustee during the settlor's lifetime is owned by the trust, not the settlor. Even where the settlor retains a life estate interest in the trust, legally the trust holds legal title to the trust property. The settlor's death terminates the settlor's life estate, but the property in the trust is not subject to probate. The trust holds legal title to the trust property, and while the settlor's equitable interest may have expired, there is no need to probate the property. The trust is still "alive," and it holds the trust property. The equitable interest may shift from one beneficiary to another, but the legal title remains the same: it is held by the trust/trustee.

While at first blush the will and the trust may appear to be mutually exclusive options, nothing could be further from the truth. While the classic trust is an *inter vivos* trust, that is not the only type of trust. In fact, the significance of the terms "*inter vivos* trust" is that the trust is created while the settlor is alive. Inasmuch as a trust is not created until it is funded, that means that the trust was funded *inter vivos*—while the settlor is alive. But one can create a testamentary trust. Juxtaposed with the term "*inter vivos* trust," it is easy to ascertain the significance of the term "*testamentary* trust." A testamentary trust is one that is not funded until the settlor's death. A clause in the will (typically the residuary clause, but not necessarily) gives the property in question to the trustee of the testator's trust, to hold and distribute pursuant to the terms of the trust. The terms of the trust then are set forth *in* the testator's will.

Note that a testamentary trust does not include one of the traditional benefits of an *inter vivos* trust. With respect to the settlor's death, not only does the property to be held by the testamentary trust *not* avoid probate, the starting assumption is that the property *must* go through probate to be subject to the terms of the testator's will giving the property in question to the testator's testamentary trust. But while a testamentary trust does not avoid probate (at least upon the settlor's death), it still offers many of the other benefits of a trust: professional management of the property in question; a degree of dead-hand control over the trust beneficiaries (if the beneficiary's interest in the trust is in the form of a conditional ongoing gift); to facilitate tax avoidance upon the death of the trust beneficiaries; to avoid probate upon the death of the trust beneficiaries; or to make choice of law decisions.

The biggest difference between an *inter vivos* trust and a testamentary trust is that the former avoid probate while the latter does not. Historically, an ancillary difference that flowed from that difference was that an *inter vivos* trust was *not* subject to probate court supervision as a general rule, while a testamentary trust was subject to probate court supervision *for the life of the trust.* Most estate planners agreed that for most clients, subjecting the trust to probate court supervision was a bad idea because it increased the costs of administration associated with the trust. The trustee had to account to the probate court on a regular basis (usually annually), and the trustee typically had a duty to get the court's approval before engaging in any non-routine transactions. A trustee of an *inter vivos* trust has no such administrative responsibilities as a general rule (absent a beneficiary making it a judicial matter). But some settlors may prefer judicial supervision of their trustee, in which case the settlor could opt for a testamentary trust. In addition, testamentary trusts were often contingent beneficiaries in a will where the hassles associated with a testamentary trust were still better than the other options (i.e., most well-drafted wills for a couple with young children will include a testamentary trust for the benefit of the children in the event there is not a surviving spouse; holding the property in trust for the minor children is arguably a better legal arrangement than having the property held by a guardian who would be subject to probate court supervision to an even greater extent than a trustee under a well-drafted testamentary trust).[3]

Even where the benefits of an *inter vivos* trust exceed the benefits of a testamentary trust, which is the case for most people considering a trust, it is difficult to transfer all of one's assets to the trust while one is alive. Some settlors are just psychologically opposed to it; some oppose the added paperwork associated with it (if you put your checking account in the trust, you no longer can sign your name to each check you write, you have to sign your name in your legal capacity as trustee: "*Carolyn Wendel O'Connell, Trustee of the Carolyn Wendel O'Connell Trust.*" And finally, only property transferred to an *inter vivos* trust while the settlor is alive is part of the *inter vivos* trust. Inasmuch as most people are constantly acquiring and disposing of property, it becomes a hassle to constantly execute new documents transferring newly acquired property to one's *inter vivos* trust. For all these reasons, and others, it is not uncommon for a settlor to transfer some of his or her property to his or her trust during his or her lifetime (typically one's larger assets that one typically does not deal with too often: title to one's house; title to one's pension plan, one's life insurance policies), but not to transfer those assets that one deals with on a regular basis and that often

---

3. *But see* note 3, after the *Clymer* case below, for an important California qualifier to this paragraph.

changes rapidly (one's checking account; maybe one's stock investments, etc.). But to the extent one has an *inter vivos* trust, and it contains the dispositive provisions of one's estate plan, it typically does not make sense to create a second, parallel estate plan in one's will. Enter the pour-over provision.

B. A Testamentary Pour-Over Provision

A pour-over provision typically is a clause in a will, but it not need be. It can be a provision in a life insurance policy designating the trust as the beneficiary, or a provision in a payment-on-death pension plan designating the trust as the beneficiary, or a similar provision in any valid testamentary instrument. The most common pour-over provision, however, is the provision in a will, where it typically is the residuary clause (again, though it need not be). Assume T's will provides in pertinent part as follows: "I give the rest, residue, and remainder to the trustee of *inter vivos* trust, to hold and distribute pursuant to the terms of the trust." First, why would a testator use such a clause? A California Court of Appeal had this to say about that question:

> The term "pour-over" is commonly used to describe a testamentary transfer to the trustee of a living trust. The assets transferred are added to and administered as part of the trust along with its existing assets. In this way, the will "pours over" into the trust. "Pour-over" also describes the incorporation by reference of the terms of an existing trust instrument into a will, resulting in the creation of a separate testamentary trust with the same terms as the existing trust. Pour-over wills are most commonly used for two purposes. First, when a revocable trust is "funded" during lifetime by a transfer of assets to a trustee, the pour-over will protects against a possible failure to transfer later-acquired assets to the trust. Second, pour-over wills are used when a revocable trust has only nominal assets during lifetime, permitting probate of property on death but avoiding public disclosure of the final disposition of such property.

Kalloger v. Normart, No. F040048, 2002 WL 31402079, at *10 (Cal. Ct. App. Oct. 25, 2002).

Note the property passing pursuant to a pour-over provision in the testator's will *does not* avoid probate upon the settlor's death. The pour-over provision applies to the property the settlor *did not* transfer to the *inter vivos* trust while the settlor was alive. Thus, upon the settlor's death, that property falls into the settlor's probate estate. Rather than creating a parallel or separate estate plan for that property, however, the settlor/testator has decided that the best course of action is simply to add that probate property to his or her *inter vivos* trust, to be held and distributed pursuant to the terms of the *inter vivos* trust. As the court noted, the pour-over provision has the advantage over creating a testamentary trust for the property that the terms of the trust remain confidential. If the testator created a testamentary trust for the property, the terms of the trust typically are in the will and hence are subject to public scrutiny following the testator's death because the will is a public document. In contrast, a pour-over provision simply directs the executor/personal representative to give the property in question (the property subject to the pour-over clause) to the trustee of the *inter vivos* trust, to hold and distribute pursuant to the terms of that trust. The terms of the trust are not in the will and need not be disclosed. Confidentiality is retained.

The problem with a pour-over provision, however, is it means that ultimately the terms of the trust control who gets the probate property, not the terms of the will. Typically a trust is not executed with Wills Act formalities. How can a document other than a will dispose of the decedent's probate property? As the California Court of Appeal's comments above indicate, historically, analysis of that question took the courts back to the "will expanding" doctrines—the doctrines that permit a testator to express intent outside of the will that can be given effect as part of the probate process: incorporation by reference and acts of independent significance. But the different possible justifications for permitting the terms of the trust to control the property in question have different legal consequences.

Incorporation by reference permits the will to incorporate the terms of the trust instrument into the will, but most courts held that if that was the doctrine used to validate the pour-over clause, it resulted in a testamentary trust that was subject to probate court supervision for the life of the trust. In essence, the decedent ended up with two trusts: (1) the *inter vivos* trust that held the property that was transferred to the trust *inter vivos* and that was not subject to probate court supervision, and (2) a testamentary trust that held the property that was transferred to the trust under the terms of the will and that was subject to probate court supervision for the life of the trust. Moreover, under incorporation by reference, amendments to the *inter vivos* trust that were executed *after* the will was executed could not be given effect. Incorporation by reference incorporates the trust instrument and the terms of the trust as they existed on the date the will was executed. So while incorporation by reference permits the court to give effect to testator's intent as expressed in a document outside the will (i.e., in the trust instrument), it does so at rather significant cost and with rather significant limitations.

Acts of independent significance, on the other hand, can be used to validate a pour-over clause as long as the referenced act—the *inter vivos* trust—has its own legal significance independent of its effect on the will. So long as the trust is funded *inter vivos* and has property in it at the time of the decedent's death, it has its own independent significance—it holds and manages the property transferred to the trust *inter vivos*. But the issue was not quite that simple, at least for some courts. First, how much property must be transferred to the trust *inter vivos* to give the trust its own "independent significance"? What if only a token amount was transferred to the trust *inter vivos*? In *In reWill of Sackler*, 548 N.Y.S.2d 866 (1989), the settlor transferred only $1.00 to the trust *inter vivos*, and then poured more than $100 million into the trust per his will. Does the *inter vivos* trust *really* have independent significance or is such nominal funding a sham that should require the trust to be executed with Wills Act formalities if it is to dispose of the probate property? And even assuming, *arguendo*, that the *inter vivos* funding is sufficient to give the trust its own independent significance, should the court nevertheless maintain jurisdiction over the property being poured over into the trust pursuant to the pour-over clause?

Notes and Problem

1. *Incorporation by reference*: With respect to validating a pour-over clause under the traditional common law doctrines, under incorporation by reference, *what* is being incorporated into *what*? What type of trust does one end up with, and why?

2. *Acts of independent significance*: With respect to validating a pour-over clause under acts of independent significance, what is the referenced act in the will? What is necessary for that "act" to have its own independent significance? How does that provide the referenced act independent significance?

3. Assume T validly executes a will. The residuary clause provides as follows: "I hereby give all my property to the trustee of my *inter vivos* trust, to hold and distribute pursuant to the terms of the trust." Thereafter the testator revokes the trust and creates a new trust instrument, but dies before funding it. What controls who gets the testator's probate property: T's will, T's trust, or the intestate scheme? Why?

C. Uniform Testamentary Additions to Trusts Act

These types of questions, and others, created risks and uncertainty with respect to the validity of testamentary pour-over clauses. To resolve the uncertainty and to facilitate the use of pour-over clauses, the Uniform Law Commission adopted the Uniform Testamentary Addition to Trusts Act ("UTATA") to create a safe harbor for pour-over clauses. Unfortunately, the "Uniform" Law is not as uniform as one might like. The Commission has disagreed over time with respect to what exactly is necessary for a pour-over clause to be valid under the Act, and a handful of states have statutorily adopted their own variation of the Act. California's version of UTATA provides as follows:

CPC § 6300. Testamentary additions to trusts

A devise, the validity of which is determinable by the law of this state, may be made by a will to the trustee of a trust established or to be established by the testator or by the testator and some other person or by some other person (including a funded or unfunded life insurance trust, although the settlor has reserved any or all rights of ownership of the insurance contracts) if the trust is identified in the testator's will and its terms are set forth in a written instrument (other than a will) executed before or concurrently with the execution of the testator's will or in the valid last will of a person who has predeceased the testator (regardless of the existence, size, or character of the trust property). The devise is not invalid because the trust is amendable or revocable, or both, or because the trust was amended after the execution of the will or after the death of the testator. Unless the testator's will provides otherwise, the property so devised (1) is not deemed to be held under a testamentary trust of the testator but becomes a part of the trust to which it is given and (2) shall be administered and disposed of in accordance with the provisions of the instrument or will setting forth the terms of the trust, including any amendments thereto made before or after the death of the testator (regardless of whether made before or after the execution of the testator's will). Unless otherwise provided in the will, a revocation or termination of the trust before the death of the testator causes the devise to lapse.

Adopting a new law, however, often has a ripple effect, creating new issues when it overlaps with existing doctrines in unexpected ways.

Clymer v. Mayo

473 N.E.2d 1084 (Mass. 1985)

HENNESSEY, Chief Justice.

This consolidated appeal arises out of the administration of the estate of Clara A. Mayo (decedent). We summarize the findings of the judge of the Probate and Family Court incorporating the parties' agreed statement of uncontested facts.

At the time of her death in November, 1981, the decedent, then fifty years of age, was employed by Boston University as a professor of psychology. She was married to James P. Mayo, Jr. (Mayo), from 1953 to 1978. The couple had no children. The decedent was an only child and her sole heirs at law are her parents, Joseph A. and Maria Weiss.

In 1963, the decedent executed a will designating Mayo as principal beneficiary. In 1964, she named Mayo as the beneficiary of her group annuity contract with John Hancock Mutual Life Insurance Company; and in 1965, made him the beneficiary of her Boston University retirement annuity contracts with Teachers Insurance and Annuity Association (TIAA) and College Retirement Equities Fund (CREF). As a consequence of a $300,000 gift to the couple from the Weisses in 1971, the decedent and Mayo executed new wills and indentures of trust on February 2, 1973, wherein each spouse was made the other's principal beneficiary. Under the terms of the decedent's will, Mayo was to receive her personal property. The residue of her estate was to "pour over" into the *inter vivos* trust she created that same day.

The decedent's trust instrument named herself and John P. Hill as trustees. As the donor, the decedent retained the right to amend or revoke the trust at any time by written instrument delivered to the trustees. In the event that Mayo survived the decedent, the trust estate was to be divided into two parts. Trust A, the marital deduction trust, was to be funded with an amount "equal to fifty (50%) per cent of the value of the Donor's 'adjusted gross estate,'... for the purpose of the United States Tax Law, less an amount equal to the value of all interest in property, if any, allowable as 'marital deductions' for the purposes of such law...." Mayo was the income beneficiary of Trust A and was entitled to reach the principal at his request or in the trustee's discretion. The trust instrument also gave Mayo a general power of appointment over the assets in Trust A.

The balance of the decedent's estate, excluding personal property passing to Mayo by will, or the entire estate if Mayo did not survive her, composed Trust B. Trust B provided for the payment of five initial specific bequests totalling $45,000. After those gifts were satisfied, the remaining trust assets were to be held for the benefit of Mayo for life. Upon Mayo's death, the assets in Trust B were to be held for "the benefit of the nephews and nieces of the Donor" living at the time of her death. The trustee was given discretion to spend so much of the income and principal as necessary for their comfort, support, and education. When all of these nephews and nieces reached the age of thirty, the trust was to terminate and its remaining assets were to be divided equally between Clark University and Boston University to assist in graduate education of women.

On the same day she established her trust, the decedent changed the beneficiary of her Boston University group life insurance policy from Mayo to the trustees. One month later, in March, 1973, she also executed a change in her retirement annuity contracts to designate the trustees as beneficiaries. At the time of its creation in 1973, the trust was not funded. Its future assets were to consist solely of the proceeds of these policies and the property which would pour over under the will's residuary clause. The judge found that the remaining trustee has never received any property or held any funds subsequent to the execution of the trust nor has he paid any trust taxes or filed any trust tax returns.

Mayo moved out of the marital home in 1975. In June, 1977, the decedent changed the designation of beneficiary on her Boston University life insurance policy for a second time, substituting Marianne LaFrance for the trustees. LaFrance had lived with the Mayos since 1972, and shared a close friendship with the decedent up until her death. Mayo filed for divorce on September 9, 1977, in New Hampshire. The divorce was decreed on January 3, 1978, and the court incorporated into the decree a permanent stipulation of the parties' property settlement. Under the terms of that settlement, Mayo waived any "right, title or interest" in the decedent's "securities, savings accounts, savings certificates, and retirement fund," as well as her "furniture, furnishings and art." Mayo remarried on August 28, 1978, and later executed a new will in favor of his new wife. The decedent died on November 21, 1981. Her will was allowed on November 18, 1982, and the court appointed John H. Clymer as administrator with the will annexed.

What is primarily at issue in these actions is the effect of the Mayos' divorce upon dispositions provided in the decedent's will and indenture of trust. In the first action, the court-appointed administrator of the decedent's estate petitioned for instructions with respect to the impact of the divorce on the estate's administration. Named as defendants were Mayo, the decedent's parents (the Weisses), and the trustee under the indenture of trust (John P. Hill).

. . .

1. *The Judge's Conclusions.*

. . .

On November 1, 1983, the judge issued his rulings of law.... The rulings that have been challenged by one or more parties on appeal are as follows: (1) the decedent's *inter vivos* trust, executed contemporaneously with her will, is valid under G.L. c.

203, § 3B, despite the fact that the trust did not receive funding until the decedent's death; (2) Mayo does not take under Trust A because that transfer was intended to qualify for a marital deduction for Federal estate tax purposes and this objective became impossible after the Mayos' divorce; (3) Mayo is entitled to take under Trust B because the purpose of that trust was to create a life interest in him, the decedent failed to revoke the trust provisions benefiting Mayo, and G.L. c. 191, § 9, operates to revoke only testamentary dispositions in favor of a former spouse; (4) J. Chamberlain, A. Chamberlain, and Hinman, the decedent's nephews and niece by marriage at the time of the trust's creation, are entitled to take under Trust B as the decedent's intended beneficiaries....

. . .

2. *Validity of "Pour-over" Trust.*

The Weisses claim that the judge erred in ruling that the decedent's trust was validly created despite the fact that it was not funded until her death. They rely on the common law rule that a trust can be created only when a trust res exists. *New England Trust Co. v. Sanger,* 337 Mass. 342, 348, 140 N.E.2d 598 (1958). Arguing that the trust never came into existence, the Weisses claim they are entitled to the decedent's entire estate as her sole heirs at law.

In upholding the validity of the decedent's pour-over trust, the judge cited the relevant provisions of G.L. c. 203, § 3B, inserted by St.1963, c. 418, § 1, the Commonwealth's version of the Uniform Testamentary Additions to Trusts Act. "A devise or bequest, the validity of which is determinable by the laws of the commonwealth, may be made to the trustee or trustees of a trust established or to be established by the testator ... including a funded or unfunded life insurance trust, although the trustor has reserved any or all rights of ownership of the insurance contracts, if the trust is identified in the will and the terms of the trust are set forth in a written instrument executed before or concurrently with the execution of the testator's will ... *regardless of the existence, size or character of the corpus of the trust*" (emphasis added). The decedent's trust instrument, which was executed in Massachusetts and states that it is to be governed by the laws of the Commonwealth, satisfies these statutory conditions. The trust is identified in the residuary clause of her will and the terms of the trust are set out in a written instrument executed contemporaneously with the will. However, the Weisses claim that G.L. c. 203, § 3B, was not intended to change the common law with respect to the necessity for a trust corpus despite the clear language validating pour-over trusts, "regardless of the existence, size or character of the corpus." The Weisses make no showing of legislative intent that would contradict the plain meaning of these words. It is well established that "the statutory language is the principal source of insight into legislative purpose." *Bronstein v. Prudential Ins. Co. of America,* 390 Mass. 701, 704, 459 N.E.2d 772 (1984). Moreover, the development of the common law of this Commonwealth with regard to pour-over trusts demonstrates that G.L. c. 203, § 3B, takes on practical meaning only if the Legislature meant exactly what the statute says concerning the need for a trust corpus.

This court was one of the first courts to validate pour-over devises to a living trust. In *Second Bank-State St. Trust Co. v. Pinion*, 341 Mass. 366, 371, 170 N.E.2d 350 (1960), decided prior to the adoption of G.L. c. 203, § 3B, we upheld a testamentary gift to a revocable and amendable *inter vivos* trust established by the testator before the execution of his will and which he amended after the will's execution. Recognizing the importance of the pour-over devise in modern estate planning, we explained that such transfers do not violate the statute of wills despite the testator's ability to amend the trust and thereby change the disposition of property at his death without complying with the statute's formalities. "We agree with modern legal thought that a subsequent amendment is effective because of the applicability of the established equitable doctrine that subsequent acts of independent significance do not require attestation under the statute of wills." *Id.* at 369, 170 N.E.2d 350.

At that time we noted that "[t]he long established recognition in Massachusetts of the doctrine of independent significance makes unnecessary statutory affirmance of its application to pour-over trusts." *Id.* at 371, 170 N.E.2d 350. It is evident from *Pinion* that there was no need for the Legislature to enact G.L. c. 203, § 3B, simply to validate pour-over devises from wills to funded revocable trusts.

However, in *Pinion,* we were not presented with an unfunded pour-over trust. Nor, prior to G.L. c. 203, § 3B, did other authority exist in this Commonwealth for recognizing testamentary transfers to unfunded trusts. The doctrine of independent significance, upon which we relied in *Pinion,* assumes that "property was included in the purported *inter vivos* trust, prior to the testator's death." Restatement (Second) of Trusts § 54, comment f (1959). That is why commentators have recognized that G.L. c. 203, § 3B, "[m]akes some ... modification of the *Pinion* doctrine. The act does not require that the trust res be more than nominal or even existent." E. Slizewski, Legislation: Uniform Testamentary Additions to Trusts Act, 10 Ann.Surv. of Mass.Law § 2.7, 39 (1963). See Osgood, Pour Over Will: Appraisal of Uniform Testamentary Additions to Trusts Act, 104 Trusts 768, 769 (1965) ("The Act ... eliminates the necessity that there be a trust corpus").

...

For the foregoing reasons we conclude, in accordance with G.L. c. 203, § 3B that the decedent established a valid *inter vivos* trust in 1973 and that its trustee may properly receive the residue of her estate. We affirm the judge's ruling on this issue.

...

4. *Termination of Trust A.*

The judge terminated Trust A upon finding that its purpose—to qualify the trust for an estate tax marital deduction—became impossible to achieve after the Mayos' divorce. Mayo appeals this ruling. It is well established that the Probate Courts are empowered to terminate or reform a trust in whole or in part where its purposes have become impossible to achieve and the settlor did not contemplate continuation of the trust under the new circumstances. *Gordon v. Gordon*, 332 Mass. 193, 197, 124 N.E.2d 226 (1955). *Ames v. Hall*, 313 Mass. 33, 37, 46 N.E.2d 403 (1943).

The language the decedent employed in her indenture of trust makes it clear that by setting off Trusts A and B she intended to reduce estate tax liability in compliance with then existing provisions of the Internal Revenue Code. Therefore we have no disagreement with the judge's reasoning. See *Putnam v. Putnam*, 366 Mass. 261, 267, 316 N.E.2d 729 (1974). However, we add that our reasoning below — that by operation of G.L. c. 191, §9, Mayo has no beneficial interest in the trust — clearly disposes of Mayo's claim to Trust A.

5. *Mayo's Interest in Trust B.*

The judge's decision to uphold Mayo's beneficial interest in Trust B was appealed by the Weisses, as well as by Boston University and Clark University. The judge reasoned that the decedent intended to create a life interest in Mayo when she established Trust B and failed either to revoke or to amend the trust after the couple's divorce. The appellants argue that we should extend the reach of G.L. c. 191, §9, to revoke all Mayo's interests under the trust. General Laws c. 191, §9, as amended through St.1977, c. 76, §2, provides in relevant part: "If, after executing a will, the testator shall be divorced or his marriage shall be annulled, the divorce or annulment shall revoke any disposition or appointment of property made by the will to the former spouse, any provision conferring a general or special power of appointment on the former spouse, and any nomination of the former spouse, as executor, trustee, conservator or guardian, unless the will shall expressly provide otherwise. Property prevented from passing to a former spouse because of revocation by divorce shall pass as if a former spouse had failed to survive the decedent, and other provisions conferring a power of office on the former spouse shall be interpreted as if the spouse had failed to survive the decedent." The judge ruled that Mayo's interest in Trust B is unaffected by G.L. c. 191, §9, because his interest in that trust is not derived from a "disposition … made by the will" but rather from the execution of an *inter vivos* trust with independent legal significance. We disagree, but in fairness we add that the judge here confronted a question of first impression in this Commonwealth.

General Laws c. 191, §9, *was* amended by the Legislature in 1976 to provide in the event of divorce for the revocation of testamentary dispositions which benefit the testator's former spouse. St.1976, c. 515, §6. The statute automatically causes such revocations unless the testator expresses a contrary intent. In this case we must determine what effect, if any, G.L. c. 191, §9, has on the former spouse's interest in the testator's pour-over trust.

While, by virtue of G.L. c. 203, §3B, the decedent's trust bore independent significance at the time of its creation in 1973, the trust had no practical significance until her death in 1981. The decedent executed both her will and indenture of trust on February 2, 1973. She transferred no property or funds to the trust at that time. The trust was to receive its funding at the decedent's death, in part through her life insurance policy and retirement benefits, and in part through a pour-over from the will's residuary clause. Mayo, the proposed executor and sole legatee under the will, was also made the primary beneficiary of the trust with power, as to Trust A only, to reach both income and principal.

During her lifetime, the decedent retained power to amend or revoke the trust. Since the trust was unfunded, her co-trustee was subject to no duties or obligations until her death. Similarly, it was only as a result of the decedent's death that Mayo could claim any right to the trust assets. It is evident from the time and manner in which the trust was created and funded, that the decedent's will and trust were integrally related components of a single testamentary scheme. For all practical purposes the trust, like the will, "spoke" only at the decedent's death. For this reason Mayo's interest in the trust was revoked by operation of G.L. c. 191, §9, at the same time his interest under the decedent's will was revoked.

It has reasonably been contended that in enacting G.L. c. 191, §9, the Legislature "intended to bring the law into line with the expectations of most people.... Divorce usually represents a stormy parting, where the last thing one of the parties wishes is to have an earlier will carried out giving everything to the former spouse." Young, Probate Reform, 18 Boston B.J. 7, 11 (1974). To carry out the testator's implied intent, the law revokes "any disposition or appointment of property made by the will to the former spouse." It is indisputable that if the decedent's trust was either testamentary or incorporated by reference into her will, Mayo's beneficial interest in the trust would be revoked by operation of the statute. However, the judge stopped short of mandating the same result in this case because here the trust had "independent significance" by virtue of c. 203, §3B. While correct, this characterization of the trust does not end our analysis. For example, in *Sullivan v. Burkin,* 390 Mass. 864, 867, 460 N.E.2d 572 (1984), we ruled prospectively that the assets of a revocable trust will be considered part of the "estate of the decedent" in determining the surviving spouse's statutory share.

Treating the components of the decedent's estate plan separately, and not as parts of an interrelated whole, brings about inconsistent results. Applying c. 191, §9, the judge correctly revoked the will provisions benefiting Mayo. As a result, the decedent's personal property — originally left to Mayo — fell into the will's residuary clause and passed to the trust. The judge then appropriately terminated Trust A for impossibility of purpose thereby denying Mayo his beneficial interest under Trust A. Yet, by upholding Mayo's interest under Trust B, the judge returned to Mayo a life interest in the same assets that composed the corpus of Trust A — both property passing by way of the decedent's will and the proceeds of her TIAA/CREF annuity contracts.

We are aware of only one case concerning the impact of a statute similar to G.L. c. 191, §9, on trust provisions benefiting a former spouse. In *Miller v. First Nat'l Bank & Trust Co.,* 637 P.2d 75 (Okla. 1981), the testator also simultaneously executed an indenture of trust and will naming his spouse as primary beneficiary. As in this case, the trust was to be funded at the testator's death by insurance proceeds and a will pour-over. Subsequently, the testator divorced his wife but failed to change the terms of his will and trust. The District court revoked the will provisions favoring the testator's former wife by applying a statute similar to G.L. c. 191, §9. Recognizing that "[t]he will without the trust has no meaning or value to the decedent's estate plan," the Oklahoma Supreme Court revoked the trust benefits as well. *Id.* at 77. However, we do not agree with the court's reasoning. Because the Oklahoma statute, like G.L. c. 191, §9, revokes dispositions of property made by will, the court stretched the doctrine of incorporation by reference to render the decedent's trust testamentary. We do not agree that reference to an existing trust in a will's pour-over clause is sufficient to incorporate that trust by reference without evidence that the testator intended such a result. See *Second Bank-State St. Trust Co. v. Pinion*, 341 Mass. 366, 367, 170 N.E.2d 350 (1960). However, it is not necessary for us to indulge in such reasoning, because we have concluded that the legislative intent under G.L. c. 191, §9, is that a divorced spouse should not take under a trust executed in these circumstances. In the absence of an expressed contrary intent, that statute implies an intent on the part of a testator to revoke will provisions favoring a former spouse. It is incongruous then to ignore that same intent with regard to a trust funded in part through her will's pour-over at the decedent's death. See *State St. Bank & Trust v. United States*, 634 F.2d 5, 10 (1st Cir. 1980) (trust should be interpreted in light of the settlor's contemporaneous execution of interrelated will). As one law review commentator has noted, "[t]ransferors use will substitutes to avoid probate, not to avoid the subsidiary law of wills. The subsidiary rules are the product of centuries of legal experience in attempting to discern transferors' wishes and suppress litigation. These rules should be treated as presumptively correct for will substitutes as well as for wills." Langbein, The Nonprobate Revolution and the Future of the Law of Succession, 97 Harv.L.Rev. 1108, 1136–1137 (1984).

Restricting our holding to the particular facts of this case—specifically the existence of a revocable pour-over trust funded entirely at the time of the decedent's death— we conclude that G.L. c. 191, §9, revokes Mayo's interest under Trust B.

6. *Nephews and Nieces of Donor.*

According to the terms of G.L. c. 191, §9, "[p]roperty prevented from passing to a former spouse because of revocation by divorce shall pass as if a former spouse had failed to survive the decedent...." In this case, the decedent's indenture of trust provides that if Mayo failed to survive her, "the balance of 'Trust B' shall be held ... for the benefit of the nephews and nieces of the Donor living at the time of the death of the Donor." The trustee is directed to expend as much of the net income and principal as he deems "advisable for [their] reasonable comfort, support and education" until all living nephews and nieces have attained the age of thirty. At that time, the trust is to terminate and Boston University and Clark University are each to receive fifty per cent of the trust property to assist women students in their graduate programs.

The decedent had no siblings and therefore no nephews and nieces who were blood relations. However, when she executed her trust in 1973, her husband, James P. Mayo, Jr., had two nephews and one niece—John and Allan Chamberlain and Mira Hinman. Before her divorce, the decedent maintained friendly relations with these young people and, along with her former husband, contributed toward their educational expenses. The three have survived the decedent.

The Weisses, Boston University, and Clark University appeal the decision of the judge upholding the decedent's gift to these three individuals. They argue that at the time the decedent created her trust she had no "nephews and nieces" by blood and that, at her death, her marital ties to Mayo's nephews and niece had been severed by divorce. Therefore, they contend that the class gift to the donor's "nephews and nieces" lapses for lack of identifiable beneficiaries.

The judge concluded that the trust language created an ambiguity, and thus he considered extrinsic evidence of the decedent's meaning and intent. Based upon that evidence, he decided that the decedent intended to provide for her nieces and nephews by marriage when she created the trust. Because the decedent never revoked this gift, he found that the Chamberlains and Hinman are entitled to their beneficial interests under the trust. We agree.

. . .

In sum, we conclude that the decedent established a valid trust under G.L. c. 203, § 3B; Mayo's beneficial interest in Trust A and Trust B is revoked by operation of G.L. c. 191, § 9; the Chamberlains and Hinman are entitled to take the interest given to the decedent's "nephews and nieces" under Trust B, leaving the remainder to Clark University and Boston University; the Weisses lack standing to remove the estate administrator; and the judge's award of attorneys' fees is vacated and remanded for reconsideration.

So ordered.

Notes and Problems

1. *Question of first impression*: Although the Massachusetts Supreme Court reversed the trial court's rulings, the Court acknowledged that the trial court was dealing with a question of first impression. What exactly was that question of first impression? How would you phrase it? Assuming the same fact pattern came up in California, would the issue be the same or different? Why?

2. *Inter vivos funding—amount*? What difference, if any, would it make if Clara Mayo (the decedent) had put $100 into the trust while she was alive? *Should* that make a difference? Why?

3. *California's approach*: As noted and discussed above, California has adopted a version of UTATA. In addition, California has abolished the rule that testamentary trusts are subject to probate court supervision for the life of the trust. Once a testamentary trust is funded, the trust is treated the same as an *inter vivos* trust in that there is no court supervision as a general rule. As envisioned and originally adopted, UTATA had two principal benefits: (1) it facilitated validating a pour-over clause, and (2) it ensured that the resulting trust was not subject to probate court supervision. Under current California law, as a general rule, no trusts, *inter vivos* or testamentary, are automatically and inherently subject to court supervision. Thus, UTATA currently only offers one benefit in California—it facilitates the creation of the trust by offering

an alternative method to validate a pour-over clause. In many states, however, testamentary trusts are still subject to probate court supervision for the life of the trust, and UTATA still offers that additional benefit in those states.

Does California's UTATA moot the old common law approaches to validating a pour-over clause? Now that you know UTATA, can you forget about the old common law approaches? The following problems may help you with your analysis of that question:

a. Assume T searches the Internet and finds a trust form she likes. She prints it out but does not sign it. Thereafter T validly executes her will. The residuary clause provides as follows: "I hereby give all my property to the trustee of my *inter vivos* trust, to hold and distribute pursuant to the terms of the trust." Thereafter T dies without doing anything else to the trust or trust instrument. What controls who gets T's property? Is the pour-over clause valid? What type of trust, if any, does T have?

b. Assume T searches the Internet and finds a trust form she likes. She prints it out but does not sign it. Thereafter T validly executes her will. The residuary clause provides as follows: "I hereby give all my property to the trustee of my *inter vivos* trust, to hold and distribute pursuant to the terms of the trust." Thereafter T signs the trust instrument but does not fund it. What controls who gets T's property? Is the pour-over clause valid? What type of trust, if any, does T have?

c. Assume T searches the Internet and finds a trust form she likes. She prints it out but does not sign it. Thereafter T validly executes her will. The residuary clause provides as follows: "I hereby give all my property to the trustee of my *inter vivos* trust, to hold and distribute pursuant to the terms of the trust." Thereafter T signs and funds the trust with $10,000. What controls who gets T's property? Is the pour-over clause valid? What type of trust, if any, does T have?

d. Assume T searches the Internet and finds a trust form she likes. She prints it out and signs it. Thereafter T validly executes her will. The residuary clause provides as follows: "I hereby give all my property to the trustee of my *inter vivos* trust, to hold and distribute pursuant to the terms of the trust." Thereafter, T amends the trust instrument but does not sign or fund it. What controls who gets T's property? Is the pour-over clause valid? What type of trust, if any, does T have? Is the amendment to the trust valid?

e. Assume T searches the Internet and finds a trust form she likes. She prints it out but does not sign it. Thereafter, T validly executes her will. The residuary clause provides as follows: "I hereby give all my property to the trustee of my *inter vivos* trust, to hold and distribute pursuant to the terms of the trust." Thereafter, T amends the trust instrument, signs it, but does not fund it. What controls who gets T's property? Is the pour-over clause valid? What type of trust, if any, does T have?

f. Assume T goes to an attorney and tells her attorney that she wants a trust and pour-over will to dispose of her estate. The attorney drafts a trust instrument and will that express T's wishes. When T returns to the attorney's office to execute the instruments, the printer prints out the will but jams just as it starts to print the trust. Inasmuch as T is there, T validly executes the will, but has to come back the following month to execute the trust. T does not fund the trust while she is alive. The residuary clause of T's will provides as follows: "I hereby give all my property to the trustee of my *inter vivos* trust, to hold and distribute pursuant to the terms of the trust." Thereafter, T dies without doing anything else to the trust or trust instrument. What controls who gets T's property? Is the pour-over clause valid? What type of trust, if any, does T have?

IV. Trust Revocability

A. Default Rule

An issue that goes hand in hand with creation of an *inter vivos* trust is whether it is revocable. If the settlor changes his or her mind, can he or she take it all back without the consent or permission of the beneficiaries or a court? Are *inter vivos* trusts revocable?

A trust may be revocable or irrevocable. Inasmuch as the settlor's intent dominates the law of trusts, it should come as no surprise that the same applies and controls the issue of whether a trust is revocable. If the settlor expressly provides that a trust is revocable, the trust is revocable. The only real issue is what should be the default approach where the trust is silent.

Because so much of the traditional law of trusts, particularly with respect to the creation of a trust, evolved out of the law of gifts, the traditional default rule with respect to the revocability of a trust should come as no surprise. As a general rule, are *inter vivos* gifts revocable? No. Accordingly, as a general rule, should *inter vivos* trusts be revocable? No. Consistent with that line of reasoning, the traditional common law approach is that a trust is presumed irrevocable unless the settlor provides otherwise. Having said that, Louisiana and California have always presumed the opposite — that the default rule should be that the trust *is revocable* unless the settlor provides otherwise.

The modern trend of trust law focuses more on the presumed intent of the average testator for its default rules. Consistent with that approach, both the Uniform Trust Code and the RESTATEMENT THIRD OF TRUSTS endorse the traditional California approach — that a trust should be presumed revocable unless the settlor provides otherwise. While not yet the majority rule, the modern trend approach to revocability is quickly being adopted in an increasing number of states.

B. Mechanics of Revoking a Trust

Assuming a trust is revocable, what should a settlor have to do to validly revoke the trust? If an *inter vivos* trust is revocable, for all practical purposes is it basically a will? If it is basically a will, should the will revocation doctrines apply and control the law of trust revocation?

Historically, inasmuch as a trust was presumed irrevocable unless the settlor provided otherwise, the general rule was that a trust was only revocable to the extent and as provided by the settlor. The settlor's intent controlled the question of how mechanically a trust could be revoked. Moreover, where the trust set forth only one method of revocation, the courts typically construed that to be the *only* method by which the trust could be revoked. Historically it was very common for an *inter vivos* revocable trust to include the following provision (or one to the same effect): "The settlor may amend, alter, or revoke the trust by an instrument in writing signed by the settlor and delivered to trustee while the settlor is still alive." Consistent with the traditional common law approach, where a trust included such an express provision, it typically was construed as the exclusive method of revoking or amending the trust. In the absence of a trust provision addressing how the trust could be revoked, any reasonable method that adequately expresses the intent to revoke should be a valid revocation. *See* Bogert's Trusts & Trustees § 1001 (2014).

As noted above, the modern trend approach to trust revocability takes more of an intent-based approach. In addition, the modern trend adopts the view that the contemporary settlor of an *inter vivos* revocable trust thinks of it as indistinguishable from a will. Under this conceptual model, the settlor typically is the initial trustee and lifetime beneficiary. The settlor still thinks of the property transferred to the trust as his or her property, technically not the trust property. The underlying assumption is that the contemporary settlor has created the *inter vivos* revocable trust as a cheaper, faster, and more confidential way of transferring one's property at death, but basically still thinks of the *inter vivos* revocable trust as functionally indistinguishable from a traditional will and therefore would prefer to be able to treat it as functionally indistinguishable from a will.

Accordingly, the Uniform Trust Code takes a wills-based approach to the revocability of an *inter vivos* trust. First, as noted above, the default presumption is that an *inter vivos* revocable trust is presumed revocable (just like a will). Second, if the trust expressly sets forth a method or methods of revocation, that/those method(s) should not be deemed the exclusive method(s) unless the trust expressly so provides. Third, whether the trust sets forth a method of revocation or not, as long as the method is not expressly made the exclusive method(s) of revoking the trust, the trust can be revoked by any method that manifests "clear and convincing evidence of the settlor's intent." UTC § 602 (c)(2)(B). Assuming the trust does not set forth an exclusive method of revocation, a subsequently executed will or codicil can revoke the trust if it expressly refers to the trust, and the will or codicil can implicitly revoke the trust by specifically devising trust property contrary to the terms of the trust. UTC § 602 (c)(2)(A). Finally, consistent with the modern trend approach to wills, if the trust sets forth an express method of revocation, the settlor need only substantially comply with the method of revocation; strict compliance is not applicable. UTC § 602(c)(1).

While a good number of states have adopted the modern trend default rule with respect to whether a trust is revocable where the trust is silent, not as many states have adopted the modern trend view as to the mechanics of revoking the *inter vivos* revocable trust. Most states have tried to loosen up the common law approach without going as far as the UTC. If the common law approach is one end of the spectrum, and the UTC is the other end, most states are somewhere in between. Where does California fall on this spectrum?

Masry v. Masry
166 Cal. App. 4th 738 (2008)

GILBERT, P.J.

How may a settlor revoke a revocable trust? Probate Code section 15401, subdivision (a)(2) provides the answer: (1) by compliance with the method stated in the trust, (2) by a writing (other than a will) signed by the settlor and delivered to the trustee during the lifetime of the settlor. Subdivision (a)(2) also tells us that its provisions do not apply if the trust instrument *explicitly* makes its language the exclusive method of revocation.

A husband and wife are trustors and trustees of a family trust. The trust provides that each of the trustors has the power to revoke the trust during their joint lifetimes by written direction delivered to the other trustor and to the trustee.

Here, husband executed a revocation of the trust but did not deliver the notice of revocation to his wife. Wife received notice of the revocation after his death.

We conclude, among other things, that the revocation provision in the trust was not explicitly exclusive, and husband's method of revocation complied with Probate Code section 15401, subdivision (a)(2). We affirm.

FACTS

In 2004, Edward Masry and appellant Joette Masry, husband and wife, created the Edward and Joette Masry Family Trust (Family Trust), which consisted of the property acquired during their marriage. Each was a trustor and trustee. Section 2.1 of the Family Trust provides for revocation. It states in pertinent part: "Each of the Trustors hereby reserves the right and power to revoke this Trust, in whole or in part, from time to time during their joint lifetimes, by written direction delivered to the other Trustor and to the Trustee."

A little over a year after the Family Trust was created, and shortly before his death, Edward executed a "Notice of Revocation of Interest in Trust and Resignation as Trustee." His purpose was to transfer his assets from the Family Trust to a new trust, the Edward L. Masry Trust (Edward Trust). He designated two of his children from a previous marriage, respondents Louis Masry and Louanne Masry Weeks, as successor cotrustees. Joette was not given notice of the revocation until two weeks after Edward's death.

Joette filed a revocation petition and a petition to ascertain beneficiaries. She argued, among other things, that Edward's revocation was invalid because she was not given notice during his lifetime. The trial court found that the Family Trust did not explicitly make delivery of the revocation to Joette, the other Trustor, during Edward's lifetime the exclusive method of revocation. The court ruled that Edward's delivery of the revocation to himself as trustee satisfied Probate Code section 15401, subdivision (b), and Family Code section 761. The trial court also ruled that respondents' civil action did not violate the no contest provision of the Edward Trust.

DISCUSSION

Revocation

How do we determine whether the trust document explicitly provides that its stated method of revocation is exclusive? We look to dictum in *Huscher v. Wells Fargo Bank* (2004) 121 Cal.App.4th 956, 18 Cal.Rptr.3d 27. Dicta may not decide a case but can be persuasive and influence later cases. *Huscher's* dictum, however, is so persuasive that it becomes the law here.

The issue in *Huscher* involved amendments to a trust under former Civil Code section 2280, the predecessor to Probate Code section 15401 enacted in 1986, but its reasoning applies to revocation. The right to revoke includes the right to modify. (*Huscher v. Wells Fargo Bank, supra,* 121 Cal.App.4th 956, 962, fn. 5, 18 Cal.Rptr.3d 27, citing *Estate of Lindstrom* (1987) 191 Cal.App.3d 375, 385, fn. 11, 236 Cal.Rptr. 376.)

Huscher chronicled and analyzed the history of Civil Code section 2280. Just before it was replaced by Probate Code section 15401, Civil Code section 2280 provided that every voluntary trust is revocable "[u]nless expressly made irrevocable by the instrument creating the trust...." (*Huscher v. Wells Fargo Bank, supra,* 121 Cal.App.4th 956, 963, 18 Cal.Rptr.3d 27.) The *Huscher* court concluded that language in trust documents that purports to revoke under Civil Code section 2280 is reasonably subject to an analysis of whether the language explicitly or implicitly makes the method of revocation exclusive. Under this analysis, one could argue that the language here, providing that notice of revocation be given by the trustor to the other trustor and the trustee, is implicitly exclusive.

But this argument is less persuasive under current Probate Code section 15401, subdivision (a)(2). *Huscher* points out that "a modification method is explicitly exclusive when the trust instrument directly and unambiguously states that the procedure is the exclusive one." (*Huscher v. Wells Fargo Bank, supra,* 121 Cal.App.4th 956, 968, 18 Cal.Rptr.3d 27.) We agree with respondents that section 2.1 of the Family Trust does not state that the method of revocation it provides is explicitly exclusive. It is simply one method of revocation in addition to that provided in Probate Code section 15401, subdivision (a)(2). Edward complied with section 15401, subdivision (a)(2), by giving notice to himself as trustee. If the language in the trust were sufficient to qualify as the explicitly exclusive method, then the language in section 15401, subdivision (a)(2) would be unnecessary.

Joette relies on *Conservatorship of Irvine* (1995) 40 Cal.App.4th 1334, 47 Cal.Rptr.2d 587. For the reasons stated in *Huscher,* the *Irvine* case is not persuasive because it relies on cases interpreting former Civil Code section 2280, which are inapposite.

The parties rely on *Gardenhire v. Superior Court* (2005) 127 Cal.App.4th 882, 26 Cal.Rptr.3d 143, but cite different parts of the opinion to support their view of the meaning of Probate Code section 15401, subdivision (a)(2).

In *Gardenhire,* the trustor was also the trustee. After the trust was created, the trustor revoked the trust by executing a will in which she disposed of all her property. The appellate court held that the trustor revoked according to the method described in the trust, "written notice signed by the Trustor and delivered to the Trustee." (*Gardenhire v. Superior Court, supra,* 127 Cal.App.4th 882, 886, 26 Cal.Rptr.3d 143.) This qualified as a writing in which the trustor gave notice to herself as trustee. Respondents point out that in this respect the notice was the same as the notice here. Like the trustor in *Gardenhire,* Edward revoked by giving notice to himself as trustee. Here the difference is that the trustor used a method provided in Probate Code section 15401, subdivision(a)(1), instead of the method provided in the trust.

Joette reads *Gardenhire* to hold that if the language of revocation in the trust is clear and express, then that is the exclusive method to revoke. *Gardenhire* states in dictum, "If the trust is not silent and instead provides a method of revocation, then Probate Code section 15401, subdivision (a)(2) is inapplicable." (*Gardenhire v. Superior Court, supra,* 127 Cal.App.4th 882, 894, 26 Cal.Rptr.3d 143.) But were we to adopt the *Gardenhire* view, Probate Code section 15401, subdivision (a)(2) would be, at best, a clarification of former Civil Code section 2280, and not a change. *Huscher's* reasoning, albeit expressed in its dictum, compels us to conclude that, absent language in the trust that its method of revocation is exclusive, the trustor has the option of revoking according to the method provided in Probate Code section 15401, subdivision (a)(2), delivering notice to himself as trustee. That there are two trustees here does not change our view. Under subdivision (a)(2), Edward's notice to himself is sufficient as notice to "the trustee."

Nor does the method of revocation here violate section Probate Code section 15401, subdivision (b). That section provides, "Unless otherwise provided in the instrument, if a trust is created by more than one settlor, each settlor may revoke the trust as to the portion of the trust contributed by that settlor, except as provided by Section 761 of the Family Code." Family Code section 761 provides, "Unless the trust instrument expressly provides otherwise, a power to revoke as to community property may be exercised by either spouse acting alone."

Joette argues that such an interpretation of Probate Code section 15401 and its subdivisions is not good public policy, because it allows a "secret" revocation and represents one spouse taking advantage of the other. It is true that had Joette been given notice of the revocation as provided in the Family Trust, she could have tried to persuade Edward to change his mind or could have made changes in the disposition of her community share of the trust property.

But married parties are permitted to dispose of their share of the community without the consent of the other spouse. And if the Legislature sees an overriding public policy argument that the method of revocation used here violates public policy, it can certainly once again amend the statute.

...

The judgment is affirmed....

Notes

1. *California approach*: If the common law approach to trust revocability is one end of the spectrum, and the Uniform Trust Code is the other end, where would you put California on that spectrum?

2. *Power to revoke versus power to amend*: As the court notes, the general rule under both the common law approach and the modern trend approach is that the power to revoke implicitly includes the power to amend, even if the power to revoke does not expressly include a statement of the power to amend.

3. *Marital trust*: It is not uncommon for a married couple or registered domestic partners to create a joint trust. Assuming it is a revocable trust (either expressly or based on California's default rule), what happens upon the death of the first spouse/ registered domestic partner? To the extent both parties put property into the trust (community property and/or separate property), should one spouse's death affect the surviving party's right to revoke?

In *Miller v. Miller*, No. H026719, 2004 WL 2601792 (Cal. Ct. App. Nov. 16, 2004), the court was faced with this issue. Damon and Hazel Miller, husband and wife, deed their home (which they had purchased with earnings acquired during the marriage) to a trust they created for their benefit during their lifetime, and upon the death of the survivor, to their two sons. The trust expressly provided that it was revocable:

> We reserve unto ourselves the power and right at any time during our lifetime to amend or revoke in whole or in part the trust hereby created without the necessity of obtaining the consent of any beneficiary and without giving notice to any beneficiary. The sale or other disposition by us of the whole or any part of the property held hereunder shall constitute as to such whole or part a revocation of this trust.

Id. at *2. Thereafter Hazel died, and Damon moved into an assisted living facility. Damon sought to revoke the trust by selling the house. The trial court ruled that Damon could neither revoke nor sell the house.

The court of appeal began its analysis by noting the default rule that unless a trust provides otherwise, community property that is transferred into a trust *inter vivos* ordinarily retains its community property characterization. In addition, the default rule is that unless a trust provides otherwise, *inter vivos* each spouse has the power to revoke over all of the community property. While the trust's express power to revoke did not address what should happen upon the death of the first spouse, the failure to address the issue meant the California default rule controlled— the surviving spouse retains the power to revoke. The only remaining issue is the scope of the power to revoke: should it be the same as it was when both spouses were alive, or does the death of the first spouse change the scope of the power to revoke?

> The appellate court in *Powell* reviewed the applicable law: "[R]evocation of a joint trust by one spouse is effective as to all community property in the trust. (Fam.Code, §761, subd. (b).) However, as to other property in the trust, revocation is effective only as to the revoking party's share of other property. (Prob.Code, §15401, subd. (b).)" (*Id.* at p. 1441.) The *Powell* court proceeded to conclude: "[T]he fact the trust assets were community property prior to Myrtle's death does not mean they retained that status at the time of revocation. At the time of Myrtle's death, Probate Code section 100 provided: 'Upon the death of a married person, one-half of the community property belongs to the surviving spouse and the other half belongs to the decedent.' (Stats.1990, ch. 79, §14, p. 470.) Thus, to the extent William and Myrtle retained reversionary property interests in the trust assets during Myrtle's lifetime by virtue of the right of revocation provided in the trust, those property interests were *transmuted* from community to separate property upon Myrtle's death. Under Probate Code section 15401, subdivision (b), William's revocation was therefore effective only as to his half of the trust corpus, as the trial court ruled. Myrtle's half was subject to disposition as provided in her will, i.e., in accordance with the provisions of the 1991 trust." (*Estate of Powell, supra,* 83 Cal.App.4th at p. 1441, italics added.)

Id. at *5. The court ruled that (1) Damon's attempted revocation of the trust was inconsistent with Damon's limited power to revoke following Hazel's death and (2) the attempted sale of the entire house was inconsistent with the sons' interest in Hazel's share, which was no longer revocable. *Id.* at *9.

4. *Marital trust—drafting for revocability and ability to amend*: A professionally drafted joint *marital revocable living trust* typically will include a clear, express statement of revocability and powers to amend. For a joint California revocable living trust, the trust document typically provides a pattern of revocability as follows:

a. *During the joint lifetimes of the settlors (the married couple or domestic partners)*: Either settlor (either spouse/domestic partner) may revoke the entire trust with respect to all of the couple's community property. With respect to either settlor's separate property, revocation is permitted only by that settlor.

b. *At the death of the first settlor (spouse/domestic partner)*: At the death of the first spouse/domestic partner, the joint trust splits into at least two parts. The surviving settlor's (surviving spouse/domestic partner) share of community property and his or her separate property is usually retained, in trust, as a new split-off revocable living trust for such survivor. Often referred to as "the survivor's trust," it remains completely revocable by such surviving spouse/domestic partner during his or her lifetime. The deceased settlor's (first to die spouse/domestic partner) share of community property and his or her separate property are either distributed outright pursuant to the dispositive provisions of the trust, or retained in a trust (or multiple trusts for more complex estates) for distribution according to its terms. In the common situation where this deceased settlor's portion of the property remains in trust (usually a new trust established by the underlying joint trust document), the terms usually provide that this trust is irrevocable.

c. *At the death of the surviving settlor (spouse/domestic partner)*: Similar to what occurs at the first settlor's death, the surviving settlor's estate may continue to be held in trust (or multiple trusts). Any such trust typically becomes, pursuant to the trust terms, irrevocable.

The ability to amend a joint marital trust is also carefully addressed in a professionally drafted document. A typical California joint revocable living trust will contain provisions for the settlors' power to amend that are, with usually one exception, consistent with those for revocation. While during the joint lifetimes of the settlors, either settlor can revoke the entire trust with respect to all of the couple's community property, the trust will usually require both for amending such portion of the trust.

Recall the will versus revocable living trust discussion at the end of Chapter 11. This is a good example of why it is usually necessary to secure the help of an estate planning attorney to assist in the "administration" of a revocable living trust at the death of the settlor or, in the case of a joint marital trust, for assistance at the death of each settlor.

5. *Marital trust—ethical issues in client representation*: As indicated, in California it is common for spouses (and domestic partners) who wish to have a revocable living trust be the vehicle for their respective dispositive wishes to utilize a joint revocable living trust. While beyond the scope of this book, the estate planning professional faces ethical issues in drafting such a document. An example of a "worst case" scenario could play out as follows: clients husband and wife discuss, together, their mutual estate plan goals and objectives in your initial meeting with them in your office. All sounds fine as they both express mutual desires to leave all of their property to the other spouse, if living, and, if not, to their children in equal shares (by consistent means). This is a fairly typical "we are in agreement" estate planning situation.

Within hours one spouse, for example, the husband, calls you and says: "I didn't want to say anything in front of my wife, but I want to change an integral part of my estate plan. I want to leave something (maybe a substantial amount of property) to someone other than my wife (in the worst case, someone in his life about which the wife knows nothing).” As the drafting attorney, you are, potentially, stuck. You have the ethical obligation of *confidentiality* to your client, the husband, but you also have the ethical obligation to *disclose* information to your client, the wife, that may be pertinent with respect to her estate planning goals and objectives. If you do not have a sufficient *engagement letter* signed by both spouses at the inception of your representation, there will be ethical problems — you are stuck with no actual, practical solution. A proper dual-representation engagement letter, agreed to by the clients, will require that the clients effectively agree to waive their right of *confidentiality* thus, each spouse knows in advance that any subsequent relevant information obtained from either spouse will be *disclosed* to the other. This will effectively obviate the inherent potential dilemma of representing both spouses whose wishes may deviate from those expressed in the initial meeting where their respective goals and objectives are expressed (and, in accordance with, drafted).

Problems

1. Settlor executed a revocable *inter vivos* trust for the benefit of her son. The trust instrument: (1) appointed Liberty National Bank & Trust as trustee; and (2) provided that following her death, all the trust property should be distributed outright to her son. Thereafter, Settlor began to have second thoughts about leaving all of the trust property to her son and none to her daughter.

   Settlor has a weak heart, and one evening she begins to have chest pains. She fears the end may be soon. She takes out a piece of paper and validly executes a holographic will that provides in part as follows: “I dissolve the living trust; I want all my property to go to my two children equally.” The settlor/testatrix wrote the holographic will approximately one hour before she died, during nonbanking hours.

   a. Has Settlor validly revoked the trust under California law? *See Gamage v. Liberty Nat. Bank & Trust Co.*, 598 S.W.2d 463 (Ky. Ct. App. 1980) (applying Kentucky law).

   b. Assume the same fact pattern as above, only this time the revocable trust is silent with respect to how it can be revoked. Has Settlor validly revoked the trust under California law?

   c. Assume the same fact pattern as above, only this time the revocable trust is silent with respect to how it can be revoked and Settlor called the trustee and informed them that she had executed the holographic will revoking the trust. Has Settlor validly revoked the trust under California law?

2. Assume the same fact pattern as Problem 1, above, only this time the trust expressly provides that the trust may be revoked “by any writing signed by the settlor and delivered to the trustee.” Following Settlor’s death, her executor presents the holographic will to the trustee. Has Settlor validly revoked the trust under California law? *See Rosenauer v. Title Ins. & Trust Co.*, 30 Cal. App. 3d 300 (Ct. App. 1973).

Chapter 13

Trust Life: Beneficiary's Perspective

I. Scope of Beneficiary's Interest

A trust is a bifurcated gift. The trustee holds and manages the trust property for the benefit of the beneficiaries. What exactly does that mean, particularly when viewed from the beneficiary's perspective?

A. Beneficiary's Interest: Mandatory versus Discretionary

A trust beneficiary's interest in the assets held by the trust is, generally, governed by the settlor's intent (i.e., the terms of the trust document itself for most trusts). More specifically, the trust document conveys to the trustee certain powers. The extent to which the trustee can exercise the powers, and the instructions for when and how they are to be exercised, are contained in various clauses in the trust. Arguably, the most critical variable in determining a beneficiary's ability to "benefit" from the trust turns on whether the interest (or the trustee's power to control such interest) is mandatory or discretionary.

Marsman v. Nasca

573 N.E.2d 1025 (Mass. App. Ct. 1991)

DREBEN, Justice.

This appeal raises the following: Does a trustee, holding a discretionary power to pay principal for the "comfortable support and maintenance" of a beneficiary, have a duty to inquire into the financial resources of that beneficiary so as to recognize his needs? If so, what is the remedy for such failure? A Probate Court judge held that the will involved in this case imposed a duty of inquiry upon the trustee....

1. *Facts....*

Sara Wirt Marsman died in September, 1971, survived by her second husband, T. Frederik Marsman (Cappy), and her daughter by her first marriage, Sally Marsman Marlette. Mr. James F. Farr, her lawyer for many years, drew her will and was the trustee thereunder.

Article IIA of Sara's will provided in relevant part:

"It is my desire that my husband, T. Fred Marsman, be provided with *reasonable maintenance, comfort and support* after my death. Accordingly, if my said husband is living at the time of my death, I give to my trustees, who shall set the same aside as a separate trust fund, one-third (1/3) of the rest, residue and remainder of my estate … ; they shall pay the net income therefrom to my said husband at least quarterly during his life; and *after having considered the various available sources of support for him,* my trustees shall, if they deem it necessary or desirable from time to time, in their sole and uncontrolled discretion, pay over to him, or use, apply and/or expend for his direct or indirect benefit such amount or amounts of the principal thereof as they shall deem advisable for his *comfortable support and maintenance."* (Emphasis supplied).

Article IIB provided:

"Whatever remains of said separate trust fund, including any accumulated income thereon on the death of my husband, shall be added to the trust fund established under Article IIC…."

Article IIC established a trust for the benefit of Sally and her family. Sally was given the right to withdraw principal and, on her death, the trust was to continue for the benefit of her issue and surviving husband.

The will also contained the following exculpatory clause:

"No trustee hereunder shall ever be liable except for his own willful neglect or default."

During their marriage, Sara and Cappy lived well and entertained frequently. Cappy's main interest in life centered around horses. An expert horseman, he was riding director and instructor at the Dana Hall School in Wellesley until he was retired due to age in 1972. Sally, who was also a skilled rider, viewed Cappy as her mentor, and each had great affection for the other. Sara, wealthy from her prior marriage, managed the couple's financial affairs. She treated Cappy as "Lord of the Manor" and gave him money for his personal expenses, including an extensive wardrobe from one of the finest men's stores in Wellesley.

…

After Sara's death in 1971, Farr met with Cappy and Sally and held what he termed his "usual family conference" going over the provisions of the will. At the time of Sara's death, the Wellesley property was appraised at $29,000, and the principal of Cappy's trust was about $65,600.

Cappy continued to live in the Wellesley house but was forced by Sara's death and his loss of employment in 1972 to reduce his standard of living substantially…. In 1972, Cappy took out a mortgage for $4,000, the proceeds of which were used to pay bills. Farr was aware of the transaction, as he replied to an inquiry of the mortgagee bank concerning the appraised value of the Wellesley property and the income Cappy expected to receive from Sara's trust.

…

In February, 1974, Cappy informed the trustee that business was at a standstill and that he really needed some funds, if possible. Farr replied in a letter in which he set forth the relevant portion of the will and wrote that he thought the language was "broad enough to permit a distribution of principal." Farr enclosed a check of $300. He asked Cappy to explain in writing the need for some support and why the need had arisen. The judge found that Farr, by his actions, discouraged Cappy from making any requests for principal.

Indeed, Cappy did not reduce his request to writing and never again requested principal. Farr made no investigation whatsoever of Cappy's needs or his "available sources of support" from the date of Sara's death until Cappy's admission to a nursing home in 1983 and, other than the $300 payment, made no additional distributions of principal until Cappy entered the nursing home.

By the fall of 1974, Cappy's difficulty in meeting expenses intensified. Several of his checks were returned for insufficient funds, and in October, 1974, in order that he might remain in the house, Sally and he agreed that she would take over the mortgage payments, the real estate taxes, insurance, and major repairs. In return, she would get the house upon Cappy's death.

Cappy and Sally went to Farr to draw up a deed. Farr was the only lawyer involved, and he billed Sally for the work. He wrote to Sally, stating his understanding of the proposed transaction, and asking, among other things, whether Margaret would have a right to live in the house if Cappy should predecease her. The answer was no. No copy of the letter to Sally was sent to Cappy. A deed was executed by Cappy on November 7, 1974, transferring the property to Sally and her husband Richard T. Marlette (Marlette) as tenants by the entirety, reserving a life estate to Cappy. No writing set forth Sally's obligations to Cappy.

The judge found that there was no indication that Cappy did not understand the transaction, although, in response to a request for certain papers by Farr, Cappy sent a collection of irrelevant documents. The judge also found that Cappy clearly understood that he was preserving no rights for Margaret, and that neither Sally nor Richard nor Farr ever made any representation to Margaret that she would be able to stay in the house after Cappy's death.

Although Farr had read Sara's will to Cappy and had written to him that the will was "broad enough to permit a distribution of principal," the judge found that Farr failed to advise Cappy that the principal of his trust could be used for the expenses of the Wellesley home. The parsimonious distribution of $300 and Farr's knowledge that the purpose of the conveyance to Sally was to enable Cappy to remain in the house, provide support for this finding. After executing the deed, Cappy expressed to Farr that he was pleased and most appreciative. Margaret testified that Cappy thought Farr was "great" and that he considered him his lawyer.

Sally and Marlette complied with their obligations under the agreement. Sally died in 1983, and Marlette became the sole owner of the property subject to Cappy's life estate. Although Margaret knew before Cappy's death that she did not have any interest in the Wellesley property, she believed that Sally would have allowed her to live in the house because of their friendship. After Cappy's death in 1987, Marlette inquired as to Margaret's plans, and, subsequently, through Farr, sent Margaret a notice to vacate the premises. Margaret brought this action in the Probate Court.

After a two-day trial, the judge held that the trustee was in breach of his duty to Cappy when he neglected to inquire as to the latter's finances. She concluded that, had Farr fulfilled his fiduciary duties, Cappy would not have conveyed the residence owned by him to Sally and Marlette. The judge ordered Marlette to convey the house to Margaret and also ordered Farr to reimburse Marlette from the remaining portion of Cappy's trust for the expenses paid by him and Sally for the upkeep of the property. If Cappy's trust proved insufficient to make such payments, Farr was to be personally liable for such expenses. Both Farr and Marlette appealed from the judgment, from the denial of their motions to amend the findings, and from their motions for a new trial. Margaret appealed from the denial of her motion for attorney's fees. As indicated earlier, we agree with the judge that Sara's will imposed a duty of inquiry on the trustee, but we disagree with the remedy and, therefore, remand for further proceedings.

2. *Breach of trust by the trustee.* Contrary to Farr's contention that it was not incumbent upon him to become familiar with Cappy's finances, Article IIA of Sara's will clearly placed such a duty upon him. In his brief, Farr claims that the will gave Cappy the right to request principal "in extraordinary circumstances" and that the trustee, "was charged by Sara to be wary should Cappy request money beyond that which he quarterly received." Nothing in the will or the record supports this narrow construction. To the contrary, the direction to the trustees was to pay Cappy such amounts "as they shall deem advisable for his comfortable support and maintenance." This language has been interpreted to set an ascertainable standard, namely to maintain the life beneficiary "in accordance with the standard of living which was normal for him before he became a beneficiary of the trust." *Woodberry v. Bunker,* 359 Mass 239, 243, 268 N.E.2d 841 (1971). *Dana v. Gring,* 374 Mass. 109, 117, 371 N.E.2d 755 (1977). See *Blodget v. Delaney,* 201 F.2d 589, 593 (1st Cir.1953).

Even where the only direction to the trustee is that he shall "in his discretion" pay such portion of the principal as he shall "deem advisable," the discretion is not absolute. "Prudence and reasonableness, not caprice or careless good nature, much less a desire on the part of the trustee to be relieved from trouble ... furnish the standard of conduct." *Boyden v. Stevens,* 285 Mass. 176, 179, 188 N.E. 741 (1934), quoting from *Corkery v. Dorsey,* 223 Mass. 97, 101, 111 N.E. 795 (1916). *Holyoke Natl. Bank v. Wilson,* 350 Mass. 223, 227, 214 N.E.2d 42 (1966).

That there is a duty of inquiry into the needs of the beneficiary follows from the requirement that the trustee's power "must be exercised with that soundness of judgment which follows from a due appreciation of trust responsibility." *Boyden v. Stevens,* 285 Mass. at 179, 188 N.E. 741. *Woodberry v. Bunker,* 359 Mass. at 241, 268 N.E.2d 841. In *Old Colony Trust Co. v. Rodd,* 356 Mass. 584, 586, 254 N.E.2d 886 (1970), the trustee sent a questionnaire to each potential beneficiary to determine which of them required assistance but failed to make further inquiry in cases where the answers were incomplete. The court agreed with the trial judge that the method employed by the trustee in determining the amount of assistance required in each case to attain "comfortable support and maintenance" was inadequate. There, as here, the trustee attempted to argue that it was appropriate to save for the beneficiaries' future medical needs. The court held that the "prospect of illness in old age does not warrant a persistent policy of niggardliness toward individuals for whose comfortable support in life the trust has been established. The payments made to the respondent and several other beneficiaries, viewed in light of their assets and needs, when measured against the assets of the trust show that little consideration has been given to the 'comfortable support' of the beneficiaries." *Id.* at 589–590, 254 N.E.2d 886. See 3 Scott, Trusts § 187.3 (Fratcher 4th ed. 1988) (action of trustee is "arbitrary" where he "is authorized to make payments to a beneficiary if in his judgment he deems it wise and he refuses to inquire into the circumstances of the beneficiary"). See also *Kolodney v. Kolodney,* 6 Conn.App. 118, 123, 503 A.2d 625 (1986).

Farr, in our view, did not meet his responsibilities either of inquiry or of distribution under the trust. The conclusion of the trial judge that, had he exercised "sound judgment," he would have made such payments to Cappy "as to allow him to continue to live in the home he had occupied for many years with the settlor" was warranted.

. . .

4. *Remainder of Cappy's trust.* The amounts that should have been expended for Cappy's benefit are, however, in a different category. More than $80,000 remained in the trust for Cappy at the time of his death. As we have indicated, the trial judge properly concluded that payments of principal should have been made to Cappy from that fund in sufficient amount to enable him to keep the Wellesley property. There is no reason for the beneficiaries of the trust under Article IIC to obtain funds which they would not have received had Farr followed the testatrix's direction. The remedy in such circumstances is to impress a constructive trust on the amounts which should have been distributed to Cappy but were not because of the error of the trustee. Even in cases where beneficiaries have already been paid funds by mistake, the amounts may be collected from them unless the recipients were bona fide purchasers or unless they, without notice of the improper payments, had so changed their position that it would be inequitable to make them repay. 5 Scott, Trusts § 465, at 341 (Fratcher 4th ed.1989). *Allen v. Stewart,* 214 Mass. 109, 113, 100 N.E. 1092 (1913). *Welch v. Flory,* 294 Mass. 138, 144, 200 N.E. 900 (1936). See *National Academy of Sciences v. Cambridge Trust Co.,* 370 Mass. 303, 307, 346 N.E.2d 879 (1976). Here, the remainder of Cappy's trust has not yet been distributed, and there is no reason to depart from the usual rule of impressing a constructive trust in favor of Cappy's estate on the amounts wrongfully withheld. . . .

. . .

5. *Personal liability of the trustee.* Farr raises a number of defenses against the imposition of personal liability, including the statute of limitations, the exculpatory clause in the will, and the fact that Cappy assented to the accounts of the trustee. . . .

The more difficult question is the effect of the exculpatory clause. As indicated in part 3 of this opinion, we consider the order to Marlette to reconvey the property an inappropriate remedy. In view of the judge's finding that, but for the trustee's breach, Cappy would have retained ownership of the house, the liability of the trustee could be considerable.

Although exculpatory clauses are not looked upon with favor and are strictly construed, such "provisions inserted in the trust instrument without any overreaching or abuse by the trustee of any fiduciary or confidential relationship to the settlor are generally held effective except as to breaches of trust 'committed in bad faith or intentionally or with reckless indifference to the interest of the beneficiary.'" *New England Trust Co. v. Paine,* 317 Mass. 542, 550, 59 N.E.2d 263 (1945), *S.C.,* 320 Mass. 482, 485, 70 N.E.2d 6 (1946). See *Dill v. Boston Safe Deposit & Trust Co.,* 343 Mass. 97, 100–102, 175 N.E.2d 911 (1961); *Boston Safe Deposit & Trust Co. v. Boone,* 21 Mass.App.Ct. 637, 644, 489 N.E.2d 209 (1986). The actions of Farr were not of this ilk and also do not fall within the meaning of the term used in the will, "willful neglect or default."

Farr testified that he discussed the exculpatory clause with Sara and that she wanted it included. Nevertheless, the judge, without finding that there was an overreaching or abuse of Farr's fiduciary relation with Sara, held the clause ineffective. Relying on the fact that Farr was Sara's attorney, she stated: "One cannot know at this point in time whether or not Farr specifically called this provision to Sara's attention. Given the total failure of Farr to use his judgment as to [C]appy's needs, it would be unjust and unreasonable to hold him harmless by reason of the exculpatory provisions he himself drafted and inserted in this instrument."

Assuming that the judge disbelieved Farr's testimony that he and Sara discussed the clause, although such disbelief on her part is by no means clear, the conclusion that it "would be unjust and unreasonable to hold [Farr] harmless" is not sufficient to find the overreaching or abuse of a fiduciary relation which is required to hold the provision ineffective. See Restatement (Second) of Trusts § 222, comment d (1959).[10] We note that the judge found that Sara managed all the finances of the couple, and from all that appears, was competent in financial matters.

There was no evidence about the preparation and execution of Sara's will except for the questions concerning the exculpatory clause addressed to Farr by his own coun-

---

10. The Restatement lists six factors that may be considered in determining whether a provision relieving the trustee from liability is ineffective on the ground that it was inserted in the trust instrument as a result of an abuse of a fiduciary relationship at the time of the trust's creation. The six factors are: "(1) whether the trustee prior to the creation of the trust had been in a fiduciary relationship to the settlor, as where the trustee had been guardian of the settlor; (2) whether the trust instrument was drawn by the trustee or by a person acting wholly or partially on his behalf; (3) whether the settlor has taken independent advice as to the provisions of the trust instrument; (4) whether the settlor is a person of experience and judgment or is a person who is unfamiliar with business affairs or is not a person of much judgment or understanding; (5) whether the insertion of the provision was due to undue influence or other improper conduct on the part of the trustee; (6) the extent and reasonableness of the provision."

sel. No claim was made that the clause was the result of an abuse of confidence. See *Boston Safe Deposit & Trust Co. v. Boone,* 21 Mass.App.Ct. at 644, 489 N.E.2d 209.

The fact that the trustee drew the instrument and suggested the insertion of the exculpatory clause does not necessarily make the provision ineffective. Restatement (Second) of Trusts § 222, comment d. No rule of law requires that an exculpatory clause drawn by a prospective trustee be held ineffective unless the client is advised independently. Cf. *Barnum v. Fay,* 320 Mass. 177, 181, 69 N.E.2d 470 (1946).

The judge used an incorrect legal standard in invalidating the clause. While recognizing the sensitivity of such clauses, we hold that, since there was no evidence that the insertion of the clause was an abuse of Farr's fiduciary relationship with Sara at the time of the drawing of her will, the clause is effective.

Except as provided herein, the motions of the defendants for a new trial and amended findings are denied. The plaintiff's claim of error as to legal fees fails to recognize that fees under G.L. c. 215, § 45, are a matter within the discretion of the trial judge. We find no abuse of discretion in the denial of fees.

The judgment is vacated, and the matter is remanded to the Probate Court for further proceedings to determine the amounts which, if paid, would have enabled Cappy to retain ownership of the residence. Such amounts shall be paid to Cappy's estate from the trust for his benefit prior to distributing the balance thereof to the trust under Article IIC of Sara's will.

So ordered.

Notes

1. *Trust as bifurcated gift*: One way to think about a trust is that it is a "bifurcated" gift. As opposed to the typical *inter vivos* outright gift, a trust is bifurcated in the following ways: (1) the "donee" is bifurcated into the trustee and the beneficiary; (2) because the gift is an ongoing gift, the property typically is split into the res/corpus (or principal) and the income it generates; and (3) at the beneficiary level the equitable interests in the trust are typically split into some combination of possessory estate and future interests.

In the *Marsman* case, Sara decided that instead of devising the property outright to her husband, Cappy, she would gift it to him through a testamentary trust. As discussed in Chapter 12, a testamentary trust is a trust created in and through a will. Typically the terms of the trust are in the will, and the trust is funded by property passing through probate. Instead of devising the property outright to Cappy, she gave legal title to Farr, to hold and manage the property for the benefit of Cappy for life, then to her daughter, Sally for life, and then to Sally's children and husband.

Each beneficiary can be given an interest in the income and/or the principal of a trust, and that interest does not have to be the same. A beneficiary's interest in a trust can be either mandatory or discretionary. Technically, whether the beneficiary's interest is mandatory or discretionary depends on whether the trustee's power with respect to the interest is mandatory or discretionary. The nature of such power is, typically, determined from the language, and instructions, of the trust document. Where the trustee's power is mandatory, the trustee *must* exercise the power for the beneficiary's benefit. Where the trustee's power is discretionary, the trustee need not exercise the power for the beneficiary's benefit; it is up to the trustee (but that discretion is far from absolute). Often the extent of discretion, like the character of the trustee's power itself, is described in the trust document by the terms and conditions, and instructions, attached to the power (i.e., trust provisions governing how, when, and in whose favor a power may be exercised).

2. *Mandatory interest*: A mandatory interest means the trustee must exercise a power to distribute or disburse property to the beneficiary in accordance with the terms of the trust. Whether a power is mandatory or discretionary depends upon the settlor's instructions to the trustee (i.e., the settlor's intent as expressed in the terms of the trust). If the terms of the trust are mandatory, no questions need to be asked and no facts need to be taken into consideration. There is no discretion. If the trustee fails to comply with the mandatory terms, the trustee will be liable for breach of trust. A court will always order a trustee to follow a mandatory instruction, which makes the beneficiary's interest in the property subject to such an instruction a mandatory interest.

One has to read the terms of each trust very carefully to ascertain the scope of a beneficiary's interest in the principal and/or income (i.e., to ascertain the nature of the settlor's instructions to the trustee). Note in *Marsman v. Nasca* that the court's opinion starts with the pertinent paragraphs from Sara's trust. With respect to Cappy's interest in the income, the trust provided as follows:

> I give to my trustees, who shall set the same aside as a separate trust fund, one-third (1/3) of the rest, residue and remainder of my estate ... ; they *shall* pay the net income therefrom to my said husband at least quarterly during his life....

(Emphasis added.) Is Cappy's interest in the income mandatory or discretionary (i.e., is this a mandatory instruction or a discretionary instruction to the trustee)?

3. *Discretionary interest*: If the settlor's instruction to a trustee is not mandatory, it is, by default, discretionary. The primary reason settlors grant the trustee some discretion is that it is impossible to see the future. Granting the trustee discretion provides flexibility. It permits—and requires—the trustee to take into consideration changes that may occur after the trust is created. A discretionary instruction requires a trustee to *think about the situation*: to take into consideration circumstances surrounding the trust and/or the beneficiary before deciding whether (and/or to what extent) to exercise a power to give the beneficiary some trust property. A mandatory instruction/power is just the opposite: no facts are to be taken into consideration in making "judgment calls," and the required action must occur regardless of the surrounding and changing circumstances.[1]

---

1. This is not to say, however, that "mandatory" powers always remain static. Trusts, especially when they are more complex or sophisticated, often contain provisions requiring mandatory trustee

4. *Discretionary interest, but a fiduciary duty*: While at first blush a discretionary interest may appear to grant a beneficiary little, if any, interest in the property in question, this is not the case. The trustee's discretion is far from absolute. A discretionary interest is an interesting interaction of complex considerations. While the discretionary nature of the interest appears to favor the trustee, keep in mind that a trustee owes each beneficiary a fiduciary duty. This fiduciary duty means the trustee must act in the best interests of the beneficiaries. The trustee *may not* act in his or her own interests or in the interests of any other party. What does it mean to say that a trustee has discretion over whether or not to exercise a power, but at the same time the trustee has a duty to act in the best interest of the beneficiary? A discretionary interest inherently includes an interesting set of contrasting considerations that make it difficult to ascertain exactly how much discretion a trustee has in a given situation.

5. *Duty to inquire*: Where a settlor grants a trustee the discretion to act, implicit in that discretion is the settlor's wish that the trustee take into consideration the circumstances surrounding the beneficiary before deciding. Not surprisingly, the courts have construed the fiduciary duty owed by the trustee to each beneficiary to mean that the trustee should have all relevant information with respect to the circumstances surrounding the beneficiary, including the most up-to-date information. Hence, the trustee's duty to inquire: the trustee must inquire into the beneficiary's situation before making his or her decision.

In addition, the fiduciary duty owed to the beneficiary means the trustee must diligently inquire into the beneficiary's situation. As the court noted, even where the beneficiary fails to respond to a trustee's inquiry, it is trustee's duty to follow up. A beneficiary may not understand the process; a beneficiary may be embarrassed to disclose his or her situation. Finding that a trustee has the duty to diligently inquire into the beneficiary's situation, even where the beneficiary is nonresponsive, follows logically from the trustee's duty to do everything in the best interest of the beneficiary. While courts are reluctant to substitute their judgment for a trustee's judgment where the beneficiary's interest is discretionary, courts arguably are the opposite when it comes to the trustee's duty to inquire: the courts tend to hold trustees to a rather high standard of inquiry.

6. *Default duty when interest is discretionary*: As the court in *Marsman v. Nasca* stated, even where a beneficiary's interest in trust property is discretionary, that does not mean the trustee's discretion is absolute. After taking into consideration the circumstances surrounding the beneficiary, the trustee has a duty to act *reasonably* and in *good faith* in deciding whether to exercise a power in favor of a beneficiary. *See* RESTATEMENT (THIRD) OF TRUSTS § 87 cmt. c (2007). Admittedly a rather soft, fact-sensitive standard, the courts and authorities have articulated a number of sub-tests to help guide the lower courts. It is an abuse of discretion if a trustee acts (or fails to

---

action based on contingencies: if a situation is "this," then the trustee must do "that," but if a particular something occurs (a contingency), the trustee must then follow a different set of instructions. Such complex or sophisticated trusts, however, are beyond the scope of this introductory class.

act) in bad faith or because of an improper motive. In addition, a trustee is liable for abuse of discretion if he or she acts "beyond the bounds of reasonable judgment ... the trustee's decision is one that would not be accepted as reasonable by persons of prudence." *Id.* Just because a court would have decided differently does not mean that the trustee has abused his or her discretion. The settlor vested his or her trust in the trustee, not the court. Now you can appreciate better why courts prefer to hold trustees accountable for procedural duties (like the duty to inquire) rather than for more substantive duties (like those inherent in the decision-making process in a discretionary interest)—the former is more of a bright-line approach.

7. *Enhanced discretion*: It is not uncommon for a settlor to grant his or her trustee "enhanced" discretion. Common expressions of the settlor's intent to grant enhanced discretion to a trustee include phrases such as "my trustee, in her sole and absolute discretion," "uncontrolled discretion" or "unlimited discretion." Despite the settlor's intent, such phrases cannot be construed literally or there would be no trust: the property would be the "trustee's" property and the trust beneficiary would have no interest or right, and any such language purporting to give the beneficiary an interest would be merely precatory. Such phrasing is also inconsistent with the fiduciary duty the trustee owes the beneficiaries. Accordingly, the courts usually construe such language as enhancing, but not eliminating, the trustee's discretion with respect to the duty to decide. The courts tend to relieve the trustee of the duty to act reasonably, but the trustee still must act in good faith. *See In re Canfield's Estate*, 80 Cal. App. 2d 443 (Ct. App. 1947).

Look back at the key provisions of Sara's trust in *Marsman v. Nasca*. Did she grant Farr enhanced discretion? By finding that Farr abused his discretion, did the court fail to give effect to that enhanced discretion?

8. *Discretion limited by trust purpose and/or power's purpose*: Contributing to the complexity of discretionary trusts is the wide spectrum of discretion a settlor can grant a trustee. At one end, it may appear that the trustee has "sole and absolute" discretion (though, as discussed above, this cannot truly be the case or there would be no trust). At the other end of the spectrum, some trusts contain a discretionary power that is greatly limited in light of the express purpose of the power. Such express purposes de facto constitute instructions to the trustee with respect to what he or she must take into consideration before deciding whether to act or not. Some purposes have become so common that they have been construed to state an ascertainable standard. The more ascertainable the standard, the more limited the trustee's discretion. The more ascertainable the purpose, the stronger the grounds for a court to second-guess a trustee's decision. Accordingly, the more ascertainable the purpose of the trust interest, the more leeway a court has to substitute its judgment for the trustee's judgment so as to prevent an abuse of discretion.

This was the situation in *Marsman* with respect to Cappy's interest in the principal. Sara's trust provided in pertinent part as follows:

> ... my trustees shall, if they deem it necessary or desirable from time to time, in their sole and uncontrolled discretion, pay over to him, or use, apply and/

or expend for his direct or indirect benefit such amount or amounts of the principal thereof as they shall deem advisable for his *comfortable support and maintenance.*"

(Emphasis added).

Cappy's interest in the principal is discretionary, and Sara gave the trustee enhanced discretion, but Sara also specifically indicated that in deciding whether to disburse some of the principal to Cappy the trustee should take into his consideration Cappy's *comfortable support and maintenance.* Courts have construed *comfortable support and maintenance* to mean that the beneficiary is entitled to distributions if necessary to maintain the standard of living the beneficiary had at the time he or she became eligible for distributions from the trust:

> This language has been interpreted to set an ascertainable standard, namely to maintain the life beneficiary "in accordance with the standard of living which was normal for him before he became a beneficiary of the trust." *Woodberry v. Bunker,* 359 Mass 239, 243, 268 N.E.2d 841 (1971). *Dana v. Gring,* 374 Mass. 109, 117, 371 N.E.2d 755 (1977). See *Blodget v. Delaney,* 201 F.2d 589, 593 (1st Cir.1953).

Marsman, 573 N.E.2d at 1030. That the trustee is to maintain the beneficiary in the standard of living to which he or she had become accustomed before becoming a beneficiary limits the trustee's discretion. As the court held, to the extent Cappy's standard of living declined below that standard, the trustee's failure to disburse more principal to Cappy was an abuse of discretion. *Id.*

Even where the trustee is granted discretion, including enhanced discretion, the trustee must keep in mind the fiduciary duty the trustee owes to the beneficiary and the settlor's intent:

> [A] trustee is "unquestionably under an obligation to give serious and responsible consideration both as to the propriety of the amounts and as to their consistency with the terms and purposes of the trust." Holyoke Natl. Bank v. Wilson, 350 Mass. 223, 227, 214 N.E.2d 42, 45. A court of equity may control a trustee in the exercise of a fiduciary discretion if it fails to observe standards of judgment apparent from the applicable instrument.

Old Colony Trust Co. v. Rodd, 254 N.E.2d 886 (Mass. 1970).

9. *Whether trustee should consider beneficiary's other resources*: Where the trustee has discretion to distribute trust income or principal to the trust beneficiary, a latent issue that can arise is whether the trustee should take into consideration the beneficiary's other resources before making the distribution. Is the trust intended to provide a floor to ensure that the beneficiary has a certain amount of support, or is the trust intended to supplement the beneficiary's resources only in the event they are insufficient? Ideally the settlor should express his or her intent with respect to this question in the trust instrument. Where the trust is silent on the issue, jurisdictions are split on the answer. The California Supreme Court has spoken on the issue: "By the weight of authority, unless the language of the trust instrument affirmatively reveals an in-

tention to make a gift of the stated benefaction regardless of the beneficiary's other means, the trustee should consider such other means in exercising his discretion to disburse the principal." *In re Ferrall's Estate*, 258 P.2d 1009 (Cal. 1953).

It is common to see trust language limiting a trustee's discretionary powers, making them effective only after certain other financial resources have been exhausted. Such limiting conditions can also be imposed on a trustee's mandatory powers, but such conditions are less common.

10. *The role of taxes in trustee powers*: Tax considerations are a dominant, if not controlling, factor that a well-advised settlor must take into consideration in deciding whether to make a power mandatory or discretionary, whether to include limitations on the trustee's dispositive powers, and/or whether to tie those limitations to an ascertainable standard. Whether federal estate and gift taxes,[2] as well as income taxes, will be imposed as a result of the testamentary transfer hinge on issues related to the trustee's powers. Often it is a matter of drafting minutia: a seemingly insignificant word or clause in a trust or other testamentary instrument may be the difference between (1) a happy client, where planning and drafting has significantly reduced tax exposure, and (2) a disgruntled client, who will be initiating a malpractice claim against the attorney because a small drafting error sent the client over the tax cliffs of despair. There can also be significant tax issues surrounding matters of who is the trustee, who may become the trustee, and what powers the settlor has in making such decisions. While these tax issues are beyond the scope of this course (they are the focus of the estate and gift tax course), we would be remiss not to at least point out the overlap with estate and gift tax.

Taxes, and a client's wish to avoid paying them, typically is an integral aspect of estate planning, whether the instrument being used is a will, a trust, or another nonprobate instrument. An attorney specializing in estate planning must have a comprehensive knowledge of the intricacies of tax law (estate and gift as well as income taxes). It is not an area in which an attorney "dabbles" without running serious risks of causing harm to the client and exposure to malpractice. Put in the context of mandatory versus discretionary, such knowledge, in real world practice, is mandatory.

Problems

1. Lotti Silliman created a trust in 1950, funding it with a farm that generated significant annual income. Her six children were named life beneficiaries and as successor trustees following her death. Article II of the trust granted the trustees power to "sell, assign, convey, exchange, and otherwise dispose of" trust assets. Article V of the trust dealt with the trust's income and principal. It provided as follows:

   The net income from the trust remaining after the payment of expenses of managing the trust and the taxes due from said trust, shall be paid annually in equal shares to the following during their lifetime.

---

2. There may also be state estate tax issues, but those are less common.

. . . .

In the making of the distribution of the annual income of this trust, the trustees shall have the right to determine what constitutes income and what constitutes corpus. They shall have the further privilege of reinvesting any proceeds from the sale of trust assets or making a distribution of such proceeds to the then beneficiaries of the trust.

From 1950 to 1997, all of the income was distributed annually from the trust. Following the death of the last of the settlor's children, the next group of successor trustees cut distribution of the trust's income to 50 percent, reinvesting the other 50 percent as corpus. One of the beneficiaries sued. With respect to the trust income, is the trust mandatory or discretionary? *See In re Trust Created by Lottie P. Silliman, dated December 29, 1950*, No. A10-590, 2010 WL 5071339 (Minn. Ct. App. Dec. 14, 2010).

2. David Geitner is a 49-year-old incompetent. John and Christine Geitner adopted him when he was young. When John died, a portion of his estate was set aside, and a guardian of the property was appointed to manage the fund. Thereafter, when Christine passed away, her will created a testamentary trust. Provision 10 of the trust governed the distribution of the trust income. Sub-paragraphs A and B of Provision 10 provided as follows:

(A) To use any part of the income from and/or corpus of said Trust which, in the sole discretion of said Trustees, may be necessary or proper for the support, maintenance, and comfort of my son DAVID R. GEITNER, so long as he lives. In making such determinations from time to time, I direct my said Trustees to take into consideration my said son's needs and the amount of income from his share in the estate of his father, the late John G. H. Geitner. I believe the income from his share in the John G. H. Geitner estate will be more than adequate for his every need and comfort, but if it is not then I decree that my said trustees shall have the power and authority, in their sole discretion, to use any part or all of the income from the trust and/or any part or all of the corpus of the trust for such purposes.

(B) During December of every calendar year following the establishment of the trust and continuing until said trust is closed as hereinafter directed, I direct my said Trustees to distribute any part or all of the income from said trust, or from the remainder thereof if any part of the corpus or income is used for the purposes set forth in sub-paragraph (A) above, which they do not use for the purposes authorized in sub-paragraph (A) above, as follows: [Section 10 then went on to list 7 alternative takers of the income.]

From 1961–1975, the income generated from David's share of his father's estate was enough to cover his expenses, and the trustee under Christine's trust distributed all of the income to the alternative beneficiaries under sub-paragraph 10. Starting in 1975, however, David's expenses increased significantly and the income from his share of his father's estate was not sufficient to cover his expenses.

The guardian had to use increasing amounts of the principal of the fund he received from his father's estate. In 1980, the guardian brought suit seeking a court order requiring the trustee to distribute some of the income to David's guardianship account for David's benefit.

Has the trustee breached the terms of Christine's trust? Is David entitled to some of the income from the trust? *See First Nat. Bank of Catawba Cty. v. Edens,* 286 S.E.2d 818 (N.C. Ct. App. 1982).

B. Scope of Discretion — Modern Trend

As noted above, where a settlor's intent is to grant the trustee discretion with respect to whether trust property should be distributed to a beneficiary, this discretion can run the spectrum from near absolute discretion to very little. The more ascertainable the standard of discretion, the easier it is for a beneficiary (or a creditor of a beneficiary) to force the trustee to exercise this discretion in his or her favor.

Strojek ex rel. Mills v. Hardin Cty. Bd. of Supervisors

602 N.W.2d 566 (Iowa Ct. App. 1999)

STREIT, P.J.

. . .

I. Background Facts & Procedure.

Marie Strojek, a mentally handicapped sixty-three-year old, has been a resident of Opportunity Village in Clear Lake, Iowa, since February 1981. Hardin County pays approximately $21,900 per year for Strojek's care at the Village. A portion of this money is used to pay for Strojek's participation at a work-activity center.

Strojek is the beneficiary of a testamentary trust established by her late father. After Strojek's mother died, her estate was divided equally between Strojek and her sister, Caroline Mills. Mills was appointed Strojek's trustee. The applicable trust provision provided:

> My trustee *shall,* from time to time, pay to or apply for the benefit of my daughter, Marie Helen Strojek, such sums from the income and principal as my trustee in the exercise of her *sole discretion* deems necessary or advisable, to provide for her proper care, support, maintenance and education. (Emphasis added.)

The trust assets included approximately $70,000 in C.D.s and bank accounts and an undivided one-half interest in a 200-acre farm. In an effort to assist the County with the costs of Strojek's care, Mills each year donated $10,000 from the trust to the County.

On July 1, 1996, the County enacted the Hardin County Mental Health Services Plan. The plan contained income and resource eligibility criteria that had to be satisfied before residents were eligible for county-sponsored benefits. In April 1997, the County informed Mills, the trustee, that Strojek no longer qualified for county assistance because her trust assets were in excess of the eligibility minimums.

Strojek filed an appeal to the Hardin County Board of Supervisors. The Board affirmed the decision, prompting Strojek to seek judicial review in district court. Without objection from either party, the district court reclassified the petition as one for writ of certiorari. The district court ruled the assets of Strojek's trust could be used to determine her eligibility for county funding, because the trust was not truly discretionary, but rather a trust for Strojek's support with a spendthrift provision. Strojek has appealed, and the County has cross-appealed.

. . .

III. The Language of the Trust Is Equivocal.

When the terms of a trust attempt to provide for the care or education of a beneficiary, courts traditionally attempted to qualify the instrument either as a support trust or a discretionary trust. The terms of a support trust require the trustee to pay or apply so much of the trust's income or principal as necessary for the beneficiary's care or education. *See* Austin Wakeman Scott, *Abridgment of the Law of Trusts* § 154 (1960) [hereinafter Scott's *Abridgment*]. Language such as "the trustee shall pay for the beneficiary's care, education, or support" is normally indicative of a support trust in that the trustee's power to apply the trust assets is limited. *Smith v. Smith,* 246 Neb. 193, 517 N.W.2d 394, 398 (1994); *see Bureau of Support v. Kreitzer,* 16 Ohio St.2d 147, 243 N.E.2d 83, 85 (1968). If considered a support trust, "the interest of the beneficiary can be reached in satisfaction of an enforceable claim ... for necessary services rendered to the beneficiary." *In re Dodge,* 281 N.W.2d 447, 450 (Iowa 1979) (quoting Restatement (Second) of Trusts § 157(b) (1959).

The terms of a discretionary trust grant the trustee complete and unfettered discretion in determining if any of the trust's income or principal should be distributed to the beneficiary. *See* Scott's *Abridgment* § 155. If considered a true discretionary trust, a "creditor of the beneficiary cannot compel the trustee to pay any part of the income or principal." Restatement (Second) of Trusts § 155(1) (1959).

The definitional distinctions between support and discretionary trusts are limpid. Provisions of particular trusts muddy these clear demarcations. When the provision is equivocal or adheres to principles common to both types of trusts, interpretative inconsistencies abound....

The parties in the present case ask this court to wade into these murky waters without even a life jacket. Each side throws out, as an aid for interpretation, only the specific language of the trust provision that supports their particular contention despite the remaining language to the contrary. Marie Strojek argues that the language of her trust grants the trustee, Mills, "sole discretion" in making distributions from the trust's assets, while ignoring the limitations placed on that discretion. The County, in turn, argues that the word "shall" in the trust language is mandatory, while ignoring the discretionary language. The equivocal nature of the provision is obvious. It blends a desire to ensure the basic support needs of a handicapped daughter with the control mechanism of trustee discretion designed to prevent wasteful depletion of the trust's assets. Any attempt by this court to hammer the language of this particular trust provision into one of these rigid categories would only breed further inconsistencies in the law.

IV. The Discretionary Support Trust: A Viable Alternative.

The state of Nebraska remedied the inherent inconsistencies of forcing equivocal trust provisions into traditional categories by creating a third category, a discretionary support trust, which addresses the equivocal provision in its entirety and best contemplates the intent of the settlor. *See In re Sullivan's Will,* 144 Neb. 36, 12 N.W.2d 148 (1943); *Smith,* 517 N.W.2d at 394.

A discretionary support trust is created when the settlor combines explicit discretionary language "with language that, in itself, would be deemed to create a pure support trust." Evelyn Ginsberg Abravanel, *Discretionary Support Trusts,* 68 Iowa L.Rev. 273, 279 n. 26 (1983) [hereinafter Abravanel]. The effect of a discretionary support trust is to establish the minimal distributions a trustee must make in order to comport with the settlor's intent of providing basic support, while retaining broad discretionary powers in the trustee. *Id.* at 290; *see Sullivan,* 12 N.W.2d at 150; 3 Austin Wakeman Scott & William Franklin Fratcher, *The Law of Trusts* § 187, at 15 (4th ed.1988) [hereinafter Scott & Fratcher] ("[I]f [a trustee] is directed to pay as much of the income and principal as is necessary for the support of a beneficiary, he can be compelled to pay at least the minimum amount which in the opinion of a reasonable man would be necessary."); *see also Kreitzer,* 16 Ohio St.2d at 150–52, 243 N.E.2d at 85–87 (reaching the same conclusion but forcing a third party creditor to seek subrogation from the trust). The rationale behind minimal support lies in the trustee's fiduciary duties to the beneficiary. Restatement (Third) of Trusts: Prudent Investor Rule § 187 cmt. d–f (1992). If a trustee abuses her discretion and violates her fiduciary duties, the beneficiary, through judicial action, may compel disbursements from the trust for minimal support. Scott & Fratcher, § 187, at 14–15. "Accordingly, the beneficiary's interest in the trust should be reachable by an attaching creditor to the same extent." Abravanel, 68 Iowa L.Rev. at 290; *see* Lawrence A. Frolik, *Discretionary Trusts for a Disabled Beneficiary: A Solution or a Trap for the Unwary?,* 46 U. Pitt.L.Rev. 335, 342 (1985) ("[T]he trustee can be required to distribute sufficient income to the beneficiary to provide at least a minimum level of support ... even if it would displace government benefits."). *But see Lang v. Commonwealth,* 515 Pa. 428, 528 A.2d 1335, 1345 (1987) (supporting the theory of discretionary support trusts, but ruling a trustee may seek public funding before the trustee must intercede). Thus, only the portion of the trust's assets necessary for the core needs of the beneficiary may be attached by third party creditors.

V. A Discretionary Support Trust Remedies the Equivocal Nature of the Trust Provision and Comports with the Intent of the Settlor.

The characterization of the Strojek trust as a discretionary support trust best remedies the paradoxical nature of the language. A discretionary support trust harmonizes the seemingly inconsistent terms of the trust. The discretionary language grants Mills wide latitude in determining Strojek's core needs, thus protecting the trust from wasteful depletion; while ensuring, by way of mandatory language coupled with support standards, that Strojek will never be left destitute. More importantly, however, the identification of this trust as a discretionary support trust best contemplates the intent of the settlor.

In interpreting wills and testamentary trusts, we are guided by well-settled principles. First, the intent of the testator is the polestar and must prevail. *In re Estate of Rogers*, 473 N.W.2d 36, 39 (Iowa 1991). Second, the testator's intent must be derived from (1) the four corners of the will, (2) the scheme for distribution, and (3) "the surrounding circumstances at the time of the will's execution." *Id.*

First, as discussed above, the four corners of the will indicate a discretionary support trust, because it resolves textual ambiguities and gives effect to each provision in its entirety. Second, the scheme of distribution suggests the creation of a hybrid trust. Under Article IV(b)(2) of the Strojek Will, Mills, the trustee, will receive the remaining assets of the trust upon her sister's death. If the trust was considered a pure discretionary trust, the trustee could completely withhold any disbursements from the trust in order to maximize the money received by her upon the beneficiary's death. We do not hint that Mills is acting upon such motivations, but it explains the settlor's use of mandatory language in crafting the provision. Mandatory language as well as defining the intended use of the trust's assets would eliminate potential abuse on the part of the trustee. Third, Strojek was born mentally handicapped and lived with her parents until she was forty-one. At the time Mr. Strojek drafted the will, Strojek's long-term needs were readily apparent. The settlor knew his daughter could not support herself or provide for her basic necessities. The settlor established the trust to prevent his impaired daughter from becoming destitute. Thus, the intent of the settlor, as gleaned from the enumerated factors, was to create a discretionary support trust.

VI. Conclusion.

The recognition of discretionary support trusts in Iowa is the next logical step in the maturation of this state's trust law. It resolves ambiguity and provides settlors a hybrid tool to effectuate their intent. Furthermore, the trust in the present case falls squarely within the definition of a discretionary support trust. It combines discretionary language with language indicative of a support trust. Assets necessary for Strojek's basic needs could be reached by Strojek or the County. Therefore, trust assets could be considered when determining eligibility for Strojek's living expenses.

The district court reached the appropriate conclusions of law, but achieved them by massaging the definition of a support trust. The finding of a discretionary support trust better supports the district court's conclusions. The evidence on record does not provide sufficient evidence for this court to determine the precise amount necessary for Strojek's care. The case is remanded for further evidentiary hearings as to these costs.

The district court's conclusions are affirmed, its rationale modified, and the case remanded for further proceedings.

Notes

1. *Traditional support trust*: Traditionally, a support trust was a trust that required the trustee to disburse as much trust property—income, and if necessary, principal—as was necessary for the beneficiary's support or education. It was a mandatory trust to the level of the beneficiary's support and/or education. But while it was mandatory to the level of the beneficiary's support and/or education, historically the beneficiary's interest was deemed nontransferable (both voluntarily and involuntarily), even in the absence of a spendthrift clause.

Historically there was only one type of support trust, and it was a type of mandatory trust. As the court noted in *Strojek*, however, settlors (either intentionally or accidentally) often included both support and discretionary language in a trust instrument, thereby muddying the waters and making it difficult for the trustee, the beneficiary, and the court to determine whether the settlor intended the beneficiary's interest to be discretionary or mandatory. A representative example of the blended and confusing phrasing led to the litigation in *Myers v. Kansas Dep't of Soc. & Rehab. Servs.*, 866 P.2d 1052 (Kan. 1994). The relevant trust provisions stated "[M]y trustee *shall* hold, manage, invest and reinvest, collect the income there from [and] pay over so much [of] the net income and principal ... as my trustee *deems advisable* for his care, support, maintenance, emergencies and welfare ...." Is that a mandatory support trust (*shall hold ... and pay over ...*) or a discretionary trust (as my trustee *deems advisable ...*)?[3]

2. *Modern trend—discretionary support trust*: The modern trend adopts a different approach to the issue—it recognizes two types of support trusts: the traditional mandatory support trust, and the modern trend discretionary support trust. As the court in *Strojek* noted, this new hybrid type of trust is mandatory to the level of support and discretionary beyond that level: "The effect of a discretionary support trust is to establish the minimal distributions a trustee must make in order to comport with the settlor's intent of providing basic support, while retaining broad discretionary powers in the trustee."

3. *California approach*: California still recognizes, statutorily, the traditional type of support trust:

CPC § 15302. Support trust

Except as provided in Sections 15304 to 15307, inclusive, if the trust instrument provides that the trustee shall pay income or principal or both for the education or support of a beneficiary, the beneficiary's interest in income or principal or both under the trust, to the extent the income or principal or both is necessary for the education or support of the ben -

---

3. The Kansas Supreme Court ruled the language created a discretionary trust rather than a support trust.

eficiary, may not be transferred and is not subject to the enforcement of a money judgment until paid to the beneficiary.

The exceptions noted at the start of the statutory provision are for certain classes of creditors who can reach the beneficiary's interest in the trust even though it is a support trust. They are the same categories of creditors who can reach a beneficiary's interest in a trust even if the trust has a spendthrift clause. To that extent, the discussion below about spendthrift clauses and creditors applies equally to a support trust in California unless otherwise noted.

4. *Transferability*: One of the issues that follows from the recognition of this "new" discretionary support trust is to what extent, if any, a beneficiary can transfer his or her interest in the trust, and to what extent, if any, a creditor of the beneficiary can reach the beneficiary's interest in the trust.

We take for granted the default property principle that a party should have the right to transfer any and all property he or she owns. Where the same person holds the legal and equitable interests in a piece of property, that principle is fairly easy to apply. If you own something, included in the bundle of rights that goes along with ownership of that property is the right to transfer it. But where the legal and equitable property interests are bifurcated, who really "owns" the property in the trust? Who really owns the property held by a trust—the trustee or the beneficiary? Should a beneficiary be permitted to transfer a merely equitable interest?

The default rule is that the default property principle of free alienability applies to a beneficiary's interest in a trust: a beneficiary can freely transfer his or her interest. That makes sense and is relatively easy to understand with respect to a mandatory interest in a trust. If the beneficiary is entitled to receive the net income quarterly, the beneficiary can transfer that interest to another party (either as a gift or by selling the right to receive the stream of income). The third party steps into the shoes of the beneficiary and receives the same rights that the beneficiary held. But what does it mean to say that a beneficiary can transfer a discretionary interest?

To the extent the beneficiary does not have the right to force the trustee to make a disbursement, does it make any sense to say that the beneficiary can transfer the interest? Courts and commentators have struggled with the issue. Is it better to say that the interest is transferable, but the third party acquires no "real" right because the beneficiary had no right to any property, or is it better just to say that a discretionary interest is nontransferable? The Uniform Trust Code and the RESTATEMENT OF TRUSTS take the former approach, (*see* RESTATEMENT (FIRST) OF TRUSTS § 155 (1935); RESTATEMENT (THIRD) OF TRUSTS § 60 TD No 2 (1999), updated (2014); UTC § 501 (amended 2010)), while one of the leading treatises on trust law, BOGERT'S TRUSTS AND TRUSTEES, takes the latter view ("If the trustee has the discretion whether to pay income or principal to the beneficiary, the beneficiary has no assignable right." BOGERT'S TRUSTS AND TRUSTEES, § 188 (2014)).

California has adopted the view that a beneficiary's interest in a discretionary trust is not a property interest, but rather is a mere expectancy. The general rule is that an expectancy is nontransferable. Thus, under California law, where a beneficiary's interest is discretionary, a beneficiary has a nontransferable property interest. The beneficiary has no rights until after the trustee has made the decision to exercise his or her discretion in favor of the beneficiary. Then and only then does the beneficiary acquire an equitable interest in the property that he or she can assert against the trustee (or that a transferee can assert if the interest is transferred). *See In re Johnson's Estate*, 198 Cal. App. 2d 503 (Ct. App. 1961); CPC § 15303(b).

Remember that a support trust is unique in that historically, as a general rule, it is treated as mandatory for certain purposes (beneficiary's interest to the level of education and/or support) but discretionary for purposes of creditors' rights (as a general rule, creditors with a money judgment cannot reach the interest in the trust). A support trust is more like a discretionary trust for purposes of whether a beneficiary can transfer his or her interest. In light of the creditors' inability to reach the beneficiary's interest in a support trust, it should come as no surprise that the beneficiary's interest in a support trust is nontransferable.

Assuming that a beneficiary can freely transfer his or her interest in a trust, to what extent (if any) can a creditor of the beneficiary reach the beneficiary's interest in the trust? Can a settlor override the default rule of transferability by expressly providing that the beneficiary's interest is nontransferable?

5. *The recurring role of taxes*: As with all areas of trusts, the issue of support trusts is heavily steeped in tax law. Well beyond the scope of this course, entire portions of a typical estate and gift tax course are dedicated to the issue of support trusts, and navigating the accompanying law is akin to walking through a minefield.

Problems

1. Ralph Nicholson's testamentary trust was for the benefit of his wife, Marguerite. She was also appointed trustee. Section II of the trust expressly provides that the trustee shall pay to Marguerite, "from time to time, and at least semi-annually, such sums of money as said executrix shall consider reasonably necessary for her support and maintenance." There was no evidence that any income was distributed to Marguerite. Upon Marguerite's death, there was $55,000 of earned but undistributed income in the trust. Marguerite's executor claimed that Marguerite's estate was entitled to the funds as the income beneficiary of the trust. The successor trustee claimed the trust was entitled to the undistributed income. Is Marguerite's interest mandatory or discretionary? Did she violate the terms of the trust? *See First Nat. Bank of Birmingham v. Currie*, 380 So. 2d 283 (Ala. 1980).

2. Settlor created an *inter vivos* trust. Paragraph (b) provides as follows:

   > The Trustees shall hold said trust estate in trust for the use and benefit of Elesabeth Ridgely Ingalls and Barbara Gregg Ingalls, both children of the Grantor's son, Robert I. Ingalls, Jr., and of such of any other descendants of said Robert I. Ingalls, Jr., as may from time to time during the continuance of the trust be living. So long as any such descendant shall be under

the age of twenty-one years, the Trustees shall use and apply for his or her support, comfort and education his or her pro rata share of the net income from said estate.

Is the beneficiary's interest mandatory or discretionary? *See Ingalls v. Ingalls*, 54 So. 2d 296 (Ala. 1951).

II. Creditor's Rights and Spendthrift Trusts

The default creditor's rights rule is that if a party can voluntarily transfer his or her property interest, a creditor can force the party to involuntarily transfer the property interest to the creditor. Should the default creditor's rights rule apply to a beneficiary's interest in a trust? If so, to what extent (if any) can a settlor opt out of the default rule by making the beneficiary's interest nontransferable?

A. Third Party as Beneficiary

In examining a creditor's right to reach a beneficiary's interest in a trust, it is important to identify whom the beneficiary is. If the beneficiary is the *settlor*, common law created one set of rules, and if the beneficiary is someone *other than the settlor*, common law created another set of rules. Inasmuch as the norm is the beneficiary is someone *other than the settlor*, the material will start with the more common scenario.

Duvall v. McGee
826 A.2d 416 (Md. 2003)

BELL, Chief Judge.

. . .

I.

James Calvert McGee ("McGee"), ... was convicted of felony-murder for his participation in a robbery that resulted in the killing of Katherine Ryon. Robert Ryon Duvall, the appellant, is the Personal Representative of the Estate of Katherine Ryon. He brought suit, in that capacity, ... against McGee, seeking both compensatory and punitive damages, ... The parties settled this action, negotiating and executing ... [a "Settlement Agreement"] pursuant to which, ... the parties agreed to the entry of judgment against McGee, and in favor of the appellant, for $100,000.00 in compensatory damages and $500,000.00 in punitive damages. The Settlement Agreement acknowledged that McGee is the beneficiary of a trust established by his deceased mother, which, at the time of the settlement, was valued at approximately $877,000.00.... Under the terms of the trust, periodic monetary payments are to be made to McGee, and to others on his behalf, by Frank B. Walsh, Jr., the Trustee of the trust ("the Trustee)," ... Another provision of the trust established what is commonly referred to as a "Spendthrift" Trust.[4] That provision prohibited McGee from alienating the trust principal ("corpus") or any portion of the income from the trust while in the hands of the Trustee, and specifically shielded both the corpus and the income from claims of McGee's creditors. The trust instrument also gives broad discretion to the Trustee to terminate the Trust at any time and pay the trust assets and any undistributed income to McGee or to any of the remaindermen to which the trust referred. The Settlement Agreement also provided that:

> "The [appellant] hereby forever releases, waives, relinquishes and abandons any rights he may have to satisfy or have paid any portion of the above-mentioned judgment by way of attachment, garnishment or any other post-judgment collection efforts directed against any periodic payments made by the Trustee of the Trust to [McGee] as the beneficiary of the Trust, or directed against any periodic payment made to any other person or entities for the benefit of [McGee]...."

Thus, it prohibited the appellant from attaching or garnishing any of the periodic payments the Trustee made to McGee from the Trust.

Having surrendered all rights to attach McGee's periodic payment from the Trust, but armed with the judgment entered pursuant to the Settlement Agreement, the appellant sought to satisfy the judgment by invading the corpus of the trust. Thus, the appellant served a Writ of Garnishment on the Trustee. Answering the Writ, the Trustee defended on the grounds that the trust was a spendthrift trust; the Trustee was not indebted to McGee; and the Trustee was not in possession of any property belonging to McGee.

Both parties moved for summary judgment. Although acknowledging that this Court, in *Smith v. Towers,* 69 Md. 77, 14 A. 497 (1888), upheld the validity of spendthrift trusts in Maryland and, thus, prohibited their invasion for the payment of debt, the appellant maintained that, over time, this Court has carved out, on public policy grounds, exceptions to the spendthrift doctrine, pursuant to which some classes of persons are permitted to invade spendthrift trusts. Noting one of the rationales of the *Smith* decision — that because "[a]ll deeds and wills and other instruments by which [spendthrift] trusts are created are required by law to be recorded in the public offices ... creditors have notice of the terms and conditions on which the beneficiary is entitled to the income of the property," 69 Md. at 89, 14 A. at 499 — the appellant argued that tort-judgment creditors should be included among those excepted, since such creditors had no opportunity to investigate the credit-worthiness of the tortfeasor

---

4. Restatement (Second) of Trusts § 152(2) (1959) defines a "spendthrift trust" as "[a] trust in which by the terms of the trust or by statute a valid restraint on the voluntary and involuntary transfer of the interest of the beneficiary is imposed...." The validity of the provision creating the spendthrift trust is not in dispute. We have stated, with regard to the prerequisites of such trusts that the creator of the trust need only manifest the intention either expressly or impliedly in the instrument creating the trust, that the beneficiaries thereunder shall be entitled to their equitable interests in the trust property, free from the claims of their creditors. *Cherbonnier v. Bussey,* 92 Md. 413, 421, 48 A. 923, 924 (1901). Both parties have argued that Sally McGee established a valid Spendthrift Trust....

prior to suffering from the tortious conduct giving rise to the claim. Furthermore, the appellant continued, the public policy of this State dictates that tort-judgment creditors be deemed a special class of creditors entitled to invade a spendthrift trust.

The trial court held:

> "Maryland law is what governs this case, however, and Maryland law is clear. A spendthrift trust may not be reached in order to satisfy the judgment in the case *sub judice*. Although the facts involving the murder of the late Ms. Ryon, and the further facts relating to the beneficiary status of the Defendant McGee, a felony murderer, are very tempting, this Court may not rewrite the law; the Maryland Legislature has the responsibility of that task, or the Appellate Courts of this State must further interpret the law.... This Court has a responsibility to apply and uphold the laws of the state as its interprets they now exist, not create new law."

Thus, the appellant's motion for summary judgment was denied and the appellees' cross-motion, granted. The appellant noted a timely appeal to the Court of Special Appeals. This Court, on its own initiative, issued the writ of certiorari to address this novel issue of Maryland law, prior to any proceedings in the intermediate court....

. . .

II.

In Maryland, it is well settled that "spend-thrift trusts" may be created....

. . .

... Acknowledging the rule favoring the free and ready alienation of property and that "the right to sell and dispose of property ... is a necessary incident of course to the absolute ownership of ... property," [*Smith v. Towers*, 69 Md. 77, 14 A. 497 (1888)] at 87, 14 A. at 498, we pointed out that "the reasons on which the rule is founded do not apply to the transfer of property in trust," *id.* at 87, 14 A. at 499, and that "[t]he law does not ... forbid all and any restraints on the right to dispose of [trust property], but only such restraints as may be deemed against the best interests of the community." *Id.* at 88, 14 A. at 499. With regard to the policy issue, we said:

> "Now common honesty requires, of course, that every one should pay his debts, and the policy of the law for centuries has been to subject the property of a debtor of every kind which he holds in his own right, to the payment of his debts. He has as owner of such property the right to dispose of it as he pleases, and his interest is, therefore, liable for the payment of his debts. But a *cestui que trust* does not hold the estate or interest in his own right; he has but an equitable and qualified right to the property or to its income, to be held and enjoyed by the beneficiary on certain terms and conditions prescribed by the founder of the trust. The legal title is in the trustee, and the *cestui que trust* derives his title to the income through the instrument by which the trust is created. The donor or devisor, as the absolute owner of the property, has the right to prescribe the terms on which his bounty

shall be enjoyed, unless such terms be repugnant to the law. And it is no answer to say that the gift of an equitable right to income to the exclusion of creditors is against the policy of the law. This is begging the question. Why is it against the policy of the law? What sound principle does it violate? The creditors of the beneficiary have no right to complain, because the founder of the trust did not give his bounty to them. And if so, what grounds have they to complain because he has seen proper to give it in trust to be received by the trustee and to be paid to another, and not to be liable while in the hands of the trustee to the creditors of the *cestui que trust*. All deeds and wills and other instruments by which such trusts are created, are required by law to be recorded in the public offices, and creditors have notice of the terms and conditions on which the beneficiary is entitled to the income of the property. They know that the founder of the trust has declared that this income shall be paid to the object of his bounty to the exclusion of creditors, and if under such circumstances they see proper to give credit to one who has but an equitable and qualified right to the enjoyment of property, they do so with their eyes open. It cannot be said that credit was given upon such a qualified right to the enjoyment of the income of property, or that creditors have been deceived or mislead; and if the beneficiary is dishonest enough not to apply the income when received by him to the payment of his debts, creditors have no right to complain because they cannot subject it in the hands of the trustee to the payment of their claims, against the express terms of the trust."

Id. at 88–89, 14 A. at 499–500.

The appellant relies on that portion of the Court's reasoning that indicates that the contract creditors are on notice, at least constructively, of the terms of the spendthrift trust prior to extending credit, along with the fact that this Court, on public policy grounds, has exempted certain obligations of the beneficiary of a spendthrift trust from the rule against attachment or garnishment of the corpus or of the income in the hands of the trustee. He also takes comfort from the position that treatise writers take with respect to the right of tort judgment creditors to satisfy their judgments from a spendthrift trust; they agree with him that it should be permitted.

In Scott on Trusts, Fourth Edition, § 157.5, while acknowledging the paucity of authority on the subject, it is stated:

"In many of the cases in which it has been held that by the terms of the trust the interest of a beneficiary may be put beyond the reach of his creditors, the courts have laid some stress on the fact that the creditors had only themselves to blame for extending credit to a person whose interest under the trust had been put beyond their reach. The courts have said that before extending credit they could have ascertained the extent and character of the debtor's resources. Certainly, the situation of a tort creditor is quite different from that of a contract creditor. A man who is about to be knocked down by an automobile has no opportunity to investigate the credit of the driver of the automobile and has no opportunity to avoid being injured no matter what the resources of the driver may be. It may be argued that the settlor can properly impose such restrictions as he chooses on the property that he gives. But surely he cannot impose restrictions that are against public policy. It is true that the tortfeasor may have no other property than that which is given him under the trust, and that the victim of the tort is no worse off where the tortfeasor has property that cannot be reached than he would be if the tortfeasor had no property at all. Nevertheless, there seems to be something rather shocking in the notion that a man should be allowed to continue in the enjoyment of property without satisfying the claims of persons whom he has injured. It may well be held that it is against public policy to permit the beneficiary of a spendthrift trust to enjoy an income under the trust without discharging his tort liabilities to others.

"There is little authority on the question whether the interest of the beneficiary of a spendthrift trust can be reached by persons against whom he has committed a tort. In the absence of authority it was felt by those who were responsible for the preparation of the Restatement of Trusts that no categorical statement could be made on the question. It is believed, however, that there is a tendency to recognize that the language of the earlier cases to the effect that no creditor can reach the interest of a beneficiary of a spendthrift trust is too broad, and that in view of the cases that have been cited in the previous sections allowing various classes of claimants to reach the interest of the beneficiary, the courts may well come to hold that the settlor cannot put the interest of the beneficiary beyond the reach of those to whom he has incurred liabilities in tort."

Bogert on Trusts and Trustees, Second Edition, Rev'd, § 224, p. 478, is to like effect....

A similar sentiment is expressed in Comment a to § 157 of the Restatement Second of Trusts, wherein it is said:

"The interest of the beneficiary of a spendthrift trust ... may be reached in cases other than those herein enumerated [alimony, child support, taxes], if considerations of public policy so require. Thus, it is possible that a person who has a claim in tort against the beneficiary of a spendthrift trust may be able to reach his interest under the trust."

Neither the argument advanced by the appellant, nor the support offered for it is persuasive.

To be sure, this Court has refused to hold, and on public policy grounds, spendthrift trusts inviolate against indebtedness for alimony arrearages, *Safe Deposit & Trust Co. v. Robertson, supra,* 192 Md. at 662–63, 65 A.2d at 296, and for child support. *Zouck v. Zouck, supra,* 204 Md. at 299, 104 A.2d at 579. Earlier, the United States District Court for the District of Maryland had reached the same result, permitting a spendthrift trust to be attached for the payment of United States income taxes. *Mercantile Trust Co. v. Hofferbert,* 58 F.Supp. 701, 705 (D.Md.1944)....

In *Robertson*, we, like 1 Scott, Trusts, § 157.1, recognized, and clearly stated, that the dependents of a spendthrift trust beneficiary "'are not "creditors" of the beneficiary, and the liability of the beneficiary to support them is not a debt.'" 192 Md. at 660, 65 A.2d at 295, quoting Scott. Scott explained that these dependents, the beneficiary's wife and children, could enforce their claim for support against the trust estate, because "it is against public policy to permit the beneficiary to have the enjoyment of the income from the trust while he refuses to support his dependents whom it is his duty to support, *id.* at 661, 65 A.2d at 295, their claim being "in quite a different position from the ordinary creditors who have voluntarily extended credit." *Id.* Focusing specifically on alimony, at issue in that case, the Court opined:

> "We think the view expressed in the Restatement[10] is sound. The reason for the rejection of the common law rule, that a condition restraining alienation by the beneficiary is repugnant to the nature of the estate granted, was simply that persons extending credit to the beneficiary on a voluntary basis are chargeable with notice of the conditions set forth in the instrument.... This reasoning is inapplicable to a claim for alimony which in Maryland at least, is 'an award made by the court for food, clothing, habitation and other necessaries for the maintenance of the wife....' The obligation continues during the joint lives of the parties, and is a duty, not a debt."

Id. at 662, 65 A.2d at 296 (citations omitted). *See, also McCabe v. McCabe,* 210 Md. 308, 314, 123 A.2d 447, 450 (1956) ("This Court has held that alimony represents a duty and not a debt.")....

Similarly, in *Zouck*, the Court drew a distinction between the considerations underlying the balance when the monetary obligation sought to be satisfied is a contract or ordinary debt and when it is child support. It noted that the monetary claim in that case was "based, in essence, upon the statutory obligation of the father, declaratory of the common law, to support his child." 204 Md. at 298, 104 A.2d at 579. *See Walter v. Gunter,* 367 Md. 386, 398, 788 A.2d 609, 616 (2002) ("This Court historically has recognized a distinction between a standard debt and a legal duty in domestic circumstances, specifically with respect to child support, and subscribes to the theory that child support is a duty not a debt."); *Middleton v. Middleton,* 329 Md. 627, 629–33, 620 A.2d 1363, 1364–66 (1993) (analyzing the debt/duty distinction with respect to parental child support obligation)....

Similarly, the obligation to pay taxes and, thus, tax arrearages, is not to be considered debt, nor is the government to be viewed as a mere creditor. Addressing and

---

10. Restatement of Trusts, § 157 provided:
"Although a trust is a spendthrift trust or a trust for support, the interest of the beneficiary can be reached in satisfaction of an enforceable claim against the beneficiary,
"(a) by the wife or child of the beneficiary for support, or by the wife for alimony;
"(b) for necessary services rendered to the beneficiary or necessary supplies furnished to him;
"(c) for services rendered and materials furnished which preserve or benefit the interest of the beneficiary."

resolving this very point, the *Hofferbert* court distinguished the public policy underlying the tax obligation and that underlying ordinary or contract debts:

> "The reasons which have actuated some courts, as in Maryland, to uphold spendthrift trust against the claims of a creditors do not necessarily apply to tax claims of the government either federal or State. The public policy involved is quite different. In the one case the donor of the property has the right to protect the beneficiary against his own voluntary improvident or financial misfortune; *but in the other the public interest is directly affected with respect to collection of taxes for the support of the government.* The imposition of the tax burden is not voluntary by the beneficiary."

Hofferbert, supra, 58 F.Supp. at 706 (emphasis added).

Ms. Ryon's estate is a mere judgment creditor of McGee, the beneficiary. The Trust simply has no legal duty to Ms. Ryon's estate and certainly no obligation to provide support. Thus the rationale underlying the decisions permitting the invasion of a spendthrift trust for the payment of alimony, child support or taxes have absolutely no applicability to the obligation in this case. Indeed, to permit the invasion of the Trust to pay the tort judgments of the beneficiary, in addition to thwarting the trust donor's intent by, in effect, imposing liability on the Trust for the wrongful acts of the trust beneficiary, is, as the appellees argue, to create an exception for "tort victims" or "victims of crime."

. . .

To be sure, the Supreme Court of Mississippi quite recently held that, "as a matter of public policy ... a beneficiary's interest in spendthrift trust assets is not immune from attachment to satisfy the claims of the beneficiary's intentional or gross negligence tort creditors." *Sligh v. First National Bank of Holmes County,* 704 So.2d 1020, 1029 (Miss.1997). There, the plaintiff and his wife brought suit against an uninsured and intoxicated motorist/defendant for injuries arising from a traffic accident which resulted in the plaintiff's paralysis. The defendant was the beneficiary under two spendthrift trust established by his late mother. Having obtained a default judgment for $5,000,000 in compensatory and punitive damages in their action alleging gross negligence, the plaintiffs sought to attach the defendant's interest under the spendthrift trusts.

In arriving at its holding, the court acknowledged the four exceptions to the rule prohibiting the invasion of a spendthrift trust enumerated in the Restatement, *i.e.,* claims: for support of child or wife; for necessaries; for "services rendered and materials furnished which preserve or benefit the interest of the beneficiary; for State or federal taxes, *id.* at 1026, quoting Restatement (Second) of Torts, § 157, and a fifth, when the trust is 'a self-settled trust, i.e., where the trust is for the benefit of the donor,' it had itself recognized *Id.,* citing *Deposit Guaranty Nat'l Bank v. Walter E. Heller & Co.,* 204 So.2d 856, 859 (Miss.1967). Conceding that § 157 of the Restatement does not list an exception for involuntary tort creditors, the court found support for its position in Comment a to that section, which, as we have seen, admits of the possibility of a tort claimant with a claim against the beneficiary of a spendthrift trust being able to reach that beneficiary's interest. *Sligh, supra,* 704 So.2d at 1026. It also was persuaded by those portions of Scott, The Law of Trusts and Bogert, Trusts and Trustees, quoted herein and to which the appellant referred us. *Id.* at 1027. Finally, the court rejected the three public policy considerations it identified from its own precedents upholding the validity of spendthrift trust provisions: "(1) the right of donors to dispose of their property as they wish; (2) the public interest in protecting spendthrift individuals from personal pauperism, so that they do not become public burdens; and (3) the responsibility of creditors to make themselves aware of their debtors' spendthrift trust protections." *Id.* at 1027.

This is the minority position, which the *Sligh* court admitted. [Citations omitted.] ...

... *Sligh* is the only case we have found, and the only case that the appellant has cited, which holds expressly that a spendthrift trust may be invaded to pay the judgment of an intentional or gross negligence tort-judgment creditor.

Sligh is no longer the law of Mississippi.[14] A mere five months after the decision in *Sligh,* by ch. 460, §2, Laws, 1998, effective March 23, 1998, the Mississippi Legislature passed the Family Trust Preservation Act of 1998. Miss.Code Ann. §91-9-503 (2003), relevant to this case, provides:

> "Beneficiary's Interest not subject to transfer; restrictions on transfers and enforcement of money judgments

> "Except as provided in Section 91-9-509, if the trust instrument provides that a beneficiary's interest in income or principal or both of a trust is not subject to voluntary or involuntary transfer, the beneficiary's interest in income or principal or both under the trust may not be transferred and is not subject to the enforcement of a money judgment until paid to the beneficiary."

...

We are not persuaded, in any event, by the reasoning of the *Sligh* court. It is true that the court acknowledged the exceptions for alimony and for child support. Missing from the court's opinion, however, is any analysis of the basis for those exceptions. The Mississippi Supreme Court, although noting the donor's intention as, perhaps, the most important public policy consideration it addressed, concluded that, because the law has generally recognized exceptions, i.e., for support, alimony, taxes, to the spendthrift doctrine, the rights of trust donors to dispose of property as they wish

---

14. *See,* 88 Calif. L. Rev. 1877, Symposium on Law in the Twentieth Century: Uniform Acts, Restatements, and Trends in American Trust Law at the Century's End. ("An almost amusing reversal of direction was the prompt 1998 legislation in Mississippi to overturn the widely acclaimed *Sligh v. First National Bank. Sligh* had introduced a policy-based spendthrift exception for the benefit of victims of a beneficiary's gross negligence or recklessness. Furthermore, lengthy and vigorous debates in the last few years have eventually led to no significant changes or trends in rules identifying privileged claimants who can penetrate the spendthrift shield. This is particularly so with reference to privileged status that applies to certain governmental claimants, and often applies to alimony and the support claims of children and spouses and to certain claims for necessities and for protection of a beneficiary's trust interest.") (citations omitted).

are not absolute. 704 So.2d at 1028. This statement, although accurate, does not analyze why the law carved out these particular exceptions, which, as the court recognized, effectively takes precedence over the trust donor's intent.

To be sure, a contract creditor is on notice as to the terms of a spendthrift trust and, on that account, is able to regulate his or her conduct in light of that information. That is not the critical basis for the exception of alimony and support from the rule, however. *Robertson* and *Zouck,* as our opinions make clear, relied heavily on the fact that the obligation was a duty and not a debt. *Robertson, supra,* 192 Md. at 660, 65 A.2d at 295; *Zouck, supra,* 204 Md. at 298–99, 104 A.2d at 579. That is also the theme that runs through *Hofferbert.* 58 F.Supp. at 705. In none of these cases was notice mentioned as a basis for the decision. That a tort-judgment creditor is not on notice that he or she will be injured and thereby will incur a loss goes without saying, but, with due respect to the near unanimous commentators,[15] that fact alone does not make the claim he or she makes in respect of the loss anything other than a debt or make its exemption from the bar of a spendthrift trust, a matter of public policy.

JUDGMENT AFFIRMED, WITH COSTS.

BATTAGLIA, J., Dissenting.

I respectfully dissent.

Katherine Ryon was beaten to death during the course of a robbery that occurred in her home. After James Calvert McGee was convicted of felony-murder for his participation in the robbery and murder of Ms. Ryon, a money judgment was entered against him pursuant to a settlement agreement, in which McGee compromised civil claims brought against him by Robert Duvall, the Personal Representative of the Estate of Ms. Ryon. The majority today concludes that Ms. Ryon's estate cannot enforce its judgment against McGee's interest in an $877,000.00 spendthrift trust established for him by his deceased mother. The majority acknowledges that claimants seeking alimony, child support, and unpaid taxes may attach a beneficiary's interest in a spendthrift trust, but concludes that the victim of a violent tort may not, reasoning that such a victim is only "a mere judgment creditor." For the reasons expressed herein, I respectfully disagree.

---

15. The Uniform Trust Act, drafted by the National Conference of Commissioners of Uniform State Laws, does not advocate including tort judgment creditors among the creditors able to invade spendthrift trusts. Section 503, "Exceptions to Spendthrift Provision," provides:

"(a) In this section, "child" includes any person for whom an order or judgment for child support has been entered in this or another State.

"(b) Even if a trust contains a spendthrift provision, a beneficiary's child, spouse, or former spouse who has a judgment or court order against the beneficiary for support or maintenance, or a judgment creditor who has provided services for the protection of a beneficiary's interest in the trust, may obtain from a court an order attaching present or future distributions to or for the benefit of the beneficiary.

"(c) A spendthrift provision is unenforceable against a claim of this State or the United States to the extent a statute of this State or federal law so provides."

The commentary to that section indicates that "[t]he drafters ... declined to create an exception for tort claimants." *See,* Comment, Uniform Trust Act § 503, 7C U.L.A 76 (Supp.2002).

. . .

The majority concedes that tort creditors do not have the benefit of notice, which, as was discussed in *Smith, supra,* is a primary purpose for not allowing the invasion of spendthrift trusts. Despite this, the majority concludes that Ms. Ryon's estate cannot reach the corpus of the spendthrift trust because its claim is nothing other "than a debt" and that "its exemption from the bar of a spendthrift trust" is not "a matter of public policy." The majority, in my opinion, is wrong.

. . .

Just as it is sound public policy to permit the attachment of a spendthrift trust for alimony, child support, and taxes, it is also as sound to permit invasion to make victims of tortious conduct whole. Indeed, a tortfeasor may be liable not only for compensatory damages, but also punitive damages, which we allow in order to "punish the wrongdoer and to deter such conduct by the wrongdoer and others in the future." *Caldor, Inc. v. Bowden,* 330 Md. 632, 661, 625 A.2d 959, 972 (1993). Consequently, to equate victims of tortious conduct with contract creditors and distinguish them from recipients of alimony, child support, and tax claims, is without merit.

As the majority concedes, spendthrift trusts are considered valid in Maryland in large part because, by virtue of filing requirements, creditors are put on at least constructive notice of the limited interest of the beneficiary of such a trust. Such notice allows creditors to protect themselves, something that Ms. Ryon could not have done. Moreover, the "duty-debt" distinction set forth by the majority as the basis for its holding is unavailing. The obligation to restitute a wrong is commensurate with the obligations to pay alimony, child support, and taxes. I agree with the commentators that "it is against public policy to permit the beneficiary of a spendthrift trust to enjoy an income under the trust without discharging his tort liabilities to others." *See* Scott on Trusts, *supra.* Consequently, I respectfully dissent.

Notes

1. *Spendthrift clauses*: While the default rule is that a beneficiary's interest in a trust is freely transferable—and thus a creditor of a beneficiary can reach the beneficiary's interest in the trust—the general rule is that the settlor's intent can trump the default rule. Where a settlor expressly provides that a beneficiary's interest in the trust is nontransferable, such a clause is commonly referred to as a "spendthrift clause." While spendthrift clauses are controversial (England, the country that invented trusts, does not recognize spendthrift clauses), in America the general rule is that a spendthrift clause is valid and enforceable. Inasmuch as a spendthrift clause is an exception to the general rule of transferability and creditors' rights, however, courts have insisted that a spendthrift clause is valid only where it prohibits both voluntary and involuntary transfers. The Uniform Trust Code requires the same. *See* UTC § 502(a) (amended 2010). Accordingly, a valid spendthrift clause means that a beneficiary cannot voluntarily transfer his or her interest to a third party and, as a general rule, a creditor

of the beneficiary cannot reach the property interest before it is distributed to the beneficiary. UTC § 501(c).

2. *Exceptions to a spendthrift clause*: While almost all jurisdictions uphold the validity of spendthrift clauses, almost all jurisdictions also recognize (either judicially or statutorily) a number of exceptions to spendthrift clauses (i.e., circumstances under which a creditor can nevertheless reach the beneficiary's interest in the trust). Different states have adopted different approaches as to when a creditor should not be subject to a spendthrift clause. The most common approach is to identify certain categories of creditors who are not subject to a spendthrift clause. A less common approach is to limit the type (and/or amount) of property that a settlor is attempting to protect with the spendthrift clause.

3. *Specific categories of creditors exempt from spendthrift clause*: For a variety of public policy reasons, most jurisdictions recognize that certain categories of creditors should not be subject to spendthrift clauses. Historically, the most common categories of creditors who are able to reach a beneficiary's interest in a trust, even if the trust has a spendthrift clause, are:

    a. minor children entitled to child support — where a court order has been entered requiring the beneficiary to pay child support, if the beneficiary falls behind in his or her child support payments, the beneficiary's interest in the trust can be reached to satisfy any child support arrearages;

    b. spouses/ex-spouses entitled to support/maintenance — most jurisdictions permit spouses/ex-spouses of a beneficiary who are entitled to receive support/maintenance payments to reach a beneficiary's interest in a spendthrift trust to satisfy any arrearages;

    c. governmental entities asserting tax liens — virtually all jurisdictions recognize that a beneficiary's interest in a trust is subject to seizure to satisfy federal or state tax liens for unpaid taxes owed by the beneficiary, even if the trust has a spendthrift clause; and

    d. creditors who have provided basic necessities — many jurisdictions permit creditors who have provided basic necessities to a trust beneficiary to reach the beneficiary's interest in a spendthrift trust in the event the beneficiary fails to pay.

These special categories of creditors cannot only reach a beneficiary's interest in a trust despite a spendthrift clause, but as a general rule they can also reach a beneficiary's interest in a support trust.

The RESTATEMENT (SECOND) OF TRUSTS recognizes the four traditional categories of "special creditors" and more. It broadens the governmental claims exception to include *any claim* by the government against the beneficiary. It also adds a fifth: creditors who have an enforceable claims against the beneficiary "for services rendered and materials furnished which preserve or benefit the interest of the beneficiary." *See* RESTATEMENT (SECOND) OF TRUSTS § 157 (1959). While this last exemption is not as well recognized as the other four, a number of states have adopted it.

Despite academic criticism of: (a) spendthrift clauses generally, and (b) the limited exceptions to them (particularly the failure to exempt tort creditors), the modern trend has been generally to reaffirm the validity of spendthrift clauses and the exceptions to them, with some nuanced differences. The RESTATEMENT (THIRD) OF TRUSTS expressly recognizes the four non-governmental categories of "special creditors" recognized by the RESTATEMENT (SECOND) and "implicitly" recognizes claims by governmental claimants and other claimants "to the extent provided by federal law or an applicable state statute." *See* RESTATEMENT (THIRD) OF TRUSTS §§ 59, 59 cmt. a(1) (2003).

The Uniform Trust Code recognizes only four of the "special creditors" who are generally exempt from the effects of a spendthrift clause: (1) children with a judgment or court order entitling them to support; (2) spouses/former spouses with a judgment or court order entitling them to support/maintenance; (3) judgment creditors who have provided services that have protected the beneficiary's interest in the trust; and (4) governmental claims (state or federal)—but only to the extent authorized by statute. *See* UTC § 503. The UTC does not expressly recognize creditors who provided basic necessities as exempt from a spendthrift clause. To the extent creditors who provide basic necessities are often public entities, however, there may not be as much difference between the RESTATEMENT approaches and the UTC as one might think at first blush—*but only to the extent* the public entity is statutorily authorized to reach the beneficiary's interest in the trust.

Finally, both RESTATEMENTS provide that their categories of excluded creditors should *not* be presumed as exclusive, while the UTC presumes that its list of excluded creditors *is* exclusive.

4. *Creditor's ability to reach trust property*: The fact that certain categories of special creditors are not subject to a spendthrift clause and can reach a beneficiary's *interest* in a trust does not mean, however, that these creditors are automatically entitled to reach *the trust property* in question. Historically, and as a general rule still, a creditor's ability to reach a beneficiary's interest in a trust simply means that the creditor steps into the shoes of the beneficiary and receives whatever interest the beneficiary had in the trust, but no more. If the beneficiary's interest is mandatory, the transferee/creditor can force the trustee to disburse the property to the transferee/creditor, just as the beneficiary could. If, however, the beneficiary's interest in the trust is discretionary, just as the beneficiary could not force the trustee to exercise his or her discretion in the beneficiary's favor, the general rule was that a transferee/creditor could not force the trustee to exercise his or her discretion in the transferee/creditor's favor. This is true whether or not the trust contains a spendthrift clause.

5. *Creditors' rights—discretionary interest*: A spendthrift clause and a discretionary interest are similar drafting options in that they make it more difficult for a creditor to reach the beneficiary's interest in a trust, but for different reasons. Spendthrift clauses constitute a complete bar to a beneficiary's ability to transfer his or her interest—a bar that de facto prevents creditors from involuntarily compelling a ben-

eficiary to transfer his or her interest (absent special creditor status). In contrast, where the beneficiary's interest in question is discretionary, it is the nature of the beneficiary's interest that makes it more difficult for the creditor to reach the trust property. Inasmuch as the beneficiary could not compel the trustee to disburse the trust property to the beneficiary, it would seem obvious that a creditor of the beneficiary should not be able to compel the trustee to disburse the trust property to the creditor.

But what if the beneficiary could have sued the trustee for abuse of discretion and prevailed (and thereby been entitled to receive some of the trust property)? Should a transferee and/or creditor of the beneficiary be able to sue the trustee for abuse of discretion and reach the trust property? To the extent the transferee/creditor steps into the shoes of the beneficiary and receives the beneficiary's interest, while the transferee/creditor could not force the trustee to exercise his or her discretion, should not the transferee/creditor have the same rights as the beneficiary to sue for abuse of discretion as it relates to the beneficiary (not the transferee/creditor)?

Jurisdictions were split on the answer to this question. While the RESTATEMENT (SECOND) OF TRUSTS is not much help, as it does not address the issue, the RESTATEMENT (THIRD) OF TRUSTS expressly addresses the issue in the comments to a section. It provides that a trustee, in deciding whether to exercise his or her discretion in favor of making a disbursement, can take into consideration that any exercise of the discretion would result in the property going to a creditor or transferee instead of the beneficiary. One can only assume that most trustees would prefer to disburse property only to a trust beneficiary, not a creditor/transferee. The RESTATEMENT (THIRD) implicitly authorizes — if not encourages — a trustee to withhold discretionary disbursements if the result would be that a creditor/transferee, and not the beneficiary, would receive the property. *See* RESTATEMENT (THIRD) OF TRUSTS § 60 cmt. e.

The Uniform Trust Code contains a section that expressly addresses the protective features of a discretionary interest in a trust. On the one hand, the UTC is more aggressive in protecting the discretionary interest from creditors' claims. The UTC expressly provides that even in the absence of an express spendthrift clause, if a beneficiary's interest is discretionary, a creditor of the beneficiary may not compel a distribution even if "(1) the discretion is expressed in the form of a standard of distribution; or (2) the trustee has abused the discretion." *See* UTC § 504(b). But the UTC goes on to create an exception for select special creditors. If: (1) the creditor is a child or spouse/former spouse entitled to support, and (2) the trustee has abused his or her discretion, then the court can order the trustee to disburse property to the creditor (in an amount that is equitable under the circumstances), whether or not the trust has a spendthrift clause. *See* UTC § 504(c).

6. *Miscellaneous additional exceptions to spendthrift clauses*: In addition to the above "special categories of creditors" exception to the enforcement of a spendthrift clause, different states have created a variety of additional — but less common — exceptions to enforcement of a spendthrift clause. Some states permit enforcement of a spendthrift

clause only against creditors' claims that seek to reach a beneficiary's interest in the trust income, but not the trust principal. In such states, creditors with enforceable claims against a trust beneficiary are free to reach the beneficiary's interest in the principal. Some states permit creditors to reach up to a certain percentage of the money due and payable to a beneficiary (principal or income), notwithstanding a spendthrift clause. Careful attention needs to be paid to each state's approach to spendthrift clauses.

7. *Court order regarding future disbursements*: Assume, *arguendo*, that neither a transferee nor a creditor has any right to reach a beneficiary's discretionary interest in a trust (i.e., because neither can force the trustee to exercise his or her discretion in favor of the transferee or creditor). Can a transferee or creditor get a court order requiring the trustee, if in the future he or she decides to exercise his or her discretion in favor of the beneficiary, to distribute the property being disbursed directly to the transferee/creditor? Or can the transferee/creditor reach the property only after it is in the beneficiary's hands? Again, the jurisdictions split over this issue.

The modern trend is decidedly in favor of permitting creditors and transferees to secure a discretionary disbursement directly from the trustee once the trustee decides to exercise his or her discretion in favor of making a disbursement. The Uniform Trust Code permits any creditors who are exempt from the spendthrift clause to obtain a court order attaching any present or future disbursements for the benefit of the beneficiary. *See* UTC § 503(c). The RESTATEMENT (THIRD) OF TRUSTS goes even further, imposing personal liability on any trustee who does not make disbursements in the exercise of that discretion to a creditor or transferee once the trustee knows of the party's right to receive it. *See* RESTATEMENT (THIRD) OF TRUSTS § 60.

8. *The California approach*: California recognizes the validity of properly drafted spendthrift clauses (CPC § 15300-01).

California's categories of "special creditors" are more limited than most jurisdictions. Statutorily, a spendthrift clause does not apply to a private creditor with judgment claims and/or public entities or officials with claims for reimbursement, for:

1. Child and/or spousal support (CPC § 15305),
2. Restitution for commission of a felony (CPC § 15305.5), and/or
3. Public support (CPC § 15306).

Judicially, California courts have also recognized that the right of the United States to collect on a federal tax lien prevails over a spendthrift provision. *See Pack v. United States*, No. CV-F-92-5327, 1996 WL 149345 (E.D. Cal. Feb. 1, 1996) (citing *Leuschner v. First Western Bank & Trust Co.*, 261 F.2d 705 (9th Cir. 1958)).

Unlike many jurisdictions, California does not grant "special creditor" status to creditors who provide basic necessities to a trust beneficiary or to creditors who protected a beneficiary's interest in the trust. Having said that, however, California recognizes the right of *any* judgment creditor to obtain a court order "directing the trustee to satisfy all or part of the judgment out of the payments to which the beneficiary is entitled under the trust instrument or that the trustee, in the exercise of the trustee's discretion, has determined or determines in the future to pay to the beneficiary." *See* CPC § 15306.5(a). The statute, however, limits the maximum amount that can be subject to such a court order to 25 percent of the amount the trustee would otherwise be disbursing. *See* CPC § 15306.5(b), (f). The statute also exempts any and all amounts the court deems necessary for the beneficiary's support or anyone the beneficiary is required to support (spouse, former spouse, or minor children).

Like most states, in California "a transferee or creditor of the beneficiary may *not* compel the trustee to pay any amount that may be paid only in the exercise of the trustee's discretion." CPC § 15303(a). Even if a *beneficiary* could have forced a disbursement based on a standard included in the discretionary power, the *transferee/ creditor* cannot. Having said that, the California statutory scheme provides the transferee/creditor some hope and rights. First, as to all transferees/creditors, if there is no spendthrift clause, and if the trustee has knowledge of the transfer or has been served by a judgment creditor, if thereafter the trustee disburses trust property to the beneficiary, the trustee may be liable to the transferee/creditor if the disbursement impairs the transferee/creditor's rights. CPC § 15303(b). Where, however, the trust contains a spendthrift provision, the spendthrift clause prevails and the trustee owes the transferee/creditor no duty.

Moreover, while the general California rule is that a transferee or creditor cannot compel a trustee to exercise a discretionary interest in the transferee/creditor's favor (even where failure to do so amounts to an abuse of discretion relative to the beneficiary), California recognizes a number of exceptions to that general rule. Basically the same categories of "special creditors" who are not subject to a spendthrift clause (one holding a claim for (i) child and spousal support, (ii) public support, or (iii) restitution for commission of a felony) may be able to reach the beneficiary's discretionary interest if: (1) the beneficiary could have compelled the trustee to disburse the trust property in question to him or her (i.e., the trustee's failure to disburse property to the beneficiary is an abuse of trust), and (2) "the court determines it is equitable and reasonable." Under such circumstances, the transferee or creditor can force the trustee to disburse the trust property to the party (and/or have the court enter an order ordering the trustee to make any future disbursements to the party). *See* CPC §§ 15305, § 15305.5, § 15306.

California has a somewhat unique and interesting component to its approach to spendthrift clauses. California is more protective of spendthrift clauses that protect income rather than principal. Notwithstanding a spendthrift clause, if principal becomes due and payable to a beneficiary, following a petition by a judgment creditor, the court has the discretion to issue an order directing the trustee to use the principal due and payable to satisfy the judgment. *See* CPC § 15301(b).

Problems

1. How would the *Duval* case come out in California? How would the *Sligh* case come out in California? What if, in *Sligh*, the defendant had only been found

liable of operating his motor vehicle negligently? Would that make any difference? Should it?

2. Settlor's trust has a standard spendthrift clause in it. It also has a provision giving the beneficiary, after reaching the age of 40, the right to demand distribution of as much of the principal of the trust as the beneficiary may desire. A creditor of the beneficiary seeks to reach the beneficiary's interest in the principal. The trustee and the beneficiary invoke the trust's spendthrift clause. The creditor invokes the beneficiary's right to demand distribution of trust property. Which clause should control, and why? *See State Central Collection Unit v. Brent*, 525 A.2d 241 (Md. 1987).

3. Settlor's trust has a standard spendthrift clause in it. Beneficiary's creditors obtain a judgment against him. The court enters an order instructing the trustee to pay beneficiary's interest in the trust income directly to beneficiary's creditors. The beneficiary consents to the income being paid directly to the creditors. The trustee invokes the spendthrift clause. Does the beneficiary's consent override the spendthrift clause? *See Lundgren v. Hoglund*, 711 P.2d 809 (Mont. 1985).

4. Settlor's trust has a standard spendthrift clause in it. The trust is for the benefit of Settlor's son. The trust provisions regarding distributions to the son are mandatory with respect to trust income, but discretionary as to the principal. Settlor's son and his wife recently divorced. Son was ordered to pay alimony to his ex-wife and child support to his children. Son has fallen behind in his payments. Can son's creditors reach his interest in the trust to satisfy his alimony and child support payments?

5. *The future*: Considering that one way to think about a discretionary interest is that even in the absence of an express spendthrift clause it de facto contains a spendthrift clause, should creditors who are not subject to an express spendthrift clause be able to reach a beneficiary's interest in a trust that is discretionary? Do the public policy considerations that support their exception from the spendthrift clause support permitting such creditors being able to force a trustee to exercise his or her discretion in their favor to satisfy a judgment they hold against the trust beneficiary?

B. Self-Settled Trusts

A self-settled trust is when a settlor creates — or causes to be created — an *inter vivos* irrevocable trust where the settlor retains an interest in the trust, typically a discretionary interest in the trust.[4] The trust also typically is an irrevocable trust, and it usually contains a spendthrift clause as well. By granting oneself a discretionary interest in the trust, the fear/concern is that the settlor is trying to put the trust assets

---

4. The trust may also include a spendthrift clause. Would that make any difference with respect to the settlor's interest if it is discretionary?

beyond the reach of his or her creditors, but still within one's own reach if one has a cooperating trustee.

Should one be permitted to create a trust to shield one's assets from one's creditors? Should it matter whether the creditors are current creditors or future creditors? If one creates an irrevocable trust, appoints an independent trustee, and retains only a discretionary right to receive any property from the trust, has the settlor retained any interest in the trust that a future creditor of the settlor should be able to reach to satisfy a judgment against the settlor?

Rush Univ. Med. Ctr. v. Sessions

980 N.E.2d 45 (Ill. 2012)

Justice THOMAS delivered the judgment of the court, with opinion.

. . .

¶ 2 BACKGROUND

¶ 3 The undisputed facts in the pleadings, exhibits and affidavits on file establish the following. On February 1, 1994, Robert W. Sessions established the "Sessions Family Trust" and provided that it was to be governed by the law of the Cook Islands. When Sessions created this trust, he placed into it his 99% limited partnership interest in Sessions Family Partners, Ltd, a Colorado limited partnership, as well as property in Hinsdale, Illinois. At the time of his death, these assets were valued at more than $16.2 million and $2.7 million, respectively. Sessions was both the settlor and a lifetime beneficiary of the trust. It was furthermore irrevocable, and it authorized the trustees to make distributions to Sessions of both income and principal for his "maintenance, support, education, comfort and well-being, pleasure, desire and happiness." The trust also named Sessions as the "Trust Protector," giving him the absolute power to appoint or remove trustees and to veto any of their discretionary actions. Sessions also had the power to appoint or change beneficiaries, by will or codicil, who would continue under the trust after his death. Finally, the trust contained a spendthrift provision that prohibited any trust assets from being used to pay creditors of Sessions or his estate.

¶ 4 Plaintiff is a charitable institution that operates a major teaching and research hospital in Chicago. In the fall of 1995, Sessions made an irrevocable pledge to plaintiff of $1.5 million for the construction of a new president's house on the plaintiff's university campus in Chicago. Sessions then executed successive codicils to his will, providing that any amount remaining unpaid on his $1.5 million pledge as of his death would be given to plaintiff on his death. On September 30, 1996, Sessions sent plaintiff another letter stating that his pledge was "made in order to induce [plaintiff] to construct a Rush University Presidential Residence." This second letter confirmed his earlier pledge as follows:

> "I agree to provide in my will, living trust and other estate planning document * * * that (1) this pledge, if unfulfilled at the time of my death, shall be paid in cash upon my death as a debt and (2) that if this pledge is unenforceable

for any reason, a cash distribution shall be made under such will, living trust or other document to [plaintiff] in an amount equal to the unpaid portion of such pledge at the time of my death."

Sessions also stated in this second letter that his pledge was binding upon his "estate, heirs, successors and assigns," except to the extent that he had paid the pledge before his death.

¶ 5 In reliance on Sessions' pledge, plaintiff constructed the president's house on its university campus in Chicago at a cost in excess of $1.5 million. The house has since been used as a residence for the president of the university and as a center for conferences and other university events. The plaintiff named the house the "Robert W. Sessions House" and held a public dedication honoring Sessions for his generosity. Sessions was present at the dedication and cut the ceremonial ribbon, and a plaque adorning the front of the house still bears his name. Sessions did not make any payments to plaintiff during his lifetime toward the $1.5 million pledge.

¶ 6 In February 2005, Sessions was diagnosed with late-stage lung cancer. He blamed plaintiff for not diagnosing the cancer sooner so that it could be treated. On March 10, 2005, about six weeks before he died, Sessions executed a new will revoking all previous wills and codicils. This new will made no provision for any payment to plaintiff toward his pledge. On April 19, 2005, six days before he died, Sessions created a second trust, the Robert W. Sessions Revocable Living Trust, and transferred to it his 1% general partnership interest in Sessions Family Partners, Ltd. This 1% interest was valued at $164,205. Shortly before his death, Sessions also made various gifts of about $200,000, which ostensibly reduced the eventual assets of his estate. Sessions died on April 25, 2005.

¶ 7 On December 15, 2005, plaintiff filed an amended claim, in the probate division of the circuit court of Cook County, against Sessions' estate to enforce the $1.5 million pledge. The estate contested plaintiff's claim, and litigation ensued. The Sessions estate was found to contain less than $100,000. Thus, on April 4, 2006, in a supplemental proceeding, plaintiff filed a three-count verified complaint against the trustees of the Sessions Family Trust that was created in 1994, seeking to reach the trust assets to satisfy the debt owed to plaintiff by Sessions. Thereafter, plaintiff moved for summary judgment against the estate on its claim in the original proceeding, and on August 31, 2006, the circuit court granted summary judgment in favor of plaintiff. The estate appealed, and the supplemental proceeding was stayed pending the outcome of the appeal. On December 3, 2007, the appellate court, in a summary order, affirmed the summary judgment in favor of plaintiff in the estate's appeal (*In re Estate of Sessions*, No. 1-07-0202, 377 Ill.App.3d 1146, 352 Ill.Dec. 148, 953 N.E.2d 84 (2007) (unpublished order under Supreme Court Rule 23)).

. . .

¶ 9 Count III of plaintiff's complaint against the trustees is the only count at issue in this appeal. That count relied upon the principle that if a settlor creates a spendthrift trust for his own benefit, it is void as to existing or future creditors and such creditors can reach the settlor's interest under the trust. Plaintiff alleged that as a creditor, it should be able to reach the assets of the trusts created by Sessions to satisfy its $1.5 million claim.

¶ 10 The circuit court entered summary judgment in plaintiff's favor on count III, finding that the Sessions Family Trust dated February 1, 1994, was void as to plaintiff's $1.5 million judgment against Sessions' estate and that the trust is liable for payment to plaintiff on the pledge....

¶ 11 The trustees appealed, ...

¶ 13 ANALYSIS

¶ 14 Before this court, both plaintiff and the Attorney General rely upon the common law rule that a person cannot settle his estate in trust for his own benefit so as to be free from liability for his debts....

. . .

¶ 20 The common law rule ... has a general purpose of protecting creditors, but it addresses the specific situation where an interest is retained in a self-settled trust with a spendthrift provision. "Traditional law is that if a settlor creates a trust for the settlor's own benefit and inserts a spendthrift clause, the clause is void as to the then-existing and future creditors, and creditors can reach the settlor's interest under the trust." Helene S. Shapo *et al.,* Bogert's Trusts and Trustees § 223, at 424–67 (3d ed. 2007). And the rule is "applicable although the transfer is not a fraudulent conveyance * * * and it is immaterial that the settlor-beneficiary had no intention to defraud his creditors." Restatement (Second) of Trusts § 156 cmt. a (1959).

. . .

¶ 24 Second, it could be said that the policy behind the common law rule is not limited solely to deterring fraud, as it prevents the distinct injustice of allowing a person to use a trust as a vehicle to park his assets in a way that preserves his own ability to benefit from those assets, while keeping them outside the reach of his present and future creditors. If the law were otherwise, "it would make it possible for a person free from debt to place his property beyond the reach of creditors, and secure to himself a comfortable support during life, without regard to his subsequent business ventures, contracts, or losses." *Schenck v. Barnes,* 156 N.Y. 316, 50 N.E. 967, 968 (1898)....

. . .

¶ 27 In an alternative argument of sorts, defendants argue that the common law rule does not come into play because plaintiff did not become a judgment creditor in relation to Sessions before he died. Defendants claim that the common law rule regarding self-settled trusts applies only to the settlor's "lifetime interest" so that once the settlor dies, the rule does not permit a creditor to reach any trust assets that could have been, but were not, distributed to the settlor during his life. Citing section 156 of the Restatement (Second) of Trusts, defendants further contend that the common law rule operates only to negate the effect of the spendthrift clause and not the entire trust.

¶ 28 Defendants' argument misapplies the legal principles it cites to the facts of the present case. We note that cases addressing similar arguments have held that the settlor's "interest" in a self-settled trust that his creditors may reach includes all income and principal that *could* have been distributed to the settlor, even when the trustee exercises complete discretion over such distributions. See Restatement (Second) of Trusts § 156(2) (1959); Restatement (Third) of Trusts § 60 cmt. f (2003). This must be distinguished from an interest that creditors may not reach: where assets contributed by the settlor are irrevocably deeded to the trust for the benefit of other beneficiaries, such as where income from the trust is payable to the settlor but principal may be distributed only to designated remaindermen after the settlor's death, in which case the settlor's "interest" includes only the trust income, and the trust principal is not subject to claims by the settlor's creditors. See *In re Brown*, 303 F.3d 1261, 1268–69 (11th Cir.2002); Restatement (Third) of Trusts § 58 cmt. e (2003). The latter situation is clearly not present here, as the trust provisions gave the trustees (who could be replaced at will by the settlor and whose every material action was subject to the veto power of the settlor as "protector" of the trust) the power to distribute both *principal and income* to the settlor, in unlimited amounts, for his "maintenance, support, education, comfort, well-being, pleasure, desire or happiness."

. . .

¶ 30 We also find unpersuasive defendants' position that creditor's rights under the common law do not extend to the assets that the trustees could have distributed to the settlor but did not distribute to him before he died. There is no conceptual difference—with respect to trust assets distributable to the settlor—between allowing the settlor to favor himself over his creditors and allowing him to favor his relatives and other heirs over his creditors. Just as the common law keeps the settlor from retaining the benefit of his assets while keeping them beyond his creditors' reach, it also requires the settlor to be "'just before he is generous.'" *In re Estate of Kovalyshyn*, 136 N.J.Super. 40, 343 A.2d 852, 859 (N.J., Hudson County Ct.1975) (quoting *Merchants' & Miners' Transp. Co. v. Borland*, 53 N.J. Eq. 282, 31 A. 272, 274 (N.J.Ch.1895)); see also 2 William Blackstone, Commentaries. Thus, we believe that if the settlor's interest in a self-settled trust is "void" as to the settlor's creditors, there is no sound reason to treat the creditors' rights as suddenly defeated the moment the settlor dies, thereby giving the commensurate economic benefit to the settlor's heirs....

. . .

¶ 36 Turning to the case before us, we find that Sessions was clearly a "debtor" of plaintiff during his lifetime and plaintiff in turn was clearly a "creditor" of plaintiff as those terms are commonly understood. A "debtor" is simply defined as "[o]ne who owes an obligation to another, esp. an obligation to pay money." Black's Law Dictionary 433 (8th ed. 2004). A "creditor" is "[o]ne to whom a debt is owed." Black's Law Dictionary 396 (8th ed. 2004). There is no question that Sessions incurred an obligation to pay plaintiff money, even if it was to be paid at the latest upon his death as a debt.

Moreover, we note that, at the very least, the facts precipitating plaintiff's claim occurred during the lifetime of Sessions, and plaintiff could therefore recover against the trust assets. See *Nagel*, 580 N.W.2d at 812. Sessions clearly incurred the obligation to plaintiff during his lifetime and we have no trouble concluding that plaintiff was a creditor for purposes of the common law trust rule invoked in this case.

¶ 37 CONCLUSION

¶ 38 ... We ... conclude that under the undisputed facts of this case, plaintiff was a "creditor" of Sessions for purposes of the common law rule. Accordingly, we reverse the judgment of the appellate court, affirm the judgment of the circuit court, and remand the cause to the circuit court of Cook County for further proceedings consistent with this opinion.

Notes

1. *Revocable trusts*: Where a settlor retains a power to revoke a trust, the property in the trust is subject to the claims of a creditor to the settlor to the extent the settlor could have revoked the trust. Even though the power to revoke is limited to the settlor's lifetime, the modern trend is to provide that if the settlor's probate assets are not sufficient to cover the claims of his or her creditors, the creditors may reach the property in the trust subject to the power to revoke even after the settlor's death and even if the power to revoke was not exercised *inter vivos* by the settlor. California has adopted the modern trend.

2. *Self-settled trusts*: To clarify, there is nothing illegal about a settlor creating an *inter vivos* trust and retaining an interest in that trust. The term "self-settled trust" is not really about the settlor's retained interest in the trust per se — it really pertains to the issue of the rights of settlor's creditors with respect to the settlor's retained interest. To the extent the settlor has retained an interest *but has structured the trust in a way that attempts to make it difficult for his or her creditors to reach his or her interest in the trust*, as a general rule, at least historically, such attempts were invalid as applied to the creditors (but the trust is otherwise still valid).

The Sessions Family Trust is a classic example of a self-settled trust. The settlor created an irrevocable *inter vivos* trust and he retained a lifetime interest in both the income and the principal for his "maintenance, support, education, comfort and well-being, pleasure, desire and happiness." No problem. But Sessions structured the trust to try to make it difficult for his creditors to reach his interest in the trust: he appointed an independent third party as a trustee, he included a spendthrift clause, and his retained interest was discretionary. Has Sessions really divested himself of all interest in the trust property, or is the trust merely a sham transaction intended and designed to put his assets beyond the reach of his creditors against public policy?

3. *Self-settled trust and spendthrift clause*: The court invoked and applied the well-recognized and general rule that with respect to a settlor's retained interest in a self-settled trust, a spendthrift clause is null and void. The spendthrift clause is still valid

as to the interest of other beneficiaries, but not with respect to the settlor's interest in the trust.

4. *Self-settled trust and mandatory interest*: Inasmuch as a spendthrift clause is null and void in a self-settled trust with respect to any interest retained by the settlor, if a settlor retains a mandatory interest, under general creditor's rights principles any creditor of the settlor would be able to reach the settlor's mandatory interest in the trust. There is no need for special treatment of a settlor's interest in a self-settled trust if the settlor's interest is mandatory (in which case it might not technically qualify as a self-settled trust, because that term typically applies only to the extent the settlor's interest is discretionary).

5. *Self-settled trust and discretionary interest*: As the court in *Nelson v. California Trust Co.*, 202 P.2d 1021 (Cal. 1949) stated:

> It is against public policy to permit a man to tie up his property in such a way that he can enjoy it but prevent his creditors from reaching it, and where the settlor makes himself a beneficiary of a trust any restraints in the instrument on the involuntary alienation of his interest are invalid and ineffective.

Any restraint in trust that directly or indirectly attempts to restrict or limit the involuntary alienation of the settlor's interest is null and void, and any and all property that the trustee could have used for the settlor's benefit is subject to the claims of the settlor's creditors. It is as if a creditor of the settlor can force the trustee to exercise his or her discretion in favor of the creditor to the full extent the trustee could have exercised it in favor of the settlor.

6. *Modern trend?*: Historically the common law approach to self-settled trusts — that they were against public policy and not permitted to shield one's assets from one's creditors — was for all practical purposes universally recognized by all states.[5] While the United States has a long history against permitting any type of self-settled asset-protecting trusts, not all common law jurisdictions share that philosophy. England, the Cook Islands, and the Bahamas have long recognized a variety of asset-protecting trusts. While a detailed examination of the approach of those countries is beyond the scope of this material, suffice it to say that asset-protecting trusts are valid in those jurisdictions so long as the creation of the trust was not in fraud of a creditor's rights at the time the property was transferred to the trust. The property can be reached only to the extent it was fraudulently transferred to the trust.

Fast forward to today, when an increasing number of American states are beginning to permit some form of asset-protecting trust (Alaska, Delaware, and a few other states were the frontrunners of this movement in an attempt to attract more trust

---

5. There were always a handful of exceptions to the common law approach; for example, trusts involving retirement plans funded under the Employee Retirement Income Security Act of 1974 (ERISA) and Individual Retirement Accounts (IRAs), but such exceptions are beyond the scope of this introductory coverage.

business to their states). Like the traditional off-shore trust accounts, so long as the creation of the trusts was not in fraud of a creditor's rights at the time the property was transferred to the trust, the asset-protecting features of the self-settled trust are valid. Currently, the number of states allowing such self-settled trusts is in the minority.[6] Such states are, in the profession, commonly referred to as "pro debtor" states (at least when it comes to the viability of such trusts). The majority of states remain consistent with the common law approach and, in this respect, are often known as "pro creditor" states. Needless to say, such trusts are controversial and it is not clear whether an actual trend has emerged (creditor law is deeply rooted in many states and changes thereto can be slow in coming). The accompanying aspect of "forum shopping" with choice of law and trust situs in attempts to create effective self-settled trusts is also a matter of some controversy.

7. *California approach*: California currently stands with the majority of states, and the law remains consistent with that of the traditional common law approach. While it is not illegal for a settlor to utilize an irrevocable trust in which he or she is a permissible discretionary beneficiary, creditors of the settlor can reach trust assets to the extent that the trustee may make distributions to the settlor. For example, if the trust language permits the trustee to make distributions "to the settlor, in the trustee's discretion, of any part or all of the trust assets," then the settlor's creditors can reach all trust assets to satisfy debts of the settlor. It is important to note that "settlor's debts" generally means all debts incurred by the settlor, irrespective of when they were incurred; debts incurred both prior to and after establishing such a trust are subject to being satisfied by assets held in trust.[7]

8. *Trust protector*: The trust protector is another modern trend development, the details of which are beyond the scope of this introductory coverage. Trust protectors arose in offshore trusts. Offshore trusts require independent third-party trustees to qualify for asset protection status, but inasmuch as settlors retain a discretionary interest in the trust, settlors would like to insure that the trustee is a cooperating trustee. The trust protector can be viewed as an attempt to give the settlor that assurance. The Sessions Family Trust gave Sessions, the settlor, "the absolute power to appoint or remove trustees and to veto any of their discretionary actions." Inasmuch as one can make a lucrative living being a cooperative trustee, a trust protector's power to remove a trustee can have some influence over a trustee, thereby making him or her more cooperative to the discretionary interests of the settlor.

The trust protector is a relatively new development and its scope is still being defined. Moreover, the trust protector has moved onshore and is increasingly being used in domestic trusts for a variety of purposes, even in jurisdictions that still follow the traditional common law approach to self-settled trusts. Trusts and estates law is

---

6. Approximately 14 states allow asset protection self-settled trusts to varying degrees.

7. Of course, transfers of assets while there are existing debts may also be subject to general "fraudulent conveyance" provisions of state law.

trying to catch up, trying to determine who can serve as a trust protector, what powers can validly be granted to a trust protector, and whether a trust protector owes a fiduciary duty to those affected by the exercise of those powers.

Problems

1. Settlor created a trust for her own benefit during her lifetime. Her interest in the income is mandatory; her interest in the principal is discretionary. The trust also has a standard spendthrift clause. Settlor and her husband recently divorced. Settlor was ordered to pay alimony to her ex-husband and child support to her children. Settlor has fallen behind in her payments. Can Settlor's ex-husband and children reach her interest in the trust to satisfy the alimony and child support payments?

2. Consider the following facts:

   On June 24, 1966, while a patient at a private mental institution, Jane M. Conant created an *inter vivos* trust. She retained the right to revoke the instrument at any time. The trust's dispositive provisions provided, in relevant part, that the trustees were to pay to or apply to the use of Conant "so much of the net income thereof, in quarterly or more frequent installments, and so much of the principal thereof, as they may deem necessary or advisable for the support and maintenance of [Conant], and accumulate and reinvest any income not so paid or applied...." On January 20, 1967, Conant was admitted to Kings Park Psychiatric Center, a part of the State Office of Mental Health, where she has resided continuously through and including the date of submission of the controversy.

   Conant is liable under the authority of Mental Hygiene Law § 43.03(a) for services furnished to her. For the period of January 1, 1985 through September 29, 1988 there is an outstanding full cost balance of $150,566.45 owed which plaintiff is now seeking to recover. Mental Hygiene Law § 43.03(a) provides that a patient and any fiduciary holding assets for that patient are jointly and severally liable for the fees owed by the patient. Here, for 20 years, only the trust income was paid to the State Office of Mental Health in partial satisfaction of the cost of care.

   During the 20-year period, plaintiff never filed any claim against defendants as the co-trustees or against the assets of the trust for payment of the unreimbursed cost of Conant's care and never sought to have the trust declared null and void under EPTL 7-3.1 until November 25, 1988, when plaintiff submitted an amended verified claim to defendants for balances due from January 1, 1985 through September 29, 1988. Defendants rejected the claim and refused to invade the principal of the trust.

   How would you characterize Conant's interest in the trust? Can the State Office of Mental Health reach Conant's interest in the trust? *See State v. Hawes*, 564 N.Y.S.2d 637 (1991).

III. Beneficiary-Compelled Termination of an Irrevocable Trust

It is easy to understand how a trust beneficiary might become frustrated with the restrictions put on his or her interest in a trust (with respect to both *when* he or she might be entitled to receive property and/or *under what conditions* he or she might be entitled to receive property). One way a trust beneficiary can try to get out from under the restrictions of the trust is to sell his or her interest. While most laypeople are not familiar with it, a market exists for people who hold a right to receive a stream of property over a period of time.[8] If a settlor creates a trust that grants a life beneficiary a mandatory interest in the income, the beneficiary would have little trouble finding a market where he or she could sell the interest in exchange for a lump sum payout (based on the life expectancy of the beneficiary, discounted to present value and then discounted again for the risk of premature death). A settlor can prevent such a transfer, however, by including a spendthrift clause. But even when there is not a spendthrift clause, the sale of one's interest in a trust is not ideal as the beneficiary typically gets only a fraction of the value of his or her interest in the trust.

All things being equal, most trust beneficiaries would have preferred an outright gift to a gift in trust. If the property had been given to the trust beneficiaries outright, both the legal and the equitable interests would be theirs. They could do whatever they wanted with the property, and they would have access and control over all of the property immediately. A gift in trust, on the other hand, gives the trust beneficiaries only a limited interest in the trust property.

If one or more of the beneficiaries are frustrated with the fact that their interests are in trust and were not distributed outright to them, should the beneficiaries be permitted to terminate the trust and have the trust property distributed outright to them? Who owns the property in a trust: the trust (per the settlor's intent), the trustee (as the agent of the settlor and as the party who holds legal title), or the trust beneficiaries (as the holders of the equitable interest)? No doubt many trust beneficiaries think they own the property in the trust, but it was the settlor's property, and the settlor expressed his or her intent by creating the trust. Would not such termination be inconsistent with the settlor's intent in creating the trust? But once a trust is created, who really owns the property in the trust? If all the trust beneficiaries agree, are they not the owners of the trust property for all practical purposes?

---

8. A beneficiary in a trust is not the only party who might hold a right to receive a stream of money over time. Sometimes settlement agreements in tort cases will be structured in such a way that a party might be entitled to receive a stream of payments over time.

In re Estate of Bonardi

871 A.2d 103 (N.J. Super. Ct. 2005)

PARRILLO, J.A.D.

...

William Bonardi died testate on March 9, 2002, survived by his wife, Donna, and his two daughters, Danielle and Jessica. At the time of his death, Danielle was eighteen-years old and Jessica was sixteen-years old. Although decedent's Will included some specific bequests to other individuals, his wife and two daughters were the primary beneficiaries under separate testamentary trusts, each made up of one-half of the residuary estate. Stephen F. Pellino, decedent's friend, was named Executor of decedent's estate and Trustee of the two testamentary trusts.

The first trust named plaintiff, Donna Bonardi, as the income beneficiary and devised the remainder to Danielle and Jessica. The second trust named the daughters as the only beneficiaries. In both instances, the daughters were not entitled to outright distribution of their interest before they reached the age of twenty-five.

Under the first trust, plaintiff's interest was subject to several terms and conditions. Paragraph TENTH of decedent's Will reads, in pertinent part:

> For the duration of the life of my wife, DONNA, the Trustee shall pay her or apply towards her benefit, all of the net income of this trust. In addition, the Trustee may pay to her or apply to her benefit such amounts of the principal of the Trust as the Trustee, in the exercise of the Trustee's absolute discretion, deems advisable for her welfare. In deciding to make such distributions of principal to or for DONNA'S benefit, the Trustee shall be guided by the following statement of my purposes and intentions: *It is my expectation that the trust income and principal will not be made available to provide primary support for the beneficiary,* as I expect that DONNA in complete or large measure will support herself. *I further direct that my Trustee shall, to the extent possible, not make payments to DONNA out of principal unless necessary, and that he rather seek to preserve the corpus, to the extent possible, for ultimate distribution to my children or survivor of them.* My Trustee shall have complete authority to make these determinations which I direct shall not be subject to legal challenge. In making determinations as to distributions of principal for DONNA'S benefit, I ask that my Trustee be mindful of the standard of living that we maintained during my lifetime. [emphasis supplied.].

Explaining the limitations imposed pursuant to this paragraph, Pellino certified that decedent had expected his wife, who had gone to school and obtained a nursing degree during the marriage, to work in the nursing field on a full-time basis after his death. According to Pellino, decedent was also concerned about "his wife's inappropriate use of alcohol" and feared "that if the estate's assets were left to Donna outright, she would continue to lead this lifestyle which he felt was inappropriate, unhealthy and against his wishes." Further, decedent "did not want the proceeds of his hard work to be used for the benefit of any future boyfriend or husband that Donna might choose." None of these concerns, however, was expressly addressed by a spendthrift provision in the trust or anywhere else in the Will.

Even so, decedent evidenced his intent elsewhere in the Will. Notably, paragraph ELEVENTH, which concerned the daughters' trust, provided that "the trust income and principal will not be made available for primary support for the beneficiary as I expect that my wife will contribute to their support...." Further, paragraph TWELFTH granted the Trustee the exclusive right to "deal with [the] corpus and the income of such trusts." Only if the accumulated income from the trust was insufficient could the Trustee invade the principal.

A dispute eventually arose between plaintiff and the Executor/Trustee over the amount necessary for plaintiff's support. Plaintiff claimed that because she was only able to work part-time due to chronic medical problems, her living expenses exceeded her income, including the amounts made available to her by the Trustee under the first testamentary trust. Essentially, she complained that Pellino was improperly withholding principal necessary for her support and requested immediate distribution of all principal in the trust.

. . .

On May 12, 2004, Danielle and Jessica Bonardi executed a waiver of their remainder interest in the trust established on behalf of their mother so that the corpus could be immediately distributed to her. Pellino, however, refused to accept the waiver. As a result, the daughters filed a motion to terminate the testamentary trust, supported by certifications stating they understood they would inherit one-half of the trust principal upon their mother's death, but believed it was in their best interest if the trust were terminated and the corpus made immediately available to their mother. At the time, both daughters were living with their mother and under the age of twenty-five: Danielle, being only twenty years old, and Jessica, eighteen.

Following oral argument, the judge granted the motion and terminated the testamentary trust, directing distribution of the daughters' remainder interest in trust principal to plaintiff, Donna Bonardi. . .

On appeal, the Executor/Trustee maintains, among other things, that termination of the testamentary trust frustrates and defeats the express intent of the testator and is, therefore, impermissible. He further argues that the judge's finding that the testator's probable intent was to the contrary was unsupported by the evidence and constituted error....

. . .

To be sure, all the beneficiaries of a testamentary trust can consent to the trust's termination if none of them is under an incapacity and continuance of the trust is no longer necessary to carry out a material purpose of the trust. *Fidelity Union, supra,* 7 *N.J.* at 566, 82 *A.*2d 191; *In re Ransom Testamentary Trust, supra,* 180 *N.J.Super.* at 120, 433 *A.*2d 834; *Restatement (Second) of Trusts* § 337 (1959). Thus, if all of the purposes of the trust have been carried out, or if the only purpose remaining unfulfilled is to confer upon certain beneficiaries interests successively in possession and in remainder, then all persons in interest, if they are *sui juris*, may jointly compel termination of the trust. *Bd. of Dir. of Ajax Electrothermic Corp. v. First Nat'l. Bank of Princeton,* 33 N.J. 456, 465, 165 A.2d 513 (1960) (*Ajax II*); 6 Alfred C. Clapp et al., *New Jersey Practice Series* § 543 (3d Ed.1982).

On the other hand:

> If a trust is created for successive beneficiaries and it is not the only purpose of the trust to give the beneficial interest in the trust property to one beneficiary for a designated period and to preserve the principal for the other beneficiary, but there are other purposes of the trust which have not been fully accomplished, the trust will not be terminated merely because both of the beneficiaries desire to terminate it, or one of them acquires the interest of the other. [*Restatement (Second) of Trusts, supra,* § 337 comment g.].

…

Further, spendthrift trusts, trusts for support of a beneficiary, and discretionary trusts cannot be terminated by consent of the beneficiaries. *Restatement (Second) of Trusts, supra,* § 337 at comments l, m, and n. This is because the material purpose of a spendthrift trust is to prevent anticipation or control of future income or corpus by the protected income beneficiary and, therefore, acceleration of the trust would directly contravene the testator's intent. *Heritage Bank-North, N.A. v. Hunterdon Medical Center,* 164 N.J.Super. 33, 36, 395 A.2d 552 (App.Div.1978). Moreover, "even if not of an express spendthrift nature, a trust nevertheless created for the primary purpose of ensuring the beneficiary's support and maintenance is not terminable by consent since such termination would obviously also contravene testamentary intent." *Ibid.* And, the fact that a trustee has the power to invade the corpus for the beneficiary's benefit does not negate a testator's intent to establish such a trust. *Id.* at 37, 395 A.2d 552. In short, "[t]he question for determination is whether the settlor had any other purpose in mind than to enable the beneficiaries to successively enjoy the trust property." *Baer v. Fidelity Union Trust Co.,* 133 N.J. Eq. 264, 266, 31 A.2d 823 (E & A 1943).

Here, a material purpose of the trust not only still remains, but would be soundly defeated by the daughters' renunciation of trust corpus in favor of their mother, the income beneficiary whose right to principal was expressly limited under the terms of the trust. First and foremost, the request is not simply to terminate the trust and accelerate distribution to the intended successive beneficiaries, but quite the opposite, to divest the remaindermen of their interest and divert the trust corpus instead to the income beneficiary. This, however, is directly contrary to the express testamentary plan, evident from the face of the language of the Will itself. As stated in paragraph EIGHTH and provided for in paragraph TENTH, the clear purpose of the trust is to preserve the corpus for the ultimate benefit of decedent's daughters "per stirpes and not per capita." Thus, if one or both of the daughters were to predecease plaintiff, their children — decedent's grandchildren — would acquire their mother's interest in the trust. However, if the relief requested were to be granted, not only would Danielle and Jessica be divested of their remainder interest, but the rights of the putative grandchildren would be defeated as well, *cf. In re Estate of Branigan*, 129 N.J. 324, 609 A.2d 431 (1992), thereby frustrating the testator's clear intent. Plainly, in this instance, acceleration and termination of the trust would have resulted in a distribution to a person other than those intended by the testator. *Cf. Ajax Electrothermic Corp. v. First Nat. Bank of Princeton*, 7 N.J. 82, 87–88, 80 A.2d 559 (1951) (*Ajax I*).

Another purpose of the trust, evidenced in paragraph TENTH, was to provide supplemental support and maintenance for plaintiff without making trust income and principal "available to provide primary support." Rather, the announced expectation was that plaintiff would "in complete and large measure" support herself and "contribute to [the daughters'] support as may be appropriate to their age and circumstance from time to time." In fact, payments out of principal were not to be made to plaintiff unless absolutely necessary for her welfare. And, in making this determination, the trustee was vested with "absolute discretion." Indeed, the express terms of the Will divested plaintiff of actual control over the estate's assets. Thus, the creation of a trust with "complete authority" in a trustee evidences testator's plain intent to deny plaintiff immediate distribution of, or control over, distribution of trust corpus. *See Heritage Bank, supra*, 164 N.J.Super. at 37, 395 A.2d 552.

It also demonstrates the testator's intent to insulate trust principal from any control exerted by the daughters during their mother's lifetime. The language of paragraph EIGHTH, which states that neither Danielle nor Jessica is entitled to her respective remainder share before she reaches the age of twenty-five, supports this construction. By selecting a specific age as the earliest time at which his daughters may receive outright distribution of principal, the testator implicitly negated their ability to affect the trust before then. Yet, when Danielle and Jessica made the mutual decision to renounce their respective remainder interests, they were only twenty and eighteen years of age respectively, living with their mother, and presumably still under her influence.... Clearly, such decision-making by those otherwise ineligible under the explicit terms of the Will contravenes the testator's plain intent. And, the expressed wishes of the testator to preserve trust corpus for the benefit of his children or their survivors simply cannot be reconciled with the family settlement struck in this case that achieves diametrically opposite results. The named remaindermen not having yet attained the age to exert control over the trust corpus, a material purpose of the trust still exists and would be completely frustrated by its premature termination and distribution of principal to plaintiff, an unintended beneficiary.

...

... The relief requested here defeats the testamentary plan, evidenced from the face of the instrument itself, and contravenes the expressed wishes of the testator.

Reversed.

Notes

1. *Trust termination*: A trust terminates naturally pursuant to the settlor's intent when all of the trust property has been disbursed pursuant to the terms of the trust. Sometimes, however, due to either changed circumstances or simple impatience, the trust beneficiaries may attempt to compel a premature termination of the trust by forcing disbursement of the trust property. That obviously gives rise to the question of when, if ever, should the beneficiaries have the power to terminate a trust.

2. *Consent of all beneficiaries*: Under the traditional common law approach, and as required by the RESTATEMENT (SECOND) OF TRUSTS, before a court will even consider premature termination of a trust, *all* trust beneficiaries must consent. *See* RESTATEMENT (SECOND) OF TRUSTS § 337(a) (1959).

Historically, obtaining the consent of *all* the beneficiaries proved more challenging than one might first assume. Often trusts are for multiple generations of beneficiaries. A trust might even include beneficiaries holding contingent interests and unborn beneficiaries. How does one get the consent of a minor or unborn beneficiary? The traditional approach has been to appoint a guardian ad litem to represent the interests of the beneficiary who lacked legal capacity, but guardians ad litem tended to analyze the proposed modification from a purely financial perspective. If the modification would adversely affect the beneficiary financially, the guardian ad litem typically would oppose the modification. Without the consent of all beneficiaries, the modification would not be approved.

The modern trend has been to facilitate obtaining the consent of the necessary beneficiaries. Guardians ad litem have been encouraged to give family harmony and family benefit as much weight, if not more weight, than purely financial considerations. In addition, the RESTATEMENT (THIRD) OF TRUSTS and the Uniform Trust Code recognize the doctrine of "virtual representation," where current beneficiaries who have substantially similar interests as other beneficiaries can represent the other beneficiaries for purposes of securing the consent of all beneficiaries. *See* RESTATEMENT (THIRD) OF TRUSTS § 65 cmt. b; UTC §§ 303–304.

California still favors the use of a guardian ad litem to represent the interests of a beneficiary who lacks capacity, or is unascertainable or unborn, but the statute expressly authorizes the guardian ad litem, in deciding whether to consent to the proposed termination or modification, to "rely on general family benefit accruing to living members of the beneficiary's family as a basis for approving a modification or termination of the trust." CPC § 15405.

3. *Unfulfilled material purpose*: The court in *Bonardi* articulates and applies what is commonly known as the *Claflin* doctrine: even where all the beneficiaries consent, they cannot force the premature termination of an irrevocable trust as long as the trust has *an unfulfilled material purpose*.[9] The settlor's intent trumps the wishes of

---

9. The name of the doctrine comes from the Massachusetts Supreme Court opinion that first articulated it. *See* Claflin v. Claflin, 20 N.E. 454 (Mass. 1889).

the beneficiaries, as long as the settlor's intent includes a material purpose that has not been fulfilled yet. If, however, the trust has no unfulfilled material purpose, and all it contains is the successive enjoyment of the equitable interests spread over time, then the beneficiaries *can* force the premature termination of the trust if all the beneficiaries consent—the beneficiaries' intent will trump the settlor's intent.

Under the *Claflin* doctrine, the issue then becomes: what constitutes an unfulfilled material purpose? That question is fact sensitive and turns on the wording of the trust and settlor's intent. As the court in *Bonardi* acknowledged, there are a handful of trust purposes that are generally recognized as per se constituting an unfulfilled material purpose. The court mentioned three widely recognized purposes that per se constitute an unfulfilled material purpose: (1) trusts that contain a spendthrift clause, (2) support trusts, and (3) discretionary trusts. In addition, most courts recognized a fourth category of trusts with a per se unfulfilled material purpose: (4) trusts where the property is not to be distributed until a beneficiary reaches a certain age. And there is a fifth category of trust purpose that can constitute an unfulfilled material purpose: (5) any trust purpose in which the court finds the purpose constitutes an unfulfilled material purpose. Obviously this last category is a very soft, fact-sensitive standard, but it provides the discretion the courts want under the *Claflin* doctrine.

In which category of "unfulfilled material purpose" would you put the court's finding in *Bonardi*?

4. *Settlor consents*: In *Bonardi*, the trust was a testamentary trust. What if the trust in question was an *inter vivos* trust? What difference, if any, should it make if the settlor consents?

If the trust is an *inter vivos trust*, and the settlor is still alive, an important variable is whether the trust is revocable or irrevocable. If it is revocable, so long as the settlor is competent, the settlor alone can revoke/terminate the trust. The discussion of whether the beneficiaries can compel a premature termination of the trust presumes an irrevocable trust.

If the trust is irrevocable, should it matter that the settlor consents? If it is irrevocable, does the settlor retain any interest in the trust? Once the settlor transfers the property to the trust, the trustee holds legal title, and the beneficiaries hold equitable title. What interest, if any, does the settlor retain? Technically, while for most purposes the settlor retains no interest in an irrevocable trust once he or she has created it, for purposes of premature termination, the courts have decided that the settlor's consent is an important variable.

Consistent with the *Claflin* doctrine, if a trust is solely a string of equitable interests spread out over time (i.e., a series of possessory estates and future interests), if all the beneficiaries consent, they should be permitted to terminate the trust prematurely. If all the beneficiaries consent, the only possible hurdle that can block the premature termination is an unfulfilled material purpose—i.e., the settlor's intent. But if the settlor is alive, and consents with the beneficiaries that the trust should be terminated, the courts have held that the settlor's consent will override any unfulfilled material purpose. In essence, the settlor has "waived" the unfulfilled material purpose. The trust can be terminated prematurely. *See* Restatement (Second) of Trusts § 338 (1957).

5. *Settlor unable to consent*: If the settlor is dead, obviously he or she cannot consent. One way to think about the issue is the trustee becomes the representative for the settlor. If all the beneficiaries consent, and the trustee consents, the trust can be terminated. Later, if any of the parties were to change his or her mind and sue, the party would be estopped based on his or her initial consent.

Being a trustee typically is a relatively lucrative position. Most trustees have a financial incentive *not* to consent. One could argue that this is the logic underlying the *Claflin* doctrine. If the trustee is blocking the premature termination for legitimate reasons, i.e., if the trust has an unfulfilled material purpose, the trustee should be permitted to block the beneficiaries even if all the beneficiaries consent. But if the trust has no unfulfilled material purpose and yet the trustee is blocking the beneficiaries' attempt at terminating prematurely, might the trustee be trying to block it just to protect his or her compensation? One could argue that the *Claflin* doctrine is nothing more than judicial regulation of a trustee's actions when faced with an attempt by the beneficiaries to terminate the trust prematurely.

6. *Modern trend*: From a theoretical perspective, the issue of premature termination of a trust is a fascinating issue because it forces one to wrestle with the question of who really owns the property in the trust. As noted above, assuming an irrevocable trust, technically the settlor no longer owns the property. For purposes of terminating a trust, who really owns the property in the trust: the trustee or the beneficiaries? One could argue that even the traditional common law approach recognizes that the beneficiaries have the stronger claim of ownership. If the trust has no unfulfilled material purpose, the beneficiaries can terminate the trust so long as all the beneficiaries consent.

The modern trend takes this basic principle, that the beneficiaries are the true owners of the trust property, and extends it a bit further than the common law did. The Restatement (Third) of Trusts continues the general rule that if all the beneficiaries consent, they can terminate an irrevocable trust unless "termination or modification would be inconsistent with a material purpose of the trust," in which case the beneficiaries can compel termination only if: (1) the settlor consents, or (2) if the settlor is dead, "with authorization of the court if it determines that the reason(s) for termination or modification outweigh the material purpose." *See* Restatement (Third) of Trusts § 65 (2003). Moreover, the comments to the Restatement (Third) provides that the traditional types of trusts that per se constituted a material purpose (a spendthrift trust, a support trust, or a discretionary trust) do not per se bar termination: "[S]pendthrift restrictions are not sufficient in and of themselves to establish, or to create a presumption of, a material purpose that would prevent termination by consent of all of the beneficiaries. This is also true, in many contexts, of discretionary provisions." *See* Restatement (Third) of Trusts § 65 cmt. e (2003).

The Uniform Trust Code likewise provides that a spendthrift provision in a trust "is not presumed to constitute a material purpose" for purposes of premature termination. UTC § 411(c). Moreover, the Uniform Trust Code permits partial termination where not all the beneficiaries consent, so long as: (a) the trust could have been terminated if all the beneficiaries had consented, and (b) the interests of the beneficiaries who did not consent are adequately protected. UTC § 411(e).

7. *Uneconomically small trusts*: Both the RESTATEMENT (THIRD) and the Uniform Trust Code permit trust termination if the size of the trust corpus has become so small that it is economically inefficient to continue the trust. *See* UTC § 414; RESTATEMENT (THIRD) OF TRUSTS § 66 cmt. d (2003). This has commonly been adopted by the states, including California. Generally, this occurs where the viability of the trust, due to the diminution in value of the trust assets, is at a point where it is just "not worth the effort" (time, expense, taxes, etc.) to keep it alive. It is common for the trust document to contain language permitting such termination. The following is an example of a portion of such a clause:

> *Power to Terminate Trust*: If the value of the trust has declined to such an amount that the Trustee deems it uneconomical, imprudent or unwise to continue to retain the principal in trust, the Trustee shall have the power to terminate the trust and to deliver the then remaining principal to, or for the benefit of, the beneficiary, or beneficiaries, then entitled to receive the income of the trust [or some other specific method of determining who should be entitled to such distribution].

Problem

Maybelle Kent established a testamentary trust for the benefit of her only child, Peggy, with Peggy's father Sidney and Title Insurance and Trust Co. appointed as co-trustees. Peggy was a 15-year-old schoolgirl at the time. The terms of the trust direct the trustees as follows:

> [T]he entire net income of said trust estate shall be held and accumulated by said trustees and reinvested by them for the beneficiaries thereof hereinafter named; provided, that any part of said net income may be paid, applied and expended by said trustees in their absolute discretion for support, care and education of plaintiff. It was also provided that when plaintiff should reach the age of 35 years, the trust estate and all accumulations thereof should be transferred and delivered to her, ...

Mabelle died in 1932. Sidney died in 1942. The year after Sidney's death, Peggy petitioned to terminate the trust. Peggy's arguments were as follows:

> [N]otwithstanding the provisions of the trust that the plaintiff should receive the entire trust estate, together with the accumulations thereof, upon reaching the age of 35, it was contemplated by plaintiff's mother at the time of the creation of said trust that should the occasion arise or circumstances exist warranting the earlier termination of said trust for the purpose of relieving

plaintiff from any undue hardship or unexpected contingency, the trust could be earlier terminated'; that such 'circumstances exist' in that when the will creating the trust was executed, plaintiff was a schoolgirl 15 years of age, living with her mother, and not capable of looking after her financial affairs; that it was contemplated by the trustor, plaintiff's mother, that if she should die before plaintiff should attain the age of 35 years, plaintiff would live with her father, Sidney R. Kent, who would provide for her independently of the trust, and therefore it would be unnecessary for plaintiff to receive the corpus of the trust prior to her attainment of the designated age; that the trustor believed that plaintiff's father, then living, would participate in the management of the trust, but by reason of his death, this is no longer possible; that the income from the trust is negligible and wholly inadequate to support plaintiff in a manner consistent with her station in life; that plaintiff's income apart from the trust is similarly insufficient; that by reason of her father's death, plaintiff is unable to have comforts and necessities and to buy a home as she could if her father were alive; that plaintiff is now 26 years of age, happily married and living with her husband, capable of managing the estate left in trust by her mother, and is desirous of purchasing a home; that 'the conditions aforesaid have arisen since the creation of the trust * * * and said situation was not contemplated by plaintiff's mother and therefore no provision was made for the same.'

Should the trust be terminated? How would you rule on Peggy's petition? *See Moxley v. Title Ins. & Trust Co.*, 165 P.2d 15 (Cal. 1946); *Larson v. Cty. of Monterey*, No. H039029, 2015 WL 7185021 (Cal. Ct. App. Nov. 16, 2015).

IV. Modification of Irrevocable Trust
A. Modifying a Trust's Dispositive or Administrative Terms

Assuming a validly created *irrevocable* trust, when, if ever, should it be modified? We saw above that if the trust is revocable, the power to revoke includes the power to amend or modify, so the settlor can still modify the trust. But what if the trust is irrevocable? Does the termination material that we just finished apply equally to proposed trust modifications?

As a general rule, the answer is "yes." If the beneficiaries have the power to terminate, the beneficiaries also have the power to amend. There is, however, one additional doctrine that the courts have historically recognized that applied only to trust modification, not trust termination.

In re Riddell

157 P.3d 888 (Wash. Ct. App. 2007)

PENOYAR, J.

¶1 The Trustee of a consolidated trust, Ralph A. Riddell, appeals the trial court's denial of his motion to modify the trust and create a special needs trust on behalf of a trust beneficiary, his daughter, Nancy I. Dexter, who suffers from schizophrenia affective disorder and bipolar disorder. Ralph's deceased father and mother each established a trust. The trusts were consolidated by the court. Upon Ralph's death, the trust will terminate and Nancy will receive payment of her portion of the trust proceeds. Ralph argues that the trial court has the power to modify the trust; that his daughter's disabilities are a changed and unanticipated condition; and that the purpose of the settlor will be preserved through the modification. We agree and remand to the trial court to reconsider an equitable deviation in light of changed circumstances and the settlors' intent that the beneficiaries receive both medical care and general support from the trust's funds.

FACTS

¶2 George X. Riddell and Irene A. Riddell were husband and wife with one child, Ralph. George's Last Will and Testament left the residue of his estate in trust for the benefit of his wife, his son, his daughter-in-law, and his grandchildren. George also created an additional trust (the Life Insurance Trust) for their benefit. Irene's Last Will and Testament left the residue of her estate in trust for the benefit of her son; her son's wife, Beverly Riddell; and her grandchildren.

¶3 The trusts contained a provision in which, upon the death of Ralph and Beverly, George and Irene's grandchildren would receive the trust's benefits until the age of thirty-five when the trusts would terminate and the trustee would distribute the principal to the grandchildren. Ralph is currently the Trustee. George and Irene are both deceased.

¶4 Ralph and Beverly have two children, Donald H. Riddell and Nancy. Both Donald and Nancy are more than thirty-five years old. Donald is a practicing attorney and able to handle his own financial affairs. Nancy suffers from schizophrenia affective disorder and bipolar disorder; by 1991 she received extensive outpatient care; and by 1997 she moved to Western State Hospital. She is not expected to live independently for the remainder of her life.

¶5 Both Ralph and Beverly are still living. Upon their death, the trusts will terminate because Nancy and Donald are both over the age of thirty-five; Nancy will receive her portion of her grandparents' trust principal, which is approximately one half of $1,335,000.

¶6 The Trustee, Ralph, filed a petition in superior court, asking the trial court to consolidate the trusts and to modify the trust to create a "special needs" trust on Nancy's behalf, instead of distributing the trust principal to her. Clerk's Papers (CP) at 4. He explained that, under the current trust, when her parents die, Nancy's portion of the principal will be distributed to her and the trust will terminate. He argued that a special needs trust is necessary because, upon distribution, Nancy's trust funds would either be seized by the State of Washington to pay her extraordinary medical bills or Nancy would manage the funds poorly due to her mental illness and lack of judgment. He argued that the modification would preserve and properly manage Nancy's funds for her benefit.

¶ 7 The trial court granted the motion to consolidate the trusts but denied the motion to modify. It stated that it did not have the power to modify the trust unless unanticipated events existed that were unknown to the trust creator that would result in defeating the trust's purpose. The trial court found that the trust's purpose was "to provide for the education, support, maintenance, and medical care of the beneficiaries" and that a modification would only "permit[ ] the family to immunize itself financially from reimbursing the State for costs of [Nancy's medical] care." CP at 54, Report of Proceedings (RP) at 4. Relying on the Restatement (Second) of Trusts, it stated that it would not allow a modification "merely because a change would be more advantageous to the beneficiaries." CP at 53; Restatement (Second) of Trusts § 66(1) cmt. b (2001). It did not issue factual findings or legal conclusions with its order but incorporated its reasoning from its oral ruling into the order.

¶ 8 Ralph moved for reconsideration, arguing that the Trust and Dispute Resolution Act, chapter 11.96A RCW (TEDRA) and the Restatement (Third) gave the trial court plenary power to handle all trusts and trust matters and the authority to modify the consolidated trust into a special needs trust. Ralph argued that, because the grandparents directed the trust proceeds to be distributed to their grandchildren when they reach the age of thirty-five, the settlors intended that their grandchildren attain a level of responsibility, stability, and maturity to handle the funds before receiving the distribution. He also argued that due to Nancy's mental illness, allowing a distribution to her would defeat the settlors' intent and the trust's purpose.

¶ 9 The trial court denied the motion for reconsideration. It again issued no factual findings or legal conclusions, but it stated that its decision was based on the findings and conclusions articulated in its oral ruling on the motion for reconsideration. On reconsideration, the trial court agreed that the Restatement (Third) of Trusts allowed the court to modify an administrative or distributive protection of a trust if, because of circumstances the settlor did not anticipate, the modification or deviation would further the trust's purpose. It then stated:

> I believe that there is a showing here that there is a circumstance that was, perhaps, not anticipated by the original settler [sic]; however, the purpose of the trust is to provide for the general support and medical needs of the beneficiaries. I think that modifying the trust in a fashion that makes some of those assets less available for that purpose than they would be under the express language of the trust presently is not consistent with the purpose of the trust.

CP at 107. The trial court reasoned that because the trust was written to provide for "medical care" and because creating a special needs trust would make some money unavailable for medical care expenses, the modification was inconsistent with the trust's purpose. CP at 101. Ralph now appeals.

ANALYSIS

...

II. TRUST MODIFICATION

¶ 12 Ralph asserts that the trial court had the authority to modify the trust under both the equitable deviation doctrine and under the plenary power granted by TEDRA. TEDRA states that it is the Legislature's intent to give courts full and ample power to administer and settle all trust matters. RCW 11.96A.020. On reconsideration, the trial court agreed that it possessed the power to modify a trust. It stated that it could modify an administrative or distributive protection of a trust if, because of circumstances the settlor had not anticipated if the modification would further the trust's purpose. The trial court understood that it possessed the ability to modify the trust.

¶ 13 Next, Ralph contends that the trial court erred in declining to modify the trust. He explains that a modification would further the trust's purpose because, if George and Irene had anticipated that Nancy would suffer debilitating mental illness requiring extraordinary levels of medical costs and make her incapable of managing her money independently, they would not have structured the trust to leave a substantial outright distribution of the trust principal to her. He contends that the settlors instead would have established a special needs trust to protect the funds because Nancy's medical bills would be extraordinary and covered by state funding.

¶ 14 Ralph explains that the settlors conditioned the distribution of trust assets on her being at least thirty-five years old, indicating that they intended that their grandchildren have a level of maturity and stability before receiving the trust distribution. Ralph asserts that given Nancy's medical conditions and inability to handle her finances independently, she will never attain a level of maturity to handle the distribution of funds; therefore a special needs trust is appropriate.

¶ 15 Niemann [Niemann v. Vaughn Cmty. Church, 154 Wash.2d 365 (2005)] is very instructive in this case. In Niemann, our Supreme Court held that trial courts may use "equitable deviation" to make changes in the manner in which a trust is carried out. Niemann, 154 Wash.2d at 378, 113 P.3d 463. The court outlined the two prong approach of "equitable deviation" used to determine if modification is appropriate. Niemann, 154 Wash.2d at 378, 113 P.3d 463. The court "may modify an administrative or distributive provision of a trust, or direct or permit the trustee to deviate from an administrative or distributive provision, if [(1)] because of circumstances not anticipated by the settlor [(2)] the modification or deviation will further the purposes of the trust." (Niemann, 154 Wash.2d at 381, 113 P.3d 463; Restatement (Third) of Trusts § 66(1) (2001)). In Niemann, the court adopted the Restatement (Third) of Trusts and noted that the Restatement (Third) requires a lower threshold finding than the older Restatement and gives courts broader discretion in permitting deviation of a trust. Niemann, 154 Wash.2d at 381, 113 P.3d 463.

¶ 16 The first prong of the equitable deviation test is satisfied if circumstances have changed since the trust's creation or if the settlor was unaware of circumstances when the trust was established. Restatement (Third) of Trusts § 66 cmt. a (2001). Upon a finding of unanticipated circumstances, the trial court must determine if a modification would tend to advance the trust purposes; this inquiry is likely to involve a subjective process of attempting to infer the relevant purpose of a trust from the general tenor of its provisions. Restatement (Third) of Trusts § 66 cmt. b (2001).

¶ 17 The reason to modify is to give effect to the settlor's intent had the circumstances in question been anticipated. Restatement (Third) of Trusts § 66 cmt. a (2001). Courts will not ordinarily deviate from the provisions outlined by the trust creator but they undoubtedly have the power to do so, if it is reasonably necessary to effectuate the trust's *primary* purpose. *Niemann*, 154 Wash.2d at 382, 113 P.3d 463. A trust settlor may possess a myriad of intentions in settling a trust, but the trial court must concern itself with their primary objective. *Niemann*, 154 Wash.2d at 382, 113 P.3d 463.

¶ 18 As stated above, we defer to the trial court's factual findings. *Niemann*, 154 Wash.2d at 375, 113 P.3d 463. In this case, the trial court did not issue formal factual findings, but it stated in the oral ruling that there was a showing of a changed circumstance in this case. This meets the first prong. The settlor's intent is also a factual question. *Niemann*, 154 Wash.2d at 374–75, 113 P.3d 463. The trial court found in its oral ruling that the "stated" purpose of the trust is to provide for the beneficiaries' education, support, maintenance, and medical care. CP at 54. Thus, it found that this trust's primary purpose was to provide for Nancy during her lifetime. Because the trust was to terminate at age thirty-five, it was also the settlors' intent that Nancy have the money to dispose of as she saw fit, which would include any estate planning that she might choose to do.

¶ 19 There is no question that changed circumstances have intervened to frustrate the settlors' intent. Nancy's grandparents intended that she have the funds to use as she saw fit. Not only is Nancy unable to manage the funds or to pass them to her son, but there is a great likelihood that the funds will be lost to the State for her medical care. It is clear that the settlors would have wanted a different result.

¶ 20 In 1993, as part of the Omnibus Budget Reconciliation Act, Congress set forth a requirement for creating special needs trusts (or supplemental trusts), intended to care for the needs of persons with disabilities and preserve government benefits eligibility while allowing families to provide for the supplemental needs of a disabled person that government assistance does not provide. Marla B. Karus, *Special Issue: Special Needs Children in the Family Court*, 43 Fam. Ct. Rev. 607, 610 (Oct.2005) (emphasis removed). The Act exempted certain assets from those assets and resources counted for the purposes of determining an individual's eligibility for government assistance. Pub.L. 103-66, § 13611(b), *codified* at 42 U.S.C. § 1396p(d)(4)(A). A supplemental needs trust is a trust that is established for the disabled person's benefit and that is intended to supplement public benefits without increasing countable assets and resources so as to disqualify the individual from public benefits. See Jill S. Gilbert,

Using Trusts in Planning for Disabled Beneficiaries, Wisconsin Lawyer (Feb.1997); *Sullivan v. County of Suffolk*, 174 F.3d 282, 284 (2nd Cir.1999).

¶ 21 In this case, the trial court was concerned with fashioning a trust for Nancy that would allow the family to shield itself for "reimbursing the State" for the costs of her medical care due to her disability. RP at 4. But in 1993, Congress permitted the creation of special needs trusts in order to allow disabled persons to continue to receive governmental assistance for their medical care. Marla B. Karus, *Special Issue: Special Needs Children in The Family Court*, 43 Fam. Ct. Rev. 607, 610 (Oct.2005); Pub.L. 103-66, § 13611(b), *codified* at 42 U.S.C. § 1396p(d)(4)(A). Special needs trusts were created in order to allow disabled persons to continue receiving governmental assistance for their medical care, while allowing extra funds for assistance the government did not provide. Given this legal backdrop, the trial court should not have considered any loss to the State in determining whether an equitable deviation is allowed. The law invites, rather than discourages, the creation of special needs trusts in just this sort of situation. The proper focus is on the settlors' intent, the changed circumstances, and what is equitable for these beneficiaries.

¶ 22 George and Irene both died without creating a special needs trust but did not know of Nancy's mental health issues or how they might best be addressed. They clearly intended to establish a trust to provide for their grandchildren's general support, not solely for extraordinary and unanticipated medical bills.

¶ 23 A special needs trust may be established by a third party or by the disabled person that would be benefited by the trust. See Barbara A. Isenhour, *Medicaid Eligibility for Long-Term Care Coverage and Special Needs Trusts*, Isenhour Bleck, P.L.L.C. (Feb. 2006). Trusts established or funded by the disabled person are subject to 42 U.S.C. § 1396p(d)(4)(A), which entitles the State to receive all remaining trust amounts upon trust termination for medical assistance paid on behalf of the disabled beneficiary. See Clifton B. Kruse, Jr., *Third Party and Self-Created Trusts Planning for the Elderly and Disabled Client*, ABA Publishing (3rd Ed.). However, the State is not entitled to receive payback upon termination of a third party special needs trust for medical assistance provided for the disabled beneficiary. See Barbara D. Jackins, *Special Needs Trusts A Guide for Trustees Administration Manual* (2005 Ed.). Here, the trust was established and funded by George and Irene Riddell for the beneficiary Nancy Dexter. It is a third party special needs trust. The trust is not subject to State assistance payback and is not required to have a payback provision.

¶ 24 We remand to the trial court to reconsider this matter and to order such equitable deviation as is consistent with the settlors' intent in light of changed circumstances.

Notes

1. *Equitable deviation*: Trust modification due to an unexpected change in circumstances is also commonly known as "equitable deviation." Most courts, the RESTATEMENT (THIRD) OF TRUSTS, and the Uniform Trust Code apply equitable deviation

not only to the dispositive provisions of a trust, but also to the administrative provisions of a trust. *See* RESTATEMENT (THIRD) OF TRUSTS §66 (2003); UTC §412. The Uniform Trust Code grants even greater discretion to a court to order administrative deviation, permitting it "if continuation of the trust on its existing terms would be impracticable or wasteful or impair the trust's administration." UTC §412(b). That standard is borrowed from the UTC's approach to cy pres, a doctrine that historically was limited to the dispositive provisions of a charitable trust. The doctrine of cy pres is covered in greater detail in Chapter 15.

2. *The traditional approach*: Under the traditional approach, before a court could modify a trust, it had to be shown that: (1) due to a change in circumstances not known to a settlor and not anticipated by him or her, (2) continuance of the trust pursuant to its original terms would defeat or substantially impair the trust purposes.

3. *The modern trend approach*: The modern trend approach lowers the bar for trust modification. The modern trend modifies the first requirement from there being an unexpected change in circumstances to simply that there be "circumstances not anticipated by the settlor"—which the notes clarify can be circumstances present at the time the trust was created but of which the settlor was not aware. As for the second requirement, instead of showing that failure to modify would frustrate the settlor's intent, all the moving party has to show is that modifying the trust would promote the settlor's intent. *See* RESTATEMENT (THIRD) OF TRUSTS §66 (2003); UTC §412.

4. *Unlawful, illegal, or against public policy*: The traditional view was that if the purpose of a trust became unlawful, illegal or against public policy, that was grounds for trust termination. *See* RESTATEMENT (SECOND) OF TRUSTS §335 (1959). The modern trend changes those into circumstances not anticipated by the settlor that justify trust modification. *See* RESTATEMENT (THIRD) OF TRUSTS §66 cmt. c (2003). The Uniform Trust Code still lists those as grounds for trust termination, UTC §410(a), but it would seem one could argue in good faith under the Uniform Trust Code that such could also constitute circumstances not anticipated by the settlor that justify trust modification, not termination.

5. *Special needs trusts*: This is the name most commonly given to trusts (generally *inter vivos* irrevocable trusts or, with less frequency, testamentary trusts resulting from an *inter vivos* revocable living trust or a testamentary trust established by a will) for a loved one who is suffering from some form of physical or mental illness. At the core of planning involving special needs trusts is that the beneficiary is someone who is hoping to qualify, or maintain eligibility, for certain government benefits. In particular, two primary government programs are at issue: Supplemental Social Security Income (often referred to as "SSI") and Medicaid/Medical health benefits ("Medical" is California's Medicaid program—federal benefits administrated by California).[10]

---

10. Medicaid/Medical is a joint state and federal-based health insurance program in addition to federal-based "Medicare." The latter is a form of federal health insurance that is available to most Americans at a certain age. However, Medicaid/Medical, is available only to certain individuals; generally, those with limited income, assets, or other financial resources. Health-related benefits provided by Medicaid/Medical are in addition to those available under Medicare and, in many instances, are

While an oversimplification, these two programs provide certain Social Security benefits and free or low-cost health coverage to millions of Americans who qualify by reason of limited sources of income and assets.

A simple *inter vivos* gift or testamentary devise (via will, revocable living trust, or otherwise) to an individual receiving SSI or Medicaid/Medical benefits (and other government benefits) will, most likely, cause such a "special needs" individual to become ineligible for continuation of these benefits. This is due to the fact that ownership (or effective ownership) of more than a minimal value of assets will disqualify an individual from such programs. So the most common iteration of the dilemma arises in estate planning: a parent may wish to provide benefits (*inter vivos* or testamentary) to a special needs child who is currently receiving or will be eligible for SSI and Medicaid/Medical, but by doing so, the child will no longer be eligible for the wide range of important life and medical benefits accorded to him or her. The typical solution is a "special needs trust." In a nutshell, an irrevocable trust is established where the special needs individual is a permissible and discretionary beneficiary. Pursuant to the trust provisions, such individual may receive distributions for a variety of purposes (ranging from living costs to recreational activities such as vacations) but the assets in the trust will not be attributed to such individual for purposes of qualifying for SSI or Medicaid/Medical.

Prior to special needs trusts coming of age in latter half of the twentieth century (California was considered on the leading edge of creating such devices in the mid-1970s), the choices for providing for someone in need were rather limited: transferring assets to such individuals (outright or in regular trust form either *inter vivos* or at one's death via a will, living trust, or in some other testamentary form) which would terminate eligibility for such government benefits or, in the harsh alternative, leave nothing to such individual (thus not affecting benefits eligibility).

A detailed explanation of what is required for a special needs trust is beyond the scope of this book. Suffice it to say that the creation of such trusts is not for the "do it yourself" market. Trust wording, in how and when trust assets may be used for the special needs beneficiary, is extremely important and missteps can cause a beneficiary to become ineligible for the aforementioned government benefits, hence defeating the purpose of such a trust.

Most special needs trusts are established by a third party, such as a parent, for a special needs individual. These are, quite logically, referred to as "third-party SNTs."[11] Can an individual concerned about his or her own future qualification for such government programs establish a personal special needs trust? Can one transfer substantially all of one's assets to an irrevocable trust with trustee discretionary powers to make distributions to the settlor, all of this in an attempt to make the settlor a "low

---

more extensive—often covering health-related items that are covered to a lesser degree or unavailable under Medicare (in-home health care is a common example of an additional benefit of Medicaid/Medical).

11. In practice, SNT is the commonly used abbreviation for special needs trusts.

income/net worth" individual who will qualify for such benefits? We have seen this type of trust before, the self-settled trust, when discussing creditor issues. The answer is a qualified yes, and such a self-settled special needs trust is commonly referred to as a "first-party SNT."

It is rather rare for an individual with substantial wealth to set up a first-party SNT just to qualify for government SSI and Medicaid/Medical benefits—an extreme case of the "benefits tail wagging the dog." More likely, a first-party SNT may be set up by an individual with special needs (who may already qualify or is soon to qualify for government benefits) and this individual is the recipient of assets by way of gift, devise/bequest/testamentary gift or inheritance, a personal injury award, etc. Faced with newly acquired assets that may preclude eligibility for SSI and Medicaid/Medical, such individual may be the settlor of a first-party SNT.

It is well beyond the scope of this book, but a first-party SNT can present some challenges. These range from delays in qualifying for such benefits for a period of time after transferring the assets in trust, to what are known as "payback" requirements. The latter is exclusive to first-party SNTs (third-party SNTs are generally not subject to this) and, put quite simply, requires that at the special needs beneficiary's death, any remaining assets in the trust be used to reimburse the state for Medicaid/Medical benefits received (or medical expenses paid on behalf of such individual) during his or her lifetime.

There are many forms of special needs trusts and accompanying complex rules relating to eligibility for government benefits. In addition, for first-party SNTs, there is some overlap with previously discussed creditor issues for self-settled trusts. Even with the many complex issues associated with special needs trusts, they can allow a special needs beneficiary to enjoy an improved lifestyle by reason of availability, as a discretionary beneficiary, of additional resources in the form of assets held in such trusts.

6. *Modification for tax reasons*: Again, while well beyond the scope of this book, modification of a trust may be precipitated for tax reasons. This is often the case when the trust is revocable or when a trust is irrevocable but when the settlor retains certain powers, directly or indirectly, to alter and amend the trust. Revocability or the settlor's retention of certain powers may prevent tax planning goals of minimizing or avoiding exposure to federal (or state) gift or estate taxes. These also might negatively affect the settlor's income tax situation. Tax-motivated modifications may include making a revocable trust irrevocable, the settlor relinquishing retained powers affecting the ongoing operation of the trust, removing the settlor as the trustee or, where applicable, preventing the settlor from becoming the trustee, or certain aspects of the settlor's ability to appoint trustees, etc.

This emphasizes the need for any attorney involved in estate planning to be well-versed in tax law. The typical estate and gift tax course is replete with horror stories of simple mistakes causing catastrophic results for tax purposes. One does not have to look too hard to find a classic blunder: your new client provides you with a trust that was drafted many years earlier by a different attorney. The goal, at the time, was to minimize estate tax exposure with respect to an asset (for example, a parcel of beachfront land in Malibu, California) that was, when the trust was drafted, worth $100,000. This was valuable at the time, but with exponential growth over the years, it is currently worth more than $25 million. Your new client comes to your office happy that they went to the trouble of setting up the trust with this parcel of land years ago so that this will no longer be included in his or her taxable estate, for estate tax purposes, at his or her death. You read the trust document and, unfortunately, have to be the bearer of bad news that the trust has a minor flaw (silent as to revocability, it gives the settlor a tax-prohibited direct or indirect power to do something, a subtle issue such as those discussed in the self-settled trust material, or some other seemingly innocuous issue), and this minor flaw means that the trust set up years ago to accomplish the client's goal of estate tax minimization does not work. Unfortunately, the trust document was ineffective for tax purposes, and this parcel of Malibu land will still be included in the client's estate for estate tax purposes, at a value of more than $25 million. Your client is no longer happy and trust modification, while possible, will still potentially expose the client to millions of dollars of unnecessary tax liability. Your client then asks for your recommendation for a malpractice attorney—a very small mistake years ago has potentially exposed the original drafting attorney to a huge malpractice lawsuit.

The RESTATEMENT (THIRD) PROPERTY: DONATIVE TRANSFERS, and the Uniform Trust Code expressly authorize trust modification to achieve tax objectives. RESTATEMENT (THIRD) PROP.: DONATIVE WILLS AND DONATIVE TRANSFERS § 12; UTC § 416. Federal tax courts, however, are not required to accept a state court-ordered trust modification.

Chapter 14

Trust Life: Trustee's Perspective

I. Overview — A Historical Perspective

While one can argue that from the beneficiary's perspective the trust has remained surprisingly unchanged over the centuries, the same cannot be said about the trust from the trustee's perspective. The typical English common law trust was funded with real property. The trustee's job was to hold the real property in trust for future beneficiaries. The purpose of the early common law trust, accordingly, was to *preserve* the trust property. Transfers of trust property to third parties were discouraged, not encouraged. Minimizing the trustee's powers and maximizing the liability of a third party who dealt with a trustee furthered the purpose of the early common law trust: to hold and preserve the trust property — the real property — for future beneficiaries.

Over time, though, the world changed from a land-based economy to a mercantile economy. The principal form of wealth changed from real property to personal property, such as stocks, bonds, certificates of deposits, annuities, savings accounts, and the like. The primary method of funding trusts likewise changed. The purpose of the modern trust changed from preserving the trust property (real property) to managing the trust property (a fund of intangible wealth). Proper management of the modern trust implicitly necessitated broad powers over the trust property, liberal authorization to invest the trust fund, and the ability to shift investments quickly as market conditions change. The trustee of a modern trust needs, and wants, to be a player in the marketplace. The nature and purpose of the modern trust were at odds with the common law trust rules with respect to: (1) a trustee's powers, (2) a third party's ability to deal with a trustee, and (3) some of the trustee's duties.

The last 50 years of the law of trusts has been marked by an ongoing attempt to bring the trust — and the law of trusts — into the twenty-first century. Traditional trust law was judicial in nature. The last several decades have seen a proliferation of statutory efforts to revise the law of trusts so as to facilitate and even promote the purpose of the modern trust: the active management of a fund of intangible wealth. If the traditional common law approach to the law of trusts represents one end of the spectrum, and the most recent statutory enactment, the Uniform Trust Code, the other end of the spectrum, where does California fall on that spectrum?

II. Trustee's Powers and Third-Party Liability for Transacting with a Trustee

A. Common Law Approach

Under the common law approach, a trustee had no inherent powers over the trust property. A trustee had only those powers expressly granted by the settlor in the trust instrument (or those powers necessarily implied in light of the trust's purpose). Moreover, once a third party knew or should have known that he or she was dealing with a trustee, the third party was charged with knowledge of the default rule: the trustee had no inherent powers and was not authorized to transfer the trust property absent express or implied authorization. For all practical purposes, the third party was charged with notice that the proposed transaction constituted a breach of trust, absent express authorization. Accordingly, a third party interested in dealing with a trustee assumed a duty to inquire into the express terms of the trust to confirm that the trustee was, in fact, authorized to engage in the proposed transaction. If the third party failed to inquire, it was charged with knowledge of the true scope of the trustee's powers. If the third party actually inquired into the express terms of the trust, it was charged with proper construction of the trust's terms. The good faith purchaser doctrine had no meaningful application to a third party who knew or should have known that it was dealing with a trustee. Accordingly, if a third party participated in a transaction with a trustee and the transaction constituted a breach of trust, for all practical purposes, the third party was strictly liable.

The traditional common law approach discouraged third parties from dealing with a trustee, and conversely, it made it difficult for a trustee to deal with third parties. This approach, however, made sense in light of the purpose of the common law trust: to *preserve* the trust property for future beneficiaries.

B. Modern Trend Approach

To the extent the purpose of the modern trust is to *actively* manage a fund of intangible wealth, (a) the trustee needs increased powers and more investment authority so as to be able to *actively* manage the trust property, and (b) third parties interested in dealing with a trustee need more protection.

1. The Trustee's Powers

As the trust evolved from its traditional purpose to its modern purpose, settlors, on an individual basis, could deal with the change in purpose by expressly granting their trustees more powers. This approach, however, was inherently limited. It is difficult, if not impossible, to anticipate all the powers a trustee might need, particularly when the nature of the trust property is likely to change over time (the longer the duration of the trust, the more difficult it is to anticipate all possible powers a trustee may need). Moreover, even if a settlor were able to predict all the necessary powers and included them in the trust instrument, third parties would still be reluctant to deal with a trustee. Under the traditional approach, dealing with a trustee involved increased transaction costs because the third party would have to inquire and ascertain the trustee's power to engage in the proposed transaction. Because the third party was charged with proper construction of the trust terms, if there was any ambiguity and the court disagreed with the third party's construction, the third party would be liable for participating in the breach of trust. If the trust were to make the transition from the common law trust to the modern trust, it would require systemic statutory changes to the law of trusts.

The modern trend has seen a number of different statutory attempts to address this transition. The early attempts were state statutes that set forth a long list of express powers a settlor could incorporate by reference. These statutes essentially maintained the common law approach but facilitated the drafting process to make it easier for a settlor to grant a trustee all necessary express powers. In 1964, the Uniform Law Commission adopted the Uniform Trustees' Powers Act (UTPA). The UTPA took more of a formula-based approach, shifting the default presumption from "a trustee has no powers" to "a trustee has all powers":

> From time of creation of the trust until final distribution of the assets of the trust, a trustee has the power to perform, without court authorization, *every act which a prudent man would perform for the purposes of the trust* including but not limited to the powers specified in subsection (c).

UTPA § 3 (emphasis added).

The most recent uniform law, the Uniform Trust Code (UTC), goes even further. The UTC grants the trustee "all powers over the trust property which an unmarried competent owner has over individually owned property." UTC § 815. Both the UTPA and the UTC permit a settlor to opt out of the modern trend approach by expressly limiting a trustee's powers in the trust instrument, but the burden is on the settlor.

Like other states, California initially adopted an exhaustive list of statutory powers that a settlor could incorporate by reference. The default, however, was still the common law approach, and the burden was on the settlor to opt out of the traditional approach by expressly incorporating the statutory powers. Ultimately, like the UTPA and the UTC, California reversed the default rule. California has a formula-based approach that automatically grants the trustee all statutory powers and all powers a trustee would need in light of the trust's purposes:

CPC § 16200. Trustee — General Powers

A trustee has the following powers without the need to obtain court authorization:

(a) The powers conferred by the trust instrument.

(b) Except as limited in the trust instrument, the powers conferred by statute.

(c) Except as limited in the trust instrument, the power to perform any act that a trustee would perform for the purposes of the trust....

Consistent with the modern trend, California places the burden on the settlor to opt out of the modern trend approach.

2. Protection for Third Parties Who Deal with a Trustee

A trustee's enhanced power would be ineffective, however, if a third party who was interested in dealing with a trustee was not granted greater protection than he or she received at early common law. The traditional common law approach: (1) required the third party to inquire into the scope of a trustee's power any time the third party knew or should have known he or she was dealing with a trustee (which increased transaction costs for third parties), and (2) held the third party to proper construction of the terms of the trust. De facto, if the transaction constituted a breach of trust, the third party was liable for participating in that breach.

The modern trend realized that the enhanced trustee's powers would be ineffective without enhanced protection for third parties. Accordingly, the Uniform Trustees' Power Act granted third parties unprecedented protection. It provides that a third party:

> is not bound to inquire whether the trustee has power to act or is properly exercising the power; and a third person, without actual knowledge that the trustee is exceeding his powers or improperly exercising them, is fully protected in dealing with the trustee as if the trustee possessed and properly exercised the powers he purports to exercise.

See UTPA § 7. Proving actual knowledge is very difficult, if not impossible. Thus, the UTPA de facto grants third parties nearly complete immunity when dealing with a trustee.

The more recently adopted Uniform Trust Code pulls back on the protection accorded to third parties interested in dealing with a trustee. The UTC essentially grants the same protection a third party would have if he or she were dealing with any other type of agent. A third party who deals with a trustee in good faith and for value is not required to inquire into the scope of a trustee's powers. Even if the transaction constitutes a breach of trust, so long as the third party acted in good faith and gave valuable consideration, the third party is not liable. UTC § 1012.

California grants third parties dealing with a trustee essentially the same degree of protection as the UTC. *See* CPC § 18100.

The goal of the modern trend statutory trust law movement has been to permit and promote the purpose of the modern trust: the *active* management of a fund of intangible wealth. At first blush, the unprecedented expansion of a trustee's powers, and enhanced protection to third parties interested in dealing with a trustee, would appear to achieve that goal. But one more important variable needed to be addressed before the modern trust purpose could be achieved: a trustee's powers are limited by the fiduciary duties the trustee owes to the trust beneficiaries. These fiduciary duties are intended to serve and protect the interests of the beneficiaries. Some of the traditional common law duties are no real obstacle to the modern trust purpose and accordingly have transitioned to contemporary trust law intact. Some traditional common law duties, however, would have been impediments to the modern approach to trusts and accordingly have been revised.

Problem

Ruth and George Dunmore created the Dunmore Family Trust. Following George's death, Ruth served as sole trustee. Pursuant to the terms of the trust, she broke the Family Trust into separate trusts (50 percent to a Survivor's Trust for her benefit that is revocable; 50 percent into three Decedent's Trusts for the benefit of her children and grandchild, and those trusts are irrevocable). Ruth continued as sole Trustee of each trust. While George was still alive, Ruth and George, acting as co-trustees, pledged the assets in the Family Trust as collateral for $12,000,000 in loans to two grandsons and their company. The borrowers have defaulted on the loans, and the banks are seeking to reach all the assets that were in the Family Trust.

Ruth claims that the she and the trusts have various claims against the grandsons and their company. She asserts that the grandsons exercised undue influence in getting them to pledge the assets for the loans and that some of the signatures on the paperwork are forged. Ruth, however, is 86 years old and is not in a position to pursue the claims. She lacks the energy and the financial resources to pursue the claims, and she was unable to find an attorney to take the claims on a contingent fee basis. Accordingly, Ruth assigned the claims to one of her sons, Steven, in exchange for valuable consideration ($1.00 plus 55% of any recovery). Another son, Sidney Jr., who is also father of the grandsons in question, objects to the proposed assignment.

Included among Sidney Jr.'s claims is that Ruth lacks the power to assign the claims. "The trust instrument gives Ruth authority to purchase, exchange, or sell any kind of property. It also gives her the authority to release any claim belonging to the trust to the extent the claim in her opinion is uncollectible." In addition, the California Probate Code grants her the power "to sell a chose of action in the same manner as personal property," and "the power to release, in whole or in part, any claim belonging to the trust."

Does Ruth have the power to assign the trusts' claims against the grandsons and their company to her son Steven? *See Dunmore v. Dunmore*, No. C063910, 2012 WL 267725 (Cal. Ct. App. Jan. 30, 2012).

III. The Office of Trusteeship

While the classic gratuitous trust is a bifurcated gift, particularly when viewed from the beneficiary's perspective, it is not a gift from the trustee's perspective. The trustee is taking on a job — an onerous job at that. The trustee is entering into a fiduciary relationship with the trust beneficiaries, a relationship where the trustee has an overriding duty to do everything in the best interests of the trust beneficiaries. Included within the overarching fiduciary relationship are a plethora of sub-duties, many of which require a certain level of skill and care, and many of which, if not performed properly, will expose the trustee to liability.

Because a trust is not a gift from the trustee's perspective, the law does not presume that an individual nominated to be a trustee will accept that nomination. A designated trustee must first accept the position—and one would be well-advised to think it over carefully before accepting. The moment an individual accepts the offer to become a trustee, he or she assumes a number of fiduciary duties that must be undertaken almost immediately. Whether a designated trustee has accepted the position is a question of the nominated party's intent, and while that intent arguably should be express, it may be implied one way or the other by the party's actions (or inactions). *See* Restatement (Third) of Trusts § 35 (2003) (updated 2014).

While a designated trustee must accept the position before he or she is held to the fiduciary duties that accompany the position, at one level a trust does not need a trustee to be valid trust. That is because the general rule is that a trust will not fail for want of a trustee.[1] If a person nominated to be a trustee declines, or if a trustee dies or is incapable of continuing, the trust is not affected. The court will appoint a successor trustee who will then assume the position and must abide by the terms of the trust.

While early English law assumed that a trustee would serve without compensation, that view did not transfer to the American system. While there is some very old authority supporting that view, the general default rule in America is that a trustee deserves compensation for such an onerous job. The question of a trustee's compensation is, however, first and foremost a question of the settlor's intent. The settlor can expressly provide whether the trustee will be compensated, and if so, at what rate. A professionally drafted trust almost always expressly provides for trustee compensation (and the method for doing so). Where the trust does not address the issue, most states have a statutory scheme that governs compensation based on the size of the trust corpus. The Uniform Trust Code provides that a trustee is entitled to "reasonable compensation," a provision that authorizes a court to override the terms of a trust to increase or decrease compensation as appropriate under the circumstances. UTC § 708.

California has adopted essentially the same approach as the UTC. *See* CPC § 15680.

Thinking back to the pros and cons of a will versus a revocable living trust at the end of Chapter 11, the disposition of the decedent's estate with a will via probate has a built-in administrative advantage of a disinterested party (the court) to supervise and ensure that the dispositive wishes and instructions of a testator's will are properly followed—that the proper assets go to the proper persons. A revocable living trust where the settlor was the initial trustee typically has a built-in administrative disadvantage in that the successor trustee who takes over the trust following the settlor's death usually functions without direct supervision—the "testamentary" dispositions of the decedent's estate are made by the new trustee. A successor trustee who lacks knowledge and has a reluctance to seek outside help (because he or she doesn't want to pay an attorney or, worse, lacks integrity) can spell disaster, the ramifications of which may be improper disposition, nonpayment of creditors, or dispositions not

---

1. There is a narrow exception for when the powers are deemed personal to the nominated party— only to be granted to and performed by the nominated person—but that exception is rarely applied. *See* Restatement (Second) of Trusts § 101 cmt. b (1959).

in conformity with trust instructions. There are remedies, but more often than not they cannot fully rectify the situation, often leaving a permanent divide among family members.

A. General Duty to Administer the Trust

The Restatement (Third) of Trusts provides that the trustee's first, and most overarching, duty is to properly administer the trust:

> (1) The trustee has a duty to administer the trust, diligently and in good faith, in accordance with the terms of the trust and applicable law.

> (2) In administering the trust, the trustee's responsibilities include performance of the following functions:

>> (a) ascertaining the duties and powers of the trusteeship, and the beneficiaries and purposes of the trust;

>> (b) collecting and protecting trust property;

>> (c) managing the trust estate to provide returns or other benefits from trust property; and

>> (d) applying or distributing trust income and principal during the administration of the trust and upon its termination.

Restatement (Third) of Trusts § 76.

Note that the Restatement (Third) of Trusts provision reflects the trustee's need to be sensitive to both the terms of the trust and the applicable law. That is because some of the law of trusts is default law that the terms of the trust can opt out of, and some of the law of trusts is binding and will prevail over conflicting trust terms. You should keep this in mind as the material moves through the various fiduciary duties. Which duties should/can a settlor opt out of, and which duties are binding on the trustee regardless of the terms of the trust?[2]

IV. The Core Duties

The Restatement (Third) of Trusts takes the position that in administering the trust there are three core duties a trustee owes the beneficiaries — all the other duties are ancillary. The three core duties are:

[1] *prudence* (so fundamental to the investment function ...),

[2] *loyalty* (often called the "cardinal" principle of fiduciary relationships, but particularly strict in the law of trusts), and

---

2. The material hinted at this issue — and has already covered it in part — when it discussed whether the terms of a trust granting a trustee "sole and absolute" discretion could actually grant a trustee that much discretion.

[3] *impartiality* (balancing the diverse interests and competing claims—concurrently and over time—of the various beneficiaries or objectives of typical modern trusts).

RESTATEMENT (THIRD) OF TRUSTS ch. 15, intro. note. It should be noted that while these duties are articulated as separate and distinct duties, they often overlap in application.

A. Duty of Loyalty

Wilkins v. Lasater
733 P.2d 221 (Wash. Ct. App. 1987)

MUNSON, Judge.

...

Nell and Fred Lasater died, testate, on June 13, 1946 and April 27, 1952 respectively. By separate wills, each created a testamentary trust funded from their half of the community property. These trusts, the provisions of which are virtually identical, provide for management by majority rule of three trustees.

The original trustees of these trusts were Lowden Jones, Elfred Lasater Nunn, and Redman Lasater. Mrs. Wilkins succeeded Mr. Jones as trustee in approximately 1955; Gary Lasater succeeded his father Redman Lasater, as trustee, after his death in 1968. Throughout the course of this action, the three trustees have included the plaintiff, Mrs. Wilkins; Mrs. Nunn, her sister; and Gary Lasater, their nephew. The three trustees are also beneficiaries of the trusts. The trusts' assets include stocks, bonds, and land which were originally part of Fred and Nell's family farm. As of 1983, the combined value of the trusts exceeded $2.6 million.

The Fred Lasater will provides in pertinent part:

> [T]he said Trustees ... shall farm and operate the lands of the estate, sell the crops, collect the income from all sources, pay taxes, insurance, interest on indebtedness and contract installments, and pay all necessary and proper expenses for labor, for the upkeep and protection of the property and for operating the same. The Trustees shall adopt rules and regulations for the efficient management of the trust property; they shall have power to sell and convey and transfer property of the trust estate ... and shall not incumber the same unless it be for the purpose of refunding existing indebtedness against the same or any portion thereof, or for the purpose of paying state inheritance taxes and federal estate taxes should there not be sufficient funds from other sources available for such payment, in which event and for which purpose, authority to mortgage is granted the Trustees. They shall not incumber the income or crops except it be for the necessary working capital in operating.

The will continues:

> The said Trustees shall have authority in their discretion … to grant unto any beneficiary or beneficiaries an advancement from the income in order to provide such beneficiary proper care and maintenance … The amounts so paid to any beneficiary shall be treated as an advancement to such one and shall be accounted for by him or her on the final distribution of the trust estate. The fact that such beneficiary at the time of being granted an advancement is also a Trustee of the estate and would otherwise pass on any advancement shall not prevent the allowance of such advancement if the other Trustees deem it proper to be made.

For purposes of this opinion, the provisions of Nell Lasater's will are identical.

For several years, the land was farmed by the individual trustees. A portion of the land was farmed from 1953 until 1969 by Mrs. Wilkins. Mrs. Nunn, likewise, farmed a portion of the land until 1972.

Gary Lasater began farming the trust land along with adjacent land which he owned independently, after the death of his father, Redman Lasater, in 1968. In 1972, Mr. Lasater entered into a 10-year lease with the trustees to farm the trust land as tenant. That lease was unanimously approved by all the trustees, including Mrs. Wilkins. Although that lease is not part of the evidence on appeal, the record indicates the lease terms provided for payment to the trusts of 33.3 percent of the grain crops on the trust land, with the tenant therefore retaining 66.6 percent of the crops. In 1982, after the lease expiration, Mrs. Wilkins, as trustee, objected to its extension. Mr. Lasater and Mrs. Nunn voted to extend the lease for 1 year over Mrs. Wilkins' objections. Consequently, Mr. Lasater continued to farm the trust land throughout the remainder of 1982.

In June 1983, Mrs. Wilkins commenced the present action, seeking an accounting of the trusts' assets, damages, and dissolution. Her complaint alleged: … (3) Mr. Lasater had breached his duty of loyalty as trustee by voting himself as tenant of trust land and by using the property for his own benefit;….

Mrs. Wilkins sought a preliminary injunction to enjoin Mr. Lasater from continuing to lease the trust land while also participating as trustee. Following a hearing on June 20, 1983, the court orally granted the injunction, stating: "The Court prohibits the trustees from entering into any additional leases or extending … the present lease or any type of renewal transaction with Mr. [Gary] Lasater … unless it is approved by the Court." …

In early 1984, the trusts and Mr. Lasater, individually, petitioned the court for approval of a lease extension for Mr. Lasater. Following a hearing, the court orally denied the extension, stating

> the trusts intended that the trustees operate the farm as princip[als], not as lessees….
>
> …
>
> … There is absolutely no exclusionary exemption in this trust permitting self-dealing between the trustees and the trust.

...

Meanwhile, Mrs. Wilkins, whose sole income was derived from the trusts, was in dire financial need; she asked the other trustees to grant her an advance from the trusts; they refused....

...

With this motion pending, the trustees met again on March 7 to consider the issue. Mrs. Wilkins was accompanied by her attorney. Following a lengthy discussion on the lease and advance and, upon the advice of her attorney, Mrs. Wilkins agreed to extend Mr. Lasater's lease through the 1987 crop year. In return, Mr. Lasater and Mrs. Nunn agreed not only to advance Mrs. Wilkins the requested funds, but also pay her other debts, as well as her attorney fees. These terms were set out in a written "stipulation" signed by the three trustees. Thereafter, Mrs. Wilkins' then attorney withdrew.

Prior to trial, Mrs. Wilkins requested court approval of her husband's attendance at trustee meetings as the other trustees had voted to exclude him. The court ordered Mr. Wilkins excluded. At trial, the issues were limited to whether: (1) the March 7 stipulation extending Mr. Lasater's lease was valid; (2) Mr. Lasater had breached various fiduciary duties while acting as both tenant and trustee; (3) the attorneys for the trusts should have declined to represent the trusts when the litigation commenced; and (4) the court properly excluded Mr. Wilkins from attending trustee meetings. Mrs. Wilkins was represented by yet another attorney at trial.

The foremost contested issues arose with respect to whether Mr. Lasater had breached various fiduciary duties while acting as lessee as well as trustee. Both sides acknowledged he technically breached a trustee's duty of loyalty by voting to extend his own lease....

...

The court concluded: (1) the March 7, 1984 stipulation was binding and the lease valid; (2) Mr. Lasater had acted properly and had breached no fiduciary duties with respect to his dealings with the trusts despite his failure to present any records.... This appeal followed with Mrs. Wilkins being represented by new counsel.

Breach of Fiduciary Duties

Initially, Mrs. Wilkins asserts Mr. Lasater breached several fiduciary duties while acting simultaneously as trustee and lessee. Under this assignment of error, she first contends the law forbids a trustee from dealing in his individual capacity with the trust property; thus, lease of trust land by a trustee is a per se breach of the duty of loyalty.

A trustee has such powers as are conferred by the terms of the trust and such "powers as are necessary or appropriate to carry out the purpose of the trust and are not forbidden". *Monroe v. Winn*, 16 Wash.2d 497, 508, 133 P.2d 952 (1943). The powers which the settlor intended to convey are gathered from the trust's language and from the nature and purpose of the trust. *Monroe*, at 508, 133 P.2d 952. Mr. Lasater and the trusts contend the provisions of the wills implicitly demonstrate the settlors contemplated the trustees leasing the land to themselves. We disagree. The wills indicate a preference, if possible, for the trustees to manage the land collectively and to farm it *as trustees.* The wills do not indicate the trustees are to lease the land to themselves in their individual capacities while also acting as trustees. Without an explicit grant of such authority, we decline to impute an intent on the part of Nell and Fred Lasater to allow conduct that ordinarily would be construed as a breach of the fiduciary duty of loyalty.

A trustee owes to the beneficiaries of the trust the highest degree of good faith, diligence, fidelity, loyalty, and integrity; a trustee must act solely in the beneficiaries' interest. *Esmieu v. Schrag,* 88 Wash.2d 490, 498, 563 P.2d 203 (1977); *In re Estate of Drinkwater,* 22 Wash.App. 26, 30–31, 587 P.2d 606 (1978). A trustee cannot deal with the trust property for his own profit or claim any advantage by reason of his relation to it, either directly or indirectly. *Tucker v. Brown,* 20 Wash.2d 740, 768, 150 P.2d 604 (1944); *In re Estate of Eustace,* 198 Wash. 142, 147, 87 P.2d 305 (1939).

This court has neither been cited to, nor found, a Washington decision involving a lessee of trust land, who also acted as trustee and additionally was a beneficiary of the trust. However, the weight of authority from other jurisdictions supports the proposition that a trustee of land is deemed to have committed a breach of loyalty by leasing trust land to himself....

. . .

Adherence to this strict construction of the duty of loyalty rests on three rationales:

First, ... it is difficult, if not impossible for a person to act impartially in a matter in which he has an interest....

... [A] trustee can not be expected to utilize his best, most objective and disinterested judgment in situations where that judgment may run counter to his own interest....

... [T]he beneficiary is deprived of that disinterested and impartial judgment to which he is entitled....

Secondly, the courts have realized that fiduciary relationships lend themselves to exploitation.... [T]he success of the trust relationship will depend on the ability of the beneficiary to trust the trustee.... The only way to insure that the beneficiary can sleep at night in free and easy reliance on the loyalty of the trustee is to remove all serious temptations to disloyalty.

Finally, ... disloyal conduct is hard to detect....

... [A] court, inquiring into his administration at a later date, cannot expect to match the trustee's knowledge.... A wide variety of determinations can generally be supported by plausible argument, and rationalizations made after the fact will generally be unassailable.

(Footnotes omitted.) Hallgring, *The Uniform Trustees' Powers Act and the Basic Principles of Fiduciary Responsibility,* 41 Wash.L.Rev. 801, at 808–11 (1966).

We likewise prefer the rule that lease of trust land by a trustee ordinarily constitutes, per se, a breach of loyalty; such a rule has the prophylactic effect of preventing the trustee from *ever* putting himself in a position where his interest could *possibly* conflict with that of a beneficiary. *Meinhard v. Salmon*, 249 N.Y. 458, 164 N.E. 545, 546, 62 A.L.R. 1 (1928). *See Magruder v. Drury*, 235 U.S. 106, 119–20, 35 S.Ct. 77, 81–82, 59 L.Ed. 151 (1914). However, this strict rule is qualified by at least three possible exceptions: (1) an express provision by the settlor allowing the trustee to lease trust property; (2) court approval of such a relationship; and (3) the beneficiaries' confirmation, ratification, or acquiescence to the trustee's dealings with the trust, with full knowledge of the relationship. *See* G. Bogert, at 241–42; *Whiteley v. Babcock, supra; Whitelock v. Dorsey, supra; Waterbury v. Nicol, supra. See also Ryan v. Plath*, 20 Wash.2d 663, 667–70, 148 P.2d 946 (1944) (rule that trustee cannot sell land to himself in his individual capacity is not absolute and may be confirmed or ratified by the beneficiaries).

Here, as noted above, the provisions of the wills do not explicitly allow the lease of the trusts' lands by a trustee and we decline to interpret them as so permitting. However, Mr. Lasater's rental of the land from 1972 to 1982 was approved by all the trustees and was apparently uncontested by the remaining beneficiaries; therefore, we decline to hold his lease during that period was a breach of the duty of loyalty. Likewise, with respect to the current lease, we conclude there is no per se breach of the duty of loyalty. Not only did Mrs. Wilkins stipulate to the lease in 1983, but the court approved it; there is no indication from the record that any other beneficiary contests the lease. Although Mrs. Wilkins assigns error to the trial court's conclusion on this issue, after careful review, we conclude her arguments are not well taken; we need not discuss that assignment further.

Nonetheless, Mrs. Wilkins also assigns error to the court's conclusion Mr. Lasater did not self-deal or otherwise breach his duty of loyalty by his actual conduct as tenant. She alleges he breached this duty as he profited from the lease of the farm land. Although Mr. Lasater testified he had not profited from the lease, he never adequately explained how he arrived at that conclusion. He admitted he had no set formula for paying a custom harvester that harvested the crops. He, likewise, admitted that although he charged the trusts hauling fees commensurate with commercial haulers, those haulers added a built-in profit to their fees. Moreover, at trial he presented no documents whatsoever demonstrating he had not, in fact, profited from the lease arrangement. In actuality, by not producing records of lease transactions, Mr. Lasater failed to render a true accounting, as required by trust law.

The burden of proof is on the fiduciary to demonstrate no breach of loyalty has been committed. *Hetrick v. Smith*, 67 Wash. 664, 667–68, 122 P. 363 (1912). In an accounting, the burden of proving the propriety of challenged transactions rests with the trustee. G. Bogert, *Trusts & Trustees* § 970, at 401 (2d rev. ed. 1983). Obscurities and doubts in the accounting will be resolved against the trustee. A. Scott, at 1399. Here, Mr. Lasater claims he was never requested to bring the records relating to his lease transaction; however, one count of this action relates to Mrs. Wilkins' request for an accounting. We further note that it is virtually impossible to disprove the fiduciary breaches alleged here without such records. The trial court apparently believed his testimony that he had not profited from the lease; this court may not substitute its judgment for that determination. *Peoples Nat'l Bank v. Taylor*, 42 Wash.App. 518, 525, 711 P.2d 1021 (1985). Nonetheless, as noted above, one claim here is for an accounting, and Mr. Lasater's self-serving testimony is insufficient to meet what we view is the increased burden of proof he bears as a fiduciary. Without documentary evidence, in the form of the underlying bills and other records, he has not met his burden of disproving that he profited from the lease.... We also note Mr. Lasater, as an interested trustee, at least technically breached the duty of loyalty by voting himself as lessee.

...

Reversed in part, affirmed in part, and remanded.

Fulton Nat'l Bank v. Tate

363 F.2d 562 (5th Cir. 1966)

JOHN R. BROWN, Circuit Judge:

...

[Steve Tate ("Steve") was serving as executor of the S.C. Tate Estate ("the Estate"). An executor owes the beneficiaries of the estate the same duty of loyalty that a trustee owes the trust beneficiaries. Steve was negotiating with the Georgia Marble Company ("Marble") to exchange some of Steve's personally owned real property for 6,100 acres of real property owned by Marble. In addition, Marble was interested in leasing some of the Estate's real property. The beneficiaries of the Estate, represented by Fulton National Bank ["the Bank"], alleged that Marble told Steve that it would agree to his property exchange (for Steve's real property) only if he also agreed to lease the Estate's real property to Marble. Steve agreed and received, personally, 6,100 acres of real estate from Marble. Both deals were closed the same day. The Bank, on behalf of the Estate beneficiaries, sued, claiming, among other things, a breach of the duty of loyalty.

The District Court appointed a Special Master to resolve the claim. The Special Master ruled that there was no breach — that there was no proof that Steve received anything in his individual capacity from the lease of the estate property to Marble. The Bank appealed, arguing that it had proved enough to at least shift the burden to Steve to prove that he did not benefit. The Fifth Circuit Court of Appeals weighed in.]

Prior to his becoming executor of the Estate, Steve proposed to Marble that Steve and Marble personally exchange certain properties and rights. Marble, however, did not accept his proposal. On April 4, 1950, Steve became the executor of the Estate which for many years had leased extensive lands to Marble under a long-term mineral lease expiring in 1959. After becoming executor, Steve persisted in his proposal for a personal exchange. At the same time, in his capacity as executor, he was negotiating with Marble over the extension of the Estate lease. Though the lease was not to expire until 1959, Marble had extensive capital tied up in mining operations on the leasehold property and had set 1956 as the deadline for securing renewal of the lease. While Steve was negotiating with Marble in the dual capacity of individual and executor, he fastidiously endeavored to keep estate business and his own personal business separate, conscious that he had to change coats rather than wear Jacob's many-colored coat. Nevertheless, during this period there was considerable friction and animosity between Steve and Marble manifested in litigation, harsh words, and even shootings. Finally, in October 1954, Steve, acting in his individual capacity, reached substantial verbal agreement with Marble on terms calling for the outright exchange of Steve's own marble lands for 6,100 acres of Marble's mountainous timber lands. However, Marble was unwilling to sign this agreement with Steve individually until a deal could be worked out on the renewal of the estate lease. Such an agreement for renewal of the estate lease was reached in February 1955, and on February 9, 1955, both the agreement between Steve individually and Marble on the exchange and the agreement between Steve as executor and Marble on the lease renewal were signed. However, showing himself to be far from oblivious to the delicate and conflicting position he was in, Steve insisted that the agreement with him individually be back-dated to October 26, 1954, the time when he felt he and Marble had reached substantial verbal agreement over the terms of his individual deal. All the beneficiaries of the Estate signed the lease renewal negotiated by Steve and subsequently received substantial benefits therefrom, but the Master found that at least one of the beneficiaries was unaware of the existence of Steve's personal agreement.

This brings us to the following pivotal fact findings by the Master:

'4. Would Georgia Marble Company have executed the personal agreement with Steve Tate without securing Steve Tate's agreement to a lease renewal satisfactory to Georgia Marble Company?

'Answer: Georgia Marble Company did not want to sign an agreement with Steve, individually, if he was going to keep on fighting them as Executor.

'5. Was Steve Tate aware of the answer to question 4?

'Answer: Yes

'* * *

'8. Had no lease renewal been before the parties, would Georgia Marble Company have executed the personal agreement in 1955?

'Answer: Apparently not.'

In other words, Steve and Marble reached agreement on the personal exchange first, but Marble refused to sign unless Steve would renew the estate lease.

The question here is whether once the Bank has shown this circumstance, the burden shifts to the fiduciary to prove that Steve made no personal profit by use of the Estate's property. This question is not simple for a number of reasons. First, general rules on the fiduciary's duty of undivided loyalty are necessarily general and offer limited help in resolving a concrete problem in this area.... Second, and perhaps manifested in the generality of the general rules, is the fact that there are two opposing policy considerations in this area which must be weighed in the individualistic scales of each concrete situation. On the one hand, there is the first commandment of fiduciary relations: thou shalt exalt thy beneficiary above all others. As expounded in the oft-quoted words of Judge Cardozo:

> "Many forms of conduct permissible in a workaday world for those acting at arm's length, are forbidden to those bound by fiduciary ties. A trustee is held to something stricter than the morals of the market place. Not honesty alone, but the punctilio of an honor the most sensitive, is then the standard of behavior. As to this there has developed a tradition that is unbending and inveterate. Uncompromising rigidity has been the attitude of courts of equity when petitioned to undermine the rule of undivided loyalty by the 'disintegrating erosion' of particular exceptions. * * * Only thus has the level of conduct for fiduciaries been kept at a level higher than that trodden by the crowd."

Meinhard v. Salmon, 1928, 249 N.Y. 458, 164 N.E. 545, 546, 62 A.L.R. 1. On the other hand, and from Judge Hand, there is the caveat that 'the law ought not make trusteeship so hazardous that responsible individuals * * * will shy away from it. * * * 'the courts should not impose impractical obligations on a trustee. Merely vague or remote possible selfish advantages to a trustee are not sufficient to prove such an adverse interest as to bring his conduct into question." *Dabney v. Chase Nat. Bank*, 2 Cir., 1952, 196 F.2d 668, 675.

With these problems in mind, we deem it appropriate to discuss the general principles governing the fiduciary's duty of loyalty.

The general rule is that 'the trustee is under a duty to the beneficiary to administer the trust solely in the interest of the beneficiary.' Restatement (Second), Trusts § 170 (1959). He violates his duty "not only where he purchases trust property for himself individually, but also where he has a personal interest in the purchase of *such a substantial nature* that it might affect his judgment in making the sale," id. comment *c* (emphasis added), and "also where he uses the trust property for his own purposes," id. comment l. Furthermore, "the trustee violates his duty * * * if he accepts for himself from a third person any bonus or commission for any act done by him *in connection with the administration of the trust*." Id. comment o. (Emphasis added.) If the trustee violates his duty of undivided loyalty, he is liable to the beneficiary for any profit thereby made. Thus, "if the trustee * * * uses trust property for his own purposes and makes a profit thereby, he is accountable for the profit so made," id. § 206 comment *j*, and if he "receives for himself from a third person any bonus or commission or other compensation for acts done by him in connection with the administration of the trust, he is accountable for the amount so received," id. comment *k*. And even though he does not breach his trust, "the trustee is accountable for any profit made by him *through or arising out of the administration of the trust*." Id. § 203 (emphasis added). However, "if the trustee enters into a transaction *not connected with the administration of the trust*, he is not accountable for a profit which may result merely because the trust property is indirectly affected thereby." Id. comment *e*. (Emphasis added.)

Although "the duties of a trustee are more intensive than the duties of some other fiduciaries," id. § 2, comment b,15 the same general rules are applicable to other fiduciaries.

This is where the law draws on behavioral psychology, where the rules of fair dealing required by equity coincide with human experience. The rules of undivided loyalty have developed as defensive responses of the common-law nervous system to impulses of self-interest. The rationale of these well-settled principles of undivided loyalty is clear:

> "It is generally, if not always, humanly impossible for the same person to act fairly in two capacities and on behalf of two interests in the same transaction. Consciously or unconsciously he will favor one side as against the other, where there is or *may be* a conflict of interest. If one of the interests involved is that of the trustee personally, selfishness is apt to lead him to give himself an advantage. If permitted to represent antagonistic interests the trustee is placed under temptation and is apt in many cases to yield to the natural prompting to give himself the benefit of all doubts, or to make decisions which favor the third person who is competing with the beneficiary."

Bogert, Trusts and Trustees § 543, at 475–76 (2d ed. 1960) (Emphasis added). See also 2 Scott, Trusts § 170 (2d ed. 1956); 4 id. § 502, at 3235–36; 54 Am. Jur. Trusts § 311-315 (1945). And in accord with this rationale, the beneficiary need only show that the fiduciary allowed himself to be placed in a position where his personal interest *might* conflict with the interest of the beneficiary. It is unnecessary to show that the fiduciary succumbed to this temptation, that he acted in bad faith, that he gained an advantage, fair or unfair, that the beneficiary was harmed. Indeed, the law presumes that the fiduciary acted disloyally, and inquiry into such matters is foreclosed. The rule is not intended to compensate the beneficiary for any loss he may have sustained or to deprive the fiduciary of any unjust enrichment. Its sole purpose and effect is prophylactic: the fiduciary is punished for allowing himself to be placed in a position of conflicting interests in order to discourage such conduct in the future. Though equity protects the beneficiary with a gentle wand, it polices the fiduciary with a big stick. The trustee must avoid being placed in such a position, and if he cannot avoid it, he may resign, or fully inform the beneficiaries of the conflict, or, upon so informing the court, request approval of his actions. Otherwise, he proceeds at his peril.

...

Superimposing ... [the language from the Georgia court opinions the court had reviewed] on the facts of this case, the inquiry here is 'whether or not Steve received anything from Marble which could be taken as a consideration for any act on his part connected with his administration of the Estate?' First, it cannot be said that Steve's personal transaction with Marble was wholly unconnected with his administration of the Estate. As individual and executor, Steve fought with Marble; Steve, as individual and executor, negotiated with the same officials of Marble at the same time over the same kind of property; as individual and executor, Steve closed both deals at the same time. And Marble wanted Steve's marble rights only if it could retain its mining facilities on the Estate lease. It was tit for tat down to the wire. Second, it cannot be said that Steve received nothing from Marble for his renewal of the Estate lease. He received Marble's acquiescence to the personal exchange, for it is clear that at least one of the reasons Marble agreed to convey 6,100 acres to Steve was Steve's agreeing as executor to renew the lease.

> ...

As a last resort, the Appellees argue that from a standpoint of policy our conclusion has a "hazardous implication." According to Appellees, "the inexorable consequence would be that in any instance in which the bank (as trustee) purchased or sold any security through the same broker for the account of any trust and contemporaneously therewith negotiated the purchase or sale of any security through the same broker for its personal portfolio, the bank would thereby open itself to surcharge in the amount of such profit as it realized on its personal transaction." This fear is simply unfounded—unfounded unless there is a connection between the fiduciary transaction and the personal one, and if there is a connection, there is and should be the fear of being brought to book.

It should now be clear that on remand of this case the burden of proceeding is on the Appellees. Furthermore, they have the burden of proving that Steve made no profit on his personal exchange, or failing in this effort, they must account for whatever profit he made.... The principal things to be determined on remand in light of the principles we have announced are: (1) whether Steve realized any profit on his personal exchange, (2) if so, how much profit did he realize, and (3) in that case, what relief is to be granted the Bank.... The trial Court will have considerable discretion in the method it chooses to handle and resolve these questions....

Reversed and remanded.

Notes

1. *Uncompromised judgment*: In theory, anytime a trustee's judgment is compromised, the duty of loyalty has been breached. The trustee's judgment may be compromised either because the trustee may personally benefit from the transaction or because the trustee has a connection to the third party "of such a substantial nature that it might affect his judgment...." RESTATEMENT (SECOND) OF TRUSTS § 170 cmt. c (1959). The sole variable affecting a trustee's decision-making process should be the best interests of the trust beneficiaries—not the interests of the trustee, and not the interests of a third party. The trust beneficiaries are entitled to the trustee's independent and objective best judgment. Anything that would compromise that judgment may constitute a breach of trust.

In the abstract, the logic behind the duty of loyalty is easy to understand. In the real world, however, the duty of loyalty is not so easy to apply. Many trustees are compensated based on the size of the trust corpus.[3] Where a trustee's power to distribute trust property is discretionary, technically, one could argue that the trustee has an interest that might affect his or her decision. Is every decision against distribution accordingly a breach of the duty of loyalty? Assessing the scope of the duty of loyalty is also difficult because trustees have personal lives to contend with. He or she must continue to interact with third parties for their own personal interests. Is a trustee absolutely forbidden from dealing with a third party who is also dealing with the trust? While that may not sound too unreasonable if the trustee is a family member for a small family trust, such a standard arguably is unworkable for a person serving as a professional trustee for hundreds of trusts and who interacts with thousands of institutions on behalf of the trusts. If a trustee is not absolutely forbidden from dealing a third party who is also dealing with the trustee in his or her personal capacity, what must be demonstrated to prove a breach of the duty of loyalty? It should not surprise you to learn that there is something of a common law versus modern trend split emerging with respect to some of these issues.

2. *Self-dealing and the common law "no further inquiry" rule*: Self-dealing occurs when the trustee personally transacts with the trust (for example, where the trustee, acting in his or her personal capacity, purchases property from the trust, or the trust purchases property from the trustee, acting in his or her personal capacity). The conflict of interest is self-evident. When the trustee purchases property from the trust, acting in his or her fiduciary capacity he or she should strive to obtain the highest possible price (for the benefit of the trust), but acting in his or her personal capacity, the trustee will strive to obtain the lowest possible price (for his or her personal benefit). It is impossible for the trustee to exercise his or her independent and objective best judgment.

Because of the obvious conflict of interest, the common law courts developed the "no further inquiry" rule. Once it is established that the trustee has engaged in self-dealing, the trustee is strictly liable. The fairness of the price and the trustee's good faith in entering into the transaction are irrelevant. The court need not inquire into such matters (hence the name of the doctrine — the "no further inquiry" rule). All that matters is that the trustee has engaged in self-dealing. Unauthorized self-dealing constitutes a per se breach of trust (breach of the duty of loyalty). The trust beneficiaries need not even prove causation. Nothing else needs to be proved.

3. *Transactions with third parties with whom the trustee is closely related or associated*: While technically not self-dealing, transactions between the trustee and third parties with whom the trustee has a personal relationship (or is closely related to) are prohibited because of the high risk that the relationship could compromise the trustee's independent and objective judgment. Accordingly, transactions with such parties are

---

3. This is particularly true for an institutional or corporate trustee as opposed to an individual trustee such as a family member or trusted family friend.

prohibited under the duty of loyalty. While such presumptions and prohibitions do not arise with respect to more independent third parties, if the trust beneficiaries can show the trustee was nevertheless "improperly influenced" in the trust's transaction with a third party, the trustee has breached the duty of loyalty. The trust beneficiaries, however, will bear the burden of proving the improper influence in such cases.

The modern trend is not to always hold the trustee strictly liable in the event of a breach of the duty of loyalty, particularly in cases involving a conflict of interest (as opposed to blatant self-dealing), but to require the complaining beneficiaries to show not only a breach of the duty, but also damages and causation. *See* UTC §§ 802(c)(4), 802(f). One scholar characterized the UTC approach as follows: "[T]he UTC largely exempts institutional trustees from the no further inquiry rule." *See* Melanie B. Leslie, *In Defense of the No Further Inquiry Rule: A Response to Professor John Langbein*, 47 WM. & MARY L. REV. 541, 543 n. 5 (and accompanying text) (2005) (see below for more discussion of this approach).

4. *Remedy*: Where there is a breach of the duty of loyalty, the trust beneficiaries can invoke the court's equitable powers to fashion an appropriate remedy. Whether a particular remedy is appropriate will depend on the facts and nature of the breach. At a minimum, the trust should be restored to where it would have been had there been no breach (this may include an award of any profits that the trust would have made but for the breach — i.e., appreciation damages). The goal is not only to make the trust beneficiaries whole, but also to deter other trustees from being tempted to breach the duty of loyalty. Traditionally, the general rule is to "disgorge" the trustee of any profit he or she has made on the deal (again, regardless of his or her good faith, the fairness of the price, causation, and/or the innocence or ignorance of the trustee). Moreover, if the trustee has purchased trust property in breach of the duty and he or she still has the property, the court may order the trustee to reconvey the property to the trust (i.e., to set aside the transaction). If the trustee has sold the property, the trust beneficiaries can seek to have a constructive trust imposed on the proceeds from the sale.

5. *Exceptions to the duty of loyalty*: As the court in *Lasater* noted, the duty of loyalty is the starting point for an analysis of the trustee's actions, but not the end point. The duty of loyalty is a default rule. A trustee *may* transact with the trust if: (1) the terms of the trust authorize it, (2) a court approves the transaction, and/or (3) the beneficiaries approve, ratify, or acquiesce in the transaction following full disclosure of all relevant information.

a. *Trust authorization*: A settlor can expressly authorize a trustee to transact with the trust property. Most courts, however, require the trust language to explicitly grant the trustee the authorization to engage in the self-dealing transaction. A trust instrument that merely grants the trustee broad powers and broad discretion with respect to the management of the trust property will generally not meet the necessary standard to authorize self-dealing. Moreover, even where a trust instrument expressly authorizes the self-dealing, that authorization does not completely absolve the trustee of his or her fiduciary duty (nor does it remove the transaction from scrutiny). The trustee must still act in good faith and must still deal with the trust fairly. The transaction remains subject to judicial scrutiny to ensure that the trustee does not abuse the authorization and loot the trust corpus: "The trustee violates his duty to the beneficiary, however, if he acts in bad faith, no matter how broad may be the provisions of the terms of the trust in conferring power upon him to deal with the trust property on his own account." RESTATEMENT (SECOND) OF TRUSTS § 170(1) cmt. t.

Even assuming, *arguendo*, that the trust contains very specific language authorizing self-dealing, it is easy to see potential problems. A less than competent trustee may not fully read or understand the trust provisions (or, worse, a trustee who understands the provisions but chooses to ignore them). If the trustee goes forward and engages in self-dealing transactions that do not comply with the trust's limited authorization, while remedies are available, practical and logistical difficulties may not fully resolve the problem. A settlor should think long and hard before authorizing self-dealing.

b. *Judicial authorization*: Self-dealing is permitted where "the court, after conducting a full adversary hearing at which all interested parties are represented, approves and authorizes the sale." *In re Scarborough Properties Corp.*, 25 N.Y.2d 553 (1969). Court approval may be appropriate where there is no real market for the trust property (a minority interest in a closely held corporation) and/or where the trust beneficiaries are split over whether the proposed self-dealing should be permitted. The court's role is to ensure that the proposed transaction is fair and just under the circumstances, that there has been full disclosure, and that the proposed transaction is in the best interests of the trust.

c. *Beneficiaries authorize*: The general rule is that the beneficiaries may authorize a trustee's proposed self-dealing if there is full disclosure to all the beneficiaries, if the beneficiaries are free from the trustee's influence, and if all the beneficiaries consent. The beneficiaries may ratify such a transaction after the fact under the same conditions.

6. *Modern trend*: Some states have modified the duty of loyalty and the duty against self-dealing to the extent that they are inconsistent with the prudent investor rule. This overlap will be examined in greater detail in the material that covers the trustee's duty to act prudently and the trustee's accompanying investment powers.

7. *Modern trend — UTC*: Professor Langbein, a leader in the trusts and estates field, has called for abolition of the "no further inquiry" rule. He argues that it is inconsistent with the purposes of the modern investment-oriented trust and that it "overdeters" and impedes a trustee's ability to aggressively and quickly respond to investment opportunities. To the extent the modern trustee is increasingly a corporate trustee, Professor Langbein has argued that the duty of loyalty that applies to corporate fiduciaries should also apply to trustees. He sees no problem with trustees profiting from transactions with the trust as long as the trustee can prove, if subsequently sued, that the transaction was nonetheless in the trust's best interests.

Professor Langbein helped draft the Uniform Trust Code, and he had some success in getting his views adopted by the UTC. The UTC distinguishes between traditional self-dealing transactions (in which the "no further inquiry" rule still applies), and conflicted transactions involving third parties. The latter transactions are only presumptively voidable, not void, and the presumption can be rebutted if:

> the trustee establishes that the transaction was not affected by a conflict between personal and fiduciary interests. Among the factors tending to rebut the presumption are whether the consideration was fair and whether the other terms of the transaction are similar to those that would be transacted with an independent party.

See UTC § 802 cmt. (2000).

Problems

1. Joel and June Eisenberg owned and operated several travel-related businesses (Air Club International, International Travel, Inc., and Aeroamerica, Inc.). They also had two minor children, Yvette and Ian. Joel was appointed guardian of the estates of the children (a guardian owes the same duty of loyalty to the minor as a trustee does to a beneficiary). Thereafter, Joel purchased a few Boeing aircraft and sold one to each of the guardianships.

   Joel then sought and received court approval to lease the planes for five years to Air Club. Joel did not disclose his interest in Air Club to the court. The following year, without court approval, Joel switched the leases from Air Club to Aeroamerica. Thereafter, Aeroamerica began to have financial problems. Aeroamerica's creditors demanded that Joel subordinate the company's obligations to the guardianships to the claims of the other creditors. Joel agreed. Three years later, Aeroamerica declared bankruptcy.

   After the Aeroamerica lease expired, Joel leased the planes to a movie company as a prop for $10,000. Joel deposited the money into Aeroamerica's account. None of the money went to the guardianship accounts. Joel then ordered that the planes be dismantled and sold for scrap parts. None of the resulting $50,000 was deposited in the guardianship accounts.

   When the children reached the age of majority they sued for breach of the duty of loyalty. Did Joel breach the duty of loyalty when: (1) he leased the planes to Air Club; (2) he switched the leases to Aeroamerica; (3) he agreed to subordinate Aeroamerica's obligations to the guardianships; (4) he leased the planes to the movie company; and/or (5) he dismantled and sold the planes? *See In re Guardianship of Eisenberg*, 719 P.2d 187 (Wash. Ct. App. 1986). What should be the measure of damages?

2. A father created two *inter vivos* trusts during his lifetime: one for the benefit of his son, and the other for the benefit of his daughter. The father was sole trustee of each trust, and each child was entitled to all income from the trusts during their lifetime. Each child also held the power to withdraw as much property from the trust as he or she deemed appropriate. Thereafter the father approached each child and explained to them that he wanted them to "sign off" on the termination

of each child's trust and the creation of a new trust. The son and daughter signed off on the withdrawal of the funds from their respective trusts without reading any of the paperwork, and the father created the new trust. Under the new trust, the father had the right to the income during his lifetime and the power to withdraw as much property from the trust as he deemed appropriate. Thereafter, the father withdrew all of the funds from the new trust. When the son realized what had happened, he sued.

Does the son have a valid claim of breach of the duty of loyalty? If so, did the son "waive" the claim by failing to read the paperwork that he signed? *See Prueter v. Bork*, 435 N.E.2d 109 (Ill. Ct. App. 1981).

3. Douglas Sachse, an attorney, was appointed trustee of the Stemler Trust. At the time, he had both a personal and a professional relationship with the primary beneficiary, Shirley Stemler. The Stemler Trust was a testamentary trust created by Dorothy Thompson's will when she died in 1978. The terms of the trust provided that Dorothy's only daughter, Shirley Stemler, was to receive the net income from the trust during her lifetime. Upon Stemler's death the trust assets were to be distributed to her then-living descendants.

    The original trust corpus was approximately $50,000. By 1990, the trust corpus has grown to approximately $90,000. In late 1990, Shirley informed Sachse that she needed the funds in the trust to start a business — Autel Corporation. Stemler had always believed that the money was her money to use as she deemed appropriate. Stemler allegedly harassed Sachse for access to the funds. Over the next few months, Sachse disbursed funds to Shirley to help start the company until there was only eight cents left in the trust account. At about this time Sachse began experiencing problems that resulted in his being admitted to a substance abuse program. Following his release, he attempted to secure a note from Shirley and Autel Corporation obligating them to repay the trust funds. Sachse admits he would not have invested any of his own funds in Autel Corporation.

    Has Sachse breached his duty of loyalty? *See Attorney Grievance Comm'n of Maryland v. Sachse*, 693 A.2d 806 (Md. Ct. App. 1997).

4. Decedent died in Los Angeles, owning several parcels of real estate. Decedent's executor also resided in Los Angeles. The devisees of some of the parcels resided in Texas. Executors essentially owe the devisees of an estate the same duty of loyalty as a trustee owes the trust beneficiaries.

    The executors wrote the devisees and advised them that there were "certain odds and ends of land" that could either be sold separately or bundled and sold together to the executors at a reasonable price; but first, the executors recommended the devisees investigate the properties. The executors requested that the devisees send an agent with the power to act to Los Angeles to investigate the situation. The devisees sent an agent with power to act, but the agent could neither read nor write. The agent brought a friend with him, who may have been a relative of the decedent. While the friend had extensive business experience, it was unclear in what capacity the friend came to Los Angeles.

After spending a week in Los Angeles, the agent agreed to authorize the sale of the real estate for $10,000 to Susan Dunlap—the wife of one of the executors. The executors sold the property to Susan, who a month later sold the land to the executors. The devisees later sued for breach of the duty of loyalty. In their complaint, they alleged that the true value of the land in question was approximately $40,000.

Did the executors breach their duty of loyalty? Did they engage in self-dealing? Does the fact that they advised the devisees in Texas to come out and inspect the properties mean they satisfied their duty? *See Golson v. Dunlap*, 14 P. 576 (Cal. 1887).

B. Duty to Be Impartial

The duty of loyalty naturally leads to the trustee's duty to be impartial. If a trust has two or more beneficiaries, the trustee has a duty to deal impartially with them, acting impartially in investing and managing the trust property and taking into account any differing interests among the beneficiaries. CPC § 16003. The trustee cannot favor one individual or class of beneficiaries over another and must still satisfy the duty of loyalty to each; hence the duty to be impartial.

Recall that the typical trust, a gratuitous trust, is a bifurcated gift. It is bifurcated three ways: (1) the trustee holds legal title, and the beneficiaries hold the equitable interest; (2) the trust property is bifurcated between the principal and the income; and (3) at the equitable level, the trust is bifurcated between the beneficiaries who hold the present interest and the beneficiaries who hold the future interest. In the typical trust, the beneficiaries who hold the present interest have a greater right to receive the income, and the beneficiaries who hold the future interest have the right to receive the principal. Because of their different interests, something of a conflict of interest arises between the interests of the present beneficiaries and the future beneficiaries. The present beneficiaries would prefer to see the trust property invested in high-risk investments that might generate greater income (but which would also put the principal at greater risk of loss), while the future beneficiaries would prefer to see the trust property invested in safer investments that would put the principal at a lower risk of loss (but which would also generate less income). Such differing interests among the beneficiaries therefore directly implicate the trustee's duty to be impartial.

Moreover, just as the duty of loyalty logically leads to the duty to act impartially, so too does the duty to act impartially logically lead to and overlap with the duty to act prudently. Where a trust has beneficiaries who are entitled to its income, the trustee needs to invest prudently so as to produce a reasonable income for the income beneficiaries while at the same time protecting and growing the principal for the future beneficiaries (i.e., the remaindermen). The RESTATEMENT (THIRD) OF TRUSTS implicitly acknowledges overlap between the duty to be impartial and the duty to act prudently when it addresses the issue as part of the Prudent Investor Rule:

§ 240. Unproductive or underproductive property

If a trustee of a trust to pay the income to a beneficiary and thereafter to distribute the principal to others holds property that produces no income or an income substantially less than an appropriate yield on the trust's investments, the trustee is under a duty to the income beneficiary either

(a) to adopt accounting, investment, and other administrative practices reasonably designed to satisfy the distribution entitlements of the income beneficiary, or

(b) to sell some or all of that property within a reasonable time.

See RESTATEMENT (THIRD) OF TRUSTS, P.I.R. Other § 240 (1992).

The RESTATEMENT (THIRD) OF TRUSTS approach parallels various tax-related concerns and doctrines. These concerns are front and center during the drafting phase of most trusts, and professionally drafted trusts often contain clauses relating to "unproductive assets" and various parties (usually income beneficiaries) having the power to demand that the trustee convert such assets to those that are "income producing." Well-drafted estate planning documents should address expressly the potential issues inherent in unproductive and/or underproductive assets.

Delaware Trust Co. v. Bradford

59 A.2d 212 (Del. Ch. 1948)

SEITZ, Vice-Chancellor.

The court is required to instruct the trustee as to the method of treatment and disposition of the net proceeds from the sale of an unproductive trust asset.

Edward G. Bradford, Jr. died December 3, 1927. Under the third item of his will he left certain property to the plaintiff, Delaware Trust Company, in trust 'to keep the same invested in good securities, and * * * to pay over the net income' to his wife for life. Under the same item, his wife was given a power of appointment either by deed or will over the trust property and in the event of her failure to exercise the power, or at the expiration of the term of appointment, the trust corpus was to be given to Yale College, a Connecticut corporation, upon certain trusts. By his will, the testator authorized the trustee to sell any of his real estate at either public or private sale.

On June 10, 1927, the testator purchased a piece of vacant land for the sum of $5,000. Upon his death, this property—then valued at $9,800.—became a part of the quoted testamentary trust, and was held as a trust asset from the testator's death on December 3, 1927 to the date of sale on September 24, 1947. During this period of 19 years, 9 months and 21 days the land was completely unproductive. In fact, it was an expense to the estate in that during this period charges amounting to $403.98 were paid thereon from the trust income.

When plaintiff as trustee sold the land on September 24, 1947, he realized, after deducting real estate commissions, the sum of $18,997.63....

Since December 3, 1927, the defendant Helen S. Bradford, as the income beneficiary for life, has acquiesced in the retention of the unproductive land by the plaintiff as trustee. In fact, she requested plaintiff not to sell the land, it being her belief that its value would in time be greatly enhanced. Plaintiff as trustee reached the same conclusion in the exercise of its independent judgment.

From 1939 to 1947, the average net annual income of the trust created by the testator and paid to the life income beneficiary amounted to $1,708.96. Plaintiff has determined from a study of its various trust accounts that a reasonable current rate of return on trust investments with diversified holdings is 3.7%.

Plaintiff has asked for the [instructions].... Thereafter, the court heard testimony on behalf of the plaintiff with respect to the facts of the case.

Where a trust is created for successive beneficiaries, and where the trust estate includes unproductive property, the trustee is ordinarily under a duty to sell the property within a reasonable time and to invest the proceeds in productive property. See 2 Scott on Trusts, § 240. The trustee here held the unproductive property for a great many years, and it is apparent from the substantial price at which it was ultimately sold that the decision of the trustee to hold the unproductive property and the request of the income beneficiary that it hold such property were fully vindicated.

Whether or not the net proceeds from the sale of unproductive trust property will be apportioned between the income beneficiary and the remainderman is one of intent. See 2 Scott on Trusts, § 241.2. If it is manifest that the testator intended the entire principal of the trust to constitute a fund, the income of which is to be for the benefit of the life beneficiary, then a duty is imposed upon the trustee to sell the unproductive property at a convenient time and to apportion the net proceeds between principal and income. However, if the trust instrument makes clear that the testator intended to deprive the life beneficiary of income from that portion of the trust represented by unproductive property, there can be no question of apportionment — it is all principal.

Generally the courts will infer that the testator intended the life beneficiary to have the benefit of income from all property in the trust unless the terms of the trust indicate otherwise. See 1 Restatement of Trusts, § 241. Consequently, where the terms of the trust are silent, the courts will direct the trustee to apportion the net proceeds from the sale of an unproductive asset between capital and income. The creator of the trust here involved showed no intent to preclude the life income beneficiary from having the benefit of income from all the trust assets. Indeed, we may infer to the contrary since the life income beneficiary was the testator's wife. Moreover, the will directed the trustee to keep the trust property invested in good securities.

I conclude that the testator intended the income beneficiary to have the benefit of the income from all the trust assets with the consequence that the net proceeds of sale should be apportioned. The fact that the income beneficiary requested the trustee to hold the unproductive asset is not important here since the trustee reached the same conclusion in the exercise of its independent judgment.

It next becomes pertinent to determine what rule of apportionment should apply here. In 1 Restatement of Trusts, § 241, the rule is set forth as follows:

"(1) Unless it is otherwise provided by the terms of the trust, if property held in trust to pay the income to a beneficiary for a designated period and thereafter to pay the principal to another beneficiary is property which the trustee is under a duty to sell, and which produces no income or an income substantially less than the current rate of return on trust investments, or which is wasting property or produces an income substantially more than the current rate of return on trust investments, and the trustee does not immediately sell the property, the trustee should make an apportionment of the proceeds of the sale when made, as stated in Subsection (2).

"(2) The net proceeds received from the sale of the property are apportioned by ascertaining the sum which with interest thereon at the current rate of return on trust investments from the day when the duty to sell arose to the day of the sale would equal the net proceeds; and the sum so ascertained is to be treated as principal, and the residue of the net proceeds as income.

"(3) The net proceeds are determined by adding to the net sale price the net income received or deducting therefrom the net loss incurred in carrying the property prior to the sale."

The rule quoted from the Restatement of Trusts has been generally followed elsewhere and will be applied here since it results in a realistic and satisfactory adjustment of adverse interests.

Where, as here, the particular trust asset has been unproductive from the very beginning of the trust, the question arises — for purposes of applying the apportionment formula — whether the 'duty to sell' commences at the inception of the trust, or at some reasonable time thereafter. While a difference of opinion apparently exists, the view that the "duty to sell" arises at the inception of the trust is supported by substantial authority. See *Edwards v. Edwards*, 183 Mass. 581, 67 N.E. 658; 2 Scott on Trusts, §241.1. See 1 Restatement of Trusts, §241, Comments a and b.

. . .

The current rate of return on diversified trust investments is shown by this trustee to be 3.7%. This rate of return will be accepted and applied in this case.

The trustee desires to be instructed as to whether in determining the net proceeds available for apportionment, the carrying charges paid out of income, as well as the capital gains tax resulting from the sale of the unproductive property, should first be deducted from the proceeds of sale.

The cost of carrying unproductive property is payable out of principal rather than income in the absence of any indication that the testator demonstrated a different intention. See 2 Scott on Trusts, §233.4. The payment of real estate taxes and insurance are such costs, and in this case should have been paid out of principal rather than income. The trustee will, therefore, pay the income beneficiary from principal the amount of income which it used to pay the taxes and insurance on the unproductive trust asset....

. . .

I conclude that the trustee should apportion the net proceeds of the sale of the unproductive real estate by ascertaining the sum which with interest thereon at the current rate of return on trust investments (3.7%) from the day when the trust was created, i.e., the date of the testator's death (December 3, 1927), to the day of the sale (September 24, 1947) would equal the net proceeds ($18,438.37). When this is done, we find that the trustee should treat the sum of $10,644.30 as trust principal and the balance, being $7,794.07, as income.

An order accordingly will be advised.

Notes

1. *Authorization to retain underperforming* assets: The income beneficiary is entitled to apportionment of the proceeds generated by the sale of the underperforming asset only if the trustee had a duty to sell the asset. Where the terms of the trust grant the income beneficiary the rents from the asset and give the trustee the power to improve the property, such clauses generally are construed as an implied authorization for the trustee to retain the asset. What if the trust terms expressly or implicitly authorize the trustee to retain the underperforming asset? If the trustee nevertheless sells the underperforming asset is the income beneficiary entitled to a share of the proceeds or should it all be allocated to principal?

2. *Duty to act impartially — default rule or binding law?* Is the duty to act impartially a default rule that the settlor can opt out of in the trust instrument, or is it a rule of law that applies regardless of the settlor's intent?

Hearst v. Ganzi

145 Cal. App. 4th 1195 (2006)

KLEIN, P.J.

. . .

This appeal involves the latest challenge by certain beneficiaries of the Hearst Family Trust (the Trust) to the actions of the Trustees thereof. The plaintiffs, who are income beneficiaries of the Trust, contend the Trustees have breached their fiduciary duty of impartiality by favoring the remainder beneficiaries over the income beneficiaries. Plaintiffs propose to bring a petition against the Trustees for breach of fiduciary duty in order to compel the Trustees to increase the income distribution to them.

. . .

The "[Proposed] Petition By Beneficiaries for Relief From Breach of Fiduciary Duty by the Trustees of the Hearst Family Trust" (hereafter, the Proposed Petition) . . . which spanned six pages, alleged in relevant part:

"A fiduciary relationship exists between the Trustees and Petitioners. The Trustees must manage the Hearst Family Trust solely in the interests of the beneficiaries. [Citations.] Pursuant to ... section 16003, the Trustees owe Petitioners a fiduciary duty of impartiality to make trust property productive for current income beneficiaries."

The Proposed Petition further alleged:

The Trust holds legal title to all the issued and outstanding common stock of the Corporation for the sole benefit of the Trust beneficiaries. In a July 18, 2003 letter, the Trustees estimated the value of the Corporation as of December 31, 2002 to be between $10.53 billion and $10.64 billion. Press accounts have estimated the value of the Corporation to be in excess of $30 billion. Based on the value range assigned by the Trustees to the common stock of the Corporation, the Trust yielded income to the income beneficiaries of 1.19 percent to 1.29 percent for the year ending December 31, 2001, and 1.24 percent to 1.25 percent for the year ending December 31, 2002.

Citing the above figures, the Proposed Petition alleged the Trustees "have breached their fiduciary duties owed to current income beneficiaries.... In at least the years 2000, 2001, and 2002, the property held by the [Trust] generated income to current income beneficiaries ... *which was substantially lower than the income normally earned by trust investments, thereby favoring the remainder beneficiaries over the current income beneficiaries of the [Trust].... [¶] ...* The Trustees' breaches of fiduciary duties have proximately caused the current income beneficiaries, including Petitioners, to suffer damages because current income beneficiaries would have received higher income in at least the years 2000, 2001, and 2002 had the Trustees not breached their fiduciary duties by failing to take steps to secure a reasonable income yield on the ... Trust. [¶] ... This Court should award damages according to proof at trial against the Trustees and in favor of all income beneficiaries as redress for the Trustees' breaches of their fiduciary duties. In addition, this Court should order that the Trustees in the future must take steps to ensure that the Trust's income is increased so that the income beneficiaries each year receive an adequate amount of income based upon the size of the ... Trust." (Italics added.)

...

DISCUSSION

...

1. *General principles.*

...

c. *A trustee's fiduciary duty, including the duty of impartiality, and a trustee's discretionary powers.*

Trustees owe all beneficiaries, including the income beneficiaries herein, a fiduciary duty. A fiduciary relationship is a recognized legal relationship such as trustee and beneficiary, principal and agent, or attorney and client. (*Persson v. Smart Inventions, Inc.* (2005) 125 Cal.App.4th 1141, 1160, 23 Cal.Rptr.3d 335.) Where a fiduciary relationship exists, there is a duty " 'to act with the utmost good faith for the benefit of the other party.' " (*Ibid.*)

The fiduciary duty of a trustee includes "the duty of loyalty (Prob.Code, 16002); *the duty to deal impartially with the beneficiaries* (Prob.Code, 16003); the duty to avoid conflicts of interest (Prob.Code, 16004); the duty to control and preserve trust property (Prob.Code, 16006; Rest.2d Trusts, 175, 176); the duty to make trust property productive (Rest.2d Trusts, 181); the duty to dispose of improper investments (Rest.2d Trusts, 230, 231); and the duty to report and account (Prob.Code, 16060)." (*Harnedy v. Whitty* (2003) 110 Cal.App.4th 1333, 1340, 2 Cal.Rptr.3d 798, italics added.)

A trustee is bound to deal impartially with all beneficiaries (16003; *Crocker-Citizens National Bank v. Younger* (1971) 4 Cal.3d 202, 219, fn. 7, 93 Cal.Rptr. 214, 481 P.2d 222; *Estate of Nicholas* (1986) 177 Cal.App.3d 1071, 1089, 223 Cal.Rptr. 410), *unless the language of the trust provides otherwise.* (§ 16000.)

Accordingly, the law in California is consistent with American Jurisprudence, which states: "Trustees owe a duty to all trust beneficiaries, and must treat all equally. *Unless the trust instrument itself provides otherwise, the trustee's duty to each beneficiary precludes it from favoring one party over another.* Thus, a trustee must act impartially with respect to all beneficiaries, doing his or her best for the entire trust as a whole. A trustee who violates his or her duties to deal impartially with all beneficiaries risks exposure to liability for breach of trust." (76 Am.Jur.2d (2005) Trusts, § 359, fns. omitted, italics added.)

In a situation where the terms of the trust give the trustee "discretion to favor one beneficiary over another[,][t]he court will not control the exercise of such discretion, except to prevent the trustee from abusing it." (Rest.2d Trusts, § 183, com. a, p. 394.)

The Restatement Second of Trusts explains: "In determining the question whether the trustee is guilty of an abuse of discretion in exercising or failing to exercise a power, the following circumstances may be relevant: (1) *the extent of the discretion conferred upon the trustee by the terms of the trust;* (2) *the purposes of the trust;* (3) *the nature of the power;* (4) the existence or non-existence, the definiteness or indefiniteness, of an external standard by which the reasonableness of the trustee's conduct can be judged; (5) *the motives of the trustee in exercising or refraining from exercising the power;* (6) *the existence or nonexistence of an interest in the trustee conflicting with that of the beneficiaries.*" (Rest.2d Trusts, § 187, com. d, p. 403, italics added.)

If discretion is conferred upon the trustee in the exercise of a power, "*the court will not interfere unless the trustee in exercising or failing to exercise the power acts dishonestly, or with an improper even though not a dishonest motive, or fails to use his judgment, or acts beyond the bounds of a reasonable judgment.* The mere fact that if the discretion had been conferred upon the court, the court would have exercised the power differently, is not a sufficient reason for interfering with the exercise of the power by the trustee. Thus, if the trustee is empowered to apply so much of the trust property as he may deem necessary for the support of the beneficiary, the court will not interfere with the discretion of the trustee on the ground that he has applied too small an amount, if in the exercise of his judgment honestly and with proper motives he applies at least the minimum amount which could reasonably be considered necessary, even though if the matter were left to the court to determine in its discretion it might have applied a larger amount." (Rest.2d Trusts, § 187, com. e, p. 403, italics added.)

. . .

a. *Plaintiffs' claim the Trustees breached their duty of impartiality by maintaining a dividend policy which effectively favors the remainder beneficiaries conflicts with Trust provisions and therefore would amount to a contest.*

The amicus curiae brief contends "California law (Prob.Code, § 16003) compels trustees to treat classes of beneficiaries impartially and there is not a word or hint in WRH's will that excuses the Trustees from these obligations."

To the contrary, the very language of the will authorizes the Trustees to treat the two classes of beneficiaries, namely, income and remainder beneficiaries, differently. The will confers discretion upon the Trustees "to decide what is income and what is corpus or principal" of the Trust, as well as "to hold funds either uninvested or invested in non-income producing securities or property in such amounts, for such periods of time and to such extent as to them may from time to time seem best...." Said provisions significantly depart from the strict statutory duty of impartiality with respect to income production for current income beneficiaries. Under the code, trustees have "a duty to administer the trust according to the trust instrument and, *except to the extent the trust instrument provides otherwise,* according to this division." (§ 16000, italics added.) Here, the trust instrument, i.e., the will, expressly provides otherwise.

Although the will permits the Trustees to depart from the strict statutory duty of impartiality with respect to income production for current income beneficiaries, *the Trustees nonetheless must exercise their discretion in good faith and are prohibited from treating the current income beneficiaries differently based on animus, bad faith or other improper motives.* (Rest.2d Trusts, *supra,* § 187, com. d.) However, there is no allegation in the Proposed Petition to the effect that the Trustees' dividend policy is grounded in bad faith or an improper motivation. There is no allegation the Trustees acted dishonestly.

The bare allegation in the Proposed Petition that the Trustees breached their fiduciary duty owed to current income beneficiaries by adhering to a dividend policy which has the effect of favoring the remainder beneficiaries over the current income beneficiaries, without more, is insufficient to state a claim for breach of fiduciary duty to overcome the no contest clause. Said allegation does not entitle the income beneficiaries to proceed with their Proposed Petition challenging the Trustees' conduct without risking forfeiture under the no contest clause.

. . .

CONCLUSION

There is no question but that the Trustees owe a fiduciary duty to all the beneficiaries of the Trust and that they are bound by statutory and case law, as well as by the terms of the governing instrument. Here, however, notwithstanding the income beneficiaries' claims the Trustees violated their fiduciary duty, abused their discretion, and breached their duty of impartiality, the claims made and the relief sought by the Proposed Petition are precluded by the language of the Trust provisions, which explicitly authorizes the Trustees to treat income and remainder beneficiaries differently.

The no contest clause herein applies to "any proceeding ... *tending in any manner or to any extent to change, annul, revoke, set aside or invalidate this my Will or any of its provisions, including but not limited to any trust created herein or hereunder or any of the provisions of any such trust....*" (Italics added.) Plaintiffs' Proposed Petition to compel the Trustees to alter their dividend policy and to hold the Trustees personally liable for breach of fiduciary duty, without more, conflicts with the terms of the instrument and therefore would amount to a contest.

The order is affirmed.

———————

Notes

1. *Fact-sensitive duty*: The trustee has a duty to be impartial between and among the different beneficiaries when investing and managing the trust property, keeping in mind the different interests of the different beneficiaries and the purposes of the trust. What that means, exactly, is a fact-sensitive determination that varies from trust to trust. The courts, however, have sent a pretty clear message that absent overriding settlor intent, the trustee has a duty to produce reasonable income for the income beneficiaries.

2. *Judicial review*: Even where the trust instrument authorizes a trustee, either expressly or implicitly, to favor one beneficiary or class of beneficiaries over another, the trustee must still act in good faith. The trustee's decisions and actions are still subject to judicial review.

3. *Remedy*: Where a trustee unreasonably delays in selling underperforming property, the trust beneficiaries can hold the trustee liable for any loss caused by the delay. *See* RESTATEMENT (FIRST) OF TRUSTS § 209 (1935).

4. *Modern trend—unitrust*: Thus far, the discussion has focused on the traditional notion of a trust: where the life beneficiary typically has an interest in the income, and the remainderman has an interest in the principal. The bifurcated interest, coupled with the trustee's duty of impartiality, has the potential to handicap the trustee's ability to prudently invest the trust property. Instead of focusing on total returns, the trustee has to focus on ensuring that the investments produce a reasonable income for the income beneficiaries. Might there be another option—another way of structuring the beneficiaries' interests so that the trustee does not need to worry about such issues?

Problems

1. Dr. Nicholas Riegler Sr., his son, Dr. Nicholas Riegler Jr., and their wives created the Doctors Riegler Trust. The trust held title to certain parcels of real estate. The trust authorized the trustees, the two doctors, to borrow money and build a medical clinic on the property, and then lease the property back to the doctors,

with rent being paid to the trust. One-half of the excessive income generated by the trust was to be paid to each wife for life. The trustees built the clinic, the doctors leased it, and the rent they paid was distributed to their wives.

Thereafter, in 1964, Riegler Jr., acting as trustee but without authority from the trust, borrowed additional funds, and with other trust funds, purchased a vacant lot for a new medical clinic he was thinking about building for his own use (the lot has produced no income whatsoever for the trust since its purchase, and it has cost the trust income due to the interest paid on the borrowed funds). In 1968, as trustee he requested court approval to borrow additional funds to purchase 57 more acres of unproductive real estate.

At about this same time, Riegler Jr. and his wife were divorcing. During the divorce proceedings, Riegler admitted that he was doing everything he could to prevent his ex-wife from getting any money out of the trust. At a hearing in 1969, the court denied Riegler Jr.'s request to borrow additional funds and chastised him for purchasing the vacant lot without authority. In response, Riegler Jr. offered to purchase the vacant lot from the trust. As of 1975, he had still not followed through on the offer, and the trust had still had not distributed any income since 1964.

Has Riegler Jr. engaged in self-dealing? Has Riegler Jr. breached his duty of impartiality to the income beneficiaries? Is Riegler Jr.'s wife/ex-wife entitled to back-income for the period in question? *See Riegler v. Riegler*, 553 S.W.2d 37 (Ark. Ct. App. 1977).

2. Clara and E.W. Bank started the Bank Lumber Co., which did quite well over the years. In 1954, Clara and E.W. decided it was time to address their estate planning needs. Clara executed a will devising the bulk of her estate to a testamentary trust. The trust appointed her husband the sole trustee, the income was to be distributed to E.W. during his lifetime, and upon his death the trust assets to be distributed to their four children. E.W. created an irrevocable trust in 1954. He transferred the bulk of his assets to the trust, including his Bank Lumber Co. stock. The distributive terms of the trust were the same as those in Clara's trust. Section 2.01 of the trust expressly authorized the trustee "[t]o retain, whether orginally (sic) a part of the trust estate or subsequently acquired ... any property, whether or not such property is ... unproductive, or of a wasting nature, all without diversification as to kind or amount."

Upon Clara's death in 1961, 375 shares of Bank Lumber Co. stock were transferred to her trust. In 1962, E.W. married Mary. They lived together until his death in 1969. He died testate, with a will leaving all his property to Mary. A few years after E.W.'s death, Mary, as executor of E.W.'s estate, sued the successor trustee claiming a breach of trust with respect to Clara's trust. She claimed that although E.W. was to receive the income from Clara's trust assets, he received less than one percent per annum of their fair market value between 1962 and 1969, when he died. Oklahoma, the state in question, had recently adopted a statute that expressly provided that upon conversion of unproductive property, the beneficiary who was entitled to receive the income shall be allocated five percent per annum for the period in which the unproductive property should have been changed.

Does Mary have a valid claim for breach of the duty of impartiality and failure to produce a fair stream of income for the income beneficiary? *See Bank v. Bank Lumber Co.*, 543 P.2d 588 (Okla. Civ. App. 1975).

In re Heller

849 N.E.2d 262 (N.Y. 2006)

ROSENBLATT, J.

In September 2001, New York enacted legislation that transformed the definition and treatment of trust accounting income. The Uniform Principal and Income Act (EPTL art. 11-A) and related statutes (L. 2001, ch. 243), including the optional unitrust provision (EPTL 11-2.4), are designed to facilitate investment for total return on a portfolio. The appeal before us centers on the optional unitrust provision, which permits trustees to elect a regime in which income is calculated according to a fixed formula and based on the net fair market value of the trust assets. We hold that a trustee's status as a remainder beneficiary does not in itself invalidate a unitrust election made by that trustee....

I.

In his will, after making certain other gifts of personal property and money, Jacob Heller created a trust to benefit his wife Bertha Heller (should she survive him) and his children. Heller provided that his entire residuary estate be held in trust during Bertha's life. He appointed his brother Frank Heller as trustee and designated his sons Herbert and Alan Heller as trustees on Frank's death. Every year Bertha was to receive the greater of $40,000 or the total income of the trust. Heller named his daughters (Suzanne Heller and Faith Willinger, each with a 30% share) and his sons and prospective trustees (Herbert and Alan Heller, each with a 20% share) as remainder beneficiaries.

Jacob Heller died in 1986, and his wife Bertha survives him. When Heller's brother Frank died in 1997, Herbert and Alan Heller became trustees. From that year until 2001, Bertha Heller received an average annual income from the trust of approximately $190,000. In March 2003, the trustees elected to have the unitrust provision apply, pursuant to EPTL 11-2.4(e)(1)(B)(I). As required by EPTL 11-2.4(e)(1)(B)(III), they notified trust beneficiaries Bertha Heller, Suzanne Heller and Faith Willinger.... As a result of that election, Bertha Heller's annual income was reduced to approximately $70,000.

Appellant Sandra Davis commenced this proceeding, as attorney-in-fact for her mother Bertha Heller, and on August 1, 2003 moved for summary judgment, seeking, among other things, an order annulling the unitrust election and revoking the letters of trusteeship issued to Herbert and Alan Heller.... Surrogate's Court ... denied the branches of her motion seeking annulment of the unitrust election itself and other relief.

Davis appealed Surrogate's Court's order, and Herbert and Alan Heller cross-appealed. The Appellate Division affirmed the order ... [and] granted leave to appeal and certified the following question to us: "Was the opinion and order of [the Appellate Division] dated August 15, 2005, properly made?" ...

II.

The 2001 legislation that forms the subject of this appeal was designed to make it easier for trustees to comply with the demands of the Prudent Investor Act of 1994. In addition to enacting EPTL article 11-A (Uniform Principal and Income Act), the Legislature both added EPTL 11-2.3(b)(5) to the Prudent Investor Act and included the optional unitrust provision, EPTL 11-2.4.

Under the former Principal and Income Act, a trustee was required to balance the interests of the income beneficiary against those of the remainder beneficiary, and was constrained in making investments by the act's narrow definitions of income and principal. A trustee who invested in nonappreciating assets would ensure reasonable income for any income beneficiary, but would sacrifice growth opportunities for the trust funds, as inflation eroded their value; if the trustee invested for growth, remainder beneficiaries would enjoy an increase in the value of the trust at the expense of income beneficiaries. Moreover, the need to invest so as to produce what the former Principal and Income Act defined as income led to investment returns that failed to represent the benefits envisaged as appropriate by settlors.

The Prudent Investor Act encourages investing for total return on a portfolio. Unless the governing instrument expressly provides otherwise, the act requires that trustees "pursue an *overall* investment strategy to enable the trustee to make appropriate present and future distributions to or for the benefit of the beneficiaries under the governing instrument, in accordance with risk and return objectives reasonably suited to the *entire* portfolio" (EPTL 11-2.3[b][3][A] [emphasis added]).

The 2001 legislation allows trustees to pursue this strategy uninhibited by a constrained concept of trust accounting income. First, the Prudent Investor Act now authorizes trustees

> "to adjust between principal and income to the extent the trustee considers advisable to enable the trustee to make appropriate present and future distributions in accordance with clause (b)(3)(A) if the trustee determines, after applying the rules in article 11-A, that such an adjustment would be fair and reasonable to all of the beneficiaries, so that current beneficiaries may be given such use of the trust property as is consistent with preservation of its value".

A trustee investing for a portfolio's total return under the Prudent Investor Act may now adjust principal and income to compensate for the effects of the investment decisions on distribution to income beneficiaries. Alternatively, the optional unitrust provision lets trustees elect unitrust status for a trust, by which income is calculated according to a fixed formula.

In a unitrust pursuant to EPTL 11-2.4, an income beneficiary receives an annual income distribution of "four percent of the net fair market values of the assets held in the trust on the first business day of the current valuation year" (EPTL 11-2.4[b][1]), for the first three years of unitrust treatment. This is true regardless of the actual income earned by the trust. Starting in the fourth year, the value of the trust assets is determined by calculating the average of three figures: the net fair market value on the first business day of the current valuation year and the net fair market values on the first business days of the prior two valuation years (*see* EPTL 11-2.4[b][2]). Income generated in excess of this amount is applied to principal.

Under the 2001 legislation, then, a trustee may invest in assets, such as equities, that outperform other types of investment in the long term but produce relatively low dividend yields for an income beneficiary, and still achieve impartial treatment of income and remainder beneficiaries. The trustee may accomplish this either by adjusting as between principal and income (*see* 14 Warren's Heaton, Surrogates' Courts, at App. 5-25–5-27) or by electing unitrust status with the result that the income increases in proportion to the value of the principal (*id.* at App. 5-14). If a trust's assets are primarily interests in nonappreciating investments producing high yields for income beneficiaries, a unitrust election may initially result in a substantial decrease in the distribution to any income beneficiary, at least until the portfolio is diversified. This case presents such a scenario.

III.

Davis argues that the trustees are barred as a matter of law from electing unitrust status because they are themselves remainder beneficiaries, and that, in any case, they may not elect unitrust status retroactively to January 1, 2002. The Appellate Division held that the legislation does not impede unitrust election by an interested trustee, that such an election is not inconsistent, per se, with common-law limitations on the conduct of fiduciaries and that the statute permits trustees to select retroactive application. We agree.

EPTL 11-2.3(b)(5), the 2001 statute that gives trustees the power to adjust between principal and income, expressly prohibits a trustee from exercising this power if "the trustee is a current beneficiary or a presumptive remainderman of the trust" (EPTL 11-2.3[b][5] [C][vii]) or if "the adjustment would benefit the trustee directly or indirectly" (EPTL 11-2.3[b] [5][C] [viii]). Tellingly, the Legislature included no such prohibition in the simultaneously enacted optional unitrust provision, EPTL 11-2.4. Moreover, in giving a list of factors to be considered by the courts in determining whether unitrust treatment should apply to a trust, the Legislature mentioned no absolute prohibitions (*see* EPTL 11-2.4[e][5][A]), and created a presumption in favor of unitrust application (EPTL 11-2.4[e][5][B]). We conclude that the Legislature did not mean to prohibit trustees who have a beneficial interest from electing unitrust treatment.

It is certainly true that the common law in New York contains an absolute prohibition against self-dealing, in that "a fiduciary owes a duty of undivided and undiluted loyalty to those whose interests the fiduciary is to protect" (*Birnbaum v. Birnbaum*, 73 N.Y.2d 461, 466, 541 N.Y.S.2d 746, 539 N.E.2d 574 [1989]). "The trustee is under a duty to the beneficiary to administer the trust solely in the interest of the beneficiary"

(Restatement [Second] of Trusts § 170[1]). In this case, however, the trustees owe fiduciary obligations not only to the trust's income beneficiary, Bertha Heller, but also to the other remainder beneficiaries, Suzanne Heller and Faith Willinger. That these beneficiaries' interests happen to align with the trustees' does not relieve the trustees of their duties to them. Here, we cannot conclude that the trustees are prohibited from electing unitrust treatment as a matter of common-law principle.

That the trustees are remainder beneficiaries does not, by itself, invalidate a unitrust election. Nevertheless, a unitrust election from which a trustee benefits will be scrutinized by the courts with special care. In determining whether application of the optional unitrust provision is appropriate, it remains for the Surrogate to review the process and assure the fairness of the trustees' election, by applying relevant factors including those enumerated in EPTL 11-2.4(e)(5)(A). Application of these factors here presents questions of fact precluding summary judgment.

. . .

Accordingly, the order of the Appellate Division should be affirmed....

Note

California: Like New York, California has adopted the Uniform Principal and Income Act and the optional provisions permitting conversion of a traditional trust into a unitrust. California Probate Code Section 16336 sets forth the conditions under which a trustee of a traditional trust is authorized (and prohibited) to make adjustments between principal and income to compensate for investments made under the California prudent investor rule. California Probate Code Section 16336.4 provides that unless expressly prohibited by the terms of the trust, the trustee may convert the trust into a unitrust. The trustee must give notice to the trust beneficiaries, and where one or more objects, can convert to a unitrust only with court approval. Following conversion to a unitrust under Section 16336.4, the income beneficiaries are entitled, annually, to four percent of the trust assets' net fair market value. Under Section 16336.5, the annual payout percentage can be adjusted to permit more flexibility, but it must be at least three percent and cannot be more than five percent. Moreover, the conversion can be ordered by the court in response to a beneficiary's request. Section 16336.6 authorizes 'reconversion' of a unitrust back to a traditional trust or to change the annual payout.

California Probate Code Section 16336.7 expressly provides that California's unitrust provisions impose no duty on a trustee to convert or reconvert a trust or even to consider converting or reconverting a trust.

Problem

Look back at Problem 2 above (preceding the *Heller* case). If that fact pattern arose today, do you think E.W. Bank would have petitioned to convert the trust to a unitrust?

C. Duty to Act Prudently

Historically, the trustee's principal job was to preserve the trust property. Under the modern trend, the trustee's principal job is to make the trust property productive. This shift from preserving the trust property to making the trust property productive corresponds with the shift from the traditional trust (which held real property) to the modern trust (which holds a fund of intangible wealth). The shift has also put increasing importance on the trustee's duty to act prudently, particularly as it applies to investing the trust property (i.e., making it productive). The duty to act prudently, however, is not limited to the trustee's investment role. Like the duty of loyalty, it applies to virtually all of the trustee's functions.

1. Articulating the Duty

While virtually every jurisdiction agrees that a trustee has a duty to act prudently in managing the trust, there are some subtle but important distinctions in how the duty is worded. Some states, and the RESTATEMENT (SECOND) OF TRUSTS, say that a trustee has the duty to act as "a man of ordinary prudence ... dealing with *his own property*" (emphasis added). Other states say that a trustee has a duty to act as "a man of ordinary prudence ... dealing with *the property of another*" (emphasis added). The Uniform Trust Code and the RESTATEMENT (THIRD) OF TRUSTS deftly avoid the issue by simply not addressing it directly: "A trustee shall administer the trust as a prudent person would, by considering the purposes, terms, distributional requirements, and other circumstances of the trust. In satisfying this standard, the trustee shall exercise reasonable care, skill, and caution." UTC § 804; *see also* RESTATEMENT (THIRD) OF TRUSTS § 77.

California essentially follows this approach, but expressly notes that the trustee's general duty to act prudently is modified by the more specific powers and duties under California's prudent investor rule:

CPC § 16040. California's prudent investor rule

(a) The trustee shall administer the trust with reasonable care, skill, and caution under the circumstances then prevailing that a prudent person acting in a like capacity would use in the conduct of an enterprise of like character and with like aims to accomplish the purposes of the trust as determined from the trust instrument.

(b) The settlor may expand or restrict the standard provided in subdivision (a) by express provisions in the trust instrument....

(c) This section does not apply to investment and management functions governed by the Uniform Prudent Investor Act, Article 2.5 (commencing with Section 16045).

2. Historical Evolution of the Investment Duties

While the trustee's duty to act prudently applies to virtually every function he or she performs, there is little doubt that, as applied to the modern trust, the duty to act prudently is most applicable to the trustee's investment function: the power and duty to invest the trust property to make it productive. At early common law, the function of the trust was to preserve the trust property. No more under the modern trend—that is not good enough. The function of the modern trust is to actively manage a fund of intangible wealth. This evolution is most evident with respect to a trustee's ability and duty to deal with the trust property.

The issue of investing trust property when the trust property is intangible wealth first arose in England, the country typically credited with creating trusts.[4] Not surprisingly, the early English response was to emphasize the importance of protecting and preserving the trust principal. So concerned were the English with protecting the trust property that only government securities and bank annuities were acceptable investments. Relatively early on the American courts rejected that approach as too conservative, but they split over the proper response to it. Under what became known as the Massachusetts rule, in *Harvard Coll. v. Amory*, 26 Mass. 446, 461 (1830), the Massachusetts Supreme Court stated:

> All that can be required of a trustee to invest, is, that he shall conduct himself faithfully and exercise a sound discretion. He is to observe how men of prudence, discretion and intelligence manage their own affairs, not in regard to speculation, but in regard to the permanent disposition of their funds, considering the probable income, as well as the probable safety of the capital to be invested.

On the other hand, the New York courts found this approach too risky for their liking. The New York Court of Appeals ruled that:

> all industrial stocks and bonds were imprudent, speculative investments for fiduciaries. Unless specifically authorized by the settlor, the trustee who invested in such securities was forced to assume the risk of any depreciation from whatever cause. General discretionary powers in the trust instrument did not authorize such so-called speculation with the trust corpus. The "legal list" in states adopting this rationale was thereby virtually confined to mortgages, corporate bonds secured by mortgage and government securities. In the absence of specific statutory or settlor authorization, many jurisdictions regularly surcharge fiduciaries for depletion resulting from investment in unsecured corporate issues.

Legal Lists in Trust Investments, 49 YALE L. J. 891, 893 (1940).

The legal list movement went on to split into two approaches. Mandatory lists absolutely prohibited any investment that was not on the approved list, absent express authorization by the settlor or a court. Permissive lists, on the other hand, listed types of investments that were presumed "safe" investments, thereby creating some-

---

4. More accurately, *inter vivos* trusts originated in England during the twelfth and thirteenth centuries, but the basic trust concept, in the form of testamentary trusts, was developed well before this under Roman law. Roman law, in the area of trusts, is "modernly" referred to as Napoleonic law. "What is Napoleonic Law?" would be a proper response to the question "What are the roots of trust law?"

thing of a safe harbor for trustees who invested in securities on the list. Such investment decisions were presumptively made prudently and in good faith.

3. The Prudent Man Approach

Over time, the Massachusetts rule prevailed over the legal list approaches and was adopted as the basis of the RESTATEMENT (SECOND) OF TRUSTS approach. The RESTATEMENT approach authorized trustees to "to make such investments and only such investments as a prudent man would make of his own property having in view the preservation of the estate and the amount and regularity of the income to be derived." RESTATEMENT (SECOND) OF TRUSTS § 227. Slowly but surely, the Massachusetts rule evolved into the prudent man rule, which was adopted in one form or another by nearly all jurisdictions by the latter part of the twentieth century.

Despite the rule's widespread adoption, courts were criticized for construing and applying the prudent man rule in a needlessly restrictive and conservative manner. Under the prudent man approach, each trust investment was viewed and analyzed in isolation: was *that particular investment decision* defensible? Viewed with 20/20 hindsight, it often was difficult to defend investment decisions that might have pushed the envelope. Moreover, because each investment decision was viewed in isolation, gains associated with other trust investments could not be used to offset any trust losses.

In addition, the courts branded certain categories of investments as "speculative," thereby creating a presumption that any investment in such categories would be imprudent. Accordingly, an imprudent investment resulting in a loss would subject the trustee to a surcharge. Although such "judicial" legal lists were more limited than their statutory predecessors, they nevertheless restricted a trustee's investment options. Furthermore, the traditional common law notion that certain trust powers could not be delegated impeded sound trust investments by limiting a trustee's ability to seek professional input.

4. The Prudent Investor Approach

The drafters of the prudent investor doctrine assert that they were simply restoring the spirit and scope of the approach first articulated in *Harvard College v. Amory* while also modernizing it to reflect and incorporate modern investment theory and practices. In addition, the Prudent Investor Act is based on an approach first adopted by the RESTATEMENT (THIRD) OF TRUSTS. *See* UNIFORM PRUDENT INVESTOR ACT prefatory note (1994), 7B U.L.A. 3 (2006).

First, the prudent investor approach embraces the portfolio theory of trust investing. No individual investment decision should be scrutinized in isolation; rather, courts should focus on whether the trust's investments are, on the whole, properly balanced. *See* UNIFORM PRUDENT INVESTOR ACT § 2(b). Consistent with the portfolio approach is the belief that there is no such thing as an inappropriately speculative investment. So long as high-risk investments are offset by low-risk investments such that the overall trust investment portfolio has an acceptable level of risk in light of the trust purposes and the circumstances surrounding the trust, in theory all possible investments are viable options (but the investments must also be suitable to the trust; i.e., the trustee should also take into consideration the settlor's objectives in creating the trust and the beneficiaries' needs and interests).

Second, an inherent byproduct of the portfolio approach to a trust's investments is the importance of diversification. Trust investment diversification ensures proper risk management, which in turn creates a presumption that a trustee's investment decisions are prudent. Diversification goes hand in hand with the modern "risk and return" approach to investment and wealth management. Prior to the prudent investor rule, there was no independent duty to diversify the trust's investments; each investment decision was viewed in isolation. The Prudent Investor Act, however, expressly provides that the trustee has a duty to diversify unless it would be prudent not to do so. *See* UNIFORM PRUDENT INVESTOR ACT § 3 (common examples of where it might be prudent *not* to diversify include where it would have significant adverse tax consequences, or in the case of a closely held family business or a family farm). Prudent investment risk management inherently includes diversification.

Third, the prudent investor approach acknowledges that managing a fund of intangible wealth is a very complicated task that increasingly calls for a high degree of skill, care, and expertise. Accordingly, the prudent investor approach advocates that a trustee should delegate the investment process to trained wealth management experts. Not only does the prudent investor approach grant the trustee the power to delegate the investment process to a third party, it arguably creates a duty for some trustees to delegate the investment process to a third party—just as a prudent investor who was not well-trained in the necessary market skills would do. *See* UNIFORM PRUDENT INVESTOR ACT § 9. But delegating the investment process does not mean a trustee can abdicate its investment duties. In delegating the investment decisions, the trustee still must act prudently:

(a) ... The trustee shall exercise reasonable care, skill, and caution in:

(1) selecting an agent;

(2) establishing the scope and terms of the delegation, consistent with the purposes and terms of the trust; and

(3) periodically reviewing the agent's actions in order to monitor the agent's performance and compliance with the terms of the delegation.

See UNIFORM PRUDENT INVESTOR ACT § 9(a). A trustee who meets the conditions set forth above with respect to delegating the trust's investment decisions will not be liable for any actions undertaken by—or investment losses incurred by—the agent. *See* UNIFORM PRUDENT INVESTOR ACT § 9(c).

Finally, the prudent investor approach acknowledges that it has the potential to be a complicated and potentially expensive approach. Trustees, however, are not free to simply turn the task of the trust's investments over to well-paid wealth management experts and then wholly abandon their responsibilities. In fact, the prudent investor approach expressly creates a duty for trustees to avoid unnecessary fees, transaction costs, and other related expenses. *See* Uniform Prudent Investor Act §7. What constitutes an "unnecessary" fee, transaction cost, or expense will depend on the realistic needs and investment goals of each particular trust, taking into consideration the purpose of the trust and the circumstances surrounding it.

Estate of Collins

72 Cal. App. 3d 663 (1977)

KAUS, Presiding Justice.

Objectors (plaintiffs) are beneficiaries under a testamentary trust established in the will of Ralph Collins, deceased. Carl Lamb and C. E. Millikan (defendants) were, respectively, Collins' business partner and lawyer. They were named in Collins' will as trustees. In 1973 defendants filed a petition for an order approving and settling the first and final account and discharging the trustees. Plaintiffs objected on grounds that defendants had improperly invested $50,000 and requested that defendants be surcharged. After a hearing, the trial court ruled in favor of defendants, and approved the account, terminated the trust, and discharged the trustees. Plaintiff beneficiaries have appealed.

FACTS

The primary beneficiaries under the testamentary trust were Collins' wife and children; his mother and father were also named as beneficiaries. General support provisions were included; the will also specifically provided that the trustees pay his daughter $4,000 a year for five years for her undergraduate and graduate education.

Paragraph (d) of the declaration of trust recited the powers of the trustees in the usual, inclusive fashion. Subparagraph (3) authorized and trustees to purchase "every kind of property, real, personal or mixed, and every kind of investment, specifically including, but not by way of limitation, corporate obligations of every kind, and stocks, preferred or common, irrespective of whether said investments are in accordance with the laws then enforced in the State of California pertaining to the investment of trust funds by corporate trustees."

Subparagraph (3) also provided: "Unless specifically limited, all discretions conferred upon the Trustee shall be absolute, and their exercise conclusive on all persons interest(ed) in this trust. The enumeration of certain powers of the Trustee shall not limit its general powers, the Trustee, subject always to the discharge of its fiduciary obligations, being vested with and having all the rights, powers and privileges which an absolute owner of the same property would have."

Collins died in 1963 and his will was admitted to probate. In June 1965, the court ordered the estate to be distributed. After various other payments and distributions, defendant trustees received about $80,000 as the trust principal. After other distributions, such as the annual $4,000 payment for the education of Collins' daughter, the trustees had about $50,000 available for investment.

Defendant Millikan's clients included two real property developers, Downing and Ward. In March 1965, Millikan filed an action on behalf of Downing and Ward against a lender who refused to honor a commitment to carry certain construction loans. In June 1965, defendants learned that Downing and Ward wanted to borrow $50,000. Millikan knew that the builders wanted the loan because of their difficulties with the lender who had withdrawn its loan commitment.

The loan would be secured by a second trust deed to 9.38 acres of unimproved real property in San Bernardino County near Upland. This property was subject to a $90,000 first trust deed; the note which secured the first trust deed was payable in quarterly installments of interest only, and due in full in three years, that is, in July 1968. The $50,000 loan to be made by defendants would be payable in monthly installments of interest only, at ten percent interest with the full amount due in 30 months, that is, in January 1968.

Defendants knew that the property had been sold two years earlier in 1963 for $107,000. Defendants checked with two real estate brokers in the area, one of whom said that property in that area was selling for $18,000 to $20,000 an acre. They did not have the property appraised, they did not check with the county clerk or recorder in either Los Angeles or San Bernardino County to determine whether there were foreclosures or lawsuits pending against the construction company. In fact, when defendants made the loan in July 1965, there were six notices of default and three lawsuits pending against Downing and Ward.

Defendants obtained and reviewed an unaudited company financial statement. This statement indicated that the Downing and Ward Company had a net worth in excess of $2,000,000.

Downing and Ward told defendants that they were not in default on any of their loans, that they were not defendants in any pending litigation, and that there had never been any liens filed on any of their projects. Defendants phoned the bank with whom Downing and Ward had a line of credit and learned that the bank had a satisfactory relationship with the builders.

Based on this information, on July 23, 1965, defendants lent Downing and Ward $50,000 on the terms described above. In addition to the second trust deed, Downing and Ward pledged 20 percent of the stock in their company as security. However, defendants neither obtained possession of the stock, placed it in escrow, nor placed a legend on the stock certificates. Defendants also obtained the personal guarantees of Downing and Ward and their wives. However, defendants did not obtain financial statements from the guarantors.

When the loan was made in July 1965, construction in the Upland area was, as the trial court said, 'enjoying boom times, although the bubble was to burst just a few months later.' From July 1965 through September 1966, the builders made the monthly interest payments required by the note. In October 1966, Downing & Ward Construction Corporation was placed in involuntary bankruptcy and thereafter Mr. and Mrs. Ward and Mr. and Mrs. Downing declared personal bankruptcies. Defendants foreclosed their second trust deed in June 1967, and became the owners of the unimproved real property. They spent $10,000 in an unsuccessful effort to salvage the investment by forestalling foreclosure by the holder of the first trust deed. In September 1968, the holder of the first trust deed did foreclose. This extinguished the trustees' interest in the property and the entire investment. In short, about $60,000 of the trust fund was lost.

The trial court made findings of fact and drew conclusions of law. As relevant, the court found that defendant trustees "exercised the judgment and care, under the circumstances then prevailing, which men of prudence, discretion and intelligence exercised in the management of their own affairs, not in regard to speculation, but in regard to the disposition of their funds, considering the probable income, as well as the probable safety of their capital." In making the loan, "the cotrustees used reasonable care, diligence and skill. The cotrustees did not act arbitrarily or in bad faith."

DISCUSSION

The trial court's finding that defendants exercised the judgment and care "which men of prudence, discretion and intelligence exercised in the management of their own affairs," reflects the standard imposed upon trustees by Civil Code section 2261. (See also, Rest.2d Trusts, §227 ('Restatement').)

Plaintiffs contend, and we agree, that contrary to the trial court's findings and conclusions, defendants failed to follow the "prudent investor" standard, first, by investing two-thirds of the trust principal in a single investment, second, by investing in real property secured only by a second deed of trust, and third, by making that investment without adequate investigation of either the borrowers or the collateral.

Although California does not limit the trustee's authority to a list of authorized investments, relying instead on the prudent investor rule (see 7 Witkin, Summary of Cal. Law (8th ed.) Trusts, §63, p. 5424), nevertheless, the prudent investor rule encompasses certain guidelines applicable to this case.

First, "the trustee is under a duty to the beneficiary to distribute the risk of loss by reasonable diversification of investments, unless under the circumstances it is prudent not to do so." (Rest., §228; see also, *Estate of Beach* (1975) 15 Cal.3d 623, 634, 125 Cal.Rptr. 570, 542 P.2d 994, fn. 9; Witkin, *supra*, at p. 5425, see generally, Uniform Management of Institutional Funds Act, Civ.Code, §§2290.1–2290.12, §2290.6.)

Second, ordinarily, "second or other junior mortgages are not proper trust investments," unless taking a second mortgage is a reasonable method of settling a claim or making possible the sale of property. (Rest., §227, p. 533.) Stated more emphatically: "While loans secured by second mortgages on land are sometimes allowed, they are almost always disapproved by courts of equity. The trustee should not place the trust funds in a position where they may be endangered by the foreclosure of a prior lien.... In rare cases equity will sanction an investment secured by a second mortgage, but only when the security is adequate and unusual circumstances justify the trustee in taking this form of investment." (Bogart, Trusts & Trustees (2d ed.) §675, p. 274.)

Third, in "buying a mortgage for trust investment, the trustee should give careful attention to the valuation of the property, in order to make certain that his margin of security is adequate. He must use every reasonable endeavor to provide protection which will cover the risks of depreciation in the property and changes in price levels. And he must investigate the status of the property and of the mortgage, as well as the financial situation of the mortgagor." (Bogart, *supra*, § 674, at p. 267.) Similarly, the Restatement rule is that "the trustee cannot properly lend on a mortgage upon real property more than a reasonable proportion of the value of the mortgage property." (Sec. 229.)

We think it apparent that defendants violated every applicable rule. First, they failed totally to diversify the investments in this relatively small trust fund. Second, defendants invested in a junior mortgage on unimproved real property, and left an inadequate margin of security. As noted, the land had most recently sold for $107,000, and was subject to a first trust deed of $90,000. Thus, unless the land was worth more than $140,000, there was no margin of security at all. Defendants did not have the land appraised; the only information they had was the opinion of a real estate broker that property in the area — not that particular parcel — was going for $18,000 to $20,000 an acre. Thus, any assumption that the property was worth about $185,000 — and therefore the $140,000 in loans were well-secured — would have been little more than a guess.

Third, the backup security obtained by defendants was no security at all. The builders pledge 20 percent of their stock, but defendants never obtained possession of the stock, placed it in escrow or even had it legended. They accepted the personal guarantees of the builders and their wives without investigating the financial status of these persons. They accepted at face value the claimed $2,000,000 value of the company shown in an unaudited statement. Defendant Millikan apparently ignored the fact that one lender had, for whatever reasons, reneged on a loan commitment to the builders.

Defendants contend that the evidence sustains the trial court's findings that they exercised the judgment and care under the circumstances then prevailing expected of men of prudence. They rely on the rule that the determination whether an investment was proper must be made in light of the circumstances existing at the time of the investment. (E.g., Witkin, *supra*, § 63, p. 5425.) That rule does not help defendants. Nothing that happened after the loan was made can change the fact that defendants invested two-thirds of the principal of the trust in a single second deed of trust on unappraised property, with no knowledge of the borrowers' true financial status, and without any other security.

We recognize, as did the trial court, that the loan was made in 1965, and defendants, some ten years later, could not be expected to recall the specifics of their investigation. But that is the point of this case turned inside out: Defendants were required to rely on faded memories because their investigation was limited to casual conversations. No documentation existed, not because it was lost, but because it was never obtained. Further, it is defendants' own fault that they filed their 'first and final account' more than eight years after assuming their duties.

Defendants seek to place themselves in the position of the trustee in *Day v. First Trust & Sav. Bank* (1941) 47 Cal.App.2d 470, 118 P.2d 51, who made investments — most of them in the 1920's — and ran into certain difficulties during the years from 1929 until 1933. Leaving aside the difference between the depression years, covered in *Day*, and the recession in the construction business in the late 1960's, an examination of some of the investments by the trustee in *Day* illustrates the difference between a prudent man and what defendants did here: A $300,000 mortgage on property appraised at $700,000 and valued in February 1933 at $555,000; a $225,000 mortgage on property appraised at $725,000; a $30,000 mortgage on property appraised at $112,000; a $35,000 mortgage on property appraised at $83,000; a $15,000 mortgage on property appraised at $37,000. (*Id.* at pp. 473–475, 118 P.2d 51.) Here defendants must be surcharged, not because they lacked prescience of what would happen, but because they both lacked and ignored information about what was happening at the time.

Plainly, defendants' conduct did not meet the prudent-investor standard. They claim, however, that the trust instrument conferred on them an "absolute discretion." Therefore, they argue, their sole obligation was not to act arbitrarily and to use their best judgment. (*Coberly v. Superior Court* (1965) 231 Cal.App.2d 685, 689, 42 Cal.Rptr. 64.)

We leave aside that even a trustee with "absolute discretion" may not "neglect its trust or abdicate its judgment," (*Coberly v. Superior Court, supra,* 231 Cal.App.2d at p. 689, 42 Cal.Rptr. at p. 67) or show a "reckless indifference" to the interests of the beneficiary. (Rest. § 222.) The record before us contains no evidence that defendants satisfied even the lesser standard of care for which they contend.

More fundamentally we do not agree with defendants' premise. While the declaration of trust may possibly enlarge the prudent-investor standard as far as the Type of investment is concerned, it cannot be construed as permitting deviations from that standard in investigating the soundness of a specific investment. This distinction is well established. Comment v. to section 227 of the Restatement reads, in part, as follows:

> 'v. An authorization by the terms of the trust to invest in a particular Type of security does not mean that any investment in securities of that type is proper. The trustee must use care and skill and caution in making the selection. Thus, if the trustee is authorized by the terms of the trust to invest in railroad bonds, he is guilty of a breach of trust if he invests in bonds of a railroad company *in which a prudent man would not invest because of the financial condition of the company.*' (Italics added.)

The provisions on which defendants rely are subparagraphs (3) and (11) to paragraph (d), quoted earlier. Neither supports their position. Subparagraph (3) merely tracks section 2261 of the Civil Code and adds that the investments listed therein are permissible "irrespective of whether said investments are in accordance with the laws then in force in the State of California pertaining to the investment of trust funds by corporate trustees." This adds nothing. Neither Civil Code section 2261 nor any other authority which we can locate authorizes different types of investments for "corporate trustees" as distinguished from amateurs. The difference is, rather, that the corporate trustee is held to a greater standard of care based on its presumed expertise. (*Estate of Beach, supra*, 15 Cal.3d 623, 635, 125 Cal.Rptr. 570, 542 P.2d 994; *Coberly v. Superior Court, supra*, 231 Cal.App.2d 685, 689, 42 Cal.Rptr. 64; Bogert, supra, § 541, p. 453.)

In any event, even if the trust instrument permitted a type of investment generally frowned on under the prudent-investor rule, it did not authorize the trustees to make it blindly. Defendants might have a point, had they purchased a well-secured second trust deed after careful investigation. Clearly, however, the nature of their investment is the least of their problems.

Alternatively, defendants rely on the language in subparagraph (11) that "all discretions conferred upon the Trustee shall be absolute, ..." This reliance, too, is misplaced.

First, viewed as an exculpatory clause, subparagraph (11) is subject to the rule of strict construction. (Rest. § 222, comment a, p. 517; Scott on Trusts, Supra, § 222.2 and cases cited.)

Second, the "absolute discretion" is "specifically limited" by the requirement that the trustee is "subject always to the discharge of its fiduciary obligations, ..."

Third, in context subparagraph (11) refers only to "discretions conferred on the Trustee" in paragraph (d) of the trust which, as noted, deals exclusively with powers, as distinguished from the degree of care with which they are to be exercised. Nor does any other part of the declaration of trust mention any relevant discretion which subparagraph (11) would make "absolute." Nowhere did the trustor say anything about a discretion not to diversify, a discretion to invest in a junior encumbrance without ability to protect against the foreclosure of a senior lien, a discretion not to make a business-like investigation of the credit and net worth of the borrower, or a discretion not to insist on an appraisal of the security given by the borrower.

The orders are reversed with directions to determine the damages to which plaintiffs are entitled.

———————

Notes

1. *Rule of law versus default duty*: The Uniform Prudent Investor Act expressly provides that the duties and standards created under the Act are default standards and duties that a settlor can opt out of if he or she so wishes: "The prudent investor rule, a default rule, may be expanded, restricted, eliminated, or otherwise altered by the provisions of a trust. A trustee is not liable to a beneficiary to the extent that the trustee acted in reasonable reliance on the provisions of the trust." UNIFORM PRUDENT INVESTOR ACT § 1(b). The issue then becomes how specific the express terms of the trust must be to constitute sufficient evidence of the settlor's intent to opt out of the Prudent Investor Act.

While in theory the Prudent Investor Act provides that it is default law that settlors can opt out of, in practice the courts have been consistently skeptical of settlors' attempts at opting out of the duties imposed by the Act. The courts have rather consistently held that generic trust language granting a trustee absolute powers and/or absolute discretion is insufficient evidence of the settlor's intent to opt out of the particular default duties imposed by the Prudent Investor Act. Even where a trust arguably contains specific language authorizing retention of specific inception assets, the courts tend to construe the language narrowly as merely authorizing the trustee to invest in the asset, not as opting out of the applicable duty to diversify. *See Wood v. U.S. Bank, N.A.*, 828 N.E.2d 1072 (Ohio Ct. App. 2005). Any attempt at opting out should be written very precisely, with detailed reference to the particular duty or duties that the settlor wishes to override, and even then the trustee should proceed carefully. Scholars are increasingly asking if the courts have not become so convinced of the wisdom of the modern portfolio theory and the duty to diversity that de facto the default duties have become mandatory (i.e., a rule of law as opposed to a default rule). The bottom line is that most courts view any attempts at opting out skeptically—and thus so should any trustee who thinks he or she is authorized to act inconsistently with the duties set forth in the Prudent Investor Act.

Finally, even to the extent that a settlor might include well-drafted and precise language in the trust opting out of the duty to diversify, there is the theoretical question of whether such intent is compatible with the essence of the modern trust. Just as with a beneficiary's discretionary interest in a trust, granting a trustee "sole and absolute" discretion is unenforceable because it is inherently inconsistent with the trustee's fiduciary duties, there appears to be growing support for a similar approach to trust terms that purport to grant a trustee "absolute" or "complete" discretion with respect to trust investments. As the court said in *Estate of Collins*: "the 'absolute discretion' is 'specifically limited' by the requirement that the trustee is 'subject always to the discharge of its fiduciary obligations,....'" Even assuming, *arguendo*, that a settlor expressly authorizes retention of inception assets that otherwise would violate the trustee's duty to diversify, while the trustee might be relieved of his or her immediate duty to diversify, just as a trustee who delegates the investment decisions still has an ongoing duty to monitor the agent's actions, a trustee who is relieved of the duty to immediately diversify still has an ongoing duty to monitor the situation. Any meaningful change in the property, the market, and/or the beneficiaries might reinstitute the duty under the trustee's more general and ongoing fiduciary obligations to do everything in the beneficiaries' best interests.

2. *Standard of care and expertise*: The general rule is that in administering a trust, a trustee is to "exercise such care and skill as a man of ordinary prudence would exercise in dealing with his own property...." RESTATEMENT (SECOND) OF TRUSTS § 174. Historically, an issue that some courts have struggled with is whether all trustees are subject to the same standard of care or whether trustees who hold themselves out as having special skills or expertise (i.e., a professional trustee) should be held to a higher standard of care (i.e., to the conduct of a reasonably prudent expert/professional trustee)? The RESTATEMENT (SECOND) OF TRUSTS expressly addressed the issue:

> The trustee is under a duty to the beneficiary in administering the trust to exercise such care and skill as a man of ordinary prudence would exercise in

dealing with his own property; and if the trustee has or procures his appointment as trustee by representing that he has greater skill than that of a man of ordinary prudence, he is under a duty to exercise such skill.

RESTATEMENT (SECOND) OF TRUSTS § 174. The modern trend is to hold a skilled/professional trustee to the higher standard, often even if the trustee did *not* "procure his appointment … by representing that he has greater skill than that of a man of ordinary prudence."

California Probate Code Section 16014 expressly addresses the issue of the standard of care to which a skilled/professional trustee is held:

CPC § 16014. Trustee's skills

   (a) The trustee has a duty to apply the full extent of the trustee's skills.

   (b) If the settlor, in selecting the trustee, has relied on the trustee's representation of having special skills, the trustee is held to the standard of the skills represented.

Has California adopted the RESTATEMENT (SECOND) approach or the modern trend approach?

3. *Duty to delegate?* An interesting question that arises under the Uniform Prudent Investor Act is whether a trustee of ordinary skill may have a duty to delegate the investment decisions to a person of greater skill. The language in the Act is more permissive than mandatory: "A trustee *may delegate* investment and management functions that a prudent trustee of comparable skills could properly delegate under the circumstances." UNIFORM PRUDENT INVESTOR ACT § 9(a) (emphasis added). Nevertheless, permitting a trustee to delegate investment decisions is such a radical departure from the traditional non-delegation approach that one cannot help but wonder if unsophisticated trustees do not have something of a de facto duty to delegate — at least if the trust assets warrant it (due to their size and/or complexity). Is that not what "a prudent trustee of comparable skills … [would do] under the circumstances?" *Id.* At a minimum, an unsophisticated trustee should think long and hard about *not* delegating the investment decisions under the prudent investor approach.

Problems

1.   Settlor created a revocable trust and conveyed approximately 1,541 shares of Enron Corporation stock to the trust. Thereafter, in 1991, she delivered a letter to the trustee (Bank of America), that directed it to retain the Enron stock. The letter went on to state: "*I hereby agree to exonerate, indemnify and hold the Bank harmless from any and all loss, damage and expense sustained or incurred by the Bank for continuing to retain these securities as assets of this account. I also relieve the Bank from any responsibility for analyzing or monitoring these securities in any way.*"

   From 1991 to 2000 the number of Enron shares in the trust increased from 1,541 to 9,500 (due to stock splits), and the value of the shares relative to the trust's overall value increased to $789,687.50 (77% of the total value of the trust assets). But what goes up must come down. The value of Enron stock proved the wisdom inherent in that old adage. "Because of declines in Enron stock value, by March 30, 2001, the shares amounted to approximately 66% of the total market value of the trust; by June 29, 2001, approximately 64%; by September 28, 2001, approximately 50%; and by December 31, 2001, approximately 2%. By the latter date, the trust contained 8,000 shares of Enron stock valued at only $4,800."

In 2003, Settlor sued Bank of America for breaching its duties to her under the prudent investor rule.

If Settlor had not written the letter directing Bank of America to retain the Enron stock, would the trustee's conduct have breached the prudent investor rule? Did Settlor's letter completely relieve Bank of America of its duties under the Prudent Investor Act? *See McGinley v. Bank of Am., N.A.,* 109 P.3d 1146 (Kan. 2005).

2. Assuming a guardian managing a ward's estate has the same duty to comply with the prudent investor rule as a trustee managing trust property, how would you analyze the following fact pattern?

    The Liebermans were involved in a serious car accident. The father was killed, and Joseph and Megan, both minors, sustained severe and permanent injuries. Megan received more than $13 million in damages, Joseph $2.5 million. They were also both awarded additional monthly payments to start when they reached the age of majority.

    On November 1, 2002, Northern Trust Co., as guardian for the two children, received $15 million. One year later, Northern Trust's first accounting showed that approximately half of the children's funds remained in the Trust's short-term investment account where the money had generated a one percent return after taxes and guardian fees.

    The Liebermans' co-guardian sued Northern Trust for breach of its investment duties. She argued that if Northern Trust had just invested the funds in the same fixed income investments that it invested the rest of the funds, it would have generated a three percent return. If Northern Trust had invested the money in a simple Dow Jones Industrial Average Mutual Fund, the return would have been more than 18 percent over the same period.

    Has Northern Trust violated its duties under the prudent investor rule? Is it relevant that Northern Trust held itself out as having particular experience and expertise with the investment and management of funds for guardianship estates? Is it relevant that the money-market fund in which Northern Trust held the funds in question is a statutorily permitted investment? *See In re Estate of Lieberman,* 909 N.E.2d 915 (Ill. App. Ct. 2009).

3. Anthony and Lottie Guest executed a family trust in 1997. The trust assets were the family home, a TD Ameritrade brokerage account, and certain personal property items (coins, jewelry). The trust was for their benefit until the death of the survivor, then the property was to be distributed outright 64 percent to their daughter and 36 percent to their grandson (the grandson is disabled and suffers from multiple sclerosis). Following the death of the settlors, the grandson agreed

that his mother should continue to manage his share of the trust, making monthly distributions to him to cover his living expenses.

About a year after the death of the second settlor to die, the daughter, acting as successor trustee, sold the family home and deposited the net proceeds (approximately $600,000) into the TD account. She then invested approximately 97.5% of the funds in the TD account the DWS High Income Series mutual fund (the DWS fund). The DWS fund consisted almost entirely of "junk bonds," which are noninvestment bonds and have ratings identifying them as "vulnerable" to default.

The trust provided in pertinent part that "the Trustees are authorized" to utilize any of the wide variety of traditional investment vehicles, including bonds, that the Trustees "in their discretion may select," and that "the Trustees have full power to invest and reinvest the trust funds without being restricted to forms of investment that the Trustees may otherwise be permitted to make by law." The daughter asserts that these provisions gave her "unbridled discretionary power to invest and distribute the Trust assets as she saw fit[.]"

Has the daughter violated the prudent investor rule? *See Guest v. Frazier*, No. B225938, 2011 WL 986200 (Cal. Ct. App. Mar. 22, 2011).

V. The Ancillary, Administrative Duties

As noted above, the RESTATEMENT (THIRD) OF TRUSTS divides the trustee's duties into two categories: the "core duties" of prudence, loyalty, and impartiality, and then the "ancillary" duties that naturally flow from and support those core duties. *See* RESTATEMENT (THIRD) OF TRUSTS ch. 15, intro. note. The core duties go to the essence of the trust—the bifurcated nature of the trust—and to the difficult decisions a trustee must make in holding and managing the trust property for the trust beneficiaries. On the other hand, the ancillary duties are more administrative and/or ministerial in nature. The ancillary duties flow from the trustee's administrative function as it relates to the bifurcated nature of the trust: (1) the trust property, and (2) the trust beneficiaries.

A. Related to the Trust Property

The trustee's primary job is to hold and manage the trust property for the benefit of the beneficiaries. Obviously prudent administration of the duty to "hold and manage the trust property" inherently includes a number of administrative duties. The trustee's ancillary duties include those administrative duties as they relate to the trust property. All of the duties can be summed up as follows: the trustee has a general duty to take care of the trust property. That phrase, however, is too general to be of much help. The following material will take a quick look at the more important administrative duties as they relate to the trust property.

1. Duty to Collect Trust Property

At first blush, the trustee's duty to collect the trust property sounds inconsistent with the requirement that a settlor fund the trust to create a trust. The funding requirement appears to put the burden on the settlor to transfer the property to the trust, while the duty to collect appears to put the burden on the trustee to go get the trust property. Not too much should be read into the phrasing. If the trust is an *inter vivos* trust, the settlor should deliver the trust property to the trustee. If, however, the trust is a testamentary trust,[5] obviously the settlor cannot deliver the property to the trustee. An agent of some sort (an executor, a personal representative, a life insurance company, a broker, etc.) must deliver the property to the trustee. Where the trustee knows or should know that someone other than the settlor is to deliver the property to the trustee, consistent with the duty of loyalty to the beneficiaries (and to a degree, the duty to act prudently), the trustee has an affirmative duty to take reasonable steps to check on the agent's conduct to ensure that the trust receives what it is legally entitled to receive and that the trust receives it in a timely manner.

Should the duty to collect apply to a successor trustee who is taking over from a prior trustee—i.e., does a successor trustee have a duty to collect the trust property from a prior trustee? *See Moeller v. Superior Court*, 16 Cal. 4th 1124, 1128, 1138 (1997).

Problems

1. An executor has a similar duty to collect the decedent's probate property.

   Charlotte Carr died testate. At the time of her death, Charlotte held a note in the amount of $200 executed by her attorney, who subsequently also served as the attorney for the executor of her estate. The executor allowed the sum to remain in the attorney's hand for some 10 years, at which point the attorney was insolvent and the estate was unable to collect. Is the executor liable to the estate beneficiaries for failure to collect the estate's assets?

2. Decedent's will created a testamentary trust. It was funded with several pieces of property that were currently occupied by tenants under valid leases. Not long after the trust was funded, one tenant refused to pay rent for several months, and another tenant in another building paid only partial rent. The trustee was worried that because of the vacancy rate in the area, it might be difficult to find replacement tenants. Accordingly, the trustee took no action against either tenant. Both properties ultimately fell into the hands of a receiver. When the receiver threatened to evict the tenants in question, both tenants resumed full rental payments. Is the trustee liable for breach of his duty to collect the trust property? *See In re McIntyre*, 48 N.Y.S. 785 (1897).

---

5. Or an *inter vivos* trust, but the trust is also to receive some at-death transfers.

2. Duty to Segregate Trust Property

Once the trust property has been delivered to the trustee, how should the trustee "hold" the property? Is the trustee free to commingle it with his or her own property, or should the trustee keep it separate and distinct from his or her own property?

Matter of Goldstick

581 N.Y.S.2d 165 (1992)

Wallach, Justice.

[The settlor, Martin Tananbaum, a multi-millionaire with interests in taxicab fleets, horse breeding, and a raceway in Yonkers, died in 1970. He established several *inter vivos* trusts and a testamentary trust for the benefit of his daughters Minnie Tananbaum ("Tananbaum") and Barbara DeGeorge ("DeGeorge"). He appointed David T. Goldstick and Florence Levine, co-trustees. In 1989, the co-trustees submitted their final accountings.]

Tananbaum and DeGeorge filed objections to the "accounts," and the trial of the issues as they proliferated consumed about 125 days and generated a 13,000 page transcript. At the conclusion the court imposed surcharges of $8.7 million in favor of the two objectants against the two trustees, and removed the latter from office. They appeal....

. . .

(3) *Surcharge on all profits from commingled real estate investments....*

(a) *The commingled investment (surcharge of $2.6 million, plus interest of approximately $1.4 million).* [Compared to other of his investments,] Goldstick met with greater success in the real estate market. He invested some $181,125 of trust funds in various real estate partnerships in which he already had a substantial interest. These enterprises yielded Goldstick, his co-venturer wife and his corporate alter egos a handsome profit of more than $2½ million. Approximately 14% of the capitalization of those partnerships came from the Tananbaum and DeGeorge trust funds. The court concluded that these huge profits were realized in part from "self-interested dealing" on the part of the trustees. Even though the trust beneficiaries profited from these investments to the extent of $158,544.32, the [trial] court, somewhat exercised over Goldstick's receipt of $2,599,292 in profits and fees from the same investment, surcharged the trustees in the full amount of those receipts....

The first duty of a trustee is that of loyalty to the beneficiaries of his trust (IIA Scott on Trusts, § 170), and he may not jeopardize that duty for his own personal benefit (*id.,* § 170.25). The trustee has a duty to segregate trust property, and should not mingle trust funds with his own (Restatement (Second) of Trusts § 179, comment *b*). Commingling trust funds with a trustee's own funds has been held a breach of trust, although such a rule is more a matter of policy than one of law (see *Matter of Lincoln Rochester Trust Company,* 201 Misc. 1008, 1013, 111 N.Y.S.2d 45). There are circumstances when commingling of the assets of several trusts may be advantageous and thus permissible, such as in consolidating and thus reducing administrative costs. However, in those situations it is incumbent upon the trustee to earmark the funds so they can be traced. A trustee is, of course, liable for dissipating commingled funds through imprudent investment. On the other hand, he is not subject to a surcharge for a breach of trust that results in no loss (III Scott on Trusts § 205).

If a trustee commits a breach of trust that results in a personal gain, he is accountable for that gain. A trustee cannot be permitted to profit through a breach of trust, even though the profit is not made at the expense of the trust estate. If a trustee makes a profit from an improper trust investment, the trust beneficiaries are entitled to that portion of the profit consisting of appreciation of misappropriated property (*Matter of Birnbaum v. Birnbaum,* 157 A.D.2d 177, 555 N.Y.S.2d 982). But where a trustee imprudently mingles his own (and perhaps another trustee's) funds in an investment that yields a profit, assuming the trust portion of the investment can be traced, the trustee should not have to disgorge his own share of those profits. In other words, any surcharge should be based on that portion of the investment identified as emanating from trust funds, rather than on the entire investment (*Provencher v. Berman,* 1st Cir., 699 F.2d 568, 570–571; *Bird v. Stein,* 5th Cir., 258 F.2d 168, 178, cert. denied, 359 U.S. 926, 79 S.Ct. 608, 3 L.Ed.2d 628; Restatement of Restitution § 210[2], and comments *b, d*).

The beneficiaries must, first of all, be able to point to some injury resulting from the improper diversion or commingling of trust assets (*Rogers v. United States,* 9th Cir., 697 F.2d 886). The challenge is in apportioning the trustee's profits between those produced by his own legitimate efforts and those resulting from the use of commingled trust assets; where there has been such a commingling the trustee normally bears the burden of identifying which property and profits should be treated as his own (Leigh v. Engle, 7th Cir., 727 F.2d 113, 138). Rather than basing the surcharge on a return of the profits related to that portion (14%) of the investment emanating from the trust, the court, in its sweeping condemnation, surcharged the trustees for the entire profit of nearly $2.6 million, even though some of that profit was earned by an entity with which Goldstick had no connection. There is no authority for that approach. The surcharge should have been limited to that portion of the profits traceable to assets invested from the trust funds.

We therefore vacate this surcharge and, in light of the necessity for a remand on other matters, also remand this aspect of the case for what may amount simply to a recomputation of the appropriate surcharge in accordance with the foregoing, although the court would be free to permit further proof by the parties in the exercise of sound discretion.

Notes

1. *Traditional approach*: The trial court's ruling, depriving the trustees of all $2.6 million in profits, is more consistent with the traditional approach to a trustee's breach of the duty to segregate. The courts were very strict in their interpretation

and application of the duty to segregate, de facto applying strict liability to any breaches. This approach was primarily intended to deter a trustee who might otherwise be tempted to commingle the trust property with his or her own property (or the property of another trust). The public policy concern underlying commingled funds is that if something happens to some of the property (say some of the investments the trustee has made do well, but some lost money), if the trustee had commingled the trust property with his or her own property, the trustee would have a conflict of interest: the trustee would want to claim that the investments that did well were investments of his or her own property, and that the investments that did poorly were the trust property investments. Analogizing the situation to a trustee's self-dealing, the traditional approach de facto applied the "no further inquiry" rule and either held the trustee strictly liable (in the case of any loss) or held that the trustee had to be disgorged of any profits realized as a result of the breach. Such a strict approach was intended to create a strong incentive for a trustee not to commingle the trust property.

2. *Modern trend approach*: The appellate court's opinion in *Goldstick* is more consistent with the modern trend approach to what constitutes a breach of the trustee's duty to segregate. The modern trend takes more of a negligence approach. The trust beneficiaries must show not only a duty and a breach, they must also show damages and causation.

In addition, as the court notes, the modern trend is not so sure the duty to segregate makes economic sense in all cases. For trustees who hold multiple trust accounts (typically professional and/or institutional trustees), there are economies of scale to permitting such trustees to commingle trust accounts, thereby saving costs of administration for each individual trust. The modern trend permits trustees to combine trust accounts for investment purposes so long as there is proper record keeping to permit each trust's beneficiaries to protect their interest. *See* RESTATEMENT (THIRD) OF TRUSTS § 84 cmt. c (2007); UNIF. TRUST CODE § 810(d). Reducing costs of administration is consistent with the trustee's duty to be prudent in administering the trust.

California's Probate Code provides as follows:

CPC § 16009. Trustee's duty to separate and identify property

The trustee has a duty to do the following:

(a) To keep the trust property separate from other property not subject to the trust.

(b) To see that the trust property is designated as property of the trust.

How would you describe the California approach? Is it more consistent with the traditional approach or the more modern trend approach?

3. Duty to Properly Care for the Trust Property

Once the trustee has possession of the trust property, common sense and the duty to act prudently dictate that the trustee take proper care of the trust property. What constitutes proper care is fact sensitive and depends on the type of property in question (real property versus personal property; tangible property versus intangible property).

Obviously different types of property require different types of care. Real property needs to be maintained—if the property starts to deteriorate, the trustee has a duty to make any necessary repairs. Intangible personal property typically requires less care, but the trustee still needs to exercise whatever care is appropriate relative to the asset. Another important variable is who has possession of the property in question. Sometimes a trust beneficiary has possession of the property in question and that, too, can affect what constitutes taking care of the property.

Because the duty to care for the trust property is more administrative and ministerial in nature, it is not uncommon for a trustee to hire one or more agents to perform the care (i.e., a gardener to cut the grass). Historically, trustees have been permitted to hire agents to take care of the more administrative and ministerial functions related to a trust, but even then the trustee cannot abdicate his or her duties. The trustee is merely delegating his or her ministerial duties. And just as in the case of a trustee who delegates the investment process under the prudent investor rule, a trustee who delegates an administrative duty still has a duty to properly select, supervise, and periodically review the conduct of his or her agents.

Problem

Della created an *inter vivos* trust, funding it with her personal residence and other assets. Upon her death, Bobo became successor trustee. He did not have much experience as a trustee. He failed to make tax and insurance payments on the house, failed to make timely mortgage payments (which resulted in five foreclosure actions against the house, costing the trust $13,000 in foreclosure fees), failed to rent the house in a timely fashion following Della's death, and after he finally rented the house, he deposited some of the rent checks in his personal account. What claims, if any, can the trust beneficiaries bring against Bobo? *See Murray v. Zajic*, No. B203119, 2008 WL 4767354 (Cal. Ct. App. Nov. 3, 2008).

B. Related to the Trust Beneficiaries

Most of the administrative duties a trustee owes to the trust beneficiaries concern one central issue: how much information, if any, does a trustee have a duty to share with the trust beneficiaries? This issue relates to one of the central issues concerning a trust: who really owns the property in the trust? One of the central features of a trust is related to these questions. Many settlors use a trust because of the privacy it provides; it is a confidential document. Unlike a will, which is probated upon the testator's death and thus becomes a public document for all to see if they wish, an *inter vivos* trust is a private document. It is not probated. As a general rule, there is no reason the document should ever be made public. For the most part, the settlor can keep private who takes under the trust and how much each beneficiary takes.[6]

---

6. *See* Chapter 11 for "privacy related" matters for a revocable living trust and why it is common to have an *abstract of trust* prepared as a separate document so as to minimize incidents of disclosure.

But how far should/does that principle extend? Can the settlor keep it confidential from the beneficiaries themselves? To what extent should the beneficiaries have a right to see the terms of the trust? To what extent should the trust beneficiaries be entitled to know what is the scope of the trust property and what the trustee is doing with the trust property? Who really owns the property in the trust?

1. Duty to Inform Party of Beneficiary Status

The first of the sub-duties related to the duty to inform is the most logical. Consistent with the duty of loyalty, a trustee has a duty to promptly inform all parties who have an interest or a potential interest in a trust of their status as a beneficiary under the trust. BOGERT'S TRUSTS AND TRUSTEES § 962, *Duty to furnish information and permit inspection* (2014). The modern trend agrees, but tries to limit the administrative burden and costs on the trustee by limiting the duty to those beneficiaries who are "fairly representative" as opposed to all beneficiaries. *See* RESTATEMENT (THIRD) OF TRUSTS § 82(1)(a). The notice should include not only their status as a beneficiary, but also their basic rights with respect to the administration of the trust and their rights to further information. *Id.* California Probate Code Section 16060 puts it rather succinctly: "The trustee has a duty to keep the beneficiaries of the trust reasonably informed of the trust and its administration."

2. Duty to Disclose Terms of the Trust

One of the reasons a settlor opts for a trust over a will is that the latter is a public document while the former is a private document. Some individuals would prefer to keep confidential who gets their property when they die—both from the public and from the takers. On the other hand, a trustee owes a fiduciary duty to each trust beneficiary. How is a beneficiary to enforce the duty if the beneficiary does not know the terms of the trust? Should a trust beneficiary have: (a) no access to the terms of the trust, (b) access only to the parts of the trust relevant to his or her interest in the trust, or (c) access to the whole trust instrument?

Fletcher v. Fletcher
480 S.E.2d 488 (Va. 1997)

COMPTON, Justice.

In this chancery proceeding arising from a dispute over an inter vivos trust, we consider the extent of a trustee's duty to furnish information about the trust instrument and about other documents relating to the trust.

... During their lifetimes, J. North Fletcher and Elinor Leh Fletcher, his wife, residents of Fauquier County, accumulated substantial assets.

Following Mr. Fletcher's death in 1984, Mrs. Fletcher executed a revocable, inter vivos "Trust Agreement" in December 1985 in which she placed all her assets. The ten-page document, containing nine articles, named her as both "Grantor" and "Trustee." In August 1993, the Grantor modified the Trust Agreement by executing a "Trust Agreement Amendment." The five-page Amendment replaced Article Six of the Trust Agreement with a new Article Six.

The Trust Agreement as amended (the Trust Agreement) contains, among other things, specific provisions for the establishment of a number of trusts upon the Grantor's death, including three separate trusts for the respective benefit of appellee James N. Fletcher, Jr., an adult child of the Grantor, and his two children, Andrew N. Fletcher, born in 1972, and Emily E. Fletcher, born in 1976 (sometimes collectively, the beneficiaries). The three separate trusts were to be in the amount of $50,000 each. The Trust Agreement appointed appellant Henry L. Fletcher, another adult child of the Grantor, and appellant F & M Bank-Peoples Trust and Asset Management Group, formerly Peoples National Bank of Warrenton, as successor Trustees to act upon the Grantor's death.

Under the Trust Agreement, the Trustees are authorized, in their discretion, to expend for the benefit of James N. Fletcher, Jr., such amounts of the net income and principal of the $50,000 trust as may be necessary to provide him adequate medical insurance and medical care during his lifetime, or until such time as the trust is depleted. In the event the trust is still in existence at Fletcher's death, then the Trustees are required to transfer and pay over to his surviving children his or her proportionate share of the balance of the remaining principal and income.

. . .

The Grantor died in June 1994. Upon her death, the Trust Agreement became irrevocable, and the successor Trustees assumed their duties. They established the three $50,000 trusts, and the beneficiaries have benefited from them.

In June 1995, beneficiary James N. Fletcher, Jr., instituted the present proceeding against the Trustees....

The plaintiff ... asserted that he "requested details from the defendants of both the December 3, 1985 trust and the trust created with the assets of that trust upon his mother's death," and that the Trustees have refused to comply with his request. He further asserted that he has been provided with only pages 1, 8 and 9 of the 1985 instrument and "two pages" from the Amendment. The plaintiff also asserted that "[w]ithout a listing of the precise terms of both trust agreements or a complete listing of the assets of these trusts," he is "unable to determine whether or not the trust estate is being properly protected."

Plaintiff also alleged that Trustee Henry L. Fletcher "has repeatedly made a point of justifying his failure to disclose the requested information ... by stating that it was his mother's request that the trust terms and dealings be kept confidential, even from the beneficiaries." Further, the plaintiff asserts that Trustee Fletcher "has failed to produce any written direction from [their mother] with respect to the confidentiality." This situation, along with other facts, according to the allegations, has resulted in "an extremely strained relationship between" the brothers.

Concluding, the plaintiff alleged that because he lacks the "relevant information" sought, "he is unable to determine whether or not either trustee is properly performing their duties as a trustee[ ] according to law." Thus, he asked the court to compel the Trustees "to provide full and complete copies of all trust instruments in their possession that relate to the two trusts referred to herein."

In a demurrer, the Trustees asserted that the bill of complaint failed to state a cause of action. In an answer, the Trustees denied that any "new trust" was created upon the Grantor's death, and asserted that the Trust Agreement remained in effect following the death. The Trustees asserted, however, that upon the death, "separate trusts were created under the express terms of the Trust Agreement," and that the plaintiff has been provided with "all provisions of the Trust Agreement relating to him and his children, along with regular accountings relating to his interest under the Trust Agreement." In sum, the Trustees denied the plaintiff is entitled to the information sought.

. . .

Subsequently, the trial court heard argument on the demurrer and, during the hearing, ruled that the plaintiff was entitled to see all provisions of the Trust Agreement. The court noted that the plaintiff's "interests as a child of" the Grantor and as "a beneficiary of her trust outweighed the arguments advanced" by the Trustees.

. . .

The Trustees contend the trial court erred in finding that the plaintiff had an absolute right to review complete copies of the Trust Agreement and in ordering them to provide plaintiff with such copies. Emphasizing that the trust instrument established three separate trusts, the Trustees argue the trial court's order "ignores the fiduciary duty of confidentiality between the Trustees and other beneficiaries under the ... Trust Agreement." Noting the use of revocable trusts in planning disposition of assets upon death, the Trustees say that following a grantor's death, "the trustees handle the trust assets for the various beneficiaries, in accordance with the grantor's instruction, in a manner appropriate for each beneficiary taking into account the unique circumstances applicable to each beneficiary."

Continuing, the Trustees observe that a grantor, as here, often "directs the trustee to segregate trust assets into separate trusts for the benefit of different beneficiaries." *See* Code § 55-19.3 (trustee may divide a trust into two or more separate trusts). According to the Trustees, "Segregation of a trust into separate trusts for different beneficiaries not only segregates the assets, but also segregates the trustee's duties to the different beneficiaries." The Trustees say that a "trustee has a continuing duty to the grantor to fulfill the trustee's obligations under the trust agreement. The trustee also has a fiduciary duty to the beneficiaries of each trust established under the agreement. The trustee's duties to the beneficiaries of each separate trust do not overlap."

The Trustees point out the plaintiff has not alleged any wrongdoing on their part "nor has he alleged that he has any interest under the ... Trust Agreement other than his interest in a separate trust established for his benefit." The Trustees state they have provided the plaintiff with copies of the portions of the Trust Agreement that pertain to the establishment and administration of the separate trusts, have submitted a copy of the Trust Agreement to the trial judge so the court may determine whether they have disclosed to the plaintiff all relevant information, and have provided regular accountings to the beneficiaries with respect to their separate trusts. The Trustees argue that the family relationship and the "specter" of disharmony, standing alone do not create a right in the plaintiff to compel disclosure. Finally, the Trustees argue "the trial court's Order compelling disclosure violates the public policy that permits individuals to ensure privacy of their affairs through the use of inter vivos trust agreements in lieu of wills."

. . .

This is a case of first impression in Virginia. The parties have not referred us to any cases elsewhere that are factually apposite, and we have found none. Nevertheless, text writers and the Restatement articulate settled principles that are applicable.

"The beneficiary is the equitable owner of trust property, in whole or in part. The trustee is a mere representative whose function is to attend to the safety of the trust property and to obtain its avails for the beneficiary in the manner provided by the trust instrument." Bogert, *The Law of Trusts and Trustees* § 961, at 2 (Rev. 2nd ed.1983). *See Shriners Hospitals for Crippled Children v. Smith,* 238 Va. 708, 710, 385 S.E.2d 617, 618 (1989) (trustee should preserve and protect trust fund for benefit of all interested in its distribution). *See also Rowland v. Kable,* 174 Va. 343, 367, 6 S.E.2d 633, 642 (1940) (trustee owes undivided duty to beneficiary). The fact that a grantor has created a trust and thus required the beneficiary to enjoy the property interest indirectly "does not imply that the beneficiary is to be kept in ignorance of the trust, the nature of the trust property and the details of its administration." Bogert, § 961, at 2.

Therefore, "[t]he trustee is under a duty to the beneficiary to give him upon his request at reasonable times complete and accurate information as to the nature and amount of the trust property, and to permit him or a person duly authorized by him to inspect the subject matter of the trust and the accounts and vouchers and other documents relating to the trust." *Restatement (Second) of Trusts* § 173 (1959). *Accord* Bogert, § 961, at 3–4; IIA Scott, *The Law of Trusts* § 173, at 462 (4th ed.1987). Indeed, "[w]here a trust is created for several beneficiaries, each of them is entitled to information as to the trust." Scott, § 173, at 464.

And, even though "the terms of the trust may regulate the amount of information which the trustee must give and the frequency with which it must be given, the beneficiary is always entitled to such information as is reasonably necessary to enable him to enforce his rights under the trust or to prevent or redress a breach of trust." *Restatement* § 173 cmt. c. *See In re Estate of Rosenblum,* 459 Pa. 201, 328 A.2d 158, 164–65 (1974).

Turning to the present facts, we observe that the appellate record fails to establish that the Grantor directed the Trustees not to disclose the terms of the entire Trust Agreement to the beneficiaries. The trust instrument, which we have examined, does not mention the subject. Although the Trustees assert the Grantor orally gave such instructions, the plaintiff questions this fact. And, there was no evidentiary hearing below to decide the matter. Thus, we express no opinion on what effect any directive of secrecy by the Grantor would have on the outcome of this case.

Recognizing the foregoing general principles of the law of trusts, the Trustees nevertheless seek to remove this case from the force of those rules by dwelling on the fact that three separate trusts were created. In essence, the Trustees treat this single integrated Trust Agreement as if there are three distinct trust documents, each entirely independent of the other, a circumstance that simply does not exist.

There is a single cohesive trust instrument based on a unitary corpus. The Trustees seek to avoid the beneficiary's scrutiny of eight pages of the Trust Agreement. They also seek to prevent review of Schedule "A," which lists the cash and securities the Grantor transferred to the trust corpus. This document was not even included in the sealed papers filed with the trial court.

The information not disclosed may have a material bearing on the administration of the Trust Agreement insofar as the beneficiary is concerned. For example, without access to the Trust Agreement (even though there are numerous separate trusts established), the beneficiary has no basis upon which he can intelligently scrutinize the Trustees' investment decisions made with respect to the assets revealed on Schedule "A." The beneficiary is unable to evaluate whether the Trustees are discharging their duty to use "reasonable care and skill to make the trust property productive." *Sturgis v. Stinson,* 241 Va. 531, 535, 404 S.E.2d 56, 58 (1991) (quoting *Restatement (Second) of Trusts* § 181 (1959)). Also, the beneficiary is entitled to review the trust documents in their entirety in order to assure the Trustees are discharging their "duty to deal impartially" with all the beneficiaries within the restrictions and conditions imposed by the Trust Agreement. *Sturgis,* 241 Va. at 534–35, 404 S.E.2d at 58.

In sum, we hold that the trial court correctly required the Trustees to disclose the information sought. Thus, the judgment appealed from will be

Affirmed.

Notes

1. *Split of authority*: There is general agreement that a trust beneficiary is entitled to see the terms of the trust so as to be able to ascertain (1) the extent of his or her interest in the trust and (2) whether the trustee has breached any duty to the beneficiary. The courts and uniform laws disagree, however, over *how much* of the trust instrument that entitles the beneficiary to see. The Uniform Probate Code takes more of a traditional view of the issue. The traditional view arguably favors the view that the settlor owns the property in the trust. The Uniform Probate Code expressly provides that a trust beneficiary is entitled to see only "the terms of the trust *which describe or affect his interest* and with relevant information about the assets of the trust and the particulars relating to the administration." *See* UPC § 7-303(b).

In contrast, the Uniform Trust Code takes more of a modern trend approach to the issue. The modern trend favors the view that the beneficiaries own the property in the trust. The modern trend expressly provides that a beneficiary who requests a copy of the trust instrument is entitled to see the entire trust instrument. UTC §813(b)(1).

2. *California approach*: California adopts more of a modern trend approach to the issue. If a beneficiary requests to see "a true and complete copy of the" terms of an irrevocable trust, the general rule in California is that the beneficiary is entitled to the whole document. *See* CPC §16061.5. If, however, the trust is revocable, the trustee's sole duty is to the party holding the power to revoke (typically the settlor), and so a trust beneficiary is not entitled to see any part of the trust until it becomes irrevocable. *See* CPC §16069(a). The material explores this point in more detail in Section V below.

3. *Default rule versus rule of law*: In *Fletcher*, the Virginia Supreme Court expressly noted that it was not addressing the issue of whether a settlor can expressly opt out of a beneficiary's right to see the terms of the trust. Is the beneficiary's right to see the terms of a trust a default rule that a settlor can expressly opt out of, or should it be a rule of law that a beneficiary has an absolute right to insist on? If a beneficiary cannot see the terms of the trust and/or the trustee's records with respect to the administration of the trust, how is a trust beneficiary supposed to protect his or her interest in the trust? *See* CPC §16068.

3. Duty to Account for Trust's Administration

To the extent the trustee's job is to hold and manage the trust property for the benefit of the trust beneficiaries, to what extent are the trust beneficiaries entitled to information about *how* the trustee is holding and managing the trust property? Should the trustee have an affirmative duty to inform the trust beneficiaries of how the trust is doing, or should the presumption be that the trustee is doing his or her job and, absent good cause, the trustee should have no duty to account to the trust beneficiaries?

Cook v. Brateng

262 P.3d 1228 (Wash. Ct. App. 2010)

BRIDGEWATER, P.J.

. . .

FACTS

¶ 2 The following facts are undisputed. Diane and John [Brateng] are siblings. In November 1995, their father, Elmer [Brateng], executed a living trust, naming himself and Diane as trustees. Elmer's health deteriorated; two years later, in November 1997, he was declared incompetent, and Diane became sole trustee of his trust.

¶ 3 With Elmer declared incompetent, the trust required Diane, the sole remaining trustee, to apply all trust property exclusively for Elmer's benefit. Specifically, the trust required Diane to "provide as much of the principal and net income of [the] trust as is necessary or advisable, in [Diane's] sole and absolute discretion, for my health, support, maintenance, and general welfare." CP at 36. The trust also required Diane to make information available to the beneficiaries:

> My trustee shall report, at least semiannually, to the beneficiaries then eligible to receive mandatory or discretionary distributions of the net income from the various trusts created in this agreement all of the receipts, disbursements, and distributions occurring during the reporting period along with a complete statement of the trust property.

CP at 60. Upon Elmer's death, the trust directed Diane, as the trustee, to divide all remaining trust property among herself, John, the Salvation Army, and the Finnish Assembly of God Church. The trust allocated to each Diane and John a 9/20th share and to each charity a 1/20th share. The trust also directed Diane to distribute the home to herself, "AS PART OF, AND NOT IN ADDITION TO, that share of [the] trust distributed to [Diane]." CP at 46.

¶ 4 In November 1997, after Elmer was declared incompetent, Diane decided to move Elmer from his home in Ilwaco, Washington, into her home in Kirkland, Washington, where she could more easily care for him. Elmer died in January 2000.

¶ 5 During the time Diane cared for Elmer from November 1997 to January 2000, she used $59,176.673 from the trust's liquid funds to pay for Elmer's medical expenses and personal expenses, as well as maintaining, repairing, and remodeling the Ilwaco home. Diane spent $20,319.75 of the trust funds to repair water damage to the Ilwaco home and to remodel its kitchen. At the time of Elmer's death, the trust had $16,439.62 in liquid funds remaining. The only other remaining trust asset was Elmer's Ilwaco home.

¶ 6 Diane kept meticulous records of her time and expenses related to caring for Elmer and her time and expenses related to driving from Kirkland to Ilwaco. She carefully recorded her time spent caring for him from 1996 to 1997—before she moved him to Kirkland—and she recorded her time spent caring for him while he lived with her in Kirkland as "24 hour In-home Care." Ex. 26. She also kept track of the fuel used to drive to Ilwaco, her meals along the way, and the cost per mile. Finally, she recorded bills that she personally paid for Elmer, recording the exact amount and method of payment. Diane's claim against the estate for acting as Elmer's care giver totaled $142,171.10.

¶ 7 Although Diane kept these meticulous records, she did not disclose her intention to claim reimbursement to John until he filed suit and requested an accounting. Before Elmer's death, Diane never discussed with John her expenses as a care giver, the value of her services as a care giver, or her decision not to encumber Elmer's Ilwaco house to pay for his care.

¶ 8 John filed suit against Diane in October 2001, which led to mediation and arbitration under the "Trust and Estate Dispute Resolution Act". John appealed the arbitrator's decision and requested a trial de novo. The trial court issued a memorandum opinion on June 20, 2008, followed by findings of fact and conclusions of law on May 26, 2009.

¶ 9 The trial court concluded that Diane, as trustee of her father's estate, had a duty to inform John that (1) she decided to claim and defer charges against Elmer's estate for providing Elmer's care, and (2) she decided not to encumber Elmer's Ilwaco house to pay for Elmer's care. The court further concluded that she breached her fiduciary duties and, thus, could not compensate herself for providing Elmer's care. The trial court awarded the Ilwaco house to Diane, but gave John a 9/20th interest in its 2007 appraised value. The court also awarded Diane a credit for one-half the value of a property adjacent to the Ilwaco house that is not part of this appeal.6 Finally, the court awarded John all of his requested fees, totaling $24,425, and awarded Diane one-half of her requested fees, or $12,358.17. The net result of the trial court's decision resulted in a $20,716.83 lien in favor of John.

ANALYSIS

I. Duty to Inform

¶ 10 Diane argues that she did not have a duty to inform John that she was claiming and deferring her charges for providing Elmer's care until his death because neither the trust nor the applicable statutes required her to provide her brother with accounting statements. She also argues, for the same reason, that she did not have a duty to inform John that she decided to refrain from encumbering the Ilwaco house to pay for Elmer's health costs. We agree.

¶ 11 A trustee, as a fiduciary, owes beneficiaries the "highest degree of good faith, care, loyalty and integrity." *Esmieu v. Schrag,* 88 Wash.2d 490, 498, 563 P.2d 203 (1977). "It is the duty of a trustee to administer the trust in the interest of the beneficiaries." *Tucker v. Brown,* 20 Wash.2d 740, 768, 150 P.2d 604 (1944). A trustee's duties and powers are determined by the terms of the trust, by common law, and by statute. *In re Estate of Ehlers,* 80 Wash.App. 751, 757, 911 P.2d 1017 (1996). At common law, Washington courts have defined a trustee's duty of care, skill and diligence to be that degree of care, skill and diligence that an ordinary prudent man exercises in similar affairs. *In re Nontestamentary Trust of Parks,* 39 Wash.2d 763, 767, 238 P.2d 1205 (1951); *Monroe v. Winn,* 16 Wash.2d 497, 508, 133 P.2d 952 (1943).

¶ 12 Diane first contends that the trust did not require her to provide John with an accounting during Elmer's life. Without any analysis, she cites the following language of the trust to support her contention:

> My Trustee shall report, at least semiannually, to the beneficiaries *then eligible to receive mandatory or discretionary distributions* of the net income from the various trusts created in this agreement all of the receipts, disbursements, and distributions occurring during the reporting period along with a complete statement of the trust property.

CP at 60 (emphasis added); Br. of Appellant at 14. The crux of her argument is that the trust language does not require Diane to provide John with an accounting because he was not "eligible" as a remainder beneficiary to receive distributions. CP at 60.

¶ 13 We ascertain a settlor's intent and purpose from the four corners of the trust instrument, construing all of its provisions together. *Templeton v. Peoples Nat'l Bank,* 106 Wash.2d 304, 309, 722 P.2d 63 (1986). Here, Diane had sole and absolute discretion to use the trust assets to provide for Elmer if he was incapacitated, as article four, section 3 of the trust stated:

> My Trustee shall provide as much of the principal and net income of my trust as is necessary or advisable, in its sole and absolute discretion, for my health, support, maintenance, and general welfare.

CP at 36. Only the trust property not distributed to Elmer during his lifetime was to be divided between Diane and John as beneficiaries. Neither Diane nor John was eligible to receive their distributions during Elmer's lifetime, as the clear intent of the trust instrument was to provide for his needs. Therefore, any mandatory accounting was primarily intended to benefit Elmer, as the sole income beneficiary; we agree with Diane that the trust did not *require* her to report receipts, disbursements, and distributions to John while Elmer was still living. The trust required Diane to provide Elmer, as the sole income beneficiary, with an accounting only upon distribution. John does not argue that Diane failed to report to Elmer.

¶ 14 Diane also correctly notes that the law did not *require* her to provide John with an accounting. Under RCW 11.106.020, a trustee must provide at least an annual accounting to "each adult income trust beneficiary ... of all current receipts and disbursements." In contrast, any beneficiary, including one holding only a present interest in the remainder of a trust, may petition the court for an accounting. RCW 11.106.040; *see Nelsen v. Griffiths,* 21 Wash.App. 489, 493, 585 P.2d 840 (1978). Lastly, a trustee has a common law duty to give a beneficiary, upon his reasonable request, complete and accurate information about the nature and amount of trust property. *Tucker,* 20 Wash.2d at 769, 150 P.2d 604. Here, because John was not an income beneficiary, RCW 11.106.020 did not compel Diane to provide him with an accounting. Because John never petitioned the court for an accounting, RCW 11.106.040 did not compel Diane to provide an accounting. And, finally, because John never requested an accounting from Diane, she did not have a common law duty to provide him with such accounting.

¶ 15 But determining that Diane was not required to provide an accounting is not dispositive of John's issues because a mandatory accounting would not have disclosed Diane's decision to defer charges and to refrain from encumbering the Ilwaco house during her father's lifetime. Here, any accounting would have revealed only those receipts and disbursements actually made. RCW 11.106.020. The plain language definition of these terms suggests that a trustee need only provide an accounting for transactions actually paid from the trust. Future contemplated transactions that have not yet occurred would not be shown on an accounting. Thus, because mandatory accounting would not have disclosed Diane's decisions to defer payment for her services rendered on her father's behalf, we turn to the more general question of whether Diane had a duty to inform John of how she was managing the costs associated with Elmer's care.

¶ 16 A trustee's duty "includes the responsibility to inform the beneficiaries fully of all facts which would aid them in protecting their interests." *Allard v. Pac. Nat'l Bank*, 99 Wash.2d 394, 404, 663 P.2d 104 (1983) (citing *Esmieu*, 88 Wash.2d at 498, 563 P.2d 203). "That the settlor has created a trust and thus required the beneficiaries to enjoy their property interests indirectly does not imply the beneficiaries are to be kept in ignorance of the trust, the nature of the trust property, and the details of its administration." *Allard*, 99 Wash.2d at 404, 663 P.2d 104. A trustee's duty includes the responsibility to inform the beneficiaries periodically of the status of the trust, its property, and how the property is being managed. *Allard*, 99 Wash.2d at 404, 663 P.2d 104. "If the beneficiaries are able to hold the trustee to proper standards of care and honesty and procure the benefits to which they are entitled, they must know of what the trust property consists and how it is being managed." *Allard*, 99 Wash.2d at 404, 663 P.2d 104.

¶ 17 *Allard* holds that a trustee has a duty to inform beneficiaries about management of the trust that significantly affects their interest or, put differently, that a trustee breaches its duty to inform when it withholds information that would prejudice the beneficiaries. *Allard*, 99 Wash.2d at 404–05, 663 P.2d 104. In *Allard*, Pacific Bank held in trust for certain beneficiaries a quarter block of property in downtown Seattle. *Allard*, 99 Wash.2d at 396, 663 P.2d 104. The property was the sole trust asset. *Allard*, 99 Wash.2d at 396, 663 P.2d 104. Under the trust provisions, Pacific Bank had full power to manage trust assets according to the judgment and care that "prudent men exercise in the management of their own affairs." *Allard*, 99 Wash.2d at 396, 663 P.2d 104. In 1978, Pacific Bank sold the downtown property before informing the beneficiaries of the sale more than a month later. *Allard*, 99 Wash.2d at 397, 663 P.2d 104.

¶ 18 The beneficiaries brought suit against Pacific Bank for breach of its fiduciary duties, arguing on appeal that Pacific Bank had a duty to inform them before selling the property. *Allard*, 99 Wash.2d at 401, 663 P.2d 104. Our Supreme Court agreed with the beneficiaries and held that Pacific Bank had a duty to inform them of the sale. *Allard*, 99 Wash.2d at 405, 663 P.2d 104. The court reasoned that, although Pacific Bank could manage trust assets without seeking the beneficiaries' consent, and although the trust provisions required Pacific Bank to furnish only an annual statement for the prior year's investments, Pacific Bank, as part of its fiduciary duties, had to inform the beneficiaries of all material facts of the downtown Seattle property transaction before the sale because such a sale was a nonroutine transaction that significantly affected the trust estate and the beneficiaries' interests. *Allard*, 99 Wash.2d at 403–05, 663 P.2d 104; *cf. In re Estate of Ehlers*, 80 Wash.App. 751, 758–59, 911 P.2d 1017 (1996) (holding that a trustee does not breach her duty of care in failing to provide timely mandatory accounting when the trustee eventually provides accounting and the untimeliness does not cause any loss to any beneficiary).

¶ 19 Here, Diane had a duty to inform John about matters that would significantly affect his interests. But unlike in *Allard*, in which selling the only trust asset significantly affected the beneficiaries' interest, providing Elmer's care was a routine practice to fulfill the trust's primary purpose, which, therefore, did not significantly affect John's remainder interest. In fact, the trust specifically gave Diane authority to "provide as much of the principal and net income of my trust as is necessary or advisable, in [her] sole and absolute discretion, for my health, support, maintenance, and general welfare." CP at 36. John could also reasonably expect that his ailing father, declared incompetent by two physicians and aged 95 at the time of his death, would require full-time care, which care could consume substantial portions, if not all, of the trust's assets.

¶ 20 Because the trust clearly provided for Diane to spend any amount of trust assets to care for Elmer, John suffered no loss whether Diane planned to defer the costs and compensate herself in the future or hire a care giver who she paid during Elmer's lifetime; he could reasonably expect those types of expenses on behalf of his incompetent and dependent father and he knew that the trust provided that Diane could pay for those expenses in her sole discretion. We hold that Diane had a duty to inform John about significant matters that affected his beneficial interest in the estate assets but that she did not breach her fiduciary duty in failing to inform John about how she was managing the routine expenses associated with Elmer's care, as John was not prejudiced by her conduct. Nor did Diane breach her duty to inform John of her management of the Ilwaco property when, without telling John, she decided not to encumber the Ilwaco house for the cost of their father's care.

¶ 21 The trust divided the remaining estate assets equally to Diane and John in 9/20th shares, with the Ilwaco home left to Diane "*as part of, and not in addition to*" her 9/20th share. CP at 46 (emphasis added) (capitalization omitted). If the value of the house exceeded Diane's 9/20th share of the remaining estate, Diane had the option of purchasing the house for any amount of value exceeding her 9/20th share of the entire estate, in effect, giving John cash payment for his interest in the estate. If Diane declined to purchase the house, the property would pass as if Elmer had died intestate.

¶ 22 It is inconsequential whether Diane took the money from the trust during her father's lifetime and encumbered the house at that time to pay herself or whether she deferred her claim for reimbursement and refrained from encumbering the house. Diane and John each had a remainder interest in the estate. If Elmer's needs during his lifetime exceeded the trust's liquid funds, Diane would necessarily have had to encumber the Ilwaco home to pay his additional expenses. If the liquid trust funds were depleted, John and Diane would be entitled to a 9/20th share of the remainder of their father's estate, here, the Ilwaco house, and Diane could purchase the house and pay John his 9/20th interest. Thus, depleting the trust's liquid funds during her father's lifetime or delaying her payment until after his death did not change the fact that, with those funds depleted, Diane would have only the option to purchase the house.

¶ 23 Further indication that John did not suffer any prejudice is that he failed to object to Diane's decisions at any point before Elmer's death, even though he had reason to know that she was maintaining the Ilwaco home, that she was Elmer's care giver, and that she would charge the estate for her care giving. John lived on property adjoining Elmer's Ilwaco home and saw Elmer visit when Diane took him there.

Diane also generally maintained the Ilwaco home and undertook repairs for water damage.

¶ 24 John also was on inquiry notice that Diane would charge the estate for caring for Elmer, as she had absolute authority to pay for his "health, support, maintenance, and general welfare." CP at 36. The trust had paid a nurse to care for Elmer before Diane took him into her home and care. When Diane started caring for him, it was certainly foreseeable that she would reasonably charge for the personal services she rendered. But John never took care of his father and never inquired about whether Diane was going to charge the estate for her care. John's failure to object, even though he had reason to know that Diane was caring for Elmer and that she would reasonably charge the estate for her services, belies his assertion now that he suffered harm as a result of her decisions.

¶ 25 We hold that Diane did not have a duty to inform John that she decided to claim and defer charges against Elmer's estate. Nor did she owe him a duty to inform him that she decided to refrain from encumbering the Ilwaco home to pay for Elmer's care.

...

Notes

1. *Duty to keep complete and accurate accounts*: Consistent with the duty of loyalty and the duty to act prudently, a trustee has a duty to maintain complete and accurate records of all of his or her activities with respect to collecting, holding, and managing the trust property. A trustee should be able to account for any and all of his or her actions and decisions.

2. *Duty to account—affirmative or responsive duty?* The nature of the trustee's duty to account has changed over time. Historically, trustees were more likely to account to a court than to a beneficiary. Testamentary trusts were subject to probate court supervision for the life of the trust, and the trustee had a duty to account, at designated intervals, to the probate court. In addition, in some states the trustee of an *inter vivos* trust likewise had a duty to account to the appropriate court at designated intervals. Thus, as a general rule, a trustee had no affirmative duty to account to a beneficiary. *See* RESTATEMENT (FIRST) OF TRUSTS § 172 cmt. c (1935). Under this more traditional approach, however, if a beneficiary requested an accounting, then the general rule was that a trustee had to account to the beneficiary (but even then, in some jurisdictions the beneficiary had to institute a judicial proceeding and convince a court that an accounting was warranted).

The modern trend has been to "privatize" the supervision of trustees. Increasingly the courts have gotten out of the "trust supervision" business. The law has shifted the burden of supervising a trustee to the trust beneficiaries. Concomitant with that shift in burden, the law has granted beneficiaries greater rights with respect to an accounting. If a beneficiary requests an accounting, the beneficiary is entitled to an accounting. Moreover, even in the absence of a request from a beneficiary, as the court's opinion in *Allard* evidences, the modern trend is to impose an affirmative duty on the trustee to inform the trust beneficiaries of any "nonroutine transaction that significantly affects the trust estate and the beneficiaries' interests." The duty to account is no longer purely ex post reactive. It is not only proactive (but still ex post), it is proactive and ex ante. To the extent trust supervision has shifted to the trust beneficiaries, they need greater information to be in a position to properly handle that responsibility. Exactly how often a trustee should account, and exactly what information should be included, depends on the facts of the situation and often is governed by state statute.

3. *Duty to account—to whom?* While the modern trend has been to expand the trustee's duty to account to the trust beneficiaries, at the same time the modern trend has tried to limit the trustee's duty to account to the trust beneficiaries so as to keep the costs of administration associated with the new duty reasonable. Most states have limited by statute the trustee's *affirmative* duty to account to either beneficiaries currently eligible to receive trust property (either mandatory or discretionary) or to "representative" beneficiaries. *See* Restatement (Third) of Trusts § 82(1)(c). Nevertheless, a trustee still has a *reactive* duty to account to *any beneficiary* who requests information or a right to inspect trust documents. *See* Restatement (Third) of Trusts § 82(2).

4. *Default rule or rule of law*: At the macro level, the duty to account is a rule of law that the settlor cannot completely opt out of. The settlor can, however, to some extent affect the specifics of the duty to account: to whom the trustee must account, how often the trustee must account, and/or what information the trustee must disclose. The settlor's intent, however, cannot violate the fundamental principle that a trust beneficiary has a right to whatever information he or she reasonably needs to protect his or her interest in the trust. *See* Restatement (Third) of Trusts § 82 cmt. a(2), e.

5. *California approach*: California imposes an affirmative duty on the trustee to account, at least annually, to any and all beneficiaries to whom trust property could be currently distributed (i.e., any beneficiary currently holding a mandatory or discretionary interest). *See* CPC § 16062. California permits the settlor to waive the trustee's affirmative duty to account, *see* CPC § 16064(a), unless the trustee is a party who raises a statutory presumption of wrongful conduct (an interested drafter, a fiduciary who caused the instrument to be transcribed, or a care custodian) and the party does not come within one of the statutory exceptions (the trustee is related by blood or marriage to the settlor or an independent attorney issues a certificate of review). *See* CPC § 16062(e). Notwithstanding settlor's intent, however, any trust beneficiary may compel an accounting if he or she can show a reasonable likelihood that a material breach of trust has occurred. *See* CPC § 16064(b).

Finally, if the trust is an *inter vivos* revocable trust, the trustee's sole duty is to the party holding the power to revoke (typically the settlor), and so a trust beneficiary is not entitled to an accounting. *See* CPC § 16069(a). The material explores this point in more detail in Section VI immediately below.

VI. To Whom Does the Trustee Owe These Fiduciary Duties?

A. Traditional Rule

A trust is a nonprobate instrument, and historically that status had legal significance. A will is a testamentary instrument. As a general rule, it has no effect until the testator's death. It transfers no property interests until the testator dies. The beneficiaries in a will hold a mere expectancy, not a property interest.

On the other hand, one of the traditional reasons an *inter vivos* trust was deemed a nonprobate transfer was that the beneficiaries receive a property interest the moment the trust is funded. The property interest may be a future interest—or even a contingent interest—but nevertheless it was a property interest that passed to the beneficiary *inter vivos*. Because the beneficiaries took an immediate property interest, the traditional approach was that a trustee owed all of the fiduciary duties to all of the beneficiaries from the moment the trust was created.

B. *Inter Vivos* Revocable Trust

The modern trend recognizes that settlors are increasingly using *inter vivos* trusts simply as a vehicle to avoid probate. In such cases the settlor tends to think that a revocable trust is nothing more than a will substitute—i.e., that it is functionally equivalent to a will except it avoids probate. If the settlor thinks that a revocable trust is functionally nothing more than a will, should the law agree—at least with respect to the issue of to whom a trustee owes his or her fiduciary duties? To the extent a revocable trust is functionally equivalent to a will, should a trustee owe no fiduciary duties to any of the beneficiaries because, as a practical matter, any interest they hold is more akin to an expectancy than a true property interest so long as the trust is revocable?

In re Estate of Giraldin
290 P.3d 199 (Cal. 2012)

CHIN, J.

A revocable trust is a trust that the person who creates it, generally called the settlor, can revoke during the person's lifetime. The beneficiaries' interest in the trust is contingent only, and the settlor can eliminate that interest at any time. When the trustee of a revocable trust is someone other than the settlor, that trustee owes a fiduciary duty to the settlor, not to the beneficiaries, as long as the settlor is alive. During that time, the trustee needs to account to the settlor only and not also to the beneficiaries. When the settlor dies, the trust becomes irrevocable, and the beneficiaries' interest in the trust vests. We must decide whether, after the settlor dies, the beneficiaries have standing to sue the trustee for breach of the fiduciary duty committed while the settlor was alive and the trust was still revocable.

...

William Giraldin and Mary Giraldin were married in 1959. When they married, William had four children and Mary had three. William adopted Mary's children. Together, they had twin sons, Timothy and Patrick. William was a successful businessman and investor and accumulated a substantial fortune.

In February 2002, William created the revocable trust at issue, the William A. Giraldin Trust (the trust), and made Timothy the trustee. William was the sole beneficiary during his lifetime. The remainder beneficiaries were Mary, who was entitled to the benefits of the trust during her lifetime, and then the nine children, who would share equally in what remained after both William and Mary were deceased. William reserved to himself specified rights, including the rights to amend or revoke the trust, to add or remove property from the trust, to remove the trustee, and to direct and approve the trustee's actions, including any investment decisions. The trust document provided that William could exercise these rights only in writing.

The trust document also provided that "[d]uring [William's] lifetime, the Trustee shall distribute to [William] that amount of net income and principal as [William] direct[s]." In the event William was declared to be incapacitated, the trustee was instructed to distribute the amount of net income and principal the trustee deemed to be appropriate to support William's "accustomed manner of living" with the understanding that "the rights of remainder beneficiaries shall be of no importance." The trust document also provided that "[d]uring [William's] lifetime, the trustee shall have no duty to provide any information regarding the trust to anyone other than [William]." After William's death, if Mary survived him, the trustee "shall have no duty to disclose to any beneficiary other than [Mary] the existence of this trust or any information about its terms or administration, except as required by law." The document also specified that William "waive[d] all statutory requirements ... that the Trustee ... render a report or account to the beneficiaries of the trust."

The trust document also states that William "[did] not want the Trustee to be personally liable for his or her good faith efforts in administering the trust estate," and that "[t]he discretionary powers granted to the Trustee under this Trust Agreement shall be absolute. This means that the Trustee can act arbitrarily, so long as he or she does not act in bad faith, and that no requirement of reasonableness shall apply to the exercise of his or her absolute discretion." William "waive[d] the requirement that the Trustee's conduct at all times must satisfy the standard of judgment and care exercised by a reasonable, prudent person. In particular, the decision of the Trustee as to the distributions to be made to beneficiaries under the distribution standards provided in this Trust Agreement shall be conclusive on all persons."

When first established, the trust contained no assets. The trust document indicated that William "had transferred and delivered to the Trustee the property described in schedule 1, attached," but the version of schedule 1 attached to the trust document was blank. It appears schedule 1 was never completed. Before establishing the trust, William had indicated the intent to invest about $4 million, about two-thirds of his fortune, in a company his son Patrick had started some years before called SafeTzone Technologies Corporation (SafeTzone). Timothy was also a part owner of the company.

In January 2002, William signed a document detailing his planned investment in the company. The day he executed the trust document, William also signed another document stating that "after the trust has been set up William A. Giraldin and Timothy W. Giraldin will begin the process of selling stock and converting assets to fulfill the investment into SafeTzone Technologies corporation of $4 million dollars." William signed other documents indicating his intent to invest the money in the company.

Between February 2002 and May 2003, William made six payments of various amounts to invest in SafeTzone, ultimately totaling more than $4 million. The company issued stock to William. After the investment was fully funded, the stock was transferred into the name of the trust. William died in May 2005. By this time, the investment in SafeTzone had gone badly, and the trust's interest in the company was worth very little.

Four of William's children, Patricia Gray, Christine Giraldin, Michael Giraldin, and Philip Giraldin (collectively plaintiffs), sued Timothy in his capacity as trustee of the trust for breach of his fiduciary duties. They alleged, in effect, that Timothy had squandered William's life savings for his and Patrick's benefit, depriving the other seven children of their benefits from the trust. Plaintiffs sought to remove Timothy as trustee and to compel him to account for his actions while acting as trustee. An amended petition alleged that Timothy should be surcharged for alleged breach of his fiduciary duties regarding the SafeTzone investment and in making loans to himself and Patrick from trust assets.

A court trial was held in October and November 2008. After the trial, the court ruled in plaintiffs' favor. It found Timothy had violated his fiduciary duty in various respects. It also found that William did not authorize many of Timothy's actions in writing as the trust required, and that William "was not sufficiently mentally competent in late 2001 and thereafter to either analyze the benefits and risks of an investment in SafeTzone ... or to authorize and direct [Timothy] to make such an investment." The court ordered Timothy be removed as trustee and that he make an accounting of the trust for the period of January 1, 2008 until his removal. Additionally, it ordered that Timothy be surcharged "for his breach of the Trust and breach of fiduciary duties owed to Decedent William G. Giraldin" in the amount of $4,376,044 for the SafeTzone investment and surcharged $625,619 for other "unsupported disbursements, distributions and loans of Trust funds...." It also ordered that Patrick return to the trust $155,000 loaned to him from trust funds.

Timothy appealed, raising several issues. The Court of Appeal additionally asked the parties to brief the question of whether, as its opinion describes it, plaintiffs had "standing to maintain claims for breach of fiduciary duty and to seek an accounting against [Timothy] based upon his actions as trustee during the period prior to [William's] death." After receiving the briefing, it found plaintiffs had no such standing. It explained that Timothy's "duties as trustee were owed solely to [William] during [the time William was alive], *and not to the trust beneficiaries.* Thus [plaintiffs], as beneficiaries, lack standing to complain of any alleged breaches of those duties occurring prior to [William's] death. Moreover, the beneficiaries have no right to compel

an accounting of the trustee's actions for the period in which the trust remained revocable [citations], and thus also lack standing to seek such relief for the period prior
to [William's] death."

The Court of Appeal also believed this action alleged a breach of Timothy's fiduciary
duty solely towards the beneficiaries rather than toward William. "In this case," the
Court of Appeal said, plaintiffs "were not purporting to pursue [William's] claims,
or to seek redress for alleged wrongs done to him. Instead, they were seeking to vin-
dicate their own distinct interests, by claiming [Timothy] had breached duties allegedly
owed *to them* during the period prior to [William's] death. We hold merely that [Tim-
othy] owed them no such duties, and thus [plaintiffs] lacked standing to assert *those
claims.* We express no opinion on the merit of any theoretical claims that might have
been asserted on [William's] behalf. None were."

The Court of Appeal reversed the trial court's judgment "without prejudice to
[plaintiffs'] right to seek a new accounting pertaining solely to the period after
[William] Giraldin's death...."

We granted plaintiffs' petition for review limited to the following question: "When
the settlor of a revocable inter vivos trust appoints, during his lifetime, someone
other than himself to act as trustee, once the settlor dies and the trust becomes irrevocable, do the remainder beneficiaries have standing to sue the trustee for breaches
of fiduciary duty committed during the period of revocability?"

II. Discussion

William created the trust during his lifetime, and he reserved the right to revoke
it. Property transferred into a revocable inter vivos trust is considered the property
of the settlor for the settlor's lifetime. Accordingly, the beneficiaries' interest in that
property is "'merely potential' and can 'evaporate in a moment at the whim of the
[settlor].'" (*Steinhart v. County of Los Angeles* (2010) 47 Cal.4th 1298, 1319, 104
Cal.Rptr.3d 195, 223 P.3d 57, quoting *Johnson v. Kotyck* (1999) 76 Cal.App.4th 83,
88, 90 Cal.Rptr.2d 99.) Thus, so long as William was alive, he had the power to divest
the beneficiaries of any interest in the trust. (See generally *Steinhart v. County of Los
Angeles, supra,* at pp. 1319–1320, 104 Cal.Rptr.3d 195, 223 P.3d 57.)

Consistent with these principles, Probate Code section 15800 provides: "Except
to the extent that the trust instrument otherwise provides..., during the time that a
trust is revocable and the person holding the power to revoke the trust is competent:

"(a) The person holding the power to revoke, and not the beneficiary, has the
rights afforded beneficiaries under this division.

"(b) *The duties of the trustee are owed to the person holding the power to revoke.*"
(Italics added.)

The italicized language from section 15800, subdivision (b), makes clear that so
long as the settlor is alive, the trustee owes a duty solely to the settlor and not to the
beneficiaries. The Court of Appeal viewed this lawsuit as alleging only that Timothy
violated a fiduciary duty towards the beneficiaries during William's lifetime. Had this
been the case, the action could simply have been dismissed on the basis that no such

duty exists. There would be no need to raise any standing question. But this case does not simply involve an alleged breach of Timothy's duty towards the beneficiaries. Although some of the trial court's order underlying this appeal was ambiguous regarding whether the court had found a violation of a duty towards the beneficiaries or towards William, a substantial thrust of this lawsuit and the trial court's order is that Timothy violated his fiduciary duty towards William during William's lifetime. To the extent, if any, that the trial court based its order on a breach of duty towards the beneficiaries during William's lifetime, we agree the court erred. No such duty exists. But to the extent the court based its order on a violation of Timothy's duty towards William during his lifetime, we must decide whether the beneficiaries have standing after the settlor's death to sue the trustee for breach of *that* duty.

The Law Revision Commission comment to section 15800 explains that the "section has the effect of postponing the enjoyment of rights of beneficiaries of revocable trusts until the death or incompetence of the settlor or other person holding the power to revoke the trust.... Section 15800 thus recognizes that the holder of a power of revocation is in control of the trust and should have the right to enforce the trust.... A corollary principle is that the holder of the power of revocation may direct the actions of the trustee.... Under this section, the duty to inform and account to beneficiaries is owed to the person holding the power to revoke during the time that the trust is presently revocable." (Cal. Law Revision Com. com., 54 West's Ann. Prob. Code (2011 ed.) foll. § 15800, pp. 644–645.)

Similarly, section 15801, subdivision (a), provides that when a beneficiary's consent may or must be given, "during the time that a trust is revocable and the person holding the power to revoke the trust is competent, the person holding the power to revoke, and not the beneficiary, has the power to consent or withhold consent." The Law Revision Commission comment to this section explains that under its rule, "the consent of the person holding the power to revoke, rather than the beneficiaries, excuses the trustee from liability as provided in Section 16460(a) (limitations on proceedings against trustee)." (Cal. Law Revision Com. com., 54 West's Ann. Prob.Code, *supra,* foll. § 15801, p. 646.)

Section 15802 provides that "during the time that a trust is revocable and the person holding the power to revoke the trust is competent, a notice that is to be given to a beneficiary shall be given to the person holding the power to revoke and not to the beneficiary." The Law Revision Commission comment to this section explains that it "recognizes that notice to the beneficiary of a revocable trust would be an idle act in the case of a revocable trust since the beneficiary is powerless to act." (Cal. Law Revision Com. com., 54 West's Ann. Prob.Code, *supra,* foll. § 15802, p. 646.)

These provisions mean that during William's lifetime, and as long as he was competent, the trust beneficiaries were powerless to act regarding the trust. A report of the California Law Revision Commission also makes this clear. "[T]he proposed law makes clear that the beneficiaries of a revocable living trust do not have the right to petition the court concerning the internal affairs of the trust until such time as the settlor, or other person holding the power to revoke, is unable to exercise a power of revocation, whether due to incompetence or death." (Recommendation Proposing the Trust Law (Dec. 1985) 18 Cal. Law Rev. Com. Rep. (1986) pp. 584–585; see 13 Witkin, Summary of Cal. Law (10th ed. 2005) Trusts, § 145, p. 710 [quoting this language].)

The question we must decide is whether the plaintiffs had standing, after William's death, to allege Timothy's breach of fiduciary duty towards William. The Probate Code does not address this question directly. That is, no section expressly states that the beneficiaries of a revocable trust either have or do not have this standing. But the code, as a whole, implies that after the settlor has died, the beneficiaries of a revocable trust may challenge the trustee's breach of the fiduciary duty owed to the settlor to the extent that breach harmed the beneficiaries' interests. As the Law Revision Commission explained, section 15800 merely *postponed* the beneficiaries' enjoyment of their rights until after the settlor's death. (Cal. Law Revision Com. com., 54 West's Ann. Prob.Code, *supra,* foll. § 15800, p. 644.)

As a general matter, the Probate Code affords beneficiaries broad remedies for breach of trust. Section 16420, subdivision (a), provides that "[i]f a trustee commits a breach of trust, or threatens to commit a breach of trust, *a beneficiary … may commence a proceeding* for any of the following purposes that is appropriate...." (Italics added.) These purposes include "[t]o compel the trustee to redress a breach of trust by payment of money or otherwise." (*Id.,* subd. (a)(3).) The Law Revision Commission comment to this section states that the "reference to payment of money in paragraph (3) is comprehensive and includes liability that might be characterized as damages, restitution, *or surcharge.*" (Cal. Law Revision Com. com., 54A Pt.1, West's Ann. Prob.Code (2011 ed.) foll. § 16420, p. 256, italics added.) Subdivision (b) of that section—which states that the "provision of remedies for breach of trust in subdivision (a) does not prevent resort to any other appropriate remedy provided by statute or the common law"— makes clear that the remedies the section affords beneficiaries are indeed broad.

Section 16462, subdivision (a), provides that "a trustee of a revocable trust is not liable *to a beneficiary* for any act performed or omitted pursuant to written directions from the person holding the power to revoke...." (Italics added.) This provision is consistent with section 15800, which provides that the trustee's duties are owed to "the person holding the power to revoke," who in this case is the settlor. If the trustee's duty is to the settlor, and the trustee acts pursuant to the settlor's directions, the trustee has violated no duty. But section 16462, including the italicized language, "to a beneficiary," also implies that if the trustee does *not* act pursuant to the settlor's directions, the trustee *may* be liable to the beneficiaries. This implication would make no sense, and section 16462 would be meaningless, if the beneficiaries have no standing, ever, to bring an action challenging the trustee's actions while the settlor was still alive. We see no textual or other basis to support the dissent's argument section 16462 only governs actions taken after the settlor has died. (Dis. opn., *post,* 150 Cal.Rptr.3d at pp. 222–223, 290 P.3d at pp. 213–214.)

Section 16069 (formerly part of section 16064) provides that the trustee need not account to the beneficiary "[i]n the case of a beneficiary of a revocable trust, as provided in Section 15800, for the period when the trust may be revoked." Timothy argues this means that he need not account to the beneficiaries ever for his actions while the trust could be revoked. The statutory language is somewhat ambiguous and may, indeed, be read as Timothy argues. But, as the cross-reference to section 15800 indicates, section 16069 must be read in context. Section 15800 provides that *during* the time the trust is revocable, the settlor has the rights afforded beneficiaries. We must read section 16069 to be consistent with section 15800. We do not read section 16069 to mean that the trustee never has to provide such an accounting, even after the trust becomes irrevocable, i.e., after the settlor's death.

. . .

Other than the Court of Appeal in this case, no California court has held the beneficiaries have no standing in this situation. Indeed, we are aware of no statute, judicial decision, or other authority, from this or any other state, denying such standing. The only California case on point has found standing. (*Evangelho v. Presoto* (1998) 67 Cal.App.4th 615, 79 Cal.Rptr.2d 146 (*Evangelho*).) In that case, the beneficiaries of a revocable trust sought, after the settlor's death, an accounting from the trustee for the period during which the trust was revocable. The trustee argued that "an accounting should not be ordered for the period when decedent was alive and the trust was revocable by decedent...." (*Id.* at p. 617, 79 Cal.Rptr.2d 146.) The Court of Appeal disagreed.

The *Evangelho* court noted that while the trustor (i.e., settlor) was alive, the trust was revocable and subject to section 15800. (*Evangelho, supra,* 67 Cal.App.4th at p. 623, 79 Cal.Rptr.2d 146.) It then explained: "The effect of this section [15800], according to the Law Revision Commission comment on this code section, is to postpone the enjoyment of the rights of the beneficiaries of revocable trusts until the death or incompetence of the settlor or the person who can revoke the trust. (Cal. Law Revision Com. com., 54 West's Ann. Prob.Code, *supra,* foll. § 15800, p. 644.) During the time the trust may be revoked, the trustee is not required to account to a beneficiary. ([Former] § 16064[, subd. (d)] [provision renumbered § 16069 by Stats. 2010, ch. 621, § 9].) [¶] The clear import of the legislative intent of section 15800 and [former] section 16064 was to postpone the enjoyment of rights under the trust law by contingent beneficiaries while the settlor could revoke or modify the trust. During the time the person holding the power to revoke is competent or alive, a trustee has no duty to account to contingent beneficiaries for the period when the trust may be revoked. When the person holding the power to revoke dies, the rights of the contingent beneficiaries are no longer contingent. Those rights, which were postponed while the holder of the power to revoke was alive, mature into present and enforceable rights under division 9, the trust law.

"Considered as a whole, the various Probate Code sections impose a duty on the trustee to protect the interests of the persons who are entitled to the proceeds of the trust. One facet of the duty is that the protected persons can compel an accounting. In the case of a revocable trust, two categories of person are protected. While the trust is revocable, the protected person is the settlor. However once the trust becomes irrevocable, such as by the death of the settlor, the beneficiaries become the protected persons. The Law Revision Commission comments explicitly speak about 'postponing the enjoyment of rights of beneficiaries of revocable trusts until the death or incompetence of the settlor or other person holding the power to revoke the trust.' (Cal. Law Revision Com. com., 54 West's Ann. Prob.Code, *supra*, foll. § 15800, p. 644.) [¶] Accordingly, the actual words of the code sections and Law Revision Commission reveal the will of the Legislature to be that only decedent as settlor could compel an accounting while she was alive and competent. But once decedent died, the right to compel the accounting set out in the code sections passed to the ... beneficiaries." (*Evangelho, supra,* 67 Cal.App.4th at pp. 623–624, 79 Cal.Rptr.2d 146, fn. omitted.)

The Court of Appeal here found *Evangelho, supra,* 67 Cal.App.4th 615, 79 Cal.Rptr.2d 146, "unpersuasive, and decline[d] to follow it." It first "note [d] the *Evangelho* court did not have the benefit of the Supreme Court's opinion in *Steinhart* [*v. County of Los Angeles, supra,* 47 Cal.4th 1298, 104 Cal.Rptr.3d 195, 223 P.3d 57], with its clear explanation of the special nature of a revocable trust, to aid in its interpretation of Probate Code section 15800." But what we said in *Steinhart* about revocable trusts was merely background regarding the legal issue before us, which was a tax question. We said nothing about revocable trusts that was not already well established.

The Court of Appeal also stressed that the trustee's duties were owed to the settlor while he was still alive. It then stated: "And if the trustee's duties are not owed to the beneficiaries at the time of the acts in question, the death of the settlor cannot make them *retroactively* owed to the beneficiaries." This statement is correct, but it does not address the question of whether the beneficiaries have standing to assert a breach of the duty towards the settlor after the settlor has died and can no longer do so personally.

The court provided a rather colorful hypothetical to illustrate its argument: "For example, if the settlor of a revocable trust learned he had a terminal disease, and was going to die within six months, he might decide that his last wish was to take his mistress on a deluxe, six-month cruise around the world—dissipating most of the assets held in his trust. The trustee, whose duties are owed to the settlor at that point, would have no basis to deny that last wish. However, if the trustee's duties were deemed to be retroactively owed to the trust beneficiaries—say, the settlor's widow and children—as soon as the settlor breathes his last breath on a beach in Bali, the trustee would find himself *liable* for having failed to sufficiently preserve *their interests* in the trust corpus prior to the settlor's death. In other words, the trustee's act, which was not a breach of any duty owed by the trustee when he committed it, would suddenly be transformed into a breach of a different duty that only came into existence when the settlor died. That is not—and cannot be—the law."

The court's argument, applied to its hypothetical facts, is correct. In that hypothetical, the trustee would have breached no duty, so would have incurred no liability. But that is not the issue we are deciding. Let us change the hypothetical somewhat. Let us assume the *trustee* himself, unbeknownst to and against the wishes of the settlor (who wishes to leave behind a large trust for his beneficiaries), goes on the six-month cruise around the world with trust funds, dissipating most of the trust assets in the process. The acts do not come to light until the settlor has died and the beneficiaries discover the trust is devoid of assets. In that situation, the trustee *would* have violated his duty to the settlor, much to the beneficiaries' harm, and, as section 16462 implies, *would* be liable to the beneficiaries. The Court of Appeal is correct that the trustee owes no duty to the beneficiaries while the settlor is alive and competent, and this lack of a duty does not retroactively change after the settlor dies. But after the settlor has died and can no longer protect his own interests, the beneficiaries have standing to claim a violation of the trustee's duty *to the settlor* to the extent that violation harmed the beneficiaries' interests. A trustee, like our hypothetical one, cannot loot a revocable trust against the settlor's wishes without the beneficiaries' having recourse after the settlor has died.

The case of *Johnson v. Kotyck, supra,* 76 Cal.App.4th 83, 90 Cal.Rptr.2d 99, illustrates the difference between the beneficiaries' standing before and after the settlor's death. In that case, the settlor, although still alive, was under the care and custody of a court-appointed conservator. The question was whether, in that situation, the beneficiary of a revocable trust was entitled to receive a trust accounting. The Court of Appeal concluded the beneficiary was not so entitled. Its analysis is instructive. The beneficiary had relied "on section 15800, which postpones the rights of trust beneficiaries 'during the time that a trust is revocable and the person holding the power to revoke the trust is competent.'" (*Id.* at p. 88, 90 Cal.Rptr.2d 99.) The court rejected this reliance. "[T]his provision does *not* mean that a trust automatically becomes irrevocable when the trustor becomes a conservatee. The Law Revision Commission comment to section 15800 explains: 'This section has the effect of postponing the enjoyment of rights of beneficiaries or revocable trusts until the death or incompetence of the settlor *or other person holding the power to revoke the trust.*' (Cal. Law Revision Com. com., reprinted at 54 West's Ann. Prob.Code (1991 ed.) foll. §15800, p. 644, italics added [by the *Johnson* court].)" (*Ibid.*) The court explained that the conservator, working with the court, was a person holding the power to revoke the trust. (*Ibid.*) It concluded, accordingly, "that section 15800 does not give a beneficiary ... any right to a trust accounting *so long as* a conservator retains authority ... to have the trust revoked and to abrogate [the beneficiary's] interest in the trust proceeds." (*Ibid.,* italics added.)

But the *Johnson* court went on to explain that the conservator might be liable to the remainder beneficiary later, after the trust becomes irrevocable, for any malfeasance. It explained that "the conservator ignores misappropriations of the conservatee's property at its own peril." (*Johnson v. Kotyck, supra,* 76 Cal.App.4th at p. 89, 90 Cal.Rptr.2d 99.) Accordingly, the court merely concluded that the beneficiary "cannot be accorded all the rights of a vested beneficiary *before* the death of the trustor [i.e., the settlor]." (*Id.* at p. 90, 90 Cal.Rptr.2d 99, italics added.) This discussion suggests that after the settlor dies, the beneficiary would have standing to complain of the conservator's actions taken before the settlor's death.

Other legal sources support finding standing after the settlor's death. Although California's law of trusts is statutory, it also draws on the common law. "Except to the extent that the common law rules governing trusts are modified by statute, the common law as to trusts is the law of this state." (§ 15002.) The Law Revision Commission comment to this section states that it refers "to the contemporary and evolving rules of decision developed by the courts in exercise of their power to adapt the law to new situations and to changing conditions." (Cal. Law Revision Com. com., 54 West's Ann. Prob.Code, *supra,* foll. § 15002, pp. 484–485.)

Consistently with section 15002, California courts have considered the Restatement of Trusts in interpreting California trust law. (See *Esslinger v. Cummins* (2006) 144 Cal.App.4th 517, 528, 50 Cal.Rptr.3d 538 [interpreting § 17200 in a way that made it consistent with the Rest.2d Trusts].) The Restatement Third of Trusts, like the Probate Code, does not expressly address the question here, but it supports the conclusion that beneficiaries do have standing after the settlor's death to sue for a trustee's breach of the duty owed to the settlor. Section 74 of that Restatement provides that while the trust is revocable, the trustee has a duty to do what the settlor directs (subd. (1)(a)), and that "[t]he rights of the beneficiaries are exercisable by and subject to the control of the settlor" (subd. (1)(b)). This section, like the similar section 15800, is inconclusive on the question before us. But the comments to this section are instructive. The comment to subdivision (1)(a), states: "A trustee is not liable to the beneficiaries for a loss that results from compliance with a settlor's direction in accordance with the terms of that direction." (Rest.3d Trusts, § 74, com. b, p. 29.) Later that comment adds, "As a practical matter, however, in the event of a surcharge action, the trustee does run a risk in relying on unwritten evidence to support a defense based on settlor direction or authorization." (*Id.* com. c, p. 30.) These comments imply that a trustee *may* be liable to the beneficiaries in at least some circumstances, which in turn implies that beneficiaries have standing to assert that liability.

One well-known treatise on trust law does address this question directly. "Consistent with the rule that the duties of a trustee of a revocable trust are owed exclusively to the settlor, at least while the settlor has capacity, the rights of non-settlor beneficiaries of a revocable trust generally are subject to the control of the settlor. Thus, as a general rule, the trustee cannot be held to account by other beneficiaries for its administration of a revocable trust during the settlor's lifetime. After the settlor's death, of course, the trustee is accountable to the trust's other beneficiaries for its administration of the trust after the settlor's death. Further, *many courts have allowed other beneficiaries to pursue breach of duty claims after the settlor's death, related to the administration of the trust during the settlor's lifetime, when, for example, there are allegations that the trustee breached its duty during the settlor's lifetime* and that the settlor had lost capacity, was under undue influence, or did not approve or ratify the trustee's conduct." (Bogert, The Law of Trusts and Trustees (3d ed. 2010) § 964, pp. 103–105, fns. omitted, italics added; see *Estate of Bowles* (2008) 169 Cal.App.4th 684, 692–694, 87 Cal.Rptr.3d 122 [considering this treatise in interpreting California trust law].) Among the cases the treatise cites to support the italicized language is *Evangelho, supra,* 67 Cal.App.4th 615, 79 Cal.Rptr.2d 146. (Bogert, *supra,* § 964, p. 105, fn. 35.)

Bogert also cites some Florida cases. (Bogert, *supra,* § 964, p. 106, fn. 35.) In *Brundage v. Bank of America* (Fla.Dist.Ct.App.2008) 996 So.2d 877, 882, the court recognized that (as in California) the trustee owes no duty to the beneficiaries of a revocable trust. "However," the court held, "once the interest of the contingent beneficiary vests upon the death of the settlor, the beneficiary may sue for breach of a duty that the trustee owed to the settlor/beneficiary which was breached during the lifetime of the settlor and subsequently affects the interest of the vested beneficiary." (*Ibid.*) Another Florida court reached a similar conclusion while applying New York law. (*Siegel v. Novak* (Fla.Dist.Ct.App.2006) 920 So.2d 89, 95.) It explained that denying standing would be "contrary to our sense of justice—a trustee should not be able to violate its fiduciary duty ... and yet escape responsibility because the settlor did not discover the transgressions during her lifetime. With an interest in the corpus of the trust after the death of their mother, the [beneficiaries] have standing to challenge the disbursements.... Without this remedy, wrongdoing concealed from a settlor during her lifetime would be rewarded." (*Id.* at p. 96, fn. omitted.)

The Uniform Trust Code is also instructive. California has not adopted the Uniform Trust Code. But it helps to illuminate the common law of trusts, which, as noted, is also the law of California except as modified by statute. (§ 15002.) One section of that code provides: "While a trust is revocable [and the settlor has capacity to revoke the trust], rights of the beneficiaries are subject to the control of, and the duties of the trustee are owed exclusively to, the settlor." (U. Trust Code (2000) § 603, subd. (a).) In substance, this provision is similar to section 15800. Like section 15800, it does not specifically address the question before us. But the accompanying comment does address the question. It expressly states what the comment to section 15800 implies: "Following the death or incapacity of the settlor, the beneficiaries *would have a right to maintain an action against a trustee for breach of trust.* However, with respect to actions occurring prior to the settlor's death or incapacity, an action by the beneficiaries could be barred by the settlor's consent or by other events such as approval of the action by a successor trustee." (U. Trust Code, com. to § 603, pp. 553–554, italics added.)

We are aware of no common law source denying standing to beneficiaries in the situation here. The cited sources strongly indicate that the common law rule is that beneficiaries do have standing after the settlor's death. Because no California statute has modified that rule, we find these sources persuasive.

. . .

Problem

Patrick Tseng was originally from China, where he was married and had several children. He immigrated to the United States and lost all contact with his family back in China. In 1954, believing his family in China to be dead, he remarried and had two children with his new wife. Patrick then learned that his family in China was still alive and he reconnected with them. Thereafter, Patrick created an *inter vivos* revocable trust with his children from his second wife appointed co-trustees. He funded the trust with assets close to $2 million, for the benefit of his second wife and all of his children. During the last six months of Patrick's life, the trustees transferred $1.8 million out of the trust. His children from his first wife in China sued, seeking more information about the terms of the trust and the transfer of the $1.8 million. The co-trustees asserted that while the trust was revocable, their only duty was to the settlor and therefore the children from China were not entitled to any information about the trust operations while the settlor was alive.

How would you rule on the request for more information about the trust, and why? *See Tseng v. Tseng*, 352 P.3d 74 (Or. Ct. App. 2015).

Chapter 15

Charitable Trusts

I. Charitable Trust Creation

A charitable trust is a particular type of trust. Inasmuch as it is a trust, the first question is whether the requirements for its creation are the same or different from the requirements to create a private trust. The key difference is that the trust must be for a charitable purpose, not for a private purpose. That obviously gives rise to a rather simple question: what qualifies as a charitable purpose?

A. Charitable Purpose

Shenandoah Valley Nat'l Bank of Winchester v. Taylor

63 S.E.2d 786 (Va. 1951)

MILLER, Justice.

Charles B. Henry, a resident of Winchester, Virginia, died testate on the 23rd day of April, 1949. His will dated April 21, 1949, was duly admitted to probate and the Shenandoah Valley National Bank of Winchester, the designated executor and trustee, qualified thereunder.

Subject to two inconsequential provisions not material to this litigation, the testator's entire estate valued at $86,000, was left as follows:

"Second: All the rest, residue and remainder of my estate, real, personal, intangible and mixed, of whatsoever kind and wherever situate, * * *, I give, bequeath and devise to the Shenandoah Valley National Bank of Winchester, Virginia, in trust, to be known as the 'Charles B. Henry and Fannie Belle Henry Fund', for the following uses and purposes:

"(a) My Trustee shall invest and reinvest my trust estate, shall collect the income therefrom and shall pay the net income as follows:

"(1) On the last school day of each calendar year before Easter my Trustee shall divide the net income into as many equal parts as there are children in the first, second and third grades of the John Kerr School of the City of Winchester, and shall pay one of such equal parts to each child in such grades, to be used by such child in the furtherance of his or her obtainment of an education.

"(2) On the last school day of each calendar year before Christmas my trustee shall divide the net income into as many equal parts as there are children in the first, second and third grades of the John Kerr School of the City of Winchester, and shall pay one of such equal parts to each child in such grades, to be used by such child in the furtherance of his or her obtainment of an education."

By paragraphs (3) and (4) it is provided that the names of the children in the three grades shall be determined each year from the school records, and payment of the income to them "shall be as nearly equal in amounts as it is practicable" to arrange.

Paragraph (5) provides that if the John Kerr School is ever discontinued for any reason the payments shall be made to the children of the same grades of the school or schools that take its place, and the School Board of Winchester is to determine what school or schools are substituted for it.

Under clause "Third" the trustee is given authority, power, and discretion to retain or from time to time sell and invest and reinvest the estate, or any part thereof, as it shall deem to be to the best interest of the trust.

The John Kerr School is a public school used by the local school board for primary grades and had an enrollment of 458 boys and girls so there will be that number of pupils or thereabouts who would share in the distribution of the income.

The testator left no children or near relatives. Those who would be his heirs and distributees in case of intestacy were first cousins and others more remotely related. One of these next of kin filed a suit against the executor and trustee, and others challenging the validity of the provisions of the will which undertook to create a charitable trust.

Paragraph No. 10 of the bill alleges:

"That the aforesaid trust does not constitute a charitable trust and hence is invalid in that it violates the rule against the creation of perpetuities."

Other heirs and distributees appeared and joined in the cause and asked that the trust be declared void and the estate distributed among testator's next of kin.

The cause was heard upon the bill and a demurrer filed by the executor and trustee. The demurrer was overruled and the contention of the heirs and distributees sustained. From decrees that adjudicated the principles of the cause and held that the trust was not charitable but a private trust and thus violative of the rule against perpetuities and void, this appeal was awarded.

The sole question presented is: does the will create a valid charitable trust?

Construction of the challenged provisions is required and in this undertaking the testator's intent as disclosed by the words used in the will must be ascertained. If his dominant intent as expressed was charitable, the trust should be accorded efficacy and sustained.

But on the other hand, if the testator's intent as expressed is merely benevolent, though the disposition of his property be meritorious and evince traits of generosity, the trust must nevertheless be declared invalid because it violates the rule against perpetuities.

"A charitable trust is created only if the settlor properly manifests an intention to create a charitable trust." Restatement of the Law of Trusts, sec. 351, p. 1099.

Authoritative definitions of charitable trusts may be found in 4 Pomeroy's Equity Jurisprudence, 5th Ed., sec. 1020, and Restatement of the Law of Trusts, sec. 368, p. 1140. The latter gives a comprehensive classification definition. It is:

"Charitable purposes include:

"(a) the relief of poverty;

"(b) the advancement of education;

"(c) the advancement of religion;

"(d) the promotion of health;

"(e) governmental or municipal purposes; and

"(f) other purposes the accomplishment of which is beneficial to the community."

In the recent decision of *Allaun v. First, etc., Nat. Bank,* 190 Va. 104, 56 S.E.(2d) 83, the definition that appears in 3 M. J., Charitable Trust, sec. 2, p. 872, was approved and adopted. It reads:

"'A charity,' in a legal sense, may be described as a gift to be applied, consistently with existing laws, for the benefit of an indefinite number of persons, either by bringing their hearts under the influence of education or religion, by relieving their bodies from disease, suffering or constraint, by assisting them to establish themselves for life, or by erecting or maintaining public building or works, or otherwise lessening the burdens of government. It is immaterial whether the purpose is called charitable in the gift itself, if it is so described as to show that it is charitable. Generally speaking, any gift not inconsistent with existing laws which is promotive of science or tends to the education, enlightening, benefit or amelioration of the condition of mankind or the diffusion of useful knowledge, or is for the public convenience is a charity. It is essential that a charity be for the benefit of an indefinite number of persons; for if all the beneficiaries are personally designated, the trust lacks the essential element of indefiniteness, which is one characteristic of a legal charity." 190 Va. at page 108....

...

In the law of trusts there is a real and fundamental distinction between a charitable trust and one that is devoted to mere benevolence. The former is public in nature and valid; the latter is private and if it offends the rule against perpetuities, it is void.

"It is quite clear that trusts which are devoted to mere benevolence or liberality, or generosity, cannot be upheld as charities. Benevolent objects include acts dictated by mere kindness, good will, or a disposition to do good * * *. Charity in a legal sense must be distinguished from acts of liberality or benevolence. To constitute a charity the use must be public in its nature." Zollman on Charities, sec. 398, p. 268.

We are, however, reminded that charitable trusts are favored creatures of the law enjoying the especial solicitude of courts of equity and a liberal interpretation is employed to uphold them. Zollman on Charities, sec. 570, p. 391; 2 Bogert on Trusts, sec. 369, p. 1129.

"Courts incline to a liberal construction in order to uphold charitable donations against the charge that they violate the perpetuity rule." Zollman on Charities, sec. 548, p. 379.

With the principle announced we are in accord. That is made certain by the quotation in *Thomas v. Bryant,* 185 Va. 845, 40 S.E.(2d) 487, 169 A.L.R. 257, which was approved in *Allaun v. First, etc., Nat. Bank, supra:*

> " 'Charitable gifts are viewed with peculiar favor by the courts, and every presumption consistent with the language contained in the instruments of gift will be employed in order to sustain them.' All doubts will be resolved in their favor." 185 Va. at page 852....

Appellant contends that the gift qualifies as a charitable trust under the definition in *Allaun v. First, etc., Nat. Bank, supra.* It is also said that it not only meets the requirements of a charitable trust as defined in Restatement of the Law of Trusts, *supra,* but specifically fits two of those classifications, *viz.:*

> "(b) trusts for the advancement of education;

> "(f) other purposes the accomplishment of which is beneficial to the community."

We now turn to the language of the will for from its context the testator's intent is to be derived. *Sheridan v. Krause,* 161 Va. 873, 172 S.E. 508, 91 A.L.R. 1067. Its interpretation must be free from and uninfluenced by the unyielding rule against perpetuities. Yet, when the testator's intent is ascertained, if it is found to be in contravention of the rule, the will, in that particular, must be declared invalid.

"Our first duty is to construe the will; and this we must do, exactly in the same way as if the rule against perpetuities had never been established, or were repealed when the will was made; not varying the construction in order to avoid the effect of that rule, but interpreting the words of the testator wholly without reference to it." *Dungannon v. Smith,* 12 Cl. and F. 546, at p. 599.

"The Rule against Perpetuities is not a rule of construction, but a peremptory command of law. It is not, like a rule of construction, a test, more or less artificial, to determine intention. Its object is to defeat intention. Therefore every provision in a will or settlement is to be construed as if the Rule did not exist, and then to the provision so construed the Rule is to be remorselessly applied." Gray's Rule Against

Perpetuities, sec. 629. Of like effect are 41 Am. Jur., sec. 13, p. 58, and *Rose v. Rose*, 191 Va. 171, 174, 60 S.E.(2d) 45.

In clause "Second" of the will the trust is set up, and by clause "Third" full power is bestowed upon the trustee to invest and reinvest the estate and collect the income for the purposes and uses of the trust. In paragraphs (1) and (2), respectively, of clause "Second" in clear and definite language the discretion, power and authority of the trustee in its disposition and application of the income are specified and limited. Yearly on the last school day before Easter and Christmas each youthful beneficiary of the testator's generosity is to be paid an equal share of the income. In mandatory language the duty and the duty alone to make cash payments to each individual child just before Easter and Christmas is enjoined upon the trustee by the certain and explicit words that it "shall divide the net income * * * and shall pay one of such equal shares to each child in such grades."

Without more, that language and the occasions specified for payment of the funds to the children being when their minds and interests would be far removed from studies or other school activities definitely indicate that no educational purpose was in the testator's mind. It is manifest that there was no intent or belief that the funds would be put to any use other than such as youthful impulse and desire might dictate. But in each instance immediately following the above-quoted language the sentence concludes with the words or phrase "to be used by such child in the furtherance of his or her obtainment of an education." It is significant that by this latter phrase the trustee is given no power, control or discretion over the funds so received by the child. Full and complete execution of the mandate and trust imposed upon the trustee accomplishes no educational purpose. Nothing toward the advancement of education is attained by the ultimate performance by the trustee of its full duty. It merely places the income irretrievably and forever beyond the range of the trust.

Appellant says that the latter phrase, "to be used by such child in furtherance of his or her obtainment of an education", evinces the testator's dominant purpose and intent. Yet it is not denied that the preceding provision "shall divide the net income into as many equal parts * * * and shall pay one of each equal parts to such child" is at odds with the phrase it relies upon. The appended qualification, it says, however, discloses a controlling intent that the 450 or more shares are to be used in the furtherance of education, and it was not really intended that a share be paid to each child so that he or she could during the Christmas and Easter holidays, or at any other time, use it "without let or hindrance, encumbrance or care." With that construction we cannot agree. In our opinion, the words of the will import an intent to have the trustee pay to each child his allotted share. If that be true,—and it is directed to be done in no uncertain language—we know that the admonition to the children would be wholly impotent and of no avail.

In construing wills, we may not forget or disregard the experiences of life and the realities of the occasion. Nor may we assume or indulge in the belief that the testator by his injunction to the donees intended or thought that he could change childhood nature and set at naught childhood impulses and desires.

Appellant asserts that literal performance of the duty imposed upon it—pay to each child his share—would be impracticable and should not be done. Its position in that respect is stated thus: "We do not understand that under the law of Virginia a court would pay money for education into the hands of children who are incapable of handling it." It then says that the funds could be administered by a guardian or under sec. 8-751, Code, 1950 (where the amounts are under $500), a court could direct payment to be made to the recipient's parents.

With these statements, we agree. But because the funds could be administered under applicable statutes has no bearing upon nor may that device be resorted to as an aid to prove or establish the testator's intent. We are of opinion that the testator's dominant intent appears from and is expressed in his unequivocal direction to the trustee to divide the income into as many equal parts as there are children beneficiaries and pay one share to each. This expressed purpose and intent is inconsistent with the appended direction to each child as to the use of his respective share and the latter phrase is thus ineffectual to create an educational trust. The testator's purpose and intent were, we think, to bestow upon the children gifts that would bring to them happiness on the two holidays, but that falls short of an educational trust.

If it be determined that the will fails to create a charitable trust for *educational purposes* (and our conclusion is that it is inoperative to create such a trust), it is earnestly insisted that the trust provided for is nevertheless charitable and valid. In this respect it is claimed that the two yearly payments to be made to the children just before Christmas and Easter produce "a desirable social effect" and are "promotive of public convenience and needs, and happiness and contentment" and thus the fund set up in the will constitutes a charitable trust. 2 Bogert on Trusts, sec. 361, p. 1090, and 3 Scott on Trusts, sec. 368, p. 1972.

The definition of the word "charity" as it appears in *Collins v. Lyon, supra,* is relied upon to sustain this position. In that decision the meaning of the word "charity" as given in *Wilson v. First Nat. Bank,* 164 Iowa 402, 145 N.W. 948, was quoted with approval as follows:

> "The word 'charity', as used in law, has a broader meaning and includes substantially any scheme or effort to better the condition of society or any considerable portion thereof. It has been well said that any gift not inconsistent with existing laws, which is promotive of science or tends to the education, enlightenment, benefit, or amelioration of the condition of mankind or the diffusion of useful knowledge, or is for the public convenience, is a charity."

Numerous cases that deal with and construe specific provisions of wills or other instruments are cited by appellant to uphold the contention that the provisions of this will, without reference to and deleting the phrase "to be used by such child in the furtherance of his or her obtainment of an education" meet the requirements of a charitable trust....

Upon examination of these decisions, it will be found that where a gift results in mere financial enrichment, a trust was sustained only when the court found and concluded from the entire context of the will that the ultimate intended recipients were poor or in necessitous circumstances.

A trust from which the income is to be paid at stated intervals to each member of a designated segment of the public, without regard to whether or not the recipients are poor or in need, is not for the relief of poverty, nor is it a social benefit to the community. It is a mere benevolence — a private trust — and may not be upheld as a charitable trust. Restatement of the Law of Trusts, sec. 374, p. 1156:

> "* * * if a large sum of money is given in trust to apply the income each year in paying a certain sum to every inhabitant of a city, whether rich or poor, the trust is not charitable, since although each inhabitant may receive a benefit, the social interest of the community as such is not thereby promoted."

In 2 Bogert on Trusts, sec. 380, we find:

> "As previously stated, gifts which are mere exhibitions of liberality and generosity, without regard to their effect upon the donees, are not charitable. There must be an amelioration of the condition of the donees as a result of the gift, and this improvement must be of a mental, physical, or spiritual nature and not merely financial. Thus, trusts to provide gifts to children, regardless of their need, or to make Christmas gifts to members of a certain class, without consideration of need or effect, are not charitable. * * *." (p. 1218.)

> "Gifts which are made out of mere sentiment, and will have no practical result except the satisfying of a whim of the donor, are obviously lacking in the widespread social effect necessary to a charity." (p. 1219.)

Of the cases relied upon in which the trust was sustained as charitable *In re Mellody (Branwood v. Haden)*, 1918, 1 Ch. 228, 87 L.J. Ch. 185, 118 L.T. 155, and *In re Estate of Nilson*, 81 Neb. 809, 116 N.W. 971, appear to be as much if not more in point with appellant's contention than any others.

In the *Mellody Case* income from the trust fund was to be used by the trustee "to provide an annual treat or field day for the schoolchildren of Turton or as many of such children as the same will provide for." It will thus be seen that the trustee had control of and administered the income from the fund and it was devoted to a supervised annual outing for school children as such. Its intended use bore a direct relationship to their schooling and education. The court held that it was a charitable trust because it (1) tended to the advancement of education, and (2) was "for purposes beneficial to a particular section of the community." Speaking of the annual treat or field day provided for, it said:

> "It may well be made, and, I doubt not, often is made, the occasion for pointing out to the children those objects of the countryside and nature about which during their school hours they have read in their books, or which they have seen in the pictures displayed upon the walls of their schoolroom. * * *."

In the *Nilson Case*, the testator, a then resident of Nebraska, recited in his will that — "Sixth. Being a native of the Tjosvold, Harmoen, Kingdom of Norway, where fishing and sailing are the chief industries, and being acquainted with the social and industrial conditions of the poorer classes of Norway, my sympathies go out to industrious and deserving servant girls, and to widows and orphans of deceased fishermen and sailors. Desiring to relieve such servant girls and widows and orphans, I give and bequeath to Akre church congregation (Akre Kirksogn) six thousand dollars, to be invested * * *", and the interest to be distributed on each "Christmas to worthy and needy servant girls and the widows and orphans of deceased sailors and fishermen who are not a public charge." (pp. 810, 811 of 81 Neb.)

The pastor of the congregation or parish, the president of the county commissioners, and the county treasurer of Akre Kirksogn, Norway, and their successors in office were designated trustees. They were peculiarly well situated to know and select who were in need of and deserving of the testator's assistance. Though the language used excludes from the class of beneficiaries those who are public charges, the context of the entire will when the trustees selected and their implied powers and discretion are taken into account sufficiently authorizes selection by them of beneficiaries from the designated class who are in need, deserving and worthy of help. The court said:

> "We are also of the opinion that the designation of the respective officers whose duty it shall be 'to carry out the provisions of this bequest' impliedly confers upon these officials the power to select from within the class the individuals who shall receive the bounty. It was, no doubt, with reference to the peculiar opportunities for knowledge as to the condition of the poor servant girls and widows and orphans afforded to these officers by virtue of their church relations that the testator selected them to execute the trust. It was impossible for him to select the individuals. He could only designate a class, and leave it to his trustees to select the individual beneficiaries of the charity, and no one seemed to him to be better fitted or to possess better qualities than those who resided among the poor people whom he wishes to help. * * *" (81 Neb. at p. 823.)

In *Goodell v. Union Association of Children, etc.*, 29 N.J. Eq. 32, a bequest of $1,000 was left to Trinity Church Sunday School with directions that it be safely invested and the interest used to secure Christmas presents for the scholars of that school. There was no indication that the recipients were to be those found to be in necessitous circumstances nor is any implied power or discretion given to limit or apply the income to such individuals. In the following language, the court declared that no charitable trust was created:

> "* * * What the gifts are to be does not appear. It does not appear that they are even to be rewards of merit, or to be used as means of inducing attendance on the part of the scholars at the school, or of promoting their good conduct there, or of inciting them to attention to religious instruction given to them there; nor whether they are to be given to all the scholars or part only. The gift is in trust, and it is not a charity in the legal sense. It is void." (29 N.J. Eq. p. 35).

...

Nor do we find any language in this will that permits the trustee to limit the recipients of the donations to the school children in the designated grades who are in necessitous circumstances, and thus bring the trust under the influence of the case styled *Appeal of Eliot,* 74 Conn. 586, 51 A. 558.

The conclusion there reached was that where a trust is set up and a class is designated as beneficiary which generally contains needy persons, the testator will be presumed to have intended as recipients those members of the class who are in necessitous circumstances.

Payment to the children of their cash bequests on the two occasions specified would bring to them pleasure and happiness and no doubt cause them to remember or think of their benefactor with gratitude and thanksgiving. That was, we think, Charles B. Henry's intent. Laudable, generous and praiseworthy though it may be, it is not for the relief of the poor or needy, nor does it otherwise so benefit or advance the social interest of the community as to justify its continuance in perpetuity as a charitable trust.

...

Here the ultimate beneficiaries of the class are not uncertain or indefinite. They are the pupils in the three designated grades of John Kerr School, and though difficulty is encountered in determining which of the inconsistent provisions of the will expresses the testator's dominant intent, yet once his true intent is ascertained the purpose of the trust is not uncertain or indefinite. It is that the school children receive their two payments on the designated times and occasions and that, as we have said, evinces no general charitable intent. No intent to apply the income to educational, charitable or eleemosynary purposes as required by the statute is disclosed.

...

No error is found in the decrees appealed from and they are affirmed.

———————

Notes

1. *The Rule Against Perpetuities*: One of the benefits of classifying a trust as a charitable trust is that it is not subject to the Rule Against Perpetuities. Saying that the trust is not subject to the Rule Against Perpetuities de facto means that the trust could last forever. If a trust does not qualify as a charitable trust, it is subject to the Rule Against Perpetuities. Historically, a private trust could not last forever—going on from generation to generation in perpetuity. The Rule Against Perpetuities essentially required a trust's future interests to vest within the lives in being at the time the trust was created, plus 21 years, or the future interest in question was invalid. Full and proper treatment of the Rule Against Perpetuities is beyond the scope of this course, but under the common law approach to the Rule Against Perpetuities, if the interest violated the Rule, it was void from the moment of its attempted creation. Hence the

claim in *Shenandoah Valley* made by the decedent's next of kin. Because the testamentary trust was in the residuary clause, if the trust failed the property would immediately fall to intestacy, where the remote heirs would take.[1]

The modern trend views the Rule Against Perpetuities with disfavor. Most jurisdictions have modified the Rule, if not abolished it. The most common modern trend approach to the Rule Against Perpetuities is to apply the "wait and see" approach. Rather than striking down a conveyance because it *might* violate the Rule Against Perpetuities, the modern trend approach prefers to wait and let the perpetuities period run before declaring a conveyance that otherwise would violate the common law approach invalid. Some jurisdictions apply the "wait and see" approach using the common law perpetuities period (lives in being plus 21 years), while other jurisdictions use a statutorily fixed number of years (typically 90 years—based on the logic that the average life in being at the time the interest was created would live 69 years, plus 21 years, which equals 90 years).

California has essentially adopted the Uniform Statutory Rule Against Perpetuities.

CPC § 21205. California rule against perpetuities

A nonvested property interest is invalid unless one of the following conditions is satisfied:

(a) When the interest is created, it is certain to vest or terminate no later than 21 years after the death of an individual then alive.

(b) The interest either vests or terminates within 90 years after its creation.

If a conveyance is valid under the traditional common law test (subpart (a)), the interest is valid under the Uniform Statutory approach. If the interest is not valid under the traditional common law approach, the courts should wait for 90 years to see if the interest either vests or terminates. The Rule Against Perpetuities is not what it used to be.

In addition to changes to the Rule Against Perpetuities, the modern trend approach to trust law has changed its approach to the requirement that a trust must have ascertainable beneficiaries. To the extent a trust fails as a charitable trust, de facto it is a private trust that historically typically would fail for lack of ascertainable beneficiaries. The modern trend, however, is to permit noncharitable private trusts that lack ascertainable beneficiaries (*see* Chapter 12). Both the Uniform Probate Code and Uniform Trust Code ("UTC") expressly permit noncharitable purpose trusts for any and all lawful purposes even though there is no ascertainable beneficiary. UPC § 2-907; UTC § 409. Such trusts may last for 21 years, but no longer. This statutory movement clarifies the legality of noncharitable purpose trusts and accordingly eliminates the

---

1. On the other hand, a well-drafted trust will not only take into consideration the Rule Against Perpetuities, it will try to have the trust last as long as permitted by the Rule. A relatively recent example of that, and of the difficulties it can pose, play a prominent role the 2011 film, *The Descendants*. In the movie, valuable family oceanfront acreage on Kauai (Hawaii) is held in a trust established generations earlier. The trust is now bumping up against the Rule Against Perpetuities. The movie examines the family dynamics that can arise in the agonizing discussions surrounding the potential sale of the trust property to a developer.

need to litigate over whether they qualify as honorary trusts and whether they are valid under the Rule Against Perpetuities.

California has adopted the core concept of the noncharitable private trust as permitted under the Uniform Probate Code.

CPC § 15211. Viability of noncharitable private trusts without a beneficiary

A trust for a noncharitable corporation or unincorporated society or for a lawful noncharitable purpose may be performed by the trustee for only 21 years, whether or not there is a beneficiary who can seek enforcement or termination of the trust and whether or not the terms of the trust contemplate a longer duration.

The interaction between the maximum trust duration permitted under California's revised Rule Against Perpetuities and California's noncharitable private trust provisions is a bit ambiguous. Where two statutory provisions overlap and are inconsistent, a general rule of statutory construction is that the more specific statutory provision controls over the more general statutory provision. It would seem that the 21-year limit in the California noncharitable purpose trust statute for noncharitable purpose trusts should control over the longer 90-year option under the California Statutory Rule Against Perpetuities.

What would be the likely outcome today if the *Shenandoah Valley* case were to arise in California?

2. *Charitable purpose — settlor's intent versus effect*: The RESTATEMENT OF THE LAW's list of charitable purposes quoted by the court in *Shenandoah Valley* is the most common starting point for analyzing whether a trust's purpose is charitable. In fact, the California statutory definition of "charitable purpose" is almost identical. CPC § 18502 (a). Where there is ambiguity with respect to whether a trust purpose qualifies as charitable, most courts will take extrinsic evidence on the issue.

As the court's opinion in *Shenandoah Valley* indicates, the settlor's subjective intent as to the trust's purpose does not necessarily control. While charitable trusts are generally considered favorably — and thus historically were treated favorably under the law (not subject to the Rule Against Perpetuities) — the courts served as something of a gatekeeper to the status of charitable trust. The requirement that the trust purpose be charitable de facto permitted the courts to regulate which trusts qualified and which did not. The settlor's intent, standing alone, does not control. The court must also agree that the trust's purpose is charitable in nature and will serve the public's interests and benefit. The purpose being served need not be one that most people would consider beneficial to the public, but the court must be persuaded that the purpose would have sufficient meaningful beneficial effect for society to warrant granting it charitable status.

In *Medical Society of South Carolina v. South Carolina National Bank of Charleston*, 14 S.E.2d 577 (S.C. 1941), the testatrix devised her home and her collection of "silver, enamels, porcelain, jade, bronzes, carpets, rugs, pictures, engravings, books, laces, kashmir shawls, and other articles of interest" in trust to her Board of Trustees to be operated as the Ross Memorial Public Museum. *Id.* at 578. After taking testimony from experts in the field, the court concluded that because the items being bequeathed to the trust were "of little or no value to the public" and because the collection could not grow, the gift lacked sufficient public benefit to qualify as a charitable trust. *Id.* at 581. As the court noted, "there can be no rule laid down for all such cases as to what is educational or of other benefit so as to constitute a public charity and, in effect, that each case must stand upon its own facts and be governed thereby." *Id.*

3. *Judicial view versus IRS view*: Whether a trust has a charitable purpose is a judicial question, not a question for the Internal Revenue Service. Technically, whether a trust qualifies as a charitable trust for tax purposes is irrelevant to the question of whether the trust qualifies as a charitable trust for judicial purposes. As a practical matter, however, qualifying a trust as a charitable trust with the Internal Revenue Service for tax purposes greatly increases the chances that the trust will also qualify as a charitable trust for judicial purposes.

4. *Mixed trust*: A "mixed trust" is one where the trustee is authorized to use the trust property for both charitable and noncharitable purposes. Depending on the details of the mixed use, the mixed trust may or may not qualify as a charitable trust.

Where the trustee has the unfettered discretion to simultaneously use the trust property for both charitable and noncharitable purposes, the courts have held that a mixed trust fails as a charitable trust. This is because, in order to qualify as a charitable trust, the trustee must be bound to use the trust property for charitable purposes only.

Whether a trust constitutes a mixed trust depends on the language in the trust instrument. Where the trustee has the discretion to choose how much of the trust property goes to the charitable purpose and how much goes to the noncharitable purpose, the trust fails as a mixed trust. Where, however, a trustee is given discretion to choose between a mixture of charitable purposes, or to choose the particular charitable purpose to which the trust property is to be applied, such a trust qualifies as a charitable trust so long as the trustee's discretion is limited to charitable purposes. The key is the authorizing language granting the scope of the trustee's discretion. Where the authorizing language expressly references charitable purposes and also includes references to noncharitable purposes (i.e., the language authorizing use of the funds for "other benevolent purposes" or "or other purposes of liberality,") the trust will likely be construed as a mixed trust, which will fail as a charitable trust. Proper drafting is critical when creating charitable trusts.

A mixed trust must be distinguished from a trust where the charitable and noncharitable interests are split over time (i.e., when the interests are successive, not concurrent). A trust that grants a life estate in an ascertainable beneficiary and a remainder interest for charitable purposes (a charitable remainder trust) does *not* constitute a mixed trust. Similarly, where the interests are reversed, a charitable income interest for a period of time, with the remainder reverting to the settlor (or other beneficiary) is, logically, known as a charitable lead trust, and does not constitute a mixed trust. The trust is valid as a private trust (assuming it meets the requirements of a private trust) for the duration of the private portion, and then the trust becomes a valid charitable trust (assuming it meets the requirements of a charitable trust) for the duration of the charitable portion.

These combinations of charitable and noncharitable split interests are a specialized area of estate planning. Notwithstanding potential conflicts of interest, attorneys who work with the charitable organization often help draft the individual's estate planning documents. So called "charitable estate planning" can assist the client with both traditional testamentary/personal goals as well as those of a charitable nature.

Finally, the most difficult mixed trust is one where the trust has, simultaneously, a valid charitable purpose and a valid private purpose. This trust should be distinguished from the "true" mixed trust in that, here, the beneficiaries of the private portion of the trust are ascertainable, as is their interest. For example, assume a settlor creates a trust for her children for life. The terms of the trust provide that the trust income is to be used for their comfortable support and maintenance, with any surplus income to be used for charitable purposes. So long as the private portion of her trust has ascertainable beneficiaries who can come into court and enforce the private portion, she arguably created two trusts, either expressly or de facto: one for charitable purposes and one for private purposes. If each portion of the trust independently meets the necessary requirements, both portions of the trust are valid. Moreover, if the court deems that sufficient standards have been given for each portion such that the trust could be divided into two trusts, the court will likely uphold the trust, as opposed to applying the general mixed trust rule and holding the trust invalid.

Problems

1. Bernie's will creates a testamentary trust "to advance the principles of socialism." Following his death, Bernie's heirs challenge the validity of the trust, claiming that it lacks a charitable purpose. How would you rule on the challenge? Assuming, *arguendo,* you concluded that the trust lacked a charitable purpose, would you void the trust immediately? *See In re Estate of Breeden,* 208 Cal. App. 3d 981 (Ct. App. 1989).

    What difference, if any, would it make if the testamentary trust had been "to advance the interests and causes of the Socialist Political Party"? *See In re Liapis' Estate,* 88 Pa. D. & C. 303 (P. Orph. 1954).

2. Catherine De Mars's holographic will contained the following residuary clause: "Any amount left go to the poor solders Leterman Hospital." Letterman General Hospital was a federally maintained facility in San Francisco for the treatment and care of soldiers, many of whom were poor. Catherine had been an active member of a relief organization that volunteered at the facility to help the soldiers. Catherine's heirs challenged the validity of the gift, arguing: (1) that the beneficiaries were too indefinite, and (2) that it lacked both: (i) a charitable purpose, and (ii) the intent to create a trust. Can the gift be construed as a valid charitable trust? *See In re De Mars' Estate,* 67 P. 374 (Cal. Ct. App. 1937).

3. Settlor created a trust and instructed the trustee to use all the net income annually for "such charitable or public uses" as the trustee deemed appropriate. Is this a valid charitable trust? What if the trust instructions authorized the trustee to use the net income annually for "human beneficence and charity"? Is this a valid charitable trust? *See In re Sutro's Estate,* 102 P. 920 (Cal. 1909).

4. Testator's will divided his estate into two funds, Fund A and Fund B, and the will directed that the assets in Fund B be sold and the proceeds be held in trust for the following purpose:

> The income of said trust, or so much of the principal as in the sole discretion of the Trustees may be deemed desirable or advisable, is to be used for the care, comfort, support, Medical attention, education, sustenance, maintenance or custody of such minor Negro child or children, whose father or mother, or both, have been incarcerated, imprisoned, detained or committed in any federal, state, county or local prison or penitentiary, as a result of the conviction of a crime or misdemeanor of a political nature.

Has testator created a valid charitable trust? *See In re Robbins' Estate,* 371 P.2d. 573 (Cal. 1962)

5. Testatrix's will provided in pertinent part as follows:

> *Second:* The ever-recurring misunderstandings between the various nations and the peoples of different races which impede human progress and lead to devastating wars, are obviously attributable, in large measure, to differences of environment and language. I believe that these handicaps can be largely overcome, if the men and women whose vocation vests in them the power to mold public opinion, make a conscious effort to that end. However, their effort will go for naught, unless based on sound education on their own part, and thorough understanding of the economics of the various countries of the world, as well as their historic, diplomatic and political backgrounds. The molding of public opinion in the United States, insofar as concerns the attitude of our citizens toward anything foreign, rests almost entirely with the press which, in turn, must depend upon editorial staffs and foreign correspondents. Based on past experience, I believe that it is fair to say that there is a woeful lack of any real education on their part in what should be the foundation of one of the most important patriotic contributions which they could make to our country and the welfare of its citizens. I have therefore long cherished the hope that I might be able to do something to help toward the correction of these conditions, and to that end I hereby give and bequeath to The Trustees of The Leland Stanford Junior University (hereinafter referred to as my 'Trustees') all of my estate and property, both real and personal and wheresoever the same may be situate, *in trust* for the foregoing purposes,—subject to the express terms and conditions hereinafter set forth:
>
> (a) My said Trustees shall establish a *Foundation of World Relations*, for the aforesaid purposes; and my said Trustees shall use and apply the net

income derived from said trust estate for the maintenance of said Foundation. My said Trustees shall, in their own discretion, determine from time to time the manner in which said net income may be best expended for said purposes, in view of the amount available therefor; and they may, if they deem such course wise, postpone the expenditure of any sums for my said trust purposes, until such time as the income available therefor shall, in their opinion, be adequate to meet such expense as may be necessary to accomplish something substantial in the said field of learing [sic] to which said trust is dedicated.

Has she created a valid charitable trust? *See In re Estate of Peck*, 335 P.2d 185 (Cal. Dist. Ct. App. 1959).

B. Unascertainable Beneficiaries

Historically, two key variables distinguished a charitable trust from a private trust. The first was that the trust had to be for charitable purposes. The second variable flows from the first. Inasmuch as a charitable trust must have a charitable purpose, and inasmuch as a charitable purpose typically is for the benefit of the public, it follows that a charitable trust should *not* have ascertainable beneficiaries. Some authorities go so far as to say that a charitable trust *cannot* have ascertainable beneficiaries. While there is some truth and benefit to thinking about the differences between private and charitable trusts in this way, as is often the case, such an articulation can be confusing in certain contexts. In reality, the issue of charitable purpose and unidentifiable beneficiaries is more a trade-off between the size of the class of potential beneficiaries and the scope of the possible benefit to the public at large— a trade-off between the direct beneficiaries and the indirect beneficiaries.

In re McKenzie's Estate
227 Cal. App. 2d 167 (Ct. App. 1964)

KINGSLEY, Justice.

Robert O. McKenzie died testate leaving a holographic will. The only portion of said will in dispute herein declares:

"I want a trust to be formed payable as a reward to the person who decides the cause of Rhomatoid [*sic*] Arthritis and a cure for the same to the satisfaction of the Medical Board of the University of Calif. at L. A."

...

... Following the trial, the court found that the above quoted will provision did not qualify as a charitable trust, and failed as a private trust for lack of an identifiable beneficiary or beneficiaries and because the interest of the beneficiary or beneficiaries violated the rule against perpetuities in that the interest or interests may not vest within the period required by law. As a conclusion of law, the court declared the aforesaid residuary clause invalid and that, "All property of decedent disposed of by the above quoted provision of decedent's last will shall go and be distributed to decedent's heirs-at-law by intestate succession." Accordingly, the trial court entered its Decree Determining Interest in Estate, ordering the residue of the said estate distributed in equal shares to the five heirs-at-law surviving the decedent.

From this determination, the Attorney General prosecutes this appeal.

At the outset, the Attorney General concedes that, unless the provision of the will in issue qualifies as a charitable trust, it is invalid for lack of an identifiable beneficiary and violation of the rule against perpetuities. On the other hand, it is well established that neither of these requirements or limitations on private trusts applies to charitable trusts. (*People ex rel. Ellert v. Cogswell* (1896) 113 Cal. 129, 45 P. 270, 35 L.R.A. 269; *Estate of Hinckley* (1881) 58 Cal. 457.)

A charitable trust has been defined as a "* * * trust for promoting the welfare of mankind at large, or of a community, or of some class forming a part of it, indefinite as to numbers and individuals." (*People ex rel. Ellert v. Cogswell, supra* (1896) 113 Cal. 129, 138, 45 P. 270, 271).

Respondents argue that the beneficiary of Mr. McKenzie's gift is one single person and not the general public; and the fact that a public benefit may arise by reason of the work of this particular individual is immaterial, citing *Estate of Kline* (1934) 138 Cal.App. 514, 32 P.2d 677.

However, "[a] trust for the prevention or cure or treatment of diseases or otherwise for the promotion of health is charitable" (Restatement of the Law of Trusts 2d, § 372; Scott on Trusts, § 372, pp. 2661–2662); and "A bequest is charitable if: (1) It is made for a charitable purpose; its aims and accomplishments are of religious, educational, political or general social interest to mankind. [Citations] (2) The *ultimate* recipients constitute either the community as a whole or an unascertainable and indefinite portion thereof. [Citations]" *Estate of Henderson* (1941), 17 Cal.2d 853, 857, 112 P.2d 605, 607, as quoted with approval in *Estate of Robbins* (1962) 57 Cal.2d 718, 722, 21 Cal.Rptr. 797, 371 P.2d 573.) The fact that the trust assets may be paid to an individual in no way deprives the trust of its charitable character if the ultimate result complies with the test of charitable purpose. (*Sheen v. Sheen* (1939) 126 N.J.Eq. 132, 8 A.2d 136; *Matter of Judd's Estate* (1934) 242 App.Div. 389, 274 N.Y.S. 902.)

In the *Judd* case, the trust provision in the will directed the trustees, "* * * out of the net income thereof to pay each year the sum of one thousand dollars to the person who, in the judgment of the trustees or other managers of said hospital, shall have made the greatest advancement toward the discovery of a cure for cancer. * * *"

The judgment of the trial court holding the above quoted provision invalid was reversed on appeal, the appellate court stating:

"The Surrogate has held the trust to be invalid because it provides for payments to persons who shall have made the greatest advancement in the discovery of, or who shall eventually have discovered, a cure for cancer. These provisions, in the opinion of the Surrogate, invalidate the trust 'because by its terms it provides plaintiff for a gift to an individual or individuals for his or their own use.' If this be the correct view, then many of the most useful benefactions of modern times are not to be classified as charitable.

"We think this conclusion proceeds upon too restricted a conception of a charitable use. In reaching it, the Surrogate considered only the immediate destination of the funds and disregarded what seems to us the dominant purpose and the wider implications of the trust. If the purpose of the trust were merely to benefit research workers in cancer, it would not be saved by reason of the useful nature of their work. [Citations.] But this involves, we are convinced, a misconception of its purpose. That purpose is the encouragement of research in the field of cancer by rewarding those who shall have been most useful in the investigation of a subject which has baffled the medical profession. It is not to be supposed that it was the intention to enrich the unidentified individuals who might happen to be successful in this research work, except as this was incidental to the achievement of a purpose to benefit mankind. The real beneficiaries are those afflicted who are expected to benefit by the research which may be stimulated by the hope of pecuniary reward. The trust is not invalid merely because it contemplates payments to individuals for their private use. That situation exists in any charitable trust which requires for the discharge of its functions the employment of compensated employees. They, too, receive emoluments 'for his or their own use.' Yet it will not be contended that such charities are created in order to compensate their employees. They are created, as was the trust here, to secure the advantage of their services in effectuating the objects of the charity. Wherever the question seems to have arisen, it has been decided in this way. [Citations.]"

By the same token, in *Sheen v. Sheen* (1939) 126 N.J.Eq. 132, 8 A.2d 136, the provision of the will directing the trustee "to establish a Trust Fund, the income of which is to be used annually for the purpose of awarding a prize to the outstanding Doctor of Medical Science in the United States for each year" was held to create a valid charitable trust. In answer to the contention that the awarding of a prize to an individual is incompatible with the trust being a charitable one, the court had this comment in reply:

> "The benefits of the award are of a two-fold nature, first, to the outstanding doctor, a sum of money as a prize or award, and secondly, an indefinite number of persons in the United States, i. e., the general public, who must necessarily receive the benefits of the development of the science of medicine attained through the study and research of members of the medical profession, not only the doctor who gets paid in part for his services, but other doctors who make research and are not fortunate enough to receive the award. The real benefits to the public and the benefits intended to be secured by the trust are the results of the study and research of the doctors of the United States, as those results are handed down to the medical profession and by them to their patients. * * *

> "Does the fact that the trust provides for a prize or award to the doctor invalidate an otherwise valid charitable trust? I think not. In 14 C.J.S. Charities § 15, p. 447, it is stated: 'A bequest of a fund for the giving of prizes and

medals for educational, medical, or literary, work, or other deeds beneficial to the general public, is a valid charitable gift.' "

We deem both the reasoning and the logic of the *Sheen* and *Judd* cases to be controlling in the situation before us. Here the natural consequences of providing a reward for the discovery of the cause and cure of rheumatoid arthritis is to stimulate research in this field. In reality, the public is the true beneficiary of what will result from the operation of this trust. The fact that a particular individual some day may qualify to receive the reward is but the instrumentality through which the benefits that will be bestowed upon the public are brought about. To consider such individual the beneficiary of the trust is to confuse the trust purpose with the means provided for achieving that purpose.

The fact that the trust provision of decedent's will does not provide for a trustee is in no way fatal to the validity of the trust. It is well settled in this state that a trust will not fail for want of a trustee. The court will appoint a trustee. (*Estate of DeMars* (1937) 20 Cal.App.2d 514, 67 P.2d 374; *Fay v. Howe* (1902) 136 Cal. 599, 69 P. 423; *Estate of Upham* (1899) 127 Cal. 90, 59 P. 315.) Nor does this trust fail by reason of the fact that the income of the trust may be accumulated for longer than the period allowed by Section 724 of the Civil Code, because charitable trusts are exempt from restrictions pertaining to accumulations. However, the matter is one that is subject to judicial supervision (Scott on Trusts, § 401.9.)

We recognize that, in addition to a possible necessity for dealing, at a future date, with the problem of accumulated income, there may arise other problems of interpretation in the event that one person may claim to have shared in the discovery of the cause but not the cure of the disease involved, while the cure may be the discovery of a second person. But these problems may, or may not, ever arise. When, and if, they do, the court can make appropriate orders in the exercise of its continuing supervisory powers over its trustee. The mere possibility of the problems does not affect the existence or the validity of the trust itself.

The decree appealed from is reversed and the matter is remanded to the trial court with directions to enter a decree sustaining the trust, appointing a trustee, and distributing the residuary estate to such trustee, such decree to reserve in the court power, on proper application, to instruct the trustee in the event any problem in interpretation of the trust or in the management of the trust estate shall hereafter arise.

Problem

Testatrix's will creates a testamentary trust. The trust provisions instruct the trustee to use the net income to maintain lots #29 and #30 and their immediate surroundings in the Wilmington and Brandywine Cemetery. The trust agreement also provides that any excess net income shall "accumulate" to be used (i) "for the renewal and replacement ... of the vaults, monuments, [and] iron fence railing," (ii) "for the defence [sic], if needful, against any attempt to condemn the property for any purpose whatsoever," and (iii) if that defense is unsuccessful, "to remove the bodies" from the burial lots "to another location." Has the settlor created a valid charitable trust? *See In re Latimer Trust*, 78 A.3d 875 (Del. Ch. 2013).

II. Standing to Enforce

Historically, one of the reasons for requiring that the beneficiaries of a private trust be ascertainable is because the court needs to know who has standing to sue to enforce the terms of the trust against the trustee. Inasmuch as the beneficiaries of a charitable trust *cannot* be ascertainable, who has standing to sue to enforce the terms of the charitable trust against the trustee?

Patton v. Sherwood

152 Cal. App. 4th 339 (Ct. App. 2007)

YEGAN, J.

. . .

Facts and Procedural History

In 2002 appellant Lowell T. Patton and his wife, Mary Lou Patton, created three CRUTs [charitable remainder unitrusts[2]] for their children.... The CRUTs named the children as income beneficiaries and named four charities as remainder beneficiaries.

The CRUTS were prepared by Attorney Matthew B. Mack of Estate Strategies for Charities, Inc. They were funded with professional minor league baseball stock valued at $2.4 million. Mack named himself administrative trustee and named Mark C. Sherwood management trustee.

Each CRUT provided that the trustor (appellant) reserved the right to change a remainder beneficiary and reserved the right remove and replace the trustees. The CRUTs required that the administrative trustee prepare annual accountings and that appellant agrees "to review and approve or object to the Accounting within ninety (90) days from the date the accounting is mailed." (CRUTS, article 5, § 5.3, subd. 5.3.5.) If the "Trustor ... objects in writing to the Accounting within ninety (90) days, then the Objector shall have one year from the date the accounting is mailed in which to bring a claim for breach of trust, petition for a court supervised accounting, or to commence an action for other remedies." (*Ibid.*)

---

2. A CRUT is one form of a charitable remainder trust. Charitable remainder trusts are, for the most part, beyond the scope of this introductory class—but a few comments may help you understand the case. As is typical with all charitable remainder trusts, a CRUT is an irrevocable trust with a non-charitable income beneficiary (e.g., one or more individuals) whose income interest lasts, pursuant to the trust terms, for some period of time (a certain number of years, or time measured by a beneficiary's life, etc.) and at such time, the trust assets are then distributed to a qualified charitable organization. In a CRUT, the income payout is measured by a specified percentage of the value of trust assets.

On February 4, 2005, appellant filed a petition to remove Mack and Sherwood as trustees. Mack and Sherwood claimed they had already resigned as trustees of one CRUT and declined to step down as trustees of the two other CRUTs until they were released from liability and awarded fees and expenses.

The trial court granted appellant's petition to remove Mack and Sherwood as trustees of the remaining CRUTs. The court appointed the Ventura County Public Guardian as successor trustee.

In a separate petition, Mack and Sherwood requested that the trial court settle their accounting, pay their fees and costs, and discharge them of liability. Appellant propounded discovery and objected to the accounting, alleging that Mack and Sherwood had charged excessive fees and breached their fiduciary duties. The trial court ruled that appellant lacked standing, relying on section 17200. The trial court said that only a trust beneficiary or trustee had standing to object to a trust accounting.

The Common Law

It is well established that the settlor of a charitable trust who retains no reversionary interest in the trust property lacks standing to bring an action to enforce the trust independently of the Attorney General. (*O'Hara v. Grand Lodge I.O.G.T.* (1931) 213 Cal. 131, 139, 2 P.2d 21; *Brown v. Memorial Nat. Home Foundation* (1958) 162 Cal.App.2d 513, 538, 329 P.2d 118.) Under the common law, the state, as *parens patriae,* superintends the management of charitable trusts and acts through its attorney general. (*Estate of Schloss* (1961) 56 Cal.2d 248, 257, 14 Cal.Rptr. 643, 363 P.2d 875; see Gov.Code, § 12598, subd. (a) [Uniform Supervision of Trustees For Charitable Purposes Act].) "Other than the Attorney General, only certain parties who have a special and definite interest in a charitable trust, such as a trustee, have standing to institute a legal action to enforce the assets of the trust. [Citations.] This limitation on standing arises from the need to protect the trustee from vexatious litigation, possibly based on an inadequate investigation, by a large, changing, and uncertain class of the public to benefited. [Citation.]" (*Hardman v. Feinstein* (1987) 195 Cal.App.3d 157, 161–162, 240 Cal.Rptr. 483.)

Settlor's Reserved Power

Appellant meritoriously argues that the settlor of a charitable trust may, under the terms of the trust instrument, reserve the power to object to a trustee accounting. In *L.B. Research and Education Foundation v. UCLA Foundation,* (2005) 130 Cal.App.4th 171, 29 Cal.Rptr.3d 710, a donor gifted $1 million to the UCLA Foundation (Foundation) to establish an endowed chair at the UCLA School of Medicine. Donor and Foundation executed a contract providing that the money would be used by qualified chair holders to support basic science research activities. (*Id.,* at p. 175, 29 Cal.Rptr.3d 710.) The contract provided that if the funds were not used for the designated purpose, the gift would revert to a contingent donee, the University of California San Francisco, School of Medicine. (*Id.,* at p. 175–176, 29 Cal.Rptr.3d 710.) Donor sued for specific performance, declaratory relief, and breach of contract alleging that Foundation had failed to provide an accounting or employ personnel meeting the criteria for the chair endowment. Foundation defended on the theory that the donor had created a charitable trust which only the Attorney General had standing to enforce. The trial court found that donor lacked standing to sue and granted judgment on the pleadings.

The Court of Appeal reversed on the theory that donor was suing on a contract subject to a condition subsequent and had standing to sue. (*L.B. Research and Education Foundation v. UCLA Foundation, supra,* 130 Cal.App.4th at p. 175, 29 Cal.Rptr.3d 710.) In dicta, the court stated that the result would be the same had the donor created a charitable trust. (*Id.,* at p. 180, 29 Cal.Rptr.3d 710.) It cited *Holt v. College of Osteopathic Physicians & Surgeons* (1964) 61 Cal.2d 750, 40 Cal.Rptr. 244, 394 P.2d 932 for the principle that "the 'prevailing view of other jurisdictions is that the Attorney General does not have exclusive power to enforce a charitable trust and that a trustee or *other person having a sufficient special interest* may also bring an action for this purpose. This position is adopted by the American Law Institution (Rest.2d Trusts, § 391) and is supported by many scholars. [Citations.]' " (*L.B. Research and Education Foundation v. UCLA Foundation, supra,* 130 Cal.App.4th, at p. 180, 29 Cal.Rptr.3d 710.)

The court in *L.B. Research & Education Foundation v. UCLA Foundation* acknowledged that statutes authorizing the Attorney General to enforce charitable trusts were enacted to provide adequate supervision and enforcement of charitable trusts. (*Id.,* at p. 181, 29 Cal.Rptr.3d 710.) " '[T]he Attorney General has been empowered to oversee charities as the representative of the public, a practice having its origin in the early common law.' [Citation.] [¶] 'In addition to the general public interest, however, there is the interest of donors who have directed that their contributions be used for certain charitable purposes. Although the public in general may benefit from any number of charitable purposes, charitable contributions must be used only for the purposes for which they were received in trust. [Citations.] Moreover, part of the problem of enforcement is to bring to light conduct detrimental to a charitable trust so that remedial action may be taken.' " (*Ibid.*)

Under the terms of the CRUTs, appellant reserved the power to change the remainder beneficiaries, remove and replace trustees, receive and object to trust accountings, "to bring a claim for breach of trust," and petition for a court supervised accounting. (CRUTS article 5, § 5.3, subd. 5.3.5.) If appellant has standing to compel an accounting, he has the associated right to object to the accounting. (Campisi and Latham, Cal. Trust and Probate Litigation (Cont. Ed. Bar 2006) § 13.40, p. 425.)

As explained in *Holt v. College of Osteopathic Physicians & Surgeons, supra,* 61 Cal.2d at pages 755–756, 40 Cal.Rptr. 244, 394 P.2d 932: "There is no rule or policy against supplementing the Attorney General's power of enforcement by allowing other responsible individuals to sue in behalf of the charity. The administration of charitable trusts stands only to benefit if in addition to the Attorney General other suitable means of enforcement are available." (Fn. omitted; see also *San Diego etc. Boy Scouts of America v. City of Escondido* (1971) 14 Cal.App.3d 189, 195, 92 Cal.Rptr. 186 ["right of the Attorney General to sue to enforce a charitable trust is not exclusive; other responsible individuals may be permitted to sue on behalf of the charity."]

Standing To Sue As A Beneficiary

Respondents argue that section 17200 trumps any reserved power in the trust instruments and that standing is jurisdictional. (See *Johnson v. Tate* (1989) 215 Cal.App.3d 1282, 1285, 264 Cal.Rptr. 68, citing *Estate of Bissinger* (1964) 60 Cal.2d 756, 764, 36 Cal.Rptr. 450, 388 P.2d 682.) Section 17200 provides that only a trustee or "beneficiary" may petition the probate court "concerning the internal affairs of a trust." (See *Esslinger v. Cummins* (2006) 144 Cal.App.4th 517, 524, 50 Cal.Rptr.3d 538 [remainder beneficiary standing].) Section 24 states: "'Beneficiary' means a person to whom a donative transfer of property is made or that person's successor in interest, *and:* ... [¶] (d) As it relates to a charitable trust, *includes any person entitled to enforce the trust.*" (Emphasis added.)

The trial court erroneously construed section 24, subdivision (d) to mean that a beneficiary must be a person to whom a donative transfer of property is made and must also be a person who is entitled to enforce the trust. It ruled that the CRUTs "contain language that suggests that a trustor may object to an accounting" but concluded that "a trust instrument cannot convey standing to a trustor to object to an accounting when the legislature has only given that authority to trustees and beneficiaries."

...

The first sentence of section 24 states that "'Beneficiary' means a person to whom a donative transfer of property is made or that person's successor in interest...." The Legislature used the word "and" to link this sentence to subparagraph (d) which states: "As it relates to a charitable trust, *includes* any person entitled to enforce the trust."

Respondents contend that the phrase "includes any person" is a qualifying clause, intended to narrow the class of beneficiaries who can object to an accounting. We reject the argument....

The word "includes" is ordinarily a word of enlargement, not limitation. (*Ornelas v. Randolph* (1993) 4 Cal.4th 1095, 1101, 17 Cal.Rptr.2d 594, 847 P.2d 560; *Oil Workers Intl. Union v. Superior Court* (1951) 103 Cal.App.2d 512, 570, 230 P.2d 71.) Here the phrase "includes any person," as used in section 24, subdivision (d), expands the class of persons who may bring an action to enforce a charitable trust. One such person is the Attorney General. (See Ross, Cal. Practice Guide, Probate (Rutter 2006) § 3.83.3, p. 3-31 [construing "any person entitled to enforce the trust" to be the California Attorney General].) Section 24, subdivision (d), includes other interested persons, otherwise it would be redundant with section 17210 which provides that the Attorney General may stand in the place of the beneficiaries to enforce the charitable trust. (See Law Revision Com. com. (1990) Enactment, reprinted at 54 West's Ann. Prob.Code (1991) foll. § 17210, p. 207; *Estate of Schloss* (1961) 56 Cal.2d 248, 257, 14 Cal.Rptr. 643, 363 P.2d 875.)

Respondents cite older cases holding that settlors/trustors have no standing to bring an action to enforce a charitable trust.... Those cases, however, predate the 1983 enactment of section 24 which provides: "Beneficiary, as it relates to trust beneficiaries, includes a person who has any present or future interest, vested or contingent, and also includes the owner of an interest by assignment or other transfer *and as it relates to a charitable trust, includes any person entitled to enforce the trust.*" (Emphasis added.) Section 24 was a new provision to the Probate Code....

...

We hold that section 24, subdivision (d) permits the settlor of a charitable trust to object to an accounting where the settlor has reserved the power in the trust instrument. Like the donor in *L.B. Research & Education Foundation v. UCLA Foundation, supra,* 130 Cal.App.4th 171, 29 Cal.Rptr.3d 710, appellant reserved the power to receive and object to accountings, to petition for a court supervised accounting, and to bring a claim for breach of trust. Our holding is not only consistent with the law, but encourages the salutary goal of making charitable donations. Charitable gifts "on condition" that the money is used for the intended gift purpose would give the trust settlor peace of mind that his or her gift will actually be used for a charitable purpose. What better way to see that the gift is delivered than to have an accounting?

The judgment (order overruling appellant's objections to the trustee accountings) is reversed. Appellant is awarded costs on appeal.

Notes

1. *Common law approach—attorney general*: As the court in *Patton* notes, the traditional common law approach granted only the attorney general standing to enforce the terms of a charitable trust. Over time, however, that approach was criticized on a number of grounds, most notably that the attorney general's office simply lacked the manpower to keep track of every charitable trust and whether the trustees were complying with the terms of those trusts. Pressure built to expand the scope of the parties who had standing to enforce the terms of a charitable trust, while at the same time there was a need to be sensitive to the counter-concern mentioned in the court's opinion: "to protect the trustee from vexatious litigation, possibly based on an inadequate investigation, by a large, changing, and uncertain class of the public to be benefited."

The common law rule is no longer the general rule. That being said, any given member of the public generally lacks standing to enforce the terms of a charitable trust. Most jurisdictions have attempted to find some middle ground—some way of recognizing that certain individuals may have a special relationship to the charitable trust that justifies granting them standing to sue to enforce the terms of a charitable trust.

2. *Co-trustee*: Obviously a trustee has an interest in the trust. He or she holds legal title. Moreover, a trustee owes a fiduciary duty to the trust. Where there is more than one trustee, a trustee can sue his or her co-trustee(s) to enforce the terms of a charitable trust against a trustee who is breaching those terms. The California Supreme Court so ruled in *Holt v. College of Osteopathic Physicians and Surgeons,* 61 Cal.2d 750 (1964). There, a majority of trustees of a charitable corporation were threatening action that arguably would constitute a breach of trust. The Court held that the corporation's minority trustees had standing to sue the majority trustees. The Court reasoned that California's Uniform Supervision of Trustees for Charitable Purposes

Act, which authorized the Attorney General to supervise charitable trusts, did not preclude trustees from having standing to bring an action to enforce the terms of the trust. Arguably, the same logic applies to a successor trustee, as so held by courts in other jurisdictions (the issue has not yet arisen in California).

3. *Beneficiary*: In a private trust, the beneficiary is the party most likely to bring a suit against the trustee to enforce the terms of the trust. Historically, a beneficiary had standing if he or she had an interest in the trust that would be or was adversely affected by the trustee's action or inaction (or proposed action or inaction).

Charitable trusts, however, are typically for the benefit of the public (or a relatively large subset of the public). It is, therefore, easy to understand the common law's reluctance to grant any and all members of the public standing to sue the trustee of a charitable trust. Offsetting the concern for "vexatious litigation," however, is the concern that granting standing only to the attorney general to enforce the terms of a charitable trust may equate to, for all practical purposes, virtually no enforcement. Accordingly, the modern trend has been to articulate a middle ground by identifying members of the public with a special relationship to the trust. Increasingly, courts are holding that those members of the public with a special interest in the charitable trust have standing to enforce the terms of the trust.

The RESTATEMENT (THIRD) OF TRUSTS expressly provides that standing includes "anyone who has a special interest in the enforcement of the trust." RESTATEMENT (THIRD) OF TRUSTS § 94(2). Having a "special interest" requires more of an interest than that the person was a potential beneficiary, but what exactly constitutes a special interest is extremely fact sensitive and remains at the court's discretion. As the official Comment to Subsection (2), note (g), states:

> The special-interest concept and its application involve a balancing of policy concerns and objectives. The special-interest requirement provides a safeguard for charitable resources and trustees by limiting the risk, and frequency, of potentially costly, unwarranted litigation; but the recognition of special-interest standing, in appropriate situations, is justified by society's interest in honoring reasonable expectations of settlors and the donor public and in enhancing enforcement of charitable trusts, in light of the limitations (of information and resources, plus other responsibilities and influences) inherent in Attorney General enforcement.

While in *Patton* the court did not expressly adopt the "special interest" approach, the court in *Patton* did acknowledge that the California Supreme Court, in a prior opinion, had noted favorably that other jurisdictions have adopted and applied the "special interest" approach. *See Holt v. College of Osteopathic Physicians and Surgeons*, 61 Cal.2d 750 (1964). One could argue that the California courts have implicitly endorsed the "special interest" approach, though neither court expressly invoked or relied on it to justify its holding.

4. *Settlor*: As a general rule, the party must have an interest in the trust to have standing to enforce the terms of a trust. If the trust is a revocable trust, the settlor

maintains an interest in the trust and thus generally has standing (though one might assume it would be easier to revoke the trust than to sue to enforce its terms against a reluctant or breaching trustee). Where a trust is irrevocable, however, the general rule is the settlor has no interest in the trust and thus has no standing.

Historically, this same logic applied to the trustee of a charitable trust. Assuming the trust was irrevocable, the settlor had no standing to enforce the terms of the trust. The modern trend, however, is moving toward granting the settlor standing if he or she has some rights under the terms of the trust. Where a settlor has retained a reversionary interest in the trust, that interest is increasingly considered sufficient to find that the settlor has standing to sue to enforce the terms of the trust. Where a settlor has retained some role in the administration of the trust, such as the settlor's right to receive and approve the accountings, as in the *Patton* case, courts are increasingly granting the settlor standing—just as the court did in *Patton*.

The RESTATEMENT (THIRD) OF TRUSTS and the Uniform Trust Code both grant the settlor standing to sue to enforce the terms of a charitable trust even in the absence of any interest in the charitable trust. RESTATEMENT (THIRD) OF TRUSTS § 94(2); UTC § 405(c). In *L.B. Research & Education Foundation v. UCLA Foundation*, 130 Cal. App. 4th 171 (Ct. App. 2005), a California Court of Appeal appeared to be rather open to that position (though the comment is, admittedly, dicta):

> A donor contributed $1 million to establish an endowed chair at the UCLA School of Medicine, which UCLA accepted along with the conditions imposed by the donor. The primary question on this appeal is whether the agreement created (1) a contract subject to a condition subsequent or (2) a charitable trust, the answer to which supposedly determines whether the donor has standing to sue UCLA and the Regents of the University of California to enforce the terms of the gift. We find there is a contract subject to a condition subsequent, not a charitable trust, and also find that, *in either event, the donor has standing to pursue this action.* Because the trial court reached a contrary result, we reverse.

Id. at 712 (emphasis added).

5. *The IRS*: Increasingly, the IRS is becoming a player in enforcing the terms of charitable trusts. The IRS has a rather large stick that it can use to get a trustee's attention: it can threaten to revoke the trust's tax-exempt status if the trustee does not comply with the terms of the trust. The IRS played an instrumental role in getting the noncomplying trustees removed by the probate court in the *Bishop Estates* case in Hawaii. *See* Rick Daysog, *IRS Wants Bishop Trustees Out*, HONOLULU STAR-BULLETIN, Apr. 28, 1999, at A-1.

III. Power to Modify — The Doctrine of Cy Pres

Because a charitable trust is not subject to the Rule Against Perpetuities, depending on the particular trust purpose there is a risk that, over time, the settlor's particular charitable purpose may become impossible or impractical—or it may even be satisfied (i.e., a trust is created to help find a cure for a disease, and a cure is found). If the trust purpose becomes impossible, impractical, or if it has been fulfilled, de facto the trust has failed. General trust law provides that where a trust fails, in whole or in part, at any time (at creation or during the life of a trust), a resulting trust should be imposed and the property should be returned to the settlor. What difference, if any, should it make if the trust in question is a charitable trust?

In re Elizabeth J.K.L. Lucas Charitable Gift
261 P.3d 800 (Haw. 2011)

Opinion of the Court by LEONARD, J.

Petitioner-Appellant Hawaiian Humane Society (HHS) appeals.... In this case, the Probate Court declined to apply the doctrine of *cy pres* to modify a charitable gift of land. The position of all parties on appeal is that the Probate Court erred in failing to apply *cy pres* to approve the proposed land transaction....

I. *BACKGROUND*

A. *The Charitable Gift*

The underlying petition in this case stems from HHS's acquisition of an interest in certain land in the Niu Valley, obtained through a charitable gift. On December 28, 1976, Elizabeth J.K.L. Lucas (Mrs. Lucas) granted HHS a 50.6183968% undivided interest in the land by way of deed. On December 30, 1982, she conveyed an additional 1.4% undivided interest in the land to HHS by way of a second deed. Both deeds contain the following use restriction:

> [F]or and as a charitable gift, [Mrs. Lucas] does hereby grant, bargain, sell and convey the property hereinafter described unto the HAWAIIAN HU-MANE SOCIETY ... so long as the same shall be used for the benefit of the public for the operation of an educational preserve for flora and fauna, to be made accessible as an educational experience for the public under the control and administration of said Hawaiian Humane Society and its successors and assigns, and, if not so used, then to State of Hawaii and its successors and assigns, for and as a public park.

Upon Mrs. Lucas's death in 1986, her remaining 47.981603% interest in the land passed through her estate to her daughter, grandchildren, and great-grandchildren (the Thompsons), all of whom have resided on the land for many years. The Thompsons formed a Hawai'i general partnership, Respondent-Appellee Tiana Partners, to which they transferred their interest in the land.

B. *Attempts to Use the Gifted Land*

After receiving the land, HHS made numerous attempts to plan a feasible use for the land in furtherance of the deed restrictions. In consultation with Tiana Partners, HHS considered many different ideas for effectuating the purpose stated in the deeds, but ultimately rejected them as physically or economically unfeasible.

In 2003, HHS commissioned a feasibility study for a proposed low-intensity development that would be accessible to the public. The study led HHS to conclude that using the land for a public educational preserve would be extremely expensive and impractical. It would require disrupting the Thompson residences and surrounding neighborhood.

During 2004 and 2005, HHS and Tiana Partners conducted a series of meetings with various community organizations, including the Honolulu Zoo, the Hawai'i Nature Center, and the Department of Education. The purpose of the meetings was to identify potential uses for the land that would be consistent with the intent of the gift, beneficial to the community, and physically and economically feasible. Due to the residential character of the surrounding neighborhood, an overriding consideration was maintaining peaceful coexistence with the Thompsons and other residents in the area. Access to the property was also a key consideration. The land is remote; much of it is steep; and it is accessible only by two residential roads. Using either road for public access would have a disruptive impact on the neighboring residents.

The State of Hawai'i (State) Department of Land and Natural Resources (DLNR) likewise determined that the land was not suitable for use as a public park. However, it determined that a portion of the land, Parcel 2, was best-suited for watershed and forest reserve purposes.

C. *Land Exchange Agreement*

HHS and Tiana Partners began considering other ways to further the intent of the original gift. On September 11, 2006, after extensive negotiations, they signed a Memorandum of Understanding (MOU). The MOU contemplates a three-way land exchange and sale between HHS, Tiana Partners, and the State. HHS and Tiana Partners agreed to convey their interests in Parcel 2 to the State. In exchange, the State would release its executory interest in the remaining parcels. HHS also agreed to convey its interest in the remaining parcels (1, 20, and 21) to Tiana Partners, free and clear of the use restriction, for $1,082,850. HHS would use the proceeds to establish a segregated fund known as the "Charles and Clorinda Lucas Educational Fund" (Educational Fund). The principal and interest would be dedicated exclusively to HHS's educational programs. These programs are designed to foster compassion and caring for all life, focusing on the interdependent relationship between animals, humans, and the environment and our role as stewards and caregivers.

The MOU conditioned the proposed land exchange upon: (1) the agreement of the State Board of Land and Natural Resources (BLNR); (2) the approval of the Hawai'i Legislature, pursuant to Hawaii Revised Statutes (HRS) § 171-50; and (3) the approval of the Probate Court. At board meetings on December 8, 2006 and December 14, 2007, the BLNR approved in principle the land exchange transaction. In December of 2007, the Legislature also approved the transaction.

D. *Petition to Approve Land Exchange*

On October 28, 2008, HHS filed a Petition to Approve Land Exchange Free and Clear of Use Restrictions (Petition) with the Probate Court. The Petition sought an order approving the proposed land transaction and eliminating the use restriction on the land. HHS maintained that the Probate Court had authority to modify the terms of the charitable gift because its stated purpose was impracticable and could not reasonably be accomplished.

The Attorney General, acting as *parens patriae,* filed a response to the Petition on November 19, 2008. He stated no objection to the relief sought and affirmed that the use restriction "has been proven demonstrably impracticable or impossible and … the relief sought in the petition is fair and reasonable and is consistent with the doctrine of cy pres." The State filed a joinder in the Petition on November 21, 2008. The Administrator of the Division of Forestry and Wildlife of the DLNR filed a declaration attesting that the DLNR had inspected and reviewed the properties described in the Petition. The DLNR "determined that these properties are not presently suitable for use as a public park, and in particular that Parcel 2 is best used for watershed and forest reserve purposes."

Laura Thompson (Thompson), Mrs. Lucas's daughter, filed a declaration attesting that Mrs. Lucas would have fully supported the land exchange "as a compromise necessary to further her deep interest in all things natural and her strong commitment to education, which can be accomplished far better through the broad reach of the Hawaiian Humane Society than in a narrow urban valley." She attested that Mrs. Lucas "was actively involved with the Hawaiian Humane Society throughout her life" and served on its Board of Directors. Mrs. Lucas fully supported its mission "to promote the bond between humans and animals and to foster the humane treatment of all animals." Thompson believed her mother was not aware of the obstacles preventing development of the land in accordance with the deeds. She believed her mother's original intent in gifting the land was "to benefit the people of Hawai'i through the work of the Hawaiian Humane Society" and to "help the Society provide an educational experience for the public."

E. *Probate Court Order and Judgment*

Following a hearing, the Probate Court entered the Order Denying Petition on May 18, 2009. The court stated the following grounds as its basis for the denial:

> 1. The deeds provide, "… for and as a charitable gift, does hereby grant, bargain, sell and convey the property hereinafter described unto the Hawaiian Humane Society, … so long as the same shall be used for the benefit of the public for the operation of an educational preserve for flora and fauna, to be made accessible as an educational experience for the public under the control and administration of said Hawaiian Humane Society, … and if not so used, then to State of Hawaii, its successors and assigns for and as a public park, …"

> 2. Even if the Court finds that the deeds create a charitable trust, the Memorandum of Understanding does not involve the use of the properties as stated in the deeds. The Memorandum of Understanding states that the Petitioner will receive cash in exchange for conveying its interest in the properties and will use the cash "… to establish a segregated fund to be known as the

'Charles and Clorinda Lucas Educational Fund,' the principle [sic] and interest of which fund shall be used exclusively to pay the costs associated with educational programs designed to foster compassion and caring for all life, focused on the interdependent relationship between animals, humans and the environment and on our roles as stewards and caregivers."

3. Mrs. Lucas' charitable purpose as stated in the deeds is to use the properties for the operation of an educational preserve for flora and fauna, to be made accessible as an educational experience for the public. The deeds also provide that if the petitioner does not use the properties for the stated charitable purpose, the properties would go to the State of Hawaii.

4. The doctrine of *cy pres* does not apply to the Petitioner since the deeds provide for an alternative if the properties are not used by the Petitioner as Mrs. Lucas intended.

On August 3, 2009, HHS filed a petition for relief from the Probate Court's Order Denying Petition. The Attorney General and Tiana Partners filed joinders in the petition for relief, and the State filed a memorandum of no opposition. All interested parties agreed that the Probate Court misconstrued the *cy pres* doctrine and that it should have approved the transaction.

On December 21, 2009, the Probate Court entered the Order Denying Relief and the Judgment. HHS timely appealed.

II. *POINTS OF ERROR*

On appeal, HHS argues that the Probate Court erred in denying the Petition and refusing to modify the terms of the charitable gift to approve the proposed land exchange. Tiana Partners filed an Answering Brief in support of HHS's position. The State filed an Answering Brief expressing its non-opposition and joinder in HHS's request for relief.

III. *STANDARDS OF REVIEW*

Hawai'i courts have not addressed the applicable standard of review for a lower court's refusal to apply the doctrine of *cy pres*. In applying an analogous doctrine to reform the terms of a private trust, the supreme court analyzed the issue as a question of law. *In re Estate of Chun Quan Yee Hop*, 52 Haw. 40, 45–46, 469 P.2d 183, 186–87 (1970). Other jurisdictions have held that whether *cy pres* applies is a question of law, reviewable *de novo*.... Accordingly, we hold that the issue of whether the doctrine of *cy pres* is applicable is a question of law, reviewable *de novo*. Once *cy pres* is determined to be applicable, the lower court has discretion in determining the appropriate modification of the charitable gift. *Obermeyer v. Bank of America, N.A.*, 140 S.W.3d 18, 22 (Mo.2004).

IV. *DISCUSSION*

A. *Cy Pres Generally*

The doctrine of *cy pres* "permits a gift for a charitable purpose which cannot, for one reason or another, be carried out as directed by the donor, to be applied 'as nearly as may be' to the fulfillment of the underlying charitable intent." 15 Am.Jur.2d *Charities* §149 (2011) (*Am.Jur.2d*). Under the doctrine's traditional formulation, three elements are required: (1) there must be property given in trust for a charitable purpose; (2) it must be impossible, impracticable, or illegal to carry out the specified charitable purpose; and (3) the settlor must have manifested a general intent to devote the property to charitable purposes. *Id.* . . .

Cy pres is only applicable to charitable trusts. *Restatement (Third) of Trusts* §67, cmt. a (2003) (*Restatement 3d*); *Am.Jur.2d* §149. Various policy considerations underlie its application. First and foremost, the doctrine stems from the inability of charitable settlors to foresee the future. *Restatement 3d*, Reporter's Notes, cmt. a (recognizing that without *cy pres*, "many charities would fail by change of circumstances and the happening of contingencies which no human foresight could provide against"). Circumstances change and contingencies frequently arise that the settlor did not or could not anticipate. This is particularly true for charitable trusts, as they may be perpetual in duration. *Id.*; Ronald Chester, George Gleason Bogert, and George Taylor Bogert, *The Law of Trusts & Trustees* §431, at 117 (3d ed. 2005) (*Bogert on Trusts*). The "needs and circumstances of society evolve over time," impacting the potential benefit of the trust. *Restatement 3d* §67, cmt. a. Rather than allowing the trust to fail, *cy pres* preserves the settlor's charitable intent by conforming the trust to the contingencies that arise. Thus "[j]ust as it is against the policy of the trust law to permit wasteful or seriously inefficient use of resources dedicated to charity, trust law also favors an interpretation that would sustain a charitable trust and avoid the return of the trust property to the settlor or successors in interest." *Id.* at cmt. b. Similarly, because charitable trusts impact a broad spectrum of the public and "are allowed by the law to be perpetual," they often merit a greater exercise of judicial discretion than a private trust. *Id.* at Reporter's Notes, cmt. a.

Courts widely recognize that the charitable purpose need not be impossible to warrant applying *cy pres*. It is sufficient that achieving the settlor's stated purpose would be impracticable or unreasonable to effectuate. *Restatement 3d* §67, cmt. c ("The doctrine of *cy pres* may also be applied, even though it is *possible* to carry out the particular purpose of the settlor, if to do so would not accomplish the settlor's charitable objective, or *would not do so in a reasonable way*.") (second emphasis added); *Bogert on Trusts* §438, at 194–96 (recognizing insufficiency of funds as basis for doctrine); *Scott on Trusts* §39.5.2, at 2717–20; §39.5.4, at 2740–41; *Am.Jur.2d* §151 (doctrine is applicable where donor's directions "*cannot beneficially* be carried into effect") (emphasis added; punctuation altered). "An impractical restriction is one that is not capable of being carried out in practice." *Am.Jur.2d* §157. If literal compliance would "defeat or substantially impair" the purposes of the trust, *cy pres* is applicable. *Restatement 2d* §399, cmt. a. The purpose of the trust becomes impaired if "the application of [trust] property to such purpose would not accomplish the general charitable intention of the settlor." 88 Am.Jur. *Proof of Facts* 3d 469, §10 (2006) (*Am.Jur. Proof of Facts* 3d).

Thus, *cy pres* is applicable where a settlor creates a charitable trust of real property to be used for a particular purpose, but the property turns out to be unsuitable for that purpose. *See Scott on Trusts* § 39.5.2, at 2724–25; *Roberds v. Markham,* 81 F.Supp. 38, 40 (D.D.C.1948) (recognizing that courts may order sale of gifted land if conditions have drastically changed or land otherwise becomes unsuitable for its dedicated purpose); *Bd. of Educ. of Rockford v. City of Rockford,* 372 Ill. 442, 24 N.E.2d 366, 369– 73 (1939) (applying *cy pres* to allow sale of land in charitable trust where its dedicated use as school became impracticable due to shifting populations, deterioration of existing building, and existence of another school that met needs of the area). In one case, for example, a settlor gifted certain land to a charity for the purpose of building a public library upon the land. *Bosson v. Woman's Christian Nat'l Library Ass'n,* 216 Ark. 334, 225 S.W.2d 336, 337 (1949). The land turned out to be unsuitable for constructing a library. *Id.* The charity reached an agreement with a county library board under which it would sell the land and use the proceeds to build a public library upon property owned by the county board. *Id.* The board agreed to operate the library for the benefit and use of the public. *Id.* at 337–38. On appeal, the court applied *cy pres* to approve the transaction. *Id.* at 338–39. It noted that *cy pres* applies where the circumstances "have changed to such an extent that in order to carry out properly the charitable intention of the donor, it is necessary to dispose of the trust property and devote the funds to the acquisition of a more suitable location[.]" *Id.* at 338 (internal quotation marks and citation omitted).

Similarly, a California court applied *cy pres* where the stated purposes of the gifted properties became impracticable. *In re Estate of Zahn,* 16 Cal.App.3d 106, 93 Cal.Rptr. 810 (1971). There, the testatrix left two residential properties to the Salvation Army. *Id.* at 811. She directed the Flower Street property to be used as a home for Christian women, and the Keniston Avenue property as a music home. *Id.* After her death, the Flower Street property was taken pursuant to eminent domain and the Keniston Avenue property was deemed unsuitable for development due to zoning issues. *Id.* at 813. The Salvation Army proposed to use the funds from the Flower Street property to erect and furnish a new building on a different site. *Id.* It further proposed to sell the Keniston Avenue property and use the proceeds to either construct a music conservatory on another site or endow a music room under construction at another Salvation Army center. *Id.*

The court confirmed that *cy pres* was applicable. *Id.* at 814. It concluded that because neither property was suitable for carrying out the testatrix's declared intentions, the lower, court "properly directed that her charitable purposes be given effect at some other suitable locations." *Id.; see also Bogert on Trusts* § 439, at 218–20 (noting that *cy pres* is applicable where trust property is taken under eminent domain).

The third element—general charitable intent—has been a source of uncertainty and reform. Under the traditional rule, *cy pres* may only be applied if the settlor possessed a general charitable intent. Am.Jur.2d § 153. His or her intent must have encompassed "something beyond the specific terms used in designating the beneficiary or purpose of the gift or how it shall be carried into effect." *Id.; see also Restatement 2d* § 399; *Bogert on Trusts* § 431, at 119; § 436, at 157–60. The donor must have had a general charitable intent, as opposed to a narrow intent to benefit only a "particular project, objective, or institution[.]" Am.Jur.2d § 153. For example, where a settlor's dominant intent is to restrict the charitable gift to the *exact* purpose specified, courts may presume that the donor would not have wanted the property to be applied to any other purpose, however closely related, even if the original purpose fails. *Restatement 2d* § 399, cmt. d. In such situations, *cy pres* is not applicable because the settlor did not have a general charitable intent. *Id.; see also Shoemaker v. Am. Sec. & Trust Co.,* 163 F.2d 585, 588 (D.C.Cir.1947) (noting that *cy pres* does not apply if the settlor's "dominant purpose has become altogether impossible of achievement"). In contrast, if the settlor's designation of a particular property or site is incidental to the dominant charitable purpose, then courts will presume that the settlor's primary intent was to dedicate the property to charitable purposes. *Shoemaker,* 163 F.2d at 589; *see also In re Wilkey's Estate,* 337 Pa. 129, 10 A.2d 425, 428 (1940) (recognizing that *cy pres* applies where "the physical location of the edifice or institution provided for in a charitable trust has been held to be of secondary importance in comparison with the general purpose for which the erection of the building or the carrying on of the charitable activity was designed"). In such cases, *cy pres* is readily applicable to effectuate the settlor's general charitable intent. *Shoemaker,* 163 F.2d at 589.

Increasingly, the "general charitable intent" requirement has shifted to an "opt-out" framework under which the settlor is presumed to have a general charitable intent unless the terms of the trust provide otherwise. *See Restatement 3d* § 67, cmt. b; Reporter's Notes, cmt. b; Unif. Trust Code § 413(a), 7C U.L.A. 509 (2006); *Bogert on Trusts* § 436, at 160 (noting that "it would seem preferable" either to employ presumption in favor of general intent or apply *cy pres* regardless of whether the settlor's charitable intent was general or specific); *but see* Am.Jur. *Proof of Facts* 3d § 6 (noting that "presumption of general charitable purpose has not yet been discussed in the reported decisions"). Commentators have noted that the "general intent" requirement is vague and difficult to apply consistently. Ronald Chester, *Cy Pres or Gift Over?: The Search for Coherence in Judicial Reform of Failed Charitable Trusts,* 23 Suffolk U.L.Rev. 41, 45–46 (1989); *accord Bogert on Trusts* § 436, at 159–60; § 437, at 183–89 (noting widespread inconsistency in applying this requirement). It turns on a fine, and often subjective, distinction between a settlor's dominant and incidental or subsidiary objectives. *See Bogert on Trusts,* § 437 at 183–89. In contrast, the opt-out rule provides a clearer delineation that avoids guesswork as to the subtleties of the settlor's intent.

Finally, in applying *cy pres,* courts must generally seek a purpose that conforms to the donor's objective "as nearly as possible." Am.Jur.2d § 157. This may be attained by limiting or modifying the objective; by diverting the funds to another use in the "same generally contemplated field"; or by directing sale of the subject property. *Id.;* Am.Jur. *Proof of Facts* 3d § 10; *Restatement 2d* § 399, cmt. p (*cy pres* allows sale of land even if "the settlor in specific words directed that the land should not be sold and that the institution should not be maintained in any other place"). In the case of a sale, the proceeds may be applied to purchase a new, more suitable site, or to further the settlor's charitable intent in another manner. *See* Am.Jur. *Proof of Facts* 3d § 21. Where a charitable gift of property is subject to use restrictions, the court may apply *cy pres* to modify or eliminate those restrictions. *Id.* at § 22; *Bogert on Trusts* § 431, at 115; *Scott on Trusts* § 39.5.2, at 2716.

In determining the appropriate modification, courts must consider a variety of factors and evidence to ascertain what the settlor's wishes would have been had he or she anticipated the circumstances. *Restatement 3d* § 67, cmt. d. Chief among them is the settlor's probable intent. *Id.* Where the settlor is deceased, this intent may be discerned from extrinsic evidence as well as the language of the trust instrument. Such evidence includes the interests and attitudes that motivated the settlor's gift; his or her involvement or interest in particular charitable institutions; and the settlor's "relationships, social or religious affiliations, personal background, charitable-giving history, and the like." *Id.; accord Bogert on Trusts* § 442, at 257–58. The language of the trust instrument is also pertinent. *Restatement 2d* § 399, cmt. d.

The modern approach to *cy pres* also emphasizes considering the efficiency and beneficial impact of the proposed use. *Restatement 3d* § 67, cmt. d. As the settlor's intent cannot be known for certain, applying *cy pres* necessarily involves some level of speculation. *Id.; accord Scott on Trusts* § 39.5.2, at 2709 (noting that courts must make "an educated guess" as to the settlor's wishes). Thus, it is generally "reasonable to suppose that among relatively similar purposes, charitably-inclined settlors would tend to prefer those most beneficial to their communities. *Restatement 3d* § 67, cmt. d (emphasis omitted; punctuation altered). To an increasing extent, courts thus seek to apply the trust property toward "a scheme which on the whole is best suited to accomplish the general charitable purpose of the donor." *Restatement 2d* § 399, cmt. b. Finally, the wishes of the trustees, the Attorney General as *parens patriae,* the beneficiaries, and other interested parties also warrant consideration. *Id.* at cmt. f; *Bogert on Trusts* § 442, at 258.

B. *Gift over Rule*

Having established the broad contours of the *cy pres* doctrine, we now turn to the heart of the issue on appeal: whether the Probate Court erred in concluding that *cy pres* is not applicable in this case. The Probate Court reasoned that *cy pres* does not apply because the deeds provide an alternative distribution in the event that the primary charitable purpose fails. It concluded that "if [HHS] does not use the properties for the stated charitable purpose, the properties would go to the State of Hawaii."

The Probate Court's rationale appears to invoke the gift over rule. A gift over is a provision that sets forth an alternative distribution in the event that the primary purpose of the charitable gift fails. Am.Jur.2d § 151. The presence of a gift over provision may potentially preclude application of *cy pres* in two ways: (1) by negating the existence of a general charitable intent, and (2) by providing an alternative distribution in the event that the settlor's original purpose fails. *Restatement 2d* § 399, Reporter's Notes, cmt. c; Am.Jur.2d § 151; *Scott on Trusts* § 39.5.2, at 2710–13; § 39.7.5, at 2795–97; 14 C.J.S. *Charities* § 56 (2011).

The first application of the gift over rule is only relevant to the traditional requirement that the settlor exhibit a general charitable intent. Under this reasoning, the gift over confirms the settlor's narrow and specific intent. 14 C.J.S. *Charities* § 56. This is especially true where the gift over is to a non-charity, such as a possibility of reverter. *Nelson v. Kring,* 225 Kan. 499, 592 P.2d 438, 444 (1979); *In re Goehringer's Will,* 69 Misc.2d 145, 329 N.Y.S.2d 516, 521 (N.Y.Surr.Ct.1972) (noting that presence of gift over provision "is a clear manifestation that [the] testator had a particular rather than general charitable intention"); *Roberds,* 81 F.Supp. at 40–42 (concluding that because deed contained possibility of reverter if land ever ceased to be used for its prescribed purpose, settlor's intent was specific to that purpose). Such a provision indicates that the settlor only wished to dedicate the property to a specific purpose and, if that specific purpose failed, to not dedicate it to charity at all. *In re Goehringer's Will,* 329 N.Y.S.2d at 521 ("[A] specific gift over will almost conclusively preclude any determination that he had other than an intent to benefit the particular charity.").

In contrast, where the gift over is to another charity or charitable purpose, many courts recognize that it confirms a general charitable intent. *See Bogert on Trusts* § 437, at 165–70; *Scott on Trusts* § 39.5.2, at 2713; *First Nat'l Bank of Chicago v. Elliott,* 406 Ill. 44, 92 N.E.2d 66, 74 (1950). Such a provision illustrates the settlor's intent to dedicate the property to charity, even if the original purpose fails. *Bogert on Trusts* § 437, at 165–70.

Here, the deeds provide an alternative charitable purpose: for the land to be used by the State as a public park. Under the traditional formulation of the charitable intent requirement, the gift over in this case confirms Mrs. Lucas's general charitable intent. Thus, regardless of the continuing viability of the general intent requirement, the gift over provision does not prevent application of *cy pres* under the first rationale.

In any event, it does not appear that the Probate Court applied the first rationale of the gift over rule. The Order Denying Petition contains no mention of general charitable intent. Instead, the Court's reasoning conforms to the second rationale. It concluded that because the deeds direct an alternative distribution, *cy pres* is inapplicable.

This second application of the gift over rule provides that *cy pres* is inapplicable as the trust property should be applied toward its alternative purpose. 14 C.J.S. *Charities* § 56. The rule reasons that the settlor foresaw the potential failure of the first purpose and accordingly provided an alternative purpose. *Id.* Thus, effectuating the alternative distribution matches the settlor's intent more closely than applying *cy pres* to maintain the first, failed purpose.

A number of cases affirm the straightforward application of this rule. In *Roberds v. Markham,* for example, the settlor conveyed property in trust to a church for its continuing operation as a church or place of worship. 81 F.Supp. at 39. The deed provided that if the property ever ceased to be used for church purposes, it would revert to the settlor's heirs and assigns. *Id.* Many years later, when the character of the surrounding neighborhood had changed and the church's population had shifted, the trustees sought to sell the property and re-erect the church at another, more suitable location. *Id.* The court concluded that because the deed contained a possibility of reverter, the settler had intended the land to revert to her heirs and assigns if its use as a church ever became impracticable or impossible. *Id.* at 40–42. It therefore did not apply *cy pres* to permit the sale. *Id.* at 42; ...

Yet this application of the gift over rule is subject to an important caveat. Where the alternative distribution is unfeasible, impracticable, or impossible, then the gift over rule does not preclude the application of *cy pres* to save the first charitable purpose. Am.Jur. *Proof of Facts* 3d § 19; 14 C.J.S. *Charities* § 56; *Restatement 3d* § 67, cmt. b. In such cases, applying the alternative purpose would likewise frustrate or substantially impair the settlor's intent. *Cy pres* is thus necessary to save the trust from failure.

...

... Fundamentally, the doctrine exists to save a charitable trust from failure while preserving the settlor's original, charitable intent. *Restatement 3d* § 67, cmt. b. Thus where both the primary and alternative charitable distributions are impracticable, courts may presume that the settlor would have intended one or both purposes to survive under application of *cy pres.*

Here, the deeds provide that if the first purpose—an educational nature preserve operated by HHS—fails, the property passes to the State "for and as a public park." This secondary purpose, however, is likewise impracticable. The DLNR determined that the land was unsuitable for use as a public park, and that only a portion of the land could be used as a forest preserve and watershed. Thus, the Legislature approved the proposed land exchange, and the State filed a joinder in HHS's Petition. Redirecting the land to the State would not effectuate Mrs. Lucas's charitable intent. Rather, it would result in the failure of the trust.... [B]oth the primary and alternative purposes of the gift are impracticable, as the land cannot feasibly be used for either purpose. The Probate Court therefore erred in concluding that the gift over rule precludes application of *cy pres.*

C. Cy Pres Applies to Approve the Proposed Land Exchange

HHS, Tiana Partners, and the State request this court to remand the case with instructions to apply *cy pres* to approve the proposed land exchange free and clear of the use restrictions. We agree that *cy pres* so applies in this case.

As discussed above, *cy pres* applies where: (1) property is given in trust for a charitable purpose; (2) it is impracticable to carry out the specified charitable purpose; and (3) the settlor manifested a general intent to devote the property to charitable purposes. *Supra* part IV(A). Here, those elements are met. Mrs. Lucas conveyed the land to HHS for charitable purposes for the use and benefit of the public. The parties do not dispute, and the evidence readily establishes, that Mrs. Lucas's specified purposes for the land are both impracticable.

The conveyance also satisfies the traditional requirement of general charitable intent. In determining whether the settlor possessed a general charitable intent, courts consider the language of the instrument, the nature and duration of the gift, the character of the recipient organization, the presence or absence of a reversionary clause, and the mode for effectuating the gift. Am.Jur.2d § 154. Courts may also consider extrinsic evidence of the settlor's probable intent. Am.Jur. *Proof of Facts* 3d § 20;

accord Bogert on Trusts § 437, at 160–73. If the settlor intended the gift to "be continued within the limits of its general purpose" rather than cease upon the failure of its specific purpose, this constitutes a general intent. *Obermeyer,* 140 S.W.3d at 24. Gifts in support of educational goals often demonstrate a general charitable intent because there is a perpetual need and use for them. *Id.; accord Bogert on Trusts* § 436, at 157.

In this case, the deeds convey the land "for and as a charitable gift" for the purpose of educating the public. They specify an alternative means of achieving the charitable purpose in the event the first method fails. The deeds thus confirm that Mrs. Lucas did not intend the trust to fail should use of the land become impracticable. *See Bogert on Trusts* § 437, at 165–70 (gift over to another charitable purpose confirms general charitable intent); *accord Scott on Trusts* § 39.5.2, at 2713; *First Nat'l Bank of Chicago,* 92 N.E.2d at 74. The declaration of Mrs. Lucas's daughter, evidencing Mrs. Lucas's probable wishes regarding the property had she been alive, further supports a general charitable intent.

Finally, the proposed land exchange closely conforms to Mrs. Lucas's original purpose. The deed restriction contemplates a nature preserve to function "as an educational experience for the public." Mrs. Lucas's daughter attested that her mother intended to generally benefit the people of Hawai'i by enabling HHS to provide "an educational experience for the public." The Educational Fund preserves those goals by promoting educational programming that focuses on the natural environment. This use of the funds also comports with Mrs. Lucas's lifelong interest and involvement with HHS. It accomplishes her probable wishes regarding the use of the land had she been aware of the obstacles preventing its development.... This unanimous accord further supports applying *cy pres* to approve the transaction. *See Restatement 2d* § 399, cmt. f; *Bogert on Trusts* § 442, at 258 (recognizing that wishes of trustees, beneficiaries, attorney general, and other interested parties warrant consideration). There is no evidence, either extrinsic or in the deeds themselves, to support a contrary conclusion.

V. *CONCLUSION*

For these reasons, we conclude that the Probate Court erred in concluding that *cy pres* is not applicable to approve the proposed transaction on the basis that the deeds provide for an alternative distribution. Accordingly, we vacate the Judgment and remand to the Probate Court to apply *cy pres* consistent with this Opinion.

Notes

1. *Logic underlying traditional approach*: As the court notes, the traditional approach to cy pres involved three elements: "(1) property is given in trust for a charitable purpose; (2) it is impracticable to carry out the specified charitable purpose; and (3) the settlor manifested a general intent to devote the property to charitable purposes." The logic underlying the doctrine is revealed by its name. Cy pres is French for "as near as possible." Inasmuch as the settlor had a general charitable intent, and within that general charitable intent a more specific charitable intent, if that particular specific

charitable intent becomes impossible or impractical, a presumption arises that the settlor would prefer the court pick another specific charitable intent "as near as possible" to the original specific intent (and within the settlor's general charitable intent) instead of having the charitable trust fail. Cy pres, however, cannot be carried out unilaterally by the trustee; it requires court approval. California has long recognized the doctrine of cy pres.

2. *General charitable intent*: Who really owns the property in a charitable trust: the settlor (or his or her heirs) or the public? How you answer that question may affect how you view the doctrine of cy pres. Once a charitable trust has been validly created, is it, for all practical purposes, the public's property? Or does the public only acquire a limited interest in the property subject to the settlor's ongoing intent and control? While that phrasing oversimplifies the issue, it offers one way to think about the issue.

The requirement of general charitable intent is consistent with the view that the settlor still owns the property in a charitable trust and therefore the settlor must consent to the proposed modification. The logic is that the settlor's more general charitable intent constitutes a form of consent to a court applying cy pres if the specific charitable intent the settlor selected becomes impossible or impractical. In that respect, cy pres is analogous to the modification doctrine as it applies to private trusts. It applies where an unforeseen change in conditions frustrates the settlor's intent. Historically, modification of a private trust also required the consent of all beneficiaries. Inasmuch as a charitable trust has no ascertainable beneficiaries, courts de facto substitute the settlor's consent for the consent of the beneficiaries. The settlor's consent is inferred from the general charitable purpose. One could even argue that implicit in the traditional cy pres doctrine is the argument that the general charitable intent is more important than the specific charitable intent.

The modern trend implicitly argues that the traditional approach accords too much weight to the element of general charitable intent. From the modern trend perspective, inferring a settlor's consent (or lack of consent) from the presence or absence of general charitable intent is: (1) too formalistic, and (2) too artificial. Some settlors likely never consider the possibility that their charitable purpose may one day become impossible or impractical. In fact, too often the task of asking what the settlor would like done if he or she had known that the specific charitable purpose would become impossible or impractical is pure speculation. Thus, the traditional common law view de facto creates a presumption against application of cy pres absent general charitable intent. The modern trend, however, implicitly argues the presumption should be in favor of cy pres absent evidence of the settlor's intent that cy pres should *not* apply. The settlor's original intent, after all, was to make a charitable gift. The modern trend approach is also consistent with the view that the public owns the property in a charitable trust—or, at the very least, that the property is closer to that end of the spectrum than the alternative (continued private ownership by the settlor or the settlor's estate/distant relatives).

As the court noted, both the Restatement (Third) of Trusts and the Uniform Trust Code abolish the requirement of general charitable intent. Instead, they create a presumption of consent and require the settlor to expressly opt out of the presumption. *See* Restatement (Third) of Trusts §67 cmt. b, reporter's notes cmt. b; UTC §413. The court states that "the opt-out rule provides a clearer delineation that avoids guesswork as to the subtleties of the settlor's intent." While that may be true going forward, does it make sense (and is it fair) to apply that approach to gifts and trusts created before the modern trend approach was articulated? Obviously, eliminating the need to prove general charitable intent will de facto increase the likelihood that cy pres will be applied. Is that merely a property grab by the public or is that actually more consistent with the settlor's original intent?

3. *Impossible, impracticable, or illegal—or inefficient?* When the court first introduces the traditional approach to cy pres, it states the standard of frustration properly. The particular charitable purpose must have become "impossible, impracticable, or illegal." Later though, when the court analyzes that element, the court uses some alternative phrasing: "impracticable or *unreasonable*...," "the property turns out to be *unsuitable*...." Is the court holding to the traditional approach, or is the court subtly shifting toward the modern trend?

The modern trend openly calls for a more relaxed standard for analyzing whether it is appropriate to apply cy pres to a particular charitable intent. The Restatement (Third) of Trusts, section 67, adds an additional economic consideration:

> Unless the terms of the trust provide otherwise, where property is placed in trust to be applied to a designated charitable purpose and it is or becomes unlawful, impossible, or impracticable to carry out that purpose, or to the extent it is or becomes wasteful to apply all of the property to the designated purpose, the charitable trust will not fail but the court will direct application of the property or appropriate portion thereof to a charitable purpose that reasonably approximates the designated purpose.

Is "wasteful" more of a subjective consideration than the others, or is it implicit in the traditional "impractical" consideration? Does it broaden the applicability of the doctrine, or is it just a better statement of what has always been implicit in the doctrine? Does it reflect a shift toward the "public ownership" end of the spectrum? If the public deems application of the trust property toward that specific charitable purpose "wasteful," is the public now free to change the purpose of the trust? Or is that just what a reasonable settlor would do if he or she were still alive and in control? Is this nothing more than a "probable intent"-type approach to unforeseen changes that may affect a charitable trust?

The Uniform Trust Code takes an even more aggressive approach to the public ownership issue of who owns property in a charitable trust as it applies to the doctrine of cy pres:

UTC §413. Cy Pres

    (a) Except as otherwise provided in subsection (b), if a particular charitable purpose becomes unlawful, impracticable, impossible to achieve, or wasteful:

        (1) the trust does not fail, in whole or in part;

(2) the trust property does not revert to the settlor or the settlor's successors in interest; and

(3) the court may apply cy pres to modify or terminate the trust by directing that the trust property be applied or distributed, in whole or in part, in a manner consistent with the settlor's charitable purposes.

(b) A provision in the terms of a charitable trust that would result in distribution of the trust property to a noncharitable beneficiary prevails over the power of the court under subsection (a) to apply cy pres to modify or terminate the trust only if, when the provision takes effect:

(1) the trust property is to revert to the settlor and the settlor is still living; or

(2) fewer than 21 years have elapsed since the date of the trust's creation.

In support of that approach, the official Comment to this Uniform Trust Code section asserts: "In the great majority of cases the settlor would prefer that the property be used for other charitable purposes. Courts are usually able to find a general charitable purpose to which to apply the property, no matter how vaguely such purpose may have been expressed by the settlor." This last comment, however, arguably supports the position that the UTC is not favoring public ownership but rather favors the settlor's intent—it just views the settlor's intent differently from the traditional common law approach. Consistent with that view, the UTC grants a settlor standing to petition a court to apply cy pres to modify the settlor's charitable trust. *See* UTC § 410(b). The UTC believes cy pres is consistent with and furthers settlor's intent, and that if the settlor were still alive, the settlor himself or herself would want to be part of the process.

The debate about whether the inefficient use of trust funds is an appropriate grounds for applying cy pres was a central issue in the California case of *San Francisco Foundation v. Superior Court*, 37 Cal. 3d 285 (1984). The California Supreme Court's statement of the facts sets the table for the examining the issue:

> The Buck trust was created by the will of Beryl Buck, a Marin County resident, who died in 1975, leaving the bulk of her estate to be held in trust and used for providing "care for the needy in Marin County" and for other charitable, religious, or educational purposes in that county.... The will names the foundation [the San Francisco Foundation] as the entity in charge of distribution [i.e., the distribution trustee] and requires that all income be distributed "not later than the end of the year following the year of receipt." ...
>
> On January 30, 1984, the foundation petitioned under Probate Code section 1120 for an order that "the Buck Trust be modified so that [after a three-year transition period] the income may be distributed throughout the entire Bay Area served by the foundation, with preference for funding from the Buck Trust to be given to grant proposals for charitable purposes in Marin County." The petition alleges that the value of the trust assets at the time of Mrs. Buck's death was $10 to $12 million with a projected annual income of "much less than $2 million," whereas the anticipated annual trust income in 1984–1987

will be at least $27 million. Exhibits before us establish that the value of the trust assets on June 30, 1983 was $360 million, and that the area served by the foundation (throughout which the petition seeks authority to distribute trust income) consists of the City and County of San Francisco and the Counties of Alameda, Contra Costa, and San Mateo, as well as Marin County.

The County of Marin responded on February 14, 1984, by filing the following: (1) A motion to remove the foundation as trustee (Prob.Code, § 1123.5), essentially on the ground that the foundation's activities in connection with its petition for modification constituted a breach of trust and rendered it unfit....

San Francisco Foundation, 37 Cal. 3d at 290–92.

The foundation's petition to modify the trust terms, and the probate court's ruling, are discussed by the California Court of Appeals in subsequent litigation involving the trust:

... In essence, the [foundation's] petition asked the court to apply the *cy près* doctrine because the size of the Buck Trust income and the relative affluence of Marin County made "it ... impracticable and inexpedient to continue to expend all of the income from the Buck Trust solely within Marin County."

In response to the petition for modification, John Elliott Cook, Marin County, and the Marin Council of Agencies filed a petition to remove the San Francisco Foundation as distribution trustee....

The petition for modification and the petition for removal of trustee were tried before the court beginning in February of 1986. After a six-month trial, the probate court issued a one hundred thirteen-page statement of decision. In its written decision, the probate court refused to apply the *cy près* doctrine to modify the Marin-only restriction. The court reasoned that all of the Buck Trust income could be spent effectively and efficiently in Marin County. Moreover, the court found that the geographic restriction in the Buck Trust was "unequivocal."

Nevertheless, the probate court found that Mrs. Buck intended that the *benefits* of expenditures made in Marin County "would and should extend beyond Marin's borders." According to the probate court, the breadth of purposes allowed in the Buck Trust also permitted the trustee to fund "major projects" in Marin County. Such major projects might include a social policy institute, an environmental research center, or a center on aging. Consequently, the statement of decision specifically provided that "Buck Trust funds may, in accordance with the terms of the Trust, be spent on projects and purposes, the benefits of which extend beyond Marin County, so long as the funds are spent in Marin County."

Estate of Buck, 29 Cal. App. 4th 1846 (Ct. App. 1994). The probate court's order did not address the petition to remove the foundation as distribution trustee, but the foundation subsequently agreed to resign.

The case gave rise to a lively academic discussion that influenced the current approach reflected in the Restatement (Third) of Trusts and the Uniform Trust Code.

Like most jurisdictions, California still follows the more traditional, common law statement of the cy pres doctrine; but at the same time, like many jurisdictions, it tends to take an increasingly liberal approach to applying the doctrine.

4. *Scope of the doctrine*: Should the court have used cy pres to save the trust in *Shenandoah Valley*? The general rule is that cy pres cannot be used to save a trust that fails to qualify as a charitable trust because it lacks a proper charitable purpose. Instead, the doctrine is used to save a charitable trust that would otherwise fail because the particular valid charitable purpose is impossible, impractical, or illegal.

If a jurisdiction has not adopted the modern trend noncharitable private purpose trust, should the courts be open to applying cy pres to benevolent trusts? Would this approach be consistent with the modern trend logic that doing so is consistent with the settlor's probable intent?

5. *The March of Dimes foundation*: The March of Dimes, a large charitable foundation, was founded in 1938 by then-U.S. President Franklin D. Roosevelt. The foundation's mission was to help eradicate polio, a disease that primarily affected children. The devastating occurrences of polio epidemics at the time made it a frightening disease for every parent. With the introduction and widespread use of the polio vaccine beginning in the mid-1950s, the disease effectively disappeared in America. Yet the March of Dimes still exists. How did the foundation's mission change over time and what is its mission today? If the foundation's legal form were that of a trust, would the doctrine of cy pres likely apply?

Problem

The Kolbs' floral business was something of an institution in Storm Lake, Iowa. The business was well known to all, and the family was well liked by all. Sadly, in the mid-1960s tragedy struck when the Kolbs' grandson was killed in a hunting accident. The Kolbs negotiated a deal with the city to create a trust to erect and maintain a fountain and garden in memory of the grandson at a specific location in one of the city's parks. The Kolbs funded the trust by deeding farmland they owned to a trust, with the net income to be used to maintain the fountain and garden.

In 2003 the City created a redevelopment proposal for the part of the city that included the park with the memorial to the Kolbs' grandson. The City proposed relocating the fountain and garden to permit the redevelopment project. The trustee sued to block the project; and in the alternative, to declare a resulting trust. The City countersued, requesting that the trustee be removed, and that the court apply cy pres. The trustee opposed cy pres on the ground that the purpose of the trust had not become impractical, unlawful, or impossible; rather the purpose was frustrated because the City simply wanted to use the land for a different purpose.

Should the court apply cy pres? *See Kolb v. City of Storm Lake*, 736 N.W.2d 546 (Iowa 2007).

Chapter 16

Powers of Appointment

I. Introduction

A. Conceptual Introduction

From an academic perspective, most students have a difficult time with powers of appointment. Having no prior experience, familiarity or conceptual understanding of what a power of appointment is, they have no sense of what it does or when it is used. In addition, the terminology surrounding powers of appointment is completely foreign to them. Accordingly, a basic conceptual understanding of the term is needed before one can begin to master the legal nuances of the doctrine.

While the term "power of appointment" may seem foreign and new, most students are familiar with its sibling doctrine: the power to revoke. In the context of a trust, the power to revoke is a power held by the settlor that provides flexibility. If a trust is revocable, and after creating the trust, certain circumstances change, the settlor can invoke the power and terminate (or modify) the trust. In essence, the power to revoke gives the settlor the ability to override the terms of the trust—to say to the trustee, regardless of the terms of the trust, "Give the trust property back to me [the settlor]." The settlor can then, if he or she wishes, create a new trust with new terms that take into consideration the changed circumstances.

In many respects a power of appointment is analogous to a power to revoke, but it is a power held by a third party (someone other than the settlor). A party holding a general power of appointment has the power to tell the trustee, regardless of the terms of the trust, to give the property to "me"—the party holding the power (or, in effect to someone else, to whom I direct—in whose favor I appoint). Just as a power to revoke grants the settlor the ability to override the express terms of the trust regarding the beneficiaries' interests, so too a power of appointment grants the party holding the power the ability to override the express terms of the trust regarding the beneficiaries' interest. Just as a power to revoke adds flexibility to a trust by permitting the settlor to override the terms of the trust if he or she deems it appropriate (presumably based on changed circumstances, but not required), so too a power of appointment adds flexibility to a trust, permitting the party holding the power to override the terms of the trust if the party deems it appropriate (presumably, but not necessarily, based on changed circumstances). Again, one initial, conceptual, way to think about powers of appointment as applied to a trust is that a power of appointment is analogous to a power to revoke in the hands of someone other than the settlor (i.e., a third party).

Technically, a power of appointment gives one party the right to direct the disposition of property legally held by another party. The typical setting is the trust. If a party holds a power of appointment, that party has the power to direct the trustee to transfer the property subject to the power in accordance with the terms of the power. A power of appointment, however, is not limited to a trust setting. It can be used in a variety of settings. How that can happen you will understand better as you become more comfortable with the concept and doctrine of the power of appointment.

Now that you understand what a power is conceptually, the technical definition is that a power exists:

> *whenever a person has the discretion to determine what persons are to receive beneficial interests in property or to determine the amount of beneficial interest in property to be received by certain persons.* Obviously, one who is the complete and unqualified beneficial owner of property has such discretion but we do not regard him as having, in addition to such ownership, a power of appointment.

A. James Casner, *Estate Planning—Powers of Appointment*, 64 Harv. L. Rev. 185, 185–86 (1950) (emphasis in original).

You will become more comfortable with that definition as you become more familiar with the concept and doctrine. A power gives the party holding the power the ability to direct who should receive property, the title of which is vested in another party. For example, assume S transfers property to T to hold in trust, for the benefit of S during S's lifetime, then to UC-Nirvana (S's alma mater). S, however, also retains a power to revoke and a power to appoint the property to whomever S wants in S's will. While S is alive, S can revoke the trust if circumstances change (or if S changes his or her mind), and upon S's death, S can override the terms of the trust and appoint the property to anyone if circumstances change (or if S changes his or her intent that UC-Nirvana should receive the property).

The power need not reside in the settlor. In practice, a power of appointment most often is granted to someone other than the settlor. For example, assume S sets up an irrevocable trust by transferring property to the trustee, T. The dispositive provisions of the trust call for income to be paid to S's daughter, D, for D's life, and at D's death the trust assets are to be distributed to S's grandchild, G (or G's estate if not then living). The trust document may also provide that D has a power of appointment, or it might be that G is given a power of appointment, or the document may give such power to T—or even to some other third party. The power of appointment may be given to almost anyone.

B. Terminology

Powers of appointment have their own unique terminology that needs to be mastered to understand the legal components. Again, although powers of appointment are not limited to trusts, that is the legal setting in which powers are most commonly associated and most commonly used. Accordingly, we will use the trust context as the backdrop for our discussion.

The party who creates the power is called *the donor*. The party who receives the power, who holds the power of appointment, and who has the power to exercise it, is called *the donee*. In practice, the donee is commonly referred to as "the power holder." While the latter is more intuitively descriptive, the term donee shall be used in this chapter.

The parties in whose favor a power can be exercised, i.e., the people who can receive the property if a power is exercised, are called *the permissible appointees, the eligible appointees, the potential appointees,* or *the objects of the power*. A party who actually has property appointed to him or her under a power of appointment is called *an appointee*.

The scope of a power can vary. There are two basic categories of powers: a general power of appointment, or a special power of appointment. The difference turns on in whose favor the power can be exercised. If the party holding the power (the donee) can exercise it by appointing the property for his or her own benefit (i.e., appoint the property to the donee, to the donee's creditors, to the donee's estate, or to creditors of donee's estate), the power is called *a general power of appointment* (often referred to in its abbreviated form: *GPA*). The class of eligible appointees may extend beyond just the donee, but so long as the donee can exercise the power for his or her own benefit (as defined above), it is a general power of appointment. De facto, a party holding a general power of appointment can give the property to anyone because he or she can give it to him or herself first and then proceed to give it to someone else.

On the other hand, a *special power of appointment* (also known as a *limited power of appointment* or *non-general power of appointment*) is any power that is not a general power (i.e., any power where the party holding the power (the donee) *cannot* appoint the property to him or herself, to the donee's creditors, to the donee's estate, or to creditors of donee's estate). Where the power of appointment is a special power of appointment, the class of eligible appointees or objects is typically rather small. The key, however, is not the size of the class of eligible appointees, but rather who is included. As long as it *excludes* the donee, the donee's creditors, the donee's estate, and creditors of donee's estate, the power is a *special power of appointment*.

Powers are not only defined by the scope of the eligible appointees or objects in whose favor they can be exercised, powers are also defined by *when* they can be exercised. Focusing on this variable, there are three basic types of powers. A power is either *presently exercisable, testamentary,* or *postponed*. The California statutory definitions do a good job of articulating the basic differences between and among these different types of powers:

CPC § 612. Types of powers

(a) A power of appointment is "testamentary" if it is exercisable only by a will.

(b) A power of appointment is "presently exercisable" at the time in question to the extent that an irrevocable appointment can be made.

(c) A power of appointment is "not presently exercisable" if it is "postponed." A power of appointment is "postponed" in either of the following circumstances:

   (1) The creating instrument provides that the power of appointment may be exercised only after a specified act or event occurs or a specified condition is met, and the act or event has not occurred or the condition has not been met.

   (2) The creating instrument provides that an exercise of the power of appointment is revocable until a specified act or event occurs or a specified condition is met, and the act or event has not occurred or the condition has not been met.

The amount of property in a fund subject to a power can vary. A power can be exercised over all the property in question, or it can be limited to a maximum percent or amount of property. In addition, the terms of a power can stipulate how often the power can be exercised: only once or more than once (e.g., quarterly or annually). It is not uncommon for a party to have a power to appoint up to five percent of the principal in a trust annually.

Finally, inasmuch as a power is discretionary, a well-drafted power typically will provide for *takers in default*. *Takers in default* are the parties who will receive the property subject to the power of appointment if the donee fails to exercise the power of appointment. Such parties should be expressly identified (either by name or by description) in the instrument creating the power.

As used in a trust, powers typically are designed to provide flexibility with respect to the trust administration. They permit the donee holding the power to de facto override the terms of the trust if they wish. Building flexibility into the power of appointment (permitting the donee to appoint up to five percent of the principal each year) adds even more flexibility to the trust.

C. Powers of Appointments — General versus Special

The law of powers of appointments is often, as with various concepts and doctrines regarding trusts, deeply entangled with the law of tax — in particular, federal estate and gift taxes. While an in-depth discussion of tax-related matters is well beyond the scope of this book, suffice it to say that the previously discussed distinction between *general* and *special* powers of appointments is at the heart of the tax issues. A *general power of appointment* can be a terrible thing for gift and estate tax purposes, whereas a power of appointment that is the more limited *special* variety usually does not create tax problems.

Ostensibly, the following is a tax case, but it nevertheless provides a good (albeit sad) illustration that may help distinguish the two types of powers of appointments.

Jenkins v. United States
428 F.2d 538 (5th Cir. 1970)

GOLDBERG, Circuit Judge:

We consider here the application of federal estate tax provisions to an unexercised and evanescent power of appointment. The executors of the estate of Martha O. Jenkins seek approval of the decision below excluding from the decedent's estate the value of certain property subject to a power of appointment. Though equitable considerations invite us to affirm the ruling below in an effort to ameliorate the apparent harshness of the tax in this particular case, legal imperatives leave us no choice but to reverse and hold that the tax must be paid.

This case grew out of the lives—and deaths—of two sisters, Ada Lee Jenkins and Martha O. Jenkins. These sisters, both of whom were unmarried, lived together in Midland, Georgia, for many years prior to their deaths. Although they owned a substantial amount of property, they lived in a simple, frugal manner. On December 23, 1958, both sisters, who were then in their seventies, executed wills. These wills were very similar in wording and provisions, each sister leaving the other a life estate coupled with a power of invasion or consumption over the testatrix's property.

On September 24, 1962, Ada Lee Jenkins died. Shortly after her sister's death Martha O. Jenkins decided that she did not wish to serve as executrix under her sister's will, and on October 4, 1962, she executed a document renouncing her designation as executrix. She apparently took no other action with regard to the will of her sister. Although she had previously been in good health, on October 10, 1962, Martha suffered a heart attack, and on the following day she died. Because of the short period of time—only seventeen days—between the deaths of the two sisters, Ada's will had not been probated at the time of Martha's death. The wills of both sisters were filed and admitted for probate on October 25, 1962. Two nephews of the sisters, Alonzo Wimberly Jenkins, Jr., and McLendon Wash Jenkins, qualified as the executors of both estates.

The will of Ada Lee Jenkins contained several provisions leaving her surviving sister a life estate coupled with a power of invasion or consumption over certain real and personal property located in Muscogee County, Georgia. Each of the relevant provisions of the will included language substantially identical to the following:

> "Should my sister, Martha O. Jenkins, survive me, then in that event, I give, bequeath and devise to Martha O. Jenkins all my right, title and interest in and to * * * [certain named property] * * * to have, hold, use and enjoy for and during her natural life, with full and unlimited power and authority to dispose of the same in fee simple by gift or otherwise at any time during her life without accountability to anyone, * * * and should my sister not dispose of my interest in said [property] during her lifetime, then on her death the

same shall pass to and become the absolute property of [a certain named re-mainderman]. * * *"

These provisions of the will led to a disagreement between the Commissioner of Internal Revenue and the executors of the estate of Martha O. Jenkins as to the amount of estate taxes due. When the executors computed and filed an estate tax return for the estate of Martha O. Jenkins, they excluded from her gross estate the value of the property in which she received a life estate with powers of invasion by her sister's will. The Commissioner, however, ruled that the value of this property must be in-cluded because Martha's powers of invasion constituted a general power of appoint-ment over such property. After paying the additional estate taxes required by the Commissioner's ruling, the executors filed a claim for a refund. When this claim was disallowed, the executors filed suit in the United States District Court for the Middle District of Georgia, seeking a refund in the amount of $26,962.73.

As plaintiffs in the district court the executors advanced four alternative contentions in support of their position that the value of the property in dispute should not be included in Martha O. Jenkins' estate for estate tax purposes. First, they contended that Martha did not have a general power of appointment because she could dispose of the property only inter vivos and not by will.... Third, they contended that Martha did not possess an exercisable general power of appointment at the time of her death because Ada's will have not yet been probated....

The district court, hearing the case on stipulated facts, entered judgment for the plaintiffs. In its opinion the court accepted plaintiffs' first and third contentions, re-jected their second contention, and did not reach the fourth. *Jenkins v. United States*, M.D.Ga.1968, 296 F.Supp. 203. The government appeals to this court. For the reasons hereinafter given, we are compelled to reject each of the plaintiffs' contentions, and we therefore reverse the judgment of the district court.

I.

Plaintiffs' first contention is that decedent did not have a general power of ap-pointment because her power could be exercised only inter vivos and not by will. We reject this contention because it involves a patent misconstruction of the relevant provisions of the Internal Revenue Code.

Section 2041 of the Code provides that the value of the decedent's gross estate shall include the value of property over which the decedent at the time of his death possessed a "general power of appointment." For estate tax purposes, therefore, property over which a decedent possessed such a power is treated as if the decedent actually "owned" the property in the conventional sense. Section 2041(b)(1) defines a "general power of appointment" as "a power which is exercisable in favor of the decedent, his estate, his creditors, or the creditors of his estate." The statutory definition is thus cast in the disjunctive. A power of appointment is a general power under § 2041(b)(1) if the donee of the power can exercise it in favor of himself or his estate or his creditors or the creditors of his estate. Professors Lowndes and Kramer have succinctly described a general power in the following language:

"A general power is a power under which the donee of the power can appoint the property subject to the power to himself, his estate, his creditors or the creditors of his estate, either directly or indirectly. It is not necessary that he be able to appoint to all four of these objects. The power will be general if it can be exercised in favor of any one of them." Lowndes & Kramer, Federal Estate and Gift Taxes § 12.5, at 262 (2d ed. 1962).

. . .

In the case at bar the decedent received by virtue of her sister's will a life estate in the property involved with an unlimited power of disposition. Thus she had the power to make inter vivos dispositions of the property, but she could not dispose of the property by will. In statutory terminology, she had the power to appoint the property to herself or to her creditors, but she did not have the power to appoint the property to her estate or to the creditors of her estate. In view of the definition contained in 2041(b)(1), the fact that decedent could appoint to herself or to her creditors was sufficient to make her power of appointment a general power. Her inability to make appointments either to her estate or to the creditors of her estate was irrelevant.

. . .

III.

Plaintiffs' third contention is that decedent did not possess an exercisable general power of appointment at the time of her death because the will of Ada Lee Jenkins had not then been probated or filed or offered for probate. Plaintiffs prevailed on this issue in the district court. 296 F.Supp. at 206–208. Our examination of this contention, however, leads us to the conclusion that it must be rejected.

We note at the outset that there is no language in the will itself which evidences a desire on the part of Ada that Martha's possession of the power of appointment was to be postponed until some time after Ada's death. On the contrary, the relevant provisions of the will are couched in terms of the moment when Martha survived Ada, i.e., the moment of Ada's death:

"Should my sister, Martha O. Jenkins, survive me, then in that event, I give, bequeath and devise of Martha O. Jenkins all my right, title and interest * * *"

The district court, however, found significance in the language of Item Sixteen of the will, which provides in part:

"*Upon the probate and admission to record* of this my will, it is my desire that my executrix, executors or executor administer my estate with the control or supervision of any Court or other authority and to that end, reposing special confidence in them, I relieve them and each of them of accountability to any Court or other authority in the administration, management and final distribution of my estate." (Emphasis added.)

The district court placed special emphasis on the first seven of the quoted words. We cannot agree, however, with the court's apparent conclusion that these words expressed a desire on the part of the testatrix to postpone her surviving sister's possession of the power of appointment. On the contrary, when these words are read in the context of the entire sentence, it is clear that they have reference only to the procedure of probating the will, and not to the timing of the passage of the power of appointment to Martha O. Jenkins.

Moreover, we find nothing in Georgia law which leads us to conclude that Martha's possession of the power would have been postponed until probate or until any other point in time later than the death of Ada. In the absence of any contrary provision in the will itself, we think it is clear that Martha received an exercisable general power at the moment of Ada's death.

. . .

We are compelled to reject plaintiffs' contention that Martha O. Jenkins could not have exercised her power of appointment prior to the probate of her sister's will. Under Georgia law she could have made conveyances of the property involved in this case at any time after her sister's death, subject only to subsequent perfection of the record title. The fact that she did not then possess a fully perfected record title is not controlling for federal estate tax purposes. The substantive powers she received at the time of her sister's death clearly came within the definition of a general power of appointment in § 2041(b)(1) of the Internal Revenue Code, and these powers were clearly exercisable at the time of her death.

. . .

Nothing in [any] ... judicial decision can relieve the decedent's estate of the burden of paying estate taxes on the value of the property embraced by her power of appointment. Both Martha O. Jenkins and Ada Lee Jenkins planned their testamentary dispositions in such a manner that the surviving sister (Martha) would be able to exercise control over the property of the testatrix (Ada) immediately upon the death of the latter. This being true, the executors of Martha's estate cannot reasonably complain when confronted by the estate tax consequences of the sisters' plan of disposition. The fact that Martha died unexpectedly very soon after the death of Ada cannot change the character of the property interest which Martha possessed. The conclusion is inescapable that Martha received an exercisable general power of appointment at her sister's death and possessed the exercisable power at her death. The estate taxes demanded by the Commissioner must therefore be paid.

. . .

The judgment of the district court is reversed.

Notes

1. *Basic tax rules for a general power of appointment*: The sad case of the Jenkins sisters illustrates the foundational estate tax law regarding general powers of appointments. If you have one, you are, for all intents and purposes, the owner of the property. In *Jenkins*, the court ruled that if a party dies holding a general power of appointment, the power is tantamount to full ownership over the applicable property.

This pseudo form of "ownership" is what causes the problems. If one has a power to appoint that is *general*, then whatever trust assets are subject to being appointed will be included in the decedent's (donee's) estate for estate tax purposes. This is often referred to as an "artificial" inclusion, as the assets are included in the decedent/donee's estate purely for estate tax purposes (i.e., the donee, having not exercised the power, does not affect the disposition of the assets upon his or her death). The assets are not subject to probate, but rather are disposed of by the underlying document.

Returning to an earlier example for illustration, assume S sets up an irrevocable trust by transferring property to the trustee, T, and the dispositive provisions of the trust call for income to be paid to S's daughter, D, for D's life, and at D's death the trust assets are to be distributed to S's grandchild, G (or G's estate if not then living). In addition, the trust document provides that D has the power to appoint all or any portion of the trust assets, at any time during life or at death through her will, to herself, her estate, her creditors, or the creditors of her estate. The power could include even more permissible appointees than this—it doesn't matter because in any of these permutations, D has a general power of appointment. Assume that D dies having never exercised this power (and she did not exercise it in her will). For estate tax purposes, the fact that D died holding a general power of appointment will result in the then-current value of all of the trust assets to be included in D's estate for estate tax purposes. Again, note that this inclusion is for tax purposes only and will not affect the trust dispositive provisions (here, distributing everything to G or G's estate).

In the alternative if, in our example, D (or in the *Jenkins* case, surviving sister, Martha) had no power of appointment whatsoever, their "life interests" would, at their death, end with the value of the life interest being zero. This would not result in any inclusion of the value of trust assets in the decedent's estate (the value of a regular life estate at the death of the life estate beneficiary is nothing). In *Jenkins* and our example, however, while the life estate extinguished any real value of the beneficiaries' interests, dying with a general power of appointment results in inclusion of the value of all trust assets in the estate for estate tax purposes.

There is no escaping the negative tax ramifications for the holder of a general power of appointment.[1] Exercising such a power at one's death and appointing it, or redirecting it, to someone, will still result in the inclusion of all such property in the decedent's estate. An *inter vivos* appointment, discussed later in this chapter, will implicate gift issues. All of this is consistent with the notion that a having a general power of appointment is tantamount to ownership of the property.

2. *Special powers of appointments and taxes:* Generally, holding only a special power of appointment will not implicate the aforementioned negative estate and gift tax issues. A trust clause giving, for example, D, the "power to appoint to anyone other

---

1. The donee of a power of appointment may, however, refuse to accept it by making a "qualified disclaimer." Just as with disclaiming a gift of an asset, such a disclaimer is tantamount to never holding the power. Disclaimers are discussed in Chapter 4.

than to D, D's estate, D's creditors, or the creditors of D's estate," is common language used to preclude the power from being the dreaded (for tax purposes) general power of appointment. Note that such a clause still provides a great deal of flexibility, which is at the heart of why someone might be given a power of appointment, without creating tax problems for the donee. All of this again raises the point that one wishing to practice in the estate planning area needs a comprehensive knowledge of tax matters (the overlap between taxes and powers of appointments is much deeper than discussed here). A trust clause giving D the "power to appoint all or any portion of the trust assets to anyone," may have been intended not to include D as a permissible appointee, but this phrasing has saddled D with a general power of appointment. Taxes notwithstanding, a clause so drafted would allow D to take all of the trust assets for herself, perhaps something unintended by the settlor. Good estate planners also need to have good drafting skills.

3. *A power of appointment in favor of the donee—but not deemed a general power of appointment?* There is one form of a power of appointment that, at first blush, may appear to be a *general* power but, utilizing previously discussed trust material, may actually be a harmless *special* power. In Chapter 13 the concept of an "ascertainable standard" was discussed (relating to discretionary powers). The *ascertainable standard* is a very important concept in tax law. Assume that in our previous example, S's trust gave D the power to appoint to herself but only if necessary for her health, education, support, or maintenance. While this is a power to appoint to oneself, the limitation by this form of ascertainable standard removes it from the tax definition of a general power of appointment.

This was also an issue in the *Jenkins* case. Excised from the case excerpt above was the argument that the power given to Martha by her sister Ada Lee was not a general power of appointment by reason of this *ascertainable standard* exception to the definition. The pertinent parts of the rather sad facts, as well as the court's analysis, are set forth below:

> Plaintiffs next advance the contention that decedent's power of appointment was not a general power because it came within the "ascertainable standard" exception found in [the statute]. This [applicable part of the law]:
>
>> A power to consume, invade, or appropriate property for the benefit of the decedent which is limited by an ascertainable standard relating to the health, education, support, or maintenance of the decedent shall not be deemed a general power of appointment.
>
> Plaintiffs make much of the fact that decedent had a substantial amount of property of her own and of the fact that she lived in an exceedingly frugal manner. Because of these facts, which are undisputed, plaintiffs contend that "there was no likelihood" that decedent would ever have exercised any of her powers of disposition over the property involved. Therefore, plaintiffs ask us to conclude, decedent's power of appointment was limited by an ascertainable standard within the meaning of the Code. We reject

this contention, as did the court below.... The district court's analysis of this issue was eminently correct, and we quote with approval from the opinion below:

> "In this connection the evidence shows that at the time of her sister's death Martha O. Jenkins was 82 years of age and was possessed of a substantial estate in her own right consisting of real and personal property having a value of approximately $150,000.00. The evidence further shows that the two sisters lived in a very conservative manner, growing their own vegetables and raising their own chickens and spending not more than about $5.00 a week for groceries. They wore black cotton dresses and would spend money on nothing unless it was absolutely necessary. It is interesting to note that they resisted until the end the urgings of their relatives that they buy themselves a television set, which fact may be regarded not only as evidence of their frugality but as a monument to their discretion.

> "The Court is convinced that Martha O. Jenkins would never have encroached upon her sister's estate to satisfy any of her own meager wants or needs, first because she had no need to do so, and second because the remaindermen named in her sister's will were the same remaindermen who were the beneficiaries under her own will later probated, but the question is not what she would have done with the property, but rather what she could have done with it." ...

The district court was correct in holding that the relevant inquiry is not what the decedent may have planned to do with the property, but rather what she was empowered to do. An ascertainable standard must be a prescribed standard, not a post-prescriptive course of action. The acting out of the standard is irrelevant, for it is the script rather than the actor which controls a decision concerning the existence of an ascertainable standard. In determining what the decedent was empowered to do, courts must look to the express language of the instrument creating the power, or to the language of the instrument as modified by state law....

In the instant case the instrument creating the power—the will of Ada Lee Jenkins—gave Martha O. Jenkins "full and unlimited power and authority to dispose of the (property) in fee simple by gift or otherwise at any time during her life without accountability to anyone." It is difficult to imagine a more unlimited, open-ended, freewheeling power than this. Moreover, Georgia law does not modify such language by implying any 'support and maintenance' limitation....

In the words of the district court, "we can only conclude that the will gave Martha O. Jenkins an unlimited right to consume or give away inter vivos any or all of her sister's property regardless of whether such encroachment was for support and maintenance or for some other purpose." ... Her complete power over the property during her lifetime was not modified by any standard other than one she might impose on herself. Thus her power was not limited by any "ascertainable standard." ...

Jenkins, 428 F.2d at 545–46.

D. Standard Applicable to Exercise

A power of appointment is a discretionary power. Recall that Chapter 13 included a discussion of discretionary trusts — trusts where a beneficiary's interest in either the principal or the income is discretionary. While a power of appointment is discretionary, and in that respect appears similar to a trustee's discretionary power to disburse trust property, an important distinction exists: a donee holding a power of appointment owes *no fiduciary duty* to the eligible appointees/objects or to anyone else. Just as a settlor can revoke or not revoke a trust as he or she wishes, with no legal concern for how the settlor's decision might affect other parties, so too with a power of appointment. The donee owes no one a fiduciary duty. The donee can exercise or not exercise the power as he or she wishes, with no legal concerns for how the donee's decision might affect any other party. There is no fiduciary duty associated with a power of appointment. It is truly at the donee's discretion, and a court has no power to review the donee's decision (so long as it does not violate the terms of the power).

II. Creation of a Power of Appointment

Whether a power of appointment has been created and, if so, *what type* of power of appointment has been created, is a question of the donor's intent.

In re Kuttler's Estate

325 P.2d 624 (Cal. Ct. App. 1958)

ASHBURN, Acting Presiding Justice.

...

Decedent died a widow on February 28, 1956, leaving three grandchildren as her sole heirs; two brothers and a sister survived her, as did Earl Hayter to whom she was engaged to marry. Her estate consisted of cash, stocks, bonds, trust deed notes, furniture and household and personal effects; also certain real property appraised at $52,500; the entire estate was valued at $143,000.

Her sister, Bertha McQuarrie, and her fiance, Earl Hayter, petitioned for probate of the holographic instrument; their application was opposed by Michael M. Kuttler as guardian for the three minor grandchildren. The objections were sustained and probate of the document was denied. It reads:

"Los Angeles 15, Calif. February 16th, — 56 To whom it may concern: If at any time I should pass on before I have a recorded Will: This is to certify that I do not want Mike Kuttler or Vera Kuttler, my deceased Sons' wives to have one thing or one cent of what I have: nor the children Joan, Bill or Nancy Ann as I never see them so I enjoy no pleasure from them.

"Notify Earl Hayter or my sister Bertha McQuarrie DO-7-7821 — for them to dispose of my belongings as they see fit. Signed Mrs. Ethel May Kuttler 2/16/56".

The trial judge ruled that the instrument is not testamentary in character, was not intended to be testamentary, was not intended to dispose of decedent's property and did not do so. From the order denying probate Hayter and McQuarrie appeal.

The effect of the instant ruling is to vest decedent's 'belongings' in the three grandchildren whom she expressly disinherited.

There is no escape from the conclusion that Mrs. Kuttler did intend this document to operation as her will. Testamentary intention is thus defined in *Re Estate of Sargavak*, 35 Cal.2d 93, 95, 216 P.2d 850, 851, 21 A.L.R.2d 307: 'The testator must have intended, by the particular instrument offered for probate, to make a revocable disposition of his property to take effect upon his death.' To this definition the court added this caution: 'It bears emphasis that we are here concerned not with the meaning of the instrument, but with the intention with which it was executed.' 35 Cal.2d at page 96, 216 P.2d at page 851.

...

... [T]he writing in question affords irrefutable internal evidence of the requisite testamentary intent. First it disinherits in explicit language decedent's only heirs (she left no children and no other grandchildren); then it confers a power of appointment upon Hayter and McQuarrie with respect to her entire "belongings."

"A power of appointment, which may be created by deed or by will, is defined, generally, as a power or authority given to a person to dispose of property, or an interest therein, which is vested in a person other than the donee of the power." *In re Lidston's Estate*, 32 Wash.2d 408, 202 P.2d 259, 265. No particular form of words is necessary to the creation of such a power. 3 Tiffany Real Property, 3d Ed., §685, p. 20; *In re Rowlands' Estate*, 73 Ariz, 337, 241 P.2d 781, 784; *In re Lidston's Estate, supra*, 202 P.2d 266; 96 C.J.S. Wills §1062 d, p. 702. Such a disposition of a testatrix' property satisfies the cases next cited, which hold that it is essential to a valid will disinheriting all or any of the heirs that it also make some valid disposition of decedent's property....

Powers of appointment have been recognized as valid in this State....

Though urged upon him, the trial judge ignored the proposition that the writing created a valid power of appointment. The question considered below was whether there was an outright gift to Hayter and McQuarrie followed by precatory words. But solution of the question of existence of a power of appointment is the proper approach to this case. The language of *In re Estate of Sloan, supra*, 7 Cal.App.2d 319, 341–342, 46 P.2d 1007, 1018, is pertinent: "As has been announced in numerous decisions the word 'precatory' is properly applied to an expression by a trustor wherein a hope, a wish, a desire, a recommendation, or a request is indicated by him. Necessarily, the words by which a precatory trust is created constitute an entreaty, and is beseeching, or suppliant, or prayerful in its nature. * * * Considering the language employed by the donor of the power in the instant matter, even by viewing it in the light of the most auspicious authorities to which the attention of this court has been directed, it is impossible to give to such language a construction which would admit of a conclusion favorable to the suggestion made by appellants to the effect that it is precatory in character. The donor's required disposition of his estate was plain, direct and conclusive. It constituted not an entreaty, nor a wish, a desire, a request, a recommendation, or anything of that sort. It is most apparent that the power created by its donor was mandatory."

The donee of a general power of appointment may exercise it in his own favor. In legal effect such a power gives him an absolute ownership....

Respondents argue that a power such as the one at bar is invalid because it delegates to another the authority to make a will for the testatrix, thus evading the statutes relating to the making of wills. The California cases above cited involve the distribution of a part of the property or less than the entire estate in decedent's property, and hold such a power to be valid. The underlying theory is that the subject matter passes from the donor's estate directly to the appointee and not from the donee or his estate. *In re Estate of Baird*, 120 Cal.App.2d 219, 227, 260 P.2d 1052; *In re Estate of Masson*, *supra*, 142 Cal.App.2d 510, 512, 298 P.2d 619; 39 Cal.Jur.2d § 3, p. 613. In one sense a power to dispose of a part of testatrix' property through an appointment to a third person does amount to the making of a will for her *pro tanto*. But the legal concept is to the contrary. There appears to be no difference in principle between a power to appoint the taker of a part of testatrix' property and a power to so dispose of all of it.

. . .

Most courts in this country which have been confronted with our present inquiry have held that general power to be valid though covering all or substantially all of decedent's estate. In *In re Tinsley's Will*, 187 Iowa 23, 174 N.W. 4, 5, 11 A.L.R. 826, the entire content of the will was as follows: "In case of any serious accident, after my just debts are paid, I direct that my aunt Miss Mary E. Clark, take entire charge of my estate for disposal as she sees fit. J. Clark Tinsley." The sixth objection to its probate was: "[I]t leaves the disposal of property to another person. The decedent did not by said instrument, and could not, delegate to an agent the power to make a will for him." It was held that this document was testamentary in character, the court saying at page 6 of 174 N.W.: "Any writing by which a person undertakes to make disposition of his property or estate to take effect after his death is testamentary in character, and, if duly signed, witnessed, and published, is entitled to admission to probate. * * * Unrestricted power of disposal is an attribute of absolute ownership. Quite in point, also, is *Cheney v. Plumb*, 79 Wis. 602, 48 N.W. 668, where the instrument was in form as follows: 'When I have done with my property, I want John R. Cheney and his wife to pay all my debts and collect my dues and dispose of my things as they think best, only I want Sarah A. Williams to have my silver spoons

* * * (and after several legacies) and remainder to keep and dispose of as they think best.' This was held sufficient to vest the property absolutely in the persons named. See also, *Benz v. Fabian*, 54 N.J.Eq. 615, 34 A. 760. And the trial court was justified in holding the instrument testamentary in form, and not a mere trust or power expiring with the death of Mary E. Clark, there is no room to doubt."

Baldwin v. Davidson, 37 Tenn.App. 606, 267 S.W.2d 756, 757, involved this clause of a will: "B. W. Davidson, Sr. shall turn over to my Sister Mrs. O. P. Brakefield my share to be distributed as she shall see fit." The word "share" referred to his interest in a certain business. This language was held to create a power of appointment which could be exercised in the donee's own favor; also held that it amounted to an absolute gift of the property to her (267 S.W.2d at pages 757–758).

Appeal of Richburg, 148 Me. 323, 92 A.2d 724. The will contained this provision: "I direct my executor to dispose of my clothing and other personal articles and effects as he in his sole discretion may deem best." 92 A.2d at page 725. This language was held to create a valid power of appointment. At page 726 of 92 A.2d the court said: "The appellant argues that assuming the executor would not take whatever property might pass under the Second Paragraph of the will to his own use, and for his own benefit, it cannot be doubted that the language thereof gives him a power of appointment over it. This Court said very recently, *In re Estate of Meier*, 144 Me. 358, 362, 69 A.2d 664, 666, 'that the power of disposition of property "is the equivalent of ownership'", and it cannot be doubted that under the terms of the Second Paragraph, the executor was given 'power of disposition' over such articles as might fit the description of property therein. The title thereto would vest in him, under the will, and remain with him until he passed it elsewhere. * * * Conceivably, he may have used the words 'dispose of' in the sense of 'destroy', assuming the property in question had no monetary value but this Court cannot rewrite the document for him, and his words have the very definite, well-established meaning in testamentary use which the appellant ascribes to them."

In re Lidston's Estate, supra, 32 Wash.2d 408, 202 P.2d 259, 261: "I further direct my Executor dispose of any balance after the aforementioned gifts have been paid according to his wise discretion." The executor proposed to distribute the property to his own wife and two other persons. The lower court held that this part of the will was not testamentary and the ruling was reversed. The difference between a power and a trust was explained at page 266, of 202 P.2d, where it was said: "No technical, special, or particular form of words is necessary for the creation of a power of appointment; if the testator's intention to confer the power appears from the entire will, full effect will be given to such intention. In Thompson, Wills, 588, § 394, the rule as supported by the authorities is stated as follows: 'No particular form of words is necessary for the creation of a power; any expression, however, informal, being sufficient if it clearly indicates an intention to give a power. All that is necessary is an indication of a clear intention to accomplish some proper purpose by the donor through the donee. It may be conferred by express words, or may be necessarily implied. * * *'" It was also remarked on that same page that: "It seems to us that as a layman the testator could hardly have used more appropriate language to express his intention to confer upon his executor the power to dispose of the residuum of the estate in a manner determinable by him."

Respondents cannot prevail upon the argument that the use of the word "notify" or the giving of Mrs. McQuarrie's telephone number in the second paragraph of the writing indicates a sense of urgency, or that deceased used the words "dispose of my belongings" in the sense of authorizing Hayter and McQuarrie to transfer her personal effects, jewelry and removable objects to a place of safekeeping in order to protect them from falling into the hands of the daughters-in-law. Nothing but speculation underlies that argument. It is true that the word 'dispose' is: "A broad any comprehensive term, with many shades of meaning, described as 'nomen generalissimum,' and standing by itself, without qualification, * * * has been said to have no technical signification." 27 C.J.S. p. 345. But it has a familiar meaning when used in wills, as is evident from the quotations of the *Richburg, Tinsley* and *Lidston* cases, supra.

What Mrs. Kuttler obviously desired was that her donees have the power to distribute her "belongings" if she should die before executing a new and formal will. To say that she wanted something less is to deny the obvious. Of course, the fact that she expected to make a later and more formal will would not detract from the testamentary character of the one in question. *Richberg v. Robbins*, 33 Tenn.App. 66, 228 S.W.2d 1019, 1022; *Henderson v. Henderson*, 183 Va. 663, 33 S.E.2d 181, 183; 1 Page on Wills (Lifetime Ed.) § 50, p. 112; 94 C.J.S. Wills § 129, p. 905.

. . .

The order of October 23, 1956, is affirmed with respect to the denial of appellant Hayter's petition for letters testamentary; in all other respects it is reversed with instructions to admit to probate the holographic document of February 16, 1956....

Notes

1. *Vested in another*: In *Kuttler*, the court makes what at first blush might sound like a strange statement: "A power of appointment, which may be created by deed or by will, is defined, generally, as a power or authority given to a person to dispose of property, or an interest therein, which is vested in a person other than the donee of the power."

The more common setting for and use of a power of appointment is in a trust. Legal title to the property subject to the power (the trust property) is vested in the trustee. Typically, someone other than the trustee will hold the power of appointment. Hence, legal title to the property subject to the power of appointment (the trust property) is vested in someone other than the donee — the title is vested in the trustee. Nevertheless, the donee has the power to override the terms of the trust and to order the trustee to disburse the trust property pursuant to the proper exercise of the power.

In *Kuttler*, the power of appointment was over the decedent's probate estate. Who holds vested title to a decedent's probate estate is a bit more complicated: "When a person dies, title to his or her property vests in the heirs or devisees, subject to administration." *Olson v. Toy*, 46 Cal. App. 4th 818, 825 (Ct. App. 1996). Upon the decedent's death, title immediately vests in the appropriate heirs or devisees, *subject to administration*. California Probate Code Section 7001 expressly so states: "The decedent's property is subject to administration under this code, except as otherwise provided by law, and is subject to the rights of beneficiaries, creditors, and other persons as provided by law." The last clause's reference to "other persons as provided by law" includes an individual holding a power of appointment over the probate estate.

2. *Creditor's rights*: A donee holding a power of appointment over property obviously has *some* rights with respect to the property. Can a donee's creditors reach the property subject to the power?

A. Special Power of Appointment

The analysis is fairly easy with respect to a donee holding a special power of appointment. A donee holding a special or limited power of appointment cannot appoint the property to him or herself, to his or her creditors, to his or her estate, or to creditors of his or her estate. In essence, a donee who holds only a limited or special power of appointment is analogous to an agent. The donee has no rights in the property per se, but as an agent can transfer the property to an eligible appointee. But just as an agent has no rights in the principal's property, so too a party holding only a special or limited power of appointment has no rights in the property subject to the power. Thus, the general rule is: creditors of a donee holding a special or limited power of appointment have no right to reach the property—neither while it is subject to appointment nor after an appointment has been made. California follows this general rule with respect to creditor's rights and a special power of appointment. *See* CPC § 681; 50A Cal. Jur. 3d *Powers of Appointment* § 44 (2015).

B. General Power of Appointment

The analysis is more complicated for creditors of a donee holding a general power of appointment. On the one hand, a donee is analogous to an agent in that he or she acts for another (the donor). Technically, a donee is *not* an agent, but conceptually it may help to think of a donee as analogous to an agent. A donee holding a general power of appointment, however, can appoint the property to him or herself, to his or her creditors, to his or her estate, or to creditors of his or her estate. For all practical purposes, is not the donee of a general power of appointment the de facto owner? The property subject to the power is analogous to money in the donee's checking account. All the donee has to do is express his or her intent to use the property and he or she will have all rights over that property. As such, should the property be treated as the donee's property for purposes of creditors' rights?

The traditional approach to the question is implicitly reflected in the terminology. The traditional approach adopts a traditional property-based view of the transaction, adopting the "gift" model of the transaction. Under the traditional "gift" model, the donor has made a gift of the power to a donee, but the donee does not "own" the property unless he or she "accepts" the gift. The clearest form of acceptance would be if the donee exercised the general power of appointment to appoint the property to him or herself. Then the property would clearly be the donee's property, and creditors of the donee could reach the property. But under the traditional "gift" model, so long as the donee does not exercise the power in favor of the donee, he or she has not accepted the property. Therefore, the donee's creditors cannot reach the property.

Kuttler reflects the modern trend. The court stated: "The donee of a general power of appointment may exercise it in his own favor. In legal effect such a power gives him an absolute ownership." If the general power of appointment gives the donee absolute ownership, should not the donee's creditors be able to reach the property even if the donee has not exercised the power in his or her own favor? Despite the language in *Kuttler*, under the modern trend general rule, creditors of a donee holding a general power of appointment over property cannot reach the property unless the donee exercises the power of appointment. It does not matter in whose favor the power is exercised — the donee or an eligible third party. The general rule is that the property is treated, by operation of law, as if it had passed through the donee's hands when the donee exercised the power, during which time the creditors' rights attached to it.

Some jurisdictions, however, have taken the modern trend to its logical extreme and deem the donee of a general power of appointment as the owner of the property even in the absence of the donee's exercise of the power (though with some conditions on when the donee's creditors may reach the property). California has adopted this approach to a general power of appointment and creditors' rights. California law basically treats the property subject to a general power of appointment presently exercisable as the donee's property:

CPC § 682. Creditor rights general power of appointment

(a) To the extent that the property owned by the donee is inadequate to satisfy the claims of the donee's creditors, property subject to a general power of appointment that is presently exercisable is subject to the claims to the same extent that it would be subject to the claims if the property were owned by the donee.

(b) Upon the death of the donee, to the extent that the donee's estate is inadequate to satisfy the claims of creditors of the estate and the expenses of administration of the estate, property subject to a general testamentary power of appointment or to a general power of appointment that was presently exercisable at the time of the donee's death is subject to the claims and expenses to the same extent that it would be subject to the claims and expenses if the property had been owned by the donee.

(c) This section applies whether or not the power of appointment has been exercised.

Problems

1. Testatrix's will devised to her daughter a farm called "Allendale" for life. The will went on to provide: "Provided, however, that the power to dispose of said real estate by will is hereby expressly granted unto my said daughter." Is the daughter's power general or special? *See St. Matthews Bank v. De Charette*, 83 S.W.2d 471 (Ky. 1935).

2. Clause II of Testator's will was intended to dispose of $600,000 of assets to take full advantage of the unified tax credit. Clause II made eight specific bequests, totaling only $260,000. Clause II went on to provide as follows:

   > In the absence of full and complete instructions from me to my Executor or Executrix, the persons to receive something under this Clause II and what each is to receive shall be appointed by my Executor or Executrix in his or her sole and absolute discretion, consistent with the stated objective of this Clause II, but this ... power of appointment shall not be used to increase or enlarge any bequest I make to any persons who serve as my Executor or Executrix, by this will or any codicil to it.

   Inasmuch as the power fails to designate a specific class of eligible beneficiaries, is the power general or special? *See Leach v. Hyatt*, 423 S.E.2d 165 (Va. 1992).

3. Testator creates a testamentary trust. The terms of the trust give Ms. Dickinson the right to receive the trust income for her life. The trust goes on to grant her a testamentary power to appoint the principal, and any undistributed income, free of trust, to such person or persons as she may designate in her will. The trust, however, also has a spendthrift clause. In light of the spendthrift clause, should the power of appointment be construed as a general or special power? *See Dickinson v. Wilmington Trust Co.*, 734 A.2d 605 (Del. Ch. 1999).

III. Exercise of a Power of Appointment

Whether a power of appointment has been properly exercised depends on the interaction of several variables: (1) the type of power of appointment; (2) the terms of the power of appointment; (3) the donor's intent; and (4) the donee's intent.

A. *Inter Vivos* — Timing of Exercise

A latent issue with respect to a presently exercisable power of appointment is whether it can be exercised in the donee's will or must it be exercised while the donee is still alive in a deed (the most common instrument used to exercise an *inter vivos* power). While a will is executed *inter vivos*, it is not effective until the testator's death for most purposes. Nevertheless, the American approach deems a will effective upon execution for purposes of revoking another will. A will is not completely testamentary in nature. For purposes of exercising a presently exercisable power of appointment, should a donee be permitted to exercise the power in his or her will?

The general rule is that a power that is "exercisable by *deed or will*" is a presently exercisable power, and a donee can validly exercise such a power in his or her will. Moreover, a power that is "exercisable by deed" is a presently exercisable power. A donor can specify that a power "exercisable by deed" cannot be exercisable by will, but absent such express intent the general rule is that a presently exercisable power can be exercised *inter vivos* in a deed or in the donee's will. An instrument that gives the donee a power to appoint the property, or a "presently exercisable power," is presumed to give a presently exercisable power that is exercisable by deed or will. *See* RESTATEMENT (THIRD) OF PROP.: WILLS & DONATIVE TRANSFERS § 17.4 (2011); CPC § 630.

B. Testamentary Power — Timing of Exercise

One of the principal reasons a settlor may use a power of appointment is to add flexibility to the administration of the trust. While the settlor is alive, he or she can retain flexibility over the trust by retaining the power to revoke the trust. If, after creating the trust, the circumstances surrounding the settlor change, or if the circumstances surrounding one or more of the beneficiaries change, the settlor can revoke the trust. If the settlor wishes, he or she can create a new trust with new terms to reflect the new circumstances and the settlor's new intent. The power to revoke provides the flexibility the settlor may want to make sure that the trust serves the settlor's changing intent. But how can a settlor build in flexibility with respect to the period after the settlor's death? Most settlors achieve that flexibility by granting a power of appointment over the property to someone they trust. Which type of power, and the scope of the power, is up to the settlor.

Carmichael v. Heggie
506 S.E.2d 308 (S.C. 1998)

GOOLSBY, Judge:

Doris Carmichael appeals a determination by the trial court that she cannot presently exercise a power of appointment to convey a fee simple interest in a tract of farm land to her son. We affirm.

Facts and Procedural Background

In his last will and testament, William Boyd Carmichael named his wife Doris executor of his estate and gave her a life estate in his undivided half-interest in an eighty-acre farm. The will also granted Doris a general power of appointment through which she could appoint the property to any appointee, including her estate, in her last will and testament. If she did not exercise the power of appointment in her will or if she predeceased William, the property was to transfer to William's then living grandchildren. The will also gave Doris, in her capacity as executor, the right to sell assets. William died, and his will was probated July 22, 1985. Doris survived her husband.

By deed dated October 14, 1994, Doris transferred her interest in the tract of land to her son Milton B. Carmichael. On December 6, 1994, she executed a will exercising the power of appointment in favor of Milton. In her will, she stated she believed the transfer had occurred with the October deed. Doris also executed a contract with Milton agreeing not to change her will in exchange for his caring for her in her old age.

Milton initiated an action for partition against Jane Heggie, who owned the other half-interest in the property. In her answer and counterclaim, Heggie questioned Milton's ownership interest in the land and requested the court interpret William's will to quiet title in the land. A guardian ad litem was appointed to protect the interest of the minor and unborn potential heirs.

The trial court held Doris could exercise the power of appointment only through her will upon her death, when the will was probated. It further found that Doris's authority as executor of William's estate did not expand her power of appointment. The deed from Doris to Milton, therefore, conveyed only a life estate *per autre vie* and no other legal interest.

Discussion

1. Doris argues the trial court erred in holding she had not exercised the power of appointment in favor of Milton. She asserts that through the execution of her will, the execution of the contract to will, and the transfer of her interest in the property, she had conveyed a fee simple interest to Milton....

Generally a contract to make a will is enforceable, provided it possesses all the essential elements of a legal contract. *Caulder v. Knox*, 251 S.C. 337, 162 S.E.2d 262 (1968). "One who contracts to will property in effect parts with his rights to act inconsistent therewith and in effect reserves to himself a life interest only." *Id.* at 346, 162 S.E.2d at 267 (1968).

We are unaware of any South Carolina cases to date specifically considering the effect of a contract to will on a testamentary power of appointment. The *Restatement (Second) of Property*, however, provides as follows:

> A donee of a power of appointment not presently exercisable cannot contract to make an appointment in the future that is enforceable by the promisee. Though the promisee cannot obtain damages or the specific property if the promise is not performed, the promisee may obtain restitution for value that the promisee gave for the promise from the person who received the value.

Restatement (Second) of Property § 16.2 (1986).

The rationale behind this rule is to fulfill the donor's intent that the selection of the appointees be made "in the light of the circumstances that may exist on the date the power becomes exercisable." *Restatement (Second) of Property* § 16.2 cmt. a (1986). Furthermore, as the *Restatement* explains, "A contract to appoint in a certain manner made prior to the date the power becomes exercisable, if valid, would defeat the donor's intent." *Id.*

We adopt the *Restatement* rule and hold Doris, as the donee of a testamentary power of appointment, may not in a contract to will bind herself to exercise the power in a certain manner. The contract to will Doris executed in favor of Milton is therefore invalid, and the trial court correctly held Doris could not make an *inter vivos* transfer of a fee simple interest in the property to Milton.

...

AFFIRMED.

Notes

1. *Testamentary/postponed power and flexibility*: From a "time of exercise" perspective, a donor has essentially three options: (1) a presently exercisable power, (2) a postponed power, or (3) a testamentary power. By picking a testamentary power, the donor has expressed his or her intent that he or she wants the donee to wait as long as possible—until the donee's death—before deciding what would be the best thing to do with the property subject to the power (i.e., before deciding whether to exercise the power, and if so, in whose favor to exercise it). This allows—and forces—the donee to take into consideration all the changes that occur during the donee's life. Hence, the RESTATEMENT's position and the court's ruling that a donee cannot *inter vivos* contract with respect to how he or she is going to exercise a testamentary power appointment. The same logic applies, though to a lesser degree, to a postponed power.

2. *Release of a power of appointment*: The presumption is that, absent express contrary intent by the donor, a donee can release a power of appointment. RESTATEMENT OF PROPERTY § 334. While a donee cannot *exercise* a testamentary power of appointment *inter vivos*, a donee can *release* a testamentary power of appointment *inter vivos*. Where an *inter vivos* contract to exercise a testamentary power would have the same legal effect as a release, the court may construe the contract as a valid release. *See Wood v. Am. Sec. & Trust Co.*, 253 F. Supp. 592, 594 (D.D.C. 1966).

A release of a power of appointment need not be complete; it can be partial. For example, a donor can create a power of appointment that may be exercised presently or testamentarily. The donee can release the ability to exercise the power presently, thereby converting it into a testamentary power, or vice versa. Another common example involves the scope of the power. A power of appointment can be either general or limited. Assume a donee holds a power that can be exercised in favor of a class that includes the donee (which would then make it a general power). The donee can release the power to appoint the property to the donee, the donee's creditors, the donee's estate, or the creditors of the donee's estate, thereby converting the power into a limited power.

3. *Testamentary exercise consistent with contract*: If a donee contracts *inter vivos* to exercise a testamentary power of appointment in a certain way (which is invalid—see above), and thereafter the donee exercises the power at time of death consistent with the contract, the general rule is that the donee's *inter vivos* contract to exercise the power that way does not affect the validity of the testamentary exercise.

4. *Donee is donor*: What if the donee in the *Carmichael* case had been the donor? If the donee grants him or herself a testamentary power of appointment, but then *inter vivos* contracts with respect to the testamentary power of appointment, should

it matter that it is the donor who holds the power? New York law provides that where the donee is also the donor, the party *can* contract *inter vivos* with respect to how the power will be exercised at time of death. The logic is that because the donee and the donor are the same party, permitting the *inter vivos* contracting with respect to the testamentary appointment is actually intent promoting because it is the same party's intent. McKinney's EPTL § 10-5.3(a) (2015).

Problem

Fred and Frances Cox executed their respective lawyer-prepared wills. Each will provided that should the decedent have a surviving spouse, all of his or her estate passed to the surviving spouse. Each will also provided that, in the event the decedent did not have a surviving spouse, his or her property went to other relatives.

Thereafter, Fred and Frances executed an *inter vivos* trust. They funded the trust with four parcels of real property. The trust expressly provided that:

> Each Settlor shall have the absolute right and power without restriction, to appoint his or her share of the trust estates including his or her share of community and separate property. Such power of appointment shall be exercisable by will and may be exercised in favor of the Settlor who is testator/trix of that particular will, or the creditors of said Settlor, or said Settlor's estate or any other person or organization.

The trust had an express provision indicating how the property subject to the power of appointment should be distributed in the event the power was not exercised.

Thereafter the testators/settlors died without revising their wills. Can a will executed before a trust granting a power of appointment be deemed to exercise the power if the will otherwise meets the requirements to exercise the power?

C. Manner of Exercise

Whether a power of appointment has been properly exercised is first and foremost a question of the *donor's* intent. One must start with the terms of the granting instrument: what type of power did the donor create, and what conditions, if any, did the donor put on the exercise?

In re Passmore

416 A.2d 991 (Pa. 1980)

ROBERTS, Justice.

This case poses the question whether donee Laura Passmore effectively exercised a power of appointment that her husband, donor Charles F. Passmore, created in her favor. Unlike the Orphans' Court Division of the Court of Common Pleas of Dauphin County, we conclude that donee did effectively exercise that power.

In 1970, donor executed a "Revocable Agreement of Trust" by which he created a revocable inter vivos trust for his own benefit as well as the benefit of donee and donee's sisters. Donor named appellee, National Bank and Trust Company of Central Pennsylvania (the Bank), as trustee. Donor provided that, upon his death, if he is survived by donee, the Bank is to divide trust principal and form two new trusts. One of the new trusts, "Trust A," is to consist of "such fractional portion of [original trust principal] that qualif[ies] for the marital deduction in determining the Federal estate tax on the estate of [donor]...." Remaining principal is to comprise the other trust, "Trust B." Donor gave the Bank discretion to pay donee income and principal from Trusts A and B. Donor also gave the Bank discretion to pay donee's sisters principal from Trust B.

Donor further provided that, upon donee's death,

> "all the property then held in Trust A shall be distributed as she may by her will appoint, making specific reference to Trust A under this Revocable Agreement of Trust. The power to make such appointment, the conditions to which it may be made subject, and the permissible beneficiaries shall be without restriction or qualification of any kind."

Donor added that, should donee "fail to exercise effectively her power of appointment over any part of the property in Trust A, the principal held in Trust A at her death shall be added to, considered part of, and administered and distributed in the same manner as the property held in Trust B." Donor created no other power of appointment in donee's favor.

Donor died in March of 1975. Donee died twenty-one months later. In her will, after directing payment of funeral expenses, donee exercised her power of appointment over Trust A principal as follows:

> "I give, bequeath and devise all of my property, of whatever nature and wherever situated, and expressly intend this act to constitute the exercise of any power of appointment which I may possess or enjoy under any Will or trust agreement executed by my husband, Charles F. Passmore, and/or the disposition of any property in which I may possess an interest as a beneficiary of a trust or otherwise am entitled to participate or share in its disposition or distribution, in trust, to be administered in a manner and for purposes hereinafter stated:...."

The "manner" of administration and "purposes" of the trust include payment of income and principal, at the named trustee's discretion, to donee's sisters. Upon the sisters' death, donee's trustee is to pay twenty-five percent of the remainder to the Blind Association of Harrisburg and seventy-five percent of the remainder to the Good Shepherd Lutheran Church of Paxtang (the Church).

In April of 1978 the Bank filed a Second and Final Account. The Bank proposed to disregard donee's exercise of her power of appointment, add Trust A principal to Trust B, and distribute the total fund in the manner donor provided in the event donee ineffectively exercised her power. The Church and the executor-trustee under donee's will took exception, claiming the Bank incorrectly disregarded donee's valid exercise of her power of appointment. The Bank and exceptants entered into a Stipulation of Facts, which included:

"9. It was Laura's intention, in executing her will ... to exercise her power of appointment over Trust A under the Charles Passmore Revocable Agreement of Trust...."

On the parties' briefs, the orphans' court entered a final decree dismissing the exceptions and holding that, under *Schede Estate*, 426 Pa. 93, 231 A.2d 135 (1967), donee's exercise of her power of appointment is ineffective for want of specific reference to Trust A in her appointment clause. Both donee's executor-trustee and the Church have appealed.

We agree with appellants that the orphans' court's reliance upon *Schede Estate*, *supra*, is misplaced. In *Schede*, the donor gave his spouse power to appoint principal of the donor's testamentary trust "unto such person or persons, excluding herself, her estate or her creditors, as my wife may by her last will and testament or any writing in the nature thereof designate and appoint by specifically referring to this Will...." The donee, who had remarried, in her will sought to exercise the power in favor of her new husband by way of the following language: "I give, devise and bequeath all of the rest, residue and remainder of my property, both real and personal of every kind and nature and of which I may have a power of appointment...." The donee in *Schede*, however, made no reference of any kind to the power of appointment her husband had created. This Court, in agreeing with the orphans' court that the donee's attempt to exercise the power was ineffective, stated:

> "the law has been clearly settled that strict and literal compliance with the terms of a special power of appointment is absolutely necessary for its valid and effective exercise. That means that the appointing instrument must specifically refer in the instant case to the power which was granted by (the donor's) will and which (the donee) seeks to exercise and execute. A general residuary clause, even if and when it included the words, 'I hereby exercise every power of appointment which I possess,' would not and does not comply with and fulfill the donor's condition and is not a valid exercise of the special power of appointment granted to (the donee)."

Schede Estate, 426 Pa. at 96, 231 A.2d at 137.

Here, however, unlike in *Schede*, donee in her will not only expressed her intention to exercise the power her husband conferred upon her but also made specific and express reference to the power her husband created. At the same time as she made a general bequest of "all of [her] property," donee deliberately "exercise(d) ... any power of appointment which [she] may possess or enjoy under any Will or trust agreement executed by [her] husband, Charles F. Passmore...." Trust A was, indeed, the only power of appointment her husband had conferred upon her.

The specific and express reference donee made here to the power her husband donor created was in full compliance with donor's expressed objective. Husband donor here, unlike in *Schede*, did not intend or mandate that donee exercise the power created only by a strict and verbatim recital of his words. What he did direct was a reasonable substantive compliance with his expressed intention that his wife identify his grant of power to her by her deliberate act. Although donor did employ language stating that donee is to "mak[e] specific reference to Trust A under this Revocable Agreement of Trust," donor immediately added that

> "[donee's] power to make such appointment, the conditions to which it may be made subject, and the permissible beneficiaries shall be without restriction or qualification of any kind."

This latter clause, like any other part of a writing, must be viewed in light of the entire instrument. See e.g., *Cahen Estate*, 483 Pa. 157, 394 A.2d 958 (1978); *Shehadi v. Northeastern National Bank of Pennsylvania*, 474 Pa. 232, 378 A.2d 304 (1977). So too, we must avoid any interpretation which would attribute to donor an intention that only a repetition of his verbatim language will satisfy the power. For such an interpretation would frustrate the objectives of donor in creating the power of appointment.

In our view, by adding both that "[donee's] power to make such appointment" and "the conditions to which it may be made subject" "shall be without restriction or qualification of any kind," donor revealed that his true objective was not to create barriers hindering attainment of the substantive goals embodied in the power of appointment. Instead, donor intended that donee identify the power by deliberate act. As Commentary discussing similar language of a donor states, here it is "quite reasonable to conclude that, although the donor, in creating the power, prescribed by a specific formality, his effective intent was merely to require sufficient formality to insure against a hasty act by the donee." V American Law of Property, Powers of Appointment § 23.44, p. 578 (Casner ed. 1952).

Consistent with the donor's intent, donee not only fulfilled donor's substantive limitations but also fulfilled donor's formal requirement of identifying and executing the power conferred. The decree of the orphans' court concluding to the contrary therefore must be reversed.

Appeal at No. 37 May Term, 1979 dismissed. Decree reversed and case remanded for proceedings consistent with this opinion. Each party pay own costs.

KAUFFMAN, Justice, dissenting.

In *Schede Estate*, 426 Pa. 93, 231 A.2d 135 (1967), this Court stated:

> For over a hundred years, the law has been clearly settled that strict and literal compliance with the terms of a special power of appointment is absolutely necessary for its valid and effective exercise. That means that the appointing instrument must specifically refer in the instant case to the power which was granted by [the donor's] will and which [the donee] seeks to exercise and execute. A general residuary clause, even if and when it included the words, "I hereby exercise every power of appointment which I possess," would not and does not comply with and fulfill the donor's condition and is not a valid exercise of the special power of appointment granted to [the donee].

Id. at 96, 231 A.2d at 137 (emphasis supplied). *See also Roger's Estate*, 218 Pa. 431, 67 A. 762 (1907); *Slifer v. Beates*, 9 S. & R. 166 (1822); *Price's Estate*, 27 Pa.Dist. 561 (O.C. Phila. Co. 1918).

Thus, the courts of this Commonwealth have long required strict and literal compliance with all conditions on form of exercise imposed by the instrument creating a power of appointment. In this case, the donor (Charles) gave the donee (Laura) a power over a certain trust (Trust A) exercisable by will only by express reference to that specific trust under the named trust agreement. Simply stated, the donee failed to comply with her donor's express instructions. Therefore, I would hold that the attempt to exercise the power of appointment was ineffective.

NIX, Justice, concurring.

I agree with Mr. Justice Kauffman that a strict reading of our decision in *Schede Estate*, 426 Pa. 93, 231 A.2d 135 (1967) would force the conclusion that the power was not effectively exercised. However, I believe the majority has elected the wise course of not being bound by the rigidity of *Schede Estate, supra*. Limitations on the manner of the exercise of a power of appointment should be recognized only where a legitimate purpose is obtained by the insistence upon literal compliance. Such was not the case here.

Notes

1. *Specific reference required*: As reflected in the court's opinion in *Passmore*, historically, if the creating instrument expressly provided that the power could be exercised only if it included an express reference to the power (or the instrument creating the power), the courts typically applied strict compliance in analyzing whether the power had been exercised. One could argue that, in some ways, the majority in *Passmore* implicitly adopted a substantial compliance approach. Such an "intent"-based approach is not too surprising given the overall movement of the law in this field.

California has statutorily addressed the degree of compliance issue as it applies to powers of appointment. How would the *Passmore* case come out in California?

CPC § 630. Compliance with donor's intent

(a) Except as otherwise provided in this part, if the creating instrument specifies requirements as to the manner, time, and conditions of the exercise of a power of appointment, the power can be exercised only by complying with those requirements.

(b) Unless expressly prohibited by the creating instrument, a power stated to be exercisable by an inter vivos instrument is also exercisable by a written will.

CPC § 631. Degree of compliance required with donor's intent

(a) Where an appointment does not satisfy the formal requirements specified in the creating instrument as provided in subdivision (a) of Section 630, the court may excuse compliance with the formal requirements and determine that exercise of the appointment was effective if both of the following requirements are satisfied:

The appointment approximates the manner of appointment prescribed by the donor.

The failure to satisfy the formal requirements does not defeat the accomplishment of a significant purpose of the donor.

(b)   This section does not permit a court to excuse compliance with a specific reference requirement under Section 632.

CPC § 632. Power requiring specific reference

If the creating instrument expressly directs that a power of appointment be exercised by an instrument that makes a specific reference to the power or to the instrument that created the power, the power can be exercised only by an instrument containing the required reference.

LAW REVISION COMMISSION COMMENTS

This section permits a donor to require an express reference to the power of appointment to ensure a conscious exercise by the donee. In such a case, the specific reference to the power is a condition to its exercise. This condition precludes the use of form wills with "blanket" clauses exercising all powers of appointment owned by the testator. The use of blanket clauses may result in passing property without knowledge of the tax consequences and may cause appointment to unintended beneficiaries....

2. *No specific reference required*: If the instrument creating the power does not require a specific reference to the power or the instrument creating the power, what should be necessary to exercise the power? Must there be a reference—any reference, but some reference—to the power? If the power is a testamentary power of appointment, should a generic residuary clause with no reference to the power be sufficient? Should it matter if the power is general or specific/limited (assuming the taker(s) under the residuary clause are eligible appointees)? What difference, if any, should it make if there is a "blanket" clause purporting to exercise any and all powers of appointment the testator may hold?

a. *Standard residuary clause plus general power of appointment*: A general power of appointment is about as close as one can get to actual ownership without it being actual ownership. All the donee has to do to get the property is accept the offer. A standard residuary clause transfers all of the testator's property that has not otherwise been transferred. Should a standard residuary clause be deemed to exercise a general power of appointment that the testator held?

i. *General rule*: The court discussed the different approaches in *First Citizens Bank & Trust Co. v. Fleming*, 335 S.E.2d 515 (N.C. App. 1985):

> In North Carolina and a minority of other states, a power of appointment upon which no restrictions are imposed is exercised by a residuary clause. G.S. 31–43; *Trust Co. v. Hunt*, 267 N.C. 173, 148 S.E.2d 41 (1966). It has been suggested that this rule was originally created to guard against the inadvertent failure of a life tenant to exercise a general power of appointment. *Trust Co. v. Hunt*, 267 N.C. 173, 148 S.E.2d 41 (1966).

> In a majority of American jurisdictions, however, residuary clauses do not exercise a power unless the power is mentioned in the residuary clause. Thus

a majority of American jurisdictions are more concerned with the inequity of inadvertent exercise of powers of appointment than of inadvertent failure to exercise powers of appointment....

ii. *California*: The California legislature has entered the debate and resolved the issue statutorily as follows:

CPC § 641. Power of appointment & general residuary clause

(a) A general residuary clause in a will, or a will making general disposition of all the testator's property, does not exercise a power of appointment held by the testator unless specific reference is made to the power or there is some other indication of intent to exercise the power.

iii. *"Some other indication of intent to exercise the power"*: What constitutes "some other indication of intent to exercise the power"? To what extent should the court be open to extrinsic evidence to provide that intent? The California Law Revision Commission Comments to Section 641 provide as follows:

Such other indication of intent to exercise the power may be found in the will or in other evidence apart from the will. Section 640 sets forth a nonexclusive list of types of evidence that indicate an intent to exercise a power of appointment. An exercise of a power of appointment may be found if a preponderance of the evidence indicates that the donee intended to exercise the power. *See Bank of New York v. Black*, 26 N.J. 276, 286–87, 139 A.2d 393, 398 (1958).

CPC § 640. Evidence of donee's intent to exercise power

(a) The exercise of a power of appointment requires a manifestation of the donee's intent to exercise the power.

(b) A manifestation of the donee's intent to exercise a power of appointment exists in any of the following circumstances:

(1) The donee declares, in substance, that the donee exercises specific powers or all the powers the donee has.

(2) The donee purports to transfer an interest in the appointive property that the donee would have no power to transfer except by virtue of the power.

(3) The donee makes a disposition that, when considered with reference to the property owned and the circumstances existing at the time of the disposition, manifests the donee's understanding that the donee was disposing of the appointive property.

(c) The circumstances described in subdivision (b) are illustrative, not exclusive.

In support of the view that the "other indication of intent to exercise the power" should include evidence other than just the terms of the will, the California Law Revision Commission Comments cite *Bank of New York v. Black*, 139 A.2d 393, 398 (N.J. 1958). In *Bank of New York*, the testator's will gave his wife (Julia Byrd) a testamentary general power of appointment over the principal of a trust that was for her benefit. The donee's bare-bones will provided in pertinent part:

Second: I give, bequeath and devise all of my estate, both real and personal, or mixed, wheresoever situated, whether in being or in expectancy, to my daughter Mary Martin Black of Warrenton, Virginia. Should my said daughter Mary Martin Black predecease me, I give, bequeath and devise all of my estate, both real and personal and mixed, in equal share to my grandsons, namely Josiah Macy, Jr., Archer Martin Macy, and Noel Everit Macy, and I hereby request said grandsons to equally share the responsibility of the care and maintenance of Aubrey Henry Martin, Jr.

Although it made no express reference to the power she held under her husband's will and even though it did not include a blanket clause purporting to exercise any and all powers of appointment she may hold, her daughter Mary Martin Black, the taker under the residuary clause, argued that the clause expressed the intent to exercise the power of appointment in her favor. The lower court found that the general residuary clause did not exercise the general power of appointment.

On appeal, the New Jersey Supreme Court began its analysis of the issue by addressing the issue of the burden of proof that should apply. The Court said the while the daughter had the burden of proving the donee's intent to exercise the power, the burden of proof was only by a preponderance of the evidence—not by clear and convincing evidence or any other standard. The Court went on to note the fact-sensitive nature of determining the testator's intent:

The meaning and intention of the testator must be determined, not by fixing the attention on single words in the will, but by considering the entire will and the surroundings of the testator when he executed the will, and by ascribing to him, so far as his language permits, the common impulses of our nature. *Torrey v. Torrey*, 70 N.J.L. 672, 59 A. 450.

Ultimately, of course, each case must be determined upon its own facts and circumstances, but the fundamental purpose of the inquiry always remains. Our primary desire is to effectuate the wishes of the deceased if they are reasonably and lawfully discoverable and adequately proven.

26 N.J. at 285.

The Court then turned to the text of the will and the circumstances surrounding its execution. The Court was particularly impressed with the very close relationship between the mother and daughter. In addition, the Court noted that the testatrix's estate totaled only approximately $25,000. The property subject to the power of appointment totaled approximately $300,000. The Court continued its analysis:

Mary and her mother were as close as human affection and esteem could bind them, and one searches in vain for a cause why, under these circumstances, without explanation, the mother, at the infirm age of 82 years, stricken with palsy and leaning more heavily upon her daughter for comfort and physical aid, should intentionally deprive her of the only sizable inheritance involved.

To the contrary, in sweeping language Julia Byrd [the testatrix] endowed Mary Martin Black "with all my estate, both real and personal, or mixed, wheresoever situated, whether in being or in expectancy * * *." Although she had the full power and authority to withdraw the whole or any part of the capital of the trust in question, she never reduced it to possession or converted it to her enjoyment. Could the fund as it thus existed be termed or regarded by her as an expectancy? Regardless of the strict legalistic definition of the phrase, the possibility that she used it to refer to the trust fund contributes something to the composite of various factors ultimately portraying the testatrix' intention.

The scrivener of Mrs. Byrd's will was a Virginia lawyer located in Warrenton. He drew the residuary clause, which by Virginia statute was sufficient to execute the power donated to the testatrix. The rule that the law of the donor's domicile governs the determination of whether the donee of a power intended to exercise it, despite the fact that the donee has a different domicile, is, to say the least, abstruse. It is said by some authorities to run contrary to legitimate expectation and has been condemned as illogical. Goodrich, Conflict of Laws, § 177 (1949); 2 Beale, Conflict of Laws, § 288.1 (1935); 5 American Law of Property, § 23.3 (1952). Withholding our judgment on the merits of this controversy over which is the more seemly choice of the law, it is enough to say that we can appreciate, at least in part, why a Virginia lawyer might regard the residuary clause in question as fully complying with Mrs. Byrd's desire to exercise her power of appointment in favor of her daughter.

. . .

It may well be that none of the incidents related above is adequate in and of itself to prove the required intention. Yet the combination of all the circumstances in their aggregate, as they integrate with one another and reflect upon the problem as a whole, is sufficient to sustain the appellant's burden of proof in the case *sub judice*.

Essential justice does not permit "a discernible intention of the testator" to be defeated. The Quantum of proof may be supplied by logical inferences if they are sufficiently persuasive to carry the necessary conviction. We accordingly, from the whole record, conclude that Mrs. Byrd intended to and did appoint the trust fund to her daughter.

26 N.J. at 291–94.

The bottom line is that, while a standard residuary clause should be presumed *not* to exercise a power of appointment, it is, to an extent, a question of testator's intent. Thus, if the court is open to extrinsic evidence of the circumstances surrounding the testator at time of execution, there is always a chance the extrinsic evidence may support a good faith argument that the residuary clause should nevertheless be construed as exercising the testator's power of appointment. That being said, one would assume such results will be rare. The rest of this discussion will accordingly focus on the terms of the residuary clause and will assume there is no extrinsic evidence to help in the analysis.

b. *Standard residuary clause plus special power of appointment*: There is an even weaker argument that a special power of appointment should be deemed exercised by a standard residuary clause that makes no express reference to the power of appointment. Many commentators argue that, conceptually, the best way to think about a special or limited power of appointment is to analogize the donee to an agent. An agent has no interest in the property in question and there is no scenario under which he or she can claim ownership. Nevertheless, if the residuary clause leaves the donee's/ testator's property to one or more eligible appointees under the limited power of appointment, should the residuary clause be deemed to have exercised the power of appointment?

The overwhelming majority rule is that a standard residuary clause does *not* exercise a special or limited power of appointment. Re-read California Probate Code Section 641. Is it limited to general powers of appointment? Might a standard residuary clause exercise a special or limited power of appointment if there is "some other indication of intent to exercise the power"?

c. *Standard residuary clause that includes blanket appointment clause*: A blended residuary clause is one that not only disposes of the testator's residuary property, but also contains a "blanket" exercise clause that purports to exercise any and all powers of appointment held by the testator. Should such a blended residuary clause, which contains a blanket exercise of any and all powers of appointment the testator may hold but makes no specific reference to any particular power of appointment, be deemed to exercise a general or limited power of appointment held by the testator?

The RESTATEMENT (SECOND) OF PROPERTY, Section 17.2, provides as follows with respect to blanket appointments:

> If the donee by deed or will manifests an intention to exercise all powers the donee has, the manifested intention includes the exercise of both general and non-general powers that are exercisable by the deed or the will.

Re-read California Probate Code Section 640 above. Are the two in agreement? Which one — the RESTATEMENT approach to blanket appointments or the California approach to blanket appointments — is broader in scope (at least expressly broader)? Re-read California Probate Code Section 632. What is the interaction between the two statutory provisions (Section 632 and Section 640)? In California, does a blanket appointments clause exercise a power of appointment that expressly requires an express reference to it?

Problem

When Mr. Wood passed away, his will created a testamentary trust. The trust granted his wife a life estate interest and a power of appointment. With respect to the power, the trust specifically provided as follows:

> [I]f my wife survives me, then she shall have the absolute power exercisable only by a written instrument other than a will delivered to the Trustee during

her lifetime to appoint any part of the principal and any undistributed income of Trust "A" in favor of herself, her estate or any person.

The trust went on to provide for how the property subject to the power should be distributed in the event Mrs. Wood failed to exercise the power.

Thereafter, Mrs. Wood began to experience some difficulties managing her affairs, so a conservator was appointed for her (but there is substantial evidence that she was still competent). The conservator, who was also a notary, prepared an instrument that expressed Mrs. Wood's intent to exercise the power of appointment under her husband's testamentary trust. Mrs. Wood exercised the instrument on November 3, 1970, and the conservator acknowledged it. Mrs. Wood instructed the conservator to deliver the instrument to her attorney with instructions that it be filed with the trustee. The conservator took the document to the office of Mrs. Wood's attorney. A few days later Mrs. Wood called her attorney's office to make sure that everything had been done to exercise the power of appointment. Her attorney assured her it had. Mrs. Wood died on November 22, 1970. The attorney did not deliver the instrument to the trustee until over a month later, on December 28, 1970.

Was the power of appointment validly exercised? *See Estate of Wood*, 32 Cal. App. 3d 862 (Ct. App. 1973).

D. Atypical Exercise Scenarios

1. Appointment in Trust; Creating a New Power of Appointment

The standard exercise scenario is where the donee, in full compliance with the power of appointment, appoints the property in question outright to an eligible appointee. That is the classic valid appointment. But what if, instead of appointing the property outright, the donee appoints the property in question to a trust for the benefit of an eligible appointee? What if, instead of appointing the property outright to an eligible appointee, the donee grants the eligible appointee a power of appointment over the property in question? If the donee could have appointed the property outright to the appointee, is it permissible to give the appointee a power of appointment over the property? Should it matter if the power is a general power or a special power (either the original power or the new power)?

The general rule is that, unless the donor expresses a contrary intent, the donee has all the same powers and rights to "give" the property to an eligible appointee as the donor would have had (so long as the ultimate possible appointees are consistent with the terms of the original power). Inasmuch as a donor could have given the property in question to an eligible taker outright, in trust, or subject to a power of appointment, the donee arguably has the same right and power. So long as the ultimate possible takers are eligible appointees of the original power, the donee can grant the property as he or she deems appropriate. Assuming a donee has a power to appoint the property among the donee's children, the donee can even appoint the property to T, a trustee, to hold and distribute the property among the donee's children as the trustee deems appropriate. Likewise, a donee of a special or limited power may exercise the power by:

(1) Creating a general power in an object of the non-general power, or

(2) Creating a non-general power in any person to appoint to an object of the original non-general power.

RESTATEMENT (SECOND) OF PROP.: DONATIVE TRANSFERS § 19.4 (1986).

Absent the donor's express contrary intent, the donee of a general power arguably has even greater power to appoint the property in question in trust or subject to a power of appointment. Inasmuch as the power is a general power, the donee can appoint the property to him or herself, and then transfer the property in trust or create a new power of appointment. Whatever the donee of a general power can do indirectly, the donee should be able to do directly. RESTATEMENT (SECOND) OF PROP.: DONATIVE TRANSFERS § 19.2-3 (1986).

2. Appointee Dies before Appointment Effective: Lapse and Anti-Lapse?

Assume a donee, D, holds a testamentary power of appointment, and the donee executes a valid will that validly exercises the power of appointment to an eligible appointee, A. Thereafter, however, the eligible appointee to whom the property was appointed, A, predeceases the donee (and the donee fails to revise his or her will). Should the doctrines of lapse and anti-lapse apply to an otherwise effective exercise of a power of appointment? Should it matter if the power was a general or special power of appointment? If it is a special power of appointment, should it matter if the appointee's issue are not eligible takers under the original power?

Dow v. Atwood

260 A.2d 437 (Me. 1969)

WILLIAMSON, Chief Justice.

This action by the Administrator ... of the Estate of Harold F. Atwood for the construction of the will and instructions for the disposition of property is reported to us on an agreed statement of facts.

We are concerned with the wills, duly probated, of Harold F. Atwood and of his widow, Leonora. The wills read:

Will of Harold:

"After the payment of my just debts, funeral charges and expenses of administration, I dispose of my estate, as follows:

First—

I, give, bequeath and devise all of my property, real, personal, and mixed, wherever found and however situated, to my wife, Leonora S. Atwood, to her so long as she lives, after which, it is my wish that she give, bequeath and devise the same to my brother, Alfred L. Atwood, to him and his heirs forever."

Will of Leonora:

"I give, bequeath and devise to Alfred L. Atwood that property which came to me under the will of my late husband, Harold F. Atwood, it being my intention to hereby appoint said property to the said Alfred L. Atwood by the exercise of the special testamentary power of appointment given to me in said will, but in nowise to appoint or bequeath to the said Alfred L. Atwood any property other than that belonging to the estate of Harold F. Atwood in which I have heretofore had a life estate."

Harold at his death on October 5, 1945 was survived by his wife Leonora, and as his heirs at law his brother Alfred L. Atwood, his sister Elizabeth A. Record, and children of a deceased brother Roger. Leonora died on September 13, 1965.

Alfred died intestate on August 19, 1965 subsequent to the execution of Leonora's will. He was survived by his wife Mary, who, as administratrix of his estate is a party to this action, and by his only heirs at law, his daughters Mary A. Rideout and Priscilla A. Norton, who also are parties herein.

. . .

The controversy is between Harold's heirs and estate (Harold's group), Alfred's heirs and estate (Alfred's group), and the Guardian Ad Litem.

The objective of the case it to determine who may be entitled to the property remaining at Leonora's death. Different solutions are urged by Harold's group, Alfred's group, and the Guardian Ad Litem.

In construing the will, our task is to find the intent of the testator and to give effect thereto if possible. We must also bear in mind the presumption against intestacy. . . .

Harold, in his will, created a life estate in Leonora with a testamentary power in her to appoint the remainder to his brother Alfred. The power of appointment under the will was a special and not a general power. Accordingly Leonora gained nothing under the will apart from her life interest and the limited right to appoint by will to Alfred. . . .

Alfred's group contends that Alfred at Harold's death and under his will acquired a vested remainder. . . .

The position of the Alfred group in our view is not found within the plain meaning of the plainly expressed provisions of Harold's will. If the testator had not intended to create a power in his widow to appoint the remainder to Alfred by her will, he could have simply given the remainder to Alfred, as suggested.

. . .

We are faced then with the disposition of the remainder, not by way of a vested interest in Alfred at the death of Harold, but upon the failure of Leonora to make an effective appointment to the only person authorized by the donor of the power.

It is immaterial for the moment whether the words "if I wish" in the will are "softened words of command", to use the phrase of Bogert, supra, Sec. 48, or precatory in meaning. See *Clifford v. Stewart*, 95 Me. 38, 45, 49 A. 52; *Jordan et al. v. Jordan et al.*, 155 Me. 5, 150 A.2d 763. In either case, at Leonora's death there was no eligible receiver. The law is well settled that an appointee under a power must be living at the effective date of the appointment. *MacBryde v. Burnett,* 45 F.Supp. 451 (D.C.Md.); 3 Restatement, Property §349; 72 C.J.S. Powers §43 b; Simes and Smith, Future Interests 2nd Ed. §§917, 984; 5 American Law of Property §§23.7, 23.46.

. . .

The Alfred group gains nothing from the operation of the anti-lapse statute. 18 M.R.S.A. §1008 reads:

> "When a relative of the testator, having a devise of real or personal estate, dies before the testator, leaving lineal descendants, they take such estate as would have been taken by such deceased relative if he had survived."

As we have seen, the power to appoint to Alfred was special and not general. Thus the rule that a general power of appointment may be considered a property interest passing under an anti-lapse statute is not applicable. *Thompson v. Pew,* 214 Mass. 520, 102 N.E. 122; *Daniel v. Brown,* 156 Va. 563, 159 S.E. 209, 75 A.L.R. 1377 and annot.; 5 American Law of Property §23.47; Restatement, Property §350; Schwartz, Future Interests and Estate Planning §13.14.

Under a testamentary special power the appointee takes from the donee and not from the donor of the power. "Lapse statutes are designed to effectuate the purpose of the testator (who, in these cases, is the donee of the power)." Simes and Smith, supra §984.

Assuming without deciding that the anti-lapse statute could apply in the case under a special testamentary power, the statute does not benefit Alfred's heirs. Alfred was not a blood relative of Leonora and therefore the anti-lapse statute would not preserve for others a gift to him under her will.

We conclude that Alfred's group took nothing under Harold's will or from the testamentary power in Leonora to appoint the property. The group of course retains any interest it may have by intestacy.

. . .

So ordered.

Notes

1. *Traditional approach*: Anti-lapse provides that where a gift lapses, if the predeceased beneficiary meets the requisite degree of relationship and has surviving issue, the gift passes to the issue of the predeceased beneficiary. There are two questions with respect to applying lapse and anti-lapse to an exercise of a power of appointment where the appointee predeceases the donee: (1) is an exercise of a power of appointment the type of "transfer" to which lapse and anti-lapse should apply? and (2) if so, who is the person with whom the appointee must meet the degree of relationship — the donor or the donee?

The general rule is that an individual must survive a decedent in order to take property from the decedent. The same default rule applies to taking under an exercise of a power of appointment. A donee cannot exercise a power of appointment in favor of a deceased appointee. Where a party who was intended to take under a testamentary power of appointment predeceased the donee/testator, the power is deemed not to have been exercised. If the predeceased appointee's estate were permitted to take, the estate could simply serve as a conduit and the property could end up being given to someone who was not an eligible taker (if the power were a special power).

As the *Dow* case indicates, historically the courts were more open to the argument that lapse and anti-lapse should apply to the exercise of a general power of appointment than to the exercise of a special power of appointment. The donee of a general power of appointment all but owns the property subject to the power. Thus, if the donee expressed the intent to exercise the power, that act was like an act of ownership. Accordingly, the property in question should be treated like any other property of the donee. So long as the appointee meets the degree of relationship with the donee, the issue of the predeceased appointee should be entitled to the property under anti-lapse.

Application of anti-lapse to an appointee of a special power of appointment, however, is more complicated. The donee is more like an agent for the donor than an owner of the property. The appointee's issue who would take in the appointee's place under anti-lapse may not be eligible appointees under the donor's power of appointment. Does it make sense to apply anti-lapse to a special power of appointment? Historically, the courts were in agreement that anti-lapse should not apply where a donee exercised a special power of appointment in favor of an eligible appointee who had predeceased the donee.

2. *Modern trend*: The modern trend has been rather critical of the traditional narrow application of anti-lapse to powers of appointment. The modern trend analogizes an exercise of a power of appointment to a devise, with the appointee being a devisee. If the devisee is an eligible appointee, and the devisee meets the requirements of the anti-lapse doctrine, the argument is that applying anti-lapse doctrine to powers of appointment is just as "intent-promoting" as it is when applied to any other type of testamentary transfer. Hence, the modern trend has been to expand application of the anti-lapse doctrines to powers of appointments. The first RESTATEMENT OF PROPERTY provided that anti-lapse applied to general powers of appointment, but was silent on the issue of whether anti-lapse should apply to special powers of appointment. RESTATEMENT (FIRST) OF PROP.: FUTURE INTERESTS § 350 (1940). The second RESTATEMENT OF PROPERTY took the position that anti-lapse should apply to both general and special powers of appointment. Moreover, it asserted that the doctrine should apply so long as the predeceased appointee met the degree of relationship with either the donor or the donee (and so long as neither expressed a contrary intent). RESTATEMENT (SECOND) OF PROP.: DONATIVE TRANSFERS § 18.5 (1984).

The 1990 version of the Uniform Probate Code followed the RESTATEMENT (SECOND) OF PROPERTY approach, applying the anti-lapse doctrine to both general and non-general powers, as well as applying it to anyone who met the degree of relationship requirement with respect to either the donor or the donee. UPC § 2-603. Under the modern trend, it is irrelevant whether the issue of the predeceased appointee are eligible takers. So long as the predeceased appointee was an eligible taker, so too are his or her issue. Inasmuch as the issue of a predeceased appointee may take indirectly under anti-lapse, the modern trend authorizes the donee to appoint the property directly to the issue where the eligible appointee predeceases the donee, even if the issue are not technically eligible takers under the terms of the power. *See* UNIF. POWERS OF APPOINTMENT ACT § 306.

The states are spread out across the spectrum between the traditional approach and the modern trend approach. California has adopted the modern trend approach:

CPC § 673. Death of appointee before effective exercise of appointment

(a) Except as provided in subdivision (b), if an appointment by will or by instrument effective only at the death of the donee is ineffective because of the death of an appointee before the appointment becomes effective and the appointee leaves issue surviving the donee, the surviving issue of the appointee take the appointed property in the same manner as the appointee would have taken had the appointee survived the donee, except that the property passes only to persons who are permissible appointees, including appointees permitted under Section 674. If the surviving issue are all of the same degree of kinship to the deceased appointee, they take equally, but if of unequal degree, then those of more remote degree take in the manner provided in Section 240.

(b) This section does not apply if either the donor or donee manifests an intent that some other disposition of the appointive property shall be made.

CPC § 674. Death of eligible appointee before exercise of special power

(a) Unless the creating instrument expressly provides otherwise, if a permissible appointee dies before the exercise of a special power of appointment, the donee has the power to appoint to the issue of the deceased permissible appointee, whether or not the issue was included within the description of the permissible appointees, if the deceased permissible appointee was alive at the time of the execution of the creating instrument or was born thereafter.

(b) This section applies whether the special power of appointment is exercisable by inter vivos instrument, by will, or otherwise.

E. Flawed Blended Exercises

As discussed briefly above, it is not uncommon for a donee holding a power of appointment to exercise his or her power of appointment by using a blanket clause in the residuary clause of his or her will (such blended exercise is not limited to residuary clauses, but this is the most common scenario under which such blending occurs). The default assumption is that the appointive property should simply be blended with the donee's/testator's own residuary property and the aggregate distributed to the takers under the terms of the clause in question. Sometimes, however, blending the two pots of property can be flawed for one reason or another (see below).

Where such blending would be flawed, the courts have developed a number of doctrines to maximize the effectiveness of the exercise and the apparent intent.

1. Selective Allocation

A fairly simple example of selective allocation to maximize the decedent's intent and to maximize the effectiveness of an exercise of a special power of appointment is where a donee blends the property over which the donee has a power of appointment with his or her own property and then gifts the aggregate to both eligible and ineligible appointees. Selective allocation essentially "unblends" the property and allocates it to the appropriate takers so as to maximize the exercise of the power of appointment and to promote the donee's intent.

For example, assume Tess has a testamentary special power of appointment over a trust that contains $200,000 to appoint the property among her children. Tess has a residuary estate that totals $300,000. Tess's validly executed will has a residuary clause that provides as follows: "I give all the rest, residue and remainder of my estate, including any property over which I hold a power of appointment, as follows: 50% to my surviving spouse, and 50% to my surviving children equally." Although Tess's will purports to give the property equally to her spouse and children, in funding the gifts the court would be sensitive to the fact that Tess's spouse is not entitled to receive any of the property subject to the special power of appointment. The court would fund the children's share first with the property subject to the special power of appointment because they are the only eligible takers of that property. That $200,000 would be allocated first to the children's $250,000. The court would then add another $50,000 out of the testator's own property to bring the total up to $250,000, the share of the property passing under the residuary clause to which the children are entitled. The court would then fund the surviving spouse's $250,000 with the remaining funds from the property that the testator owned in her own name. Selective allocation is used to ensure that only eligible parties receive the appropriate property while at the same time allocating to maximize the effectiveness of the gifts in question.

2. Capture

Assume Tess has a presently exercisable general power of appointment over a trust that contains $500,000, to appoint as she deems appropriate among her parents' children (including herself or her estate). Tess has a residuary estate that totals $100,000. Tess's validly executed will has a residuary clause that provides as follows: "I give all the rest, residue and remainder of my estate, including any property over which I hold a power of appointment, as follows: the property over which I hold a power of appointment to my brother Bob, and the residue of my estate to my surviving children equally." Tess's brother Bob predeceased Tess, and he has no surviving issue. What, if anything, should come of Tess's attempt to exercise the general power of appointment?

The court was presented with a similar scenario in *Fiduciary Trust Co. v. First National Bank of Colorado Springs, Colorado*, 181 N.E.2d 6 (Mass. 1962). The court stated in pertinent part:

It is a recognized principle in the law of property that where the donee of a general power attempts to make an appointment that fails, but where, nevertheless, the donee has manifested an intent wholly to withdraw the appointive property from the operation of the instrument creating the power for all purposes and not merely for the purposes of the invalid appointment, the attempted appointment will commonly be effective to the extent of causing the appointive property to be taken out of the original instrument and to become in effect part of the estate of the donee of the power.' Fiduciary Trust Co. v. Mishou, 321 Mass. 615, 624, 75 N.E.2d 3, 9, and cases cited. This so called principle of 'capture' (Amerige v. Attorney General, 324 Mass. 648, 656, 88 N.E.2d 126) which, 'like some other principles applicable to general powers of appointment, owes its origin to the conception that the grant of a general power is in itself almost tantamount to a grant of ownership' (Old Colony Trust Co. v. Allen, 307 Mass. 40, 42, 29 N.E.2d 310, 311) has no application in cases of special powers, where the ineffectively appointed property passes to takers in default of appointment (Thayer v. Rivers, 179 Mass. 280, 290, 60 N.E. 796; Hooper v. Hooper, 203 Mass. 50, 58–59, 89 N.E. 161; see Old Colony Trust Co. v. Richardson, 297 Mass. 147, 155, 7 N.E.2d 432, 121 A.L.R. 1218) or, in some cases, to the objects of the power where there are no takers in default provided.

Id. at 7–8.

A blended residuary clause is generally presumed to manifest an intent by the donee to exercise sufficient dominion and control over the property subject to the general power of appointment to subject it to the capture doctrine.

California recognizes the capture doctrine. *See* CPC § 672(b).

IV. Failure to Exercise a Power of Appointment

As noted at the start of the chapter, because a power of appointment is discretionary and thus may never be exercised, a well-drafted power of appointment will provide for who should take in the event the power is not validly exercised. Where a power of appointment has such a provision, it controls whether the power is a general power or a special power. Where there is no express "takers in default" clause addressing who should take in the event the power is not validly exercised, who should take?

Remember the power of appointment terminology. The party who creates the power is called the "donor." The party to whom the power is given is called the "donee." The power terminology is based on the "gift" model, except it is deemed that there is no acceptance unless the donee "exercises" the power (and even then, in the case of a special power of appointment, the donee is deemed not to have ever held any interest in the property). If the gift model is the controlling model, if the power is not exercised and the "gift" is not accepted, the interest still belongs to the donor. Donor's intent should control. In the absence of an express "takers in default" clause, the donor should be presumed to have retained whatever he or she did not expressly give. The starting assumption for who should get the property subject to the power of appointment if the power was not completely exercised and if there was no express "takers in default" clause is the property should pass through the donor's estate— but that is only the starting point.

Crawford v. Crawford

296 A.2d 388 (Md. 1972)

SINGLEY, Judge.

The case was heard below on an agreed statement of facts, which may be briefly summarized. Mrs. Crawford married Francis I in 1905. There were two sons: Francis J. Crawford (Francis II), born in 1909, and Francis III (Francis Albert Crawford, Jr.), born in 1914. When Francis I died in 1922, he was 59 years of age; Mrs. Crawford was 36; Francis II, 13, and Francis III, seven. The year 1935 was of consequence, because in that year Francis III, the younger son, would attain age 21.

In 1940, Francis II married Hollus Field (Hollus), one of the appellees, and together they moved to one of the farms. They had one son, Francis J. Crawford, III (Francis IV), who is also an appellee. Francis II continued to farm the place which he occupied until his death in 1967, survived by his widow, Hollus, and by Francis IV. Thereafter, Hollus and Francis IV remained on the farm until Mrs. Crawford gave them notice to vacate in 1969. During the interim, Francis II and Hollus had built a barn, a silo and a loafing barn, at least partly at their expense, and had erected or maintained the fencing and gates. Except for one year, however, Mrs. Crawford had paid the taxes.

The chancellor concluded, quite rightly, we think, that by a true and proper construction of the will of Francis I, Mrs. Crawford took an estate *durante viduitate*, an estate during widowhood, which is a life estate subject to a special limitation, ... an estate which would be terminated by the widow's death or remarriage. Despite the inartistic manner in which the will was drafted, this much is palpably clear.

A troublesome aspect of the matter flows from the circumstance that there is no express limitation over in remainder upon termination of the estate during widowhood, and the remainder would pass in intestacy should Mrs. Crawford fail to exercise her power to divide, unless a limitation over can be implied.

. . .

In the instant case, at the time of the death of Francis I, Mrs. Crawford and Francis II and Francis III were the primary objects of the testator's bounty. In *McElroy v. Mercantile-Safe Deposit and Trust Co.*, 229 Md. 276, 283–284, 182 A.2d 775 (1962), we reviewed the well-settled rules of construction, the distillation of which is that the general intent of the testator is in every case the controlling consideration. It certainly could be argued that Francis I intended to vest a remainder in Francis II and Francis III which would come into possession in undivided one-half shares upon the remarriage or the death of Mrs. Crawford. The question is, under what circumstances may a limitation over be implied?

V American Law of Property § 23.63, at 644–645 (1952) deals with the situation where A devises a life estate to B and gives B a narrowly restricted power to appoint the remainder among the children of A:

> "The situation last considered includes a typical so-called 'special' power of appointment. The donor of such a special power, having a general intent to benefit the members of the designated class of permissible appointees, may foresee the possibility that the donee will fail to exercise the power. If he does foresee it, the donor likely will include in the instrument creating the power an express gift in default of appointment and the gift in default likely will be in favor of the class of persons designated as permissible appointees. On the other hand, it may not occur to the donor of such a power that the donee may fail to exercise it. In that event there will be no express gift in default of appointment and, if the donee should die not having exercised the power, the question whether the appointive property passes to the members of the class of permissible appointees or to the donor's heirs or residuary devise(e)s will be raised. That question is considered in this Section.

> "As a general proposition, it seems clear that the appointive property should pass, in such a situation, to the designated class of permissible appointees. The donor of the special power of appointment has (1) a general intent to benefit the members of the specified class of permissible appointees and (2) an intent that the apportioning of the appointive property within the class shall be within the discretion of the donee of the power. The fact that the donee has failed to apportion the property within the class should not defeat the donor's intent to benefit the class. Accordingly the appointive property should pass to the class and an equal division of it among the members of the class seems to be the closest approximation to the intent of the donor."

. . .

The preferable view would seem to be that the result will be accomplished by implying a gift over to the permissible appointees in default of the exercise of the power of appointment where there is no specific limitation over in favor of the appointees, … Section 367(2) of the Restatement, Property, at 2030, states that before a gift over can be implied the power must be expired. Either the remarriage of Mrs. Crawford or her death would result in expiration of the power. Restatement, Property, supra, § 367 comment d, at 2033; *Wilks v. Burns*, 60 Md. 64 (1883); 3 Tiffany, The Law of Real Property, supra, § 707, at 77.

Alternatively, the proposition may be implemented and the same result reached by treating the special power of appointment as an imperative power which will be executed by the courts in the event of the termination of the prior estate without an exercise of the power by the donee, see Restatement, Property, supra, § 367, comment c, at 2032; Miller, supra, § 256, at 733; Kales, Estates, Future Interests § 637, at 730–

32 (1920); 2 Simes & Smith, Future Interests §§ 1032–1033, at 495–506 (2d ed. 1956); Moser, Some Aspects of Powers of Appointment in Maryland, 12 Md.L.Rev. 13, 20 (1951);2 Simes, Powers in Trust and the Termination of Powers by the Donee, 37 Yale L.J. 63 (1927)....

We now turn to the meaning of the phrase "... said Real Estate to be divided as aforesaid and not sold prior to A D 1935." The chancellor concluded that this was a special power of appointment vested in Mrs. Crawford in the exercise of which she could divide the farms between Francis II and Francis III....

We are inclined to accept and expand the conclusion reached below. What we think Francis I intended was that Mrs. Crawford should have only the narrowly restricted power to divide the farms between Francis II and Francis III either by deed of appointment or by the terms of her own will.

. . .

To hold otherwise would result in an intestacy, which should be avoided if sound reason permits, ...

Notes

1. *Special power of appointment*: Inasmuch as a special power of appointment grants a donee such little control and interest over the property subject to the power of appointment, in the event of a failure to exercise the power of appointment, the donee's estate has no real claim to the property. Typically, however, a special power of appointment is to a limited class of eligible appointees. In the event of a failure to exercise the power of appointment, should the property in question be treated as property of the donor and pass through the donor's probate estate, or should the property in question be treated as an implied gift by the donor to the eligible appointees and be distributed equally to the eligible appointees? As the court's opinion in *Crawford* evidences, even under the traditional approach, where the eligible class is limited in size, the courts tended to imply a gift to the eligible appointees in the event the donee failed to appoint the property (or, in the alternative, the courts deemed the power an "imperative power" and exercised it for the donee).

The modern trend approach to failed appointments with no express default takers continues that approach, expanding it to provide that even where there is an express "takers in default" clause, if it fails for some reason, the implied gift to the eligible takers kicks in. But under both the modern trend and the traditional approach, if the class of eligible takers is not small and well-defined, a court would be hard-pressed to not return the property to the donor's estate under the failed gift reasoning.

2. *General power of appointment*: Inasmuch as a general power of appointment grants a donee almost complete control over the property subject to the power of appointment, in the event of a failure to exercise the power of appointment, should the property in question be treated as property of the donor and pass through the

donor's probate estate, or should the property in question be treated as an implied gift by the donor to the donee and pass through the donee's estate?

The more traditional approach was to return the property to the donor's estate under the failed gift reasoning. The modern trend is to give the property to the donee's estate under a variation of the implied gift theory based on the nearly complete gift theory inherent in a general power of appointment.

Index

693